Comparing Financial Systems

Comparing Financial Systems

Franklin Allen and
Douglas Gale

The MIT Press
Cambridge, Massachusetts
London, England

First MIT Press paperback edition, 2001

This book was set in Palatino by Windfall Software using ZzTEX and was printed and bound in the United States of America.

Library of Congress Cataloging-in-Publication Data

Allen, Franklin, 1956–
Comparing financial systems / Franklin Allen and Douglas Gale.
p. cm.
Includes bibliographical references and index.
ISBN 0-262-01177-8 (hc : alk. paper), 0-262-51125-8 (pb)
1. Finance. 2. Comparative economics. I. Gale, Douglas.
II. Title.
HG173.A433 2000
332—dc21 99-30173
CIP

10 9 8 7 6 5 4 3

To Chloë, James, and Toby

Contents

Preface

In 1994 we published a book entitled *Financial Innovation and Risk Sharing*. We made the argument there that the degree of incompleteness in market structure, particularly the structure of financial markets, should be thought of as being endogenously determined. In the models we proposed, agents choose the design of securities subject to various constraints such as transaction costs. An important issue is what are the appropriate transaction costs and other frictions such as asymmetric information that should be included. This led us to the issue of how financial systems in different countries operate, which is the subject of this book. Even among economically advanced countries, a large range of systems is observed. How can these systems be understood? Why do some countries have significant stock markets while others do not? Is the structure of the banking system important? Is one system best, or does each have advantages and disadvantages? These are just some of the questions that immediately come to mind when comparing financial systems in different countries.

We are not the first to compare financial systems in different countries, and we owe a large debt to those who have considered these issues before. Rather than using conventional theory to try to understand differences in financial systems, our approach has been to develop new theories to provide insights into these differences. Along the way we have written a number of papers, which have been published in various journals. These are referenced throughout the book.

Many people have helped us during the writing of this book. We are grateful for the many comments and suggestions that we have received in seminars and at conferences. Numerous people have provided written comments on earlier drafts of the book and on the related papers. In particular, we thank Linda Allen, Michael Brennan, Serdar Dinç, Xavier Freixas, Gary Gorton, Akiyoshi Horiuchi, Jan Krahnen, Michael Magill,

José Marin, Ernst Maug, Lubos Pastor, Martine Quinzii, Jean-Charles Rochet, A. Subrahmanyam, Anjan Thakor, and numerous anonymous referees. We are particularly grateful to Jun Qian (QJ) for excellent research assistance and to Stephanie Hogue for her help in preparing the manuscript. Finally, we thank the National Science Foundation and the Wharton Financial Institutions Center for financial support.

Comparing Financial Systems

I Setting the Stage

1 Comparing Financial Systems

1.1 Objectives

Many economists view markets as the ideal mechanism for allocating resources. The most important markets in this respect are the stock market and other financial markets. In the United States and United Kingdom, where many of the ideas concerning the desirability of markets were developed, financial markets are indeed important, and at first sight this characterization seems appropriate. However, there are a number of serious problems with this view of the world. The first is that in most countries, stock markets are unimportant. Financial markets are primarily markets for government debt. Often the external funds firms need for investing are obtained from banks. A second problem is that in all countries, including the United States and United Kingdom, internally generated funds are very important. In the industrialized nations, they are far more important than external finance raised through markets and banks. And third, the ideal of frictionless markets is rarely achieved in practice. In fact, one of the arguments we make in this book is that intermediaries are needed to overcome the informational barriers to participation in markets and thus enable firms and investors to exploit markets effectively.

A comparison of different countries' financial systems thus indicates that the focus of standard economic models on financial markets as a means of allocating resources is misplaced. The aim of this book is to outline a more nuanced view. We seek to develop theories that better capture how resources are allocated in practice and understand the normative properties of different financial systems.

Financial systems are crucial for the allocation of resources in a modern economy. They channel household savings to the corporate sector and allocate investment funds among firms. They allow intertemporal

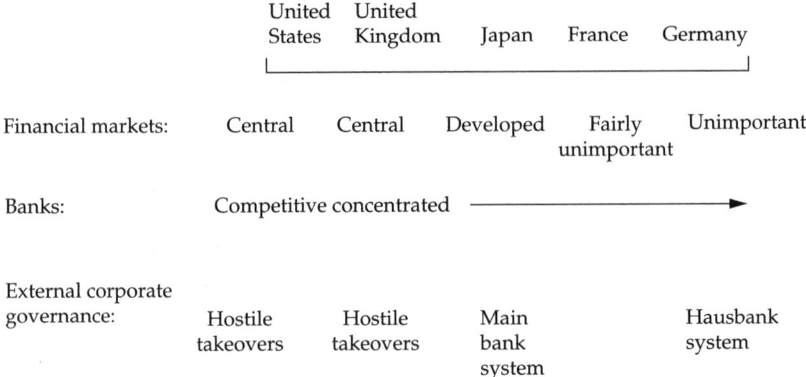

Figure 1.1
Overview of financial systems

smoothing of consumption by households and expenditures by firms. They allow both firms and households to share risks.

These functions appear to be common to most developed economies. When we look at different countries, however, we observe very different financial systems, which we describe in some detail in later chapters. Here we only need to take account of some broad comparisons, summarized in figure 1.1. The United States and Germany can be viewed as polar extremes. In the United States financial markets play an important role in allocating resources, while in Germany they are relatively unimportant. (When we refer to "financial markets," we mean organized markets for securities such as stocks, bonds, futures contracts, and options.) Instead, in Germany banks play by far the most important role. The three major universal banks—Deutsche, Dresdner, and Commerzbank—dominate the allocation of resources in the corporate sector. In contrast the United States has long pursued a vigorous policy of promoting competition among banks. As a result, the banking system is less concentrated than in Germany, particularly with regard to providing services to the corporate sector. Universal banking is prohibited by the Glass-Steagall Act, so the commercial and investment banking sectors have been separate.

As figure 1.1 indicates, other major industrial countries fall in between these two extremes. In the United Kingdom financial markets have a long history and also play a central role, but in contrast to the United States, the domestic banking industry is highly concentrated, with four major banks—Barclays, National Westminster, Midland, and

Lloyds—traditionally dominating the market. Although there is no equivalent to the Glass-Steagall Act and universal banking is allowed, commercial and investment banking are in practice separate in the United Kingdom. Japan has sophisticated financial markets, but for most of the past fifty years, a concentrated banking system has played the dominant role in allocating resources. Finally, France is much like Germany in that banks have traditionally dominated and markets have been unimportant for the corporate sector. The main difference in France is that the government has been much more important than in other countries through its direct ownership of major banks and other financial institutions at various times.

The differences in institutions and markets across countries also have implications for corporate governance. In the United States and United Kingdom, the equity markets provide a market for corporate control. In particular, the possibility of takeovers is assumed to be a device for disciplining managers. A raider can buy up the shares of a badly managed company, replace the management, and make a capital gain. Hostile takeovers are legally possible in Japan and Germany, but they do not occur in practice. It has been widely suggested that monitoring by the banks performs the same external oversight role as hostile takeovers. In Japan this is known as the main bank system, and in Germany it is called the hausbank system.

Why do these different countries have such different financial systems? Do their economies have different needs, resources, and technologies that require different financial systems? Are different financial systems performing different functions, or do they constitute different ways of doing the same thing? Can we say that one system is "better" than another?

The current trend is toward market-based systems. As a matter of policy, France has deliberately chosen to increase the importance of financial markets since the mid-1980s. Japan is planning a "Big Bang" reform of its financial system to make it more efficient and enable the Tokyo markets to compete with those in New York and London. The European Union is moving toward a single European market, which will increase competitiveness and exposure to financial markets. Latin American countries, such as Brazil, are implementing changes to create U.S.-style financial systems.

Why are so many countries, with different histories, environments, and populations, converging on a single financial paradigm? Is there any reason to think that financial systems based on sophisticated, competitive financial markets dominate all others? There are at least two explanations for the almost universal popularity of financial markets at this time. The first is that government intervention has become discredited. The popularity of government intervention in the 1950s and 1960s can be traced back to the market failures of the 1929 Wall Street crash and the Great Depression of the 1930s. To many people today, it appears that government failures are at least as important a problem as market failures. The second reason is that economic theory, particularly that pertaining to financial markets, has stressed the effectiveness of markets in allocating resources. For example, in discussing financial deregulation in France, Melitz (1990, p. 397) noted, "As one contemplates the panoply of measures that took effect in France from late 1984 to the end of 1986, there is no doubt that the changes were inspired by a general vision. This was no mere lifting of controls: new instruments were created; new markets were added, including markets in futures; and the importance of permitting every individual agent to hedge his risks was clearly recognized. The whole program smacks of a close acquaintance with the principles of the theory of finance."

We are interested in understanding the role of financial markets and financial intermediaries in different national economies. As economists, we bring to our task an intellectual training that places markets at the center of the study of economic phenomena. For some, markets define the subject matter of economics. For most of us, complete and competitive markets represent an ideal allocation system characterized by the fundamental theorems of welfare economics. The theory of asset pricing, which is the most highly developed part of financial economics, is also a theory of markets. The theory of finance that Melitz refers to as inspiring the program for reform of the French financial system is a theory of markets. It seems natural to begin by looking at the financial systems we find in the world in terms of the extent to which each conforms to or deviates from the ideal of complete, perfectly competitive markets.

This is not the only way to frame these issues, however. As every economist knows, the ideal world of Arrow-Debreu-MacKenzie (ADM) markets leaves out of account a number of factors that have become an increasingly important part of economics in the past few decades:

- The incentive problems that arise between employers and employees, managers and shareholders, financial institutions and their customers.

- The difficulties that arise in financial markets when information is asymmetrically distributed.
- The transaction costs and moral hazard that prevent the existence of more than a small fraction of the number of markets envisaged by the ADM model.
- The lack of perfect competition that results from long-term financial relationships or the existence of powerful financial institutions.

These issues are central to an understanding of finance, since much of financial practice and theory deals with the attempt to overcome agency problems, incomplete markets, transaction costs, and lack of information. One could argue that the ADM ideal is the last place to look for guidance on financial issues.

Despite its limitations, the classical theory makes a powerful case for the role of markets whenever the imperfections caused by market power, asymmetric information, and incentive problems are not too great. However, the theory does not give us any reason to think that financial markets are the solution to all problems. What remains is to develop a better understanding of the potential for market failure and the role for financial intermediaries in helping markets to achieve the potential indicated by the classical theory. We try to elucidate the strengths and weaknesses of financial markets and other institutional arrangements. In doing so, we have identified a number of trade-offs, outlined below, that seem to us to be central in understanding the historical development of financial systems and the way to improve their performance and design.

It is important to stress from the outset what this book does not attempt to do. It is not meant to be a synthesis and survey of existing theories of banking. Freixas and Rochet (1997) have already provided an excellent book doing this. Moreover we do not seek to provide a comprehensive survey of work on the design of financial systems. Recent insightful contributions include Baliga and Polak (1995), Boot and Thakor (1997a, 1997b), Bhattacharya and Chiesa (1995), and Hauswald (1996). Nor do we cover the large and growing literature on finance and development or the literature on capital market imperfections and investment except where they are relevant to the topic at hand. (For excellent surveys of these literatures, see Levine 1996 and Hubbard 1998, respectively.) Instead, we seek to develop new theories based on a broad comparison of different countries' financial systems.

1.2 Background

The historical development of financial systems was heavily influenced by the problems associated with financial markets, especially financial crises. In chapter 2 we discuss the evolution of the financial systems in five countries that we have chosen to focus on: the United States, United Kingdom, France, Germany, and Japan. In each country we see that market failures have shaped the evolution of the financial system. In some cases, the response has been to regulate financial markets; in others the response was to rely on banks and other institutions at the expense of markets.

Chapter 3 describes the current institutions and markets in these countries. The financial system in all countries transforms household savings into investment funds for firms, but the roles of financial markets and financial institutions differ in importance, as do the types of assets held by households. In the United States and the United Kingdom, households hold securities that are marked to market. In Germany and Japan, with their greater reliance on banks and other institutions, households hold fixed claims on financial institutions. As a result, one important difference among these countries is the extent to which households are exposed to risks originating in changes in market values. There are also features that are common to all the financial systems in these countries. One is the importance of internal finance: the amount of investment financed by retained earnings is much greater than that financed by external sources, regardless of the relative importance of markets and institutions.

In chapter 4 we discuss the different ways in which countries deal with the problem of corporate governance. The relative importance of financial markets and financial institutions makes a difference here too. In the United States and the United Kingdom, the market for corporate control is assumed to play an important part in disciplining managers and forcing high corporate performance. A company that is badly managed or underperforming can be taken over and the management replaced or the direction of the company changed. This mechanism is not actively used in other countries, however. In Germany, many companies are not publicly traded and those that are are controlled by block shareholdings, so hostile takeovers are difficult. In Japan, cross-shareholdings perform the same function of preventing hostile takeovers. An alternative suggestion is that close relationships with banks—the hausbank in Germany and the main bank in Japan—

provide a substitute for control by the market. Although there has been a lot of theoretical support for these ideas, the empirical evidence is weak. Nonetheless, each of these economies has performed well in spite of the ambivalent evidence of effective corporate governance.

In chapter 5 we review some attempts to build a more realistic theory by assuming that markets are perfectly competitive but incomplete. These models are of some value in understanding the limitations of financial markets. Ultimately, however, theories based on the absence of transaction costs, information problems, and other frictions are not a satisfactory representation of actual markets, and we have to consider new ways of modeling these frictions.

Having set the stage in part I, the rest of the book argues that financial institutions, intermediaries and firms, solve market failures and compensate for the limitations of financial markets. Any comparison of financial markets and financial institutions involves complex trade-offs. The current moves toward market-based financial systems may be desirable. In the period from 1865 to 1914, when the U.S. financial system was market based and unfettered by regulation, the United States went from having a gross domestic product (GDP) per head comparable to Germany and France but less than that of the United Kingdom, to being by far the richest country per capita in the world. On the other hand, the United States was beset with financial crises throughout this period. This instability did not cease until the regulations of the early 1930s were imposed in response to the Great Crash of 1929 and the banking crisis of 1933. There are other ways of dealing with market failures. The suppression of financial markets that has historically occurred in countries such as France and Germany has been one response. The strict regulation of the financial system that has occurred in the United States and the self-regulation that has been characteristic of the U.K. financial system are others. We seek to develop a fuller understanding of the attributes of different financial systems by examining these developments as a response to the limitations of financial markets.

1.3 Competition versus Risk Sharing

The ideal of competitive markets underlies the antitrust law and a good deal of economic policy in the United States. In financial markets, competition among investors and firms performs a number of roles. It ensures that risks are spread widely. It also ensures there is informational efficiency so assets are priced accurately and these prices provide effective signals for resource allocation. The theoretical foundation for competition policy comes from the classical theorems of welfare economics, which assume the ADM environment of complete markets, symmetric information, no agency problems, and so on, and from industrial organization theories that were originally developed with nonfinancial industries in mind. For many practical purposes the ADM setting is irrelevant, and the transposition of models from nonfinancial to financial settings begs the question of whether the financial sector works in the same way as the nonfinancial sector. When markets are imperfect in various ways, there are important trade-offs between competition and other objectives such as efficiency and stability. Since one of the frequent arguments in favor of financial markets is that they are more competitive than financial institutions, questioning whether competition is a good thing may lead one to question the value of markets.

In the banking sector, competition ensures that the banking industry operates efficiently and shares the returns of that efficiency among all sectors of the economy. As figure 1.1 indicates, the United States banking sector is the only one of the five that we investigate that is not dominated by a few large banks. The European countries developed concentrated nationwide banking systems with extensive branch networks in the nineteenth century. In contrast, the United States explicitly rejected this structure in the nineteenth century and has actively encouraged competition by regulation and antitrust law ever since. As we pointed out, the theoretical arguments for the competitive ideal are based on models that may not be appropriate in the financial sector, especially when imperfections such as asymmetric information, incompleteness of markets, and moral hazard are taken into account. The example of the European financial systems suggests that some countries at least have not been persuaded by the theoretical arguments.

In part II we reconsider a number of different aspects of competition in relation to financial markets and financial institutions. One of the most important functions of a financial system is to achieve an optimal allocation of risk bearing. One of the conditions for optimal risk sharing is that markets be "complete." Unfortunately, markets are not in reality complete and so we must seek a second-best solution.

As we document in chapter 3, one of the drawbacks of a market-based system is that investors are exposed to market risk, that is, fluctuations in asset values caused by changes in market information and investors' beliefs. Market-based systems (the United States and the

United Kingdom) expose households to more risk than do institution-based systems (Germany and Japan). This immediately raises the question of who bears the risk. The answer we provide in chapter 6 is that intermediaries can eliminate the risk through intertemporal smoothing, thus providing insurance to investors who would otherwise be forced to liquidate assets at disadvantageous prices.

This is an example of how the incompleteness of markets gives rise to a role for institutions. If markets were complete in the ADM sense, it would be possible for individual investors to insure themselves against this risk. Since markets are incomplete, there is a demand for risk sharing that can be provided by long-lived institutions. Second, even if there were markets, this risk is normally considered nondiversifiable. To eliminate the risk one needs not just markets for cross-sectional risk sharing but a different pattern of accumulation. If markets were complete, this accumulation of reserves would occur automatically in response to intertemporal prices. Since they are not complete, intermediaries must make these decisions instead.

In fact, financial markets can destroy risk-sharing opportunities. In markets, investors constantly rebalance their portfolios to earn the highest rate of return. Intertemporal smoothing requires that investors accept lower returns than the market offers in some periods in order to get higher returns in others. A financial institution that has to compete with financial markets will face disintermediation when the market return is higher than the smoothed return, even though the insurance provided by financial institutions would make everyone better off than they would be without it. Unless institutions can be shielded from competition, it may be impossible to offer welfare-improving insurance against fluctuations in market returns.

One of the arguments for markets is that they economize on and disseminate information that is needed for efficient decision making. Market-based financial systems are characterized by dispersed information (publicly traded companies are required to reveal more information than privately held companies), and dispersed shareholdings give a large number of people an incentive to gather information on firms and monitor their performance. These arguments seem to suggest that market-based financial systems, such as those in the United States and United Kingdom, have a clear informational advantage over intermediary-based systems, such as those in France and Germany. However, this advantage is not immediately clear from casual observations of these countries' financial systems. As we argue throughout, the situation is more complex when actual imperfections are taken account of. One of the drawbacks of market-based systems is the well known free-rider problem. If information is going to be revealed by the market, no one has an incentive to collect it. For this reason, competitive financial markets may be characterized by underinvestment in information. Intermediaries with block shareholdings, as in Germany, or close relationships with a small number of firms, as in Japan, may have a better incentive to gather information and monitor firms and can efficiently internalize the fixed costs of doing so. Whether they actually do so is another matter.

What these simple comparisons overlook is the fact that markets and intermediaries may be dealing in different kinds of information. What markets do well is to collect and aggregate diverse opinions. Intermediaries and other financial institutions can benefit from increasing returns to scale in processing standardized information, but may have less success dealing with uncertainty, innovation, and new ideas. The contrast between markets and intermediaries can be carried too far, however. We have already suggested that intermediaries may be necessary for the successful functioning of markets. Recent developments in venture capital firms and the private equity market blur the distinction between intermediaries and markets.

For all these reasons, explored in some detail in chapter 7, the comparison of markets and intermediaries and their informational properties is not easily resolved. Welfare analyses involving information are notoriously difficult, so it is not surprising that no straightforward conclusions can be drawn.

In chapter 8, we look at some issues of competition policy that arise in financial systems. U.S. policy for a long time actively discouraged the development of branch networks. This led to a very large number of small banks. It was argued this was desirable because it ensured that markets were competitive and banks had incentives to operate efficiently. We develop a model where depositors bear transaction costs of searching among banks. It is shown that taking account of these radically changes conventional results. In this case, the equilibrium with a multitude of single branch banks is the same as the monopoly equilibrium. In contrast, a duopoly with two large banks with extensive branch networks leads to the perfectly competitive solution. Another key issue is risk taking. It is well known that agency problems give rise to risk-shifting behavior. Competition may exacerbate these problems by increasing the incentives to "go for broke." In this sense, competition may increase the instability of the financial sector and create inefficiency through excessive risk taking.

There is also a tension between the goals of competition and stability. The U.S. financial system experienced frequent financial crises during the latter part of the nineteenth century and the early part of the twentieth century. This was not the case in Europe. Although frequent before this time, by the middle of the nineteenth century, the European central banks, and the Bank of England in particular, had developed their techniques of intervention to such an extent that banking panics were essentially eliminated.

Many historical financial crises were accompanied by recessions and depressions. The financial system plays a central role in the economy, and it came to be widely believed that financial systems are fragile in the sense that small shocks may start a contagion that eventually destabilizes the whole system. In the past, financial systems have been prone to periodic crises, and maintaining the stability of the system has often been one of the top priorities of financial policymakers. This sometimes leads to a mentality of maintaining stability at all costs, which may not be the optimal policy. In chapter 9 we initially study a model with banks alone in which optimal risk sharing actually requires crises in the banking system. The point here is that some shocks cannot be avoided, and the futile attempt to prevent an inevitable adjustment to one of these shocks will exacerbate the consequences of shocks and lead to a misallocation of risks.

This is not the end of the story, because this analysis is based on a financial system with banks alone. We go on to introduce markets for financial assets held by the banking system. Unfortunately, this innovation does nothing to remedy the situation. In fact, it makes it worse. Troubled intermediaries, seeking to find liquidity by selling their assets on the market, simply reduce the value of their assets, thereby making their problems worse. The mere existence of a market does not provide liquidity to the system as a whole, nor does it ensure that liquidity will be available to the banking sector on reasonable terms. We show that a central bank can intervene and prevent this type of collapse in prices. This intervention is welfare improving in the sense that it makes everybody better off.

Banking panics are not the only type of financial crisis that have been important historically. There are a number of historical episodes where the prices of stocks and real estate have risen to great heights and then collapsed dramatically. These collapses often appear to spill over into the real economy because people default and the collateral for loans is based on the peak asset prices. Recent examples of this type of incident are the bubbles and subsequent recessions in Japan, Finland, Norway, and Sweden. In the second part of chapter 9, we consider the role of monetary policy and the credit system in creating the conditions for a crisis. When asset purchases are financed by the financial system, it is possible for bubbles to be created, which then lead to the possibility of financial crises, since the assets on which the expansion of credit is based are overvalued and further expansion of credit may be necessary to sustain the value of these assets. When expansion stops, the bubble pops, and the financial system is left with losses that may threaten its stability. Unfortunately, both market-based and intermediary-based systems seem to be prone to these crises. Sensible regulation and credit policies are the only safeguard.

One way of distinguishing financial markets and financial intermediaries is by the kind of relationship that is formed when two parties enter into a financial transaction. In a market it is distant: once the security is issued and purchased, it is very difficult to change it. With an intermediary, it is more intimate: the number of parties is small (two), and this allows a contract to be adjusted as circumstances change. This may be an advantage or a disadvantage. When there are moral hazard problems, the commitment that dealing with a market allows may create an incentive for the agent to make better decisions ex ante. On the other hand, in a risk-sharing problem, continuous renegotiation may be a substitute for writing a very complex contract. These issues are discussed in chapter 10. We illustrate some of these ideas in a discussion of the U.S. private equity market. This "market" consists of limited partnerships that have some of the features of an intermediary.

1.4 The Role of the Firm

No discussion of the financial system of a country is complete without mentioning the corporate sector. The corporate sector provides many of the securities traded by the financial sector, and the returns to these securities depend on the performance of the companies that make up the corporate sector. The financial sector has a role in corporate governance because it allocates control rights and assists in the design of the securities that are used. It also provides information on company performance that guides managers and investors. Perhaps the most important reason for regarding the corporate sector as part of the financial system is that in the presence of imperfections in the financial sector, companies internalize financial tasks themselves. This is most obvious in internal finance, where the firm provides from its own resources the funds needed for investment rather than turning to external sources of finance. There are other ways in which the firm internalizes the functions of a financial institution, from diversification to hedging to corporate control. For all these reasons, no sharp line can be drawn between the theory of the firm and the theory of finance.

The theory of the firm that has been developed since the early 1980s stresses the agency relationship between owners and managers and poses the problem of controlling the manager as the central theoretical issue. As we have noted, a careful comparison of financial systems is not very supportive of existing governance theories. Markets for corporate control simply do not exist in some countries, and the evidence for the monitoring role of banks is weak. In addition, the reliance on internal finance in each of the countries underlines the fact that managers are largely autonomous of outside sources of finance. It seems that a theory of the firm as an autonomous entity is needed to complement the theory of the firm based on agency and corporate control.

Chapter 11 starts by considering why this kind of separation of ownership and control may in fact be desirable. External controls involve costs as well as benefits, and a certain degree of autonomy on the part of management may be beneficial for the firm. For example, if managers have superior information about the way in which the firm ought to be run, it may be optimal to give them free rein to make use of that information, even if the managers' interests are not perfectly aligned with those of the owners.

We typically think of the firm as one of the beneficiaries of the financial system, but not part of the financial system itself. However, in an imperfect world in which markets are incomplete and intermediaries suffer from agency problems, the firm itself can act as a financial institution. That is, it takes over the functions of a financial institution to compensate for the limitations of financial markets and financial intermediaries.

One example of this phenomenon is the role of internal finance. With complete markets, we can assume that firms pay all earnings to shareholders and that financial markets or intermediaries provide firms with the funds they need for investment. In practice, asymmetric information and agency costs restrict the role of external finance and make it a costly alternative to internally generated funds. Quantitatively, internal finance is a more important source of funds than debt or equity for investment. The problem with this state of affairs is that there is no reason to think that the resulting allocation of funds for investment is optimal. Firms that are cash rich may be poor in opportunities for investment and vice versa, so the external finance constraint appears to be a source of inefficiency. What this simple argument overlooks is the possibility that firms that have an excess of cash can acquire other firms and, conversely, that firms that have too little cash can sell themselves to those that have too much. In other words, the firm redefines itself to achieve a better allocation of resources and increase value. This kind of situation is considered in the second part of chapter 11.

Another justification for internal finance is the asymmetry of information between managers and shareholders. Even if managers' interests are not perfectly aligned with those of shareholders, it may still be second-best optimal to give managers a large amount of discretion in the running of the firm. The reason is simply that tying their hands through restrictive corporate governance procedures prevents them from exploiting their informational advantage on their own behalf, but it also prevents them from exploiting it on the behalf of shareholders as well. Shareholders may be better off allowing managers a free hand to appropriate some rents if they increase the value of the firm sufficiently. An example is presented in chapter 11.

In Japan, the separation of ownership and control is perhaps the most extreme. There are no hostile takeovers. Boards are large and ineffective and dominated by the president of the company. The banks intervene only when a firm is in financial distress. In many ways Japanese firms are like nonprofits in the United States. Despite this, many of these Japanese firms have been very successful over a long period of time. Toyota, Sony, and Matsushita, to name but a few, are world leaders in their industries. Moreover the shareholders in Japanese companies have done well in the long run. The return on the NRI 350 index (Nomura Research Institute stock market index of 350 Japanese stocks) since the early 1970s is about the same as the return on the Standard & Poor's 500 during that period. (From the first quarter of 1971 until the third quarter of 1995, the annual growth rate of the NRI 350 was 12.16 percent. Over the same period, the annual growth rate of the S&P 500 was 12.17 percent.) This same view of the firm as an independent entity is true in other countries, although perhaps to a lesser degree. As we document in chapter 4, in the United States the nonprofit sector is thriving and large, with nonprofits often successfully competing directly with for profits. Their external governance mechanism are weak or nonexistent, and yet they seem to operate fairly efficiently.

These examples provide a challenge to conventional theories of firms as profit-maximizing entities. In chapter 12 we consider a different approach. We see the firm as a self-organizing entity that can solve its own incentive problems. The firm is influenced by many groups of stakeholders—managers, shareholders, customers, suppliers, workers—and requires the cooperation of all these groups in order to succeed. Although different groups have different interests, they all have a common interest in the growth and prosperity of the firm. In chapter 12 we study some examples of ways in which the firm develops its own autonomous objectives that are not identifiable with those of any individual. Managers have to cooperate in running the firm, and by mutual monitoring can overcome the agency problems that have been the focus of the traditional literature on the manager-shareholder conflict. Instead of leading to shirking, this form of cooperative autonomy leads to farsighted concern with the success of the firm, because the welfare of each individual manager depends on being able to attract new, young managers into the firm, which is possible only if the firm has a viable future. This simple idea is an example of the way in which self-interested stakeholders are led to cooperate in behaviors that lead to success for the firm rather than myopic exploitation or rent seeking.

1.5 Intermediaries and Markets

The contrast between the U.S. and German financial systems suggests that markets and intermediaries are alternatives that perform more or less the same functions but in different ways and perhaps with different degrees of success. One important area in which they perform differently is where people have diversity of opinion and there is genuine disagreement about the optimum decision. One of the advantages of the market, discussed in chapter 13, is that it allows investors to agree to disagree. Economizing on information through the delegated monitoring inherent in intermediation inevitably requires investors to submerge their disagreements and accept a compromise, one that may not satisfy most of them. As a result, markets may have a significant advantage over intermediaries in situations where diversity of opinion is important, such as the financing of new technologies. However, in general, the more one examines the limitations of markets and the reasons that markets are used in some situations and not in others, the less adequate the either-or perspective appears. In fact, it appears that intermediaries are becoming increasingly essential to the efficient exploitation of increasingly complex markets.

The tremendous innovation in financial markets that has occurred in the past two decades in the United States and the explosion in the volume of trade that followed has been narrowly focused. Essentially it has been providing better risk-sharing opportunities for financial institutions (and their customers). This is not surprising when one considers the expertise that is needed to operate in these markets, but it is hard to reconcile with the traditional theory of asset markets. To put it another way, the familiar advice, "If you don't understand it, don't buy it," is hard to reconcile with the standard model of expected utility-maximizing behavior. The traditional theory builds in so much information along with its standard rationality postulates that an investor with rational expectations would want to participate in all of these markets. On the other hand, we do not necessarily want to drop the rationality assumption as an organizing principle. This presents us with a dilemma.

Chapter 14 develops an approach to model the informational costs of using markets and to explain in terms of rational behavior, but somewhat nonstandard informational structures, why markets are costly to use and why participation in these markets is limited as a result.

The role of intermediaries, then, is to make it possible for individuals to gain some of the benefits of markets without bearing prohibitive costs. Part of this can be done by economizing on the costs of acquiring information. This can be seen as the traditional advising role of intermediaries. The intermediary acquires information at a fixed cost and then shares it with its customers at a nominal marginal cost. But this transmission may not be the most important role of intermediaries. Much of the information is hard to transmit, and if the intermediary takes on the role of agent for the customer and makes decisions on his behalf, there is the problem of how the intermediary knows what is good for the customer without the latter's understanding how the market works. One possibility is that intermediaries can repackage securities in a way that requires less information to evaluate. Another is that intermediaries can make implicit contracts with customers to ensure them against some of the uncertainty they face in trading an unfamiliar security. These ideas are explored in chapter 15.

1.6 Trade-offs

A number of themes tie the book together. One is that the same functions may be performed by quite different markets or institutions in different countries, so one has to look at the financial system as a whole in order to get an idea of how well the system performs these functions.

Another theme concerns the tension between the (ex post) efficiency associated with competitive financial markets and the superior risk sharing associated with financial systems based on large financial institutions. In order for financial markets to exist, there has to be a certain amount of depth—that is, large numbers of traders and a large volume of trade. These are circumstances in which competition flourishes. Financial markets are attractive because they minimize the role of the middleman and provide the best terms to those providing investment funds and those trying to raise funds. Firms and individuals who deal with a financial institution are often at a disadvantage, however, because of differences in size or because of the holdup problems that arise from asymmetric information in a long-term relationship.

The drawback of market-based financial systems is that markets are incomplete. There are fixed costs of setting up markets, which can be recovered only when a minimum critical size is reached, so many small markets are not viable. Other markets are not viable because of asymmetric information, moral hazard, or something else. Financial systems based on institutions can overcome these problems by offering made-to-measure risk-sharing contracts. Furthermore, there is a sense in which incomplete financial markets actually expose individuals and firms to greater risk, because assets that are marked to market may fluctuate for reasons that have little or nothing to do with their fundamentals. In fact, financial institutions, by avoiding the use of markets, may be able to offer risk-smoothing services that markets cannot. Finally, competition from markets may undermine the risk sharing that institutions offer, since there will be states of nature in which the returns offered on the market diverge from those offered by institutions engaged in offering risk-sharing contracts. Then there will be disintermediation, which may prevent the coexistence of competitive markets and institutions, so there are a number of trade-offs between the (ex post) efficiency of financial markets and the risk sharing provided by financial institutions.

Another theme concerns the tension between the competitiveness of financial systems characterized by financial markets and an unconcentrated banking sector and the stability of financial systems characterized by a few dominant institutions. Competition among banks may lead to risk-taking behavior because banks are fighting for market share (which introduces nonconvexities into their preferences) or because it lowers profit margins, reducing the value of future earnings and the associated incentive to avoid bankruptcy. Also, the presence of markets for assets, which offers helpful liquidity when an individual bank suffers a small shock, may turn into a disadvantage when it forces banks to liquidate assets at fire-sale prices, thus reducing asset values and worsening the position of depositors compared to a situation in which the banks' assets were relatively illiquid. Similarly, competition may require large numbers of small banks, which are more prone to financial contagion. These are just some of the ways in which a financial system that encourages competition may incur costs that can be avoided in a bank-based or institution-based system.

Information plays a central role in many of the topics we discuss. Markets and intermediaries deal with information in different ways. Markets are known to be effective mechanisms for aggregating information; intermediaries economize on the costs of gathering information by replacing many monitors with one delegated monitor. Which is more effective depends on the kind of information that is being acquired. Intermediaries may be more effective in eliminating duplication of information gathering and processing, which is likely to be relevant when everyone agrees on what information needs to be collected and how it should be processed. But there are also situations in which individuals agree to disagree, and everyone has to make up his or her own mind. This may be the case when new technologies are being evaluated or when a unique decision has to be made. Competitive markets may be better at dealing with this kind of information.

Another theme is the autonomy of the modern corporation. One of the major concerns of corporate finance is the design of mechanisms for corporate control—in other words, how to make managers do what shareholders want. Markets and banks can provide corporate oversight, but firms themselves can develop structures to solve the oversight problem. We argue that in some cases, external control may not be optimal. In any case, some degree of autonomy seems to be the norm and does not appear to be incompatible with success.

When external sources of finance do not provide the firm with all the funds it needs, the firm can resort to self-finance. This is often regarded as a bad thing. Either the cost of self-finance is greater than the cost of obtaining funds in the market or self-finance is seen as symptomatic of an agency problem, because the manager is undertaking investment that the market does not want to finance. We know there are conditions under which external sources provide efficient finance, but these are restrictive. The fact that internal finance is so dominant in many successful economies suggests that it may be optimal under certain circumstances. In this sense, the firm can be regarded as a "financial" institution that overcomes the limitations of financial markets in the same way that intermediaries do.

A final theme concerns the role of intermediaries in making markets work. We have stressed the advantages of financial institutions as if they were a substitute for markets, but one of their most important functions is a supporting role. Markets are a wonderful invention, but they require a great deal of sophistication on the part of investors. When the participation costs of acquiring information are substantial, the second-best solution may be to develop alternative institutions that economize on the participation costs. In this book, we try to find a way of thinking about the informational and other barriers to using markets effectively. Intermediaries are one of the solutions. In the end, it is not a question of markets *versus* intermediaries but rather of markets *and* intermediaries.

A comparison of different types of financial system is complex, and there are no simple answers. A wide range of different systems is observed in practice, each with advantages and disadvantages. What is important in analyzing financial systems is understanding the major trade-offs. Figure 1.2 shows the ones that we have emphasized. We can see the different financial systems of the United States and Germany as two extremes. The United States has a competitive, market-based system, which is prone to instability. Large amounts of information are disseminated publicly, but the free-rider problem blunts the incentives to gather the information. The market for corporate control imposes some external restraints. At the other extreme is Germany, with a concentrated, intermediary-based financial system that provides risk sharing and stability. Not much information is disseminated publicly, but the private incentives to gather information are large because the free-rider problem is eliminated. Finally, the external constraints on firms

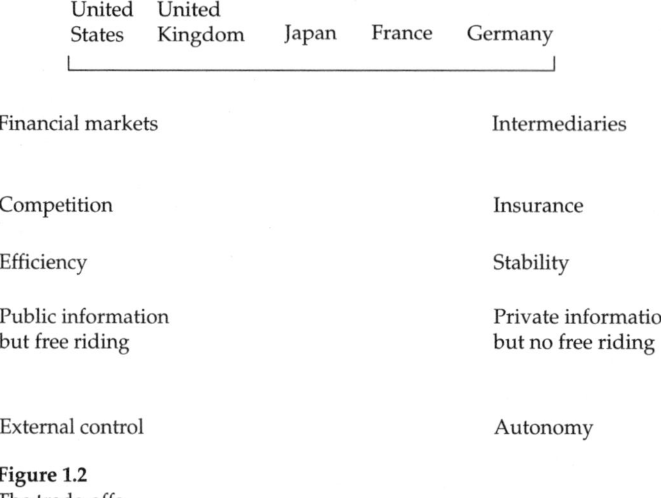

Figure 1.2
The trade-offs

are probably weaker than in the United States, and this gives firms greater autonomy. The other countries lie in between. The United Kingdom is close to the United States in terms of its reliance on markets but differs in its tolerance of concentration in the financial sector and the relative laxness of its regulatory environment. Japan and France are closer to Germany in their tolerance of concentration, lack of reliance on markets, and weakness of external mechanisms of governance. Finally, it is likely to be a combination of markets *and* intermediaries that are important everywhere as markets become increasingly sophisticated.

By historical accident, much of the academic research on financial systems has been undertaken in the United States and United Kingdom. This has perhaps led to a bias toward market systems. At the very least we hope that this book will convince readers that the study of comparative financial systems and the role of institutions in overcoming market failures is important, and there is no theoretical presumption that intermediated systems are inferior.

References

Baliga, S., and B. Polak. (1995). "Banks versus Bonds: A Simple Theory of Comparative Financial Institutions." Cowles Foundation working paper No. 1100, Yale University.

Bhattacharya, S., and G. Chiesa. (1995). "Financial Intermediation with Proprietary Information." *Journal of Financial Intermediation* **4,** 328–357.

Boot, A., and A. Thakor, (1997a). "Financial System Architecture." *Review of Financial Studies* **10,** 693–733.

———. (1997b). "Banking Scope and Financial Innovation." *Review of Financial Studies* **10,** 1099–1131.

Freixas, X., and J. Rochet. (1997). *Microeconomics of Banking*. Cambridge, MA: MIT Press.

Hauswald, R. (1995). "Financial Contracting, Reorganization and Mixed Finance: A Theory of Banking Systems." Working paper, University of Maryland.

Hubbard, R. G. (1998). "Capital Market Imperfections and Investment." *Journal of Economic Literature* **36,** 193–225.

Levine, R. (1997). "Financial Development and Economic Growth: Views and Agenda." *Journal of Economic Literature* **35,** 688–726.

Melitz, J. (1990). "Financial Deregulation in France." *European Economic Review* **34,** 394–402.

2 The Historical Development of Financial Systems

The development of a financial system is essential to permit economies to exploit the gains from trade fully. Without a financial system, goods must be bartered on spot markets, and each family has to finance capital accumulation from its own resources, an extreme case of internal finance. As financial systems become more developed, more of the gains from trade can be captured, including the benefits from risk sharing, diversification, insurance, intertemporal smoothing, an efficient allocation of investment within and across industries, larger-scale investment opportunities, and regional and international trade. This chapter briefly describes the historical development of financial systems and provides an institutional background for the subsequent analysis.

2.1 Early Financial Systems

One of the earliest financial systems was developed in Mesopotamia. This financial system gradually increased in sophistication from the third to the middle of the first millennium B.C.[1] Initially barley and silver served as a means of payment and unit of account. Over time silver was increasingly used and by the seventh century B.C. had become the sole money. Loans were made during this period by landowners and merchants, as well as temples and royal treasuries, for consumption needs and providing seeds for planting. If a borrower defaulted, he or his family could be forced into the servitude of the lender. Barley and silver were deposited for safekeeping with certain families, but the deposits were not relent to others, so the families were not bankers in the modern sense.

The Greeks, and in particular the Athenians, created a financial system that went beyond having a means of payment and simple loans. This financial system started to develop around the sixth century B.C.

and reached substantial refinement by the fourth century B.C. Silver coins were used as the means of payment. The main financial institutions were money changers and banks. There were numerous different types of coin from other Greek cities and Persia in circulation, which created the need for money changers. Banks that accepted deposits and made loans began to operate in the late fifth century B.C. Loans were usually made for consumption and were secured by valuables. As for financial instruments, there were some mortgages. There were also "bottomry loans," a combination of a loan and an insurance contract, that provided a method of financing foreign trade. The provider would supply funds to finance a voyage; in the event of a shipwreck or some other catastrophe, repayment was waived. These loans thus had some of the characteristics of equity. To prevent fraud, the lender or one of his representatives often went on the voyage.

The financial system of the Roman empire during the first centuries B.C. and A.D. was more advanced than that of Athens in some dimensions. Gold and silver coins were used, and the geographical extent of the empire meant that money changers played an important role. There were money lenders who made consumption loans to the wealthy who were living beyond their means, to the poor, and to small farmers who had had a temporary setback. Bankers took deposits, made loans, and transferred coins within the empire. The other type of financial institutions that existed at this time were tax-farm companies, which groups of wealthy individuals formed in order to collect taxes on behalf of the government. The most important financial instruments were mortgage loans, consumer loans, and loans from landlords to tenants. Bottomry loans also played an important part in financing seaborne trade.

These early examples illustrate the important characteristics of the first stage of development of financial systems:

- Financial instruments are limited to precious metals or metallic coins.
- Loans are made to individuals with consumption needs, to allow agricultural production, and to finance trade.
- Financial intermediaries are limited to money changers, money lenders, and banks.

Financial systems did not go beyond this first stage until the thirteenth century A.D. During medieval times, international trade in western Europe was conducted in fairs that were held every few months. Among the well-known ones were those at Champagne, Geneva, and

Besançon.[2] At these fairs payments were originally made by barter, precious metals, or bullion. The next stage was the development of a system in which each merchant would record claims and liabilities arising during the fair. At the end of the fair, an official would validate the claims and liabilities recorded. This system considerably reduced the exchange of bulky coins since only net payments had to be made.

In the thirteenth century, the Northern Italians took this clearing of books one step further and developed bills of exchange, a debt instrument drawn on the buyer of goods that promised payment of a specified amount in the buyer's home town at some date in the future. In the simplest case, it could be sold for cash by the seller to another trader who needed funds for purchases in the buyer's home town. In more complicated cases, there could be a whole chain of transactions in a variety of different places before the bill of exchange eventually returned to the original issuer. The prohibition on usury imposed by the Roman Catholic church meant that bills of exchange could not be discounted. To get around this problem, the exchange rate specified in the transaction was usually such that there was a de facto discount. The innovation of bills of exchange was a great success and helped to spur the development of banks in the modern sense.

It was in Tuscany, in particular in Florence, Siena, and Lucca, that banks were first established after the Middle Ages; they subsequently spread to Venice and Genoa. These banks became skilled in transferring the monies associated with international trade and the Roman Catholic church and spread networks throughout Europe. Banking practices developed substantially during this early period. In the fourteenth century, the Bardi and Peruzzi banks of Florence grew to substantial size. They helped to finance the English side of the Hundred Years' War but were bankrupted when Edward III defaulted on them in 1348. In the fifteenth century, the Medici bank of Florence reached a level of sophistication that was not surpassed until the nineteenth century.

Other characteristics of modern financial systems also developed in Northern Italy at this time. Maritime insurance became important, and other types of insurance such as life insurance were introduced. Double-entry accounting systems were developed. Some governments such as that of the Florentine Republic borrowed significant amounts, and the debt claims against them were transferable. To a limited extent, partnerships and companies issued equity-like instruments, some of which were traded. Thus, the second stage of financial development was reached:

• Financial instruments are more varied and include trade credit, mortgages, and government and corporate securities.

• Financial institutions include early types of bank and insurance companies.

• Trading of government and corporate claims is limited and occurs in informal markets.

Florence, the premier financial center in the fourteenth and fifteenth centuries, lost this role in the 1520s when Francis I of France seized Florentine property in Paris, Lyons, and Bordeaux in 1521 and then defaulted on Florentine bankers in 1529. Venice took over for a short time until 1557, when Genoa replaced it. In 1620 Northern Italy ceased to be the major center for trade and banking, and Amsterdam started a long period of financial dominance. These changes in the relative importance of financial centers were usually caused by financial crises that were triggered by a default due to a war or some other political incident, rather than natural events such as a bad harvest or an epidemic of disease.

Two important developments occurred in Amsterdam that helped it to establish its preeminence: the establishment of an organized stock market as part of the Amsterdam Bourse and the founding of the Bank of Amsterdam, which became a model for public banks set up by governments. The Amsterdam Bourse had its own specialized building from 1608 onward. Initially it was primarily a market for commodities, and the market for securities was relatively unimportant. The only company issues traded were those of the United East India Company and West India Company; the other securities were government debt of various types. Nevertheless, the market soon developed sophisticated trading practices. De la Vega (1688) described the use of options and futures contracts and indicated that trading was fairly active.

The Amsterdam Bourse was an important institutional development because it contained the first formal stock exchange. Prior to that, securities had been traded in informal markets. Interestingly, one reason the Bourse became renowned was because of the tulip mania of 1636–1637, when the prices of tulips rose quickly to enormous heights before collapsing dramatically. It caused considerable disruption because many speculators had borrowed the funds for their investment and went bankrupt.

The Bank of Amsterdam, established in 1609, was not the first public bank but was patterned after the Bank of Venice, which was founded in 1587.[3] Its main purpose was to facilitate payments. All bills of exchange over 600 florins had to be paid at the bank from accounts based on guilders of constant silver content. It did not make loans except occasionally to the City of Amsterdam, the province of Holland, and the United East India Company. Deposits paid no interest but were guaranteed by the City of Amsterdam. The bank was an instant success. Most large merchants in Amsterdam and many foreign merchants had accounts there because of the ease of payment that the bank allowed. It essentially became a clearing-house for European international trade because of the importance of bills of exchange drawn on it.

The Bank of Amsterdam was a public bank; it took deposits and made exchanges, but it did not provide credit except occasionally. Adam Smith asserted, apparently correctly for much of its history, that for every guilder circulated as bank money, there was a guilder on deposit at the bank. In 1614 the City of Amsterdam founded the Bank of Lending, which was authorized to make loans. Although it did not flourish, it did provide a precedent for the Bank of Sweden, which was founded in 1656 and taken over by the Swedish government in 1668.[4] This was important because it was the first central bank. It was divided into two departments: the exchange department, which operated like the Bank of Amsterdam with 100 percent reserves, and the lending department, which was responsible for loans and did not have full reserves. The Bank of Sweden was also the first bank to issue bank notes. It had a strong incentive to do this; its specie reserves were copper, an extremely cumbersome means of payment. By the beginning of the eighteenth century, the third stage of financial systems had been developed:

- Financial markets are more formalized.
- Governments are more involved in financial systems through institutions such as central banks.

The years 1719–1720 were a watershed for the development of financial systems because of the occurrence of two interlinked events: the South Sea Bubble in England and the Mississippi Bubble in France. It can be argued that it was these events, and the differing long-term reaction to them in the two countries, that led to the development of two distinctly different types of financial system: the stock market–oriented Anglo-Saxon model and the bank-oriented continental European model.

2.2 Market-oriented Systems

Both the United Kingdom and the United States developed stock market–oriented systems, although the banking systems in the two countries have different histories resulting from different traditions concerning the concentration of power.

The United Kingdom

Prior to the end of the seventeenth century, the financial system in the United Kingdom had not developed beyond the second stage. There were informal markets for government debt and for the securities of the few corporations that then existed. In 1694 the Bank of England was founded, to help the government market debt to finance the Nine Years' War with the French, ongoing since 1688. Unlike the Bank of Amsterdam and other similar banks in Europe, which were usually government owned, the Bank of England was a private institution whose purpose was to make a profit. Initially it provided the government with £1.2 million in exchange for an annual interest payment of £100,000. It was also authorized to issue bank notes to serve as a substitute for gold in large transactions.

In 1711 the South Sea Company was set up, ostensibly to undertake trade in the South (Atlantic) Sea. It also provided competition to the Bank of England by undertaking to fund a portion of the government's debt in exchange for a payment to the company. In the first six months of 1720, the stock of the South Sea Company became the focus of feverish speculation, and its price rose more than sevenfold. This dramatic rise led to a large number of other stock issues by promoters who also hoped to profit from price appreciation. At the height of the speculation in June 1720, the Bubble Act was passed, designed to prevent these other promotions from diverting resources away from the South Sea Company. It tried to do this by making it necessary to have a royal charter, which could be obtained only by an act of Parliament, to form a joint stock company. The Bubble Act did not prevent a dramatic fall in the price of South Sea stock, and by the end of the year, it was not much above the level it had started the year at. As in the Amsterdam Bourse's tulip mania of the previous century, many who had borrowed to speculate on the price rise were bankrupted by the sudden fall.

The aftermath of the bubble lasted for many years. In particular, the Bubble Act was not repealed until 1824, and until then it had the effect of creating a barrier to company formation. Only a few companies in addition to the Bank of England, the South Sea Company, and the East India Company were traded in the London capital markets. The companies that were formed under the Bubble Act, such as the canal companies, mostly traded in informal markets in the provincial cities.

Although the London capital market did not develop as a source of funds for companies, it did become an important source of funds for the government. The English fought many wars during the eighteenth and early nineteenth centuries, and the need to finance these led to a financial revolution. Dickson (1967) has argued that the ability of the English to fund their government debt so effectively was an important factor in allowing them to defeat the French regularly for over a century despite the fact that the population of England was roughly a third that of France. The sophistication that the London capital markets developed as a result of this financial revolution allowed London to take over from Amsterdam as the major financial center at the end of the eighteenth century.

The London Stock Exchange was founded in 1802. As the nineteenth century progressed, the importance of the London Stock Exchange as a source of funds for companies steadily increased. The repeal of the Bubble Act in 1824 and the freedom to form companies without specific parliamentary approval, introduced in 1856, resulted in a significant expansion of the number of publicly listed firms. The development of the railways in Britain and the rest of the world and the large demand for capital that resulted were also an important contributory factor to the growth of the exchange.

The banking system also developed dramatically in the nineteenth century. For some time after its foundation in 1694, the Bank of England had to compete with other institutions for its privileges at the periodic renewal of its charter. In 1742 it was granted a monopoly over note issue in England except for private banks. These private banks fell into two groups: the London banks, based in London, and the country banks, based outside London. Because of the Bank of England's role, London became the clearing center for the nation, so country banks needed to have London branches. In order to compete, London banks needed to have branches outside the capital. As the nineteenth century progressed, banks consolidated into nationwide networks. By the beginning of the twentieth century there were essentially five major national banks.

One important characteristic of the banking system that developed was that it did not engage in long-term lending to industry. It frequently provided short-term loans and on occasion rolled these over. Some banks lent to industry during the first part of the nineteenth century, but these usually did not survive the periodic liquidity crises. Instead industry relied on internal finance and markets for raising funds. For small firms, the informal market of family and friends was particularly significant; for large firms, stock exchanges were.

The Bank of England came to play an increasingly important role in guaranteeing the stability of the banking system during the nineteenth century. The last true panic was the Overend, Gurney and Company crisis of 1866. After that time, it was clear that the Bank of England would step in and provide the necessary liquidity in times of crisis, and systemic runs were subsequently avoided.

Although the events of World War I resulted in New York's replacing London as the major financial center, the United Kingdom has remained a stock market–oriented financial system. It is also the location of the offices of a very large number of foreign banks that participate in the various Euro markets. Domestically, the banking system remains highly concentrated, with nationwide branching networks, and does not lend long term to industry.

The United States

The United States has rather a different banking history than most other industrialized countries do. As Roe (1994) and others have documented, the reasons are largely due to a different political history. Alexander Hamilton was influenced by British experience with the Bank of England and after the Revolution advocated a large federally chartered bank with branches all over the country. This led to the foundation of the First Bank of the United States (1791–1811) and later the Second Bank of the United States (1816–1836). There was considerable distrust of the concentration of power these institutions represented. In a report on the Second Bank, John Quincy Adams wrote, "Power for good, is power for evil, even in the hands of Omnipotence."[5] The controversy came to a head in the debate on the rechartering of the Second Bank in 1832. Although Congress passed the bill, President Jackson vetoed it, and the veto was not overturned. Since then, there has been a strong bias toward decentralization of the banking system and an aversion to powerful institutions of any kind.

Throughout the nineteenth century the U.S. banking system was highly fragmented. Unlike every other industrializing country, the United States failed to develop nationwide banks with extensive branch networks. Prior to the Civil War, states were free to regulate their own banking systems, and there was no national system. Many states adopted a "free banking" system, which allowed free entry. There were serious banking panics in 1837 and 1857, both followed by depressions and significant economic disruption.

The Civil War, which began in 1861, and the need to finance it significantly changed the role of the federal government in the financial system. The National Bank Acts of 1863 and 1864 set up a national banking system and granted limited powers to banks. In particular, the 1864 act was interpreted as confining each to a single location. When the question of whether banks could hold equity arose, the Supreme Court ruled that since the 1864 act had not specifically granted this right, they could not.

The creation of the national banking system did not prevent the problem of panics and the associated economic disruption and depressions. There were panics in 1873, 1884, 1893 and 1907. After the crisis of 1907, a European banker summed up European frustration with the inefficiencies of the U.S. banking system by declaring the United States was "a great financial nuisance."[6] Finally, in 1913 the federal reserve system was created.

The organization of the federal reserve system differed from that of a traditional central bank like the Bank of England. It had a regional structure and decentralized decision-making power. During the years after its creation, it did not develop the ability to prevent banking panics. In 1933 another major banking panic led to the closing of banks for an extended period just after Roosevelt took office. The problems of the banking system led to the Glass-Steagall Act of 1933, which introduced deposit insurance and required the separation of commercial and investment banking operations. The Banking Act of 1935 extended the powers of the federal reserve system and changed the way it operated. These reforms finally eliminated the occurrence of banking panics almost seventy years after this had happened in the United Kingdom.

Just as wars between England and France in the eighteenth century helped to develop the London capital markets, the U.S. Civil War helped to develop New York's markets. In addition, the prohibition on banks' holding equity under the Supreme Court's interpretation of the National Bank Act of 1864 and the general weakness of the banking system helped to strengthen the role of financial markets. During World War I, the part that the New York markets played in financing all parties, but particularly the British and the French, ensured that New York supplanted London as the leading financial center. During the four years leading up to 1917, the United States went from being a net debtor of between $3 billion and $4 billion to a net creditor of $5 billion. Great Britain had taken many centuries to achieve a similar position.[7]

The Great Crash of 1929, like the South Sea and Mississippi bubbles two centuries before, had a significant effect on the development of U.S. markets. Although it led to the creation of the Securities and Exchange Commission (SEC) and the regulation of financial markets, the importance of markets was in the end increased. The Glass-Steagall Act together with continuing support for restrictions on interstate banking ensured that banks were restricted even more than markets. It can also be argued that the creation of the SEC helped to ensure the integrity of the markets. Continued financial innovation in terms of the introduction of organized options and financial futures markets has helped to strengthen the market orientation of the U.S. financial system.

Although the crash of 1987 was of greater magnitude than that of 1929, it did not have an effect on the real economy. Nevertheless, it does illustrate that crises can still occur in financial markets even though banking panics appear to have been eliminated.

2.3 Bank-Oriented Systems

The reaction to the Mississippi Bubble in France, which occurred at about the same time as the South Sea Bubble, was also the introduction of heavy regulation of the stock market. Whereas the United Kingdom repealed the Bubble Act at the beginning of the nineteenth century, the French did not ease restrictions on stock markets until the 1980s (see chapter 3). Their experience has substantially affected the development of financial systems in continental Europe. This section starts by considering the French financial system from the Mississippi Bubble onward and then considers developments in Germany and other European countries and Japan.

France

The Mississippi Bubble was intimately connected to the activities of a Scotsman, John Law, who had been forced to leave Scotland after killing the husband of his mistress in a duel. He developed proposals for a bank that could issue notes without 100 percent reserves and went around the capitals of Europe trying to persuade governments to adopt them. Eventually, in 1716, he persuaded the French regent to allow him to undertake this scheme. The Bank Générale, set up soon after, opened branches in the provinces and made a limited note issue. In 1718, the bank was reorganized as the Banque Royale and given the right to issue notes, with the only limit being set by the regent rather than the level of reserves. It was subsequently merged with the Compagnie d'Occident (the Louisiana or Mississippi Company). Similarly to the South Sea Company, shares in this merged entity became the subject of intense speculation. Their price rose in a spectacular fashion before crashing dramatically.

France's experience with the Mississippi Bubble profoundly affected the subsequent development of the stock market and banks. After the collapse, an official Bourse was set up to allow the market in company shares to be regulated. The French Revolution led to the closing of the Bourse and the suppression of public companies. Although the Bourse subsequently reopened, markets for company securities did not develop significantly through the nineteenth century and most of the twentieth. An example of the Paris Bourse's lack of sophistication in this regard was the fact that the first bonds to finance French railways were issued between 1842 and 1845 on the London Stock Exchange. Not until it became clear that the bonds were bought primarily by French investors were subsequent issues made in Paris. However, bonds were much less important and banks much more important in providing funds for railways than in the United Kingdom. Another factor impeding the development of stock markets was the ease with which the French press could be bribed. This made it difficult for investors to obtain objective information and made manipulation a severe problem.

John Law's Banque Royale severely retarded the development of banks for many years. One indication of this was the reluctance of subsequent institutions to use the title "bank." With the exception of the Bank of France, the central bank founded in 1800, banks used the terms *caisse*, *crédit*, *société*, or *comptoire* in their official names.

In 1838 Jacques Laffite, a former governor of the Bank of France, founded the Caisse Générale du Commerce et de L'Industrie. Its purpose was to lend long term to industry. It failed in 1848, a year after Laffite's death, but the idea was resurrected by the Pereire brothers with the support of Louis Napoleon. In 1852, shortly after Louis Napoleon became emperor of the Second Empire, they opened the Crédit Mobilier, which played a large part in financing French railways and other public works. Economic historians have hailed it as "a major innovation and discontinuity in the finance of not only France but of Europe as a whole" (Kindleberger 1993, p. 111). Cameron (1961) emphasized that it served as the prototype for industrial banks in Germany and the rest of Europe.

Other banks were set up around this time by the government to lend to specific sectors and fill gaps in the credit structure. The Crédit Foncier (1852) and the Société de Crédit Agricole (1860) were formed to provide lending for building and agriculture. Deposit banks such as Crédit Lyonnais (1863) were also formed during this period to provide loans to industry. They fairly rapidly developed branch networks throughout France.

Although these institutions had as their initial aim the provision of loans for industry, they ended up to varying degrees providing short-term commercial loans to firms and speculating in foreign bonds. It was in Germany that the system of banks lending to industry took deeper root.

Germany

Unlike Britain and France, Germany was politically fragmented during most of the nineteenth century. Prior to its unification in 1871, it was made up of at least thirty principalities, republics, and kingdoms, which ranged in size from cities like Frankfurt to large states like Prussia. At the beginning of the nineteenth century, there were at least four major financial centers in Germany: Frankfurt, Cologne, Hamburg, and Berlin. The most important financial institutions at this time were family-dominated private banks: the Rothschilds in Frankfurt, the Oppenheims in Cologne, Heine and Warburg in Hamburg, and Bleichröder in Berlin.

Joint stock banks were not introduced until the middle of the nineteenth century, when the Schaffhausen'schen bank was created in Prussia in 1848 and given wide powers. There followed a wave of bank formation building on this model from 1850 to 1857, halted by a financial crisis in 1857, but with a second wave from 1866 to 1873, spurred by the unification of the country and the creation of a single currency. Many of the German bankers of this period had spent time in France and were influenced by the French experience with the Crédit Mobilier.

Thus, the Dresdener bank was specifically set up to pursue industrial lending. Other banks, such as the Commerzbank of Hamburg and the Deutsche Bank of Berlin, were set up to help provide finance for foreign trade but soon turned to financing industry when they found it difficult to challenge the dominance of the British and the French in the international arena.

Financial markets in Germany were undeveloped at this time relative to those in Britain. Joint stock companies were rare in Germany prior to 1850. The markets that did exist, primarily in Frankfurt and Berlin, were mostly for various forms of government debt, for loans to princes, towns, and foreign states. The financial market in Berlin did play some role in financing German railways, but this did not develop into extensive financing of industry.

Links between banks and industry grew substantially during this period. Banks were represented on the boards of companies, and industrialists held seats on the boards of banks. This interlinkage was widespread but not universal. Some firms like Thyssen and Stinnes in the iron and steel industry and some industries such as chemicals avoided this type of involvement. Most firms, though, relied primarily on bank financing and internal finance. Presumably the existence of cartels in many industries (which were legal at this time) enhanced the profitability of firms and made internal finance that much easier. The close relationship between banks and firms led to the development of the hausbank system, where firms form a long-term relationship with a particular bank and use them for most of their financing needs. There is a continuing debate over how much control banks had over these companies, and it appears that their influence varied from firm to firm.

From the second wave of bank formation around the time of unification until the beginning of the twentieth century, German banks formed national networks just as in England and France. If anything, this process went somewhat more quickly than elsewhere.

The great industrial banks were not the only ones that developed during the nineteenth century. The Landschaften (land companies) were created as mortgage banks in Prussia in the first decades of the century. These banks are not profit maximizing but are operated in the public interest, with boards appointed by local and regional governments. Cooperative banks were set up around the middle of the century to provide rural credit for peasants and to help small shopkeepers and tradesmen and are operated in the interest of depositors. These institutions have formed a significant part of the German banking system from the time of their foundation.

Considerable disruption was caused by the Allies' attempt to break up the large German banks at the end of World War II. These attempts were ultimately unsuccessful. The different units reunited after the occupation ended, and the pattern of big banks intimately tied to industry and financial markets playing an insignificant role, except for government debt, soon resumed. The isolation of Berlin did mean that the financial center shifted from Berlin to Frankfurt, though.

The relative importance of banks and financial markets in Germany has to be viewed in the context of another fact: that relatively few companies are publicly traded. A very large part of the equity in Germany is privately held by wealthy families.

Other European Countries

In continental Europe, the nineteenth-century French and German examples were more influential than those of England and the United States. Spain followed the French system when the Bank of Isabella II was founded in 1844, patterned after Jacques Laffitte's Caisse Générale. After a bout of stock speculation and a financial crisis in 1847, legislation was passed that made the formation of joint stock companies much more difficult and thus deterred the use of markets for the finance of industry. In 1856 a credit company act allowed the development of banks structured like the Crédit Mobilier, and the Pereire brothers formed a Credito Mobiliaro. A number of other French-financed banks were set up, as well as many domestically financed ones. These banks provided the funds for the development of railways in Spain during the boom of 1854–1866. The investments were not successful because industry did not develop in tandem. After the railways were built, they were not used very much because of a lack of demand for moving freight and passengers.

Italy saw two waves of formation of foreign banks during the nineteenth century. In the 1860s these were mainly French subsidiaries, and in the 1890s they were German. The investments made in the 1860s were not very successful, whereas those in the 1890s were, and Italy advanced substantially. Capital markets did not develop very much at all during this period. When the foreign banks faced domestic crises and withdrew, they left a lack of domestic institutions to provide finance. After World War I, the Italian government stepped in to fill the void and used the Istituto per la Ricostuzione Industriale (IRI, or Italian Reconstruction Finance Corporation) to help provide finance for industry. The state has played an important role in providing funds for Italian industry ever since.

In northern Europe, the German system was the most influential. In Austria, Switzerland, and Sweden, German-style banks developed close ties with industry. In Sweden one interesting difference was that most capital invested in banks was in the form of long-term deposits rather than short-term deposits that were rolled over. In all these countries, financial markets were primarily for government debt.

Japan

The German and Japanese financial systems are often mentioned together as having typical bank-based financial systems when these are contrasted with Anglo-Saxon market-based systems. In fact the historical development of the two countries' financial systems and the role of the government has been significantly different. In Germany, the hausbank system developed in the private sector, whereas in Japan the government was instrumental in the development of the main bank system.[8]

After the Meiji restoration in 1868, the Japanese government sought to establish a modern industrialized economy and introduced Western types of financial institutions. Entry into the banking industry was easy, and there was little government regulation. Banking panics occurred three times in the 1920s: in 1920, 1923, and most seriously in 1927. A new banking law that went into effect in January 1928 was introduced to correct this problem. The Ministry of Finance was responsible for administering the new law. In order to reduce the large number of banks that then existed, they adopted the principle of one bank in one prefecture, whereby banks were given a monopoly in a limited area. The necessary reduction in the number of banks was achieved through mergers, and Bank of Japan loans were used to facilitate this process. The government thus began to become directly involved in the financial system before the start of the war with China and the United States.

In the 1930s financial markets, and particularly the issue of shares, played a relatively important role in funding industry. Between 1931 and 1940, shares provided 31.7 percent of funds, bonds 4.3 percent, loans from private financial institutions 27.3 percent and retained earnings 37.0 percent. After the war the proportion provided by shares was much smaller, on the order of 5 to 10 percent, and the proportion provided by institutions and retained earnings increased substantially.[9]

During the early stage of wartime control, from 1937 to 1941, the Temporary Law of Fund Adjustment of 1937 extended government involvement. The authorities' permission was required for all firms above a certain size to increase their equity base or merge. Perhaps more important, the law controlled loans to firms that were categorized as "favored," "permitted," or "proscribed." Major banks belonging to the *zaibatsu* groups resisted this government control because they did not want to concentrate their loans to (favored) munitions companies, which they regarded as a poor risk. The government moved to counter this resistance and gradually introduced a system of central control of financial resources, with the Bank of Japan playing a pivotal role. This process culminated in the Munitions Companies Designated Financial Institutions System in January 1944, under which each munitions company was assigned a major bank to take care of the firm's financial needs. According to Hoshi, Kashyap, and Loveman (1994) many of these relationships subsequently developed into the postwar main bank system.

The adjustment in the financial system after the war inevitably involved government intervention in deciding which assets and which liabilities could be written off by financial institutions. The need to reconstruct the economy also led to substantial involvement by the government. The government became directly involved in allocating funds to industry through the foundation of the Reconstruction Financing Bank (RFB) in 1947. It allocated credit to the industries that it perceived to be crucial to Japan's postwar construction: coal mining, electric power, iron and steel, and marine shipping. In 1951 the RFB's role was assumed by the Japan Development Bank (JDB), which continued to lend to the same key industries as the RFB. After 1960 its role was extended to support the government's industrial policy.

The General Headquarters of the Allied Occupation (GHQ) wanted Japan to develop U.S.-style securities markets that focused on long-term lending, with banks undertaking short-term lending. However, as a practical matter, implementing this plan when a well-established banking system was already in place was very difficult. The main problem the banking system faced was the issue of maturity transformation. Firms needed long-term funds so that they could invest and grow without continually worrying about short-term factors. Investors, particularly households, wanted safe and liquid deposits. To help overcome this problem, the Law of Long-Term Credit Banks, introduced in 1952, allowed some special banks to raise funds by issuing long-term debentures rather than taking short-term deposits. These banks were then able to lend long term.

The wartime system of credit allocation established a close relationship between firms and banks. This, together with the other postwar developments, led to the development of the main bank system. The main characteristics of this system are the long-term relationship between a bank and its client firm, the holding of both debt and equity by the bank, and the active intervention of the bank should its client become financially distressed. It has been argued that this main bank relationship ensures that the bank acts as a delegated monitor and helps to overcome the agency problem between managers and the firm.

In addition to directly intervening in the allocation of capital through the RFB and JDB, the government intervened in the financial system by holding interest rates at low levels during the 1950s and 1960s. This had a number of effects, including providing rents to banks and some transfer of income from banks to industrial firms. The transfer of rents to banks helped ensure their solvency and contributed to the stability of the system.

The Japanese government thus intervened much more in the financial system than was the case in the United States, United Kingdom, France, or Germany. Horiuchi (1995) argues that most of the direct allocation of funds was to industries such as coal mining, agriculture, forestry and fisheries, and marine transportation. These were not in the vanguard of Japan's industrial development. The JDB became involved in lending for the industrial policy promoted by the Ministry for International Trade and Industry (MITI). Although they succeeded in supporting some "winners," such as numerical control machine tools, they also rejected many others, such as requests for support from Toyota and Sony.

The majority of funds were provided not by government-controlled banks such as the JDB but by private banks. Although the government did try to affect the private sector's allocation of funds, there is not much evidence that they succeeded in altering the course of investment, with a few exceptions such as coal mining and shipbuilding.

In the mid-1960s the Japanese government wanted to gain international recognition by, for example, joining the Organization for Economic Cooperation and Development (OECD). In order to do this, they needed to relax their regulation of the financial system. Over the years, this relaxation has gathered pace. Financial markets have steadily become more important as the restrictions on issuing bonds have been relaxed. At the same time, main bank relationships have come under heavy strain, and the system has begun to break down as large firms increasingly are able to rely on financial markets to raise funds.

As financial markets became more important in the 1980s, stock prices rocketed, and in the last five years of the decade rose sevenfold. A similar phenomenon occurred in the real estate market. In 1990 prices in both markets collapsed. This episode provides another recent example of the fragility of financial markets.

2.4 Implications

The history recounted above has a number of implications for the analysis of financial systems that follows in subsequent chapters.

1. *A wide range of different systems has existed in industrialized countries.* At one level there is clearly a distinction between the market-oriented systems of the United Kingdom and the United States and the bank-oriented systems of France, Germany, and Japan. However, even within these categorizations are important differences. For example, for political reasons, the United States, unlike the United Kingdom and other European countries, failed to develop a nationwide banking system with a few major banks. Financial markets for company shares did not develop in France or Germany. Instead banks undertook the role of providing finance to industry. In France, the relationship between banks and industry did not develop in quite as successful a way as in Germany, where these ties have been strong and intimate. As another illustration, in Japan the government had a significant effect in the development of the main bank system through its wartime controls. In contrast, the hausbank system in Germany developed without government intervention.

This range of systems raises the important welfare issue of determining which is the best system in particular circumstances. Do financial systems make a substantial difference to economic welfare? Or are they simply veils that have little effect? Given the importance of internal finance in most countries, it could be argued that institutional differences in the financial system are immaterial. This is one of the fundamental questions posed in comparing financial systems.

2. *Imperfections are important.* The historical development of financial systems illustrates the importance of capital market imperfections. Many, if not most, of the events described are difficult to understand in terms of standard frictionless models, that is, models of perfectly competitive markets with symmetric information and no transaction costs. Even the most advanced financial systems are far from the frictionless models that have been widely used in finance. Financial markets did not develop spontaneously. The earliest financial transactions involving loans and transfers through time were handled by institutions. It was not until relatively late, when the Amsterdam Bourse was founded at the start of the seventeenth century, that anything like a formal market existed.

It can be argued that transaction costs, asymmetric information, and other imperfections are of primary importance, and most systems have been much closer to the extreme where no financial markets exist at all than to a frictionless world. Although frictionless models may be a useful benchmark and starting point for analysis, they are of little use in providing insight into the operation of actual financial systems. Thus, a primary aim of this book is to develop simple tractable models that capture the effects of various frictions and provide insights into the operation of actual financial systems.

3. *Financial systems are fragile and crises are endemic.* One of the most striking features of all the financial systems is their instability. From the earliest development of financial institutions, there have been problems of failure and runs. From the earliest introduction of formal financial markets there have been problems with speculative bubbles. These crises have had a dramatic effect on the development of financial systems.

In contrast, financial crises and speculative bubbles do not appear in frictionless models. The idea that markets are efficient and the invisible hand operates well has had a powerful influence in recent years. This idea starkly contrasts with the history of financial systems, where, from the tulip mania, to the South Sea and Mississippi bubbles, the Great Crash of 1929, black Monday in 1987, and the collapse of the "bubble economy" in Japan in 1990 there appear to have been enormous problems.

Another strand of the literature has tried to understand these events in terms of irrational behavior of various kinds. Although bounded rationality and other forms of irrationality are clearly of some importance, it is not clear they are of primary importance. Of all the markets that exist, financial markets provide the strongest incentives for participants to undertake careful analysis and exhibit rational behavior. Another theme of this book is to pursue the alternative of trying to understand the fragility of financial systems in terms of imperfections rather than irrational behavior.

4. *Governments and central banks apparently have an important role to play.* A number of financial systems have operated in the absence of government and central bank intervention. An example is the United States from the time that the Second Bank of the United States closed in 1836 until the National Bank Act of 1863. Scotland also had experience with free banking in the seventeenth and eighteenth centuries. There has been a significant debate about the success of these experiments. However, the fact that they did not persist and that even the most market-oriented economies such as the United States have dispensed with them suggests a number of market failures that require intervention to be solved. One of the aims of the book's focus on imperfections is to try to gain a better understanding of the nature of the market failures that justify government intervention in financial systems.

A related issue is whether intervention by the government is the only or the best way of correcting market failures. One of the interesting features of many financial systems is the variety of nonprofit organizations that exist.

Notes

1. See Goldsmith (1987) for an account of early financial systems. This section draws heavily on this source.

2. See Kindleberger (1993).

3. The Bank of Venice was initially called the Banco di Rialto.

4. The establishment of the Nobel Prize in Economics was to mark the tercentenary of this event.

5. Timberlake (1978, p. 39).

6. Studenski and Krooss (1963, p. 254).

7. Ibid., p. 284.

8. This section draws heavily on Horiuchi (1995).

9. Ibid., table 2, p. 96.

References

Cameron, R. (1961). *France and the Economic Development of Europe (1800–1914)*. Princeton, NJ: Princeton University Press.

Dickson, P. (1967). *The Financial Revolution in England: A Study in the Development of Public Credit, 1688–1756*. New York: St. Martin's Press.

Goldsmith, R. (1987). *Premodern Financial Systems: A Historical Comparative Study*. Cambridge: Cambridge University Press.

Horiuchi, A. (1995). "Financial Sector Reforms in Postwar Japan: An Overview." Working paper, University of Tokyo.

Hoshi, T., A. Kashyap, and G. Loveman. (1994). "Financial System Reform in Poland: Lessons from Japan's Main Bank System." In M. Aoki and H. Patrick (eds.), *The Japanese Main Bank System: Its Relevancy for Developing and Transforming Economies*. New York: Oxford University Press, 592–633.

Kindleberger, C. (1993). *A Financial History of Western Europe*. 2d ed. New York: Oxford University Press.

Roe, M. (1994). *Strong Managers, Weak Owners*. Princeton, NJ: Princeton University Press.

Studenski, P., and H. E. Krooss. (1963). *Financial History of the United States*. 2d ed., New York: McGraw-Hill.

Timberlake, R. (1978). *The Origins of Central Banking in the United States*. Cambridge, MA: Harvard University Press.

de la Vega, J. P. (1688). *Confusion de Confusiones*. Translated by H. Kallenbenz. Cambridge, MA: Kress Library Series of Publications, Kress Library of Business and Economics, Harvard University.

3 Institutions and Markets

We have argued that differing reactions to the instability associated with financial markets led to two broad types of financial system—one market based and the other bank based. This chapter considers the institutions and markets that are available to investors and firms in the United States, United Kingdom, Japan, France, and Germany.[1]

Table 3.1 compares the relative importance of banks and markets in these countries. It can be seen that the United States is at one extreme and Germany at the other. In the United States banks are relatively unimportant, with a ratio of assets to GDP of only 53 percent, about a third that of Germany at 152 percent. On the other hand, the U.S. ratio of equity market capitalization to GDP at 82 percent is three times that of Germany at 24 percent. Japan and the United Kingdom are interesting intermediate cases; both banks and markets are important. In France banks are important, and markets are less so.

Table 3.2 shows the total gross financial assets owned by the household sector in the five countries broken down by the form in which

Table 3.1
International comparison of banks and markets, 1993 (billions of dollars)

	GDP	Banking assets (BA)	BA/GDP	Equity market capitalization (EMC)	EMC/GDP
United States	$6,301	$3,319	53%	$5,136	82%
United Kingdom	824	2,131	259	1,152	140
Japan	4,242	6,374	150	2,999	71
France	1,261	1,904	151	457	36
Germany	1,924	2,919	152	464	24

Source: Barth, Nolle, and Rice (1997, Table 1).

Table 3.2
Total gross financial assets ultimately owned by the household sector

Country	$ billion	Value relative to GDP	% held directly by households	% held by pension funds (public and private)	% held by insurance companies	% held in mutual funds, etc.
United States	20,815	3.00	58	17	13	10
United Kingdom	3,107	2.97	40	24	27	7
Japan	12,936	2.71	71	10	16	3
France	2,689	1.90	62	2	17	19
Germany	2,900	1.46	67	4	20	5

Note: Aggregation of direct asset holdings, pension fund assets, assets of insurance companies, and assets in mutual funds and other collective investment schemes at the end of 1994.
Source: Miles (1996, Table 4, p. 21).

they are held. Except for the United Kingdom, most assets are owned directly by households. In the United Kingdom pension funds and insurance companies are much more important than in the other countries. In France and Germany and to some extent Japan, pension funds are relatively unimportant. Table 3.3 shows the total portfolio allocation of assets ultimately owned by the household sector. In the United States and United Kingdom, equity is a much more important component of households assets than in Japan, Germany, and France. For cash and cash equivalents (which includes bank accounts) the reverse is true. Table 3.4 shows the direct holdings of financial assets by private individuals. Equity is particularly important in the United States and to some extent in the United Kingdom. It is relatively unimportant in the other countries. Cash and cash equivalents are relatively unimportant in the United States. Bonds are fairly unimportant in the United Kingdom and Japan.

In a series of important papers Mayer (1988, 1990) has documented how firms obtain funds in a number of different countries. Table 3.5, which is from Mayer (1990), indicates some of his findings: in all countries except Japan, retentions are the most important source of finance. In Japan loans are the most important, but retentions are a close second. Loans are also important in the other countries. Markets are not an important source of funds. Corbett and Jenkinson (1996, 1997) provide more recent evidence for the United Kingdom, United States, Japan, and Germany. They also find that firms are mostly internally financed and markets are fairly unimportant.

The characterization of financial systems as market based or intermediary based is a useful starting point, but as Tables 3.1 to 3.5 indicate, the issues are more complex than this simple taxonomy suggests.

Table 3.3
Portfolio allocation of total financial assets ultimately owned by the household sector (% of total)

Country	Cash and cash equivalents	Domestic bonds	Domestic equity	Foreign bonds	Foreign equity	Loans and mortgages	Real estate[a]	Other	Total
United States	19	27	36	1	9	3	1	4	100
United Kingdom	24	10	39	2	13	1	4	7	100
Japan	52	12	11	1	1	6	1	15	100
France	38	30	13	3	3	2	1	10	100
Germany	36	31	11	5	2	4	1	9	100

Note: Aggregation of direct asset holdings, pension fund assets, assets of insurance companies and funds in collective investment schemes (mutual funds, unit trusts, investment trusts, etc.) at the end of 1994.
a. Includes only property held for investment purposes, not direct ownership of residential property by households.
Source: Miles (1996, Table 5, p. 22).

Table 3.4
Private individuals' direct financial assets (% of total)

Country	Cash and cash equivalents	Domestic bonds	Domestic equity	Foreign bonds	Foreign equity	Loans and mortgages	Other	Total
United States	27.2	17.6	39.8	0.3	10.2	1.6	3.3	100
United Kingdom	55.8	8.6	24.9	0.1	4.1	—	6.5	100
Japan	64.1	5.9	9.4	0.2	0.1	0.0	20.3	100
France	43.5	23.0	14.0	2.3	2.4	3.1	11.7	100
Germany	52.2	23.1	10.0	3.5	1.0	0.0	10.2	100

Note: Direct asset holdings excluding all pension assets, insurance policies, and collective investment schemes (mutual funds, unit trusts, investment trusts, etc.) at the end of 1994.
Source: Miles (1996, Table 6, p. 22).

Table 3.5
Unweighted average gross financing of nonfinancial enterprises, 1970–1985 (% of total)

	United States	United Kingdom	Japan	France	Germany
Retentions	66.9	72.0	33.7	44.1	55.2
Capital transfers	.0	2.9	.0	1.4	6.7
Short-term securities	1.4	2.3	N.A.	.0	.0
Loans	23.1	21.4	40.7	41.5	21.1
Trade credit	8.4	2.8	18.3	4.7	2.2
Bonds	9.7	.8	3.1	2.3	.7
Shares	.8	4.9	3.5	10.6	2.1
Other	−6.1	2.2	.7	.0	11.9
Statistical adjustment	−4.1	−9.4	N.A.	−4.7	.0
Total	100.1	99.9	100.0	99.9	99.9

Source: Mayer (1990, Table 12.3, p. 312).

3.1 The United States

The United States has a very different financial history from other large industrialized countries. A strong distrust of the power involved in large financial institutions caused a bias toward decentralization of the banking system. Throughout the nineteenth century, the U.S. banking system was highly fragmented, and unlike European industrializing countries, the United States failed to develop nationwide banks with extensive branch networks. As table 3.1 indicated, banks are less important and markets more important than in other countries. A brief overview of current U.S. institutions and markets is provided in table 3.6.

Commercial banks are primarily engaged in providing short-term finance to firms and consumers. The range of services that they provide is limited by regulation. The Glass-Steagall Act of 1933 prevented commercial banks from underwriting securities. These restrictions have been gradually relaxed. In April 1987, Bankers' Trust, Citicorp, and J. P. Morgan were the first commercial banks to set up Section 20 subsidiaries to undertake underwriting activities.[2] They have subsequently been followed by many other banks. Approval is given on a case-by-case basis. The main requirement is that the subsidiary's revenues for these activities does not exceed 10 percent of total gross revenues. Firewalls preventing the flow of information between the Section 20 subsidiary and other parts of the bank are mandated.

Commercial banks' activities in insurance and real estate are also limited. Banks may engage in credit, life, and disability insurance agency

Table 3.6
Institutions and markets in the United States

Banking system	
Commercial banks	Provide short-term lending to firms, residential real estate loans, agricultural loans, and loans to other financial institutions. The Glass-Steagall Act prohibited commercial banks from undertaking investment banking activities but prohibitions have relaxed in recent years.
Savings and loans and thrifts	Traditionally have provided mortgages and other consumer loans. Many have a mutual structure, so depositors are shareholders.
Pensions	
Public	All workers are covered. Pensions are linked to average earnings. Low replacement ratio.
Private	Primarily cover largely defined benefit based on final salary. Indexation provisions rare (5 percent of private schemes); discretionary increases common. Defined-contribution plans growing in importance.
Insurance	Life insurance companies provide tax-advantaged savings vehicles with an insurance component. Property and casualty companies primarily provide insurance, and assets for investment are a by-product. Many insurance companies have a mutual structure.
Financial markets	
Stock markets	There are three major exchanges: the NYSE, AMEX, and NASDAQ. They have traditionally been a significant source of primary funds through initial public offerings (IPOs).
Debt markets	These are an important source of funds for the federal, state, and local governments, as well as for firms.
Derivative markets	Commodity futures markets date from the late nineteenth century. Financial options and futures markets were founded in the early 1970s and have become very liquid. Over-the-counter markets for swaps and other derivatives have significant volume.

and underwriting activities. Federal regulations also allow banks to engage in general insurance agency activities in towns with a population of fewer than 5,000. With regard to real estate, banks can engage only in purchases of premises necessary for undertaking their business. Finally, commercial banks are not able to invest in the equity of nonfinancial firms except in special cases, such as when a firm goes bankrupt and loans are transformed into equity interests.

The historical restrictions on banks' crossing state boundaries have been eased recently. The Riegle-Neal Interstate Banking and Branching Efficiency Act of 1994 set up a timetable for relaxing the rules. States had the option to opt in early and permit interstate banking from

September 1994 onward. States also had the ability to opt out and prevent bank mergers provided they did so before the end of May 1997. After this date, banks were essentially unrestricted with regard to interstate banking except in states that opted out or imposed other restrictions. The full effects of this law on the structure of the banking industry have still to be realized.

Savings and loans and thrifts were originally founded to provide mortgages to consumers. Many were founded as mutuals, so the depositors owned the institution. In recent years a significant number have "demutualized" and changed to shareholder-owned organizations. Traditionally these institutions were restricted to taking short-term deposits at low interest rates and lending long term at higher interest rates. The industry went through severe problems in the 1970s and early 1980s. The steep rise in interest rates that occurred as a result of the high inflation in those years meant that they were left with low-yielding loans that did not allow them to pay the higher short-term rates necessary to retain deposits. In order to try to ease the problems they faced, regulations limiting the range of their activities were relaxed. This had the unfortunate effect of exacerbating the problem since some institutions started to try to solve their financial difficulties by undertaking high-risk investments.

The pensions provided through the social security system in the United States are funded on a pay-as-you-go basis with a buffer fund invested in government debt to smooth short-term fluctuations. The system covers all workers. Pensions are linked to average earnings. The ratio of the social security pensions to earnings, termed the *replacement ratio*, is low.

Private pensions are given a number of tax advantages. Contributions and asset returns are tax free, and only benefits are taxed. The main regulation imposed on the way pension funds can be invested is the "prudent man" rule. This requires that managers carry out sensible portfolio diversification, and there are no specific limits on portfolio distributions. The Employee Retirement-Income Security Act of (ERISA) of 1974 imposed a number of regulations on the provision of pensions by firms, setting minimum standards for vesting of pensions and imposing requirements for the funding of pensions. The act also set up the Pension Benefit Guarantee Corporation (PBGC), which guarantees the benefits of funds in default. The ERISA requirements for funding pensions provide protection for the PBGC. Higher premiums for the PBGC are charged on underfunded schemes. Private pension schemes cover about 46 percent of the workforce.

As Table 3.2 indicates, the assets of pension funds are quite significant and constitute 17 percent of households' total assets. The asset allocation of pension funds (both private and public) are shown in table 3.7. It can be seen that the majority of the funds, 52.4 percent, are in equities with the other important category being bonds with 27.4 percent of assets.

Insurance companies activities' can be divided into two areas: life insurance and property and casualty insurance. As with banking, the U.S. insurance industry is heavily regulated. In addition to providing life insurance contracts of various types, life insurance companies also sell annuity contracts, manage pension plans, and provide accident and health insurance. Many of the contracts they provide are essentially tax-advantaged savings vehicles. The assets of life insurance companies are therefore large. Property insurance involves insuring against losses related to real property, and casualty insurance is mainly concerned with protection against legal liability. Since property and casualty insurance does not involve providing savings vehicles, the amount of assets generated is smaller. As table 3.2 indicated, the holdings of insurance companies are significant and constitute 13 percent of households' assets. The portfolios of insurance companies are shown in table 3.8. In the United States most of the investments are fixed income, with bonds and mortgages accounting for 74 percent of assets. Total equity holdings are relatively small, with 14.9 percent of assets.

The U.S. financial markets are varied and deep. There has been extensive financial innovation since World War II, which accelerated in the 1970s and 1980s. This financial innovation has helped to strengthen the market orientation of the financial system by introducting new financial products such as various mortgage-backed securities and other securitized assets, as well as derivative instruments such as swaps and complex options. These have all had a virtual explosion in volume. At the same time, new exchanges for financial futures, options, and other derivative securities have appeared and become major markets.

As table 3.3 shows, the financial assets of households are mostly in equities, with 45 percent of the total, and bonds, with 28 percent. Cash and cash equivalents are relatively unimportant at 19 percent, and the other remaining categories are even smaller. Over the long term, there has been a shift away from individuals' holding equity directly toward intermediaries holding it. Much of this has been transferred into indirect holdings through pension and mutual funds. Figure 3.1 shows the proportion of equity owned by individuals, and figure 3.2 shows how the institutional share has changed. The share of pension

Table 3.7
Allocation of pension assets, private schemes plus assets of state schemes, (% of total)

Country	Cash and cash equivalents	Domestic bonds	Domestic equity	Foreign bonds	Foreign equity	Loans and mortgages	Real estate	Other	Total
United States	5.5	25.5	44.7	1.9	7.7	3.0	2.7	9.0	100
United Kingdom	2.6	8.9	54.4	2.7	21.0	0.0	7.8	2.5	100
Japan	29.1	46.1	11.4	3.5	3.1	6.3	0.6	0.0	100
France	6.6	54.4	25.3	4.6	1.6	2.1	2.2	3.2	100
Germany	14.8	38.8	5.2	3.5	1.4	29.5	4.2	2.5	100

Source: Miles (1996, Table 7, p. 23).

Table 3.8
Portfolio composition of insurance companies, end of 1994 (% of total)

Country	Cash and cash equivalents	Domestic bonds	Domestic equity	Foreign bonds	Foreign equity	Loans and mortgages	Real estate	Other	Total
United States	3.9	62.2	14.5	0.3	0.4	11.5	2.4	4.7	100
United Kingdom	3.6	17.1	45.9	3.0	13.9	2.0	7.8	6.7	100
Japan	12.7	16.0	19.0	2.9	4.9	36.0	5.5	3.0	100
France	4.9	57.1	18.0	4.5	1.8	2.0	9.1	2.7	100
Germany	1.8	59.8	10.1	6.5	2.5	12.7	5.8	0.8	100

Source: Miles (1996, Table 8, p. 23).

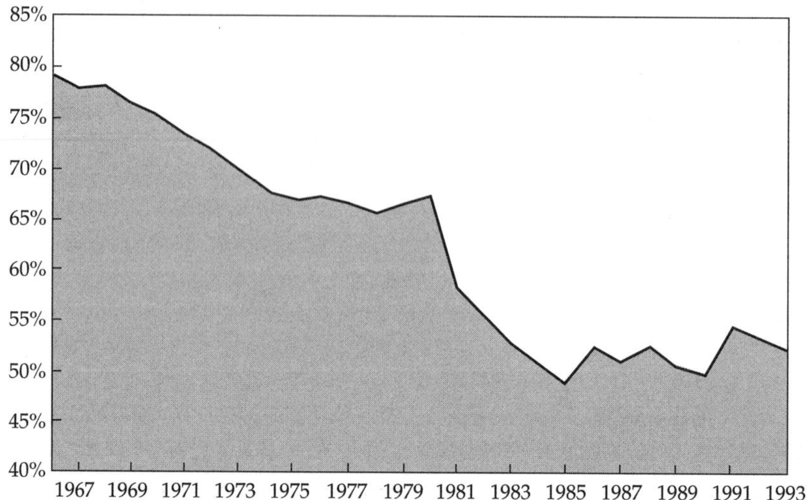

Figure 3.1
Individual ownership of corporate equity, United States, 1966–1993. *Source:* Board of Governors of the Federal Reserve System, Flow of Funds Accounts.

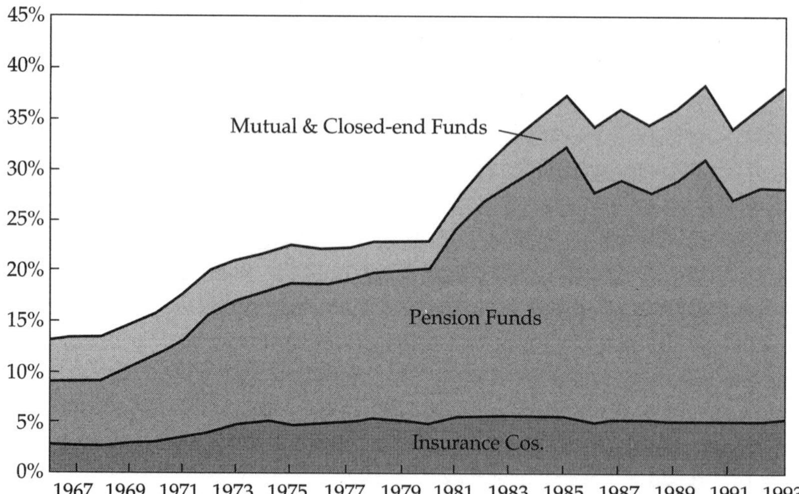

Figure 3.2
Selected institutional share, United States, 1966–1993. *Source:* Board of Governors of the Federal Reserve System, Flow of Funds Accounts.

funds and mutual funds to a large degree has risen to replace the fall in individual holdings. The assets of insurance companies have remained constant during this period.

In addition to the question of how individuals hold their savings, there is also the important issue of how firms raise their funds. Table 3.5 shows the sources in terms of retentions, capital transfers, short-term securities, loans, trade credit, bonds, and shares for the period 1970–1985. It can be seen that retentions are by far the most important, with loans, trade credit, and bonds also being significant.

3.2 United Kingdom

An overview of the U.K. financial system is given in table 3.9. Apart from the size and structure of the banking sector, the financial system in the United Kingdom resembles that in the United States in the sense that markets play an important role, although the U.K. system is characterized by much less regulation.

The City of London has traditionally been a major center for international banking and finance. The foreign and domestic sectors of the banking industry are roughly equal in size. This large foreign presence may partly explain the large ratio of banking assets to GDP indicated in table 3.1. With some exceptions, such as Citibank, foreign banks are not involved with the domestic sector. Although there is no equivalent to the Glass-Steagall Act, the domestic sector is divided into commercial banking and investment banking (or merchant banking, in U.K. terminology).

Commercial banking has traditionally been dominated by the big four clearing banks: Barclays, National Westminster, Midland, and Lloyds. These are essentially universal banks, and they provide a wide range of banking services to consumers and firms; some have moved into life insurance, travel services, real estate, and trust management. They also offer underwriting and other services through wholly owned subsidiaries. The regulations on the activities they can undertake are limited. The only restriction with regard to securities activities is that gilt-edged market making must be conducted through a subsidiary. There is not even a restriction requiring firewalls between different parts of the bank. For insurance subsidiaries, they cannot count their investment as part of their capital, but apart from that, insurance activities are unrestricted. Real estate investments are unregulated. Banks can invest in the equity of nonfinancial firms and vice versa.

Table 3.9
Institutions and markets in the United Kingdom

Banking system	
Commercial banks	This sector has traditionally been dominated by the big four clearing banks: Barclays, National Westminster, Midland, and Lloyds.
Foreign banks	London's role as an international financial center means that the foreign sector is roughly the same size as the domestic sector. With a few exceptions, such as Citibank, foreign banks are not involved with the domestic market.
Building societies	The primary role of these institutions historically was to provide mortgages. Deregulation allowed them to expand their activities into other banking activities. This has prompted many to change from a mutual form into banks in recent years.
Pensions	
Public	Covers all residents, with a lump sum for everybody. There also exists a component linked to average earnings during working life, but this can be opted out of. Low replacement ratio.
Private	Largely defined benefit based on final salary. Provisions for total or partial indexation are common (75 percent of participants).
Insurance	Provided by bank subsidiaries as well as insurance companies. The industry is highly fragmented and lightly regulated. Lloyds exchange is important for domestic and international syndicates.
Financial Markets	
Stock markets	Important for domestic and overseas companies. Large number of companies listed. Source of primary funds through IPOs.
Debt markets	Important for government debt and bank debt. The domestic bond market has been replaced by the less regulated Eurobond market based in London.
Derivative markets	Active financial futures and options exchanges.
Other markets	Large foreign exchange markets and markets for precious metals such as gold.

The investment banks developed separately from the commercial banks. Historically, they were merchants engaged in international trade and discounted bills to finance this trade. Over time they moved into traditional investment banking activities such as underwriting, investment management, merger and acquisition services, and financial advisory work.

The final part of the banking sector is the building societies. Like the S&Ls in the United States, these were originally formed to help people buy homes by supplying mortgages. Many were mutual organizations. Their activities have been fairly closely regulated by the Building Societies Commission. These regulations have gradually been relaxed, and they have essentially become competitors to the big four. Many have changed from being mutual organizations to shareholder-owned banks.

The state pension system covers all residents. The basic component is small in size. There is also an earnings-related component to supplement the basic rate. However, it is possible to contract out of this earnings-related part and replace it with a private pension scheme.

Private pensions are popular in the United Kingdom. As in the United States the contributions and asset returns are untaxed, and only benefits are taxed. However, any lump-sum component of the benefits is untaxed. The portfolios that pension funds invest in are subject to a "prudent man" rule and are also limited to a 5 percent self-investment limit. There are a number of recent restrictions on funding. The only part of private pensions that is guaranteed is a minimum that everybody must receive. Coverage is high, with 50 percent of the workforce participating in company schemes.

Pension funds constitute a large proportion, 24 percent, of households assets, as table 3.2 indicates—significantly larger than in other countries. Table 3.7 shows that equities constitute a very large proportion, 75.4 percent, of pension fund assets. Bonds and real estate are relatively insignificant.

The insurance industry, like banking, is fairly lightly regulated. Unlike the domestic banking industry, it is not dominated by a few large players and is quite competitive. A unique feature of the British insurance industry is the Lloyds exchange, which started as a major center for marine insurance and subsequently developed into a center for other types of insurance. Recently, Lloyds has suffered heavy losses in its insurance business. Some investors in Lloyds, alleging fraudulent behavior on the part of underwriters, refused to cover their part of the losses and resorted to legal action against Lloyds. The future of Lloyds is unclear. Similarly to pension funds, insurance companies represent a much larger proportion of household assets at 27 percent than is the case in other countries, as shown in table 3.7. They also invest significantly more in equities, 59.8 percent, than insurance companies do in other countries.

As in the United States, financial markets in the United Kingdom are sophisticated. In addition to extensive domestic listings of firms, many foreign firms are listed in London. Bond and money markets are important. Markets for short-term instruments such as commercial bills, gilts, bank bills, and commercial paper are liquid. The Eurobond market is based in London and is very liquid. The market for long-term gilts is also liquid. Exchange-based derivatives markets were established in the 1980s and have grown quickly. The foreign exchange market is the largest in the world. Markets for precious metals, particularly that for gold, are also important.

Table 3.3 shows that the large holdings of equity by pension funds and insurance companies and their overall importance result in equity's being a majority (52 percent) of household assets, even more than in the United States. Cash and cash equivalents are significant at 24 percent but much less so than in Japan, France, and Germany. Bonds at 12 percent are also relatively unimportant.

With regard to how firms raise funds in the United Kingdom, table 3.5 indicates that retentions (72.0 percent) are by far the most important source. Apart from loans (21.4 percent) all other sources are relatively unimportant.

3.3 Japan

The Japanese financial system has changed significantly over the years. Before World War II, both markets and banks were important. After the war, banks were predominant, but in recent years markets have steadily become more important. Table 3.10 gives a summary of the current form of Japan's institutions and markets.

The banking sector in Japan can be divided into banks that focus on short-term lending, banks that lend only long term, and banks that do both. The so-called ordinary banks, the counterparts of commercial banks in other countries, provide a range of services to consumers and firms, both large and small. Most of their lending is relatively short term. Trust banks provide a range of services, but unlike ordinary banks they also lend long-term to corporations. Long-term credit banks raise funds by issuing bonds that mature in one to five years and lend the money long and medium term mainly to large corporations.

In addition to these shareholder-owned banks, there is also a large cooperative sector of credit unions and credit associations that cater to the needs of small business and are owned by their members. Credit associations are much like ordinary banks in terms of the range of services they offer, except they can give loans only to their members and are restricted to a particular geographical area. Both credit unions and associations have national organizations that redistribute the funds from surplus areas to deficit areas. There is a similar system of agricultural cooperatives.

Table 3.10
Institutions and markets in Japan

Banking system	
Commercial (or "ordinary") banks	Includes city banks, regional banks, and second-tier regional banks. They provide short-term credit to large corporations, small business loans, and consumer lending.
Trust banks	These provide a range of services, including ordinary banking services, long-term loans to corporations, asset management, investment advisory services, and custodian services.
Long-term credit banks	These use the funds raised from medium- and short-term debentures to provide long- and medium-term loans, mainly to large corporations.
Cooperatives	Credit associations and credit unions provide banking services to small business firms. Agricultural counterparts provide services to farmers.
Postal savings system	Large government-sponsored system that sells insurance and provides savings accounts.
Pensions	
Public	Partly lump sum and partly linked to average earnings over working life, but scheme members can contract out if they wish. High replacement ratio. Partially funded.
Private	Largely defined benefit based on years of service and final basic salary. Often taken as a lump sum.
Insurance	Life insurance is significantly more important in Japan than other countries. Large life insurance companies are mostly mutuals.
Financial markets	
Stock markets	The Tokyo Stock Exchange is the most important and is a sophisticated market.
Bond markets	Bond markets for the debt of central and local governments, of financial and nonfinancial firms are all significant. Japanese firms issue a large number of convertible and warrant bonds.
Derivative markets	Financial options and futures markets are active.

Although Japan is not unusual in having a postal savings system, it is unusual in having one with such large assets. The reason for its success in attracting deposits is that it has many branches, in the past it has been granted various tax advantages, and there is a government guarantee of its funds. At the end of March 1993 postal savings accounts represented 16.7 percent of personal financial assets. In addition post offices sell insurance, and the assets arising from this accounted for a further 6.4 percent of personal financial assets. These funds are invested in the Trust Fund Bureau and are used to finance Japan's treasury investment and loans program, which consists of loans to small businesses, agricultural and forestry operations, and various public works projects like public highways, housing, and hospitals. In recent years some of the funds have also been invested in the security markets.

Japanese banks are fairly heavily regulated. The nature of the regulation is similar to that in the United States because of the influence of the occupation forces after World War II. Banks are generally not allowed to underwrite securities. They can underwrite bonds in a subsidiary but are allowed to own more than 50 percent of such a subsidiary only with the permission of the Ministry of Finance. They cannot sell or underwrite insurance or invest in real estate except for their premises. Unlike banks in the United States, Japanese banks can own up to 5 percent of the equity of nonfinancial firms. The reverse is even less restricted; nonfinancial firms may own banks.

The social security system grants pensions that are high relative to average earnings. It is also generous in that it starts at age sixty for both men and women. In the other countries considered, pensions start at age sixty-five except for the United Kingdom, where women obtain pensions at age sixty and men at age sixty-five (this difference will be phased out in the coming years). The state pension system is unusual among the countries considered in that it is only partially a pay-as-you-go system since part of the liabilities is funded. The assets that have been accumulated for this purpose are invested in the same way as the funds of the postal savings system. At the end of March 1993, the funds put aside for this purpose were equivalent to about 9.5 percent of personal financial assets. The state pension has two components—one that everybody receives and one related to average earnings over the working life. The earnings-related part can be contracted out of by participants and replaced with a private pension.

Private pension systems in Japan are largely defined benefit based on years of service and final salary. Indexation is rare except for any component replacing social security. Contributions are tax free. Unlike the other countries considered, asset returns are taxed. Benefits are also taxed except for any part paid as a lump sum. As a result, they are often taken as a lump sum. Funding of private pension schemes is optional. The guidelines for investing the funds are that there can be a maximum of 30 percent invested equity, 20 percent in property, 30 percent in foreign securities, and 10 percent in any one company. The benefits are insured under a provision of the wage payment law.

Table 3.2 indicates that 10 percent of household assets are held by pension funds, significantly more than in France and Germany but less than in the United States and United Kingdom. Table 3.7 shows that a surprisingly high proportion (29.1 percent) of these assets is held in cash and cash equivalents, with 49.6 percent in bonds and relatively little in equities at 14.5 percent.

Life insurance firms in Japan hold a significant number of assets compared to those in other countries. In addition to providing life insurance and long-term savings vehicles, they also lend a significant amount of their funds long term to firms. Another important part of their activities is that they manage corporate pension funds. The funds from insurance are managed jointly with those for corporate pensions. An interesting feature of life insurance companies in Japan is that most large ones are mutuals. Property and casualty insurance companies are also significant players in the Japanese financial system, but they are not as important as the life insurance companies. Insurance companies hold a significant proportion of household assets (16 percent from table 3.2). It can be seen from table 3.8 that a high proportion (12.7 percent) is again in cash and cash equivalents and a moderate amount in bonds (18.9 percent) and equity (23.9 percent). A much larger proportion (36.0 percent) is in loans and mortgages than in other countries.

Although banks have played a dominant role in the financial system for most of the period since World War II, this did not stop the development of fairly sophisticated financial markets. There are eight stock exchanges, with the Tokyo Stock Exchange by far the most important. There is also an over-the-counter market, which has become more important in recent years. As table 3.1 indicated, the total capitalization of stocks is large compared to other countries. During the 1960s and 1970s the valuation of Japanese stocks in terms of measures such as the price-to-earnings ratios and dividend yield were comparable to other countries. However, during the bubble years of the 1980s price/earnings (P/E) ratios became very large, and dividend yields fell to low levels. Even after the bubble burst, these measures did not revert to their prebubble levels. Part of the difference in P/E ratios is due to differences in accounting conventions, but even the adjusted figures are still significantly higher than in other countries.

The debt markets in Japan are also well developed. The money markets involve a broad range of instruments, including government debt, intermediaries' debt, and commercial paper. They expanded rapidly during the period 1985–1990, but this growth has subsequently slowed. At the end of 1994 government bonds constituted the majority of bonds traded in Japan. Also significant were the debentures issued by banks, government-guaranteed bonds, and corporate bonds. One of the characteristics of Japanese bond markets that stands out is the large number of convertible and warrant bonds that were issued in the 1980s during the bubble. As a result of the collapse of the bubble in the 1990s, most of the warrants were not exercised, and the convertibles were not converted.

In the 1980s the Japanese derivative markets became important in terms of volume. The most active futures and options are on the market indexes. Options on individuals stocks are not yet traded. After the bursting of the stock market bubble in 1990, the argument was made that trading in derivatives had contributed to the collapse. As a result, the regulation of derivatives trading increased. This raised the cost of transacting substantially, and as a result a significant volume of trading migrated to the Singapore International Monetary Exchange (SIMEX). More recently there has been some deregulation to try to make trading less costly.

It can be seen from table 3.3 that households' holdings of assets are very different compared to the United States and United Kingdom. Cash and cash equivalents, which includes bank accounts, are very large, at 52 percent of assets. Bonds at 13 percent and equity at 12 percent are not very important. In the long run individual holdings of equity have fallen even more dramatically than in the United States. Figure 3.3 shows the fall from 1953, when it was above 50 percent, until

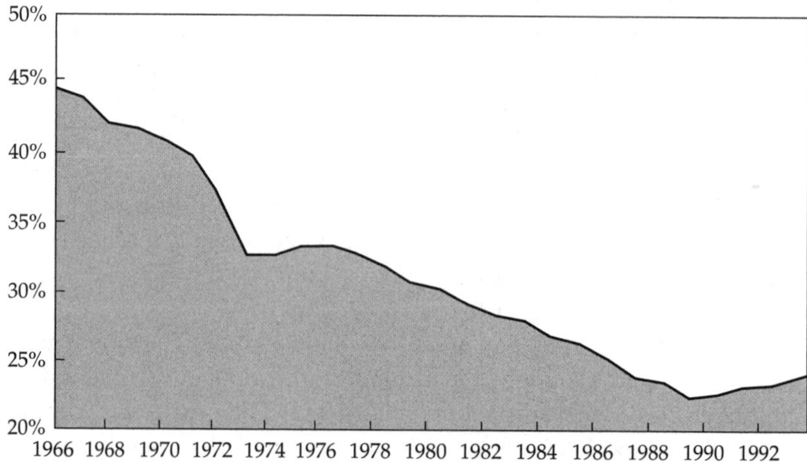

Figure 3.3
Individual ownership of TSE corporate equity, Japan, 1966–1993. *Source: Tokyo Stock Exchange 1994 Fact Book.*

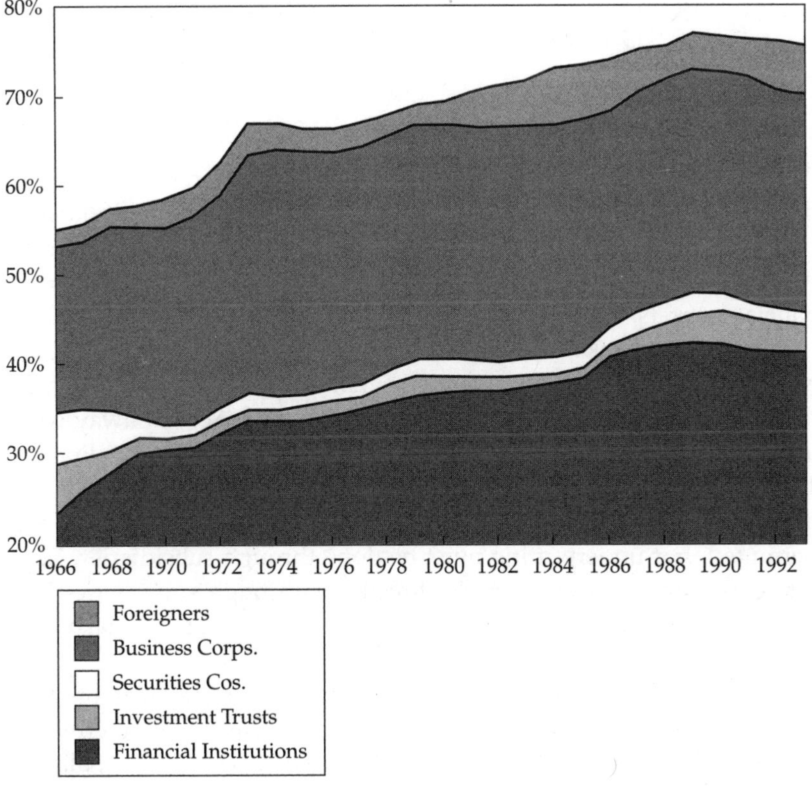

Figure 3.4
Selected institutional share, Japan, 1966–1993. *Source: Tokyo Stock Exchange 1994 Fact Book.*

1993, when it was about 20 percent or so. As figure 3.4 demonstrates, this fall in individual ownership has mainly been offset by an increase in the holdings of banks, insurance companies, and business corporations. Investment trusts, or the equivalent of mutual funds in the United States, have if anything fallen in size. This can perhaps be explained by the terrible performance of these funds. In a careful study of mutual fund performance, Cai, Chan, and Yamada (1997) found that between January 1981 and December 1992, the average annual rate of return of 800 open-type mutual funds was 1.74 percent, while that of the market was 9.28 percent. Regardless of the benchmarks and performance measures employed, they find strong evidence of underperformance in Japanese mutual funds.

The pattern for raising funds in Japan is somewhat different from the United States and United Kingdom. Table 3.5 shows that loans are the most important source, at 40.7 percent, but retentions are also important, at 33.7 percent.

3.4 France

An overview of the French financial system is given in table 3.11. Traditionally France has had a bank-based financial system and markets played an unimportant role. However, in the 1980s, the government made a conscious effort to reform the financial system and bolster financial markets. Bertero (1994) provides an account of the changes.

Prior to 1984 banks were regulated based on the principle of specialization. For example, there were deposit banks, investment banks, and medium- and long-term banks. The 1984 Banking Act did away with these specializations. Now, banks are relatively unregulated in France. They are unrestricted in their securities activities, and no firewalls are mandated. With regard to insurance products and services, sales are permitted, but underwriting must be done through subsidiaries. Real estate investments can be made directly or through subsidiaries but must be limited to 10 percent of the bank's incomes. Commercial banks can invest in nonfinancial firms and vice versa.

One feature of commercial banks in France that is unique among the five countries considered is the fact that many have been alternately nationalized and privatized. Until 1982 three banks were nationalized: Société Générale, Crédit Lyonnais, and Banque Nationale de Paris. After the election of a socialist government in 1982, a majority of banks were put under the control of the state. After five years this policy of nationalization was reversed, and many banks were returned to the private sector.

Although commercial banks are the most important sector in the banking system, mutual and cooperative banks are also significant. The Crédit Mutuel has the aim of providing credit to individuals with a modest income. Each person participating in the mutual company has one vote in the overall decision-making process. The Crédit Coopérative is a system of cooperative banks. They can receive credit from everybody but must lend the majority of their funds to members, cooperative companies, mutualist companies, mutualist insurance companies, associations, and public collectives. The Crédit Maritime Mutuel has the role of providing banking services to the craft fishing and marine farming sector, and the Crédit Agricole Mutuel aims to provide loans to farmers at reasonable rates. The Crédit Populaire provides credit to

Table 3.11
Institutions and markets in France

Banking system	
Commercial banks	Since 1945 there have been waves of nationalization and privatization. Until 1982, three banks were nationalized: Société Générale, Crédit Lyonnais, and Banque Nationale de Paris. After the election of a socialist government in 1982, many banks were nationalized, but five years later this policy was reversed and many banks were privatized.
Mutual and cooperative banks	There are various kinds of mutual banks with different specific purposes. For example, the aim of the Crédit Agricole Mutuel is to provide loans to farmers at reasonable rates. There is typically a pyramid structure with local, regional, and national levels.
Savings banks	These have the important privilege that interest is tax free up to a certain level of savings. Loans can be made only to individuals or bodies whose principal activities are neither industrial nor commercial.
Pensions	
Public	Covers all workers. Pensions linked to average earnings during working life. High replacement ratio.
Private	These are rare. A minority of industries have occupational schemes.
Insurance	Can be provided by universal banks as well as insurance companies.
Financial markets	
Stock markets	The most important exchange is the Paris Bourse, but there are six other regional exchanges. The Paris market grew significantly in the 1980s and 1990s and is now one of the major markets in Europe.
Debt markets	There is a significant market for government debt as well as for banks. There is also an important commercial paper market.
Derivative markets	The Marché à Terme International de France (MATIF) was founded in 1986 and quickly became one of the most important futures markets in Europe. The Marché des Options Négotiables de Paris (MONEP) started in 1987 and became one of the most important options exchanges.

the trade sector and small and medium-sized industries. These mutual and cooperative banks tend to have a pyramid structure with local, regional, and national organizations. In terms of their importance for the distribution of means of payment, they were in aggregate 64 percent of that of commercial banks in 1992.

The savings banks in France are identified by their trademark L'Ecureuil (Squirrel). They have the privilege of offering accounts up to a certain size where the interest is tax free. The loans that the savings banks make are only for the benefit of individuals or entities whose principal activity is neither industrial nor commercial. Relative to commercial banks, their importance in 1992 was 30 percent in terms of the distribution of the means of payment. In addition to the Ecureuil savings bank network, there is a large postal savings bank, which is roughly the same size.

The state pension system in France is a generous one with a replacement rate of 47 to 65 percent and universal coverage. Contributions are tax free, but benefits are taxed. Private pensions are very limited. As table 3.2 indicates, the proportion of household assets held by pension funds is only 2 percent. The main reason is that funded company schemes have been forbidden. Moreover, book reserve funding is subject to tax discrimination. Some mutual societies provide pension through group life insurance policies, but these have to follow insurance regulations, which require that they invest at least 34 percent in state bonds and a maximum of 40 percent in property and 5 percent in shares of foreign insurers. Table 3.7 indicates that the majority of assets, 59.0 percent, are in fact held in bonds, with 26.9 percent held in equities.

The assets that insurance companies hold in France are a substantial portion of household assets. As table 3.2 indicates they represent 17 percent of the total. Their investments are primarily in bonds, which constitute 61.6 percent of their assets, as shown in table 3.8. Bonds are the next most important asset, with 19.8 percent of the total.

French financial markets, particularly those for equities and derivatives, have developed greatly since the beginning of the 1980s. For example, between 1981 and 1991, the total market capitalization on the Paris Bourse went up by a factor of 5.8—transactions by a factor of 25. In addition to the bourse in Paris, there are six others in Lyon, Marseille, Bordeaux, Nantes, Lille, and Nancy. The reform of January 23, 1991, created a single national market so that stocks could be traded at any exchange, not just at the exchanges where they had been admitted for negotiation. In addition to this reform, another important change in 1991 was the completion of a computerized trading system. This is the CAC (Cotation Assistée en Continu) system.

Derivatives markets, set up in the mid-1980s, were an immediate success. The Marché à Terme International de France (MATIF) effectively started operations in February 1986. The initial listing was a notional bond futures contract. The set of listings was subsequently expanded to include a range of interest rate futures, options contracts, a futures contract on the CAC 40, and a number of commodities contracts. The MATIF soon came to rival the London International Financial Futures Exchange (LIFFE). The Marché des Options Négotiables de

Paris (MONEP) was set up by the Paris Bourse for trading in stock and index options in September 1987. It also was successful and is now one of the leading stock options exchanges in Europe.

A high proportion of funds (62 percent) are held directly by households in France (see table 3.2). Very little (2 percent) is held by pension funds, while insurance companies are important (17 percent). Collective investment schemes such as mutual funds have a substantial presence, with 19 percent of assets, much higher than in any other country. Table 3.3 indicates that most of households' investments are in cash and cash equivalents (38 percent) and bonds (33 percent). Very little is in equities (16 percent).

The source of funds in France is primarily retained earnings. As shown in table 3.5 these constitute 44.1 percent of the total. Loans are a close second, with 41.5 percent. Interestingly, shares are the next biggest category, with 10.6 percent. This is the largest among the countries shown.

3.5 Germany

Germany is very different from the other countries in that banks play a far more important role and markets much less of a role than in the other countries (see table 3.1). The ratio of banking assets to GDP in 1993 was 152 percent, while the ratio of equity market capitalization to GDP was only 24 percent. A brief overview of the German financial system is provided in table 3.12.

The commercial banks in Germany are universal banks. The big three—Deutsche, Dresdner, and Commerzbank—provide a whole array of services to both firms and consumers. On the firm side, they provide both short- and long-term loans. They can also hold equity in firms and so can provide equity finance. On the consumer side, they provide a wide range of products, including the provision of savings instruments, loans, and life insurance products. For the last, Deutsche has its own insurance subsidiary, while the other two big banks have formed strategic alliances with major insurance firms.

Other types of bank in addition to the major universal banks are important in Germany. Savings banks were originally set up to provide credit and savings vehicles to the poor. The funds were used to provide mortgages and finance local and regional investments. They continue to undertake these roles. The savings bank system has a three-tier structure. There are over seven hundred local savings banks at the base,

Table 3.12
Institutions and markets in Germany

Banking system	
Commercial banks	Includes the three major banks: Deutsche Bank, Dresdner Bank, and Commerzbank. These are universal banks that engage in a full range of activities, including taking deposits, granting loans and mortgages, providing life insurance, underwriting security issues, and investing directly in securities, including equities.
Savings banks	These are not profit-maximizing entities but are operated in the public interest. There are three tiers: local savings banks, state savings banks, and the central savings bank.
Cooperative banks	The depositors are the shareholders. As with savings banks, there is a three-tier structure with local, state, and central levels.
Pensions	
Public	Covers all workers. Pensions linked to average earnings during working life. High replacement ratio.
Private	Largely defined benefit based on flat-rate benefit. Indexation mandatory. For tax reasons, financed mainly in the form of book reserves.
Insurance	Provided by universal banks as well as insurance companies. In contrast to banking, the industry is heavily regulated. Insurance is usually provided by groups because there has traditionally been a prohibition on cross-subsidization across lines.
Financial markets	
Stock markets	Seven regional exchanges, with Frankfurt being the most important. Relatively few companies are listed. These markets have traditionally been an insignificant source of funds for firms.
Debt markets	Important source of funds for all levels of government as well as for banks. Not important for nonfinancial firms.
Derivative markets	These are undeveloped. Financial options and futures markets opened only in 1990, and the volume of trade has remained unimportant.

above them are twelve regional banks that the local banks belong to, and at the top is a central organization that the regional banks belong to. Savings banks can be set up only by local authorities, such as municipalities and districts, and these founders act as their guarantors.

The credit cooperatives were originally founded to help weakly capitalized commercial enterprises. They are mutual organizations owned by their depositors. Like the savings bank, they have a three-tier structure. There are three regional central banks as well as a central organization.

An interesting feature of the German banking sector is that a majority of the organizations (in terms of assets) are not standard profit-maximizing entities. Savings banks, which account for 36 percent of total banking assets, do not maximize profits. Also, the cooperatives, which constitute another 15 percent of total banking assets, are owned by their depositors. Although all countries have a range of ownership forms in their financial system, Germany is perhaps unique in the degree to which organizations have different forms.

Banks in Germany face relatively few regulatory restrictions. The underwriting of securities is unrestricted and can be undertaken directly by the bank; there is no need to set up a subsidiary. Moreover, firewalls are not mandated. The insurance activities of banks are restricted somewhat. They can be conducted as a principal only through subsidiaries that are regulated by the Insurance Supervisory Office in the same way as insurance firms. A bank may conduct insurance activities as an agent without restriction. Real estate activities are permitted. The book value of investment in equity and real estate may not exceed the bank's liable capital. However, investment in real estate through subsidiaries is unlimited. Banks may hold equity in nonfinancial firms and vice versa.

Germany's social security system provides pensions to all workers. These state pensions are linked to average earnings during working life. The replacement ratio is high. There is also an extensive private pension system. Private plans are usually defined benefit and provide a flat benefit. Inflation indexing is mandatory. One special feature of the German pensions is how they are taxed at the corporate level. Pensions funded by book reserves are given special advantages. Firms are allowed discretionary use of the funds accumulated on the firm's balance sheet in this way free of tax. As a result, very few funds in Germany are invested in anything other than book reserves of the firm. In addition, benefits booked this way are insured by the Pension Guarantee Association. As in France, very few assets are held by pension funds. As indicated by table 3.2, they constitute just 4 percent of household assets. For those funds held externally, there are guidelines on how they can be invested. There is a maximum limit of 20 percent in equity, 5 percent in property, and 4 percent in foreign securities. As shown in table 3.7 equities in fact constitute only 6.6 percent of pension assets. Bonds represent 42.8 percent and loans and mortgages are 29.5 percent.

The insurance industry in Germany is much more heavily regulated than the banking industry. The Insurance Supervisory Office requires that funds be invested according to the requirements of security, profitability, mixing, and spreading, with liquidity assured at all times.

More than 80 percent of the insurance companies' assets are placed with the banks. Although insurance companies can invest in equities, this type of investment plays a very small role in their portfolios. An important feature of the German insurance industry is the legal requirement that life insurance be separate from other forms of insurance. The supervisory authority has extended this to other insurance lines. As a result insurance tends to be offered by groups with many consolidated subsidiaries. The assets held by insurance companies are significant, representing 20 percent of household assets (see table 3.2). From table 3.7 it can be seen that 66.3 percent of these investments are in bonds and only 12.6 percent are in bonds.

Financial markets are relatively undeveloped in Germany compared to most other industrial countries, and few households participate directly in the markets. The lack of prohibitions on insider trading makes participation by unsophisticated investors unattractive. In addition, the availability of mutual funds is less than in other countries, and other indirect means of holding stock are limited. Overall, German investors have a limited range of equity instruments to invest in.

The debt markets are more important than the stock markets. Most of the debt and notes traded are issued by federal, state, or local governments, government entities, banks, and other intermediaries. The amount of debt issued by German industrial firms in German markets is very small and constitutes less than 0.5 percent of bonds outstanding. Some large firms borrow in the Euro-deutschemark markets, but the total amount is less than 2 percent of total domestic debt.

Futures and options markets in Germany are of little practical importance. The Deutsche Termin Bourse, Germany's first futures and options exchange, opened only in 1990, and volume has not been particularly high.

Table 3.2 indicates that Germany is very like France in terms of the asset holdings of households. The main difference is that less (5 percent) is held in mutual funds and other collective investment schemes. The allocation across assets shown in table 3.3 is like France, the most being in cash and cash equivalents (36 percent) and bonds (36 percent). Equity is fairly unimportant (13 percent).

Germany is much more like Japan and France in terms of firms' raising funds than the United States or United Kingdom. Table 5 indicates that retentions are the single most important source (55.2 percent), but bank loans are also important (21.1 percent).

3.6 Conclusion

A country's financial system is often characterized as being market based or bank based. The data presented in this chapter indicate that the nature of this distinction is a complex issue and can be viewed in a number of different ways. From the perspective of households, there is a clear difference between the assets held in the United States and United Kingdom and those held in Japan, Germany, and France. In the Anglo-Saxon countries, equity is a significant proportion of households' holdings. In the United States direct and indirect holdings (via pension funds, insurance companies, and mutual funds) are important. Overall, equity constitutes 45 percent of household assets. In the United Kingdom indirect holdings (pension funds and insurance companies) are more important than in the United States. The total of 52 percent of household assets in equity is even higher than in the United States. This contrasts sharply with Japan, France, and Germany, where the corresponding figures from table 3.3 are 12 percent, 16 percent, and 13 percent. In these countries the type of assets held instead are cash and cash equivalents and bonds. In Japan 52 percent of assets are held in cash and cash equivalents and 13 percent in bonds, while in France it is 38 percent and 33 percent, respectively, and in Germany, 36 percent in both. The implications of these different asset holdings are that in the United States and United Kingdom households bear significant risk, while in Japan, Germany, and France they bear relatively little risk.

Another observation that follows concerns the nature of decisions that individuals in the different countries make. In France, Germany, and Japan the fact that individuals invest indirectly through intermediaries means that the nature of the decisions they must make are different from individuals transacting in markets directly. The intermediaries can structure products so that they are easily understood. It is interesting to note that although still high, individual participation in the stock market in the United States has been falling. As figure 3.2 illustrated, the share of pension funds and mutual funds has risen to compensate for this fall. Thus, individuals in all countries are becoming less involved in transacting directly in financial markets.

When viewed from the prospective of firms' raising funds, the distinction between market-based and bank-based systems is much less clear-cut. There are some differences in how firms obtain their funds.

Perhaps the most striking point about table 3.5, however, is that in all countries except Japan, retained earnings are the most important source of funds. External finance is simply not that important.

In the case of internal versus external finance, it is important to distinguish between the developed world and the emerging countries. Although it is true for all the countries considered and for most other developed countries that internal finance dominates external finance, this is not the case for emerging countries. Singh and Hamid (1992) and Singh (1995) show that in a range of countries, external finance is more important than internal finance. Moreover, equity is the most important financing instrument and dominates debt. This interesting difference between the industrialized nations and the emerging countries has received little attention so far.

Notes

1. The sources used for this chapter are Barth, Nolle, and Rice (1997), Davis (1992, 1996), Durieux, Serieyssol, and Stephan (1995), Hayakawa (1996), Miles (1996), Pestieau (1992), Saunders and Walter (1994), and Walter and von Rosen (1995). Except where otherwise stated, the figures used are obtained from these sources.

2. A Section 20 subsidiary is an investment banking subsidiary of a bank holding company that can deal directly in activities that are ineligible from the standpoint of the Glass-Steagall Act of 1933, such as underwriting debt and equity. The name Section 20 comes from the Glass-Steagall Act of 1933, which prohibited banks from affiliating with a company "engaged . . . principally [in the] issue, flotation, underwriting, public sale, or distribution at wholesale or retail or through syndicate participation of stocks, bonds debentures, notes or other securities."

References

Barth, J., D. Nolle, and T. Rice. (1997). "Commercial Banking Structure, Regulation and Performance: An International Comparison." Economics Working paper 97-6, Comptroller of the Currency.

Bertero, E. (1994). "The Banking System, Financial Markets, and Capital Structure: Some New Evidence from France." *Oxford Review of Economic Policy* **10,** 68–78.

Cai, J., K. Chan, and T. Yamada. (1997). "The Performance of Japanese Mutual Funds." *Review of Financial Studies* **10,** 237–273.

Corbett, J., and T. Jenkinson. (1996). "The Financing of Industry, 1970–1989: An International Comparison." *Journal of the Japanese and International Economies* **10,** 71–96.

———. (1997). "How Is Investment Financed? A Study of Germany, Japan, the United Kingdom and the United States." *Manchester School of Economic and Social Studies* **65** (Supplement), 69–93.

Davis, E. P. (1992). "The Development of Pension Funds in the Major Industrial Countries." In Jørgen Mortensen (ed.), *The Future of Pensions in the European Community* (pp. 107–131). London: Brassey's.

———. (1996). "An International Comparison of the Financing of Occupational Pensions." In Z. Bodie, O. Mitchell, and J. Turner (eds.), *Securing Employer-Based Pensions: An International Perspective* (pp. 244–248). Philadelphia: University of Pennsylvania Press.

Durieux, G., M. Serieyssol, and P. Stephan. (1995). *French Financial Markets*. Abington, U.K.: Gresham Books.

Frankel, A., and J. Montgomery. (1991). "Financial Structure: An International Perspective." *Brookings Papers on Economic Activity*, 257–310.

Hayakawa, S. (1996). *Japanese Financial Markets*. Abington, U.K.: Gresham Books.

Institute of Fiscal and Monetary Policy. (1996). *Socio-Economic Systems of Japan, the United States, the United Kingdom, Germany and France.* Tokyo: Ministry of Finance.

Mayer, C. (1988). "New Issues in Corporate Finance." *European Economic Review* **32**, 1167–88.

———. (1990). "Financial Systems, Corporate Finance, and Economic Development." In R. G. Hubbard (ed.), *Asymmetric Information, Corporate Finance and Investment* (pp. 307–332). Chicago: University of Chicago Press.

Miles, D. (1996). "The Future of Savings and Wealth Accumulation: Differences Within the Developed Economies." London: Global Securities Research and Economics Group, Merrill Lynch.

Pestieau, P. (1992). "The Distribution of Private Pension Benefits: How Fair Is It?" In *Private Pensions and Public Policy* (pp. 31–50). Paris: OECD.

Saunders, A., and I. Walter. (1994). *Universal Banking in the United States: What Could We Gain? What Could We Lose?* New York: Oxford University Press.

Singh, A. (1995). *Corporate Financial Patterns in Industrializing Economies: A Comparative International Study.* Technical Paper 2. Washington, D.C.: International Finance Corporation.

Singh, A., and J. Hamid. (1992). *Corporate Financial Structures in Developing Countries.* Technical Paper 1. Washington, D.C.: International Finance Corporation.

Walter, N., and R. von Rosen. (1995). *German Financial Markets.* Abington, U.K.: Gresham Books.

4 Corporate Governance

In most countries, including the United States, the United Kingdom, Japan, Germany, and France, managers of corporations are ultimately legally responsible to the shareholders. In their seminal book, Berle and Means (1932) argued that in practice, managers did not pursue the interests of shareholders but instead pursued their own. The contractual aspect of the firm together with the problem Berle and Means highlighted led to the development of the agency approach to corporate governance by, among others, Coase (1937), Jensen and Meckling (1976), Fama and Jensen (1983a, 1983b), and Hart (1995). An excellent survey is contained in Shleifer and Vishny (1997). The main issue that has been focused on in this literature is how shareholders can ensure that managers pursue their interests.

One of the themes of this book is that this focus is too narrow. In practice, the issue of corporate governance is more complex. In Germany, the system of codetermination means that shareholders are not the only group the managers of the corporation are responsible to; employees are also formally represented in the governance process. In the other countries, the situation is more complex than the legal responsibility suggests. A number of stakeholders have an influence that varies across countries. In this chapter we are concerned with the relationship between how corporations operate in practice and the agency theories of corporate governance in the literature. In chapter 11 we argue that provided the interests of the firm and the manager are somewhat aligned, separation of ownership and control can be optimal in a second-best world. In chapter 12 we develop an alternative approach to organizations where incentives for the efficient use of resources are provided without external monitoring.

In the next section we consider the actual operation of corporate governance in the five countries. We start with a discussion of the legal definition of corporations in each country and the restrictions on shareholding. The operation of various possible governance mechanisms in these situations is then addressed. In the United States and United Kingdom, the mechanisms for ensuring that managers operate in the interests of shareholders are the strongest, and most managers do profess this as their aim. Internal and external governance systems are usually cited as being responsible for this. The main internal governance system is the board of directors, and the main external governance system is the market for corporate control. The effectiveness of these mechanisms has been widely questioned. There seems to be some evidence, particularly in recent years, that boards of directors are dominated by management, and the CEO in particular. Although stock market prices of acquirers and acquirees rise in aggregate when mergers and takeovers are announced, the evidence is mixed regarding studies of the ex post profitability of acquisitions based on accounting data.

At the other end of the spectrum is Japan, where managers' expressed goal is to pursue employment stability for workers rather than dividends for shareholders. The operation of the standard corporate governance mechanisms of the board of directors and the market for corporate control are such that the objective of implementing value creation for shareholders is not pursued. The boards of directors are typically large, unwieldy groups dominated by insiders. The prevalence of cross-holdings of shares in Japan means that even though there are no legal impediments to hostile takeovers, they do not occur. It has been widely argued that the main bank system has substituted for the standard Anglo-American corporate governance systems. In this system, a large bank, which is a major provider of funds to the firm, monitors its activities and ensures that the funds loaned are sensibly invested. If the firm encounters problems, the main bank can discipline management where necessary and provide the funds needed to see the firm through difficult times or liquidate it. Financial deregulation in the 1970s and 1980s increasingly allowed large Japanese firms to obtain funds from the bond market. As a result, the main bank system no longer seems to be as important for many of these firms.

Germany and France are intermediate cases, where the interests of shareholders are pursued but not exclusively. The interests of other stakeholders, in particular employees, are important. In Germany, the system of codetermination formalizes this balance of interests since both the shareholders and the employees are represented on the supervisory board. In France, the attendance of employee representatives at board meetings as observers and extensive government ownership of industry have had a similar effect. In both countries, complex patterns of share ownership by holding companies and cross-holdings severely limit the market for corporate control, as in Japan. Although hostile takeovers are legally permissible, they are very rare.

Corporations represent only one type of economic organization. The other major forms are family businesses, worker cooperatives, state-owned firms, and nonprofit enterprises. Governance mechanisms for these alternative forms of organization provide an interesting contrast to corporations. Family businesses more closely approximate the neoclassical ideal of a firm operated in the interests of its owners. Competition between family-owned businesses and corporations may help ensure an efficient allocation of resources. The governance of worker cooperatives and state-owned firms raises similar issues to those dealt with in standard theories of public choice. Finally, there are nonprofit organizations, which represent a significant portion of economic activity in all the countries considered.

This chapter also considers the governance issues raised by nonprofits. They provide a particularly interesting case because they are the organizations that perhaps have the least outside pressures on their operation. Despite this, nonprofit organizations in many cases compete directly and successfully with for-profit corporations. For example, in the United States both types of institution own significant numbers of hospitals. In some sectors nonprofits dominate even though entry by for-profit organizations is quite possible and would at first sight appear to be profitable. As an illustration, it is quite possible to set up for-profit educational institutions. Language education in the United States and many other countries is provided by for-profit institutions. However, this seems to be one of the few areas of education where for-profits successfully compete. Advanced education for degrees is overwhelmingly provided by nonprofit and government-financed universities, with no serious for-profit providers of degrees and higher degrees despite the apparent heavy subsidy for research provided by liberal arts students in private universities. It would appear that a for-profit institution operating without these subsidies should be fairly profitable.

The tremendous differences in the way that corporations operate in different countries, together with the vast range of successful nonprofit organizations, suggest that the standard view of governance is rather narrow. We believe that a much broader notion of the firm, both profit and nonprofit, is required. In chapters 11 and 12 we develop theories that are applicable in a wider range of institutional forms.

4.1 Different Concepts of the Corporation

This section starts with a discussion of the legal definitions of the firm in the five countries, looks at regulatory restrictions on share ownership and the resulting differences across countries, considers the governance mechanisms analyzed in the literature, and concludes with a discussion of whose interests are pursued in practice.[1]

Legal Definitions of the Firm

The precise legal details of the corporation differ somewhat across countries. The origins of company law in the United States and United Kingdom are shared, so they are similar. The managers have a fiduciary duty to the shareholders. In other words, they have a strong legal requirement to act in the interests of shareholders. A classic illustration is provided by a case involving the Ford Motor Company early in its history. Henry Ford announced a special dividend but said that it would be discontinued in the future in order to allow funds to be diverted for the benefit of employees. One of the major shareholders sued on the grounds that the corporation exists for the benefit of shareholders and the management did not have the right to pursue the interests of workers. The Ford Motor Company lost the case. (Subsequently it appeared that Henry Ford's announcement was designed to manipulate the stock price so that he could purchase blocks at a lower level than would otherwise be necessary.)

The official channel through which shareholders influence company affairs is the board of directors, which is elected by the shareholders, with there typically being one vote per share. Sometimes multiple classes of shares exist, with the main difference between classes being in terms of the number of votes each share has attached to it. The board of directors consists of a mix of outside directors and inside directors who are the top executives in the firm. It is rare that the chief executive officer (CEO) is not on the board. In both the United States and the United Kingdom the CEO can act as chair of the board of the directors. Once elected, the board of directors specifies the business policies that the firm will pursue. The role of management is to implement the policies that the board has determined. Shareholders have very little to say beyond electing directors. For example, it is the directors who decide on their own compensation without any input from shareholders.

A committee of outside directors determines the senior management's compensation. Except in unusual circumstances, such as a proxy fight, the outside directors are nominated by the incumbent management and thus typically owe their allegiance to the CEO. Table 4.1 shows the total number of directors and for the United States, United Kingdom, and Japan (in parentheses) the number of outside directors for a typical sample of large firms in each of the countries. The size of boards is roughly the same in the United States and the United Kingdom—usually around ten to fifteen people. In the United States a majority are typically from outside the firm, while in the United Kingdom a minority are.

Japan resembles the United States in terms of the legal form of corporations because of the heavy influence of the U.S. Occupation Forces on the legal system and the structure of institutions after World War II. Some important differences do exist, however. In the past, nonfinancial corporations faced elaborate restrictions that prevented them from establishing holding companies. One of the changes in the ongoing reform of the Japanese financial system, the so-called Japanese Big Bang, is to allow nonfinancial corporations to form holding companies. The rights of Japanese shareholders are in theory greater than those of shareholders in the United States and United Kingdom. For example, in Japan it is easier for shareholders to nominate directors directly and elect them. Also, management remuneration must be decided at general meetings of shareholders. These differences in rights and the role of the shareholders meeting have led to a unique feature of Japanese corporate life, the *sokaiya,* racketeers who demand payment in exchange for not disrupting shareholders' meetings.

Despite these differences in shareholders' rights, the structure of Japanese boards of directors is such that shareholders do not in fact have much influence. It can be seen from table 4.1 that the size of Japanese boards is much larger than in other countries. There are a handful of outside directors, but they have very little influence; the overwhelming majority of directors are from inside the company. Their number is such that they include many people in addition to the most senior members of management. The nominations of individuals for positions as a director are essentially controlled by the company's CEO. This, together with the unwieldy size of the board and its composition, means that CEOs hold tremendous power. Provided the financial position of a Japanese corporation is sound, it is essentially the CEO and those closest to him who control the company's affairs.

Table 4.1
Number of members on boards of directors

United States			United Kingdom			Japan			France			Germany		
Ford	15	(10)	Glaxo	16	(7)	Toyota	60	(1)	Saint Gobain	16		Hoechst	21	11
IBM	14	(11)	Hanson	19	(8)	Hitachi	36	(3)	AGF	19	(5)	BASF	28	10
Exxon	12	(9)	Guinness	10	(6)	Matsushita	37	(6)	Usinor Sacilor	21	(5)	Robert Bosch	20	11
Mobil	16	(10)	British Airways	10	(6)	Nissan	49	(5)	Alcatel Alsthom	15		Krupp	22	7
Philip Morris	16	(4)	Allied Domecq	12	(4)	Toshiba	40	(3)	Elf Aquitane	11		Bayer	22	11
RJR Nabisco	9	(6)	Grand Metropolitan	14	(1)	Honda	37	(3)	Renault	18		Daimler Benz	20	8
Texaco	13	(11)	BTR	10	(4)	Sony	41	(6)	Thomson	8		Volkswagen	20	7
Johnson & Johnson	14	(12)	Associated British Foods	7	(1)	NEC	42	(5)				Thyssen	23	27
GAP	11	(8)	British Steel	8	(0)	Fujitsu	36	(7)				Siemens	20	15
						Mitsubishi Electric	37	(3)						
						Mitsubishi Motors	43	(4)						
						Mitsubishi Heavy Industries	43	(3)						
						Nippon Steel	53	(1)						
						Mazda	45	(8)						
						Nippon Oil	22	(0)						

Note: Figures in parentheses for the United States are outside directors, for the United Kingdom nonexecutive (outside) directors, for Japan outside directors (including cross directorships), and for France directors from the government. For Germany the first column represents the members of the supervisory board, and the second is the members of the Management Board.
Source: Institute of Fiscal and Monetary Policy (1996, Chart III-3-3, p. 69).

Germany's system of codetermination is very different from that of the United States, United Kingdom, and Japan. Pistor (1996) notes that it arose in the late nineteenth century from an attempt to overcome the contradiction between the reality of industrialization and liberal ideas about the self-determination and the rights of individuals. Its legal origins date from 1891 when an amendment to the law on entrepreneurial activities (*Gewerbeordnung*) provided that workers' councils could be established on a voluntary basis. The Weimar Constitution formally recognized codetermination, but the principle was suppressed by the Nazis. It steadily reemerged after World War II, and currently the most important legislation governing it is the Co-determination Act (*Mitbestimmungsgesetz*) of 1976. This generally applies to companies with more than two thousand employees.

Firms to which it applies have two boards: the supervisory board and the management board. The supervisory board is the controlling body, with half of its representatives elected by shareholders and half by the employees (Schneider-Lenné 1992, Prowse 1995). The shareholders' general meeting elects the shareholder representatives. Two-thirds of the employee representatives work for the company, and the other third are trade union representatives. The supervisory board elects a chairman and deputy chairman from its members. A majority of two-thirds of the votes is required for a candidate to be elected. If this is not attained in two polls, the shareholders elect the chairman from among themselves, and the employee representatives similarly elect the deputy. As a result, the chairman is usually from the shareholder side, and the deputy chairman is from the employee side. In the event of a tie in the voting of the supervisory board, the chairman has a casting vote. It is in this sense that shareholders have ultimate control. However, members of the supervisory board legally represent the interests of the company as a whole and not just the groups they represent. It can be seen from table 6.1 that supervisory boards are typically just over twenty people in size and so are slightly bigger than boards in the United States and United Kingdom but smaller than in Japan.

The management board is appointed by the supervisory board. Nobody can be a member of both boards, and cross-company board memberships are restricted. The management board is responsible for the operation of the company, and the supervisory board supervises its activities. The management board provides information to the supervisory board, a situation that can obviously lead to abuse because management has an incentive to distort the information so that it looks as though the firm is doing better than is actually the case. However, this problem is often mitigated by the chairman of the supervisory board being a retired former CEO of the company with wide experience of its operations and many informal contacts. Table 4.1 shows that the management board is usually fairly small—smaller than the supervisory board and the boards in other countries.

The German system provides an interesting contrast to the Anglo-American and Japanese systems. It is often argued that the dual board system better represents outside shareholders and ensures that management must take account of their views. In addition, employees' views are also represented, and their bias is presumably to ensure the long-run viability of the firm.

France's system contains elements of both the Anglo-American and the German systems. There are two types of boards of directors, and firms can choose which to have. The first type, which is more common, is single tiered, as in the Anglo-American system. The board elects the président directeur-général (PDG) who is like a CEO but is more powerful. He or she has the sole right to represent the company and is the only person who can delegate this power. Single-tiered boards mostly consist of outside directors, who are shareholders and representatives from financial institutions with which the firm has transactional relationships. As in the Anglo-American model, the board determines business policies, which are then carried out by the PDG and management.

The second type of board has two tiers, as in Germany. The conseil de surveillance is like the German supervisory board except that employees do not have the right to representation. However, one unique feature of the French system makes it more akin to the German one: with single-tiered and two-tiered boards, workers' representatives have the right to attend board meetings as observers in all companies with at least fifty employees. The conseil de surveillance appoints the directoire, who have responsibility for the management of the company. One of the members of the directoire is designated président de directoire by the others.

The size of boards is roughly similar to the United States. Complete or partial government ownership of corporations is more prevalent than in other countries, and as table 4.1 indicates, in some cases this translates into government representation on boards (figures in parentheses are directors from the government).

Regulatory Restrictions and the Pattern of Share Ownership

In addition to having different legal structures for the firm, the countries also place differing restrictions on the holding of shares by financial institutions and nonfinancial corporations (see table 4.2). These restrictions have had important implications for the countries' patterns of share ownership, which are shown in table 4.3.

Restrictions on institutional holdings of shares are one area where the United States differs significantly from the United Kingdom. In the United States the Glass-Steagall Act prevents banks from holding equity stakes in companies except in unusual circumstances, such as when the firm has gone bankrupt. Insurance companies are regulated by state laws. The most significant regulation is that of New York State, which affects a large proportion of companies not only because many companies are based there but also because other states tend to follow their lead. Historically, New York regulations prevented insurers from holding any equity. However, in more recent times, life insurance companies have been able to hold a limited amount. Mutual and pension funds are also restricted in the amount of any single stock they can own to ensure diversification. It can be seen from table 4.3 that these regulations have meant that the pattern of share ownership in the United States is significantly different from the pattern in other countries. Only a small amount of equity, 6 percent, is held by financial institutions, whereas in the other countries, the average holding is 29 percent. Instead, the proportion owned by individuals is much higher than elsewhere, and the proportion owned by mutual and pension funds is higher than in Japan, Germany, and France. The main restriction on the holding of shares by nonfinancial corporations in other firms is the requirement that this not restrict competition in any way. This has been interpreted fairly strictly. In a famous case the U.S. Supreme Court forced Dupont to sell its 25 percent holding in General Motors and cut all other ties. The United States's 14 percent ownership of shares by nonfinancial corporations is much lower than in Japan, Germany, and France but comparable to the United Kingdom.

It can be seen from table 4.2 that the United Kingdom has far fewer formal regulations than the United States does. Banks can hold equity if they wish and need obtain permission from the Bank of England only if they are purchasing large blocks. Insurance companies are limited only by the need to diversify, which is a self-imposed limitation. With regard to holdings of nonfinancial corporations, the only limitation

Table 4.2
Regulations on shareholding of financial institutions and nonfinancial corporations

	United States	United Kingdom	Japan	France	Germany
Banks	Banks: Cannot hold shares of other corporations (Glass-Steagall Act). Bank holding companies: Holdings are limited to a maximum of 5 percent of the shares of nonfinancial corporations Trusts: Holdings are limited to a maximum of 10 percent of the fund's assets in any one company's shares.	No Special regulations on holdings. However, in the case of large-volume acquisitions of shares, advance permission of the Bank of England is required. A report to the Bank of England is required when exposure (all claims including shares invested) exceeds 10 percent of a bank's total capital.[a]	Under Article 11 of the Anti-Monopoly Law holdings are limited to 5 percent of the total number of issued shares of a domestic company.	The holding of shares of any single nonfinancial corporation is limited to a maximum of 15 percent of the bank's capital. Total holdings of all shares cannot exceed 60 percent of all the bank's capital.	Holdings greater than 10 percent are permitted, but only up to the value of the bank's capital.[a]
Life insurance companies	Varies by state. For instance, under New York State law (which applies to 60 percent of all insurance companies), investments must be less than 20 percent of assets or a maximum of 50 percent of surpluses. Holdings of the shares of any single company are limited to 2 percent of total assets.	Voluntary self-limitation of holding of stock in any single company (normally 2.5 percent of assets), for the purpose of portfolio diversification. A maximum (normally 5 percent of assets) is imposed on the amount of stock in any single company which a pension fund or insurance company can hold on its own.	Under the Anti-Monopoly Law, holdings are limited to a maximum of 10 percent of the total number of issued shares of any single company.		Holding of shares up to 20 percent of total assets is permitted.

Table 4.2 (continued)

	United States	United Kingdom	Japan	France	Germany
Other insurance companies	Prohibition on holding a noninsurance company in its entirety.	Same as above.	Same as above.		No regulations.
Mutual funds	Tax penalty imposed on holdings in excess of 10 percent of the stock of any single company.	Under laws regulating financial services, holding of stock for the purpose of controlling a company is prohibited.	No regulations.		No regulations.
Pension funds	Under the Employee Retirement Income Securities Act, investment diversification is required. Holdings in excess of 10 percent of the pension fund's own stock are prohibited.	Same as for insurance companies.			No regulations.

Table 4.2 (continued)

	United States	United Kingdom	Japan	France	Germany
Other	Holding of stock that results in restricting competition is prohibited.	Under the City Code on Takeovers and Mergers, the mutual holding of shares the purpose of which is to prevent the transfer of control of stock is prohibited.	Establishment of holding companies is prohibited (Article 9 of the Anti-Monopoly Law). A subsidiary whose parent company owns more than half of its stock cannot hold stock in its parent company (Commercial Code Article 211 [2]). When one company controls another through shareholdings, the controlled company has no voting rights with respect to the controlling company's stock (Commercial Code, Article 241 [3]).	A company can hold a maximum of 10 percent of the total number of issued shares of another company. Subsidiaries can also hold up to 10 percent of the stock of parent companies but cannot vote.	A subsidiary whose parent company owns more than half of its stock cannot hold stock in its parent company. Mutual holding of shares is possible, but voting rights are limited to 25 percent of all voting rights, even when a company owns more than 25 percent of the stock of another company. Establishment of holding companies is permitted (in the case of pure holding companies and management holding companies).

Table 4.2 (continued)

	United States	United Kingdom	Japan	France	Germany
Other (*continued*)			A corporation that engages in nonfinancial business and has capital assets worth at least 10 billion yen, or net assets worth at least 30 billion yen, is prohibited from holding shares in domestic companies exceeding the value of its capital or net assets, whichever is greater (Anti-Monopoly Law, Article 9 [2]).[b]		

a. The United Kingdom and Germany are scheduled to make modifications to their regulations as EU integration progresses.
b. Japan is scheduled to make changes to its laws on holding companies as part of the "Big Bang" reform of its financial system.
Source: Institute of Fiscal and Monetary Policy (1996, Chart III-2-3, p. 60).

Table 4.3
Comparison of shareholders by sector (% of total)

	Individuals	Pension funds	Financial institutions	Nonfinancial corporations	Public sector	Foreign individuals and institutions	Other
United States	50	20	5	14	0	5	6
United Kingdom	20	31	30	3	4	12	
Japan	23		41	25	1	4	6
France	34		23	21	2	20	
Germany	17		22	42	5	14	

Note: Data are for 1990 except for France, which are for 1992.
Sources: Prowse (1995, Table 2, p. 13) for the United States and Institute of Fiscal and Monetary Policy (1996, Chart III-2-1, p. 59), for the other countries.

is that firms must not mutually hold each other's shares to prevent a transfer of control. The difference in ownership patterns that this creates relative to the United States is that financial institutions hold more and individuals less. Compared to Japan, Germany, and France, the holding of shares by nonfinancial corporations is much less and the holdings of pension funds much greater.

As tables 4.2 and 4.3 indicate, Japan, Germany, and France are all somewhat similar in terms of the regulatory restrictions on holding shares and the patterns of ownership. In all three countries, banks can hold the equity of companies. There are regulations on the proportions of the equity of firms that banks can hold in Japan. In Germany and France there are restrictions on holdings of equity relative to bank capital. Holding companies were traditionally not permitted in Japan. In Germany and France there are limitations on the percentages of firms that can be owned.

Complex interactions of holding companies occur in both Germany and France. Van Hulle (1996) contains an account of European holding groups. Figure 4.1 gives the ownership structure of Daimler-BenzAG as an example. Each level of the "tree" in figure 4.1 shows the companies, individuals, or groups who own the company in the level immediately above and the percentage of the shares held by each. Thus, Daimler-Benz is held by Deutsche Bank (28.5%), Mercedes Holding (25.23%), Kuwait (14%), and a large group of small shareholders (32.5%). Here the interactions between firms are necessarily somewhat more subtle than in Japan because of their complexity, but they have similar effects.

Governance Mechanisms

The literature describes a number of ways in which shareholders can ensure that managers act in their interests. The most important of these are the board of directors, executive compensation, the market for corporate control, concentrated holdings and monitoring by financial institutions, debt, and product market competition. We consider each of these in turn.

Board of Directors

The board of directors is, in theory at least, the first method that shareholders have to control managers and ensure the company is run in their interest. The way that boards are chosen and structured differs in significant ways across countries. In the United States and United

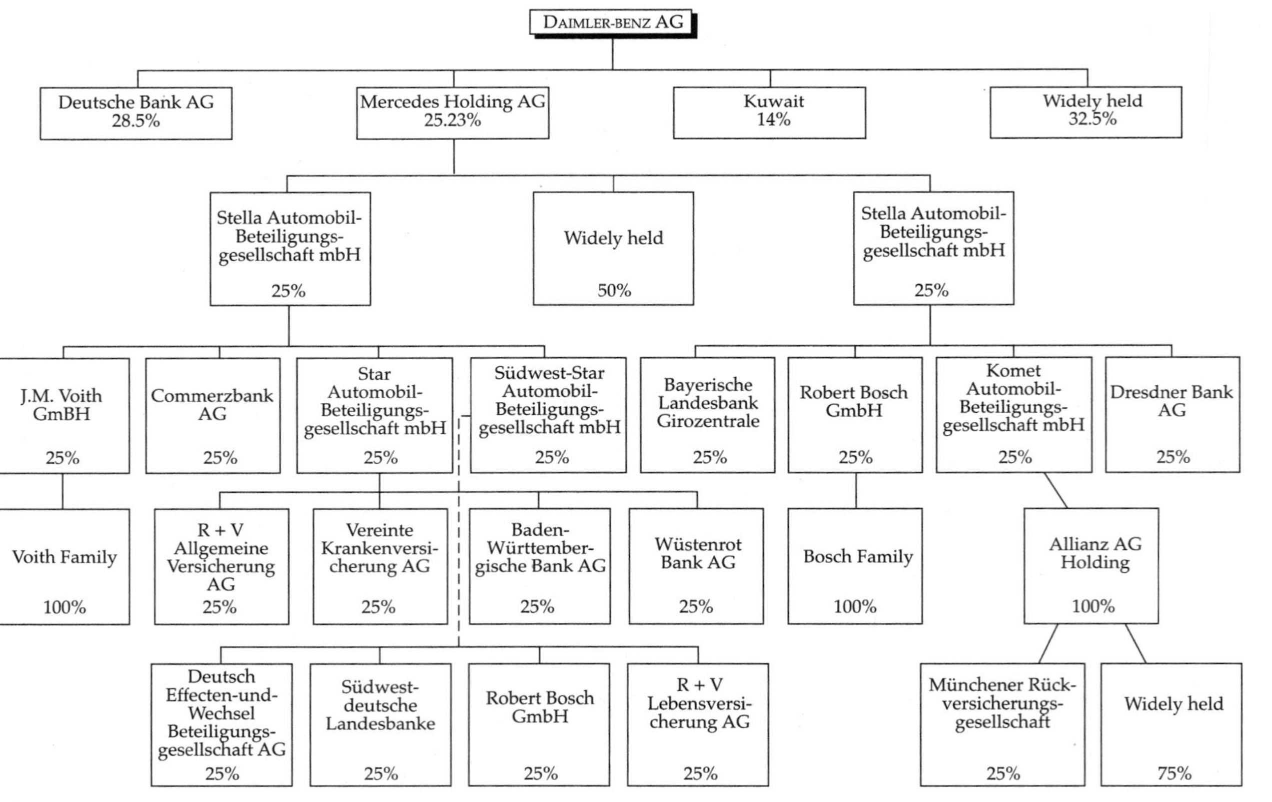

Figure 4.1
Ownership tree of Daimler-Benz AG. *Source:* Prowse (1995).

Kingdom, shareholders elect directors and have to rely on them to set business policies and supervise management. A balance of inside and outside directors on the board is supposed to ensure the board is at the same time knowledgeable about the company and independent from management. The extent to which this theory works in practice is widely debated. Since management, and in particular the CEO, effectively determines who is nominated for the board, it is not entirely clear that the board is as independent as it might be. Mace (1971), Weisbach (1988), and Jensen (1989) document the weakness of United States boards in disciplining managers, and Bhagat and Black (1998) survey the literature on the relationship between board composition and firm performance. The evidence indicates that boards with a majority of independent directors do not perform better than firms without such boards, although having a moderate number of inside directors appears to be associated with greater profitability.

In Japan the independence of the board of directors is accentuated by the large size of boards, the very limited number of outside directors, and the extreme power of the CEO to determine nominations for directors. Although shareholders in theory have more power to control the board of directors than in other countries, this does not mean much in practice.

The two-tiered nature of German boards represents an attempt to formalize the different roles of outside and inside directors since the supervisory board consists of people outside the current management while the management board consists of serving managers. Informational problems are minimized by including former managers on the supervisory board, a practice that dilutes the independence of the supervisory board. If the supervisory board contains former managers, how separate from current management can it be in practice? Typically the current management, will have been chosen by the former management, and many of the policies they will be implementing will have originated with previous regimes. Another complication is that the supervisory board has employee representatives. It is interesting to note that in France where both single-tiered and two-tiered boards are possible, single-tiered boards tend to predominate.

Although the structure of boards is so different across countries, the limited empirical evidence available suggests that they are equally effective or ineffective at disciplining management. Kaplan (1994a, 1994b) has conducted studies of the relationship between management turnover and various performance measures in Japan, Germany, and the United States. His findings indicate a similar relationship in each of the countries. Kang and Shivdasani (1995) confirm these results for Japan and provide evidence on the effectiveness of different types of governance mechanisms. Among other things, they find that the presence of outside directors on the board has no effect on the sensitivity of top executive turnover to either earnings or stock price performance. In contrast, concentrated equity ownership and ties to a main bank do have a positive effect. For Germany, Franks and Mayer (1997a) find a strong relationship between poorly performing companies and turnover on management boards but not with turnover on supervisory boards.

Executive Compensation

An additional method of ensuring that managers pursue the interests of shareholders is to structure compensation appropriately. Diamond and Verrecchia (1982) and Holmstrom and Tirole (1993) have developed models where the interaction of capital markets and contingent compensation achieves this. Provided investors have an incentive to gather information and stock market prices partially reflect this, incentives can be provided by making managers' compensation depend on the company's stock price. Examples of the form this dependence can take are direct ownership of shares, stock options, and bonuses dependent on share price. Provided stock prices contain enough information about the anticipated future profitability of the firm, fairly effective automatic incentive systems to ensure that managers maximize shareholder wealth can in theory be designed.

Stock prices are not the only contingency that can be used to motivate managers. Accounting-based performance measures are also frequently used. The advantage of stock price is that it is not as easily manipulable by management as accounting data. In addition to making compensation directly contingent, there is the possibility of dismissal for bad performance. If other firms perceive that the performance was due to incompetence, the manager may find it difficult to find another job and so may bear a large penalty. On the other hand, managers who perform extremely well may be bid away at higher compensation levels to other companies. The managerial labor market thus also plays an important part in providing incentives to managers.

In addition to providing incentives for increased effort, contingent compensation may have another less desirable effect. There is a danger that if executive compensation is sensitive to stock price and executives have limited downside risk, they will have an incentive to take excessive risks. They benefit greatly from good performance, but the penalties for poor performance are limited.

There has been some debate about the optimal sensitivity of executive compensation to stock price in practice. Jensen and Murphy (1990) confirm previous findings of a positive relationship between executive pay and performance in the United States and estimate that CEO compensation varies by about $3 for every $1,000 change in firm value. They suggest that this figure is much too small. Haubrich (1994) has calibrated an appropriately designed principal agent model that takes into account risk aversion and argues that a small sensitivity is optimal for reasonable parameter values. For other countries, the number of empirical studies is small. Kaplan (1994a, 1994b) considers the sensitivity of pay and dismissal to performance in Germany and Japan and he finds that they are similar to the United States in this respect.

The dramatic increase in executive compensation in the United States in recent years, partly in response to arguments such as those of Jensen and Murphy, has led to the opposite concern of whether boards of directors have been captured and are paying themselves exorbitant amounts. It is interesting to note that there is a considerable difference in levels of compensation across countries. In the United States executive compensation is very high. At the other extreme, Japan executives appear to earn a small fraction of what their counterparts in the United States earn. The United Kingdom, Germany, and France lie in between these two extremes.

The Market for Corporate Control

Manne (1965) has argued that an active market for corporate control is essential for the efficient operation of capitalist economies. It allows able management teams to gain control of large amounts of resources in a small amount of time. Inefficient managers are removed and replaced with people who are better able to do the job. The existence of a market for corporate control also provides one means of disciplining managers. A firm that is pursuing policies that do not maximize shareholders' wealth can be taken over and the managers replaced.

The market for corporate control can operate in three ways: proxy contests, friendly mergers, and hostile takeovers. In proxy contests, a group of shareholders try to persuade the remaining shareholders to act in concert with them and unseat the existing board of directors. For example, somebody who wishes to change a firm's policies can have herself and others with similar views voted onto the board of directors at a shareholders' meeting. In order to do this, she solicits proxies from other shareholders, which allows her to vote their shares. Proxy fights are usually difficult to win because holdings are often spread among many people. As a result they do not occur very frequently in any of the countries under consideration. (For recent theoretical analyses of proxy fights that throw some light on the problems involved with shareholder voting, see Bhattacharya 1997, Yilmaz 1997, and Maug 1998.)

Friendly mergers occur when both firms agree that combining them would be value creating. The transaction can occur in a number of ways—for example, an exchange of stock or a tender offer by one firm for the other firm's stock. Friendly mergers and takeovers occur in all the countries under consideration and account for most of the transaction volume that occurs. Prowse (1995) reports that in the United States, friendly transactions constituted 82.2 percent of transactions, in the United Kingdom 62.9 percent, and in the rest of Europe 90.4 percent.

The third way in which the market for corporate control can operate, through hostile takeovers, occurs when there is conflict between the acquirers and acquirees over the price that should be paid, the effectiveness of the policies that will be implemented, and so forth. Hostile tender offers allow the acquirers to go over the heads of the target management and appeal directly to their shareholders. This mechanism is potentially very important in ensuring an efficient allocation of resources in the way Manne (1965) suggested. However, as Hansmann (1996) points out, hostile tender offers first appeared in 1956 and were not widely used until the 1960s, so they are relatively recent. Corporations with widely held shares had been commonplace for many decades before that. It is not clear that hostile tender offers have induced a significant change in the efficiency with which corporations are managed.

Grossman and Hart (1980) have pointed to a problem with the operation of this mechanism of corporate governance that is consistent with the latter observation. Existing shareholders will have a strong incentive to free-ride on raiders who plan to increase the value of the firm. On the one hand, if the price the raider offers is below the price that the new policies will justify and the shareholder believes the offer will succeed, then there is no point in tendering. However, in that case, the offer will not succeed. On the other hand, if the raider offers a price above the current value and the shareholder believes that the offer will not succeed, then it will be worth tendering his shares. But then the offer will succeed. In both cases, the shareholder's beliefs are inconsistent with equilibrium. The only equilibrium is one in which the raider's offer price is equal to the price the new policies will justify. In that case, the raider's profit will be zero, before allowing for any costs incurred in undertaking the bid. If these costs are included, the profit will be negative, and there will be no incentive to attempt a takeover.

A number of solutions to the free-rider problem have been suggested. Grossman and Hart's (1980) solution is that corporate charters should be structured so that raiders can dilute minority shareholders' interests after the takeover occurs. This means the raider can offer a price below the posttakeover value of the firm to him and the bid will still succeed. Existing shareholders will know that if they retain their shares, the raider will dilute their interest. Shleifer and Vishny (1986) pointed out that if the raider can acquire a block of stock before attempting a takeover at the low pretakeover price, there will be a profit on this block even if all the remaining shares are purchased at the full price justified by the raider's plans. Burkart (1995) shows that it is privately optimal for a large shareholder to overbid, and this can lead to possible losses and inefficiencies.

In addition to the Grossman and Hart free-rider problem, there are a number of other problems with the operation of the market for corporate control. The second problem arises because of competition among bidders. Suppose there are substantial (sunk) costs of identifying a takeover target initially. Once the takeover bid is announced, other raiders will realize it is an attractive target and will bid. This competition will eliminate any profits by ensuring the target will sell at its full value. This means the initial bidder will realize a loss if the initial costs of identifying the target are taken into account. Unlike the free-rider problem, allowing ex post dilution will not have the desired effect of providing an incentive for takeovers. Competing raiders will take into account the benefits of dilution and include them in their bids. In contrast, owning a block of stock purchased at the pretakeover price will allow a raider to make a profit.

The third problem in the operation of the market for corporate control is the possibility of management entrenchment. Managers may be incompetent and want to prevent a takeover to preserve their jobs. There are a number of ways they can achieve this. First, they have a significant informational advantage over outside raiders. By using this appropriately, they may be able to thwart takeover attempts. For example, they may plausibly claim that the raider is not offering enough and the firm would be better to continue under current policies or wait for another bidder. Second, there are a number of antitakeover tactics that they can use—for example, poison pills, staggered election of directors, and dual class recapitalizations. Poison pills involve issuing rights to shareholders to buy stock in the company at a significantly reduced price in the event of a takeover. Staggered elections of directors ensure that only a fraction of directors, often one-third, can be replaced in any year, so even if a raider acquires all the votes, it will still take some time to acquire control of the board. Dual class recapitalizations involve issuing a second class of share with superior voting rights and requiring they be exchanged for regular shares before being sold. This ensures that votes become concentrated in managers' hands.

Despite all these problems, hostile takeovers do occur fairly frequently in the United States and United Kingdom. Prowse (1995) points out that in the United States, almost 10 percent of companies that belonged to the Fortune 500 in 1980 have since been acquired in a transaction that was hostile or started off as hostile. For the United Kingdom, Franks and Mayer (1992) report thirty-five successful hostile bids made over two years in the mid-1980s. This is much higher than in Germany, France, or Japan. In Germany, Franks and Mayer (1993) report that there have only been three hostile takeovers between 1945 and 1994 and analyze them. They document a substantial market in share stakes (1997a), but their analysis suggests such sales do not perform a disciplinary function. In Japan Kester (1991) argues that there have been no hostile takeovers among large firms in that period. In France hostile takeovers are also rare.

Why do these differences in the number of hostile takeovers between the United States and United Kingdom and the other countries exist? A common belief is that it is because of regulatory restrictions. In fact, there are few explicit restrictions on takeover attempts in Germany, France, or Japan. In some ways, the regulations are more conducive to takeovers than in the United States and United Kingdom. For example, the threshold at which a large equity stake must be disclosed in Germany is 25 percent, compared to 5 percent in the United States and United Kingdom. This suggests that the barriers caused by Grossman and Hart's free-rider problem and competition among bidders are less significant in Germany. Rather than regulatory restrictions, a more plausible explanation for the difference in the occurrence of takeovers across countries is the prevalence of cross-shareholdings in Japan and the structure of holding companies and cross-shareholdings in Germany and France, which make it difficult to acquire the necessary number of shares.

Another important issue is the extent to which the market for corporate control leads to an improvement in efficiency in the way Manne's (1965) argument suggests it should. There have been numerous empirical studies of takeovers in an attempt to understand whether they create value. Jensen (1993) estimates the total increase in the stock market value of target firms in the United States from 1976 to 1990 was $750 billion. In contrast, it seems that the increase in value for bidding firms was zero and possibly even negative. Overall, the stock market data suggest that total value (the sum of the targets' values and bidding firms' values) did increase significantly, although there is an issue of whether this was caused by the mergers and takeovers or was simply a reflection of a previous undervaluation in the stock market. Another possibility, suggested by Shleifer and Summers (1988), is that gains from takeovers may be the result of violating implicit contracts with workers and other suppliers.

A number of studies have used accounting data to attempt to identify the reason that the value of the targets increased. For example, Ravenscraft and Scherer (1987) and Herman and Lowenstein (1988) have found little evidence that operating performance improves after takeovers. Franks and Mayer (1996) found for a sample of U.K. firms that hostile takeover targets did not underperform before acquisition but were subject to the redeployment of assets afterward. There are some studies (Kaplan 1989; Bhagat, Shleifer, and Vishny 1990; Kaplan and Weisbach 1991; Healey, Palepu, and Ruback 1992, 1997) that do find changes and improvements in operations that can at least partially explain takeover premia, so the evidence is mixed.

Concentrated Holdings and Monitoring by Financial Institutions

Stiglitz (1985) has argued that one of the most important ways that value maximization by firms can be ensured is through concentrated ownership of the firm's shares. In the extreme case, one person or a single family owns the firm, and there are significant incentives to maximize its value. At the other extreme, shares are held by a large number of people, with no single person holding a large stake; in this case nobody has an incentive to monitor the management and ensure they are running the firm in shareholders' interests. In an intermediate case, one or more shareholders own a large stake, and many small shareholders have a few shares. In this situation, the large shareholders may have an incentive to monitor the firm's management and ensure they maximize share value. Shleifer and Vishny (1986), Huddart (1993) and Admati, Pfleiderer, and Zechner (1994) model equity-financed firms that have one large shareholder and a fringe of smaller ones. In all of these models, more wealth commitment by owners increases monitoring and firm performance. Shleifer and Vishny find that firm value increases with the large shareholder's holding but this need not be true. In Huddart and Admati, Pfleiderer, and Zechner, the reverse can occur because the large shareholder is risk averse.

A number of recent theoretical analyses have reconsidered important aspects of concentrated ownership. Burkart, Gromb, and Panunzi (1997), in considering the costs and benefits of monitoring by large shareholders, show that such monitoring may restrict the misuse of resources ex post but may also blunt ex ante managerial initiative. There is a trade-off between control and initiative. Bolton and von Thadden (1998a, 1998b) develop a framework to analyze the trade-off between liquidity and control. Large blocks result in incentives to monitor but also lead to a lack of liquidity. Pagano and Röell (1998) consider the trade-off between public and private ownership and monitoring. With private ownership, there is monitoring because of shareholder concentration but no liquidity. Public ownership results in the costs of going public and less monitoring but greater liquidity.

The differences in concentration of share ownership in the different countries are illustrated in table 4.4. This shows the percentage of outstanding shares owned by the largest five shareholders in the United States, United Kingdom, Japan, and Germany for a sample of large nonfinancial companies. The United States and United Kingdom have relatively low concentration, while Japan and particularly Germany have a high concentration. Table 4.5 shows the frequency of majority ownership and identity of the majority shareholder. In the United Kingdom in particular, and the United States to some extent, majority ownership is mainly due to family and individual holdings of large blocks. Often the founding family retains a significant amount of the shares after the firm has gone public. In Japan majority ownership is less frequent. The difference there between the concentration indicated by the largest five shareholders and majority ownership is probably due to the constraint on holdings by banks and insurance companies of 5 percent and 10 percent, respectively, of the shares in any one firm. In Germany, majority

Table 4.4
Summary statistics of ownership concentration of large nonfinancial corporations, percentage of outstanding shares owned by the largest five shareholders

	United States	United Kingdom	Japan	Germany
Mean	25.4	20.9	33.1	41.5
Median	20.9	15.1	29.7	37.0
Standard deviation	16.0	16.0	13.8	14.5
Minimum	1.3	5.0	10.9	15.0
Maximum	87.1	87.7	85.0	89.6
Mean firm size (millions of US$, 1980)[a]	3,505	1,031	1,835	3,483
Mean firm size (millions of US$, 1980)[b]	1,287	N.A.	811	1,497

Note: Samples: United States, 457 nonfinancial corporations in 1980; United Kingdom, 85 manufacturing corporations in 1970; Japan, 143 mining and manufacturing corporations in 1984; and Germany, 41 nonfinancial corporations in 1990.
a. Measured by total assets.
b. Measured by market value of equity.
Source: Prowse (1995, Table 9, p. 25).

ownership, like the holdings of the largest five shareholders, is particularly high. Franks and Mayer (1997b) provide evidence that ownership is also highly concentrated in France.

The importance of equity ownership by financial institutions in Japan and Germany and the lack of a market for corporate control in these countries has led to the suggestion that the agency problem in these countries is solved by financial institutions' acting as the outside monitor for large corporations.

In Japan this system of monitoring is known as the main bank system. According to Teranishi (1994) and Hoshi, Kashyap, and Loveman (1994), this system grew out of the close relationships between banks and firms that were fostered by the way credit was allocated during World War II. The main characteristics of this system are the long-term relationship between a bank and its client firm, the holding of both debt and equity by the bank, and the active intervention of the bank should its client become financially distressed. It has been widely argued that this main bank relationship ensures that the bank acts as a delegated monitor and helps to overcome the agency problem between managers and the firm. Hoshi, Kashyap, and Scharfstein (1990a, 1990b, 1993)

Table 4.5
Frequency of majority ownership and the identity of the majority shareholder (%)

	United States	United Kingdom	Japan	Germany
Frequency of majority ownership[a]	10.8	9.8	8.4	25.1
Identity of majority owner[b]				
Individual	5.1	6.7	2.1	6.4
Financial institution }		0	3.6	3.7
Nonfinancial firm }	5.7	1.8	2.7	8.7
Other[c] }		1.3	N.A.	6.4

a. Number of majority-owned firms as a percentage of total number of firms in the sample. For the United States, number of majority-owned firms identified from the total of all listed companies.
b. Number of firms majority owned by a certain shareholder class as a percentage of all firms in the sample.
c. Includes foreign and government majority-owned companies. For Japan, foreign-owned companies are subsumed in the other categories.
Source: Prowse (1995, Table 10, p. 29).

provide evidence that the main bank system helps firms by easing liquidity constraints and reducing agency costs. They also document that firms reduced their bank ties in the 1980s as access to the bond market became easier. In contrast, Hayashi (1997) finds no evidence that main bank ties ease liquidity constraints. He suggests the results of Hoshi, Kashyap, and Scharfstein are probably due to the poor quality of their capital stock estimate. Kang and Shivdasani (1997) find that companies restructure to a greater extent in response to adverse circumstances the greater the ownership of the main bank. Aoki and Patrick (1994) provide a number of studies suggesting that until recently, the effectiveness of the main bank system has been high. Ramseyer (1994) provides a dissenting view that the traditional emphasis in the literature on the importance of this system in achieving effective corporate governance is too strong. He argues that if the system really worked in the way described, explicit contracts should be used much more than they are in practice. Overall, the main bank system appears important in times of financial distress but less important when a firm is doing well.

In Germany the data on concentration of ownership probably understate the significance of the banks' effective position. The reason is that many bank customers keep their shares on deposit at banks and allow banks to exercise proxies on their behalf. As a result banks control a higher proportion of voting equity and have more representation on boards of large industrial enterprises than their direct holdings suggest. A 1978 Monopoly Commission study found that of the top one hundred corporations, banks controlled the votes of nearly 40 percent of the equity and were represented on two-thirds of the boards. German banks thus tend to have very close ties with industry and form long-run relationships with firms. This is known as the hausbank system. A number of studies have provided evidence on the effectiveness of the outside monitoring of German banks. Elston (1993) finds that firms with strong ties to a bank are not as liquidity constrained as firms with weaker ties. Cable (1985) and Gorton and Schmid (1996) find evidence that firms with a higher proportion of equity controlled by banks have better performance. This evidence is consistent with the hypothesis that bank involvement helps the performance of firms, but it is also consistent with the hypothesis that banks are good at picking winners.

A number of issues concerning the effectiveness of banks as outside monitors arise in the case of Japan and Germany. The first is that banks are themselves subject to the same agency problems as firms. Charkham (1994, p. 36) points out that in effect, the big three banks essentially control themselves: "At general meetings in recent years, Deutsche Bank held voting rights for 47.2 percent of its shares, Dresdner for 59.25 percent and Commerzbank for 30.29 percent." In addition, other large shareholders are often widely held themselves. Schreyögg and Steinman (1981) compare a sample of three hundred large German firms according to whether there is concentration in terms of direct ownership or ultimate ownership, taking into account the holding company structure. They find that in terms of ultimate ownership, there is significantly less concentration. The problem is illustrated by figure 4.1. Although it would appear at first sight that Daimler-Benz has concentrated ownership, the shareholders are themselves held by groups.

Diamond (1984) has referred to this as the problem of "who monitors the monitor." In his model he suggests that intermediaries can overcome this problem by having a diversified portfolio and promising a fixed return to depositors. If the intermediary does not monitor then it will be unable to pay the promised return to depositors. Prowse (1995) suggests a number of problems with the application of Diamond's argument to Japanese and German banks. First, the effect of deposit insurance is not considered. Second, in addition to debt, banks in these countries also have equity holdings, which have significant nondiversifiable risk associated with them. This means a bank can claim that bad outcomes are due to this risk rather than a lack of monitoring.

Hellwig (1991), an early critic of the view that banks provide effective monitoring of firms in Germany, argued that close relationships between banks and firms involved costs as well as benefits for the firm. Banks acquire private information about the firm, which they can use to extract rents. Using historical sources, he argued that firms have an incentive to seek autonomy from banks as quickly as possible. In more recent work, Hellwig (1998) argues that intermediaries and firms are often involved in a collusive relationship whose aim is to limit the power of outsiders. In this model, firms and intermediaries cooperate to share control, not necessarily to promote effective management of the firm.

Edwards and Fischer (1994) have argued that in Germany, the corporate governance role of banks has been overemphasized in the literature. They provide a variety of evidence that banks do not have the degree of influence as lenders, shareholders, or voters of proxies that is usually supposed. For example, they find that the number of votes controlled in a company is only weakly related to the number of representatives the bank has on the supervisory board.

Wenger and Kaserer (1998) point to the examples of Metallgesellschaft and Daimler-Benz as extreme examples of the failure of the German corporate governance system. Metallgesellschaft had losses of over $1 billion when it wound up a large position in oil futures. This position had been undertaken as part of a plan to sell home heating oil in the United States at a fixed price. It appears that the supervisory board, despite being chaired by a representative of Deutsche Bank, did not fully understand the strategy until they were forced to by the sequence of events that unfolded. In the late 1980s and early 1990s Daimler-Benz adopted a strategy of becoming a conglomerate despite the fact that United States auto companies had already been unsuccessful with this strategy. Although Daimler-Benz's supervisory board was chaired by Deutsche Bank's CEO, there was no attempt to prevent what subsequently turned out to be a significant waste of resources.

La Porta, Lopez-de-Silanes, and Shleifer (1999) consider the incidence of widely held corporations in twenty-seven wealthy economies, including those that are the focus of this book. They find that with the exception of countries such as the United States and United Kingdom, where minority investors are well protected, corporations are not widely held but instead are controlled by families or the state. Another exception is Germany, where banks play a significant role in the governance of some large corporations through their ownership of shares.

La Porta, Lopez-de-Silanes, Shleifer, and Vishny (1998) suggest a possible reason for the common occurrence of large blocks of stock that is different from the standard monitoring explanation. They find a negative correlation between the extent of minority shareholder protection and concentrated equity ownership. The implication is that the easiest way to prevent abuse of minority shareholders when legal protection is poor is to hold large blocks of stock.

Debt

An important strand of the corporate governance literature has focused on the role of debt as a means of disciplining managers. Grossman and Hart (1982) were the first to argue that managers could precommit to work hard by using debt rather than equity. Similarly, Jensen's (1986) free cash flow theory suggested that debt could be used to prevent managers from squandering resources. In the late 1980s and early 1990s it was widely argued that leveraged buyouts (LBOs), whereby managers or other groups purchased firms using a large proportion of debt financing, were a response to agency problems. However, debt can have undesirable as well as desirable effects on managers' behavior. Jensen and Meckling (1976) pointed out that managers have an incentive to take risks and may even accept projects that destroy value if significant amounts of debt are used. Myers (1977) pointed to the debt overhang problem, whereby firms may forgo good projects if they have significant debt outstanding. The reason is that for a firm facing financial distress, a large part of the returns to a good project go to bondholders.

One of the concerns of the literature on debt has been how lenders can ensure that borrowers actually make repayments on the debt they issue. One of the standard answers has been reputation. For example, Eaton and Gersovitz (1981), Allen (1983), and Diamond (1989) provide models of debt where reputation plays an important role in ensuring repayment. Bulow and Rogoff (1989) point out that reputation alone often will not work.

Hart and Moore (1998) and Hart (1995) have stressed the importance of the right to liquidate in the event of default as a method of ensuring repayment. The threat of liquidation ensures that some funds can always be extracted except in the final period. Their theory and its extensions provide a plausible theory of entrepreneurial firms but are not directly applicable to corporations because outside equity cannot be used. Fluck (1998) has shown how this framework can be extended to allow for outside equity by incorporating a right for equity holders to dismiss management and using infinite lived equity.

Perhaps the most important weakness of the argument that debt is important for ensuring corporate governance in corporations is the fact that retained earnings are the most important source of finance for corporations, as we saw in chapter 3. In most countries, debt is not as important. Typically large corporations do not have a problem in meeting their debt payments.

Product Market Competition

It has been argued (see, e.g., Alchian 1950 and Stigler 1958) that competition in product markets is a powerful force for solving the agency problem between owners and managers. If the managers of a firm waste or consume large amounts of resources, the firm will be unable to compete and will go bankrupt. There is little doubt that competition, particularly internationally, is a powerful force in ensuring effective corporate governance.

Competition between different organizational forms may be helpful in limiting efficiency losses. If a family-owned business has the sole objective of maximizing share value, it may force all the corporations in that industry to do the same. Hart (1983) has developed a model with two types of firm: traditional profit-maximizing ones he terms *entrepreneurial* and *managerial* firms that are operated by managers pursuing their own interests. Managerial effort and input prices are substitutes. The more effort the manager puts in, the lower are costs and the higher are profits. Managerial effort and input prices are unobservable; only profits can be observed and contracted on. A shirking manager can thus claim that profits are low because input prices were high. This means there is managerial slack. Using the assumption that managers are infinitely risk averse at a particular level of income, Hart is able to show that aggregate output is lower and price is higher than in the first best case where everything can be contracted upon. The amount of managerial slack depends on the amount that input prices are correlated across firms. It is demonstrated that with perfect correlation, the incentive effect on managers will be greater the higher the proportion of firms that are entrepreneurial. Scharfstein (1988) shows that if the manager's marginal utility of income is strictly positive (as opposed to being infinitely risk averse at a particular level of income), increased competition can increase rather than reduce managerial slack.

Schmidt (1997) addresses a related question in a model without hidden information. He observes that increased competition may threaten the survival of a firm by forcing it into bankruptcy and asks what effect this may have on managerial slack. Schmidt's model assumes that the manager is risk neutral and wealth constrained and that he receives a penalty (lost rents, forgone opportunities) when his firm goes bankrupt. The manager is required to engage in efforts that reduce expected future costs. After he has made the effort, the actual costs are observed and the owner decides whether to liquidate the firm. Greater competition lowers the price that the firm receives for its output and, other things being equal, increases the risk that the owner will find it optimal to liquidate the firm.

Schmidt shows that greater competition has two effects on the manager's optimal effort. The first is the threat-of-liquidation effect that we would expect. This has two components: the direct component that the manager has a directly increased incentive to work harder to avoid liquidation and an indirect component, since the cost to the owner of providing incentives to take high effort is reduced. The threat-of-liquidation effect unambiguously raises managerial effort.

The second effect is ambiguous and results from the fact that increased competition reduces profits and may reduce the benefits of a cost reduction. As a result, the owner may be disinclined to pay the manager the high rents necessary to achieve a cost reduction. If the value of a cost reduction is decreasing in the degree of competition, the net effect of increased competition may be to lower managerial effort. The second effect occurs only if the manager is paid more than his reservation level, that is, the income he can get in his next best alternative occupation. Schmidt (1997) cites a special case of his model that is studied by Aghion, Dewatripont, and Rey (1995). In their model, the manager is always paid his reservation level, and so the effect of increased competition is unambiguous.

Scharfstein (1988) and Schmidt (1997) demonstrate that increased competition does not necessarily reduce managerial slack. However, the agency perspective they take is rather narrow. Competition seems likely to involve many other factors rather than just inducing managerial effort. For example, managers at the top level in a company act like entrepreneurs in the sense that they choose the direction of the firm and asssign crucial tasks to their subordinates. In dynamic markets with constantly changing prices, products, and markets, they identify new opportunities and coordinate the managerial team as it seeks to exploit these opportunities. In such cases, it may not be possible to say with any degree of confidence ex ante which managements will succeed and which will fail. It is precisely in this case that competition in the product market can be important. In the absence of valuable information on the part of shareholders and effective means of controlling management decisions, competition among companies both reveals which managements are the best and at the same time disciplines them. The company with the strongest management will develop the best products, produce the highest earnings and growth, and drive companies with weaker management out of business—or at least leave them with a much smaller share of the market.

Given that product market competition has often been claimed to be one of the more plausible governance mechanisms and the wide range of possible ways it may influence governance, it is surprising how little formal analysis has been done in this area. Much work remains to be done on this topic.

Explaining Cross-Country Differences in Corporate Governance

Why are there such marked differences in corporate governance in different countries? Prowse (1990, 1995) has stressed that governance develops subject to legal and regulatory constraints. Roe (1994) has argued that in understanding the different structure of corporate governance across countries, it is important to consider political factors in the development of the legal system and regulation. In particular, he argues that the United States chose to have a financial system where the power of financial institutions such as banks and insurance companies was very limited. As a result, they could not play a significant role in corporate governance. In Germany and Japan, a different political climate allowed financial institutions to become involved in corporate governance.

Political factors are important without a doubt, but there is a question of the extent of their importance. The United Kingdom presents an interesting contrast to the United States. It has a similar separation of ownership and control in corporations but very different financial institutions. In particular, the banking system is concentrated, and although the Bank of England has wide powers of intervention, there are few if any explicit restrictions on the activities that banks may undertake, as Table 4.2 indicates. Nevertheless, banks have chosen not to become involved in corporate governance. Insurance companies have also not been barred from playing an important governance role but have not done so. If banks and insurance companies in the United Kingdom chose not to become involved in corporate governance, then the same might be true in the United States if the banks and insurance companies there had had the ability to become involved. This comparison is difficult to reconcile with the idea that it is politics and legal and regulatory constraints that is the sole determinant of differences in corporate governance across countries.

Whose Company Is It in Practice?

How important are these differences in governance mechanisms? To what extent are managers in the different countries constrained by governance mechanisms to act in shareholders' interests? One view is that governance mechanisms do not constrain firms very much, at least in some countries. For example, managers in Japan do not appear to view themselves as working for the shareholders. This is illustrated by the mission statement of Asahi Breweries contained in the box. The statement is revealing in that shareholders are apparently fairly unimportant in their stated goals. They appear only in the final section and apparently seem fairly unimportant: "We at Asahi . . . desire to fulfill our responsibilities to the stockholders and the local communities in which we operate."

The view that Japanese corporations have relatively little responsibility toward their shareholders is confirmed in surveys of managers. Figure 4.2 shows the choices of senior managers at a sample of major corporations in the five countries between two alternatives:

1. *A company exists for the interest of all stakeholders.*
2. *Shareholder interest should be given the first priority.*

In Japan the overwhelming response by 97.1 percent of those asked was that all stakeholders were important. Only 2.9 percent thought shareholders' interests should be put first. At the other end of the spectrum, managers in the United States and United Kingdom by majorities of 75.6 percent and 70.5 percent, respectively, stated that shareholders were the most important stakeholders. Germany and France are more like Japan in that 82.7 percent and 78 percent, respectively, viewed the firm as being for all stakeholders.

Box 4.1
Corporate Philosophy of Asahi Breweries, Ltd.

We at Asahi Breweries, Ltd., through our business activities including alcoholic and nonalcoholic beverages, food and pharmaceuticals, wish to contribute to the health and well-being of people the world over. By thus contributing to society as a whole, the company seeks to attain the trust and confidence of the consumer and develop still further.

1. *Consumer Orientation* Identifying the best interests of consumers, we endeavor to meet their demands by creating products suited for contemporary tastes and lifestyles.
2. *Quality First* Open to consumer opinion of our products, we consistently enhance quality level and extend technological capabilities in order to market the finest products in the industry.
3. *Respect for Human Values* Our Company firmly believes that human beings are the core of the business, and follows the principle of human values through developing human resources and implementing fair personnel management. Each employee is encouraged to fully utilize his or her own potential, and work to realize an open, positive thinking corporate culture.
4. *True Partnership Between Labor and Management* Our Company aims to strengthen harmonious relations between labor and management based on mutual understanding and trust. Both parties work hand in hand for corporate development as well as the welfare of all employees.
5. *Cooperation with Business Associates* We seek to build strong relations with all our business associates and affiliates in a spirit of co-existence and co-prosperity based in mutual trust. At the same time, we are determined to accept and fulfil our responsibilities as the core of the Asahi group of companies.
6. *Social Responsibilities* We at Asahi, through securing and expanding the base of our operations, desire to fulfill our responsibilities to stockholders and the local communities in which we operate. Also in carrying out business activities, we sincerely observe the moral principles of management based on social standards.

Source: Asahi Breweries, Ltd. Case, 1989, Harvard Business School, 9-389-114.

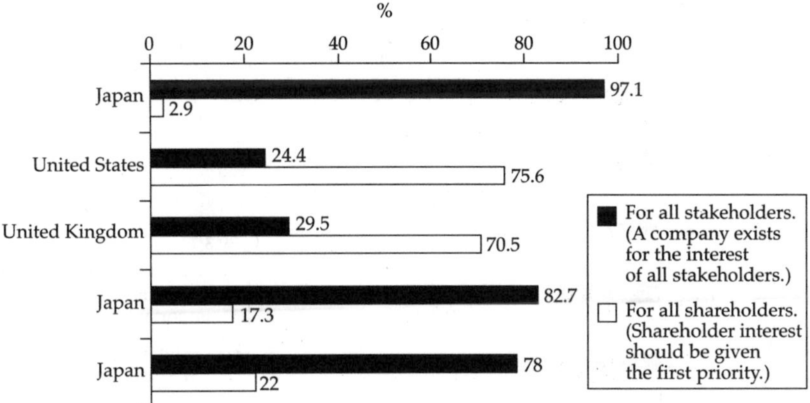

Figure 4.2
Whose company is it? *Source:* Yoshimori (1995, pp. 33–44).

The same survey also asked the managers what their priorities were with regard to dividends and employee layoffs. They were asked to choose between two alternatives:

1. *Executives should maintain dividend payments, even if they must lay off a number of employees.*

2. *Executives should maintain stable employment, even if they must reduce dividends.*

Figure 4.3 shows the results. As before, there is a sharp difference between Japan and the United States and United Kingdom, with Germany and France closer to Japan but not quite as extreme.

The evidence on managers' views of the role of the firm is upheld by the way that wages are structured in the different countries. In the United States and United Kingdom wages are based on the nature of the job done; employees' personal circumstances generally have no effect on their compensation. In Japan and Germany, it is common for people to be granted family allowances and special allowances for small children. In France, vacation allowances are common. These differences underline the fact that in the United States and United Kingdom, the firm is designed to create wealth for shareholders, whereas in Japan and to some extent Germany and France, it is a group of people working together for their common benefit.

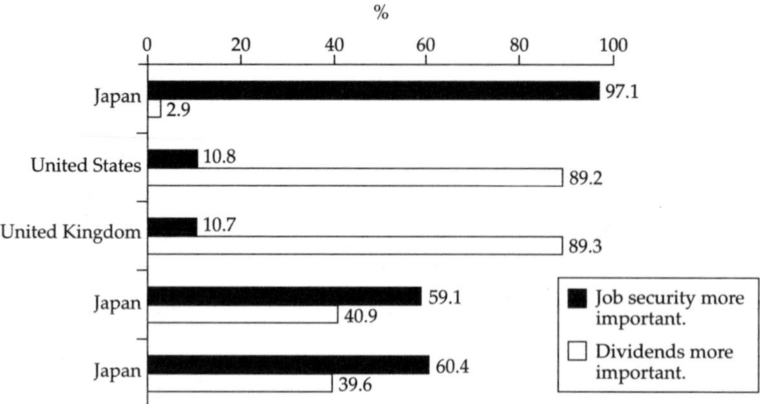

Figure 4.3
Job security or dividends. *Source:* Yoshimori (1995, pp. 33–44).

These differences in the role of the firm, together with the limited evidence on the effectiveness of internal and external governance mechanisms, raise the issue of whether the traditional agency view of the firm is the most useful way to think about it. Before turning to this issue, we consider the operation of nonprofit organizations where, even in the United States and United Kingdom, the specific goal of the organization is different from pursuing profit.

4.2 Nonprofits and Mutuals

Traditional neoclassical theory recognizes two types of organization: the profit-maximizing firm and the government. In reality the range of organizational forms encountered in most countries is significantly greater. Some of these, such as workers' cooperatives, represent a negligible portion of economic activity; others are significant. Nonprofit firms are important in many countries. In the United States nonprofits are important in health care, education, social services, and cultural activities. Where they compete directly with for-profit organizations. Table 4.6 shows the main sectors where taxable and tax-exempt organizations coexist and the relative shares of each (see also James and Rose-Ackerman 1986 and Hansmann 1996). In the sectors shown, both forms of organization coexist and successfully compete.

Table 4.6
Service industries where taxable and nontaxable firms coexist, United States totals 1992

SIC Code	Kind of business or operation	Taxable firms[a]		Tax-exempt firms[b]		Tax-exempt firms' share of total	
		Establishments (number)	Receipts[c] ($1,000)	Establishments (number)	Revenue[d] ($1,000)	Establishments (%)	Revenue (%)
Health services							
8011	General medical clinics	4,736	12,590,420	3,187	16,548,253	40	57
8021	Dental clinics	604	351,169	115	73,640	16	17
805	Nursing and personal care facilities	14,954	33,989,607	5,925	15,220,487	28	31
8062	General medical and surgical hospitals	704	24,162,290	4,920	254,391,214	87	91
8063, 9	Specialty Hospitals	699	6,920,685	797	25,344,022	53	79
808	Home health care services	8,045	10,413,844	2,215	5,713,903	22	35
809	Misc. health and allied services, n.e.c.	11,457	9,604,620	6,492	7,122,298	36	43
Educational services							
823	Libraries	232	30,141	1,572	527,347	87	95
824	Vocational schools	4,615	3,892,230	1,052	548,601	19	12
829	Schools and educational services, n.e.c.	9,888	3,320,018	3,659	1,897,224	27	36
Social services							
83	Total	59,123	13,349,165	81,726	53,671,936	58	80
835	Child day care services	35,327	5,269,980	15,970	3,691,637	31	41
832,3,6,9	Other social services	23,796	8,079,185	65,756	49,980,299	73	86

Table 4.6 (continued)

		Taxable firms[a]		Tax-exempt firms[b]		Tax-exempt firms' share of total	
SIC Code	Kind of business or operation	Establishments (number)	Receipts[c] ($1,000)	Establishments (number)	Revenue[d] ($1,000)	Establishments (%)	Revenue (%)
R&D, management and related services							
8731	Commercial physical and biological research	3,826	11,788,343	344	4,978,474	8	30
8732	Commercial economical, sociological and educational research	5,165	6,138,318	536	352,374	9	5
8734	Testing laboratories	4,540	4,763,614	164	371,169	3	7
8741	Management services	19,733	21,728,354	453	598,290	2	3
8742	Management consulting services	33,762	22,628,984	342	326,373	1	1
8743	Public relations services	5,103	2,890,250	205	63,935	4	2
8748	Business consulting services, n.e.c.	12,628	4,573,223	694	1,258,292	5	22
Amusement, recreation, and related services							
7922	Theatrical producers and misc. services	4,255	4,433,701	1,669	1,296,809	28	23
7929	Bands, orchestras, actors and other entertainers and entertainment groups	5,831	4,191,788	1,420	1,522,885	20	27
7991	Gymnasiums and athletic clubs	1,697	880,109	183	145,255	10	14
7997	Membership sports and recreation clubs	7,275	5,018,717	7,452	5,609,613	51	53

Table 4.6 (continued)

		Taxable firms[a]		Tax-exempt firms[b]		Tax-exempt firms' share of total	
SIC Code	Kind of business or operation	Establishments (number)	Receipts[c] ($1,000)	Establishments (number)	Revenue[d] ($1,000)	Establishments (%)	Revenue (%)
841	Museums and art galleries	356	134,612	2,749	2,602,725	89	95
842	Arboreta and botanical or zoological gardens	119	57,085	329	595,818	73	91
7032	Sporting and recreational camps	1,840	603,079	1,205	373,727	40	38

Note: For detailed definition of terms, refer to the source.

a. The two classifications are based on the federal income tax filing requirement for the establishment or organization. Establishments that indicated that all or part of their income was exempt from federal income tax under provisions of section 501 of the IRS code were classified as tax exempt; establishments indicating no such exemption were classified as taxable. All government-operated hospitals were classified as tax exempt.

b. The basic dollar volume measure for taxable service establishments inludes receipts from customers or clients for services rendered, from the use of facilities, and from merchandise sold during 1992, except for health practitioners and legal, architectural, engineering, and surveying services, which reported on a cash basis. Receipts are net after deductions for refunds and allowance for merchandise returned by customers. They do not include taxes collected from customers and remitted directly to a local, state, or federal tax agency, nor do they include income from contributions, gifts, grants, dividends, interest, and investments or sale or rental of real estate.

c. Basic dollar volume measure for tax-exempt firms. Includes revenue from customers or clients for services rendered and merchandise sold during 1992. Also included is income from interest, dividends, gifts, grants, rents, royalties, and so forth. Receipts from taxable business activities of firms exempt from federal income tax (unrelated business income) are also included in revenue. Revenue does not include taxes collected and directly paid, sale of real estate, investments, or other assets.

d. N.E.C.: Not elsewhere classified.

Source: U.S. Department of Commerce, Bureau of the Census, The 1992 Census of Service Industries.

The industries where nonprofits compete with for profits have particularly interesting implications for corporate governance. As we have seen, standard views of corporate governance based on the agency theory of the firm suggest that governance mechanisms involving monitoring by outsiders are crucial in ensuring that organizations are run efficiently. However, in the sectors in table 4.6, nonprofits compete quite successfully with for profits. The formal governance mechanisms in these nonprofits appear very weak. There is no market for corporate control, and there are typically self-perpetuating boards of trustees and directors who usually receive little, if any, compensation for their oversight facilities. However, these firms are able to compete successfully with for-profit entities that are subject to the full rigors of the market for corporate control and other disciplining devices.

The financial sector provides a particularly interesting example of the coexistence of different organizational forms. Hansmann (1996) points out that in the nineteenth century in the United States, mutual savings banks were a highly successful form of organization. The term *mutual* in their title is misleading since, in fact, they are legally nonprofits. The depositors do not have the right to vote on the affairs of the bank, which is governed by a self-perpetuating board. Of course, mutual organizations where the depositors formally control the organization are also important in the financial sector. Mutual savings and loans have this structure. In the insurance industry, mutual organizations are also important. Nonprofits and mutuals have played a significant role in the financial sector not only in the United States but also in many other countries.

4.3 Conclusion

Since Berle and Means (1932) pointed to the separation of ownership and control in the modern corporation, the literature on corporate governance has concentrated on the agency problem between shareholders and managers. It has been widely agreed that the board of directors is an ineffective way of overcoming this problem. The focus instead has been on external governance mechanisms.

In the United States and United Kingdom the main external mechanism is the market for corporate control. The three ways in which this operates are through proxy contexts, friendly mergers, and hostile takeovers. Like boards of directors, proxy contests are also widely agreed to be ineffective as a means of disciplining managers. Friendly mergers allow efficiency gains to be made but do not solve the agency problem. This leaves hostile takeovers as the main way in which managers can be disciplined. However, as Hansmann (1996) points out, these are a relatively recent invention and were not widely used until the 1960s. The efficiency of firms did not apparently change much at this juncture. There are also theoretical problems with the operation of the takeover mechanism, such as the Grossman and Hart (1980) free-rider problem. Finally, the empirical evidence is mixed. There are increases in stock market values as a result of mergers and takeovers, but it is not clear why these increases occur. The evidence from studies of accounting data suggests that changes in operating efficiency are hard to find. Alternative explanations are that the increase in stock values is due to a recognition by the market of previous undervaluation or a transfer from other stakeholders, as Shleifer and Summers (1988) suggested.

In Japan and Germany, the absence of a market for corporate control has led to an alternative theory of how the agency problem is overcome. In Japan, it has been suggested that the main bank system performs this role. The idea is that a firm's major bank, which is typically also a holder of a block of equity, can exercise considerable influence. In Germany, the hausbank system operates in a similar way. The main difference is that in addition to loans and the direct ownership of equity, German banks are also able to vote the proxies of customers' shares. How effective are these mechanisms in ensuring that managers pursue shareholders' interests? At a theoretical level there is an issue of why the banks should undertake the role of pursuing shareholder value maximization. As with the corporations themselves, they are public companies, and there seems no reason that they do not also suffer from an agency problem. An illustration is the fact that the managers of the big three German universal banks have proxies for such a large proportion of their own bank's shares that they have effective voting control. At an empirical level, the evidence for the effectiveness of this type of system is that when a firm does have financial problems, its main bank or hausbank does intervene and the firm is able to do better than firms in a similar situation that do not have a link to a bank. Apart from situations of financial distress, there is little evidence of involvement.

Another focus of the literature on corporate governance has been on the use of debt finance as a mechanism for overcoming the agency problem. Grossman and Hart (1982), Jensen (1986), and others argue that by forcing the firm to pay out large amounts of their earnings as interest on debt, managers are precommitting to work hard and avoid squandering shareholders' money. Again this argument is not entirely persuasive. Empirically the problem is that the most common form of finance is retained earnings. Debt is relatively little used. Most corporations have very little difficulty meeting their interest payments.

One other factor often invoked as ensuring effective corporate governance is product market competition. With a few notable exceptions such as Hart (1983), little attempt has been made to analyze this effect. Since competition is an important factor in many industries, it may be that it has a significant role to play.

All five countries have many types of private organization other than for-profit corporations, including nonprofit firms. The governance mechanisms for these organizations provide additional insights. There is no market for corporate control and no external monitoring by financial institutions. The only apparent external oversight is through boards of trustees and directors. Despite this lack of a solution to the agency problem, these organizations are able to compete with for-profit corporations.

To summarize, the standard corporate governance mechanisms that are the focus of much of the literature do not appear to work very effectively. However, despite this lack of outside discipline and monitoring, most firms seem to operate fairly efficiently. In all five countries many firms compete effectively in international markets, and their shareholders have historically received high rates of return. Many nonprofits also compete effectively with for-profit organizations. In chapters 11 and 12 we develop theories of the firm consistent with these observations.

Notes

1. Much of the information that is used comes from Charkham (1994), Prowse (1995), and from the 1996 report of a study group at the Institute of Fiscal and Monetary Policy of the Japanese Ministry of Finance.

References

Admati, A., P. Pfleiderer, and J. Zechner. (1994). "Large Shareholder Activism, Risk Sharing, and Financial Market Equilibrium." *Journal of Political Economy* **102,** 1097–1130.

Aghion, P., M. Dewatripont, and P. Rey. (1995). "Competition, Financial Discipline, and Growth." Working paper, Université Bruxelles Libre.

Alchian, A. (1950). "Uncertainty, Evolution, and Economic Theory." *Journal of Political Economy* **58,** 211–221.

Allen, F. (1983). "Credit Rationing and Payment Incentives." *Review of Economic Studies* **50,** 639–646.

Aoki, M., and H. Patrick. (1993). *The Japanese Main Bank System: Its Relevance for Developing and Transforming Economies*. New York: Oxford University Press.

Berle, A., and G. Means. (1932). *The Modern Corporation and Private Property*. New York: Commerce Clearing House.

Bhagat, S., and B. Black. (1998). "The Uncertain Relationship Between Board Composition and Firm Performance." In K. Hopt, M. Roe, and E. Wymeersch (eds.), *Corporate Governance: The State of the Art and Emerging Research*. New York: Oxford University Press.

Bhagat, S., A. Shleifer, and R. Vishny. (1990). "Hostile Takeovers in the 1980's: The Return to Corporate Specialization." *Brookings Papers on Economic Activity,* 1–72.

Bhattacharya, U. (1997). "Communication Costs, Information Acquisition, and Voting Decisions in Proxy Contests." *Review of Financial Studies* **10,** 1065–1097.

Bolton, P., and E. von Thadden. (1998a). "Blocks, Liquidity, and Corporate Control." *Journal of Finance* **53,** 1–25.

———. (1998b). "Liquidity and Control: A Dynamic Theory of Corporate Ownership Structure." *Journal of Institutional and Theoretical Economics* **154,** 177–223.

Bulow, J., and K. Rogoff. (1989). "A Constant Recontracting Model of Sovereign Debt." *Journal of Political Economy* **97,** 155–178.

Burkart, M. (1995). "Initial Shareholdings and Overbidding in Takeover Contests." *Journal of Finance* **50,** 1491–1515.

———, D. Gromb, and F. Panunzi. (1997). "Large Shareholders, Monitoring, and the Value of the Firm." *Quarterly Journal of Economics* **112,** 693–728.

Cable, J. (1985). "Capital Market Information and Industrial Performance." *Economic Journal* **95,** 118–132.

Charkham, J. (1994). *Keeping Good Company: A Study of Corporate Governance in Five Countries.* Oxford: Clarendon Press.

Coase, R. (1937). "The Nature of the Firm." *Economica* **4,** 386–405.

Diamond, D. (1984). "Financial Intermediation and Delegated Monitoring." *Review of Economic Studies* **51,** 393–414.

———. (1989). "Reputation Acquisition in Debt Markets." *Journal of Political Economy* **97,** 828–862.

Diamond, D., and R. Verrecchia. (1982). "Optimal Managerial Contracts and Equilibrium Security Prices." *Journal of Finance* **37,** 275–287.

Eaton, J., and M. Gersovitz. (1981). "Debt with Potential Repudiation: Theoretical and Empirical Analysis." *Review of Economic Studies* **48,** 289–309.

Edwards, J., and K. Fischer. (1994). *Banks, Finance and Investment in Germany*. Cambridge: Cambridge University Press.

Elston, J. (1993). "Firm Ownership Structure and Investment: Theory and Evidence from German Panel Data." Unpublished manuscript.

Fama, E., and M. Jensen. (1983a). "Separation of Ownership and Control." *Journal of Law and Economics* **26,** 301–325.

———. (1983b). "Agency Problems and Residual Claims." *Journal of Law and Economics* **26,** 327–349.

Fluck, Z. (1998). "Optimal Financial Contracting: Debt versus Equity." *Review of Financial Studies* **11,** 383–418.

Franks, J., and C. Mayer. (1992). "Corporate Control: A Synthesis of the International Evidence." IFA Working Paper No. 165-92, London Business School.

———. (1993). "German Capital Markets, Corporate Control and the Obstacles to Hostile Takeovers: Lessons from Three Case Studies." Working paper, London Business School.

———. (1996). "Hostile Takeovers and the Correction of Managerial Failure." *Journal of Financial Economics* **40,** 163–181.

———. (1997a). "Ownership, Control and the Performance of German Corporations." Working paper, London Business School.

———. (1997b). "Corporate Ownership and Control in the U.K., Germany, and France." *Journal of Applied Corporate Finance* **9 (Winter),** 30–45.

Gorton, G., and F. Schmid. (1996). "Universal Banking and the Performance of German Firms." Working Paper 5453, National Bureau of Economic Research, Cambridge, MA.

Grossman, S., and O. Hart. (1980). "Takeover Bids, the Free-Rider Problem, and the Theory of the Corporation." *Bell Journal of Economics* **11,** 42–64.

———. (1982). "Corporate Financial Structure and Managerial Incentives." In J. McCall (ed.), *The Economics of Information and Uncertainty.* Chicago: University of Chicago Press.

Hansmann, H. (1996). *The Ownership of Enterprise.* Cambridge, MA: Harvard University Press.

Hart, O. (1983). "The Market Mechanism as an Incentive Scheme." *Bell Journal of Economics* **14,** 366–82.

———. (1995). *Firms, Contracts and Financial Structure.* Oxford: Clarendon Press.

Hart, O., and J. Moore. (1998). "Default and Renegotiation: A Dynamic Model of Debt." *Quarterly Journal of Economics* **113,** 1–41.

Haubrich, J. (1994). "Risk Aversion, Performance Pay, and the Principal-Agent Problem." *Journal of Political Economy* **102,** 258–276.

Hayashi, F. (1997). "The Main Bank System and Corporate Investment: An Empirical Reassessment." Working paper 6172, National Bureau of Economic Research, Cambridge, MA.

Healy, P., K. Palepu, and R. Ruback. (1992). "Does Corporate Performance Improve After Mergers?" *Journal of Financial Economics* **31,** 135–175.

———. (1997 Summer). "Which Takeovers Are Profitable? Strategic or Financial?" *Sloan Management Review,* 45–57.

Hellwig, M. (1991). "Banking, Financial Intermediation, and Corporate Finance." In A. Giovannini and C. Mayer (eds.), *European Financial Intermediation* (pp. 35–63). Cambridge: Cambridge University Press.

———. (1998)."On the Economics and Politics of Corporate Finance and Corporate Control." Working paper, University of Mannheim.

Herman, E., and L. Lowenstein. (1988). "The Efficiency Effects of Hostile Takeovers." In J. Coffee, Jr., L. Lowenstein, and S. Rose-Ackerman (eds.), *Knights, Raiders, and Targets: The Impact of the Hostile Takeover.* New York : Oxford University Press.

Holmstrom, B., and J. Tirole. (1993). "Market Liquidity and Performance Monitoring." *Journal of Political Economy* **101,** 678–709.

Hoshi, T., A. Kashyap, and G. Loveman. (1993). "Financial System Reform in Poland: Lessons from Japan's Main Bank System." In M. Aoki and H. Patrick, *The Japanese Main Bank System.* New York: Oxford University Press.

Hoshi, T., A. Kashyap, and D. Scharfstein. (1990a). "Bank Monitoring and Investment: Evidence from the Changing Structure of Japanese Corporate Banking Relationships." In R. G. Hubbard (ed.), *Asymmetric Information, Corporate Finance and Investment.* Chicago: Chicago University Press.

———. (1990b). "The Role of Banks in Reducing the Costs of Financial Distress in Japan." *Journal of Financial Economics* **27,** 67–68.

———. (1993). "The Choice Between Public and Private Debt: An Analysis of Post-Deregulation Corporate Finance in Japan." Working paper 4421, National Bureau of Economic Research, Cambridge, MA.

Huddart, S. (1993). "The Effect of a Large Shareholder on Corporate Value." *Management Science* **39,** 1407–1421.

Ibbotson Associates. (1996). *Stocks, Bonds, Bills and Inflation 1996 Yearbook.* Chicago: Ibbotson Associates.

Institute of Fiscal and Monetary Policy. (1996). *Socio-Economic Systems of Japan, the United States, the United Kingdom, Germany and France.* Tokyo: Ministry of Finance, Japan.

James, E., and S. Rose-Ackerman. (1986). *The Nonprofit Enterprise in Market Economics.* New York: Harwood Academic Publishers.

———. (1989). "The Eclipse of the Public Corporation." *Harvard Business Review* **67,** 60–70.

———. (1993). "The Modern Industrial Revolution, Exit, and the Failure of Internal Control Systems." *Journal of Finance* **48,** 831–880.

Jensen, M., and W. Meckling. (1976). "Theory of the Firm: Managerial Behavior, Agency Costs and Ownership Structure." *Journal of Financial Economics* **3,** 305–60.

Kang, J., and A. Shivdasani. (1995). "Firm Performance, Corporate Governance, and Top Executive Turnover in Japan." *Journal of Financial Economics* **38,** 29–58.

———. (1997). "Corporate Restructuring During Performance Declines in Japan." *Journal of Financial Economics* **46,** 29–65.

Kaplan, S. (1989). "The Effects of Management Buyouts on Operating Performance and Value." *Journal of Financial Economics* **24,** 581–618.

———. (1994a). "Top Executives, Turnover, and Firm Performance in Germany." *Journal of Law, Economics, and Organization* **10,** 142–159.

———. (1994b). "Top Executive Rewards and Firm Performance: A Comparison of Japan and the United States." *Journal of Political Economy* **102,** 510–546.

Kaplan, S., and M. Weisbach. (1991). "The Success of Acquisitions: Evidence from Divestitures." *Journal of Finance* **47,** 107–138.

Kester, C. (1991). *Japanese Takeovers: The Global Contest for Corporate Control.* Boston: Harvard Business School Press.

La Porta, R., F. Lopez-de-Silanes, and A. Shleifer. (1999). "Corporate Ownership Around the World." *Journal of Finance* **54,** 471–517.

La Porta, R., F. Lopez-de-Silanes, A. Shleifer, and R. Vishny. (1998). "Law and Finance." *Journal of Political Economy* **106,** 1113–1156.

Mace, M. (1971). *Directors, Myth and Reality.* Boston: Harvard Business School Press.

Manne, H. (1965). "Mergers and the Market for Corporate Control." *Journal of Political Economy* **73,** 110–120.

Maug, E. (1998). "How Effective Is Shareholder Voting? Information Aggregation and Conflict Resolution in Corporate Voting Contests." Working paper, Duke University.

Myers, S. (1977). "Determinants of Corporate Borrowing." *Journal of Financial Economics* **5,** 147–175.

Pagano, M., and A. Röell. (1998). "The Choice of Stock Ownership Structure: Agency Costs, Monitoring and the Decision to Go Public." *Quarterly Journal of Economics* **113,** 187–225.

Pistor, K. (1996). "Co-determination in Germany: A Socio-Political Model with Governance Externalities." Paper presented at the *Conference on Employees and Corporate Governance.* Columbia Law School, Nov. 22, 1996.

Prowse, S. (1990). "Institutional Investment Patterns and Corporate Financial Behavior in the United States and Japan." *Journal of Financial Economics* **27,** 43–66.

———. (1995). "Corporate Governance in an International Perspective: A Survey of Corporate Control Mechanisms Among Large Firms in the U.S., U.K., Japan and Germany." *Financial Markets, Institutions and Instruments* **4,** 1–63.

Ramseyer, J. M. (1994). "Explicit Reasons for Implicit Contracts: The Legal Logic to the Japanese Main Bank System." In M. Aoki and H. Patrick (eds.), *The Japanese Main Bank System.* New York: Oxford University Press.

Ravenscraft, D., and F. Scherer. (1987). *Mergers, Selloffs and Economic Efficiency.* Washington, D.C.: Brookings Institution.

Roe, M. (1994). *Strong Managers, Weak Owners: The Political Roots of Corporate Finance.* Princeton: Princeton University Press.

Scharfstein, D. (1988). "Product Market Competition and Managerial Slack." *RAND Journal of Economics* **19,** 147–155.

Schmidt, K. (1997). "Managerial Incentives and Product Market Competition." *Review of Economic Studies* **64,** 191–214.

Schneider-Lenné, E. (1992). "Corporate Control in Germany." *Oxford Review of Economic Policy* **8,** 11–23.

Schreyögg, G., and H. Steinmann. (1981). "Zur Trennung von Eigentum und Verfügungsgewalt—Eine Empirische Analyse der Beteiligungsverhältnisse in Deutschen Grossunternehman." *Zeitschrift fur Betriebswirtschaft* **51,** 533–556.

Shleifer, A., and L. Summers. (1988). "Breach of Trust in Hostile Takeovers." In A. Auerbach (ed.), *Corporate Takeovers: Causes and Consequences,* (pp. 33–36). Chicago: University of Chicago Press.

Shleifer, A., and R. Vishny. (1986). "Large Shareholders and Corporate Control." *Journal of Political Economy* **94,** 461–488.

———. (1997). "A Survey of Corporate Governance." *Journal of Finance* **52,** 737–783.

Stigler, G. (1958). "The Economies of Scale." *Journal of Law and Economics* **1,** 54–71.

Stiglitz, J. (1985). "Credit Markets and the Control of Capital." *Journal of Money, Credit and Banking* **17,** 133–152.

Teranishi, J. (1994). "Loan Syndication in War-Time Japan and the Origins of the Main Bank System." In M. Aoki and H. Patrick (eds.), *The Japanese Main Bank System.* New York: Oxford University Press.

Van Hulle, C. (1996). "On the Nature of European Holding Groups." Working paper 9609, Department of Applied Economics, Katholieke Universiteit, Leuven.

Weisbach, M. (1988). "Outside Directors and CEO Turnover." *Journal of Financial Economics* **20,** 431–460.

Wenger, E., and C. Kaserer. (1998). "The German System of Corporate Governance—A Model Which Should Not Be Imitated." In S. Black and M. Moersch (eds.), *Competition and Convergence in Financial Markets—The German and Anglo-American Models* (pp. 41–48). Amsterdam: North-Holland Elsevier Science.

Yilmaz, B. (1997). "Strategic Voting and Proxy Contests." Working paper, University of Pennsylvania.

Yoshimori, M. (1995). "Whose Company Is It? The Concept of Corporation in Japan and the West." *Long Range Planning* **28,** 33–44.

5 The Limitations of Markets: The Classical View

There is sometimes an assumption in discussions of financial systems that financial markets are the new cutting edge of financial technology and that countries that lack a highly developed system of financial markets are somehow "backward" or "underdeveloped." This view is based on ideas that are as old as economics itself and are deeply ingrained in the traditional theory of finance.

In this chapter we review some of the classical theory of finance based on the theory of general competitive equilibrium. This review provides some tools that will be used in later chapters, but it also serves to indicate the limitations of some traditional models of finance and hence motivate the approaches adopted in the following chapters. We begin the review with the Arrow-Debreu-McKenzie (ADM) model and then pass on to the model of general equilibrium with incomplete markets (GEI), originally intended as a more realistic version of the ADM model. The GEI model has its uses and serves as a valuable counterexample to many of the classical results derived from the ADM model. However, the notion of market incompleteness is only a metaphor for the many imperfections that affect markets in the real world. While it is true that many of the markets envisaged by the ADM theory do not exist in practice, it is also true that many of the markets that do exist do not resemble the competitive markets of the GEI model. In particular, they do not have a single market-clearing price at which a homogeneous commodity is traded. "Incomplete markets" is at best a metaphor for a broad range of frictions found in most financial markets. These frictions are essential to understanding the role of intermediaries in making markets possible, for intermediaries serve to overcome both the incompleteness of markets and the frictions in the markets that do exist. After surveying the literature on the incomplete markets approach, we will conclude that in order to understand the limitations of actual markets, it is not enough to understand incompleteness; we have to allow a role for frictions in markets and for intermediaries as institutions that help overcome these frictions.

5.1 The Arrow-Debreu-Mackenzie Paradigm

The modern theory of asset pricing is essentially an application of arbitrage theory, sometimes described as the law of one price. It is a special case of Adam Smith's notion of the invisible hand, formalized by the fundamental theorems of welfare economics, which demonstrate the possibility of using the price mechanism to decentralize efficient allocations. The modern version of this theory was developed by Arrow, Debreu, and Mackenzie and now forms the basis of the standard theory of asset markets. The classical papers on the ADM complete markets model are Arrow and Debreu (1954) and McKenzie (1954, 1959); Mas-Colell, Whinston, and Green (1995) provide a good survey of the theory. Asset-pricing theory has been remarkably successful, and financial economists can feel justifiably proud of their field's accomplishments. Nonetheless, the whole edifice is based on an idealized set of assumptions. In this chapter we take a closer look at the foundations of the theory and find that there are reasons for thinking that it is at best a rough approximation to reality. This is particularly true when we consider the role of the complete markets assumption.

It is often said that prices provide economic agents with all the information they need in order to make the "right" choices—"right" in the sense that they maximize the individual agents' objectives, utility in the case of a consumer and profits in the case of a producer, and in the sense that the choices are mutually compatible, that is, the markets clear. The agents' choices are "right" in the deeper sense that no other attainable allocation could make some agents better off without making some agents worse off. The market has produced an outcome that is maximal with respect to the (partial) Pareto ordering.

More concretely, consider an economy with ℓ commodities indexed by $h = 1, \ldots, \ell$. The commodity space is $\mathbf{R}^\ell$, the ℓ-fold product of the real line, and every bundle of commodities can be represented by a vector $x = (x_1, \ldots, x_\ell)$ in $\mathbf{R}^\ell$.

There is a finite number of types of producer $j = 1, \ldots, n$, and a continuum of each type. For simplicity and without any essential loss of generality, we normalize the measure of producers of each type to equal one. Each type of producer j is characterized by a production set $Y_j \subset \mathbf{R}^\ell$.

There is a finite number of types of consumer $i = i, \ldots, m$ and a continuum of each type. The measure of consumers of each type is normalized to equal one. Consumers of type i are allowed to choose any nonnegative commodity bundle $x_i \in \mathbf{R}^\ell_+$ as a possible consumption bundle. Each has an initial endowment $e_i \in \mathbf{R}^\ell_+$ of commodities and an initial endowment $0 \leq \bar{t}_{ij} \leq 1$ of the shares of producers of type j. Their preferences are represented by a utility function $u_i : \mathbf{R}^\ell_+ \to \mathbf{R}$.

This idealized setting gives a picture of perfectly functioning markets in which intermediaries are not needed. Every agent enters into unbrokered exchanges with respect to all commodities. Each (type of) producer j chooses a production plan y_j to maximize its profits $p \cdot y_j$, subject to the technological constraint $y_j \in Y_j$. Each (type of) consumer i chooses a consumption bundle $x_i \in \mathbf{R}^\ell_+$ to maximize $u_i(x_i)$ subject to the budget constraint $p \cdot x_i \leq p \cdot e_i + \sum_{j=1}^{n} \bar{t}_{ij}\pi_j$, where π_j denotes the equilibrium profits of producer j. In equilibrium, markets clear, that is,

$$\sum_{i=1}^{m} x_i = \sum_{j=1}^{n} y_j.$$

The result of this unbrokered interaction is Pareto efficient under some mild monotonicity conditions. And under some equally well-known convexity assumptions, there is a partial converse: any Pareto-efficient allocation can be decentralized as an equilibrium with lump-sum transfers. These are the fundamental theorems of welfare economics. (For precise statements, see any microeconomic theory text, such as, Mas-Colell, Green, and Whinston 1995.)

This picture of the perfectly functioning market system rests on an infrastructure of assumptions that we shall investigate in more detail. For the moment, we highlight the complete markets assumption. The ADM model incorporates time and uncertainty by redefining commodities so that the same physical good delivered in different states of nature or at different dates is treated as a different commodity. This reinterpretation of the model leads to a proliferation of commodities and markets, but leaves the theory otherwise unchanged. Thus, the same simple formal structure accounts for a theory of risk sharing and intertemporal allocation, the central concerns of financial economics, without substantial change. This impressive piece of magic rests on the heroic assumption that there exists at some initial date a market and a market clearing price for every conceivable commodity, now and in the future, where commodities are distinguished by every circumstance on which their delivery can be made contingent.

As an illustration, consider a two-period version of the economy in which there is a finite number of states $s = 1, \ldots, S$ at the second date. At the first date $t = 0$, individuals have no information about the state; at the second date $t = 1$ they all observe the realization of the true state of nature. There is a single consumption good, which serves as both an input and output for the production processes. Since we distinguish commodities by the state and date in which they are delivered, there are $S + 1$ different contingent commodities: consumption at the first date and consumption in each of the S states at the second date. A commodity bundle is an $S + 1$-vector $(x_0, x_1, \ldots, x_S)$, where x_0 is the amount of the consumption good at date 0 and x_s is the amount of the consumption good at date 1 in state $s = 1, \ldots, S$. The set of all possible commodity bundles is identified with the linear vector space $\mathbf{R}^{S+1}$. Then the production set of producer j is a subset $Y_j \subset \mathbf{R}^{S+1}$, and the consumption set of consumer i is $\mathbf{R}_+^{S+1}$. The definition of equilibrium is unchanged, except for the interpretation.

The possibility of using the price mechanism to decentralize efficient decisions has important implications for the theory of the firm and corporate finance.

- *Value maximization.* There is an unambiguous objective for the firm: the maximization of the firm's value. This is the essentially unique objective that leads firms to make the right choices regarding production and financing decisions.
- *Decentralization.* Efficient allocation of resources can be decentralized to value-maximizing managers of individual firms. In the same way, capital budgeting within the firm can be decentralized by requiring managers of different divisions or units to make decisions that maximize net present values.
- *Shareholder unanimity.* There is unanimity about the behavior of the firm. All shareholders, regardless of their risk and time preferences, will agree that the firm should maximize value. With complete markets, maximization of the shareholder's individual welfare requires maximization of his wealth. This occurs for all shareholders if and only if the value of the firms in which they hold shares is maximized.
- *Modigliani-Miller theorem.* It follows that financing decisions are irrelevant. There is a generalized Modigliani-Miller theorem in operation,

since the law of one price implies that the value of the sum of the claims on the firm is equal to the value of its production plan.

There are, of course, alternative versions that apparently weaken the strength of the complete markets assumption. The theory of continuous-time finance based on the pioneering work of Merton (1969, 1971, 1973a, 1973b) and Black and Scholes (1973) has shown how continuous trading of a limited set of securities can span a high-dimensional commodity space. The work of Harrison and Kreps 1979; Kreps 1981) examines in detail the correspondence between complete markets and continuous trading of a limited set of assets. In these versions, markets are effectively complete: markets are not literally complete in the sense that there is a market for every contingent commodity at some initial date, but there are enough markets to guarantee that the allocations achieved are the same as the allocations that would be achieved with complete markets. This is a beautiful and powerful extension of the ADM model and one that has found extensive practical application in the modern theory of finance, but it too rests on strong assumptions:

- Continuous trading is extremely demanding. In the Harrison-Kreps theory, agents trade at prespecified discrete intervals in order to approximate complete markets, but in the Black-Scholes model, trading is literally continuous and the volume of trade is infinite as a result. If transaction costs are significant, as they tend to be in practice, continuous trading will be extremely expensive, and this alone may prevent the achievement of complete markets.
- Even in frictionless markets, the degree of rationality required to operate such dynamic trading strategies is a heavy assumption.
- The relationship between the amount of uncertainty and the number of securities that must be traded is subtle. As the work of Duffie and Huang (1985) has shown, for each additional dimension of the stochastic process that represents the underlying uncertainty, there must be an additional security traded. Furthermore, the complete-markets result of Harrison and Kreps holds only if the stochastic process satisfies certain regularity assumptions.
- In practice, it is common to make functional-form assumptions (Brownian motion, logarithmic utility) to allow closed-form solutions. This kind of restriction, which is inevitable in applied work, disguises the special nature of the general framework.

• Although the number of markets in operation is greatly reduced, their informational function is taken over in equilibrium by the agents themselves. Although the agent appears to be using only spot markets for the assets he trades, in order to derive the optimal trading strategy he needs to know the spot prices that would obtain in those spot markets at every date and in every state of nature that might occur. In other words, he needs to know the equilibrium prices in the spot markets contingent on every state of nature, even though he will never actually observe most of those prices. The agents are responsible for creating a complete set of virtual markets in their heads to replace the complete set of markets from the ADM model.

This criticism, originally leveled by Nagatani (1975) at the theory of Arrow securities (Arrow 1964), reminds us that equilibrium with self-fulfilling expectations requires a great deal of information and rationality on the part of the agents. The theory of continuous-time finance saves us from the obvious criticism of the ADM that we do not in practice observe complete markets, but it does not substantially weaken the strength of the complete-markets assumption. Whether markets are actually complete or virtually complete (because agents implicitly calculate the prices that would be generated by the ADM markets), we are in fact assuming that agents make use of a colossal amount of information without bearing any explicit costs. Once the costs of acquiring information are recognized and incorporated in the theory, things can be expected to change a lot. We return to the informational assumptions of the classical theory of markets in chapter 14, which investigates the costs of using markets. For the moment, we make a first cut at understanding incomplete markets by assuming that some markets are simply "missing" and that in every other respect the usual assumptions are all satisfied. In the next section, we describe a simple example of an economy with incomplete markets. Then we use this example to illustrate how some of the central implications of the ADM model for finance must be revised when markets are no longer complete.

5.2 Equilibrium with Incomplete Markets

We take as our starting point the two-period economy. When markets are incomplete, the fundamental theorems of welfare economics fail, or at least need to be reinterpreted. Implicit in the ADM definition of equilibrium is the assumption that all trade occurs at a single date, before consumption and production occur, and that every agent can trade future goods contingent on each state of nature. If the set of markets for contingent commodities is incomplete at the initial date, the resulting equilibrium may not be efficient.

In the rest of this section, we develop a simple example of general equilibrium with incomplete markets (GEI). The concepts used here are drawn from the extensive literature developed in the 1960s and 1970s (Diamond 1968; Dreze 1974; Grossman and Hart 1979; Hart, 1975, 1977, 1979a, 1979b 1980; Radner 1972; for a comprehensive treatment of the theory, see Magill and Qunzii 1996). As a simple illustration, suppose that goods can only be traded on spot markets at each date and that the only securities that can be traded, again on spot markets, are (proportionate) shares in the activities of various producers.

We now have a larger set of commodities in some sense, and yet the incompleteness of markets at the initial date means that individuals have fewer opportunities to trade than they did in the ADM model. In addition to the $S + 1$ contingent commodities, which are traded on spot markets in the different states $s = 0, 1, \ldots, S$, there are shares in the n different types of firms. However, there are more than n different kinds of shares. Firms are distinguished by both their type and the production plans they choose. In general, consumers of different types will want to own shares in firms with different production plans, even if the type of firm is the same. In effect, the market provides consumers with tailor-made securities. When markets are complete, shares are redundant securities from the point of view of risk sharing. Consumers use contingent commodities to achieve an optimal allocation of risk. Shares are simply a component of wealth. When markets are incomplete, shares are used to achieve the optimal allocation of risk and consumption and saving. Consumers care not just about the value of the shares (the value of the production plan), but also about the production plan itself. This means that we have to distinguish firms by their production plans as well as their types.

The number of potential securities is infinite, since there is an infinite number of different production plans that can be chosen. However, we can simplify the problem of describing an equilibrium by noting that as long as the production sets are convex, there is no loss of generality in assuming that a fraction t_{ij} of producers of type j all choose the same production plan y_j^i and that consumers of type i only hold shares in the producers of type j who choose this production plan. To see this, note that if two or more consumer types held shares in the same production plan, we could simply divide them up among different producers and treat the common production plan as if it were consumer specific. Conversely, if a consumer wanted to hold shares in several different production plans of type j producers, we could find a single production plan that would give the consumer the same consumption. (This assumes the production sets are convex.) In what follows, we assume that there is a specific production plan y_j^i for each type of consumer i and each type of producer j. With this assumption we have $S+1$ contingent commodities and mn securities.

Wealth is transferred between dates and states by holding shares, so in addition to the choice of a consumption bundle, each consumer has to choose a portfolio of shares to purchase at the first date. The portfolio of type i consumers is denoted by $t_i = \{t_{ij}\}_{j=1}^n$, where $t_{ij} \geq 0$ is the number of shares of a type j producer in the portfolio. Note that we are ruling out short sales in this definition of equilibrium. This turns out to be an important assumption.

Consumption at date 2 is determined by the portfolio chosen at date 1, via the budget constraint. In state $s > 0$, his (real) wealth is $e_{is} + \sum_{j=1}^n t_{ij} y_{js}^i$ and, if the consumer is not satiated with respect to consumption in any state, he must consume his entire wealth. Thus, his consumption in state $s > 0$ is equal to his wealth:

$$x_{is} = e_{is} + \sum_{j=1}^{n} t_{ij} y_{js}^i.$$

A consumer's utility is determined entirely by choices made at the first date. In an obvious notation, we can write

$$u_i(x_i) = u_i(x_i^0, e_i^1 + t_i \cdot y^{i1}) \equiv u_i^*(x_i^0, t_i; y^i).$$

The decision problem of the consumer at the first date is to choose a consumption level x_i^0 and a portfolio t_i to solve

$$\max u_i^*(x_i^0, t_i; y_i)$$

$$\text{s.t. } p^0 x_i^0 + q \cdot t_i \leq p^0 \ell_i^0 + q \cdot \bar{t}_i,$$

taking as given the prices (p^0, q) of goods and shares and the production plans chosen by all the producers.

By not allowing the consumers to buy shares in all the producers, we are anticipating the fact that in equilibrium, consumers of type i will not want to buy shares in the production plans $\{y_j^k : k \neq i\}$. We need to ensure that in equilibrium they do not want to do so. This will be done implicitly through the pricing of shares. One of the equilibrium conditions will be that shares are priced in such a way that only consumers of type i want to buy shares in y_j^i.

In equilibrium, shares will be owned by the types of consumers that value them most. Let us suppose the individual utility functions are C^1 on an open set containing the consumption set $\mathbf{R}^{S+1}$ and that the derivatives $\partial u_i(x_i)/\partial x_{is}$ are positive for all s and x_i. Then define $\mu_{is}(x_i)$ for any $x_i \in \mathbf{R}^{S+1}$ by putting

$$\mu_{is}(x_i) = \frac{\partial u_i(x_i)/\partial x_{is}}{\partial u_i(x_i)/\partial x_i^0}, \forall s = 1, \ldots, S.$$

Since we have a separate budget constraint in each state s we can choose the consumption good to be the numeraire in the first period, that is, normalize prices in state $s = 0$ so that $p^0 = 1$ in what follows. In equilibrium, one share in the future production plan y_j^{i1} will be evaluated by consumers of type i using the marginal rates of substitution $\mu_i(x_i)$: if consumers of type i hold a positive amount of the shares in y_j^{i1}, then the price must equal their marginal valuation; in other words, it must satisfy

$$q_j = \mu_i(x_i) \cdot y_j^{i1},$$

and, for every other type of consumer k,

$$q_j \geq \mu_k(x_k) \cdot y_j^{i1}, \forall k = 1, \ldots, m.$$

Note that the price does not depend on the consumer's type i; this is because we are going to assume that the producers are value maximizing, so the values of a unit share in any producer of type j must be the same in equilibrium. If type i consumers do not hold a positive number of shares in y_j^{i1}, then q_j may be greater than $\mu_i(x_i) \cdot y_j^{i1}$.

Now suppose that a new production plan y^1, one not offered in equilibrium, is introduced into the economy by a producer. Since a single producer has measure zero, this production plan can make no difference to the allocation of resources in the economy. Hence, the consumption bundles and marginal rates of substitution of the different consumer types remain unchanged. The value of the new production plan, that is, the maximal amount of first-period consumption that any consumer would give up for it, must be

$$MV(y^1) = \max_{i=1,\dots,m} \{\mu_i(x_i) \cdot y^1\},$$

where MV stands for "market value." Then the decision problem faced by each producer of type j is to choose a production plan $y \in Y_j$ to maximize $MV(y^1) + y^0$.

Now we can give a more formal definition of equilibrium.

Definition 5.1 An equilibrium consists of an m-tuple of consumption and portfolio plans (x_i^0, t_i), an mn-tuple of production plans (y_j^i), and a vector of share prices q such that, for every i,

1. (x_i^0, t_i) *maximizes* $u_i^*(x_i^0, t_i; y^i)$ *subject to the budget constraint* $x_i^0 + q \cdot t_i \leq e_i^0 + q \cdot \bar{t}_i - \sum_j \bar{t}_{ij} \sum_k t_{kj} y_j^{k0}$;
2. y_j^i *maximizes* $MV(y_j^{i1}) + y_j^{i0}$ *subject to* $y_j^i \in Y_j$, *for every* j;
3. $q_j \geq MV(y_j^{i1})$ *for all* i *and* j, *with* $MV(y_j^{i1}) = \mu_i(x_i) \cdot y_j^{i1}$ *if* $t_{ij} > 0$, *where* $MV(y^1) = \max_{i=1,\dots,m}\{\mu_i(x_i) \cdot y^1\}$ *for any production plan* y;
4. $\sum_i t_i = \mathbf{1}$ *and* $\sum_i x_i^0 = \sum_i e_i + \sum_j \sum_i t_{ij} y_j^{i0}$.

The value of the firm in (1) is net of the cost of investment, which is reflected in the term $\sum_j \bar{t}_{ij} \sum_k t_{kj} y_j^{k0}$ in the budget constraints of the initial shareholders. Despite the simplicity of the model, this definition of equilibrium appears rather complicated, even though it simply requires that consumers maximize utility, that producers maximize value, and that markets clear. Part of the complexity arises from the fact that we have to allow for the valuation of new securities that are not actually observed in equilibrium, and to do so we have to build into the definition of equilibrium some analysis of the consumer's portfolio behavior, that is, the first-order conditions for an optimal portfolio.

We note in passing that condition (3) ensures that there is no loss of generality in assuming that consumers of type i hold no shares in any production plan y_j^k for $k \neq i$.

Now that we have described an equilibrium with incomplete markets, we are ready to discover how many of the standard results of finance continue to hold.

5.3 Efficiency

It is clear that a GEI allocation will not typically be Pareto efficient in the usual sense. Ignoring boundary conditions, Pareto efficiency requires that marginal rates of substitution be equalized across individuals, that is, $\mu_i(x_i) = \mu_j(x_j)$ for all i and j. With a limited number of linearly independent securities to trade, there is no reason to think that this criterion will be satisfied, and it is easy to show by example that it will not be satisfied in most cases.

It is often argued that this efficiency criterion is inappropriate for an economy with incomplete markets. The incompleteness of markets is the result of transaction costs or other frictions to which a central planner might also be subject. For this reason, one should constrain the central planner to make use of the transaction technology when attempting to improve on the equilibrium allocation. In the present case, this leads to a concept of constrained Pareto efficiency. An equilibrium allocation is said to be constrained Pareto efficient if there does not exist an attainable allocation consisting of first-period consumption, production plans, and portfolios that Pareto dominates the equilibrium allocation. Constrained Pareto efficiency characterizes the equilibrium in the sense that every equilibrium allocation is constrained Pareto efficient and every constrained Pareto-efficient allocation can be decentralized as an equilibrium with lump-sum transfers. Using standard arguments, one can show that the equilibrium allocation defined above is constrained Pareto efficient. (See Gale 1982 for a proof.)

This result is quite special. In particular, it is not robust to the introduction of more than two periods or more than a single good at each date. Hart (1975), for example, has shown that an economy with two goods, two periods, and no uncertainty, in which goods can be traded only on spot markets, can have multiple Pareto-ranked equilibria.

A much deeper result, due to Geanakoplos and Polemarchakis (1986), shows that in a two-period, pure exchange model with a fixed set of linear securities denominated in terms of goods, equilibrium is generically inefficient in a very strong sense. More precisely, it is shown that if markets are effectively incomplete and there are two or more goods at each date, then it is generically possible to make all agents better off by redistributing goods and securities at the first date. With two or more goods, changes in the allocation of goods and securities at the first date have an effect on prices at the second date. These endogenous price changes, which are not taken into account by agents making decisions in the first period, create pecuniary externalities. With complete markets, pecuniary externalities do not "matter" because marginal rates of substitution are all equalized, but with incomplete markets they do. This is what makes it possible for all the agents to be made better off.

When there is only one good at each date, as in our example, there are no relative prices at the second date. There is thus a unique relationship between first-period decisions and second-period allocations, and no possibility of pecuniary externalities. Clearly this is a very special case and one that should be treated with caution.

5.4 Spanning, Value Maximization, and Decentralization

One of the most important lessons of the ADM model is the sufficiency of prices (or the information contained in prices) as a guide for efficient decision making. In the ADM model, everyone observes a complete vector of contingent-commodity prices, and these prices are used for the valuation of everything in the economy. In particular, the firm's production plan is valued like any other commodity bundle, using the prices for contingent commodities. In the GEI model, on the other hand, we use the functional $MV(y^1)$ to value the firm, and $MV(y^1)$ evidently contains a lot more information (parameters) than an ordinary price vector. So it is not clear whether we have achieved the same degree of decentralization in a GEI model as we have in an ADM model. An interesting question is how much (or how little) information the producers need in order to choose the right production plans and thus, indirectly, provide the right securities for the consumers.

In presenting the definition of equilibrium, we treated the producers as if they understood how much each consumer would pay for a small amount of each security that could be produced (cf. Hart 1979b, 1980). This idea can be elaborated by imagining a two-stage game in which producers make choices of production plans in the first period and consumers trade securities in the second. Corresponding to every choice of production plans in the first period, there is a distinct subgame in the second. In each of these second-period subgames, there will be equilibrium prices for each of the securities produced. The price functional $MV(y^1)$ is just a reduced-form representation of these subgame-equilibrium prices, and the assumption that each producer knows the prices of every conceivable security is just an assumption of rational expectations about the subgame that results when a new security is introduced. (This is essentially the idea behind the model in Hart 1979b.)

The alternative interpretation is that the auctioneer simply calls out the prices of all the securities, at which producers can sell as much as they want of each security.

In practice, however, the assumption that so much information is available for free seems a little stringent. For this reason, theorists have looked for simplifying assumptions under which producers could use the information available about the prices of actually traded securities in order to infer the equilibrium price of a nontraded security. One example of this approach applies to securities that are spanned by the existing set of traded securities.

Our model of equilibrium assumes that consumers can only hold nonnegative amounts of each security, that is, $t_{ij} \geq 0$ for every (i, j). In the traditional account of spanning, on the other hand, it is implicitly assumed that unlimited short sales are allowed. In that case, the set of available portfolios must include $Z = \{\sum_{ij} t_{ij} y_j^{i1}\}$, the linear subspace of $\mathbf{R}^S$ spanned by the future production plans $\{y_j^i\}$. The usual no-arbitrage condition requires that the price of a security $z = \sum_{ij} t_{ij} y_j^{i1} \in Z$ must be equal to $\sum_{ij} t_{ij} MV(y_j^{i1})$, since otherwise it would be possible to construct a riskless arbitrage, a violation of the conditions for equilibrium. This means that any security in the linear subspace Z can be priced by arbitrage. In order to infer the price functional MV on Z, it is sufficient to know the prices of the traded securities $\{y_j^{i1}\}$. As long as the producer wants to choose a production plan in the span of the set of traded securities, he can calculate the equilibrium price of the new security from the prices he observes in the market. However, if the producer wants to venture outside the span of the set of traded securities, then linearity no longer applies, and the calculation is more complicated.

Furthermore, if we assume that every agent has strictly positive consumption $x_i \gg 0$, then the first-order conditions for equilibrium imply that $q_j = \mu_k(x_k) \cdot y_j^{i1}$ for every k and (i, j), from which it follows immediately that

$$MV(z) = \mu_k(x_k) \cdot z = \sum_{ij} t_{ij} \mu_k(x_k) \cdot y_j^{i1}$$

for every k and (i, j). In other words, individual marginal valuations agree on the subspace Z. For this reason, consumers are interested only in the value of the security, not its individual characteristics, as long as it belongs to Z. This also explains why maximizing value and decentralizing decisions are the "right" thing to do—that is, consumers all agree that this is the right thing to do. Of course, since all consumers have tailor-made securities, the issue of unanimity, which played such a large role in the research into incomplete markets in the 1970s, is more or less irrelevant here.

Since the theory works out so neatly in the case where there are no short-sale constraints, it may be wondered why we introduced them into our model of GEI. The problem is that without short sale constraints, the theory is not well behaved. First, there are problems establishing the existence of equilibrium without placing exogenous bounds on the agents' portfolios. The work of Duffie and Shaefer (1985, 1986) suggests that this kind of nonexistence is a pathological phenomenon. A more serious problem, however, is the fact that without short-sale constraints, Allen and Gale (1988, 1992) have shown that introducing a security outside the span of the already traded securities violates the perfect-competition assumption. More precisely, introducing a small amount of a new (nonredundant) security has a large impact on the economy and thus gives even a small producer a significant amount of market power. In that case, the price-taking assumption is not justified. This issue will be discussed in more detail below. For the moment, we retain the no-short-sale constraint.

Since portfolios are required to be nonnegative, the set of portfolios is the convex cone K spanned by the set of traded securities, that is,

$$K = \left\{ \sum_{ij} t_{ij} y_j^{i1} : t_{ij} \geq 0 \right\}.$$

Any security in K can be obtained by purchasing a portfolio with suitable nonnegative weights of each security. This puts an upper bound on the price that can be obtained for the security $y^1 = \sum_{ij} t_{ij} y_j^{i1}$. In fact, the definition of the equilibrium price functional $MV(y^1)$ implies that it must be convex:

$$\begin{aligned} MV(y^1) = \mu_k(x_k) \cdot y^1 &= \sum_{ij} t_{ij} \mu_k(x_k) \cdot y_j^{i1} \leq \sum_{ij} t_{ij} \max_k \{\mu_k(x_k) \cdot y_j^{i1}\} \\ &= \sum_{ij} t_{ij} MV(y_j^{i1}). \end{aligned}$$

It is easy to see that in some cases, we may well have $MV(y^1) < \sum_{ij} t_{ij} MV(y_j^{i1})$, which implies that the producers will perceive that if they were to offer the security y^1 for sale, they would receive less than the cost of synthesizing it in the market. This possibility depends crucially on the assumption that short sales are not allowed. If it were possible to take short positions in all traded securities, then the no-arbitrage condition would require $MV(y^1) = \sum_{ij} t_{ij} MV(y_j^{i1})$ exactly.

The interesting question is whether a producer can use the information from the prices of traded securities to figure out the market price that he would receive for a security in K. In other words, is there a subset of K whose elements can be expressed as nonnegative linear combinations of the traded securities and whose equilibrium value is the same linear combination of the prices of the traded securities? If markets are effectively complete, so that the marginal rates of substitution $\mu_i(x_i)$ are equalized for all consumer types, then the subset of securities that can be priced by arbitrage is the whole of K. Typically, markets will not be effectively complete, and the set of securities that can be priced by arbitrage is smaller. Let A denote the set of securities that can be priced by arbitrage, let Z_i denote the set of securities in the portfolios of consumers of type i, and let $K(Z_i)$ denote the nonnegative cone of elements of Z_i. Since $MV(y^1) = \mu_i(x_i) \cdot y^1$ for all $y^1 \in Z_i$, it is clear that $MV(y) = \sum_{ij} t_{ij} MV(y_j^i)$ for any $y \in K(Z_i)$, so $K(Z_i) \subseteq A$. We can even extend this argument a little further by letting

$$Z_i' = \{y_j^{k1} : MV(y_j^{k1}) = \mu_i(x_i) \cdot y_j^{k1}\}$$

be the set of traded securities that are optimal for a consumer of type i and then noting that $K(Z_i') \subseteq A$.

On the other hand, if $y^1 \in K(Z_i') \backslash K(Z_k')$ and $y^{1\prime} \in K(Z_k') \backslash K(Z_i')$, then for any $0 < \lambda < 1$,

$$MV(\lambda y^1 + (1-\lambda) y^{1\prime}) < \lambda MV(y^1) + (1-\lambda) MV(y^{1\prime}),$$

so we cannot even extend arbitrage pricing to the convex hull of $\cup_{i=1}^m K(Z_i)$.

How should we interpret these spanning conditions? What do we learn from the fact that producers can price securities by arbitrage? One interpretation is that the producers do not need to know the true price functional $MV(y^1)$. They only need to know the prices of traded securities, and from that they can work out the prices of the nontraded securities. In a sense this is true, but possibly misleading. First, they can do this only for the set of securities in A, and thus they need to know A before they start. This may be informationally demanding—as demanding as knowing $MV(y^1)$ to begin with.

Second, they need to know the right spanning securities to use, since there may be more than one nonnegative linear combination that will generate the security to be priced, and not all linear combinations may give the right price.

In the classical ADM theory, the vector of commodity prices reveals all the information that producers need to know in order to maximize profits (value of the firm). Furthermore, producers can observe these prices in markets, where the complete set of contingent commodities is being traded. When markets are incomplete, things are more complicated. In order to achieve even constrained efficiency, producers have to form more or less complicated conjectures about how the value of their firms will change in response to this or that change in the production plan. In some cases, where the spanning conditions are satisfied, these conjectures can be formed by looking at the value of other firms (though even this is a nontrivial task). In other cases, even this may not be enough, and the producer may have to guess the marginal valuations of different types of investors in order to make the correct conjecture. In any case, the more complicated the objective function needed for efficient decision making is, the more difficult it is to decentralize decisions.

Note that here we have discussed only decentralization among firms, although the classical theory allows for decentralization within firms as well (if the firm consists of divisions with additive production sets, maximizing profits in each division is necessary and sufficient for profit maximization in the firm as a whole). With incomplete markets, there is no simple theory of decentralization within the firm. We return to these issues in chapter 7.

5.5 Shareholder Unanimity

In our model of equilibrium with incomplete markets, there is complete unanimity by definition. Each producer has identical shareholders who must therefore agree about what the firm ought to do. We achieve this outcome by assuming a very large number of producers of each type and they produce tailor-made securities. This is a kind of "Tiebout hypothesis" applied to finance rather than local public goods. These assumptions, originally identified by Hart (1977), are natural in a world of perfect competition, but they are nonetheless quite strong. If the number of firms were limited, unanimity might not be assured, and that would lead to conflicts among shareholders.

Grossman and Hart (1979) have developed a theory of the firm designed to deal with exactly this issue, though it has proved somewhat intractable. Their focus was on developing an account of producer behavior that would guarantee a limited form of decentralization (constrained efficiency). When consumers of several different types hold shares in the production plan of a single firm, the producer must attempt to maximize a weighted sum of their marginal rates of substitution. Using the notation of the preceding model, if the representative consumer of type i holds a share t_{ij} in the production plan y_j, then producer j must choose y_j to maximize

$$\sum_i t_{ij}\mu_i(x_i) \cdot y_j^1 + y^0.$$

This is a somewhat complicated objective function, and from a positive point of view, it is not clear that the producer will find it easy to use.

Even if we can assume that the producer does use this objective function, the problems do not end there. In a multiperiod context, the identities of a given firm's shareholders will change from period to period as the shares are bought and sold. It turns out that later shareholders may want to change the plans of earlier shareholders, thus introducing a form of time inconsistency.

Whether the "financial Tiebout hypothesis" holds in practice is an interesting empirical question. There is a large number of publicly traded companies, and it may be that the number of different types of consumers is not so great but that they can distribute themselves among firms in a way that allows for something close to unanimity. As far as we know, this question remains unexplored. In any case, from a purely theoretical point of view, the Grossman-Hart theory raises some problems, since they require that the number of firms (not just firm types) be fewer than the number of consumer types in order to generate a lack of unanimity. This emphasis on the finiteness of the number of firms makes the assumption of perfect competition a little strained.

5.6 Security Design and the Relevance of Corporate Finance

One of the properties of the ADM model that does not transfer to incomplete markets is the irrelevance of corporate finance decisions—the Modigliani-Miller theorem. The fact that different consumers have different marginal rates of substitution across states ensures that they will value the same security differently. For this reason, the value of the firm will not be independent of the claims issued against the production plan.

Suppose that the producer has chosen a production plan y_j that will be sold in equilibrium to consumers of type i. Then the value of the shares in equilibrium will be $q_j = \mu_i(x_i) \cdot y_j^1$. The equilibrium conditions require that no other consumer type k is willing to pay more for these shares, so that $q_j \geq \mu_k(x_k) \cdot y_j^1$ for any $k = 1, \ldots, m$. However, there may be a way of marketing tranches of y_j^1 to different clienteles in a way that increases the total value of the firm. For example, choose z_1 and z_2 to solve the problem

$$\max MV(z_1) + MV(z_2)$$

$$\text{s.t. } z_1 + z_2 = y_j^1.$$

It is always the case that $MV(z_1) + MV(z_2) \geq MV(y_j^1)$, and if $MV(z_1) + MV(z_2) > MV(y_j^1)$, then the producer would do strictly better to split the firm—issue two claims promising to pay z_1 and z_2, respectively, and sell them to the consumer types who value them most highly.

If there were no costs of issuing new claims, then we would soon end up with effectively complete markets. This kind of arbitrage is profitable as long as there are two types of consumers, each of whom values a part of the firm more highly than any other type. To preserve the incompleteness of markets, Allen and Gale (1988) assumed fixed costs of introducing securities. Then as long as the valuations of different consumers are not too different in equilibrium, the process of introducing new claims will stop before markets are complete.

Note that the restriction on short sales is crucial to supporting this kind of incentive to introduce securities. If consumers are allowed to make unlimited short sales, then it will be possible to make an arbitrage profit as long as the value of the sum of the claims is different from the value of the whole firm. Suppose that some producers of type j issue two securities and some issue only one (traditional equity shares). The two classes of firms have different financial structures, but they cannot have different values in equilibrium. If they did, a speculator could buy a one-security firm, short the claims of the two-security firm, and make a profit. Since the issuers of two securities need an increase in value to compensate for the cost of the additional security, we cannot have an equilibrium in which different producers choose different financial structures. However, if a producer thinks that by issuing only a single security, he can take a free ride on the others and get the same value, then we cannot have an equilibrium in which everyone chooses a two-security financial structure.

There is something fundamentally wrong with the notion of a perfectly competitive market with unlimited short sales when there are fixed costs of issuing securities. What lies at the bottom of the problem is the assumption of price-taking behavior. We have argued (Allen and Gale 1992) that perfect competition (price-taking behavior) does not make much sense when unlimited short sales are allowed. However small a single producer may be, he has a large effect on the market when he introduces a new security if unlimited short sales are allowed. Although the producer himself is providing a negligible amount of the security, by allowing others to trade the security, he is introducing a new market that may have a nonnegligible effect on the equilibrium. Put another way, although the new security is in zero net supply, the open interest may be nonnegligible.

In this case, it is possible to rescue the competitive model by assuming that short sales are not allowed. When short sales are not allowed, the open interest in the security is limited to the amount supplied by the producer, which is a negligible amount if the producer is negligible. In this way, the effect of each producer remains negligible in equilibrium. Many markets have zero net supply by definition. For example, in options markets there must be "short sales" in order to have any trade at all. In such cases, it is not clear how to rescue the competitive assumption. Simply opening such a market is going to have a big effect, and we need a theory of equilibrium with imperfect competition to account for this.

Allen and Gale (1992) develop a two-stage model of security design with imperfect competition. In the first stage, firms simultaneously choose optimal financial structures. In the second stage, competitive investors bid for the securities issued in the first stage. The equilibrium supply of securities is determined in a Nash equilibrium of the first-stage game. Then, taking the supply of securities as given and allowing unlimited short sales, prices adjust to clear the competitive securities markets in the second stage. Letting the number of firms increase without bound does not bring us back to perfectly competitive pricing, however. Imperfect competition is essential to allow firms to recover the cost of issuing complex securities.

5.7 Modeling Imperfect Markets

The fact that the model of equilibrium with incomplete information is badly behaved when we allow unlimited short sales and financial innovation alerts us to the fundamental incompatibility of the assumptions of perfect competition, in the sense of ADM, and the factors that explain the incompleteness of markets in the first place. What this suggests is that merely assuming that some markets are missing does not lead to a credible theory of incomplete markets. If we think about the other reasons that markets are incomplete, this observation becomes quite obvious.

The category of transaction costs includes not just the cost of recording and verifying the transaction, but the much more important costs of learning to make optimal decisions and thinking about the optimal transaction in any particular context. Given the uncertainty that attends any commitment to trade in the distant future and the difficulty of collecting and analyzing information that might be relevant to such transactions, it is not surprising that the number of transactions that are undertaken for the distant future is small. In fact, they appear to be limited to long-term debt and certain types of supply contracts. Similarly, the costs of making transactions contingent on unlikely and very minutely defined states of nature are likely to outweigh the benefits. These costs, of course, are present in markets that do exist and may be important determinants of the kind and volume of trades that go on there. Whether the markets exist or not, transaction costs are something that should be taken into account in modeling them.

It is well known that *adverse selection* may limit trade or even prevent a market from operating at all (cf. Akerlof's lemons problem in Akerlof 1970). Insurance markets and credit markets are prime examples. What is true for these markets is clearly true for financial markets in general. Corporate finance has taken on board the adverse selection problem, but it has not had much impact on the theory of asset markets. The important point is that markets with adverse selection behave very differently from markets without adverse selection. The GEI model, which assumes that some markets are missing but otherwise maintains the assumptions of the ADM model, is not consistent with the presence of adverse selection. Even the rational expectations model, which at least introduces asymmetric information, deals only with uncertainty about states of nature, not the characteristics of individual goods or traders. To account for any of these things requires a market with a different structure. (For an attempt to deal with adverse selection in general equilibrium see Gale 1992.)

Many risks cannot be insured because of the attendant moral hazard problems. It is hardly surprising that there are no private markets in which one can insure against future unemployment or business failure, since these risks depend so much on decisions made by the insured. The same kinds of moral hazard affect the financial transactions that we do observe, whether it is the moral hazard on the part of the CEO of a company in which an investor has just bought stock or moral hazard on the part of the investment banker who is advising his purchase. Markets that are affected by moral hazard will behave very differently from the Walrasian markets of the ADM and GEI models. Careful modeling of these problems is required to understand the uses and limitations of financial markets.

Many contracts are introduced in futures and options exchanges only to disappear after a few months because of lack of interest. It takes a certain minimum volume of transactions to provide adequate liquidity and cover the fixed costs of running a market. These factors, which are important in explaining the absence of many markets, also affect the operation of markets that do survive. They need to be explicitly modeled if we are to understand the efficiency properties of these markets.

As we argued in chapter 1 and again in this chapter, the rationale for unregulated competitive markets is based on an ideal case, formalized in the ADM model. Once imperfections such as transaction costs and asymmetric information are introduced, the efficiency of the market mechanism is no longer guaranteed. Regulation and other forms of government intervention are one answer to market failures, but there are alternatives. The development of financial institutions such as intermediaries can take the place of "missing markets," as can different ways of organizing the financial functions of firms.

The limitations of the ADM model as a description of reality go beyond the mere absence of markets, however. The markets that do exist are characterized by many of the frictions listed. The structure of these markets has been adapted to cope with transaction costs, adverse selection, moral hazard, illiquidity, and fixed costs of participation. Instead of trading a homogeneous commodity at a single market-clearing price, these markets allow agents to negotiate contracts, often through intermediaries, taking into account asymmetric information about the nature of the transaction. In these "markets," information is exchanged, relationships are established, bargaining and renegotiation occur, search takes place (individuals are matched), innovation and security design are undertaken, and institutional forms are established. The following chapters deal with the broad theme of how the invisible hand of the market—in the sense of firms and individuals pursuing private goals—copes with the limitations of financial markets, narrowly defined. In particular, although in some cases intermediaries and markets are seen as alternative mechanisms for the allocation of resources, in many cases intermediaries play a crucial role in making markets work by reducing the costs of participating in the market for individual firms and investors.

References

Akerlof, G. (1970). "The Market for 'Lemons': Quality Uncertainty and the Market Mechanisms." *The Quarterly Journal of Economics.* **84,** 488–500.

Allen, F., and D. Gale. (1988). "Optimal Security Design." *Review of Financial Studies* **1,** 229–263.

———. (1992). "Arbitrage, Short Sales, and Financial Innovation." *Econometrica* **59,** 1041–1068.

Arrow, K. (1964). "The Role of Securities in the Optimal Allocation of Risk-Bearing." *Review of Economic Studies* **31,** 91–96.

Arrow, K., and G. Debreu. (1954). "Existence of Equilibrium for a Competitive Economy." *Econometrica* **22,** 265–290.

Black, F., and M. Scholes. (1973). "The Pricing of Options and Corporate Liabilities." *Journal of Political Economy* **81,** 637–654.

Diamond, P. (1967). "The Role of a Stock Market in a General Equilibrium Model with Technological Uncertainty," *The American Economic Review* **57,** 759–776.

Duffie, J. D., and C. Huang. (1985). "Implementing Arrow-Debreu Equilibria by Continuous Trading of Few Long-lived Securities." *Econometrica* **53,** 1337–1356.

Duffie, J. D., and W. Shafer. (1985). "Equilibrium in Incomplete Markets: I—A Basic Model of Generic Existence." *Journal of Mathematical Economics* **14,** 285–300.

———. (1986). "Equilibrium in Incomplete Markets: II; Generic Existence in Stochastic Economies." *Journal of Mathematical Economics* **15,** 199–216.

Dreze, J. (ed.). (1974). *Allocation Under Uncertainty: Equilibrium and Optimality.* Proceedings from a workshop sponsored by the International Economic Association. New York: Wiley.

Gale, D. (1982). *Money in Equilibrium.* Cambridge: Cambridge University Press.

Geanakoplos, J., and H. Polemarchakis. (1986). "Existence, Regularity, and Constrained Suboptimality of Competitive Allocations When the Asset Market Is Incomplete." In W. Heller, R. Starr, and D. Starrett (eds.), *Essays in Honor of Kenneth J. Arrow.* Vol. 3. *Un-*

certainty, Information, and Communication (pp. 65–95). New York: Cambridge University Press.

Grossman, S., and O. Hart. (1979). "A Theory of Competitive Equilibrium in Stock Market Economies." *Econometrica* **47,** 293–329.

Harrison, J. M., and D. Kreps. (1979). "Martingales and Arbitrage in Multiperiod Securities Markets." *Journal of Economic Theory* **12,** 381–408.

Hart, O. (1979a). "Monopolistic Competition in a Large Economy with Differentiated Commodities." *Review of Economic Studies* **46,** 1–30.

———. (1979b). "On Shareholder Unanimity in Large Stock Market Economies." *Econometrica* **47,** 1057–1083.

———. (1980). "Perfect Competition and Optimal Product Differentiation." *Journal of Economic Theory* **22,** 279–312.

Kreps, D. (1981). "Arbitrage and Equilibrium in Economies with Infinitely Many Commodities." *Journal of Mathematical Economics* **8,** 15–35.

Leland, H. (1974). "Production Theory and the Stock Market." *Bell Journal of Economics* **5,** 125–144.

Magill, M., and M. Quinzii. (1996). *Theory of Incomplete Markets.* Cambridge MA: MIT Press.

Mas Colell, A., M. Whinston, and J. Green. (1995). *Microeconomic Theory.* New York: Oxford University Press.

McKenzie, L. (1954). "On Equilibrium in Graham's Model of World Trade and Other Competitive Systems." *Econometrica* **22,** 147–161.

———. (1959). "On the Existence of General Equilibrium for a Competitive Market." *Econometrica* **27,** 54–71.

Merton, R. (1969). "Lifetime Portfolio Selection Under Uncertainty: The Continuous-Time Case." *Review of Economics and Statistics* **51,** 247–57.

———. (1971). "Optimum Consumption and Portfolio Rules in a Continuous-Time Model." *Journal of Economic Theory* **3,** 373–413.

———. (1973a). "Theory of Rational Option Pricing." *Bell Journal of Economics* **4,** 141–183.

———. (1973b). "An Intertemporal Capital Asset Pricing Model." *Econometrica* **41,** 867–887.

Nagatani, K. (1975). "On a Theorem of Arrow." *Review of Economic Studies* **42,** 483–485.

Radner, R. (1972). "Existence of Equilibrium of Plans, Prices, and Price Expectations in a Sequence of Markets." *Econometrica* **40,** 289–303.

II

Competition Versus Insurance

6 Intertemporal Smoothing

In the early 1970s, most industrialized countries were adversely affected by a sharp rise in oil prices. This oil shock had a dramatic effect on the stock market valuations of firms. Figure 6.1 shows the effect on the real value of shares listed on the New York Stock Exchange (NYSE): prices fell by almost half compared to their value at the peak in 1972. As we saw in chapter 3, households in market-based economies have considerable exposure to market fluctuations. According to the data presented, in the United States and United Kingdom equity constituted about half of households' financial assets. The collapse in share prices caused by the oil shock thus had a severe negative impact on the wealth of households. Any households that were forced to liquidate stocks after market prices fell would have suffered from lower consumption over the remainder of their lives. Retirees in particular would have been affected in this way.

In the bank-based economies of Japan, Germany, and France, the effect was very different. In these countries, only a small portion of households' financial assets are in the form of equity, and a much greater proportion is held in claims on intermediaries, which are not marked to the market. In Japan over half of household financial assets were held in the form of cash and bank accounts, while in Germany, and France the amount held in this form was only slightly less. In all three countries the amount of equity held was relatively small and constituted less than one-sixth of assets. The effect of the oil shock was thus rather different. Since the claims on intermediaries were fixed in nominal terms, the households in Japan, Germany, and France did not suffer a fall in wealth like their counterparts in the United States and United Kingdom and would not have been forced to reduce their consumption. Somehow the bank-based financial systems were able to smooth the oil price shock rather than pass it on to investors.

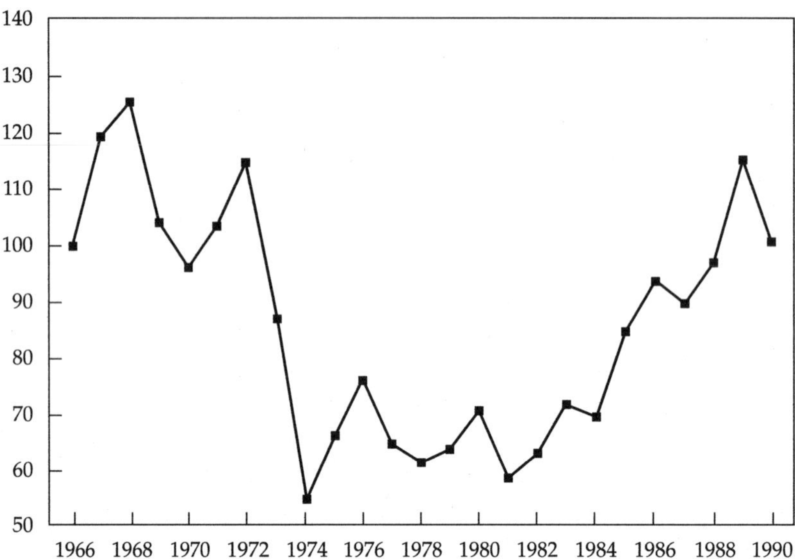

Figure 6.1
The variation of real U.S. stock prices, 1966–1990

In the 1980s the situation was reversed. The economies of most industrialized countries performed relatively well, and stock markets boomed, as illustrated for the United States by figure 6.1. Investors in the United States and United Kingdom who held stocks were able to achieve higher-than-expected returns and could use these returns to finance a higher level of consumption. The dissaving generation in Japan, Germany, and France did less well by comparison. Since their savings were placed with intermediaries, such as banks, on which they held fixed claims, there was no windfall gain for them.

The effect of the oil shock on the United States and other stock markets is an example of what is usually considered a nondiversifiable risk. The shock causes highly correlated changes in most stock values, so investors cannot avoid the risk by holding a diversified portfolio. Nonetheless, these episodes illustrate that the risks borne by individuals in market-based and bank-based financial systems can be very different, even when the countries are subjected to similar shocks.

As we have noted, there is often a presumption that economies with highly developed financial markets are necessarily better able to allocate resources and share risks. Yet there is a sense in which economies with fewer choices of financial instruments can offer superior risk sharing. As our example illustrates, financial systems in which a large amount of wealth is held in the form of bank deposits may shield households from fluctuations in the value of assets that are marked to market. Of course, households in the United States and United Kingdom can hold bank deposits as well, but the returns may not be as good. The problem is that banks in market-based systems have to compete with financial markets, and competition from markets may prevent banks and similar institutions from providing risk smoothing to households. In other words, either banks have to pass on risks to households or they have to hold safer assets, which earn lower returns. Before we consider these complications, there is a much more immediate question that has to be faced: How do different financial systems cope with risk? If the United States and United Kingdom economies have similar risk characteristics to those of Japan, Germany, and France, how can the latter's bank-based financial systems avoid the risk that is reflected in the United States stock market prices shown in figure 6.1? To answer this question, we first have to think about the way that risk sharing is traditionally treated in the theory of markets.

Traditional financial theory has little to say about hedging nondiversifiable risks. It assumes that the set of assets is given and focuses on the efficient sharing of these risks through exchange. For example, the standard diversification argument requires individuals to exchange assets so that each individual holds a relatively small amount of any one risk. Risks will also be traded so that more risk-averse people bear less of the risk than people who are less risk averse. These strategies do not eliminate macroeconomic shocks, which affect all assets in a similar way. We call this kind of risk sharing cross-sectional risk sharing, because it is achieved through exchanges of risk among individuals at a given point in time.

Departing from the traditional approach, this chapter focuses on the intertemporal smoothing of risk. Risks that cannot be diversified at a given point in time can nevertheless be averaged over time in a way that reduces their impact on individual welfare. One hedging strategy for nondiversifiable risks is intergenerational risk sharing, which spreads the risks associated with a given stock of assets across generations with heterogeneous experiences. Another strategy involves asset accumulation in order to reduce fluctuations in consumption over time. Both of these strategies are examples of the intertemporal smoothing of asset returns.

In standard financial models with fixed asset supplies and a single time period, nondiversifiable risk is unavoidable, and someone has to bear this risk. Such models implicitly overlook possibilities for intertemporal smoothing. At the other extreme, in an ideal ADM world, cross-sectional risk sharing and intertemporal smoothing are undertaken automatically because markets are complete and there is complete participation in those markets. Neither the standard financial models, which assume a fixed set of assets, nor the idealized ADM model, which does not explicitly deal with institutions, provide much insight into the relationship between the structure of a country's financial system and the stock of assets accumulated. In particular, they do not tell us how a country's reliance on financial markets or intermediaries affects its ability to smooth asset returns by changing its dynamic accumulation path. The opportunities for engaging in intertemporal smoothing may be very different in market-based and bank-based financial systems. What we argue here is that incomplete markets do not provide for effective intertemporal smoothing, but that long-lived financial institutions such as banks can do so, as long they are not subject to competition from financial markets. Competition from financial markets can lead to the unraveling of intertemporal smoothing provided by long-lived institutions. In good times individuals would rather opt out of the banking system and invest in the market, so in the long run, intertemporal smoothing by banks is not viable in the presence of competition from markets.

This chapter considers the consequences of intertemporal smoothing for economic welfare. It also considers positive issues such as asset pricing in a model with incomplete markets. In practice, markets may not be complete in the ADM sense for a wide variety of reasons, including moral hazard, adverse selection, transaction costs, and incomplete participation. For simplicity we consider an economy with an overlapping generations structure, which results in incomplete participation. This is a tractable paradigm for the analysis of intertemporal smoothing and captures many of the features common to a wide range of models of market incompleteness.

Our analysis is related to a number of strands of the literature. First, Scheinkman (1980), McCallum (1987), and others have shown that incorporating a long-lived asset rules out the possibility of overaccumulation. This work is not concerned with risk. In contrast, our chapter analyzes how the risk arising from the dividend stream of long-lived assets is not eliminated by financial markets but can be eliminated by an intermediary. Second, Qi (1994) extends the Diamond-Dybvig model to an overlapping generations model. In his model there is no aggregate risk and no role for intertemporal smoothing. Bhattacharya and Padilla (1996), Bhattacharya, Fulghieri, and Rovelli (1998) and Fulghieri and Rovelli (1998) also compare the performance of markets and intermediaries in achieving an efficient intertemporal allocation of resources in an overlapping generations model. There is again no aggregate uncertainty in their models, and they do not consider intertemporal smoothing. Third, Gordon and Varian (1988) consider how governments can implement policies such as social security to allow intergenerational risk sharing in the context of a model with a single asset. They do not consider market allocations and asset pricing or the role of intermediation, which are the focus of this chapter. Fourth, Demange and Laroque (1995) consider a model with a sequence of generations who care only about their own welfare and not about future generations. They investigate how the introduction of incomplete stock markets and government taxes and subsidies can improve all generations' welfare in such a setting. Again they do not focus on intermediation.

We outline a simple example to fix ideas and describe a standard overlapping generations (OLG) model used in Allen and Gale (1997) with two assets: a risky asset in fixed supply and a safe asset that can be accumulated over time. Then we show that under certain conditions, the safe asset is never held in the market equilibrium; in fact, it is dominated by the risky asset. Next we show that intertemporal smoothing can lead to a higher level of average expected utility than is possible in the market equilibrium. We show that the market equilibrium is not ex ante Pareto efficient: there exist allocations with intertemporal smoothing that make all generations better off ex ante compared to the market equilibrium. We use this inefficiency to suggest that intertemporal smoothing could be implemented by a long-lived intermediary. We continue the theme of a market failure by introducing a refinement of the usual notion of Pareto efficiency and arguing that the market equilibrium is not efficient. Then we show that the intertemporal smoothing provided by a long-lived intermediary is fragile and that competition from financial markets can lead to disintermediation, which causes the smoothing mechanism to unravel. Formal proofs are contained in the appendix.

6.1 Incomplete Risk Sharing: An Example

We begin with a simple example to illustrate how incomplete markets create an opportunity for an intermediary to improve welfare in a dynamic economy. There is an infinite number of periods $t = 0, 1, 2, \ldots$ and a sequence of overlapping generations. At the first date $t = 0$ there is an initial old generation that lives for one period, and at every date t there is a new generation that lives for two periods. We can assume that each generation consists of a continuum of identical agents and normalize the number of agents to unity. We refer to these agents as investors or depositors, depending on whether we think of the economy as making investments through financial markets or through banklike intermediaries, respectively.

At each date there is a single good, which can be invested or consumed. Investors/depositors are endowed with $e > 0$ units of the consumption good in their youth. They do not consume when they are young, but instead invest their endowment to provide for consumption in their old age. Their utility from consumption is $u(c)$, where $u'(c) > 0$ and $u''(c) < 0$.

There are two assets. The first is an asset in fixed supply with time-varying returns. In even-numbered periods $t = 0, 2, 4, \ldots$ the payoff is r_H, and in odd-numbered periods $t = 1, 3, 5, \ldots$ the payoff is r_L with $r_H > r_L > 0$. The initial old generation owns the aggregate supply of the durable asset, which is normalized to equal one unit. The second asset is a storage technology. One unit of consumption at date t can be transformed into one unit of consumption at date $t + 1$. The amount of storage is determined endogenously by the investment decisions of the agents.

There is no uncertainty in this economy once time begins, but we take the perspective of an agent in an initial position, behind the veil of ignorance, who does not know whether she will be born in an even- or an odd-numbered generation. The two events are assumed to be equally probable. To the extent that the consumption and utility of even and odd generations are different in equilibrium, the agent faces risk in the initial position. Furthermore, it is not possible to insure against this risk, since agents cannot trade before they are born and it is impossible to insure the risk after the uncertainty is resolved.

This is the basic incompleteness of markets that occurs whenever agents are initially uncertain what role they will play in the economy, and it obviously prevents optimal ex ante sharing of risk. Although the example is very simple, there is some value in rehearsing the details of this story because it makes clear the logic of the dynamic stochastic model presented in the following section.

The Allocation with Financial Markets

Consider what happens when there are competitive financial markets. The young generation uses its endowment e to purchase assets in financial markets. We focus here on a stationary equilibrium, where asset prices and consumption depend on only whether the date is even or odd. Let P_H denote the price of the durable asset in terms of consumption in even periods when the payoff is r_H, and let P_L denote the price in odd periods when the return is r_L. The price of storage is taken to be one with no loss of generality.

In even-numbered periods the young generation looks ahead to the next period, when the payoff will be r_L and the price P_L. The representative investor buys x_L units of the durable asset and buys s_L units of storage. The portfolio (x_L, s_L) must solve the optimization problem:

$$\begin{aligned} \max_{(x_L, s_L)} \quad & u[(r_L + P_L)x_L + s_L] \\ \text{s.t.} \quad & e = P_H x_L + s_L \\ & x_L, s_L \geq 0. \end{aligned}$$

Similarly, in odd-numbered periods their optimization problem is:

$$\begin{aligned} \max_{(x_H, s_H)} \quad & u[(r_H + P_H)x_H + s_H] \\ \text{s.t.} \quad & e = P_L x_H + s_H \\ & x_H, s_H \geq 0. \end{aligned}$$

In equilibrium, the market-clearing condition for the durable asset requires

$$x_L = x_H = 1.$$

The first-order conditions are:

$$(r_L + P_L - P_H)u'[(r_L + P_L)x_L + s_L] \geq 0$$

$$(r_H + P_H - P_L)u'[(r_H + P_H)x_H + s_H] \geq 0.$$

It can straightforwardly be seen that the only possible solution is:

$$s_L = s_H = 0$$

$$P_L = P_H = e.$$

The consumption of any generation depends on whether it is old in an even-numbered period, in which case consumption is $c_H = e + r_H$, or an odd-numbered period, in which case consumption is $c_L = e + r_L$.

An Intermediated Financial System

Suppose next that there is an intermediated financial system. For simplicity, assume that there is only one intermediary. It is a mutual organization and is run in the interest of depositors. Since the intermediary is the only game in town, each generation must become depositors in the intermediary if they want to provide for future consumption. The intermediary takes the endowments of the young generation of depositors and either invests them in storage or pays them out to the current old generation of depositors. The intermediary also determines the returns that will be paid to depositors, and these returns may differ from the returns earned on the assets held by the intermediary.

The intermediary could implement many allocations. In particular, it could choose to implement the market allocation. However, it can also use the storage technology to transfer from even-numbered generations to odd-numbered generations. After $t = 0$, if it desired, it could even do the reverse and transfer from odd-numbered generations to even-numbered generations. We are assuming that welfare is calculated with people assigning an equal probability to being in an even-numbered generation compared to an odd-numbered generation. Since the intermediary is a mutual organization run in the interests of depositors, we assume that in its objective function, it weights even and odd generations equally. In other words, its objective function is:

$$U(c_H, c_L) = 0.5u(c_H) + 0.5u(c_L),$$

where c_H is the consumption in even periods and c_L is the consumption in odd periods. In maximizing the welfare of depositors, it should therefore choose

$$c_H = c_L.$$

This is easily done since it can invest in the storage technology firms to carry over returns from the even-numbered periods to the odd-numbered periods. Suppose $T = (r_H + r_L)/2$. By investing T in the storage technology in even-numbered periods and 0 in odd-numbered periods and transferring e from young to old every period, it is possible to equate payouts to depositors in every period. Given the welfare perspective adopted, everybody will be better off ex ante with this allocation than in the market allocation.

A Comparison

Consider a numerical example with

$u(c) = \ln(c), e = 1, r_L = 0.1$ and $r_H = 0.9$.

In the equilibrium with financial markets, consumption and utility alternate between

$c_L = 1.1, u_L = 0.1$

and

$c_H = 1.9, u_H = 0.64.$

On average, utility is $\overline{u} = 0.37$.

In the case of the intermediated economy, the intermediary would invest 0.4 in each even-numbered period in the storage technology and pay it out in the following odd-numbered period. It would transfer 1 from young to old every period. It would pay out the same amount each period so $c_H = c_L = 1.5$ and $u(c_H) = u(c_L) = 0.41$ so average utility is $\overline{u} = 0.41$.

Comparing the allocation with financial markets to the allocation with intermediation, it is clear that the intermediated economy leads to a superior allocation of resources. The (monopoly) intermediary maximizes the ex ante welfare of depositors. In contrast, with financial markets, the prices of securities do not provide signals that lead to as high a level of welfare for investors as for depositors in the intermediated system.

To generate a Pareto improvement in this model, we have to adopt the perspective of an agent in the initial position and assume that agents cannot insure against the uncertainty that they face in this position. The intermediary is able to provide insurance ex post by making transfers that act as a substitute for missing markets. Of course, any kind of noncontractible uncertainty will cause a loss of welfare, and any institutional arrangement that provides insurance against this risk will improve welfare. The reason we think this example is relevant to the comparison of financial markets and financial intermediaries is that markets by definition expose investors to fluctuations in market values. In an economy where assets are not marked to market, because financial markets do not exist, financial intermediaries can smooth returns and insure investors against this risk. To show how this works, without appealing to the fictional initial position, we need a model in which there is uncertainty about asset returns.

6.2 The Model

We use a standard, infinite-horizon, OLG model as a vehicle for the analysis of intertemporal smoothing of risk. Time is divided into a countable number of dates $t = 1, 2, \ldots$, and a new generation is born at each date t. Each generation consists of an equal number of identical agents, so there is no loss of generality in treating each generation as if it consists of a single representative agent. There is an initial old generation, which lives for one period; each subsequent generation lives for two periods.

There is a single good available for consumption in each period, and an agent born at date t has an endowment of e units of the good when young and nothing when old.

There are two types of assets, a safe asset and a risky asset, which are held to provide for future consumption. The supply of the risky asset is normalized to unity and is initially owned by the old generation. The risky asset lasts forever and pays a dividend of y_t units of the consumption good at each date t. The only exogenous uncertainty in this economy comes from the stochastic process y_t. We assume that y_t is independently and identically distributed and nonnegative, with a positive and finite expectation and variance.

The safe asset is represented by a storage technology, which converts one unit of the consumption good at date t into a unit of consumption at date $t+1$. None of the safe asset is owned by the initial old generation, so $s_0 = 0$.

Agents choose their investments to maximize their von Neumann-Morgenstern expected utility. Their risk preferences are represented by the additive utility function

$$U(c_1, c_2) = u(c_1) + v(c_2),$$

where c_i is the agent's consumption in the ith period of life. The functions $u(\cdot)$ and $v(\cdot)$ satisfy the usual properties: both are twice continuously differentiable, increasing, and strictly concave.

The special features of this model are chosen for the sake of simplicity. In particular, the OLG structure is a metaphor for all the other sources of market incompleteness that may arise in practice.

6.3 Market Equilibrium

Let $x_t \geq 0$ denote the amount of the risky asset and $s_t \geq 0$ the amount of the safe asset held by the young generation at date t. For simplicity, we do not allow short sales, but nothing is changed in equilibrium if short sales are allowed, as we explain at the end of the section. The agent's first-period budget constraint restricts the sum of his first-period consumption and the value of his portfolio to be equal to his first-period endowment:

$$c_{1t} + s_t + p_t x_t = e,$$

where p_t is the price of the risky asset at date t. The second-period budget constraint restricts his second-period consumption to be equal to the portfolio's liquidation value plus the dividend on the risky asset:

$$c_{2t+1} = s_t + p_{t+1} x_t + y_{t+1} x_t.$$

At every date the agents know the present and past values of asset returns. In other words, the (common) information set is $y^t \equiv \{y_1, \ldots, y_t\}$. Since an agent's decision can at most depend on the information available to him, his choice of (x_t, s_t) is a function of y^t, that is, it is adapted to the stochastic process $\{y_t\}$. Asset prices and consumption satisfy the same condition since they are functions of the agents' portfolio decisions. At each date the representative agent chooses his portfolio to maximize his expected utility, conditional on the available information and subject to the period budget constraints.

An equilibrium consists of a sequence of portfolios $\{(s_t, x_t)\}$ and prices $\{p_t\}$, adapted to the stochastic process $\{y_t\}$, and satisfying the following conditions. First, at each date t, the portfolio $(s_t, x_t) \geq 0$ chosen by the representative young agent solves the problem:

$$\begin{aligned} \max \quad & E_t[u(c_{1t}) + v(c_{2t+1})] \\ \text{s.t.} \quad & c_{1t} + p_t + s_t = e \\ & c_{2t+1} = s_t + (y_{t+1} + p_{t+1})x_t. \end{aligned}$$

Second, the market for the risky asset must clear, that is, $x_t = 1$ for every date t. In what follows, we focus our attention on Markov equilibria, that is, equilibria with the property that the endogenous variables (p_t, s_t, x_t) are functions of the contemporaneous shock y_t. A Markov equilibrium is said to be stationary if this functional relationship is time invariant:

$$(p_t, s_t, x_t) = f(y_t), \forall t.$$

Although the safe asset would seem to be a useful hedge against the uncertainty generated by the risky asset, it turns out that this is not the case. Since the returns to the risky asset are assumed to be independently and identically distributed, the representative young agent in a stationary Markov equilibrium solves the same decision problem at each date, regardless of the state in which he is born, and since the old supply the risky asset inelastically, the equilibrium price is constant and nonstochastic. The net return to holding the risky asset in such an equilibrium is $r_t = y_{t+1} + p_{t+1} - p_t = y_{t+1}$, and, since y_{t+1} is nonnegative and sometimes positive, the safe asset is clearly dominated and will never be held in equilibrium.

Proposition 6.1 There exists a stationary, Markov equilibrium $\{(p_t, s_t, x_t)\}$ in which the price of the risky asset is a constant $p_t = p$ and the demand for the safe asset is $s_t = 0$ at every date t if $\sup u'(\cdot) > \inf v'(\cdot)$.

Proof See the chapter appendix.

The assumption that $\sup u'(\cdot) > \inf v'(\cdot)$ is needed to ensure that there exists a positive rate of return at which the representative young agent wants to transfer wealth from the first to the second period of his life. Otherwise there is no (constant) asset price at which the young agent is willing to hold the risky asset and a stationary equilibrium cannot exist.

To illustrate the operation of the market equilibrium, consider the following example:

$$U(c_1, c_2) = \ln(c_1) + \ln(c_2)$$

$$e = 1$$

$$y_t = \begin{cases} 0 & \text{w.pr. } 1/2 \\ 1 & \text{w.pr. } 1/2. \end{cases}$$

For this case it can be shown that the stationary equilibrium price is $p_t = 0.5$ and the allocation of consumption in equilibrium is

y_t	c_{1t}	c_{2t}
0	0.5	0.5
1	0.5	1.5

The levels of expected utility attained are $E[v(c_{21})] = -0.14$ for the initial generation and $E[U(c_{1t}, c_{2t+1})] = -0.84$ for each subsequent generation. The long-run average expected utility is therefore also -0.84.

In this example, the risky asset is very attractive. It can be bought in youth for 0.5 and sold for the same amount in old age; it also pays nonnegative dividends, which are 1 half of the time. Since the risky asset is so attractive, investors sacrifice consumption in youth in order to be able to consume in old age. They consume only 0.5 in youth but in old age consume 0.5 or 1.5 with equal probability, or 1 on average.

It has been assumed so far that no short sales are allowed. This assumption can be dropped at no cost, however, since the equilibrium allocations would be exactly the same if short sales were allowed. The existence of a representative agent and the fact that net asset holdings must be nonnegative in equilibrium together ensure that no short sales can actually take place in equilibrium, even if they were allowed. Furthermore, market clearing requires $x_t = 1$, so the short-sale constraint is never binding for the risky asset. The short-sale constraint $s_t \geq 0$ for the safe asset may be binding in equilibrium. If it is, then we need to introduce a price $q_t < 1$ for claims to the safe asset in order to clear the market at zero net supply.

The model can also be extended to allow for (random) endowments (e_{1t}, e_{2t}) in both periods of an agent's life. In this case, the safe asset may sometimes be used in equilibrium. However, it is always true that $s_t = 0$ with positive probability in a stationary Markov equilibrium. Furthermore, by restricting the distribution of e_{1t}, we can ensure that the conclusion of proposition 6.1 continues to hold. In any case, financial markets do not eliminate the risk created by random fluctuations in endowments and asset returns. Similarly, if the return on the safe asset is positive or it is possible that $y_t < 0$, the yield on the risky asset will no longer be uniformly higher than the yield on the safe asset and some of the safe asset may be held in equilibrium. Again, however, financial markets will not eliminate risk. In the next section, we shall see feasible allocations in which risk is almost entirely eliminated in the long run.

6.4 Intertemporal Smoothing

In a stationary, Markov equilibrium, the safe asset is not used to hedge against the uncertainty of the risky asset's return. However, in an infinite-horizon economy, almost all of the risk can be eliminated through a program of accumulating buffer stocks of the risk-free asset. This is simply an application of a well-known theorem of Schechtman (1976). Schechtman considered the problem of an individual who has a risky income ω_t and wants to maximize the expected value of his long-run average utility:

$$E\left\{\lim_{T\to\infty} T^{-1}\sum_{1}^{T} u(c_t)\right\}.$$

The individual cannot borrow but is able to self-insure by investing in a safe asset (storage technology). Consider the following policy: at each date t, the individual, who has accumulated savings s_{t-1}, consumes $E\omega_t$ if this is feasible and $\omega_t + s_{t-1}$ otherwise. Then the individual's savings at date t will be

$$s_t = \max\{\omega_t + s_{t-1} - E\omega_t, 0\}.$$

Let $M_T \equiv \#\{t \le T | s_t = 0\}$ be the (random) number of periods that this process spends at the boundary in the first T periods. The renewal theorem tells us that if the random variables $\{\omega_t\}$ are independently and identically distributed, then, with probability 1, M_T/T converges to 0 as

T approaches infinity. Since the individual's consumption is less than $E\omega_t$ only when $s_t = 0$, this implies that the individual's consumption is equal to $E\omega_t$ for all but a negligible fraction of the time, and his long-run average utility will converge to $u(E\omega_t)$ almost surely.

The same policy works in our framework. Suppose that a planner wants to maximize the long-run average of the expected utilities of the different generations. To this end, the planner accumulates part of the economy's total endowment using the storage technology. Let s_t denote the accumulated savings at the end of date t, and let $\omega_t \equiv e + y_t$ denote the total endowment of the economy at date t. Then by following the policy of setting

$$s_t = \max\{\omega_t + s_{t-1} - E\omega_t, 0\},$$

we can provide the two generations at each date with a total consumption equal to $\bar{\omega} \equiv E\omega_t$ in almost every period, with probability one. The planner will divide the consumption between the two generations in a way that maximizes the typical generation's utility. If we let

$$(c_1(w), c_2(w)) \equiv \arg \max_{c_1+c_2=w} u(c_1) + v(c_2),$$

and put $U^*(w) \equiv u(c_1(w)) + v(c_2(w))$, then we have shown that the planner can achieve

$$E[\lim_{T\to\infty} T^{-1} \sum_1^T u(c_1(\min\{\bar{\omega}, \omega_t + s_{t-1}\}) + v(c_2(\min\{\bar{\omega}, \omega_{t+1} + s_t\}))]$$

$$= U^*(\bar{\omega}).$$

Proposition 6.2 There exists a feasible policy $\{s_t\}$ that ensures with probability one that all but a negligible fraction of generations are able to achieve the expected utility level $U^*(\bar{\omega})$.

The utility level $U^*(\bar{\omega})$ is at least as great as the level achieved in the market equilibrium on average. In fact, this must be true for any feasible allocation in which the long-run average consumption levels of the old and young are well defined. Let $\{(c_{1t}, c_{2t})\}$ be a feasible consumption process, and suppose that

$$\bar{c}_i \equiv \lim_{T\to\infty} T^{-1} \sum_1^T c_{it}$$

is well defined. Then, by concavity,

$$
\begin{aligned}
E\left[\lim_{T\to\infty} T^{-1}\sum_1^T\{u(c_{1t})+v(c_{2t+1})\}\right]
&\le E\left[u\left(\lim_{T\to\infty} T^{-1}\sum_1^T c_{1t}\right)+v\left(\lim_{T\to\infty} T^{-1}\sum_1^T c_{2t+1}\right)\right]\\
&= E[u(\bar{c}_1)+v(\bar{c}_2)]\\
&\le u(E\bar{c}_1)+v(E\bar{c}_2).
\end{aligned}
$$

Now, we have assumed that $\{(c_{1t}, c_{2t})\}$ is feasible so, with probability one,

$$
T^{-1}\sum_1^T(c_{1t}+c_{2t}) \le T^{-1}\sum_1^T \omega_t \to \bar{\omega}.
$$

From this it follows that $E\bar{c}_1 + E\bar{c}_2 \le \bar{\omega}$, which in turn implies that $u(E\bar{c}_1)+v(E\bar{c}_2) \le U^*(\bar{\omega})$, and from this we conclude that

$$
E\left[\lim_{T\to\infty} T^{-1}\sum_1^T\{u(c_{1t})+v(c_{2t+1})\}\right] \le U^*(\bar{\omega}).
$$

The inequality will be strict when $\{(c_{1t}, c_{2t})\}$ corresponds to the market allocation, since the agents' risk preferences are strictly concave in old age and the variance of y_t is strictly positive. This result can be summarized as follows.

Proposition 6.3 For any feasible allocation $\{(c_{1t}, c_{2t}, s_t)\}$ for which long-run average consumptions are well defined,

$$
E\left[\lim_{T\to\infty} T^{-1}\sum_1^T\{u(c_{1t})+v(c_{2t+1})\}\right] \le U^*(\bar{\omega})
$$

and the inequality is strict if $\{(c_{1t}, c_{2t}, s_t)\}$ is the market equilibrium allocation.

In the example from the previous section, $\bar{\omega}=1.5$ and the additive logarithmic utility function implies that the long-run average expected utility is maximized by setting $c_1(w)=c_2(w)=\bar{\omega}/2=0.75$. In this case,

$U^*(\bar{\omega}) = -0.58$, which compares favorably with the long-run average expected utility in the market equilibrium $E[U(c_{1t}, c_{2t+1})] = -0.84$.

Propositions 6.2 and 6.3 extend immediately to the case where there are both random endowments (e_{1t}, e_{2t+1}) and random asset returns y_t, as long as we assume that the aggregate endowments $\omega_t \equiv e_{1t} + e_{2t} + y_t$ are independently and identically distributed.

6.5 Ex Ante Efficiency and the Genesis of Intertemporal Smoothing

We have seen that a long-lived agent, or a planner who maximized the long-run average of expected utility, might behave very differently from the successive generations in the OLG model, who maximized their own expected utility over a two-period horizon. The former would have an incentive to accumulate large stocks of the safe asset in order to provide insurance against rate of return risk, whereas the latter have no incentive to hold the safe asset at all in a stationary, Markov equilibrium.

This raises the question of whether there is some sort of market failure, some form of inefficiency, in the equilibrium described in proposition 6.1. In order to consider this question, we have to be more precise about how we define the welfare of an individual agent. There are two salient definitions. The first identifies the individual's welfare with her expected utility $E[U(c_{1t}, c_{2t+1})|y^t]$, conditional on the information that is available when she is born. In effect, it treats the "same" individual born at two different information sets as two different individuals. The second definition identifies the individual's welfare with her unconditional expected utility $E[U(c_{1t}, c_{2t+1})]$, implicitly assuming that there is only one individual born at any date, regardless of the information available at that date.

Correspondingly, there are two notions of Pareto efficiency, ex ante and ex post, depending on whether we take into account the state in which an agent is born. A feasible allocation is ex post efficient if it is impossible to increase the ex post expected utility $E[U(c_{1t}, c_{2t+1})|y^t]$ of some generations without reducing the ex post expected utility of other generations. On the other hand, a feasible allocation is ex ante efficient if it is impossible to increase the ex ante expected utility $E[U(c_{1t}, c_{2t+1})]$ of some generations without reducing the ex ante expected utility of other generations. We consider efficiency initially using the ex ante notion and then using the ex post notion.

It is easy to see that a market equilibrium allocation will not be ex ante efficient in general, because agents are not allowed to trade before they are born. Hence, all trades are undertaken by an agent after the state in which she is born has been revealed. In other words, the birth state y^t is a "preexisting condition," against which an agent cannot insure. However, a planner could provide such insurance by making appropriate transfers between the old and the young at each date. Thus, even without making use of the storage technology, the planner could achieve a Pareto improvement from the ex ante point of view. However, the expected utility of the typical generation will be even higher if intergenerational smoothing is carried out, accumulating reserves of the safe asset and using them to smooth fluctuations in consumption. Intergenerational risk sharing by means of transfers between the old and young at each date does not remove the aggregate uncertainty caused by the randomness of the aggregate endowment. Intertemporal smoothing eliminates this uncertainty at no cost in terms of long-run average consumption.

Although it is easy to see that intertemporal smoothing can increase long-run average expected utility, some care must be taken about the way in which intertemporal smoothing is introduced in order to ensure that *each* generation is better off ex ante compared to the equilibrium allocation. Consider the policy described in the previous section. Under that policy, $c_{1t} + c_{2t} = \bar{\omega}$ when $\omega_t + s_t \geq \bar{\omega}$ and $c_{1t} + c_{2t} = \omega_t + s_t$ otherwise. In the market equilibrium, $c_{1t} + c_{2t} = e + y_t$ in all periods. Since $s_0 = 0$, it follows that if the intertemporal smoothing scheme were implemented at the first date, either the initial old generation or the initial young generation or both would be worse off in an ex ante sense compared to the market allocation. A similar argument applies in subsequent periods. In order to achieve an ex ante Pareto improvement, intertemporal smoothing has to be introduced in two stages. The first stage achieves an increase in expected utility by means of intergenerational risk sharing (transfers), which allows the planner to accumulate some of the endowment in the form of reserves of the safe asset without making any generation worse off. Once reserves are sufficiently large, it is possible to switch to a policy of intertemporal smoothing and make every generation better off ex ante than it would be with intergenerational risk sharing alone.

To see how the first stage is implemented, consider some necessary conditions for ex ante efficiency. If the equilibrium is ex ante efficient, it must be impossible to make both generations at date t better off by reallocating consumption at that date. That means that the equilibrium consumption allocation (c_{1t}, c_{2t}) must solve the maximization problem

$$\max \quad E[\lambda u(c_{1t}) + (1-\lambda)v(c_{2t})]$$
$$\text{s.t.} \quad c_{1t} + c_{2t} = \omega_t \equiv e + y_t,$$

for some constant $0 \leq \lambda \leq 1$. A necessary condition for this to be true is that

$$u'(c_{1t})/v'(c_{2t}) = \text{constant}$$

with probability one. In the market equilibrium $c_{1t} = e - p_t$ is nonstochastic, whereas $c_{2t} = p_t + y_t$ is stochastic, so the necessary condition for ex ante Pareto efficiency cannot be satisfied and the market equilibrium is ex ante inefficient. In fact, it is possible to find an ex ante Pareto-preferred allocation by making stationary transfers contingent on the contemporaneous asset returns. Let $\tau(y_t)$ be the transfer from young to old at period t when the asset return is y_t and define the new consumption allocation by putting $\hat{c}_{1t} = c_{1t} - \tau(y_t)$ and $\hat{c}_{2t} = c_{2t} + \tau(y_t)$. For an appropriate specification of the transfer function $\tau(\cdot)$,

$$E[v(\hat{c}_{21})] > E[v(c_{21})]$$

and

$$E[u(\hat{c}_{1t}) + v(\hat{c}_{2t+1})] > E[u(c_{1t}) + v(c_{2t+1})]$$

for every date t. By continuity, the same will be true if we reduce the consumption of the young at each date by a constant amount $\eta > 0$ and add this amount to the stock of the safe asset, so that by period t we have accumulated $s_t = \eta t$. Hence by using intergenerational transfers, an arbitrarily large level of reserves can be built in preparation for switching to the intertemporal smoothing program.

Let S denote the target level of reserves accumulated in the first stage, and let T denote the end of the first stage, that is, choose T so that $s_T = S$. To show that a Pareto-improving scheme with intertemporal smoothing can be implemented, the following lemma is needed.

Lemma 6.1 For any $\epsilon > 0$ there is a level of initial reserves S sufficiently large that, starting the intertemporal smoothing plan at date T the probability of $s_t = 0$ at any $t \geq T$ is less than ϵ.

Proof See the chapter appendix.

In the short run, this is obvious because it will take some time to run down the reserves to 0. In the longer run, it is not so obvious that the probability of running out of reserves is uniformly small at all future dates. The lemma follows from the fact that reserves follow a random walk when $s_t > 0$ and are expected to increase when $s_t = 0$. This means that reserves are expected to increase on average without limit under the intertemporal smoothing policy. Although the event $s_t = 0$ will occur infinitely often, the probability that it happens at any fixed date t is becoming vanishingly small as t approaches infinity.

The fact that the probability of the event $s_t = 0$ is bounded by ϵ for each future generation means that the ex ante expected utility of any generation living after date T is at least $(1 - \epsilon)U^*(\bar{\omega})$, which is greater than the equilibrium ex ante expected utility $E[U(c_{1t}, c_{2t+1})]$ for ϵ sufficiently small. Thus, generations $t \geq T$ will prefer the intertemporal smoothing plan ex ante to their market allocation. There is a problem with the generation born at date $T - 1$ since this generation does not get the full benefit of intergenerational risk sharing but has its second-period consumption reduced on average. To compensate this generation, we make a one-time transfer out of the reserves. With this adjustment, every generation is ex ante better off.

Furthermore, since the first stage with intergenerational sharing is finite in length, the analysis below shows that the long-run average expected utility will converge to $U^*(\bar{\omega})$. All this can be summarized in the following result.

PROPOSITION 6.4 The market equilibrium allocation is ex ante Pareto inefficient. There exists an attainable allocation with intertemporal smoothing, which provides every generation with higher ex ante expected utility and achieves the long-run average expected utility $U^*(\bar{\omega})$.

The existence of an allocation that improves ex ante welfare for all generations compared to the market equilibrium can be illustrated in the context of the numerical example used above. In the initial stage, the market allocation is altered by intergenerational transfers:

$$\tau(y_t) = \begin{cases} 0.1125 & \text{if } y_t = 0 \\ -0.275 & \text{if } y_t = 1 \end{cases}.$$

When $y_t = 0$, the old receive a transfer of 0.1125 from the young, and when $y_t = 1$, the young receive a transfer of 0.275 from the old. These transfers ensure that the expected utility of the initial generation is

Table 6.1
Equilibrium consumption and utility

Generation born at	c_{1t}	c_{2t+1}	$E[U(c_{1t}, c_{2t+1})]$
$T-1$	0.5	$\begin{cases} 0.5 \text{ w.pr. } 0.5 \\ 0.75 \text{ w.pr. } 0.5 \end{cases}$	−1.18
T	$\begin{cases} 0.5 \text{ w.pr. } 0.5 \\ 0.75 \text{ w.pr. } 0.5 \end{cases}$	$\begin{cases} 0.5 \text{ w.pr. } 0.25 \\ 0.75 \text{ w.pr. } 0.75 \end{cases}$	−0.88
$T+1$	$\begin{cases} 0.5 \text{ w.pr. } 0.25 \\ 0.75 \text{ w.pr. } 0.75 \end{cases}$	$\begin{cases} 0.5 \text{ w.pr. } 0.25 \\ 0.75 \text{ w.pr. } 0.75 \end{cases}$	−0.78

slightly greater than the market equilibrium level of −0.84. They also allow an addition to reserves of 0.028 to be extracted from each generation except the initial one, while still leaving them slightly better off than the market allocation.

To see how the second stage operates, consider the effect on the ex ante expected utilities of the generations around date T if intertemporal smoothing were implemented at date T and there were no reserves at that date, as shown in table 6.1. We assume that the generation born at date $T-1$ simply receives the market allocation when it is young. The generation born at date $T+1$ is clearly better off than in the equilibrium, but generations $T-1$ and T are worse off. If there were positive reserves at date T, $s_t > 0$, the generations born after T would be even better off. For the generation born at $T-1$, a transfer of 0.21 in their youth at date $T-1$ would be sufficient to make them better off than in the market equilibrium. For the generation born at date T, a transfer of 0.03 would be sufficient. Hence the total reserves at the time of the transition must be at least 0.24. Remembering that the initial generation and generation $T-1$ do not help build reserves, this implies that the initial stage must last at least six periods, so $T=7$.

Comparing the paths of utility in this ex ante Pareto-superior allocation with that in the market equilibrium, it can be seen that the first six generations in this example have slightly higher utility, but all subsequent generations are significantly better off. The long-run average expected utility is −0.58, compared to −0.84 in the market equilibrium. Note also that the average expected utility is significantly greater than can be achieved with intergenerational transfers alone. The consumption allocation that maximizes long-run average expected utility through intergenerational transfers with no accumulation of reserves is

$$c_{it} = \begin{cases} 0.5 & \text{w. pr. } 0.5 \\ 1.0 & \text{w. pr. } 0.5 \end{cases}$$

for $i = 1, 2$, which gives expected utility of $E[U(c_{1t}, c_{2t+1})] = -0.69$.

At the start of the section, we pointed that there exist two notions of efficiency, depending on whether we take into account the state in which an agent is born. Ex ante efficiency, which proposition 6.4 focused on, takes the expectation of utility across all possible states. An alternative view is that of ex post efficiency, where an individual's welfare is conditional on the information available when he is born. The discussion of lemma 6.1 provides insights into ex post expected utility in the model when intertemporal smoothing is adopted. Aggregate consumption is $\bar{\omega}$ if and only if $s_t > 0$ and $\Pr[s_t = 0] \to 0$ as t approaches infinity. Hence, ex post expected utility will converge to $U^*(\bar{\omega})$ in probability as t approaches infinity. In other words, except when reserves are low, the ex post expected utility of each generation will be $U^*(\bar{\omega})$, which is higher than in the market equilibrium. As t becomes large, the probability of reserves being low and a generation being worse off ex post than in the market equilibrium becomes vanishingly small. In fact, in the long run all but a negligible fraction of generations can be made better off ex post. We pursue this issue further in the next section.

We have so far studied the existence of allocations that allow the introduction of intertemporal smoothing *and* an ex ante Pareto improvement over the market allocation, without specifying the institutional framework that implements them. The existence of such allocations suggests a story of how intertemporal smoothing by intermediaries might come into existence. Given the opportunity to make individuals better off, some institution will try to exploit that opportunity and capture part of the surplus. One possibility is that a long-lived intermediary is set up to provide insurance against uncertain returns by averaging high and low returns over time. Such an intermediary could hold all the assets and offer a deposit contract to each generation. Initially the intermediary offers intergenerational insurance. Later, after accumulating large reserves, the intermediary can offer almost all generations a constant return on deposits, independent of the actual returns.

Some degree of market power will be required to ensure that individuals participate in this scheme, as we shall see. This market power may arise naturally, or it may be the result of government intervention. For example, the government may give the intermediary an exclusive license in order to achieve an ex ante Pareto improvement.

An important issue concerns the objective function that financial intermediaries in Japan, Germany, and France pursue in practice and whether this is consistent with intertemporal smoothing. Simple profit maximization will not be sufficient to support intertemporal smoothing. It is interesting to note that in all these countries there is a wide variety of types of institution in the financial sector other than profit-maximizing firms, including mutual organizations and nonprofits as well as publicly owned institutions.

Germany provides a particularly interesting example. Among the universal banks, only the commercial banks, which have about a quarter of total banking assets, are ostensibly profit maximizing. Even among these, however, it is not clear that profit maximization is an appropriate description of the actual objective they pursue. As we pointed out in chapter 4, banks vote the proxies of a large number of stocks that they hold on behalf of customers. The managers of the big three banks—Deutsche Bank, Dresdner Bank, and Commerzbank—vote enough of the proxies for their own banks that they have effective control. In recent years, Deutsche Bank held voting rights for 47 percent of its shares, Dresdner for 59 percent, and Commerzbank for 30 percent (Charkham (1994, p. 36). The forces ensuring these banks maximize profit for shareholders as opposed to pursuing some other objective are weak or nonexistent.

The remaining types of universal bank in Germany are explicitly not profit maximizing. Savings banks, which hold about a third of total banking assets, were originally set up to provide credit to the poor and finance local and regional investments. The cooperative banks have a mutual structure in which the depositors are shareholders. The managers of all these institutions have a great deal of autonomy.

In Japan, all institutions have a high degree of autonomy. To the extent there is outside interference, it is from a firm's main bank. However, banks themselves are not subject to this influence. In France, the government has been heavily involved in terms of ownership of banks and other financial institutions. In this case there is also explicitly a deviation from profit-maximizing behavior.

In the cases where banks and other intermediaries are not profit maximizing, there is an interesting question as to what the objective function that they pursue is. One possibility is that they are concerned with the survival of the institution to ensure that employment will go forward. In this case, they may build up reserves in good times and run them down in bad times so that they are engaging in intertemporal smoothing. Although this may not be exactly the same as the optimal policy described in the previous section, it may still be a substantial improvement over the market allocation. The question of what objective functions firms and institutions maximize when external governance is weak or nonexistent is considered at greater length in chapter 12.

6.6 Almost Uniform Pareto Efficiency

We have shown that at least from an ex ante perspective, the market equilibrium is inefficient. In fact, we can go further than this. What proposition 6.4 demonstrates is that by transferring income between periods to smooth consumption as much as possible, almost every generation will be made better off by a nonnegligible and uniform amount. Thus even in an ex post sense, nearly everybody is made significantly better off by introducing intertemporal smoothing. For almost all social welfare functions, this will be an improvement. In this section we introduce a refinement of the Pareto criterion to capture this notion: an almost uniform Pareto improvement. We shall argue that under a mild refinement of the standard concept of Pareto efficiency, an allocation is not efficient if it is possible to make an almost uniform Pareto improvement.

Our starting point is the well-known fact that if utility functions are concave, every Pareto-efficient allocation maximizes a weighted sum of utilities. More precisely, a feasible policy $\{s_t\}$ is Pareto efficient if there exists a nonnegative sequence of numbers $\{\lambda_t\}$ such that $\{s_t\}$ solves the problem

$$\begin{aligned} \max \quad & \sum_t \lambda_t u(c_t) \\ \text{s.t.} \quad & c_t = y_t + s_t - s_{t-1} + e \\ & s_t \geq 0, c_t \geq 0, s_0 = 0 \end{aligned} \tag{6.1}$$

One can think of the objective function as a Bergson-Samuelson welfare function

$$W(u_1, u_2, u_3, \ldots) = \sum_t \lambda_t u_t \tag{6.2}$$

in which the welfare weights $\{\lambda_t\}$ determine how much each generation's welfare "counts" in the calculation of social well-being.

There has long been a debate on the appropriate weights to apply to different generations. Pigou (1932, chap. 2) suggests that utilities that are closer in time are weighted too heavily by individuals and society should adopt a different weighting scheme. Ramsey (1928, p. 543) argued in favor of equal weights for all generations: "We do not discount later enjoyments in comparison with earlier ones, a practice which is ethically indefensible and arises merely from the weakness of the imagination." The equal weighting Ramsey advocated has become one of the standard approaches in a variety of contexts, including optimal growth, environmental issues, and taxation (see Svensson 1980). Another standard approach is to discount utilities so that future generations are weighted less than current ones (see Koopmans 1967). In this section we take an intermediate position between these two standard approaches. Our refinement of Pareto optimality imposes a lower bound on the weights assigned to different generations. In other words, any weights are allowed except that no generation can be given an arbitrarily small weight in the social welfare function. This restriction is designed to capture a minimalist notion of equity across generations.

The welfare function W defined by equation 6.2 is said to be uniformly weighted if there exists a number $B \leq 1$ such that

$$\frac{1}{B} \leq \lambda_t \leq B, \forall t. \tag{6.3}$$

At one extreme, when B equals 1, the implied welfare function is equally weighted. As B becomes larger, a wider range of weights is allowed, and as B becomes arbitrarily large, most schemes with positive weights are allowed. The crucial restriction is that the ratios of weights λ_{t+h}/λ_t for different generations t and $t+h$ remain bounded, and bounded away from 0. This is precisely what is *not* possible if the market equilibrium allocation is to be a solution of a welfare maximization problem like equation 6.1. If the market equilibrium allocation solves equation 6.1 it can be shown that the welfare weights must be extremely unequal. In fact, we shall shortly see that the ratio of the weights λ_{t+h}/λ_t converges to 0 as the distance between generations h diverges to 1. This is the sense in which the Pareto efficiency of the market equilibrium allocation appears to be rather extreme, and this is why we consider the restriction to uniform welfare functions fairly mild. This refinement of the Pareto criterion motivates two immediate corollaries. The first makes precise the sense in which the equilibrium allocation is not efficient. A feasible policy $\{s_t\}$ is called *uniformly Pareto efficient* if it solves the maximization problem (equation 6.1), and the welfare function is uniformly weighted. To ensure that this restriction has some cutting power, we keep B fixed as the horizon T is allowed to increase without bound.

PROPOSITION 6.5 Suppose that the equilibrium allocation described in Proposition 6.1 is a solution of equation 6.1 for the welfare weights $\{\lambda_t\}$. Then there exists a number $0 < \rho < 1$ such that for every generation t, $\rho\lambda_t > \lambda_{t+1}$. Consequently, for any B and h sufficiently large,

$$\lambda_{t+h}/\lambda_t \leq \rho^h/B < 1/B, \tag{6.4}$$

so the market equilibrium allocation is not uniformly Pareto efficient.

Proof See the chapter appendix.

The proposition shows that as the distance between generations grows large, the relative disparity in their welfare weights grows without bound. More precisely, $\lambda_{t+h}/\lambda_t \to 0$ as $h \to \infty$. Clearly this is inconsistent with the uniform weighting property (see equation 6.3), which requires that $1/B \leq \lambda_{t+h}/\lambda_t \leq B$, for all values of t and h, and this explains why the market equilibrium allocation fails to be uniformly Pareto efficient.

In the example, considered in the previous section, $\rho = 0.92$, so that the weighting of each generation in the social welfare function underlying the market equilibrium allocation falls quite rapidly and it is not necessary for generations to be far apart to have widely different weights. It can be argued there is no good rationale for this property, and from a welfare point of view, it might be argued that a more equal weighting would seem to be at least as reasonable. The second corollary shows that the intertemporal smoothing policy is uniformly Pareto efficient, at least in the limit as $T \to \infty$. To show this, we first need to extend our definition slightly. Call a feasible policy $\{s_t\}$ *uniformly Pareto efficient in the limit* if there is some bound B, and a uniform weighting scheme $\{\lambda_t\}$ such that for any ε and all T sufficiently large,

$$\frac{1}{T}\sum_{t=1}^{T} \lambda_t u(c_t) > \frac{1}{T}\sum_{t=1}^{T} \lambda_t u(c_t') + \varepsilon,$$

where $c_t = y_t + s_t - s_{t-1} + e$ and $c_t' = y_t + s_t' - s_{t-1}' + e$, for $t = 1, \ldots, T$, and as usual $s_0 = s_0' = 0$. Note that two properties are being combined in our notion of uniform efficiency in the limit. First, although a policy may be dominated for each finite horizon T, it catches up in the limit as T diverges to ∞. Second, we are comparing long-run weighted averages of utility rather than weighted sums of utilities. With this definition, we can now state the result.

PROPOSITION 6.6 The policy $\{s_t\}$ described in proposition 6.3 is uniformly Pareto efficient in the limit.

The result follows from the fact that the policy described in proposition 6.1 maximizes the long-run average expected utility of all the generations. Putting $\lambda_t = 1$, for all t, obviously satisfies the required bounds for any $B > 1$, and for this specification of the welfare function, the policy must eventually overtake any other.

6.7 Competition Between Intermediaries and Financial Markets

A commonly heard argument is that financial markets are desirable because of the risk-sharing opportunities they provide. It is well known that this is correct as far as cross-sectional risk-sharing opportunities are concerned, but the results of the preceding sections suggest that this argument ignores the possibilities for intertemporal risk smoothing. We have shown in the context of a simple OLG model that an intermediated financial system can make every generation better off than it would be with financial markets alone. In this interpretation, financial markets and intermediaries are not simply veils thrown over a fixed set of assets. They actually determine, in conjunction with other factors, the set of assets accumulated by the agents in the economy. By adopting one or another set of institutions, the economy is placed on a different trajectory, with important implications for risk smoothing.

A natural question that arises is whether it is possible to combine the cross-sectional risk-sharing advantages of financial markets with the intertemporal risk-smoothing advantages of an intermediated system. There is a significant obstacle in the path of trying to combine the two types of systems. Risk sharing of the kind discussed in this chapter implies some form of arbitrage opportunity. Taking advantage of arbitrage opportunities is rational for the individual, but it undermines the insurance offered by the intermediary. For this reason, an open financial system may not be able to provide intertemporal risk smoothing, although it provides a tremendous variety of financial instruments.

One way to illustrate the effect of competition from financial markets is to consider the effect of opening up a relatively small, closed, and intermediated financial system to global financial markets. Initially the small country's financial system is monopolized by a cartel of banks that engage in intertemporal smoothing without the threat of competition. After opening the small country's financial system, the banks now face the constraint that individuals can opt out and invest in global markets instead. The assumption that the country is small relative to the rest of the world implies that prices in the global market are not affected by the financial system of the small country or its investors' decision to participate in the risk-sharing mechanism provided by the intermediary.

Let $\{(p_t, s_t, x_t)\}$ be the equilibrium in the global market, and let $\{(c'_{1t}, c'_{2t}, s'_t)\}$ be the optimal allocation implemented in the small country. The global equilibrium represents a benchmark for the welfare of investors in the absence of a long-lived intermediary, as well as an outside option for the individuals when the intermediary is in operation. We assume that all investors in the small country make use of the intermediary. Since the intermediary can always replicate the investment opportunities available through the market, there is no loss of generality in this assumption.

Disintermediation can take several forms, depending on whether investors are able to make side trades while taking advantage of the intermediary. We assume that the intermediary can enforce exclusivity, which means that an agent who wants to trade in the market is unable to make use of the intermediary at all. This assumption makes disintermediation less attractive and produces a weaker constraint on the intermediary's problem of designing a risk-smoothing scheme. We can show that even this weak constraint on the intermediary is sufficient to rule out any welfare improvement from intertemporal risk smoothing. Alternative (stronger) specifications of the disintermediation constraint would only strengthen this result.

The disintermediation constraint (DC), which ensures that people do not abandon the small country's risk-sharing mechanism once they have access to global markets, can be stated as follows: for any history $y^t = (y_1, \ldots, y_t)$ the allocation $\{(c'_{1t}, c'_{2t}, s'_t)\}$ satisfies

$$E[u(c'_{1t}) + v(c'_{2t})|y^t] \geq \max_{(x,s)\geq 0} E[u(e - p_t) + v(x(y_t + s))|y^t].$$

The expression on the right is the maximum expected utility an agent born at date t could obtain from trading on the open market. The expression on the left is the expected utility offered by the risk-sharing mechanism. The crucial point is that both expressions are conditioned on all the information available at date t. An agent makes his decision whether to join the risk-sharing mechanism after he has observed y^t.

The possibility of disintermediation implies that an intermediated financial system in a small, open country does not allow any improvement in expected utility over that obtained by investors in global financial markets. To prove this result, we need two additional assumptions. The first rules out the possibility of a welfare-increasing Ponzi scheme. We assume there exists a constant K such that if $U(c_{1t}, c_{2t+1}) \geq U(e, 0)$, then $c_{1t} \geq -K$ and $c_{2t+1} \geq -K$ with probability one. Since the utility level $U(e, 0)$ is always attainable, an agent's expected utility must be at least this high in equilibrium, and that means his consumption will be bounded below with probability one. The second assumption is purely technical: we assume that the random asset return y_t assumes a finite number of values. Under these assumptions, we can show that the equilibrium allocation is ex post Pareto efficient, and so there is no feasible allocation that makes any generation better off without making some generation worse off ex post. The DC requires each generation to be at least as well off ex post as it was under the equilibrium allocation and hence no better off.

Proposition 6.7 If the allocation $\{(c'_{1t}, c'_{2t}, s'_t)\}$ is feasible and satisfies the disintermediation constraint, then each agent is ex post no better off under $\{(c'_{1t}, c'_{2t}, s'_t)\}$ than he would be in the market equilibrium $\{(p_t, s_t, x_t)\}$.

Proof See the chapter appendix.

To understand proposition 6.7, it is helpful to think about the policy used in proposition 6.2. That policy provides the two generations at each date with a total consumption equal to the lesser of $\bar{\omega}$ and the sum of the actual return and the reserves held by the intermediary, so that the total amount consumed each period is

$$c'_{1t} + c'_{2t} = \min\{\bar{\omega}, y_t + s'_{t-1} + e\}.$$

If the reserves held by the intermediary endowment are very low (close to zero), the expected utility of an agent must be lower than in the market equilibrium. Compared to the equilibrium allocation, she loses the high returns from the risky asset when $y_t > \bar{\omega}$ and still suffers the probability of loss when $y_t < \bar{\omega}$. Any generation will be better off only if it inherits a large reserve from the previous generation. This will be true most of the time, but occasionally a generation will be born when reserves are low, and that generation will be worse off ex post. If that generation can opt out of the risk-sharing mechanism, the whole scheme will break down, leaving us in the situation described by proposition 6.7.

To see this in the context of the numerical example, suppose that reserves are at zero at date T^*. If intermediation is initiated or continued and intertemporal smoothing were implemented, the allocation of consumption would be as in table 6.1, with $T = T^*$. The young generation (born at T^*) would obtain $E[U(c_{1T^*}, c_{2T^*+1})] = -0.88$. However, with markets they would obtain the usual market allocation, which gives $E[U(c_{1T^*}, c_{2T^*+1})] = -0.84$. Hence when there are no reserves, the young generation will prefer the competitive market allocation and will defect if given the opportunity. This is why some monopoly power is important in establishing and maintaining intermediation. Building up the reserves necessary to start intertemporal smoothing requires intergenerational transfers initially. Access to competitive financial markets ensures that this type of risk reduction will not be feasible. Any allocation of consumption offered by an intermediary must match the market and give the young generation $E[U(c_{1T^*}, c_{2T^*+1})] = -0.84$. This means that an intermediary cannot improve on the market.

Proposition 6.4 implies that ex ante expected utility will be higher for all generations in an intermediated economy than in an economy with financial markets only. Incomplete financial markets do not allow intertemporal smoothing, while intermediaries in principle can, provided that investors do not have ready access to financial markets. This suggests that intermediary-based economies may be worse off by allowing access to financial markets. This result may have important policy implications for the European Union and other regions considering liberalizing access to global financial markets.

6.8 Conclusion

Our formal analysis has focused on a simple, overlapping-generations model. This benchmark is meant to illustrate the absence of intertemporal smoothing that can result from incomplete markets and to show how an intermediated financial system can eliminate the resulting inefficiencies. It is important to stress that the overlapping-generations structure is chosen because of its tractability. We believe that there are many other types of incompleteness that lead to the absence of intertemporal smoothing.

In our model, investors have a short time horizon, and this means that they do not self-insure. Individuals live more than two "periods," but whether self-insurance can realistically be achieved in a single individual's lifetime is questionable. In the first place, the number of independent shocks may be small. We can think of the Great Depression as being one shock and the boom of the 1950s and 1960s as another. With this interpretation, the number of periods each generation lives through is small. In addition, there are life cycle considerations that may prevent households from self-insuring. For example, the desire to purchase a house and provide an education for their children means that many households do not start saving for retirement until fairly late in life. For both of these reasons, the possibilities for self-insurance may be limited.

Demange (1996) considers a similar model but with overlapping generations that each live for three periods rather than two. She shows that three types of equilibrium are possible. When the return on the safe asset is low, the investment in the safe asset is zero, similarly to above. The volatility of asset prices depends on the amount the middle-aged group saves and can be high. If the return on the safe asset is high, it is held in equilibrium and price volatility is low. When the return on the safe asset is intermediate between these two extremes, the investment in the safe asset depends on the level of asset prices. Constantinides, Donaldson, and Mehra (1997) have also considered an overlapping-generations model with agents who live for three periods. They show that with borrowing constraints, simulations based on reasonable parameter values produce results consistent with the equity premium puzzle.

Finally, note that incomplete market participation will not be a problem when agents have a bequest motive that causes successive generations to act like a single infinitely lived individual. There is some evidence that in the general population, bequest motives and risk sharing within extended families are limited (see Altonji, Hayashi, and Kotlikoff 1992; Hayashi, Altonji, and Kotlikoff 1996). The issue here is whether the wealthy, who own most of the capital, have a sufficient bequest motive for intertemporal smoothing not to be a problem. Altonji, Hayashi, and Kotlikoff (1992) point out that wealthy individuals are underrepresented in the data sets most commonly studied in this area, and we are unaware of any evidence regarding this group specifically.

In the introduction, we used the comparison of Germany and the United States to suggest that different financial systems deal with nondiversifiable risk in different ways. The model shows that it is theoretically possible for an intermediated financial system to achieve a higher level of welfare than a market-based system. It is tempting, then, to compare the U.S. and German financial systems in the light of this example. It is often suggested that German banks hold high levels of hidden reserves, which they rely on when asset returns are low. Even if this form of intertemporal smoothing is limited by comparison with the theoretical schemes considered above, it may nonetheless be an improvement over competitive financial markets in terms of reducing nondiversifiable risk. Thus, the German financial system, with its reliance on financial intermediaries, may have some advantages over the U.S. system, which relies more on financial markets.

Given this interpretation, proposition 6.7 has important policy implications. It suggests that opening the German financial system to foreign competition—for example, by creating a single European market in financial services—could threaten intertemporal smoothing and make Germans worse off in the long run. Of course, risk sharing is not the only consideration in the choice of optimal financial systems. Other important issues are discussed in subsequent chapters.

6.9 Appendix

Proof of Proposition 6.1

Suppose that $(s_t, x_t) = (0, 1)$ for every t. Then the necessary and sufficient conditions for the optimality of this portfolio are:

$$u'(e - p_t)p_t = E_t[v'(p_t + y_t)(p_t + y_t)]$$

$$u'(e - p_t) \geq E_t[v'(p_t + y_t)].$$

If these conditions are satisfied with $p_t = p_{t+1} = p$, then $\{(s_t, x_t, p_t)\}$ is a stationary, Markov equilibrium. Substituting $p_t = p_{t+1} = p$ in the first-order conditions, it is clear that the first condition implies the second. Hence, we only need to find a solution to the equation

$$u'(e - p) = E[v'(p + y_t)(p + y_t)/p] \leq E[v'(p + y_t)]E[(p + y_t)/p].$$

Since $u'(\cdot), v'(\cdot) > 0$, the left-hand side is clearly less than the right when p is sufficiently small. On the other hand, for p sufficiently large, the right-hand side must exceed the left; otherwise, taking the limit as $p \to \infty$, and noting that $E[(p + y_t)/p] \to 1$, we have

$$\sup u'(\cdot) \leq \inf v'(\cdot),$$

a contradiction. Thus, for some intermediate value of p, the first-order condition must be satisfied, and this value of p is the equilibrium asset price.

Proof of Lemma 6.1

Recall that $s_{t+1} = \max\{0, s_t + \omega_t - \bar{\omega}\}$, so that $E[s_{t+1}|s_t] \geq s_t$. Define $f(s) = \frac{1}{s+1} \in [0, 1]$ for any $s \geq 0$. Then

$$\begin{aligned} E[f(s_{t+1})|s_t] &\geq f(E[s_{t+1}|s_t]) \\ &\geq f(s_t) \end{aligned}$$

since f is convex and decreasing. Putting $F_t \equiv f(s_t)$, $\{F_t\}$ is a bounded supermartingale, so by the Martingale convergence theorem, $F_t \to F_\infty$ almost surely as $t \to \infty$. Since ω_t has positive variance, it is clear that $F_\infty = 0$, almost surely. Convergence almost surely implies convergence in measure, so for any $\epsilon > 0$, there is a finite T such that

$$\Pr[F_t < \epsilon] > 1 - \epsilon, \forall t > T.$$

Suppose that we want to start the intertemporal smoothing plan at date T when the reserves have grown to $s_T = S$. We have shown that for any $\epsilon > 0$, there is a $T' > T$ such that $\Pr[s_t = 0] < \epsilon$ for all $t > T'$. Keeping ϵ and T fixed, it is clear that by making S sufficiently large, the probability that $s_t = 0$ for any $T \leq t \leq T'$ can be made less than ϵ. Then we have shown that for any $\epsilon > 0$, there is a level of initial reserves S sufficiently large that, starting the intertemporal smoothing plan at date T, the probability of $s_t = 0$ at any $t \geq T$ is less than ϵ as required.

Proof of Proposition 6.5

We begin by establishing the inequality of equation 6.4. The sequence {y } is initially assumed to be independently and identically distributed. Suppose that a policy $\{s_t\}$solves the problem

$$\max \quad \sum_t \lambda_t u(c_t)$$

$$\text{s.t.} \quad c_t = y_t + e + s_t - s_{t-1}.$$

The first-order conditions for the choice of c_t for this problem imply

$$\lambda_t u'(c_t) = \mu_t$$

and for the choice of m imply

$$\mu_t \geq E_t[\mu_{t+1}],$$

where μ_t is the Lagrange multiplier associated with the constraint and E_t denotes the expectation operator conditional on the information available at date t. Suppose that $\{(x_t, s_t)\}$is an attainable allocation with the property that $s_t = 0$ for every t. Recall that $y_t \leq A$ with probability 1. Then

$$\lambda_t u'(e + y_t) \geq E_t u'(e + y_{t+1})$$

for every realization of y_t, which implies that

$$\frac{\lambda_t E_t[u'(e + y_{t+1})]}{\lambda_{t+1} u'(e + A)} \geq \frac{1}{\rho},$$

where $\rho < 1$ can be chosen independent of t because the process $\{y_t\}$ is assumed to be independently and identically distributed.

An alternative proof follows from the fact that an almost uniform Pareto improvement is possible. Let $\{c_t\}$be the consumption sequence generated by the policy defined in the proof of proposition 6.3. Let

$$\eta = u(Ey_t + e) - Eu(y_t + e) > 0.$$

Then for any $\varepsilon > 0$, there exists a $\bar{T}$ such that $T > \bar{T}$ implies

$$\#\{0 \leq t \leq T \mid Eu(c_t) < Eu(y_t + e) + \eta\} < \varepsilon T.$$

For any B-uniform sequence $\{\lambda_t\}$, where $B \geq 1$ is fixed but arbitrary, and for all $T > \bar{T}$,

$$\begin{aligned} \frac{1}{T}\sum_{t=1}^{T} \lambda_t Eu(c_t) &\geq \frac{1}{T}\sum_{t=1}^{T} \lambda_t \left(Eu(y_t + e) + \eta\right) - \varepsilon Bu(Ey_t + e) \\ &\geq \frac{1}{T}\sum_{t=1}^{T} \lambda_t Eu(y_t + e) + B^{-1}\eta - \varepsilon Bu(Ey_t + e) \\ &> \frac{1}{T}\sum_{t=1}^{T} \lambda_t Eu(y_t + e) \end{aligned}$$

for ε sufficiently small. This shows that the equilibrium allocation is not uniformly efficient for any fixed but arbitrary B.

Proof of Proposition 6.7

Index the values of y_t by $s = 1, \ldots, S$, and let $c_1 \in \mathbf{R}$ and $c_2 \in \mathbf{R}^S$. Then we can write the expected utility of an agent who consumes c_1 in the first period and c_{2s} in the second period if state s occurs as $u(c_1) + V(c_2)$, where $V(c_2) \equiv \sum_{s=1}^{S} \pi_s v(c_{2s})$. Let $C \subset \mathbf{R} \times \mathbf{R}^S$ be a compact set such that $c \in C$ implies that

$$u'(c_1) \geq \sum_{s=1}^{S} \pi_s v'(c_{2s}),$$

and for any $c \in C$, let

$$\Delta(c) = \{\delta \in \mathbf{R} \times \mathbf{R}^S | u(c_1 + \delta_1) + V(c_2 + \delta_2) \geq u(c_1) + V(c_2)\}.$$

From the concavity of $u(\cdot)$ and $v(\cdot)$ and the gradient inequality, it follows that

$$u'(c_1)\delta_1 + \sum_{s=1}^{S} \pi_s v'(c_{2s})\delta_{2s} \geq 0.$$

Then $c \in C$ implies that

$$\max \delta_{2s} \geq -\delta_1.$$

We now prove a slightly stronger result.

Lemma 6.2 For any $\epsilon > 0$, $c \in C$ and $\delta \in \Delta(c)$, there exists $\lambda > 1$ such that $\delta_1 \leq -\epsilon$ implies that $\max \delta_{1s} \geq \lambda \delta_1$.

Proof The proof is by contradiction. Suppose that contrary to what we want to prove, for some $\epsilon > 0$ and any $\lambda > 1$ we can find $c \in C$ and $\delta \in \Delta(c)$ such that $\delta_1 \leq -\epsilon$ and $\max \delta_{2s} < \lambda \delta_1$. Then we can find a sequence (c^k, δ^k) such that, for each k, $c^k \in C$, $\delta^k \in \Delta(c^k)$, $\delta_1^k \leq -\epsilon$ and

$$\lim_{k \to \infty} \max_s \delta_{2s}^k / |\delta_1^k| = 1.$$

C is compact, so there exists a convergent subsequence of $\{c^k\}$. Since u and v are concave, there is no loss of generality in assuming that $\delta_1^k = -\epsilon$. Then $\{\delta^k\}$ is bounded above and $\delta^k \in \Delta(c^k)$ implies it is bounded below as well, so $\{\delta^k\}$ has a convergent subsequence as well. There is no loss of generality, then, in taking $\{(c^k, \delta^k)\}$ to be a convergent sequence with a limit, (c^0, δ^0) say. By continuity,

$$u'(c_1^0) \geq \sum_s \pi_s v'(c_{2s}^0),$$

$$u(c_1^0 + \delta_1^0) + V(c_2^0 + \delta_2^0) \geq u(c_1^0) + V(c_2^0)$$

and $\max \delta_{2s}^0 = -\delta_1^0$. However, the second inequality and the strict concavity of u and v imply that

$$u'(c_1^0)\delta_1^0 + \sum_{s=1}^{S} \pi_s v'(c_{2s}^0)\delta_{2s}^0 > 0,$$

which contradicts the other two relations.

Now, turning to the proof of proposition 6.5, let $\{(c_{1t}, c_{2t}, s_t)\}$ denote the equilibrium allocation, and let $\{(c'_{1t}, c'_{2t}, s'_t)\}$ denote another feasible allocation that satisfies the disintermediation constraint. Suppose that $s_t = s'_t = 0$ for every date t. Let $\delta_t \equiv (c'_{1t}, c'_{2t+1}) - (c_{1t}, c_{2t+1})$ denote the difference in generation t's consumption in the two allocations. The equilibrium allocation satisfies

$$u'(c_{1t}) \geq E[v'(c_{2t+1})|y^t], (c_{1t}, c_{2t+1}) \geq 0, c_{1t} \leq e, \text{ and } c_{2t} \leq e + y_t.$$

The first inequality is the first-order condition, the second holds by assumption, and the last two follow from the budget constraints and the fact that $p_t = p_{t+1}$. If we define C by putting

$$C = \{(c_1, c_2) \in \mathbf{R}_+ \times \mathbf{R}_+^S | u'(c_1) \geq E[v'(c_2)], c_1 \leq e, c_2 \leq e + \max y_s,$$

then it is clear that $(c_{1t}, c_{2t+1}) \in C$ for every t. Furthermore, $\delta_t \in \Delta(c_{1t}, c_{2t+1})$ for each t. Hence, the conditions of the lemma are satisfied.

Suppose that contrary to what we want to prove, some generation is ex post better off under the alternative allocation than it would be in equilibrium. Without loss of generality, we can assume that generation 1 is better off. Since the initial generation is no worse off and there is no possible gain from using the storage technology, the improvement in generation 1's welfare must come from a transfer from generation 2, which implies that in some state(s), $\delta_{12} < 0$. Since generation 2 is ex post no worse off, there must be some state in which $\delta_{22} \geq -\lambda\delta_{12}$ for some $\lambda > 1$. The increase in generation 2's second-period consumption can come only from a reduction in generation 3's first-period consumption, and since $\delta_{13} = -\delta_{22} \geq \delta_{12}$, our lemma implies that $\delta_{23} \geq -\lambda\delta_{13} \geq -\lambda^2\delta_{12}$ in some state(s). Continuing in this way, we can find a sequence of states

$(y_1, y_2, \ldots)$ such that at each date t, generation t reduces its first-period consumption by $-\lambda^{t-1}\delta_{12}$ and increases its second-period consumption by at least $\lambda^t\delta_{12}$. Since $\lambda > 1$, this will become infeasible in finite time.

Now suppose that there may be changes in the holding of the safe asset. Other things being equal, an increase in storage will have the effect of reducing the first-period consumption and increasing the second-period consumption of a given generation by the same amount, but will not reduce the ratio λ in the inequalities above. The preceding argument will continue to hold, with δ_{2t+1} interpreted as the transfer of consumption between generations $t+1$ and t. Again, there is no feasible sequence of transfers that will make some generation better off ex post without making some other generation(s) worse off.

References

Allen, F., and D. Gale. (1997). "Financial Markets, Intermediaries, and Intertemporal Smoothing." *Journal of Political Economy* **105,** (1997) 523–546.

———. (1995). "A Welfare Comparison of Intermediaries and Financial Markets in Germany and the U.S." *European Economic Review* **39,** 179–209.

Altonji, J., F. Hayashi, and L. Kotlikoff. (1992). "Is the Extended Family Altruistically Linked? Direct Tests Using Microdata." *American Economic Review* **82,** 1177–1198.

Bhattacharya, S., P. Fulghieri, and R. Rovelli. (1998). "Financial Intermediation Versus Stock Markets in a Dynamic Intertemporal Model." *Journal of Institutional and Theoretical Economics* **154,** 291–319.

Bhattacharya, S., and A. J. Padilla. (1996). "Dynamic Banking: A Reconsideration." *Review of Financial Studies* **9,** 1003–1032.

Charkham, J. (1994). *Keeping Good Company: A Study of Corporate Governance in Five Countries.* Oxford: Clarendon Press.

Constantinides, G. M., J. B. Donaldson, and R. Mehra. (1997). "Junior Can't Borrow: A New Perspective on the Equity Premium Puzzle." Working paper, University of Chicago.

Demange, G. (1996). "Wealth Distribution and Asset Prices." Working paper, Départment et Laboratoire d'Economie Théorique Appliquée (DELTA).

Demange, G., and G. Laroque. (1995). "Incentive Constraints, Capital Accumulation, and Intergenerational Risk Sharing." Working paper, Départment et Laboratoire d'Economie Théorique Appliquée (DELTA).

Fulghieri, P., and R. Rovelli. (1998). "Capital Markets, Financial Intermediaries, and Liquidity Supply." *Journal of Banking and Finance* **22,** 1157–1179.

Gordon, R. A., and H. R. Varian. (1988). "Intergenerational Risk Sharing." *Journal of Public Economics* **37,** 185–202.

Hayashi, F., Altonji J., and L. Kotlikoff. (1996). "Risk Sharing Between and Within Families." *Econometrica* **64,** 261–294.

Koopmans, T. C. (1967). "Objectives, Constraints, and Outcomes in Optimal Growth Models." *Econometrica* **35,** 1–15.

McCallum, B. T. (1987). "The Optimal Inflation Rate in an Overlapping-Generations Economy with Land." In W. A. Barnett and K. J. Singleton (eds.), *New Approaches to Monetary Economics.* Cambridge: Cambridge University Press.

Pigou, A. C. (1932). *The Economics of Welfare.* 4th ed. London: Macmillan.

Qi, J. (1994). "Bank Liquidity and Stability in an Overlapping Generations Model." *Review of Financial Studies* **7,** 389–417.

Ramsey, F. (1928). "A Mathematical Theory of Savings." *Economic Journal* **38,** 543–559.

Schectman, J. (1976). "An Income Fluctuation Problem." *Journal of Economic Theory* **12,** 218–241.

Scheinkman, J. (1980). "Notes on Asset Trading in an Overlapping Generations Economy." Working paper, University of Chicago.

Svensson, L. (1980). "Equity Among Generations." *Econometrica* **48,** 1251–1256.

7 Information and Resource Allocation

The way in which information is acquired and used to allocate resources is possibly one of the most critical differences between market-based and bank-based financial systems, and considerable attention has been paid to this topic in the context of financial markets. In contrast, relatively little work has been done analyzing how information is acquired and resources allocated when banks and insurance companies are the predominant providers of finance. At first sight, it might seem that economies with liquid stock markets and many publicly quoted companies would be more effective at allocating resources than economies with a few large intermediaries and a small number of publicly quoted companies. Publicly quoted companies have to provide more information about their operations than private companies do, and the prices of those companies are themselves informative. So it might seem that the more markets there are, the better. This chapter considers the merits of this type of argument.

We consider three different ways of thinking about the role of financial market prices in allocating resources: prices as indicators of value and scarcity, the statistical use of prices to analyze risk, and prices as aggregators of information. Prices are traditionally thought of as indicators of value and scarcity. This view, which we summarize, asserts that prices provide sufficient information for the efficient allocation of resources. Prices can also be used as data to estimate asset-pricing relationships, such as the capital asset pricing model (CAPM), which firms use for decision making. Asset markets readily provide such data, but the information may also be generated in other types of financial systems. A third role of prices is to reveal agents' private information. Under certain conditions, this information is aggregated in prices and becomes publicly available for resource allocation.

These three roles of prices are well known, and much of the information in this chapter is provided to set the stage for the analysis, in the latter stages of the sections, of the advantages and disadvantages of different institutional frameworks. Our specific focus is on the costs and benefits of having information revealed by prices. It is often assumed that economies with highly developed financial markets, which provide information aggregated in prices, are superior to economies that lack sophisticated financial markets. The first point we make is that under certain conditions, private information can be completely revealed through a loan market as well as through an equity market. Thus, intermediary-based and market-based systems can be equally efficient under certain conditions. The presumption that information is lost or used inefficiently in intermediated economies is not based on purely theoretical analysis. Nonetheless, there do exist conditions under which intermediation can suppress information, but the way in which this occurs is subtle and requires careful analysis. We show, by means of a simple example, that intermediation can prevent the exploitation of private information to achieve the first best, but this result depends on the distribution of information among agents, that is, on who has the information to begin with. These examples do not by any means exhaust the subject, which clearly raises more questions than can be answered here, but it indicates that the comparison of informational efficiency in financial systems requires more research than it has been given to date.

An important point, which is well known but often disregarded in discussions of financial systems, is that informational efficiency and welfare (Pareto) efficiency are quite different things. In the comparison of stylized financial systems, we deliberately impose assumptions that guarantee that full revelation of information through market prices or in some other way leads to the first best. In other words, informational efficiency is equivalent to Pareto efficiency. In general, this need not be true. For example, in order to reveal information, prices have to fluctuate with changes in underlying information, but price fluctuations themselves are costly to the extent that they impose risk of uninsured changes in wealth on investors. We analyze the trade-off between allocative efficiency and risk sharing in the context of an example where more information leads to better investment decisions, but at the cost of more price variability. This is a reminder of the general theory of the second best: starting from a situation in which several conditions for Pareto efficiency are not satisfied, satisfying one of the conditions for

Pareto efficiency can make everyone worse off. Again, welfare comparisons of financial systems are hazardous, even in simplified theoretical settings.

7.1 Prices and Decentralization

The first role of prices as indicators of scarcity and value is the standard neoclassical view of prices that originated with Adam Smith's notion of the invisible hand. The modern version of this theory is captured in the ADM model and the fundamental theorems of welfare economics. If markets are complete and various other restrictions are satisfied, markets allow a Pareto-efficient allocation of resources. When firms maximize their value and individuals maximize their utility, resources are not wasted. Nobody can be made better off without making somebody else worse off.

The neoclassical theory of resource allocation, which culminated in the ADM theory, was initially developed under the assumption of perfect certainty. Under these conditions, decision making is relatively simple. Every agent knows the future values of the relevant prices and interest rates, so maximizing the value of the firm is a purely technical exercise. Debt finance and equity finance are equivalent. The main informational role of financial markets is to provide the term structure of interest rates. Stock markets are informationally redundant since the value of the firm can easily be calculated from the prices of inputs, outputs, and interest rates.

How firms should make investment decisions to maximize their value is the subject of capital budgeting. Over the years, it has become a mainstay of the curriculum in most business schools, expounded in numerous textbooks for many years (Brealey and Myers 1996; Ross, Westerfield, and Jaffe 1996). According to the methodology outlined in these books, managers first need to derive the stream of cash flows $\{C_t\}_{t=0}^{T}$ that will accrue to shareholders over time, including the initial cost of the investment C_0. This is done using various types of information. Projections based on accounting data generated within the firm usually play an important part. Once the cash flows have been calculated, they are discounted at the opportunity cost of capital for each period, r_t. This gives the net present value (NPV) of the investment:

$$NPV = C_0 + \frac{C_1}{1+r_1} + \frac{C_2}{(1+r_2)^2} + \cdots + \frac{C_T}{(1+r_T)^T}.$$

NPV is obviously maximized by accepting positive NPV projects and rejecting negative NPV projects. There are a number of other capital budgeting methods, such as internal rate of return (IRR) and profitability index (PI), which are widely used and are equivalent to NPV if correctly applied. We will focus on NPV.

The discount rates, $\{r_t\}_{t=1}^{T}$, that should be used are found from the term structure of interest rates. Since there is no uncertainty, markets are complete as long as every agent can borrow and lend at these rates. Then there is unanimous agreement among the shareholders about the optimal policy for the firm. Shareholders should simply tell the managers to follow the NPV rule (or an equivalent). If all managers follow this rule, the allocation of resources within the economy will be Pareto efficient. Futhermore, the actual mechanics of decentralizing decisions from shareholders to managers are simple. The information that shareholders need to convey to managers is minimal. The shareholders do not need to tell the managers anything except to "maximize NPV." In particular, they do not need to tell the managers their preferences or the discount rates that should be used. The managers can observe the term structure of interest rates themselves.

NPV is not only a useful way for shareholders to decentralize decision making to managers. It is also an excellent way to decentralize within the firm. Managers at the head office do not need to convey huge amounts of information to subsidiaries. They too can simply ask their subordinates to maximize NPV. If all divisions of a firm do this, then the overall value of the firm is maximized. The move by many firms in recent years to decentralize by having profit centers is essentially based on this type of logic. The popularity of internal management systems using economic value added (EVA®), which is based on these types of ideas, indicates their practical importance (see, for example, Stern, Stewart, and Chew 1995, and Glassman 1997).

Of course, all this ignores the agency problems that were discussed in chapter 4 and will be discussed in subsequent chapters. In particular it assumes that it is easy to ensure that managers do maximize NPV. This abstraction from agency problems will be maintained throughout the rest of the chapter. However, it is perhaps worth noting in passing that even with regard to solving the agency problem, this type of decentralization is advantageous. The methods to be followed are fairly straightforward, and it can be relatively easily checked ex post whether the correct procedures were in fact implemented by managers.

The neoclassical model of resource allocation with certainty thus provides a practical framework for implementing decentralization from shareholders to management and within the firm. Moreover, it can be justified as being desirable for both shareholders and society as a whole. Since the only external financial data required are contained in the term structure of interest rates, the method can be applied in any institutional context where there are financial markets or intermediaries. However, the case of uncertainty requires more stringent assumptions.

If markets are complete, then the theory developed for the neoclassical model under the assumption of certainty carries over to the case of uncertainty more or less unchanged. Decentralization from shareholders to management and within the firm can again be straightforwardly achieved. Maximization of value is a technical exercise provided that the equilibrium prices of all inputs and outputs are known. Again, stock markets are informationally redundant, since the value of the firm can easily be calculated from the prices of the (contingent) inputs and outputs.

If markets are complete, uncertainty has no effect as far as firms are concerned. A firm buys all its inputs and sells all its outputs on a contingent basis, before any uncertainty is resolved. Consequently the firm's profits and market value are known for sure at the initial date when all decisions are made.

The restrictiveness of the complete-markets assumption limits its usefulness as a model for the decentralization of investment decisions. In chapter 5 we showed that under certain conditions, value maximization is sufficient for constrained Pareto efficiency when markets are incomplete. However, the value of the firm depends in a complex and nonlinear way on the choice of the firm's production plan and the marginal valuations of the shareholders. How does the firm gain the knowledge necessary to make these investment decisions? In very special cases, such as the Diamond (1967) model with multiplicative uncertainty, the relationship between the value of the firm and investment is linear, so it is enough to know the stock price in order to maximize the value of the firm. In general, things are more complicated.

In contrast, corporate finance textbook expositions of capital budgeting techniques offer a much simpler method of calculating the effect of an investment decision on the value of the firm. It simply replaces the stream of cash flows above with a stream of expected cash flows,

$E[C_t]$ and calculates the present value using a discount rate from an asset pricing model estimated from historical price data. The conditions under which this method is valid are reviewed in the next section.

7.2 Risk, Decentralization and Institutions

A significant part of the literature on financial economics has been devoted to a particular model, the CAPM. Its great advantages are that it is conceptually simple, has some empirical plausibility, and is relatively easy to use in practice for capital budgeting. Fama and Miller (1972) and Fama (1976) provide an excellent account of the traditional justification of this type of approach. Suppose the statistical distribution of stock prices is represented by a normal distribution. (The tails of the distributions that are actually observed are fatter than the normal, so this is an approximation.) Given normality, von Neumann-Morgenstern expected utility can be expressed as a function of the mean and variance of an investor's portfolio. By making a variety of other assumptions (see below), it is possible to derive the simple relationship

$$Er = r_F + \beta(Er_M - r_F),$$

where Er is the expected return on a stock, r_F is the risk-free rate, β is the covariance between the return on the stock and the return on the market (which is a portfolio consisting of all the stocks available weighted by value) divided by the variance of the market, and Er_M is the expected return on the market.

Initially, empirical studies such as Fama and McBeth (1973) provided some support for the validity of the CAPM. This, combined with its practical simplicity, has led to the widespread use of the CAPM. More recent and more sophisticated tests have been less favorable (see Ferson 1995 for a survey). Nevertheless, the CAPM has continued to be widely used, particularly as a means of finding discount rates for capital budgeting.

Although there is a vast theoretical literature on the CAPM (see Ingersoll 1987 for a good account), most of it assumes a fixed quantity of stock and a fixed amount of investment. CAPM-type models with endogenous investment in a general equilibrium framework are rare. One example is Geanakoplos and Shubik (1990), who investigate the efficiency of resource allocation when the CAPM is embedded in a general equilibrium model with uncertainty (see also Magill and Quinzii 1996, 1998). Geanakoplos and Shubik show that the conditions required for the CAPM to hold are quite special and the conditions for efficiency under the CAPM are more special still. It is sufficient for Pareto efficiency that, among other things, there be only one consumption good in each state of nature and that investors have quadratic utility functions. If either of these assumptions is relaxed, then efficiency is no longer guaranteed. Hence, even if the CAPM holds because, say, stock returns are normally distributed, an efficient allocation of resources is not necessarily obtained.

Of course, the deficiencies of assuming quadratic utility are well known. In particular, the range of wealth for which investors have a positive marginal utility of consumption is limited, and within this range an increase in wealth leads to a reduction in the amount held in risky assets. The assumption of a single good is also problematic. However, Geanakoplos and Shubik are able to show that if redistributions of income do not affect relative commodity prices very much, the allocation with decentralized investment decisions is constrained Pareto efficient.

Although the theoretical underpinnings are based on special assumptions and the empirical support for the CAPM is questionable, the popularity of the CAPM is not surprising. The methodology provides a practical way for firms to decentralize their investment decisions from shareholders to managers and from head office to divisions. Our main interest in this section is to see how the CAPM can be used in different institutional frameworks. Three different scenarios are considered: a stock market economy, an intermediated economy, and an economy dominated by family firms. We think of the stock-market economy as corresponding to the United States In recent times, at least, some firms in practically every industry are listed. We think of the intermediated economy as being like the United States in the nineteenth century or some European economies in the twentieth century. In this case, finance is provided by intermediaries such as banks and insurance companies. There is a stock exchange, but only the intermediaries are listed. They make loans to firms and have equity investments in them. The economy dominated by family firms is meant to capture some of the features of emerging economies, such as those in Latin America, where a few wealthy families own all the firms in the economy. Before considering each of these possibilities we review the CAPM theory.

A CAPM framework

We consider a special case of the economy discussed in chapter 5. There are two dates, 0 and 1, with one consumption good at each date. At date 0 it is either consumed or used as the input for production, and at date 1 it is the output and is consumed. At date 1 there are S states of nature, which occur with probability π_s. All consumers and producers agree on the probabilities. The consumption good is distinguished by the date and state in which it is delivered, so there are $S+1$ different contingent commodities, consumption at date 0, and consumption in each of the S states at date 1.

There are m types of consumers, $i=1,\ldots,m$, and n types of producers, $j=1,\ldots,n$. There is a nonatomic continuum of consumers and producers and, for simplicity, a unit measure of each type.

Each consumer of type i has a consumption set $\mathbf{R}_+^{S+1}$ with generic element x_i, an initial endowment of commodities e_i, an endowment of shares $\bar{t}_i=(\bar{t}_{i1},\ldots,\bar{t}_{in})$, and a utility function $u_i:\mathbf{R}_+^{S+1}\rightarrow\mathbf{R}$. We write $x_i=(x_i^0,x_i^1)$ and $e_i=(e_i^0,e_i^1)$, where e_i^0 and x_i^0 are the first-period endowment and consumption of consumer i and $e_i^1=(e_{is})$ and $x_i^1=(x_{is})$ are vectors of endowments and consumption at date 1 in the S states.

Each producer of type j has a production set $Y_j\subset\mathbf{R}_-\times\mathbf{R}_+^S$ and chooses a production plan $y_j=(y_j^0,y_j^1)$ to maximize its net market value $y_j^0+MV(y_j^1)$ where y_j^0 is the input at date 0, y_j^1 is the vector of outputs y_{js} and $MV(y_j^1)$ is the date 0 market value of y_j^1. The inputs and outputs of all the n producers are denoted by the matrix y.

It is convenient to recognize that a consumer's utility is determined by his date 0 consumption x_i^0 and his portfolio of securities t_i. Hence a consumer maximizes $u_i(x_i)=u_i(x_i^0,e_i^1+\sum_j t_{ij}y_j^1)\equiv u_i^*(x_i^0,t_i;y)$.

As before, the marginal rates of substitution, or marginal valuations as they will be referred to below, are denoted

$$\mu_{is}(x_i)=\frac{\partial u_i(x_i)/\partial x_{is}}{\partial u_i(x_i)/\partial x_i^0}.$$

The consumption good at date 0 is taken as numeraire, and if consumers of type i hold a positive amount of shares, then the value of the stock of producer j, q_j, is given by the weighted sum of the outputs at date 1 where the weights are the marginal valuations

$$q_j=\mu_i(x_i)\cdot y_j^1.$$

Two changes are made in the definition of equilibrium offered in chapter 5:

- *Unlimited short sales.* In chapter 5 we prohibited short sales by requiring portfolios to be nonnegative. Here, a consumer is allowed to choose any portfolio $t = (t_1, \ldots, t_n) \in \mathbf{R}^n$ subject to the usual budget constraint and the requirement that $x_i \in \mathbf{R}_+^{S+1}$.
- *One plan per producer type j.* In chapter 5 we allowed producers of a given type j to choose different production plans for different types of consumers. Here we assume that all producers of type j choose the same production plan y_j in equilibrium. In fact, there is no loss of generality in this, since we can always split types to allow for more choices of plans.

With these changes and using the notation introduced in chapter 5, an equilibrium consists of an m-tuple of consumption and portfolio plans (x_i^0, t_i), an n-tuple of production plans (y_j), and a vector of share prices q such that, for every i,

(x_i^0, t_i) maximizes $u_i^*(x_i^0, t_i; y)$ subject to the budget constraint $x_i^0 + q \cdot t_i \le e_i^0 + q \cdot \bar{t}_i - \sum_j \bar{t}_{ij} y_j^0$.

y_j maximizes $y^0 + MV(y_j^1)$ subject to $y_j \in Y_j$, for every j.

$q_j = MV(y_j^1) = \mu_i(x_i) \cdot y_j^1$ for all j.

$\sum_i t_i = \mathbf{1}$ and $\sum_i x_i^0 = \sum_i e_i^0 + \sum_j y_j^0$.

A number of special assumptions on consumer preferences and endowments are required to turn this into a CAPM:

- *Quadratic preferences.* Suppose to begin that each consumer has preferences that are additively time separable and quadratic at the second date:

$$u_i(x_i) = v_i^0(x_i^0) + \sum_{s=1}^{S} \pi_s(x_{is} - \frac{1}{2} b_i x_{is}{}^2),$$

where $b_i > 0$ is a constant.

- *No nontraded risks.* We assume that consumers have no initial endowments at the second date: $e_i^1 = 0$ for all i.
- *Monotonicity.* Preferences are assumed to be monotonic so the marginal utility of consumption is positive on the range of feasible

consumption bundles: $1 - b_i\omega_s > 0$ for all i where $\omega_s = \sum_j y_{js}$ for each s. Thus, ω_s is the payoff of the market portfolio in state s.

- *Interior equilibrium.* In equilibrium, all consumers are assumed to be in the interior of their consumption sets: $x_i \gg 0$ for all i.

These assumptions are quite restrictive, and although some of them can be weakened, they remain extremely special. The limitations of the CAPM will be discussed later. First, we derive some well-known properties that allow us to present a neat theory of producer behavior.

With quadratic preferences, the marginal valuation functions can be written as

$$\begin{aligned}\mu_{is}(x_i) &= \frac{\partial u_i(x_i)/\partial x_{is}}{\partial u_i(x_i)/\partial x_i^0} \\ &= \frac{\pi_s(1 - b_i x_{is})}{\partial v_i^0(x_i^0)/\partial x_i^0} \\ &= \pi_s(\bar{a}_i - \bar{b}_i x_{is}), \forall s = 1, ..., S,\end{aligned}$$

where

$$\bar{a}_i = \frac{1}{\partial v_i^0(x_i^0)/\partial x_i^0}, \bar{b}_i = \frac{b_i}{\partial v_i^0(x_i^0)/\partial x_i^0}.$$

Since unlimited short sales are allowed, the first-order conditions for an optimum to the consumer's problem have the form

$$q_j = \sum_s \pi_s \mu_{is}(x_i) y_{js}, \forall i, \forall j.$$

Then for any consumers i and k, we have

$$\begin{aligned}0 &= \sum_s \pi_s[\mu_{is}(x_i) - \mu_{ks}(x_k)]y_{js} \qquad (7.1) \\ &= \sum_s \pi_s[\bar{a}_i - \bar{a}_k - (\bar{b}_i x_{is} - \bar{b}_k x_{ks})]y_{js}.\end{aligned}$$

To exploit this condition, we need an assumption concerning the returns to investment in stocks:

- *Existence of a safe asset.* If we regard y_j^1 as a column vector and let A be the $S \times n$ matrix with the production plans for columns, then span A denotes the linear subspace of $\mathbf{R}^S$ consisting of linear combinations of production plans. We say that there is a safe asset if $\mathbf{1} \in \text{span } A$, and we assume that such an asset exists.

Since $\mathbf{1}$ belongs to span A and x_i^1 and x_k^1 belong to span A, it is clear that

$$\mu_i(x_i) - \mu_k(x_k) = (\bar{a}_i - \bar{a}_k)\mathbf{1} - \bar{b}_i x_i^1 + \bar{b}_k x_k^1 \in \text{span } A$$

(where $\mu_i(x_i)$ and $\mu_k(x_k)$ are the vectors of marginal valuations $\mu_{is}(x_i)$ and $\mu_{ks}(x_k)$). There must exist a portfolio $\hat{t} = (\hat{t}_1, \ldots, \hat{t}_n)$ such that

$$\mu_i(x_i) - \mu_k(x_k) = \sum_j \hat{t}_j y_j^1.$$

Multiplying equation 7.1 by $\hat{t}_j$ and summing over all j yields

$$\begin{aligned} 0 &= \sum_j \sum_s \pi_s[\mu_{is}(x_i) - \mu_{ks}(x_k)]\hat{t}_j y_{js} \\ &= \sum_s \pi_s[\mu_{is}(x_i) - \mu_{ks}(x_k)] \sum_j \hat{t}_j y_{js} \\ &= \sum_s \pi_s(\mu_{is}(x_i) - \mu_{ks}(x_k))^2, \end{aligned}$$

which implies that $\mu_i(x_i) - \mu_k(x_k) = 0$ for any i and k. But this implies that the equilibrium is not merely constrained efficient; it is actually Pareto efficient. Thus we have proved the following result.

Proposition 7.1 Under the maintained assumptions, any equilibrium of the CAPM including a safe asset is Pareto efficient.

We can derive the next result as a corollary of the Pareto efficiency of equilibrium. For any i and k, we have

$$\begin{aligned} &\mu_i(x_i) - \mu_k(x_k) = 0 \\ &\quad \Longrightarrow \bar{a}_i\mathbf{1} - \bar{b}_i x_i^1 = \bar{a}_k\mathbf{1} - \bar{b}_k x_k^1 \\ &\quad \Longrightarrow x_i^1 = \frac{\bar{a}_k - \bar{a}_i}{\bar{b}_i}\mathbf{1} - \frac{\bar{b}_k}{\bar{b}_i} x_k^1 \\ &\quad \Longrightarrow \omega^1 = \sum_i \frac{\bar{a}_k - \bar{a}_i}{\bar{b}_i}\mathbf{1} - \sum_i \frac{\bar{b}_k}{\bar{b}_i} x_k^1, \end{aligned}$$

where the last line is obtained by summing over i and noting that $\sum_i x_i^1 = \omega^1$ where ω^1 is the payoff of the market portfolio. Thus, we have proved the mutual fund theorem.

Proposition 7.2 Under the maintained assumptions, in any equilibrium of the CAPM including a safe asset, the date 1 consumption of consumer k can be represented as a linear combination of the safe asset with payoff $\mathbf{1}$ and the market portfolio with payoff ω^1, that is,

$$x_k^1 = \gamma_k \mathbf{1} + \delta_k \omega^1.$$

Pricing stocks is particularly easy in the CAPM. Not only do agents agree on what the firm should do, they actually have the same marginal valuations in each state so they will price any newly introduced security in the same way. Moreover, from the Pareto efficiency theorem, we know that this kind of pricing must lead to an efficient set of securities, that is, maximizing value using the common marginal valuations will lead to a Pareto-efficient allocation. Let $Q(y^1)$ denote the value of a new security (production plan). Then using the common marginal rates of substitution to value the security

$$\begin{aligned}
Q(y^1) &= \sum_s \pi_s(\bar{a}_i - \bar{b}_i x_{is}) y_s \\
&= \sum_s \pi_s(\bar{a}_i - \bar{b}_i(\gamma_i + \delta_i \omega_s)) y_s \\
&= \sum_s \pi_s(\bar{a}_i - \bar{b}_i \gamma_i - \bar{b}_i \delta_i \omega_s) y_s \\
&= (\bar{a}_i - \bar{b}_i \gamma_i) E[y^1] - \bar{b}_i \delta_i E[\omega^1 y^1] \\
&= aE[y^1] - bE[\omega^1 y^1]. \qquad (7.2)
\end{aligned}$$

The coefficients of this pricing formula are independent of i as the last step indicates since everybody's marginal rate of substitution is equal in each state. Hence the value of any security is just a linear combination of the expected payoff and the covariance with the market portfolio, where the coefficients depend on the equilibrium but not on the particular security.

It is helpful at this stage to see how equation 7.2 can be transformed into the standard form of the CAPM, which is stated in terms of percentage returns rather than absolute payoffs. The gross percentage return on the risk-free asset is $1 + r_F$, on the market portfolio with payoff ω^1 is $1 + r_M$, and on a security with payoff y^1 is $1 + r$. Without loss of generality, units are chosen so that the date 0 value of the market portfolio is 1 and the expected payoff is $E[\omega^1] = 1 + Er_M$. Applying equation 7.2 to the risk-free asset with $y^1 = 1$ invested so the payoff is $y^1 = 1 + r_F$ with certainty gives

$$1 = [a - b(1 + Er_M)](1 + r_F).$$

Similarly, applying equation 7.2 to the market portfolio so $y^1 = \omega^1$ gives

$$1 = a(1 + Er_M) - bE[(\omega^1)^2].$$

Solving these last two expressions simultaneously and using $E[(\omega^1)^2] = Var(\omega^1) + (1 + r_M)^2$, it can be shown that

$$a = \frac{1}{1 + r_F} + b(1 + Er_M)$$

$$b = \frac{1}{1 + r_F} \frac{(Er_M - r_F)}{Var(\omega^1)}.$$

Substituting back into equation 7.2 and simplifying with $E[\omega^1 y^1] = Cov(\omega^1, y^1) + (1 + Er_M)E[y^1]$, it follows that

$$Q(y^1) = \frac{1}{1 + r_F} \left[E[y^1] - (Er_M - r_F) \frac{Cov(\omega^1, y^1)}{Var(\omega^1)} \right].$$

Finally, using $Var(\omega^1) = Var(r_M)$ (which follows since the value of the market portfolio is normalized to 1), $E[y^1] = (1 + Er)Q(y^1)$, and $Cov(\omega^1, y^1) = Q(y^1)cov(r_M, r)$, this simplifies to the standard form

$$Er = r_F + \beta(Er_M - r_F),$$

where $\beta = Cov(r_M, r)/Var(r_M)$.

The attraction of the CAPM is that in order to make efficient decisions, that is, decisions that are both optimal from the point of view of shareholders and socially efficient, a manager needs to pay attention to only three pieces of information: expected return, the covariance of returns with those of the market portfolio, and the risk-return trade-off. We next consider how this approach can be used to decentralize decision making among various levels of management. But first, we stop to review some of the limitations of the CAPM:

No untraded risk. The assumption that $e_i^1 = 0$ means that the only uncertainty individual consumers face relates to the outcome of the investments they make in the securities purchased at date 0. If there are few securities, there are few sources of risk. Thus, we begin with as many assets as we have sources of risk, so it is perhaps not surprising that markets are effectively complete and that risk sharing is efficient. This assumption can be weakened, to allow for the case where $e_i^1 \neq 0$, as long as e_i^1 belongs to the span of A, but it is still a restrictive (nongeneric) assumption. Presumably nontraded risks are one of the major sources of incomplete (inefficient) risk sharing, though perhaps not for rich investors who earn most of their income from stocks.

Unlimited short sales. Although the proof above requires unlimited short sales, it can be seen that provided $Er_M > r_F$, everybody will hold some amount of the market portfolio and short sales constraints will not bind for stocks in the equilibrium considered. As far as the safe asset is concerned short sales may occur in equilibrium (i.e., there may be borrowing) so this assumption cannot be relaxed without changing the pricing relationship.

Mean-variance analysis. In the reduced form of the CAPM, it is often assumed that any model with preferences that depend only on the mean and variance of the asset returns has the CAPM properties. However, as Geanakoplos and Shubik show, this is not true as far as the Pareto efficiency property is concerned. Different versions of mean-variance preferences give rise to the mutual fund theorem and the familiar pricing formula, but only the quadratic version or other special cases such as normal returns and exponential utility give Pareto efficiency. Hence, from a normative point of view, the theory is more special than even the usual CAPM. Of course, the really important question is how good an approximation mean-variance preferences are in the first place. Clearly if there were some nonlinearity in the marginal utilities, then even the assumption that risk is limited to the holding of assets would prevent incomplete risk sharing. The key feature of the CAPM is that marginal valuation vectors can be spanned by the asset set. If there were some other set of assumptions that ensured this property, those assumptions would produce the same results as the CAPM. Finally, Fama (1965) has shown that stock returns on the NYSE have "fatter tails" than a normal distribution and are better represented by a two-parameter symmetric stable distribution. A similar theory to the CAPM can be derived in this case (see Fama and Miller 1972). Again Pareto efficiency presumably will hold only in special cases.

Safe asset. The three results stated above have analogues for the case where there is no safe asset. Essentially the risk-free asset is replaced by a zero-beta portfolio (see Black 1972). For the purposes of some of the analysis below, the limitations on the data available mean that identifying a zero-beta portfolio may be problematic, so a safe asset is assumed to exist.

Capital Budgeting in Alternative Institutional Frameworks

Stock Market Economy

In developing the CAPM, no explicit set of institutions was described. The CAPM is perhaps most easily understood in terms of a stock market economy, with all stocks quoted on the stock exchange. There is also a market for bonds. Bonds take the role of the risk-free asset, and the interest rate on bonds determines the risk-free return. In this case, there is a considerable amount of information publicly available in the form of prices and interest rates. This information can be used in a number of ways.

The current stock prices of firms allow us to calculate discount rates for evaluating projects. It follows from our earlier analysis that the value of a firm with production plan $y_j = (y_j^0, y_j^1)$ is given by $MV(y_j^1) + y_j^0$, where

$$MV(y_j^1) = \frac{E[y_j^1]}{1 + Er_j}.$$

If the stock is sold net of the initial input y_j^0, then the stock price is simply $MV(y_j^1)$. Given an estimate of $E[y_j^1]$ and the stock price $MV(y_j^1)$, it is easy to back out Er_j. The accuracy of this process depends critically on the accuracy of the estimate of $E[y_j^1]$ and since predicting the future is never easy, this may not be a robust way of obtaining an estimate of Er_j.

An alternative procedure, which avoids the need to estimate $E[y_j^1]$, is to make use of the history of stock prices to estimate the CAPM. The model presented in the previous section has two dates. However, if we assume that the history of the stock market consists of repeated trials of the model and that the process is stationary, the data generated by the stock market can be used to estimate the CAPM. There are, of course, many statistical issues involved in any practical attempt to use historical data to estimate the CAPM (see, for example, Fama 1976). However, in principle it is possible to estimate the model and to find β's for particular firms and industries. These can be used, together with an estimate of $Er_M - r_F$ based on historic data and a value of r_F from the bond market, to calculate Er_j.

PROPOSITION 7.3 The manager of a type j firm can maximize the welfare of shareholders by choosing investments to

$$\max \; NPV = C_0 + \frac{EC_1}{1 + Er_j},$$

where C_0 is the cost of the investment, EC_1 is the expected cash flow, and Er_j is the expected return on stocks of type j in the market and is given by the CAPM

$$Er_j = r_F + \beta_j(Er_M - r_F).$$

In this economy, the financial markets play an important role in providing the historical information that managers need to make efficient investment decisions in the following sense. They give r_F directly and provide the data from which β_j, and hence Er_j, can be estimated. Of course, in making the capital budgeting decision, the managers must estimate the expected cash flow EC_1 from the investment. This is usually a difficult problem and cannot be avoided. However, by using historical stock market data to estimate the CAPM and find a discount rate, the problem of estimating firms' expected future cash flows to back out a discount rate from the current stock price has been eliminated. The CAPM methodology is also preferable to simply looking at historical rates of returns on stocks because the current risk-free rate may be different from the rate in the past.

Decentralization within the Firm

Many large corporations have tens of thousands of employees. Some of the largest, such as General Motors and IBM, have turnovers equivalent to the GDPs of reasonably sized countries. Managing these large organizations is an extraordinarily difficult task. One possibility is to have a hierarchical centrally managed organization. In this case, large amounts of information must be transferred from head office to the divisions and vice versa. This includes but is not limited to the information that senior managers at the head office need to make ongoing decisions. They would then send out detailed instructions to the divisions on how to proceed. An alternative to this type of centralized command and control organization is decentralization into autonomous divisions. One way that such decentralized divisions can be coordinated is to let them operate on their own with little oversight. At best managers of divisions will decide on what they think is desirable for the organization as a whole. At worst they will pursue the interests of their own division.

Another alternative is to decentralize and tell the division managers to maximize NPV. This provides a ready benchmark that can be understood throughout the organization, and it avoids the need for large amounts of information to be transferred between the head office and the divisions. Perhaps the greatest advantage of the CAPM framework and this type of capital budgeting methodology is that it provides a practical way for the shareholders to delegate decisions to managers. The shareholders do not need to provide explicit instructions other than to "maximize NPV." They do not need to convey their degree of risk aversion, anything else about their preferences, or anything about the discount rate the managers should use in evaluating projects. Propositions 7.1 through 7.3 indicate that in the setting described, the allocation of resources will be Pareto efficient.

Implicit in the preceding discussion is the assumption that each firm operates in a single industry. However, the theory can readily be extended to conglomerates that have divisions in multiple industries provided there are no technological externalities between the divisions. Given enough independence between divisions, the financial markets provide the information that allows firms to decentralize investment decisions to divisions. All that is necessary to calculate the β for each division of the conglomerate is that in each industry there are some firms that are listed on the stock exchange. Knowledge of their prices provides the necessary information to estimate β's.

Proposition 7.4 In the CAPM framework, firms with additively separable technologies can maximize their shareholders' welfare by splitting operations into divisions and instructing the managers of each division to maximize NPV.

The assumptions needed for decentralization within the firm are strong, however. We must assume that each division operates as a separate firm. More precisely, the production possibility set of the conglomerate is the sum of the production possibility sets of the individual divisions and the individual production possibility sets are independent of one another. For example, these assumptions would not be satisfied in a corporation where services such as advertising, financial accounting, information technology, and so forth were provided to divisions from the head office. Without these assumptions, there is no simple decentralization theory.

Furthermore, even if the conglomerate is effectively a collection of separate firms, the fact that most divisions are not listed and publicly traded as separate firms may have an effect on the quality of the information available. For example, in empirical studies, financial economists often use pooled data sets, that is, they assume that all the firms in an industry have the same value of β and pool the data on all these firms to calculate an estimate of β from the time series of prices. They do this because, assuming their assumption is correct, more data give a more precise estimate. Clearly, having fewer firms listed in the industry (because some are divisions of multi-industry conglomerates) will reduce the precision of the estimate of β. While it may be possible in principle to implement the CAPM when only a few firms in an industry are quoted, in practice it may be very difficult because of the quality and quantity of the data available.

An Intermediated Economy

The use of the CAPM for capital budgeting is usually assumed to take place in a stock market economy because the availability of historical stock price series makes it easy to estimate the CAPM. However, it may also be possible to implement it in economies with different institutional structures. The CAPM requires everyone to hold some combination of the risk-free asset and the market portfolio, but there are many institutional frameworks that allow one to do this. Also, since the structure of the optimal portfolio is so simple, the information needed to make optimal decisions is also limited. This allows us to extend the capital budgeting methodology to different institutional frameworks.

Suppose, for example, that finance is provided to firms through intermediaries, such as banks or insurance companies, the intermediaries are the only entities that are listed on the stock exchange, and in addition to this limited stock market, there is also assumed to be a market for risk-free bonds. A financial system satisfying these properties is referred to as an *intermediated economy.* Examples of intermediated economies include a number of countries, such as the United States in the nineteenth century, some European economies in the twentieth century, and a number of emerging economies today. This model also has some relevance for less extreme financial systems, such as Germany and France, where the number and value of companies listed is significantly smaller than in the United States and United Kingdom.

The capital budgeting methodology can be applied to an intermediated economy as long as the limited amount of information required by the CAPM is available.

PROPOSITION 7.5 Provided that firms' managers have enough information to find the discount rate corresponding to the CAPM discount rate Er_j and maximize NPV using this discount rate, the allocation of resources will be the same as with a stock market where every firm is listed, as in proposition 7.3.

To see why this result holds, we start with the simplest case, where the intermediaries finance their investments by issuing equity and then make equity investments in firms. Later, we will use a Modigliani-Miller type of argument to suggest that issuing risk-free deposits or equity-linked insurance contracts as well as equity will not change the results. Similarly, financing the intermediaries by using debt as well as equity will not make a difference. For the moment, suppose the intermediaries are essentially like mutual funds, which issue equity to purchase equity. There are constant returns to scale up to a maximum size. There is free entry, and this maximum size is such that there are many intermediaries and the market is competitive. At date 0, the intermediaries issue equity to investors. They use the funds obtained to purchase the firms from entrepreneurs initially and to provide the funds for investment after the managers have made an investment decision.

If the discount rates the managers use are the same as in proposition 7.3, the production decisions will be the same. By holding the stocks of the intermediaries, investors are able to hold the market portfolio. Given the CAPM framework assumed, this is optimal for them, and it follows from the mutual fund theorem, proposition 7.2, which shows it is optimal to hold some combination of the market portfolio and the risk-free asset. The investors' portfolio holdings will be identical to the stock market economy, where all firms are listed separately.

Having seen how resources are allocated in the case where the intermediaries are mutual funds, it is straightforward to extend the result. Changing the form of the intermediary will not alter the result, provided the financing of the intermediaries and firms does not alter risk-sharing opportunities. For example, if the intermediaries are banks and issue risk-free deposits as well as equity to finance themselves, then a Modigliani-Miller type of argument ensures that the allocation of resources is the same as in the stock market economy. Since there is a risk-free asset, investors will simply substitute deposits for the risk-free asset or vice versa. Similarly, if an insurance company issues an equity-based asset, there will be no change in the allocation. Since everybody's overall portfolio is some combination of the risk-free asset and the market portfolio, this equity-based asset will simply be held by everybody in the right ratio so that it constitutes part of the market portfolio. A similar result will hold if the firms finance themselves by debt and equity rather than using only equity.

The crucial issue raised by proposition 7.5 is how managers have enough information to find the discount rate Er_j appropriate to their industry. In a stock market economy, the necessary information is provided by the market in a readily accessible form. The risk-free rate r_F can be found from the bond market. Historical data can be used to estimate $Er_M - r_F$ and β_j. In an intermediated economy, r_F can again be found from the bond market. The information concerning $Er_M - r_F$ and $Var(r_M)$ can be obtained from the stock prices of the intermediaries. Since the intermediaries are effectively like mutual funds and together hold the market portfolio, it is possible to use historical data on their returns to estimate Er_M and $Var(r_M)$. This can be done in the same way as in the full stock market economy, except that the number of stocks will be much fewer. It is interesting to note that in a study of U.S. stock prices from 1802 to 1987, Schwert (1990) found that the mean and standard deviation of returns were remarkably stable through time despite the fact that the number of stocks increased from twelve bank stocks at the start to over fifteen hundred, representing a broad range of industries, by the end of the period.

The most difficult task is to calculate $Cov(r_M, r_j)$, which together with $Var(r_M)$ can be used to find β_j. A historical series of r_M can be found from the stock market. The main problem is to find a series of r_j. Since there are no stock market data available for the industry, internally generated data must be used instead. The managers should use accounting data to calculate the amount generated for owners, that is, the free cash flow, in each period and work out the return r_j this corresponds to. This data series can then be used for the stock market returns r_j and hence β_j, and the appropriate discount rate Er_j can be found. It is an empirical issue how good the estimates of the β_j's obtained in this way are compared to those obtained from stock market data. However, at least in theory, both a stock market economy and an intermediated economy can do equally well.

An Economy Dominated by Family Firms

In a third type of economy, which we call a family-dominated economy, it is assumed that a few families own all the wealth, and there is a competitive bond market that determines the risk-free rate. The main change is that there is now no stock market at all. However, there is a primary market at date 0 where the wealthy families can buy whole firms. The families then make their investment decisions and receive the payoffs from the firms they own. This is again an idealized case. However, it can be thought of as corresponding to some emerging countries' financial systems, such as some of those in Latin America where wealth is very unequally distributed and financial intermediaries and markets are undeveloped.

PROPOSITION 7.6 Provided the firms' managers have enough information to find Er_M, can calculate the CAPM discount rate Er_j, and maximize NPV using this discount rate, the allocation of resources will be the same as with a stock market where every firm is listed, as in proposition 7.3.

The point here is that even if there is no active stock market, privately held firms can allow their owners to hold a share of the market portfolio through diversification across the most important industries of the economy. This result follows in the same way as proposition 7.5. Instead of buying the market portfolio by purchasing intermediaries in the limited stock market, the families must buy the market portfolio in the primary equity market. Just as before, all the families will end up with some combination of the market portfolio and the risk-free asset.

The key issue is again how the managers can obtain the information needed to find the discount rate. In the stock market economy, all the historical information required was provided by the market. In the intermediated economy, stock market data could be used to find r_M and Er_M, but internally generated data had to be used to find β_j and hence Er_j. The family-dominated economy requires that everything except the risk-free rate r_F be found internally. If there is enough internally generated information on the returns to individual divisions within the family-owned enterprise, this may be possible in principle, but the difficulty of putting it into practice could be substantial.

Assessing the Value of the CAPM

As far as the decentralization of decisions from shareholders to managers is concerned, the results are similar in the three cases considered. Shareholders only need to instruct managers to maximize NPV; they do not need to convey information about their preferences or their discount rates. Managers can obtain the historical information they need to estimate the CAPM and find appropriate discount rates from financial markets or internally. It is a practical issue as to which provides the best estimates for decision making. As far as decentralization within the firm is concerned, the institutional frameworks are not identical. In the case of the stock market and intermediated economies, it is possible to decentralize without having information flows between the head office and the divisions. The necessary information can be obtained from markets or within the division. In the family-dominated economy, this is not the case. The head office and divisions will need to communicate so that information about the returns on the market portfolio can be disseminated throughout the organization.

The asset pricing model focused on here is the CAPM. There are, of course, many other asset-pricing models, such as Ross's (1976) APT and, more recently, Fama and French's (1993) three-factor model. Although these pricing models may have advantages empirically, they are not as attractive theoretically. The CAPM provides a theory of decentralization where, at least in the form assumed above, it is optimal for shareholders to tell managers to maximize NPV. In other asset-pricing contexts, it is not clear that this is a sensible strategy for shareholders to follow.

This section has ignored the agency problem of how shareholders ensure that managers maximize NPV rather than pursue their own aims. Solving the agency problem in capital budgeting decisions is a very important but relatively underexplored topic. Early analyses of the intrafirm allocation of resources when there are information and incentive problems are provided by Harris, Kriebel, and Raviv (1982), Antle and Eppen (1985), Holmstrom and Ricart i Costa (1986), and Thakor (1990). They showed that a variety of constraints on division managers such as transfer pricing and capital rationing can help to overcome the agency problem. More recently, Harris and Raviv (1996, 1998) and Stein (1997) have developed models of the agency problem that explain many of the features of capital budgeting processes that are actually observed in practice. These include initial spending limits and the back-and-forth negotiations to verify division managers' claims as well as "picking-the-winner," where the head office intervenes directly in the allocation of funds. Narayanan (1985) and Berkovitch and Israel (1997) have provided theories to explain the optimality of capital budgeting techniques that are *not* equivalent to maximizing NPV.

Finally, we cannot overemphasize the restrictiveness of the CAPM model. One reason that it is possible to implement the capital budgeting methodology in various institutional settings is that the information called for by the CAPM is relatively limited. This follows from the restrictive assumptions of the CAPM itself, not least the assumption that everyone agrees about the true distribution for each random variable. With diversity of opinion, informational problems can be much more complex, however, and this may be the reason that different institutional structures matter. We return to these issues in chapter 13.

7.3 Informational Efficiency, Investment, and Risk Sharing

The third important role of prices is as aggregators of information. One of the questions that received considerable attention in the 1960s and 1970s is the extent to which stock markets are informationally efficient and reflect the available information. The notion implicit in much of this research is that if stock prices were informationally efficient, they would provide a good mechanism for allocating investment resources, a view well exposited by Fama (1976, p. 133): "An efficient capital market is an important component of a capitalist system. In such a system, the ideal is a market where prices are accurate signals for capital allocation. That is, when firms issue securities to finance their activities they can expect to get 'fair' prices, and when investors choose among the securities that represent ownership of firms' activities, they can do so under the assumption they are paying 'fair' prices. In short, if the capital market is to function smoothly in allocating resources, prices of securities must be good indicators of value."

Extensive evidence was provided during the 1960s and 1970s that markets are efficient in the sense that investors pay "fair" prices, and it is not possible to make excess returns above the reward for bearing risk using information that is publicly available. This is termed *semistrong form efficiency.* There was some evidence that even using information that is apparently private, it is not possible to make excess returns. This is termed *strong-form efficiency*. More recently, studies have not been as supportive. (For surveys of the empirical literature on efficient markets, see Fama 1970, 1991, and Hawawini and Keim 1995.)

Grossman (1976) developed a theoretical model to show how private signals obtained by investors could become incorporated in prices so that apparently private information became public. If an investor has favorable information, he will buy the security and bid up its price; if he has unfavorable information, he will sell it and bid down the price. Grossman was able to show that under certain conditions, prices aggregate all the economically relevant private information. This result provides a theoretical underpinning for the notion of prices as aggregators of information and led to a large literature on information revelation (Grossman and Stiglitz 1976, 1980, Hellwig 1980, Diamond and Verrecchia 1981; for surveys see Grossman 1981 and Admati 1989; an important more recent contribution is Jackson 1991).

The large number of publicly listed firms in the United States, together with extensive disclosure requirements, means that a great deal of information about firms' activities is released. In addition to this publicly available information, many analysts work for mutual funds, pension funds, and other intermediaries and gather private information. The empirical evidence on efficient markets suggests that much of this information is reflected in stock prices. Taken together, this can be interpreted as evidence that U.S. stock markets do an effective job of allocating resources efficiently.

On the other hand, in some countries, such as Germany and other continental European countries, relatively few companies are listed, and accounting disclosure requirements are limited, so very little information is publicly available. In addition, the number of analysts that follow stocks is small, so only limited private information is incorporated in prices. The implication would appear to be that the financial systems in these countries do a poor job of allocating resources compared to the United States.

As we have argued in this chapter, however, there may be substitutes for the information revealed by prices, in which case the mere existence of more price data in the United States may not be a decisive point in favor of a market-oriented system. On the other hand, there is a cost to having stocks publicly quoted. There is considerable evidence that U.S. stock prices are very volatile. The traditional explanation for this volatility is the arrival of new information about payoff streams and discount rates (see Fama 1970 and Merton 1987), although it may also result from the uninformative activity of "noise" traders, that is, traders who are irrational or are motivated by liquidity motives. The volatility of stock prices can cause considerable variability in the consumption of investors who liquidate stocks to finance their consumption. If investors are risk averse, noisy consumption is clearly undesirable.

In a well-known paper Hirshleifer (1971) pointed out that the release of information could destroy valuable risk-sharing opportunities. Allen (1983) and Laffont (1985) investigated this in the context of security markets and showed that more information could make people worse off because the added price volatility increases consumption variability. Jacklin and Bhattacharya (1988) showed that bank deposits can be more desirable than equity mutual funds for similar reasons.

In this section, we investigate the trade-off between the value of information as a guide to resource allocation and its harmful effects on risk sharing. In financial systems like Germany's, few companies are publicly quoted and little information is revealed by the companies that are. This lack of information, which may be bad from the point of view of efficient decision making, may be a good thing from the point of view of risk sharing.

A Representative Agent Model

Suppose there are two dates and a single good that can be used for investment or consumption at each date. There is assumed to be a large number of economic agents, who can be thought of as entrepreneurs, each of whom has an endowment $e > 0$ of the consumption good at the first date and none at the second. The endowment of the good can either be consumed or used as an input to a risky production process. Let c denote first-period consumption and k investment in production, so the entrepreneur's budget constraint is

$$c + k = e.$$

The entrepreneur's output in the second period is

$$y = \theta f(k),$$

where $f(k)$ is a neoclassical production function satisfying $f'(k) > 0$ and $f''(k) < 0$ for all k and $\theta \geq 0$ is a common productivity shock, which is a random variable with mean $E[\theta]$ and $Var[\theta] > 0$. Each entrepreneur has some private information about the productivity of the production process. The private signal received by entrepreneur i is

$$\theta_i = \theta + \varepsilon_i,$$

where ε_i is an independently and identically distributed error term with $E[\varepsilon_i] = 0$ and $Var[\varepsilon_i] > 0$. Suppose that $u(c)$ is the period utility function and that it satisfies $u'(c) > 0$ and $u''(c) < 0$. The entrepreneur solves the following decision problem:

$$\max_{c,k} \quad u(c) + E[u(\theta f(k))|\Phi_i]$$

$$\text{s.t.} \quad c + k = e,$$

where Φ_i is entrepreneur i's information set.

Informational Autarky

As a benchmark, consider the case in which agents make their investment decisions simultaneously, without observing one another's actions, so each entrepreneur's decision can only be based on his private signal θ_i.

The first-order condition for the decision problem, which is necessary and sufficient for the solution, is

$$u'(e - k) = E[u'(\theta f(k))\theta f'(k)|\theta_i].$$

This equation uniquely determines the optimal value of k as a function of θ_i.

Clearly the agent is better off having the information about θ_i because it allows him to make a better decision. This is true even if he is risk averse. The result follows from a revealed preference argument. For any choice of k and any value of θ_i

$$u(e - K_A(\theta_i)) + E[u(\theta f(K_A(\theta_i))|\theta_i] \geq u(e - k) + E[u(\theta f(k)|\theta_i],$$

where $K_A(\theta_i)$ is the optimal choice conditional on θ_i (the A stands for "autarky"). Suppose an entrepreneur were to ignore his signal and just choose some value of k irrespective of θ_i. Taking expectations of both sides of the previous expression with regard to θ_i, it follows that for any choice of k,

$$E[u(e - K_A(\theta_i)) + u(\theta f(K_A(\theta_i))] > u(e - k) + E[u(\theta f(k)].$$

The inequality is strict because u and f are strictly concave and $Var[\theta]$ and $Var[\varepsilon_i]$ are both positive. The entrepreneur is better off using the information.

Rational Expectations Equilibrium

In the previous subsection each agent acted independently. Now suppose that there exists a stock market. Entrepreneurs can invest part of their endowment in the market and raise funds for their productive activity from the market. At first sight, it might seem that such a market would be redundant since every entrepreneur can self-finance. In fact this is not the case. The market plays an important role because its equilibrium return on equity aggregates the entrepreneurs' information so they can all make better investment decisions. Let r be the return on equity—that is, one unit of the good today is exchanged for a promise to pay r units tomorrow.

Suppose for the moment that θ is known (in equilibrium, it will be revealed by the market price). The decision problem of the representative entrepreneur is

$$\max_{c,b,k} \quad u(c) + u(\theta f(k) - r(k-b))$$

$$\text{s.t.} \quad c + b = e,$$

where b is the amount invested in the stock market. Market clearing in the stock market requires that

$$k = b,$$

and the budget constraint implies that $c = b - k$. An equilibrium therefore consists of the investment $k = K_I(\theta)$ and return on capital $r = R_I(\theta)$, where I stands for the "informative" equilibrium, such that $(c, b, k) = (e - K_I(\theta), K_I(\theta), K_I(\theta))$ solves the decision problem above for each value of θ.

Since agents observe only their private signal and the return $r = R_I(\theta)$, they will know θ only if $R_I(\theta)$ is a sufficient statistic for θ, that is, if $R_I(\theta)$ is monotonically increasing or decreasing. We assume this in what follows. Then the ordered pair $(R_I(\theta), K_I(\theta))$ is a rational expectations equilibrium (REE) relative to the initial information structure: $R_I(\theta)$ is sufficient for θ, so all the information is revealed by the equilibrium return function. Conversely, since there is a large number of agents, the private signals $\{\theta_i\}$ are sufficient for θ, so the return function $R_I(\theta)$ does not contain more information than is possessed by the agents collectively.

The agents are better off in an REE than they were in informational autarky. Since θ is more informative than θ_i in the sense of Blackwell (i.e., θ_i equals θ plus "noise"), they are able to make better decisions. For any values of θ and θ_i

$$u(e - K_I(\theta)) + u(\theta f(K_I(\theta))) \geq u(e - K_A(\theta_i)) + u(\theta f(K_A(\theta_i))),$$

so integrating over θ and θ_i we have (using the strict concavity of u and f and the positive variances of θ and ε_i),

$$E[u(e - K_I(\theta)) + u(\theta f(K_I(\theta))] > E[u(e - K_A(\theta_i)) + u(\theta f(K_A(\theta_i))].$$

In fact the REE equilibrium implements the first best allocation, so there is no conflict between risk sharing and allocative efficiency.

This last result is true only because there is a single representative agent. There are no potential gains from risk sharing because the REE eliminates the asymmetric information associated with private signals. In the next subsection, we distinguish two types of agents and analyze the optimality of risk sharing between them.

Before turning to that topic, however, we note that the optimal risk sharing studied here could be implemented by a variety of institutional arrangements. We have explicitly discussed the way in which an economy with a capital market achieves optimal risk sharing, but the same could be done by a competitive banking system. If banks took deposits from producers and relent them to producers at the same interest rate, the demand for loans and supply of deposits would determine the equilibrium return, which would also reveal the true state of the world. In this case, the intermediaries are merely performing the role of markets in a different guise.

The results of this section can be summarized in the following.

PROPOSITION 7.7 The REE equilibrium in a stock market or in a bank loan market implements the first best allocation. There is full allocative efficiency, and risk sharing is optimal since there is only type of agent.

Inefficiency with Heterogeneous Agents

Suppose now that there are two types of agents, investors and producers. Investors have an endowment e of the good in the first period and none in the second. They maximize the expected utility of consumption $v(c) + v(c')$, where c is present consumption, c' is future consumption, and v is the period utility function. The producers have no endowment, but can raise capital on the market to invest in production as before. For simplicity, it is assumed that they consume only in the second period.

Let r be the return demanded on capital, and suppose that a representative producer knows the true value of θ. Her decision problem is

$$\max_k \theta f(k) - rk,$$

for which the necessary and sufficient condition is

$$\theta f'(k) = r.$$

The investors solve the decision problem

$$\max_{c,b} \quad v(c) + v(rb)$$

$$\text{s.t.} \quad c + b = e,$$

for which the necessary and sufficient condition is

$$v'(e-b) = v'(rb)r.$$

Using the market-clearing condition $k = b$, we can combine the two first-order conditions to get

$$\theta f'(k) = r = \frac{v'(e-k)}{v'(rk)}.$$

Any solution to these equations is a competitive equilibrium for the economy, for a given value of θ, though it is not necessarily unique. Let $(K_H(\theta), R_H(\theta))$ denote a solution pair, where H stands for the "heterogeneous" equilibrium. Then $(K_H(\theta), R_H(\theta))$ is an REE if $R_H(\theta)$ is monotonically increasing or decreasing in θ, as we shall assume.

The welfare properties of this REE are quite different from those of the REE with a single representative agent. Although information revelation still leads to an ex post optimal allocation of investment, the uncertainty generated by the revelation of θ imposes risk on both agents that may not be optimal ex ante. In fact we can show the following.

PROPOSITION 7.8 If $f(k) = k$, $K_H'(\theta) < 0$, and the producers are risk neutral, the REE equilibrium is Pareto inferior to the equilibrium with no information.

Proof The ex ante expected utility of the representative producer in the REE equilibrium is

$$E[u(\theta f(K_H(\theta)) - R_H(\theta)K_H(\theta))],$$

and the expected utility of the representative investor is

$$E[v(e - K_H(\theta)) + v(R_H(\theta)K_H(\theta))].$$

When the production function is linear, that is, $f(k) \equiv k$, then

$$R(\theta) \equiv \theta,$$

and the producer's profit is

$$\theta f(K_H(\theta)) - R_H(\theta)K_H(\theta) = \theta K_H(\theta) - \theta K_H(\theta) = 0$$

for all θ. The investor's expected utility is

$$\begin{aligned} E[v(e - K_H(\theta)) + v(R_H(\theta)K_H(\theta))] &= E[v(e - K_H(\theta)) + v(\theta K_H(\theta))] \\ &< v(e - E[K_H(\theta)]) + v(E[\theta K_H(\theta)]) \\ &< v(e - E[K_H(\theta)]) + v(E[\theta]E[K_H(\theta)]) \end{aligned} \tag{7.3}$$

where the first inequality follows from the concavity of $v(c)$, that is, Jensen's inequality, and the second inequality follows from the fact that $E[\theta K_H(\theta)] < E[\theta]E[K_H(\theta)]$ since $K_H(\theta)$ is decreasing.

Now consider an equilibrium in which there is no information about the realization of θ. Since the representative producer is risk neutral, her objective function is

$$E[\theta k - rk].$$

Choosing k to maximize this implies that the equilibrium return on capital must satisfy $r = E[\theta]$ and the producer's expected profits are 0. When $\theta < r = E[\theta]$ the producer makes a loss, and when $\theta > r = E[\theta]$ she makes a profit. On average they cancel out.

The equilibrium choice of the investor must solve

$$\max_{c,b} \quad v(c) + v(E[\theta]b)$$
$$\text{s.t.} \quad c + b = e.$$

as before, but there is now no risk for the investor, since his return is fixed independent of the realization of θ. In fact, comparing his expected utility in the REE with his expected utility in the equilibrium with no information, we see, using equation 7.3, that

$$E[v(e - K_H(\theta)) + v(R_H(\theta)K_H(\theta))] < v(e - E[K_H(\theta)]) + v(E[\theta]E[K_H(\theta)])$$
$$\leq \max_b \{v(e - b) + v(E[\theta]b)\}.$$

Since the producer is indifferent between the two equilibria, the REE equilibrium is Pareto inferior to the equilibrium without information.

Note the three assumptions that are needed to prove this result:

- The production technology is linear, so there are no profits for the producer in the REE.
- The investment in the REE declines as productivity rises, so the investor is getting negative insurance in the REE.
- The producer is risk neutral, so there are no expected profits for the producer in the equilibrium without information, and the investor can shift all the risk to the producer.

The first and third assumptions are standard and need no discussion. The second assumption requires that as the rate of return earned by the investor goes up, the amount saved goes down. This arises naturally in many examples of utility functions as a result of an income effect. As the rate of return increases, the investor is better off and so is able to consume more in the early period. Consider as an illustration the family of utility functions with constant relative risk aversion:

$$v(c) = \frac{1}{1+\alpha} c^{1+\alpha}.$$

Then $K_H(\theta)$ solves

$$\max_k \left\{ \frac{1}{1+\alpha}(e-k)^{1+\alpha} + \frac{1}{1+\alpha}(\theta k)^{1+\alpha} \right\}.$$

The necessary and sufficient condition for a solution is

$$(e-k)^{\alpha} = (\theta k)^{1+\alpha}\theta,$$

which implies

$$e = k(1 + \theta^{\gamma}),$$

where $\gamma = 1 + \frac{1}{\alpha}$. Note that $\gamma > 0$ if and only if $\alpha < -1$ and that the right-hand side is increasing in θ if and only if $\gamma > 0$. Thus, $K_H(\theta)$ is decreasing if and only if $\alpha < -1$.

In general, this result suggests that the uninformative equilibrium is likely to be better from a welfare economics perspective if:

• The producer is not gaining from the information revealed in the REE (because her profits are low) and

• The investor is not gaining from the information revealed in the REE (because his allocation depends on θ in a way that provides negative insurance) and

• The allocation of risk is close to optimal in the uninformative equilibrium (because the less risk-averse party is bearing most of the risk).

The proposition starkly demonstrates that there is no presumption that more information leads to a better outcome, even if that information is useful for productive efficiency. This has important implications for financial systems. It suggests that countries such as Germany and France, where accounting information about companies is not freely available and there are few analysts following companies, are not necessarily at a disadvantage compared to countries such as the United States and United Kingdom, where the reverse is true. Allocative efficiency is offset by the fact that investors bear a lot of risk.

In this section, we have not so far distinguished between stock markets and banks. As in the previous section, they are essentially equivalent. We now extend the model in order to gain some insight into how stock markets and banks aggregate information differently.

Many Industries

So far we have considered the case where producers have private information about a common productivity shock. In other words, we have been assuming there is only one industry. Now we consider the case where there are a number of different industries, and each industry has a different productivity shock. Ex ante it is unknown which are going to be the more productive industries and which the less productive. This situation imposes risk, and the issue is how to deal with it. As before, agents are either producers and investors, and production decisions are made by producers after information is revealed.

We simplify the analysis by eliminating aggregate risk. There is assumed to be a continuum of producers with unit measure in each industry. There is a continuum of industries that are indexed by their productivity θ_j. Specifically, each industry has a distinct value of θ_j drawn from the same continuous uniform distribution on the range 0 to $\overline{\theta}$. The law of large numbers ensures that the ex post cross-sectional distribution is the same as the ex ante probability distribution.

Suppose initially that each producer observes his own industry's value of θ_j and chooses k to solve the problem,

$$\max_k \theta_j f(k) - rk.$$

Then a producer in an industry with productivity parameter θ_j will choose $K(\theta_j, r)$, as before. Since the measure of entrepreneurs is 1, the total investment in the industry is $K(\theta_j, r)$. The total investment across industries will be

$$K(r) = \int K(\theta_j, r) d\theta_j.$$

Investors provide the capital as in the previous subsection. The return on capital r is determined by the equation

$$v'(e - K(r)) = v'(rK(r))r.$$

Since there is no ex ante aggregate uncertainty, r is determinate, and the investors face no risk. Their expected utility is

$$v(e - K(r)) + v(rK(r)).$$

The ex ante welfare of the producers in the industry with productivity θ is simply

$$E[u(\theta f(K(\theta, r)) - rK(\theta, r))].$$

Although the producers face uncertainty (and do not like it) there is no possibility of making them better off by suppressing information. As in the representative agent case, information can only help here. If information is suppressed, it will reduce welfare.

We next consider what happens if information is dispersed among producers and investors. We start with the case where it is dispersed among the producers. This is similar to the case considered in previous subsections. An entrepreneur i in industry j with productivity θ_j observes $\theta_{ji} = \theta_j + \varepsilon_i$ with the usual assumptions regarding ε_i. If there is a market for the stock of each of the entrepreneurs in the industry, then as before θ_j will be revealed and there will be allocational efficiency. A type θ_j producer could sell his profits on the market at a price q, say. If the sum of the agents' information is sufficient for θ_j and if θ_j is revealed by the price, then in a diversified economy we would have

$$rq = rQ(\theta_j) = \theta_j f(K(\theta_j, r)) - rK(\theta_j, r).$$

Since $Q'(\theta_j) > 0$ this price will in fact reveal the full information required to make the optimal investment $K(\theta_j, r)$.

Banks can perform the same task of information aggregation. Now, the sum of information in the industry is sufficient for θ_j and the demand for loans in the industry will be sufficient for θ_j, so if the bank can give this information back to the individual producers, by, for example, the bank's specifying the amount it is willing to loan to each producer, then full information will be revealed and every producer in the industry will choose $K(\theta_j, r)$.

In many situations, the producers may not have all the information that is necessary to make an optimal decision. Although producers may be expected to be well informed about some things, it is unlikely that they will have complete information, especially in the case of new industries or industries where lot of change is going on. One of the functions of the market is that it provides many individuals with an incentive to become informed and then put their private information to work in the market. The information from investors reflected in stock prices may be useful even to well-informed managers. To analyze this type of situation, we next focus on the case where associated with every producer there is an idiosyncratic shock $\theta_{ji} = \theta_j + \varepsilon_i$, but now instead of being observed by the entrepreneur, it is observed by investors.

If there is a stock market, then, just as in the case where producers possess the information about θ, the prices will be fully revealing. It does not matter which side of the market the information comes from. With a bank serving as the intermediary, it is no longer the case that the two are equivalent, however. Whereas a bank can conceivably observe the aggregate demand for loans in an industry (or equivalently its share of it), it cannot observe the aggregate supply to an industry. All banks will simply offer deposit accounts at rate r, and all deposits will be homogeneous. Hence, the information of investors will be lost in a financial system with banks, whereas it will be revealed in a stock market system. Thus, with different types of industry, informational efficiency depends on the particular institutional and informational structure.

Proposition 7.9 With many industries, each with a different productivity shock, the equivalence of a stock market and intermediated economy depends on who has the information. If producers have the information, the two are equivalent. If investors have the information, it will be revealed by a stock market but not by a banking system.

While in much of the rest of this chapter, stock market and intermediated economies have theoretically been equivalent, this is not the case here. The homogeneity of deposits in terms of their all paying the same rate of interest means that investors' information cannot be conveyed by a banking system, while it can be conveyed by a stock market.

Related Literature

There has been a large literature on the welfare properties of models where there is some form of "noise" or "liquidity" trading and prices are partially revealing. Much of this literature is concerned with the desirability of allowing insider trading. One view is that insider trading involves the informed benefiting at the expense of the uninformed. Another view is that insider trading is desirable because it leads to prices' being more informative, which improves the allocation of investment. (For a variety of positions and analyses of insider trading, see Glosten 1989, Manove 1989, Ausubel 1990, Fishman and Hagerty 1992, Leland 1992, Bernhardt, Hollifield, and Hughson 1995, and Bhattacharya and Nicodano 1995.)

Other authors have analyzed what happens when one group of traders is better informed than another, either because they have paid to acquire information or they are simply endowed with superior information. Bernardo and Judd (1997) analyze a version of the Grossman and Stiglitz (1980) model with pure exchange using numerical techniques and show that everybody would be better off without information. Dow and Rahi (1997) analyze a parametric model with investment in productive assets by firms. They derive closed-form solutions for all agents' utilities, and this allows a nice characterization of the trade-off between risk sharing and investment.

A third strand takes a security design approach to analyze the relationship between incomplete markets and information revelation. This literature has identified three effects of security design on welfare when agents are endowed with different information: spanning, adverse selection, and insurance destruction (i.e., the Hirshleifer effect). In general, welfare improves with spanning and is reduced with adverse selection and insurance destruction. Taking the number of assets as given, Rahi (1995) finds that it is constrained Pareto efficient to issue information-free securities as a way to minimize the adverse selection problem. Marín and Rahi (1998) generalize the analysis of the previous paper and show that under certain conditions, its main conclusion is reversed. In particular, they identify conditions on the primitives of the economy for which it is Pareto efficient to issue "speculative securities." These are securities whose payoff explicitly depends on private information sunspots (i.e., a random shock unrelated to endowments and preferences about which some agents have private information). Finally, Marín and Rahi (1997) consider the effect of endogenizing the number of assets in this type of model and build a theory of (endogenous) market incompleteness. They find that under certain conditions, the introduction of a new security makes all agents worse off because it provides new information that destroys insurance opportunities. The two devices these last two papers focus on—the incorporation of asymmetric information sunspots and the reduction of the number of tradable securities—inject noise in the price system in a way that less information is revealed and, consequently, fewer insurance opportunities are destroyed.

A fourth part of the literature considers the role of prices in inducing efficient investment in the context of financial systems. Jacklin and Bhattacharya (1988) compare the role of equity markets and bank deposit contracts in ensuring efficiency. They show that the desirability of each depends on the attributes of the underlying investments and the information available. Boot and Thakor (1997a, 1997b) compare various aspects of different financial systems. The important characteristic of financial markets in their models is that stock prices reveal information, and this is what differentiates them from banks. Their first paper analyzes the development of financial systems and shows that banks will predominate early in their history, while the informational advantages of markets may allow them to emerge subsequently. The second shows that financial innovation occurs more with separated commercial and investment banking than with universal banking. Subrahmanyam and Titman (1999) are interested in the development of financial systems and also characterize stock markets by the information revelation of prices. They show that there can be interesting interactions between information that is acquired fortuitously by investors and information that is paid for. Similarly to Pagano (1993), it is shown that with a fixed cost for investors to participate in primary equity markets, a high-participation equilibrium with many new issues and a low-participation equilibrium with few new issues can both exist.

Finally, a number of papers consider the feedback role of stock prices in providing incentives when there is an agency problem between shareholders and managers. Holmstrom and Tirole (1993) consider how compensation contracts can be conditioned on stock prices to give effort incentives. Dow and Gorton (1997) consider how good investment incentives can be provided to managers when stock prices contain information managers do not have.

References

Admati, A. (1989). "Information in Financial Markets: The Rational Expectations Approach." In S. Bhattacharya and G. M. Constantinides (eds.), *Financial Markets and Incomplete Information: Frontiers of Modern Financial Theory* (Vol. 2, pp. 139–152). Totowa, NJ: Rowman and Littlefield.

Allen, F. (1983). "A Normative Analysis of Informational Efficiency in Markets for Risky Assets." Working paper, Nuffield College, Oxford.

Antle, R., and G. D. Eppen. (1985). "Capital Rationing and Organizational Slack in Capital Budgeting." *Management Science* **31,** 163–174.

Ausubel, L. M. (1990). "Insider Trading in a Rational Expectations Economy." *American Economic Review* **80,** 759–776.

Berkovitch, E., and R. Israel. (1997). "To NPV or Not to NPV: Why Net Present Value Leads to *WORSE* Capital Budgeting Decisions Than Other Criteria." Working paper, University of Michigan.

Bernardo, A. E., and K. L. Judd. (1997). "Efficiency of Asset Markets with Asymmetric Information." Working paper, UCLA.

Bernhardt, D., B. Hollifield, and E. Hughson. (1995). "Investment and Insider Trading." *Review of Financial Studies* **8,** 501–543.

Bhattacharya, S., and G. Nicodano. (1995). "Insider Trading, Investment, and Welfare: A Perturbation Analysis." Working paper, London School of Economics.

Black, F. (1972). "Capital Market Equilibrium with Restricted Borrowing." *Journal of Business* **45,** 444–454.

Boot, A., and A. Thakor. (1997a). "Financial System Architecture." *Review of Financial Studies* **10,** 693–733.

———. (1997b). "Banking Scope and Financial Innovation." *Review of Financial Studies* **10,** 1099–1131.

Brealey, R., and S. Myers. (1996). *Principles of Corporate Finance.* 5th ed. New York: McGraw-Hill.

Diamond, P. (1967). "The Role of a Stock Market in a General Equilibrium Model with Technological Uncertainty." *American Economic Review* **57,** 759–776.

Diamond, D., and R. Verrecchia. (1981). "Information Aggregation in a Noisy Rational Expectations Economy." *Journal of Financial Economics* **9,** 221–235.

Dow, J., and G. Gorton. (1997). "Stock Market Efficiency and Economic Efficiency: Is There a Connection?" *Journal of Finance* **52,** 1087–1129.

Dow, J., and R. Rahi. (1997). "Informed Trading, Investment, and Welfare." Working Paper 97/3, European University Institute.

Fama, E. F. (1965). "The Behavior of Stock Market Prices." *Journal of Business* **38,** 34–105.

———. (1970). "Efficient Capital Markets: A Review of Theory and Empirical Work." *Journal of Finance* **35,** 383–417.

———. (1976). *Foundations of Finance.* New York: Basic Books.

———. (1991). "Efficient Capital Markets, II." *Journal of Finance* **46,** 1575–1617.

Fama, E. F., and K. French. (1993). "Common Risk Factors in the Returns on Stocks and Bonds." *Journal of Financial Economics* **33,** 3–56.

Fama E., and J. MacBeth. (1973). "Risk, Return, and Equilibrium: Empirical Tests," *Journal of Political Economy* **81,** 607–636.

Fama, E. F., and M. Miller. (1972). *The Theory of Finance.* New York: Holt, Rinehart and Winston.

Ferson, W. (1995). "Theory and Empirical Testing of Asset Pricing Models." In R. A. Jarrow, V. Maksimovic, and W. T. Ziemba (eds.), *Handbooks in Operations Research and Management Science, Vol. 9: Finance* (pp. 145–200). Amsterdam: North-Holland.

Fishman, M., and K. Hagerty. (1992). "Insider Trading and the Efficiency of Stock Prices." *Rand Journal of Economics* **23,** 106–122.

Geanakoplos, J., and M. Shubik. (1990). "The Capital Asset Pricing Model as a General Equilibrium with Incomplete Markets." *Geneva Papers on Risk and Insurance Theory* **15,** 55–72.

Glassman, D. (1997). "Contracting for Value: EVA® and the Economics of Organizations." *Journal of Applied Corporate Finance* **10,** 110–123.

Glosten, L. (1989). "Insider Trading, Liquidity, and the Role of the Monopolist Specialist." *Journal of Business* **62,** 211–235.

Grossman, S. (1976). "On the Efficiency of Competitive Stock Markets Where Traders Have Diverse Information." *Journal of Finance* **31,** 573–585.

———. (1981). "An Introduction to the Theory of Rational Expectations Under Asymmetric Information." *Review of Economic Studies* **48,** 541–549.

Grossman, S., and J. Stiglitz. (1976). "Information and Competitive Price Systems." *American Economic Review* **66,** 246–253.

Grossman, S., and J. Stiglitz. (1980). "On the Impossibility of Informationally Efficient Markets." *American Economic Review* **70,** 393–408.

Harris, M., C. Kriebel, and A. Raviv. (1982). "Asymmetric Information, Incentives, and Intrafirm Resource Allocation." *Management Science* **28,** 604–620.

Harris, M., and A. Raviv. (1996). "The Capital Budgeting Process, Incentives and Information." *Journal of Finance* **51,** 1139–1174.

——. (1998). "Capital Budgeting and Delegation." *Journal of Financial Economics* **50,** 259–289.

Hawawini, G., and D. Keim. (1995). "On the Predictability of Common Stock Returns: World-Wide Evidence." In R. A. Jarrow, V. Maksimovic, and W. T. Ziemba (eds.), *Handbooks in Operations Research and Management Science, Volume 9: Finance* (pp. 497–544). Amsterdam: North-Holland.

Hellwig, M. (1980). "On the Aggregation of Information in Competitive Markets." *Journal of Economic Theory* **22,** 477–498.

Hirshleifer, J. (1971). "The Private and Social Value of Information and the Reward to Inventive Activity." *American Economic Review* **61,** 561–574.

Holmstrom, B., and J. Ricart i Costa. (1986). "Managerial Incentives and Capital Management." *Quarterly Journal of Economics* **101,** 835–860.

Holmstrom, B., and J. Tirole. (1993). "Market Liquidity and Performance Monitoring." *Journal of Political Economy* **101,** 678–709.

Ingersoll, J., Jr. (1987). *Theory of Financial Decision Making.* Totowa, NJ: Rowman and Littlefield.

Jacklin, C., and S. Bhattacharya. (1988). "Distinguishing Panics and Information-Based Bank Runs: Welfare and Policy Implications." *Journal of Political Economy* **96,** 568–592.

Jackson, M. (1991). "Equilibrium, Price Formation, and the Value of Private Information." *Review of Financial Studies* **4,** 1–16.

Laffont, J. (1985). "On the Welfare Analysis of Rational Expectations Equilibria with Asymmetric Information." *Econometrica* **53,** 1–29.

Leland, H. (1992). "Insider Trading: Should It Be Prohibited?" *Journal of Political Economy* **100,** 859–887.

Magill, M., and M. Quinzii. (1996). *Theory of Incomplete Markets.* Cambridge, MA: MIT Press.

——. (1998). "Equity, Bonds Growth and Inflation in a Quadratic Infinite Horizon Economy." Working paper, University of Southern California.

Manove, M. (1989). "The Harm from Insider Trading and Informed Speculation." *Quarterly Journal of Economics* **104,** 823–845.

Marín, J., and R. Rahi. (1997). "Information Revelation and Market Incompleteness." Working paper, London School of Economics.

——. (1998). "Speculative Securities." Working paper, London School of Economics.

Merton, R. (1987). "On the Current State of the Stock Market Rationality Hypothesis." In R. Dornbusch, S. Fischer, and S. Bossons (eds.), *Macroeconomics and Finance: Essays in Honor of Franco Modigliani.* Cambridge, MA: MIT Press.

Narayanan, M. (1985). "Observability and the Payback Criterion." *Journal of Business* **58,** 309–323.

Pagano, M. (1993). "The Flotation of Companies on the Stock Market: A Coordination Failure Model." *European Economic Review* **37,** 1101–1125.

Rahi, R. (1995). "Optimal Incomplete Markets with Asymmetric Information." *Journal of Economic Theory* **65,** 171–197.

Ross, S. (1976). "The Arbitrage Theory of Capital Asset Pricing." *Journal of Economic Theory* **13,** 341–360.

Ross, S., R. Westerfield, and J. Jaffe. (1996). *Corporate Finance.* 4th ed., Chicago: Irwin.

Schwert, G. W. (1990). "Indexes of U.S. Stock Prices from 1802–1987." *Journal of Business* **63,** 399–426.

Stein, J. (1997). "Internal Capital Markets and the Competition for Corporate Resources." *Journal of Finance* **52,** 111–133.

Stern, J., G. Stewart III, and D. Chew, Jr. (1995). "The EVA® Financial Management System." *Journal of Applied Corporate Finance* **8,** 32–46.

Subrahmanyam, A., and S. Titman. (1999). "The Going Public Decision and the Development of Financial Markets." *Journal of Finance* **54,** 1045–1082.

Thakor, A. (1990). "Investment 'Myopia' and the Internal Organization of Capital Allocation Decisions." *Journal of Law, Economics and Organization* **6,** 129–154.

8 Competition in Banking

8.1 Attitudes toward Competition

The genius of American banking is competition. And the more competition the better. You look at every other major country and they only have a handful of banks that account for most of the business.

—William Proxmire, chairman of the United States Senate Banking Committee, 1986

As the historical comparison of different countries' financial systems in chapter 2 illustrated, the development of the banking sector in the United States differed from that of other industrialized countries. The United States has a history of promoting competition in all sectors of the economy, and in the financial sector, the support for competition has been particularly vigorous. Distrust of power in the hands of large financial institutions very early led to restrictions on the ability of banks to expand geographically or to diversify into other activities. Subsequent perceived abuses led to the Glass-Steagall Act of 1933, which separated commercial and investment banking. Financial markets have been closely regulated by the SEC from its foundation in 1933 to maintain competition, and the Justice Department has been vigilant in preserving competition in the banking sector using antitrust policy.

In other countries, including those with market-oriented systems and those with bank-oriented systems, the banking sectors became highly concentrated many years ago. For example, in England banks developed nationwide networks during the latter part of the nineteenth century, so that by the beginning of the twentieth century, there were essentially only five major banks. Other industrialized countries also experienced consolidation and the development of nationwide networks

Table 8.1
International comparison of banking concentration[a]

Country	Number of commercial banks	Population per bank	Three-firm concentration ratio (%)
France	425	135,365	63.6
Germany	330	245,379	89.5
Japan	150	831,760	28.3
United Kingdom	491	118,328	29.1
United States	10,971	23,508	13.3

a. The percentage of total banking system assets accounted for by the three largest banks.
Source: Barth, Nolle, and Rice (1997, table 3).

around this time. In many cases, governments actively encouraged this change. Table 8.1 shows the number of commercial banks, the population per bank, and the three-firm concentration ratio in 1993 in France, Germany, Japan, the United Kingdom, and the United States. The table shows the dramatic differences in concentration that have resulted from their different historical experiences. The United States has many more banks, less population per bank, and a much lower concentration ratio than any of the other countries.

Why have there been such different views on the desirability of different banking structures historically? What are the trade-offs between competition and concentration? What is the optimal degree of competition? These questions have been given some urgency because of moves toward increased competition in the European Union (EU) and Japan. The EU has committed to remove barriers across banking markets in order to have a completely integrated banking market on both the demand and supply sides (see Cerasi, Chizzolini, and Ivaldi 1997). In Japan one of the underlying principles of the "Big Bang" financial reform is to increase competition in the financial sector.

The traditional (U.S.) view is that competition is a good thing in any industry, and behind this view is the assumption that competition in the banking sector is just like competition in any other industry. The economic arguments in favor of competition have mostly been transplanted from the industrial organization literature (see, e.g., Alhadeff 1954, Fischer 1968, Rhoades 1982, Gilbert 1984, Freixas and Rochet 1997). It is argued that competition ensures that costs are minimized and the prices of banking services are such that resources are allocated efficiently. In other words, competition promotes efficiency and shares the benefits of the financial system with the rest of the economy. On the other hand, concentration allows banks to operate inefficiently and to exploit other sectors of the economy.

The literature on efficiency in banking is vast; most of it has focused on issues of X-inefficiency, efficient scale of production, and so forth and does not treat the banking industry as different from any other industry (see, e.g., Berger and Mester 1997 for a survey and Berger, Leusner, and Mingo 1997 for a recent empirical study). Banks are assumed to have a production technology and an efficient frontier like any other firm or industry. The crucial question is whether the assumptions of the standard models of competition are appropriate for the banking sector.

To the extent that there are economies of scale in banking and other financial services, concentration may be necessary to achieve the benefits of large-scale operation. Similarly, concentration may be necessary for Schumpeterian reasons to promote investment in new technologies. But on balance, the arguments in favor of competition seem to have won the day.

So the question arises why other countries have taken such a different path in the past with respect to competition in the banking sector. A related question is what should be done in the future. Are the moves in the EU and Japan toward more competition desirable? Is the consolidation in the U.S. banking industry likely to lead to an improvement? In this chapter we consider some of the limitations of the arguments in favor of (perfect) competition in banking and suggest that the less competitive organization of the banking sector found in other countries may have some advantages.

The traditional economic rationale for competition in banking appears to be borrowed from the industrial organization (IO) literature. Well-known models of imperfect competition have been used to show how profit-maximizing firms can exploit their market power to increase profits by restricting output and raising prices. More precisely, when the number of competing firms is small, output is below the perfectly competitive level, and prices are above the perfectly competitive level, with a consequent loss of consumer and producer surplus. By contrast, as the number of firms grows without bound, it can be shown that under certain conditions the market equilibrium converges to perfect competition. Translating these findings from manufacturing industries to the financial sector, it is argued, large numbers of competing banks are needed to ensure efficiency. If banks acquire market power, they can exploit it to charge higher interest on loans, pay lower interest on deposits, and distort the savings and investment decisions of consumers and producers. Similarly, by charging excessive fees for banking services, they raise the costs of transactions and distort the exchange decisions of consumers and producers. Finally, lack of competition may cause banks to operate within the limits of their technical capacity, so-called X-inefficiency.

Even in the standard IO setting, these arguments have their limitations. For example, in models of Bertrand competition, it is possible to support a perfectly competitive outcome with only two firms. If the Bertrand model is a good approximation to the nature of competition in the financial sector of the economy, we may not need thousands of banks to support a reasonable degree of competition. One can argue too on Schumpeterian grounds that some degree of monopoly is required to provide firms with the ability and incentive to make investments in new technology. Then there is a trade-off between dynamic efficiency, which requires a small number of banks, and static efficiency, which requires a large number of banks. In this chapter we go further and explore some alternative models of competition that may be more appropriate for the banking sector than the models developed with other industries in mind. In particular, we focus on the relationship between size and competition, the relationship between risk-taking behavior and competition, and nonprofit-maximizing behavior.

8.2 Competition and Networks

Financial services are different from other commodities in a number of respects. Models that serve well to describe other industries may not be appropriate for the banking sector or, more generally, for the financial services sector. For the same reason, the nature of competition in banking may be different from other industries. Traditional opposition to concentration in banking is based on the twin fears of monopoly power and X-inefficiency, where the welfare analysis of these two problems has been based largely on models borrowed from the IO literature, models intended to describe nonservice industries.

In this section, we explore a model of competition in the banking sector that suggests that small banks may be less aggressively competitive than large banks. It will not be possible to do more than sketch the central idea here. Our objective will be achieved if we convince readers that it is not clear what the right model of competition is and that this issue is worth thinking about.

The model we present exploits two types of imperfections arising from asymmetric information. The first is the presence of lock-in effects. Information is costly for both banks and their customers, whether borrowers or depositors, and once relationship-specific investments in information have been made, the parties may find themselves locked in to the relationship. For example, a borrower having incurred a fixed cost of revealing its type to a bank will suffer a loss if it switches to another bank. In addition there is the well-known "lemons effect," which arises if the borrower leaves the bank with which it has been doing business for many years. These lock-in effects will be modeled by simply assuming that there is a fixed cost of switching banks. As is well known (see, e.g., Diamond 1971), switching costs give the bank a degree of monopoly power, even if the bank is not large.

There are other reasons that banks are monopolistic competitors. For locational reasons their services are not perfect substitutes. Differences in size and products and specialized knowledge also make them imperfect substitutes. Here, we focus on the lock-in effect.

The second essential imperfection arises from the fact that a bank's customers have incomplete information about the services it offers and the prices at which these services are offered at the time when the relationship is begun. In fact, the smaller the bank is, the less likely it is that the bank's reputation will be an adequate source of information about the quality and prices of the bank's products.

A third important feature of our model is the fact that banks offer a variety of services. The simplest example is the case of a bank with a large number of branches. Since customers have different preferences over branch location, branches at different locations are offering different services. This means that a bank with many branches is offering a bundle of different services to their customers.

Location is not the only dimension along which banks differ, of course. They offer different menus of accounts, or concentrate on different types of lending business; they attract a different mix of retail or wholesale funds; they may diversify into nonbank products such as insurance or mutual funds. Location is a convenient metaphor for these different dimensions.

By exploiting these three features of the model—lock-in effects, limited information, and product diversity—we can reverse the usual presumption that greater concentration leads to more efficient outcomes.

The Model

There is a finite set of locations indexed by $\ell = 1, \ldots, L$, and at each location there are two banking offices, $j = 1, 2$. Time is divided into an infinite number of discrete periods, $t = 1, 2, \ldots$. There is a large number of individuals allocated exogenously to the different locations. Each period, these individuals have a demand for a unit of banking services that provides them with a surplus v. The value of banking services to individuals is distributed according to the distribution function $F(v)$, that is, $F(v)$ is the fraction of the population with valuation less than or equal to v.

At each date, consumers are randomly assigned to a new location. They have an equal probability of arriving at any location, and we assume that the number of locations is so large that the probability of returning to the same location is negligible and can be ignored. This is an extreme assumption, to be sure, but it serves to eliminate inconvenient and apparently unimportant complications. Each location is also assumed to receive a representative sample of the different types of individuals, so whatever the number of individuals at a given location, the distribution of types is $F(v)$.

For simplicity, banks are assumed to have a zero marginal cost of providing banking services. Profit is thus identical to revenue.

At each date, the market is assumed to clear as follows. First, the individuals who have gathered at a particular location choose which bank to patronize. They do this before they know the price that the bank will charge. Next, the bank sets the price for its product (the interest rate on loans or deposit accounts, or the fees for other bank services). Finally, consumers make one of three choices: to purchase the current bank's services at the quoted price, switch to the other bank, whose price by now has been fixed, or do without the services of a bank. There is a fixed cost $c > 0$ of switching from one banking office to the other.

We consider two limiting cases of bank organization. In the first, which we call *unitary banking*, each bank has a single branch. In other words, each banking office represents an independent bank. In the second case, which we call *branch banking*, there are only two banks, each owning one branch in each location. That is, all the banking offices are organized into two large networks. Regardless of the form of organization, we use the term *banking office* to denote the smallest unit of the bank, whether it constitutes the entire bank or a branch of a larger bank network.

Individuals are assumed to observe only what happens at their own bank in each period, and since they move to a different location in each period, they have no knowledge of the previous behavior of the bank they are patronizing in the current period. The banks themselves are assumed to condition their behavior in each location on their experience at the same location. This maintains an informational symmetry between the unitary and branch banking forms of industrial organization (i.e., unitary banking and branch banking), since in each case only local information is being used to condition the (local) pricing decision.

Unitary Banking

In this form of IO each bank consists of a single office. A bank sets the price of its product in each period to maximize the present value of profits. In the static version of this model, the unique equilibrium involves each banking office's choosing the monopoly price. More precisely, suppose that there is a unique price p_M such that

$$p_M(1 - F(p_M)) \geq p(1 - F(p)), \forall p.$$

A bank will clearly never want to charge more than p_M. If the two banks at some location happen to charge prices $p \leq p' \leq p_M$, where $p < p_M$, the bank charging p can always raise its price by ϵ without losing any customers because of the fixed cost of switching. This will clearly increase its profits, so the only equilibrium is for both banking offices to charge p_M.

In a dynamic context, things are generally more complicated because of the possibility of supporting a different equilibrium by means of punishment strategies. Under the maintained assumptions, however, there is no possibility of using such strategies to increase the set of equilibria. Because individuals observe only what happens at their own locations and never return to the same location, nothing that a banking office does in the current period will be observed by individuals who will visit that location in the future. Further, since banks at other locations do not condition their behavior on what happens at this location, there is no possibility of the bank's future customers' being indirectly informed of a deviation through another bank's reaction to this bank's current deviation. Our informational assumptions have effectively severed any possible feedback from a current change in price to a future change in demand, so the argument used in the static model continues to apply. We conclude that the unique, subgame perfect equilibrium of the unitary banking game consists of each bank, in each location, charging the monopoly price p_M in every period. Consumers whose valuation v is greater than p_M will purchase banking services; those whose valuation is less than p_M will not. The equilibrium is inefficient for the usual reason: the monopoly price is too high and the monopoly quantity is too low.

Branch Banking

Now suppose that banking offices are formed into two large networks. Each bank has one branch in each of the locations. Although consumers move from location to location, they can stay with the same bank if they wish. The possibility of staying with the same bank generates a plethora of other equilibria. We describe one such equilibrium to illustrate the possibilities.

In each period at each location, half the customers patronize each of the banks. Along the equilibrium path, the banks charge a price $p = \varepsilon > 0$ in every period. If, in any period, one of the banking offices has deviated from the equilibrium strategy, all the customers will leave the bank that last deviated and henceforth patronize branches belonging to the other bank. The banks continue to charge the same price. If no bank deviated but some of the customers deviated in the past, the banks continue to charge the same price and the customers continue to patronize the two banks equally. The profits (for a single banking office) from deviating last one period and are less than or equal to $(p_M - \varepsilon)(1 - F(p_M))$; on the other hand, it loses the profits from these customers in each future period until they all disappear from the game. Customers last only a finite number of periods, but if the number of locations is large, they will be around on average for a very long time. Each period, a fraction ℓ^{-1} of the customers dies and is replaced. The equilibrium profits lost by a single banking office's deviation are equal to $[\varepsilon/(1 - \ell^{-1})(1 - \delta)](1 - F(\varepsilon))$. For δ sufficiently close to 1 and ℓ sufficiently large, the profits from deviating are less than the profits of the equilibrium strategy. This shows that under branch banking, it is possible to support equilibria that are "more efficient" than the unique equilibrium in the case of unitary banking, where "more efficient" means that the sum of consumers' and producers' surplus is greater.

How should we interpret these results? The lock-in effects in the banking sector may be substantially greater than in most service industries and may be one of its distinguishing features. Small banks with a limited range of services and a limited geographical presence may have a greater incentive to exploit the lock-in effect than a large bank, because the large bank is always competing for the customer's future business, in another product line or another location. When we take into account the Schumpeterian arguments for large-scale production and the positive effects of concentration on financial stability, it begins to appear that there may be substantial costs attached to the American infatuation with competition.

Reputation and Competition: A Broader View

The ideas sketched above can be applied to other contexts in which there is repeated interaction between banks and individuals. In particular, we can apply it to situations in which the interaction between banks and individuals in each period and at each location can be modeled by an arbitrary game.

As before, there is a finite set of locations, $\ell = 1, \ldots, L$, and at each location there are two banking offices, $j = 1, 2$. Time is indexed by $t = 1, 2, \ldots$. In the case of branch banking, there are two players, $j = 1, 2$. In the case of unitary banking, there are $2L$ players indexed by the ordered pairs (j, ℓ).

There is a large number of individuals allocated exogenously to the different locations. An individual lives for L periods and spends each period in a different location. These individuals are identical except for the order in which they visit the different locations. Thus, an individual's type is just a sequence of locations $\theta = (\ell_1 \ldots, \ell_L)$, and we assume that in each generation there are equal numbers of each possible type and in each period they are distributed uniformly across locations, independent of their previous experience, except for the restriction that an individual cannot visit the same location twice.

At each date and in each location, individuals first decide which banking office they want to "play" with. Once they have made this decision, they are committed to playing only with that banking office for the rest of the period. This assumption produces a lock-in effect analogous to the previous model. Once the individuals have chosen a banking office, a normal-form game Γ is played. The players of Γ comprise a bank B and a representative customer C. Each player $i = B, C$ has a finite strategy set S_i and a payoff function $u_i : S \to \mathbf{R}$, where $S \equiv S_B \times S_C$ is the set of strategy profiles. Since there is a continuum of customers, the number of customers matters. For simplicity, we assume that the bank's payoff is linear in the number of customers, so if the strategy profile is $s = (s_B, s_C)$ and the number of customers is n, then the bank's payoff is $u_B(s)n$ and the representative customer's payoff is $u_C(s)$. The normal-form game is defined by $\Gamma = (N, S, u)$, where $N = (B, C)$ and $u = (u_B, u_C)$. Note that the definition of the game does not include the number of customers, which is an endogenous variable. We need to know the number of customers in order to calculate the payoffs in the stage game but not to calculate the set of Nash equilibria of Γ.

As before, the informational assumptions are crucial to the outcomes. In each period, each individual knows his own personal history, that is, the locations he has visited in the past and the actions chosen by the banks and individuals at those locations when he visited them. Since each individual occupies a different location in each period, he knows nothing of the past behavior of the banks in his present location and consequently cannot condition his current behavior on that information. We may as well assume that the banks have complete information. The informational assumptions about the banks will not turn out to be very important. The imperfect information of the individuals is crucial, on the other hand. From the point of view of a unitary bank, it means that its current actions will have no effect on its future payoffs, since in each period the actions of the individuals it is currently playing against must be independent of the bank's past actions.

Since banks and individuals play the game Γ repeatedly, albeit with different partners, this is a cousin of the well-known repeated-game model of long-term relationships. The argument used to establish the existence of a larger equilibrium set, containing superior equilibria, is familiar from the literature on the "folk theorem" for repeated games (Fudenberg and Tirole 1991, chap. 5). If we think of the model of banks and their customers as a kind of repeated game, then it is not surprising that we get a kind of folk theorem for branch banking and an anti–folk theorem for unitary banking, for branch banking, under the maintained assumptions, allows for long-term relationships and unitary banking does not.

Unitary Banking

The payoff to an individual born at date t is the discounted sum of his period payoffs: $\sum_{k=1}^{L} \beta^{k-1} u_C(s_{t+k-1})$, where s_{t+k-1} is the strategy profile in the stage game played in his kth period. For a bank, the payoff is the discounted sum of payoffs in each period: $\sum_{t=0}^{\infty} \beta^{t-1} u_B(s_t) n_t$, where n_t denotes the number of individuals playing the game with the bank in period t.

Now consider the decision problem of a typical individual. The individual may condition his actions in the current period on his personal history, and since there may be a nonnegligible set of agents with the same history, this could cause some dependence of the equilibrium play of the game on past behavior. To rule out this possibility, we consider only equilibria in which all individuals behave in the same way in any given play of the stage game Γ. Then their behavior must be measurable with respect to the common knowledge partition, that is, the finest partition that is coarser than each individual's information partition. This means that we can write their action as a function of the period, bank, and location—that is, for any given (j, ℓ, t), the behavior of every individual playing that stage game is the same $f(j, \ell, t) \in S_C$.

With these assumptions, we can show that any Nash equilibrium of the unitary banking game must involve playing a Nash equilibrium of the stage game Γ in each period. First consider the behavior of the banks. Since nothing in the past is common knowledge, the actions of the individuals must be independent of anything other than time. Then, since the banks anticipate no effect of their current actions on their continuation payoffs, they must choose an action that maximizes their current period payoff, taking as given the number of individuals. In other words, they must choose an action that is a best response in the static game Γ to the action chosen by the individuals.

For the individuals' part, their action must be a best response to the mixed strategy chosen by bank, and since their action is uncorrelated with the action chosen by the bank (by our assumption), it too must be a best response in the static game. This proves that any Nash equilibrium of the dynamic game involves playing a Nash equilibrium of the (static) stage game in every period and location.

Branch Banking

In the branch banking game, by contrast, individuals play against the same bank, albeit in different locations, in every period. It is easy to see that a larger set of equilibria can be supported. Clearly every equilibrium of the unitary banking game has its counterpart here. To show that the set of equilibria is larger, it is sufficient to construct some very simple equilibria in which the same action is chosen by every player in every play of the stage game, along the equilibrium path. Suppose that there exists a profile $s' = (s'_B, s'_I) \in S$ that is strictly preferred by the individuals to any equilibrium of the stage game and yields positive profits to the banks. We assume that s'_I is a best response to s'_B for the individuals in the stage game Γ. Clearly it is optimal for the individuals to choose s'_I as long as the banks are expected to play s'_B. If one of the banks deviates, we assume that all the individuals who observe the deviation patronize the other bank from then onward, unless there is a deviation by that bank, in which case they revert to the first bank, and so forth. A deviation by one of the banks may increase the bank's payoff in the short run, but the number of customers must drop in the long run, and given a sufficiently short period length, this must be to the bank's disadvantage. More precisely, at any information set, if the bank has a positive measure of customers at some location, it should play s'_B. If it plays any other strategy, it anticipates losing those customers in the future and, hence, any positive continuation payoff it might get in the future. Since there is no countervailing advantage from the deviation, as long as the continuation payoff is great enough, the bank will be deterred from deviating.

8.3 Competition and Risk Taking

When firms are debt financed, managers acting in the shareholders' interests have an incentive to take excessive risks, because the debt holders bear the downside risk while the shareholders benefit from the upside potential. This is the well-known problem of *risk shifting* or *asset substitution*, and it is particularly acute in the banking sector where a large proportion of the liabilities are in the form of debt (deposits). An interesting example of this is provided by the U.S. experience. Keeley (1990) argues that deregulation of the banking industry in the 1970s and 1980s led to an increase in competition and a reduction in banks' profits. This in turn greatly increased the incentive for banks to undertake risk-taking behavior. His empirical findings strongly support this thesis.

Risk shifting affects not only the distribution of returns between shareholders and debtholders. It is sometimes argued that the deadweight costs of bankruptcy are large in the banking sector. The failure of one bank may cause the failure of other banks and begin a kind of contagion that disrupts the financial system and raises the costs of intermediation in the economy as a whole. Financial fragility is one of the central concerns of regulators and provides another reason for bank regulators to pay attention to the incentives the managers may have to take excessive risks. (We discuss this further in chapter 9.)

For both of these reasons, it is important to consider the potential for risk shifting when analyzing competitive behavior in banking. It turns out that the risk-shifting problem is exacerbated by competition. Other things being equal, greater competition reduces the profits or quasi-rents available to managers or shareholders, or both. As a result, the gains from taking excessive risks become relatively more attractive, and this increases the incentive to exploit the nonconvexity in the payoff function. Any analysis of the costs and benefits of competition has to weigh this effect against the supposed efficiency gains of greater competition.

To illustrate these ideas, we consider the problem faced by a banking regulator who controls entry into the banking industry by granting charters to a limited number of banks. We use a model of Cournot competition, in which banks choose the volume of deposits they want, subject to an upward-sloping supply of funds schedule. Having more banks will tend to raise the equilibrium deposit rate and increase the tendency to shift risks. What is the optimal number of charters? Should the regulator restrict competition by granting only a few charters or encourage competition by granting many?

A Static Model

Suppose that the regulator has chartered n banks, indexed $i = 1, \ldots, n$. Each bank chooses a portfolio consisting of perfectly correlated risks. This assumption is equivalent to assuming that the risk of each investment can be decomposed into a common component and a purely idiosyncratic component. If there is a very large number of investments, the purely idiosyncratic components can be pooled perfectly. Then the idiosyncratic risks disappear from the analysis, and we are left with a common component representing the systematic risks.

A portfolio is characterized by its size and rate of return. The bank's investments have a two-point return structure: for each dollar invested, bank i will receive a return y_i with probability $p(y_i)$; with probability $(1 - p(y_i))$ they pay a return 0. The bank chooses the riskiness of its portfolio by choosing the target return y_i on its investments. The function $p(y_i)$ is assumed to be twice continuously differentiable and satisfies

$$p(0) = 1, p(\bar{y}) = 0, \text{ and } p'(y_i) < 0, p''(y_i) \leq 0, \forall 0 < y_i < \bar{y}.$$

The higher the target return is, the lower is the probability of success and the more rapidly the probability of success falls. Because the investments have perfectly correlated returns, the portfolio return has the same distribution as the returns to the individual investments.

Let $d_i \geq 0$ denote the total deposits of bank i, which is by definition the total number of dollars the bank has to invest. (For the moment, we ignore bank capital.) There is an upward-sloping supply-of-funds curve. If the total demand for deposits is $D = \sum_i d_i$, then the opportunity cost of funds is $R(D)$, where $R(D)$ is assumed to be a differentiable function satisfying

$$R'(D) > 0, R''(D) > 0, R(0) = 0 \text{ and } R(\infty) = \infty.$$

We assume that all deposits are insured, so the supply of funds is independent of the riskiness of the banks' portfolios. Deposit insurance is modeled further below.

The payoff to bank i is a function of the riskiness of its own portfolio and the demand for deposits of all the banks:

$$\pi_i(\mathbf{y}, \mathbf{d}) = p(y_i)[y_i d_i - R(D)d_i],$$

where $\mathbf{d} = (d_1, \ldots, d_n)$ and $\mathbf{y} = (y_1, \ldots, y_n)$. Note that we have ignored the cost of deposit insurance to the bank in calculating its net return.

Since a bank can always ensure nonnegative profits by choosing $d_i = 0$, it will always earn a nonnegative expected return in equilibrium, that is, $y_i d_i - R(D)d_i \geq 0$. There is no need to introduce a separate limited-liability constraint.

In a Nash-Cournot equilibrium, each bank i chooses an ordered pair (y_i, d_i) that is a best response to the strategies of all the other banks. Consider an equilibrium $(\mathbf{y}, \mathbf{d})$ in which each bank i chooses a strictly positive pair $(y_i, d_i) \gg 0$. As a necessary condition for a best response, this pair must satisfy the following first-order conditions:

$$p(y_i)[y_i - R(D) - R'(D)d_i] = 0$$

$$p'(y_i)[y_i - R(D)]d_i + p(y_i)d_i = 0.$$

Assuming the equilibrium is symmetric, that is, $(y_i, d_i) = (y, d)$ for every i, the first-order conditions reduce to

$$y - R(nd) - R'(nd)d = 0$$

$$p'(y)[y - R(nd)] + p(y) = 0,$$

and this implies that

$$-\frac{p(y)}{p'(y)} = y - R(nd) = R'(nd)d.$$

Given our assumptions on $p(y)$, an increase in y reduces $-p(y)/p'(y)$. Suppose that there are two symmetric equilibria, (y, d) and (y', d'). Then $y > y'$ implies that $R'(nd)d < R'(nd')d'$, which, given our assumptions on $R(D)$, implies that $d < d'$ and $R(nd) < R(nd')$. Then clearly $y - R(nd) > y' - R(nd')$, contradicting the first equation. So there is at most one solution to this set of equations, which determines both the size and the riskiness of the banks' portfolio in a symmetric equilibrium.

Proposition 8.1 Under the maintained assumptions, there is at most one symmetric equilibrium $(y^*, d^*) \gg 0$ which is completely characterized by the conditions

$$-\frac{p(y)}{p'(y)} = y - R(nd) = R'(nd)d.$$

What can we now say about the effect of competition on risk taking?

Suppose that we identify the degree of competitiveness of the banking sector with the degree of concentration. In other words, the larger the number of banks, the more competitive the banking sector is. A first attempt at answering the question would involve increasing n ceteris paribus and observing how the riskiness of the banks' behavior changes.

With a fixed supply-of-funds schedule $R(\cdot)$, it is most likely that the volume of deposits will remain bounded as n increases. More precisely, if we assume that $R(D) \to \infty$ as $D \to \infty$, then it is clear that $D \to \infty$ is inconsistent with equilibrium, and this implies that $d \to 0$ as $n \to \infty$. This in turn implies that $R'(nd)d \to 0$, from which it immediately follows that $y - R(nd) \to 0$ and $p(y) \to 0$, or in other words, that y and $R(nd)$ both converge to $\bar{y}$.

Proposition 8.2 If $R(D) \to \infty$, then in any symmetric equilibrium, $y - R(nd) \to 0$ and $y \to \bar{y}$ as $n \to \infty$.

The effect of increasing competition is to make each bank much smaller relative to the market for funds, and this in turn reduces the importance of the price effect (the $R'(nd)d$ term) in the bank's decision. As a result, banks behave more like perfect competitors and will increase their business as long as profits are positive. Equilibrium then requires that profits converge to zero, and this implies that banks have extreme incentives for risk taking. In the limit as $n \to \infty$, they will choose the riskiest investments possible in an attempt to earn a positive profit.

Effect of Replicating the Market

This exercise is enlightening but somewhat artificial since it assumes that we are dealing with a market of fixed size and increasing the number of banks without bound in order to achieve competition. Normally one thinks of perfect competition as arising in the limit as the number of banks and consumers grows without bound. One way to do this is to replicate the market by shifting the supply-of-funds function as we increase the number of banks. Suppose that the rate of return on deposits is a function of the deposits per bank:

$$R = R(D/n).$$

In effect, we are assuming that as the number of banks is increased, the number of depositors is increased proportionately, so that the supply of funds in relation to a particular bank is unchanged.

The effect of this change in the model is to make it more like the traditional model of a market in which, as the number of firms increases, the effect of any firm supply on the price of the product becomes vanishingly small. Here the effect of any bank's demand for deposits on the equilibrium deposit rate becomes vanishingly small in the limit as the number of banks becomes unboundedly large. To see this, note that the first-order conditions become

$$y - R(d) - R'(d)dn^{-1} = 0$$

and

$$p'(y)[y - R(d)] + p(y) = 0.$$

As before, we can ensure that d remains bounded as $n \to \infty$ by assuming that $R(d) \to \infty$ as $n \to \infty$. Then the last term on the left-hand side of the first equation will vanish as $n \to \infty$, leaving a limiting value of (y, d) that satisfies $y = R(d)$. Substituting this in the second equation tells us that $p(y) = 0$. In other words, as the number of banks increases, the profit margins fall to zero, with the result that banks choose riskier and riskier investments.

PROPOSITION 8.3 If $R(D) \to \infty$, then in any symmetric equilibrium, $y - R(d) \to 0$ and $y \to \bar{y}$ as $n \to \infty$.

This is a highly stylized model, so the results have to be taken with a grain of salt; nonetheless, they illustrate clearly the operative principle, which is that competition, by reducing profits, encourages risk taking.

In this case, we have constant returns to scale in banking, so that in the limit, when there is a large number of individually insignificant banks, profits must converge to zero. In other words, banks will expand the volume of their deposits and loans until the deposit rate approaches the expected return on investments. But this gives them an extreme incentive to shift risks to the depositors or the deposit insurance agency, since it is only by doing so that they can get positive profits at all.

With constant returns to scale, zero profits is always a necessary condition of equilibrium in a competitive industry. However, there are other ways of ensuring the same outcome even if constant returns to scale are not assumed. We replicated the market by increasing the number of banks and potential depositors in the same proportion. This is an interesting thought experiment, but it is not the same as the comparative static exercise that the regulator is undertaking. Presumably the regulator has to choose n optimally, taking as given the supply-of-funds schedule. Suppose that m is the number of depositors and n the number of banks. Then the market supply-of-funds schedule can be written $R(D/m)$ if $R(\cdot)$ is the individual supply-of-funds schedule. When m is very large, the supply of funds is elastic, other things being equal, so the banks will take the marginal cost of funds as being equal to the average cost $R(D/m)$. However, increasing the number of banks n in relation to m will force profits down. If d remains bounded away from zero, the average cost of funds must increase to ∞, and if d goes to zero, profits will also go to zero. In this way, the regulator can achieve the effects of free entry, but there is no need to do this in order to ensure competition. Competition, in the sense of price-taking behavior, follows from having a large market, that is, a large value of m, independent of whether n is large. Clearly the regulator does not want to drive profits to zero if it can be helped, because of the incentives for risk taking that that creates.

Deposit Insurance

The preceding analysis assumes that all deposits are insured and that the costs are not borne by the banks. This is clearly unrealistic, so it makes sense to consider explicitly the cost of deposit insurance. We assume that the premium for deposit insurance is set before the banks choose their strategies and that it is the same for each bank, independent of the strategy chosen. In equilibrium, the premium accurately reflects the cost of deposit insurance provided by a risk-neutral insurer.

Let π denote the premium per dollar of deposits. Then the objective function of bank i is $p(y_i)(y_i - R(D) - \pi)d_i$, and the first-order conditions in a symmetric equilibrium in which banks choose the strategy (y, d) will be:

$$y - R(d) - \pi - R'(d)dn^{-1} = 0$$

$$p'(y)[y - R(d) - \pi] + p(y) = 0.$$

In equilibrium, the premium must be set so that the expected return on deposits is equal to the return demanded by depositors:

$$R(d) = p(y)(R(d) + \pi).$$

Substituting $\pi = [(1 - p(y))/p(y)]R(d)$ into the first-order conditions yields

$$y - R(d)/p(y) - R'(d)dn^{-1} = 0$$

$$p'(y)[y - R(d)/p(y)] + p(y) = 0.$$

Let (y^n, d^n) be a symmetric equilibrium when there are n banks and suppose that $(y^n, d^n) \to (y^0, d^0)$ as $n \to \infty$. Then the first-order conditions imply that

$$\lim_{n\to\infty} y^n - R(d^n)/p(y^n) = 0,$$

which is possible only if $y^n \to \bar{y}$ and $p(y^n) \to 0$, as before.

Efficiency

Let us leave distributional questions to one side for the moment, although historically they have been at the center of the arguments for competition in banking, and suppose that the regulator is interested only in maximizing surplus. Reverting to the constant-returns-to-scale case, two necessary conditions for Pareto optimality are that the average cost of funds be equal to the expected return on investments and that the expected return on investments should be a maximum:

$$R(D/m) = p(y)y$$

$$p(y)y \geq p(y')y', \forall y' \in [0, \bar{y}].$$

Neither of these conditions will hold in equilibrium when m and n are very large. The first condition requires that the volume of deposits expand until the cost of funds equals the expected value of investments. However, when the market is highly competitive, we have $y - R(D/m) \cong 0$, so that $p(y)y - R(D/m) < 0$. As we also saw, the second condition cannot be satisfied in equilibrium, since as the market grows large $(m, n \to \infty)$, we have $y \to \bar{y} < \infty$ and $p(y) \to 0$, so $p(y)y \to 0$. This is not only suboptimal but the worst possible outcome because it minimizes the total surplus.

Suppose instead that we hold the value of m fixed and adjust n to maximize total surplus, taking the equilibrium values $(y(n), d(n))$ as given functions of n determined by the equilibrium conditions

$$y - R(nd/m) - R'(nd/m)dm^{-1} = 0$$

and

$$p'(y)[y - R(nd/m)] + p(y) = 0.$$

A "small" change in n will increase the expected revenue by

$$\{p'(y(n))y(n) + p(y(n))\}ny'(n) + p(y(n))y(n)$$

and the cost by

$$R(nd(n)/m)\{nd'(n) + d(n)\},$$

so a necessary condition for an (interior) optimum is

$$\{p'(y(n))y(n) + p(y(n))\}ny'(n) + p(y(n))y(n) = R(nd(n)/m)\{nd'(n) + d(n)\}.$$

This can be rewritten as

$$p(y(n))y(n) - R(nd(n)/m)d(n) = \{p'(y(n))y(n) + p(y(n))\}ny'(n) + R(nd(n)/m)nd'(n),$$

where the left-hand side is the expected surplus generated by a single bank and the right-hand side is the change in expected revenue per bank as n increases plus the change in the cost per bank of the funds borrowed. Since the left-hand side is positive, the right-hand side must be positive too. But we know that the second term on the right must be negative since adding more banks reduces the volume of business each bank does, so the first term on the right is positive. We know that $y'(n)$ is negative—increased competition leads to increased risk taking—so the term in braces must be negative. Assuming that $p(y)y$ is concave in y, this tells us that n will be chosen so that $y(n)$ is greater than the value that maximizes expected revenue. On the other hand, it will not, as we have seen, be as great as the value under free entry, since it is never optimal to let $n \to \infty$. It may, in fact, be optimal to let the number of banks remain quite small.

A Dynamic Analysis

The same arguments extend immediately to a dynamic environment as long as we assume that the banks play the short-run strategy at each date. Suppose there are a countable number of dates, $t = 1, 2, \ldots$. At each date, the n banks play the same game as before, choosing the level of deposits d_{it} and the quality of their investments y_{it}. For simplicity, we ignore the complication of deposit insurance. This is a game of complete and perfect information, so a strategy for a bank is a sequence of functions $f_i = \{f_{it}\}$, where each function f_{it} maps the history of the game at that date into a feasible choice. Suppose that we focus on the Markov perfect equilibrium in which a bank's action at date t is independent of the history of the game up to that point. In that case, the action will be time invariant, and the bank's payoff from the continuation game V will also be time invariant. The payoff at any date will be

$$\pi_i = p(y_i)[y_i d_i - R(D)d_i + \beta V],$$

where β is the discount factor and V is the payoff from the continuation game. Note that the continuation payoff V is also multiplied by the probability of success. If the bank fails, it ceases operation and will not receive any profits in the future. This raises the question of what happens to the number of banks over time. As a stopgap, we assume that as soon as one bank fails, the government issues a license to another bank. This maintains the stationarity of the model but is not entirely satisfactory. However, with this assumption, the results from the static case are immediately replicated in the dynamic setting. The first-order condition for the choice of y_i becomes

$$0 = p'(y_i)[y_i d_i - R(D)d_i + \beta V] + p(y_i)d_i.$$

In a stationary equilibrium,

$$V = \{p(y_i) + \beta p(y_i)^2 + \beta^2 p(y_i)^3 \ldots\}(y_i - R(D))d_i$$
$$= p(y_i)\{\beta p(y_i)/(1 - \beta p(y_i))\}(y_i - R(D))d_i,$$

so the first-order condition reduces to

$$0 = p'(y_i)K[y_i - R(D)] + p(y_i),$$

where

$$K = 1 + \frac{\beta^2 p(y_i)^2}{1 - \beta p(y_i)} > 1.$$

The same results go through. As $y_i - R(D) \to 0$, $p(y_i) \to 0$. The only difference is that the convergence is slower because of the presence of future earnings, which will be lost in the event of a bank failure.

Things would be even simpler if the bank were allowed to continue in spite of its failure to repay the debt. The anticipated future profits are higher, but they have no effect on current choices. The bank behaves in exactly the same way as in the static model.

We have sketched one possible equilibrium, and not necessarily the most plausible one. As is well known, there are many equilibria in repeated games when the discount factor β is close to 1. In this case, in order to have an effective discount factor close to 1, we need to ensure that $p(y_i)$ is close to 1 as well. That is, the game we have described is not a repeated game, because of the possibility of bank failure, but it has the properties of a repeated game if banks are taking a small amount of risk, so the continuation probability is close to 1. Suppose that this is the case; that is, consider parameter values for which the Cournot equilibrium involves little risk. Then some of the equilibria that can be supported may involve more risk taking than the benchmark and some may involve less. For example, let (y_M, d_M) denote the monopsony outcome, that is, the level of deposits per bank and the choice of portfolio that maximizes joint profits. This will provide a higher equilibrium payoff than the competitive (Cournot) outcome. If the discount factor is sufficiently close to 1, the following equilibrium reversion strategy will support this outcome as a subgame perfect equilibrium: simply assign every bank the action (y_M, d_M) as long as there is no deviation and a return to the time-invariant Cournot strategy as soon as one bank deviates. Will this strategy involve more or less risk taking? Because the value of the continuation game is higher than before, an examination of the first-order condition makes clear that the (individually and socially) optimal portfolio will be less risky than before. Collusion, by raising profits, reduces the incentive for risk taking.

On the other hand, using the same arguments we could find an equilibrium that supports greater risk taking. Just because profits are higher and there is a threat of returning to the noncollusive Cournot outcome, banks may be compelled to take more risk than they would like. As long as the cost of the additional risk does not entirely offset the gain from colluding on the demand for deposits, banks will not deviate from this implicit agreement.

Precisely because there are so many possible stories, this is not an entirely satisfactory account of bank behavior. A model that had a unique equilibrium would be more appealing. Also, since there is no direct connection between the choices of the bank today and the size of the bank tomorrow (i.e., this is not a stochastic game), we miss one of the interesting reasons for adopting a risky strategy: the desire to grow. We consider these issues in the next section.

8.4 Dynamic Competition

In the last section we saw how the limited liability of managers and shareholders in a modern banking corporation produces a convex objective function, which in turn leads to risk-shifting behavior. This kind of behavior is most likely to occur when the bank is "close to the water line," that is, when the risk of bankruptcy is imminent. For banks that are not in immediate danger of bankruptcy, the risk-shifting argument may be less relevant. However, even if a bank is not near the water line, there may be other reasons for thinking that its objective function is convex. Consider, for example, the winner-takes-all nature of competition. When banks compete for market share, the bank that ends up with the largest share may be able to exploit its market power to increase profitability. In this case, the profit function may be convex in market share—that is, doubling market share may more than double profits. Another reason is the presence of increasing returns to scale. If larger banks have lower average costs, then profits will be a convex function of the size of the bank. Either of these possibilities will give the bank an incentive to take riskier actions, even when the bank is not in immediate danger of bankruptcy.

These incentives for risk-taking behavior are naturally studied in a dynamic context. Suppose that a group of banks are competing over time. Their activities are constrained by the minimum capital ratio, so the only way to expand is to acquire more capital. Because of agency costs or the adverse signaling effects, it may be expensive for banks to raise capital from external sources, so they try to accumulate capital by retaining earnings. The relative size of the bank matters, because it gives the bank a competitive edge over other banks. Because their reduced-form profit functions are convex and they are constrained by their capital, the game is a race to see who can accumulate capital or market share fastest.

When banks compete to capture greater market share or to reap economies of scale, they consider not only the effect of their actions on immediate profits but also on their future position in the market. How the bank's current actions will affect its future position in the market depends on the nature of the risks and the behavior of the other banks. Even if the profit function is convex only when the bank is close to the bankruptcy point, the objective function may be convex over a much wider region because the objective function incorporates or discounts future possibilities that are still far away. This may influence the shape of the bank's objective function globally, through backward induction.

We begin by considering the case of a pair of duopolists who compete for market share. It is not clear a priori whether competition or concentration leads to more risk taking. If the market is concentrated, the future profits are greater, but this may mean that banks compete more aggressively for the dominant position in the market, leading to more risk taking early on but less risk taking once they have achieved a solid position.

A Duopoly Model

There is a finite number of dates, $t = 1, 2, \ldots, T$ and a pair of banks, $j = A, B$. We model competition as a stochastic game in which the states are the set of market positions, indexed by $i = 0, 1, 2, \ldots, I$. The market position summarizes everything that banks care about, and in particular, the market share is a linear function of the state—more precisely, the market share of bank A is $x_i \equiv i/I$ and the market share of bank B is $1 - x_i = (I - i)/I$.

Payoffs depend only on market share. If the state is i, there is a flow of utility equal to u_i for bank A and v_i for bank B. Payoffs are increasing in market share, so $u_i < u_{i+1}$ and $v_i > v_{i+1}$ for all $i < I$.

There is a finite set of actions that the banks can choose, and a strategy for bank A (resp. Bank B) is a sequence of functions $\{f_{At}\}$ (resp. $\{f_{Bt}\}$) that map the history of the game up to that date into a feasible action. In practice, we shall restrict attention to Markov strategies, in which the bank's action depends on only the state of the game at that date. A Markov strategy for bank A (resp. B) can be represented by a sequence $a = \{a_{it}\}$ (resp. $b = \{b_{it}\}$), where a_{it} is the action chosen by bank A at date t in state i. By restricting attention to Markov strategies, we are refining the set of equilibria.

Suppose that a strategy profile (a, b) has been chosen. The evolution of the game is determined by a stationary transition probability $p : I^2 \times A^2 \to [0, 1]$, where $p_{ik}(a_{it}, b_{it})$ denotes the probability of a move from position i to position k when the actions chosen by the banks are (a_{it}, b_{it}). Let U_{it} denote the continuation payoff of bank A in state i at date t. Then

$$U_{it} = \sum_k p_{ik}(a_{it}, b_{it})(u_k + U_{kt+1}),$$

and V_{it} is defined similarly.

This is a game of complete and perfect information. A Markov perfect equilibrium consists of a pair of Markov strategies (a, b) such that for every (i, t), the strategies maximize the player's continuation payoff, given the strategy of the other player.

Competing for Market Share

To say anything about the incentives for risk taking, we need to impose some more structure. Suppose that each bank has two actions, a safe action S and a risky action R. Then a strategy indicates whether a bank chooses to play safe or risky at each date in each state of the market. To simplify further, we assume that the state adjusts by at most one position in any single period. If the state is i at date t, then the state will belong to the set $\{1 - i, i, i + 1\}$ at date $t + 1$. The probability of movement to either of the adjacent positions depends on the choices of the two banks, and we make the following assumptions.

1. If both banks choose S, the market position does not change.
2. Suppose that both banks choose R. If $0 < i < I$, then the market position at the next date is $i - 1$ with probability p, i with probability $1 - 2p$,

and $i+1$ with probability p. If $i=0$ (resp. $i=I$), then the position at the next date is i with probability $1-p$ and $i+1$ (resp. $i-1$) with probability p.

3. If one bank chooses R and the other chooses S, then the rules are the same as in case 2, except that the probability p is replaced by q, where $0<q<p<1/2$.

Thus, risk taking by one or more banks leads to a mean preserving spread in the market position, and the variance is increasing in the number of banks choosing the risky action. The incentives for taking risk depend on the shape of the payoff functions U and V. Whatever action is chosen by the rival bank, the distribution of next period's market position when a bank chooses R is a mean preserving spread of the distribution when the bank chooses S. Thus, if u and U are convex, the bank will prefer R; if u and U are concave, the bank will prefer S.

As a benchmark, consider the case where the instantaneous payoff is linear in the market position: $u_i = a(i/I)$ and $v_i = a(I-i)/I$, for all i where a is the constant $1/I$ (choosing this constant simplifies the calculations). This specification gives the bank neither a preference for nor an aversion to risk-taking behavior. However, both arise naturally from the dynamic analysis of the game. Figure 8.1 shows the continuation payoff for bank A at the first date, in a symmetric Markov perfect equilibrium. For the purposes of this simulation it was assumed that there were 21 states ($I=20$) and 2,000 dates ($T=100$). The transition probabilities are $p=0.3$ and $q=0.25$. The continuation payoffs for banks A and B are symmetric because $V_{it} = U_{I-i,t}$ so we can refer to the one diagram for both.

What we see clearly from figure 8.1 is that when a bank's market share is low, its objective function is convex, and it has an incentive to take risk; when its market share is high, its objective function is concave, and it has an incentive to avoid risk. The critical value of market share is $i^*/I = 0.45$; when a bank's market share is above 0.45, it will choose S, and when it is below 0.45, it will choose R. This means that when the market shares of the two banks are very unequal, one below 0.45 and one above 0.55, one chooses R and the other chooses S, and the probability of moving up or down is q. When both have intermediate market shares, between 0.45 and 0.55, they both choose S and there is no movement.

Figures 8.2 and 8.3 show the continuation payoffs for bank A in a symmetric equilibrium when the instantaneous payoff function takes the form

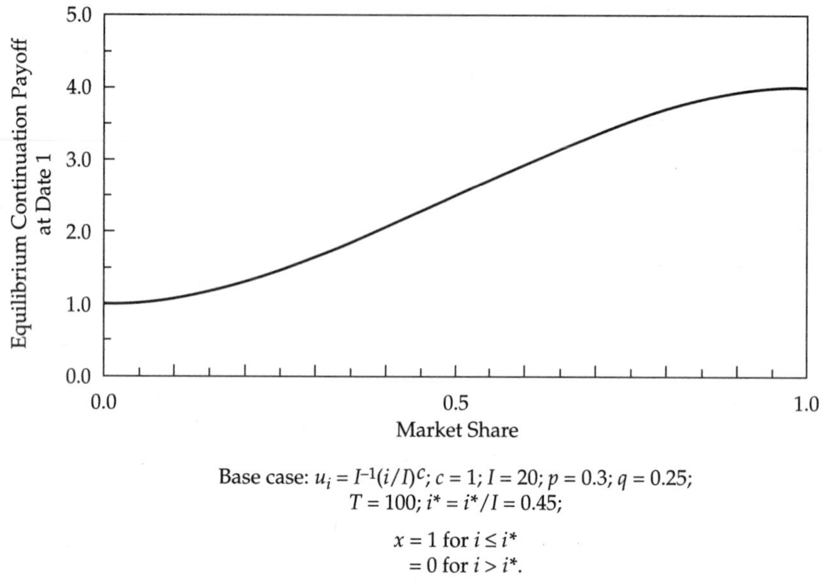

Figure 8.1
Reflecting barriers: symmetric equilibrium

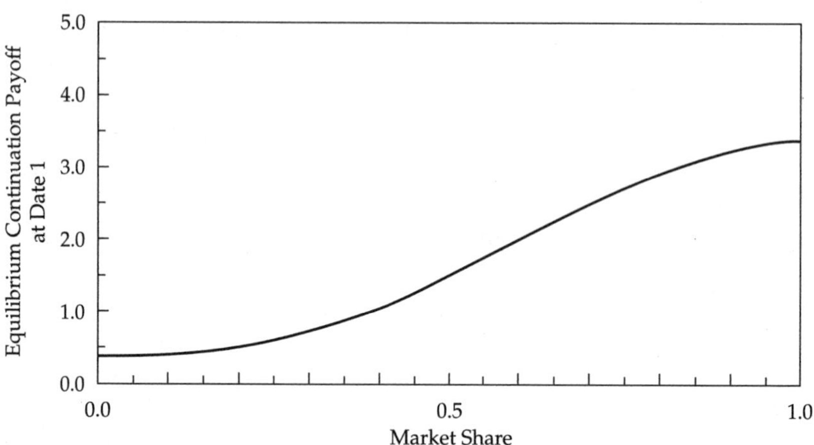

Figure 8.2
Reflecting barriers: symmetric equilibrium with $c = 2$ and $i^* = 0.6$

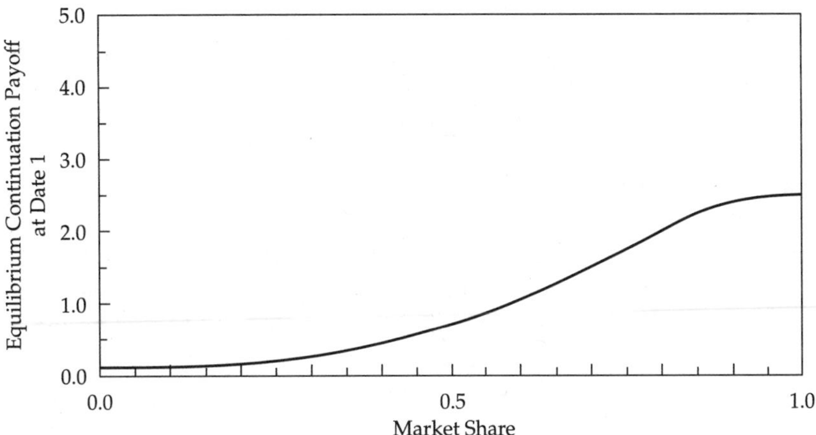

Figure 8.3
Reflecting barriers: symmetric equilibrium with $c = 4$ and $i^* = 0.7$

$$u_i = a(i/I)^c,$$

and $c > 1$ is chosen to introduce greater convexity. The rest of the parameters are the same as in the previous case. In figure 8.2 we assume $c = 2$, and in figure 8.3 we assume $c = 4$. In both cases the convex region has increased in size, so we should expect that the risky action will be chosen more often. In fact, the critical value of market share is $i^*/I = 0.6$ in figure 8.2 and $i^*/I = 0.7$ in figure 8.3, so at least one of the banks chooses R for any state, and for intermediate states both choose R. The intermediate values of market share correspond to the intervals $[0.4, 0.6]$ in the case of figure 8.2 and $[0.3, 0.7]$ in the case of figure 8.3. But note that there is still a concave region, in spite of the fact that the instantaneous payoff function is convex everywhere.

The explanation for the shape of the continuation payoff function in all three cases comes from the rules for changing the state. More precisely, the stochastic process defined by the equilibrium play of the game has reflecting barriers. As we will explain in more detail, when a bank's market share hits zero, it does not go out of business; at worst it will remain at zero for some periods before bouncing back. This nonconvexity is like having increasing returns in the neighborhood of zero. Similarly, when a bank's market share hits 100 percent, it must eventually bounce back, and this is like having locally decreasing returns.

Consider the linear model $c = 1$, and suppose that at least one of the banks chooses R. Let s_t denote the (random) state at date t. The symmetry of the stochastic process implies that $E[s_{t+1}|s_t] = s_t$, whenever the state i is strictly between the boundaries 0 and I, and the fact that the instantaneous utility function is linear implies that the expected future payoff is the same as the current payoff. On the boundaries, things are different. When $i = 0$, $E[s_{t+1}|s_t] > s_t$ since the market position cannot get any lower but it may be higher, and the expected future utility is greater than the current utility. When $i = I$, $E[s_{t+1}|s_t] < s_t$, since it cannot get any higher but it may be lower, and the expected utility next period is less than the current utility. This suggests a convexity (resp. concavity) in the continuation payoffs when the market position is close to $i = 0$ (resp. $i = I$). Furthermore, because the continuation payoffs incorporate the possibility of movement from an interior position $0 < i < I$ to a boundary position, the curvature generated at the extreme values will be transmitted to the interior, thus producing the logistic shape that we see so clearly in figures 8.1 through 8.3.

This argument can be made more precise if we consider an example that is somewhat simpler than the duopoly model. Suppose that the bank gets a payment of i whenever it is in state i and the state has a fixed probability p of moving up or down in each period, with reflecting barriers at the boundaries. The expected future profits of the bank in state i in period t are denoted by f_{it} and defined by the equation

$$f_{it} = i + \sum_k p_{ik} f_{kt+1}$$

for $i = 0, \ldots, I$ and $t = 1, \ldots, T$, where the transition probabilities $\{p_{ik}\}$ are defined in the usual way. At the last date, we define $f_{i,T+1} = 0$ and $f_{i,T} = i$, for all i. At the second last date, a straightforward calculation shows that

$$f_{i,T-1} = \begin{cases} 2i & \text{for } 0 < i < I \\ p & \text{for } i = 0 \\ 2I - p & \text{for } i = I \end{cases} .$$

In other words, the function $f_{\cdot,T-1}$ is convex in the region near $i = 0$, linear between $i = 0$ and $i = I$, and concave in the region near $i = I$. If we continue this calculation backward, we find that the regions of strict concavity and strict convexity grow until they meet in the middle. (Since we have fixed the transition probability parameter p, the process is symmetric.) The proof is by induction. Suppose that for some $t, f_{\cdot,t}$ is a symmetric function that is convex in the region $i \leq I/2$ and concave in the region $i \geq I/2$. Then the same is true for the function $f_{\cdot,t-1}$. Thus, we can show that all the functions $f_{\cdot,t}$ have the logistic shape shown in figures 8.1 through 8.3. Things are slightly more complicated in the calculations required to produce the figures: there the transition probabilities are endogenous and depend in a nontrivial way on the state. This is why the critical value of market share that triggers the switch from R to S is not always 1/2.

Competition with Absorbing Barriers

Once we realize the importance of reflecting barriers, it is natural to ask what would happen if we made some other assumption. Suppose, for example, that we assumed absorbing barriers. In this case, a bank that achieves zero market share goes out of business; its rival retains the whole market forever. Formally, we retain all the assumptions of the last section, except that when the market position is $i = 0$ (resp. $i = I$), the position remains the same in the next period, with probability one. The continuation payoffs are shown in figures 8.4 through 8.6 for the utility functions with the parameter values $c = 1, 2, 4$ respectively. Here we see that continuation payoffs retain the shape of the instantaneous payoff function. When u_i is linear, so is U_{it}; when u_i is convex, so is U_{it}. It is easy to see why this should be so. Consider the linear case. From the specification of the transition probabilities and the recursive equation for the continuation payoffs, we have

$$U_{it} = \begin{cases} 0 & \text{if } i = 0 \\ I^{-1} + U_{I,t+1} & \text{if } i = I \\ i/I^2 + p(U_{i-1,t+1} + U_{i+1,t+1}) + (1 - 2p)U_{i,t+1} & \text{if } 0 < i < I. \end{cases}$$

Now if $U_{i,t+1}$ is linear, say, $U_{i,t+1} = \alpha_{t+1} i$ for some $\alpha_{t+1} > 0$, this reduces to

$$U_{it} = \begin{cases} 0 & \text{if } i = 0 \\ I^{-1} + \alpha_{t+1} I & \text{if } i = I \\ i/I^2 + \alpha_{t+1} i & \text{if } 0 < i < I, \end{cases}$$

so $U_{i,t}$ is also linear; in fact, $U_{i,t} = \alpha_t i$, where $\alpha_t = \alpha_t + I^{-1}$.

Reflecting barriers generate risk-taking and risk-avoiding behavior in a way that absorbing barriers do not. The leads to an interesting point. When we considered risk-shifting behavior, it was the possibility of

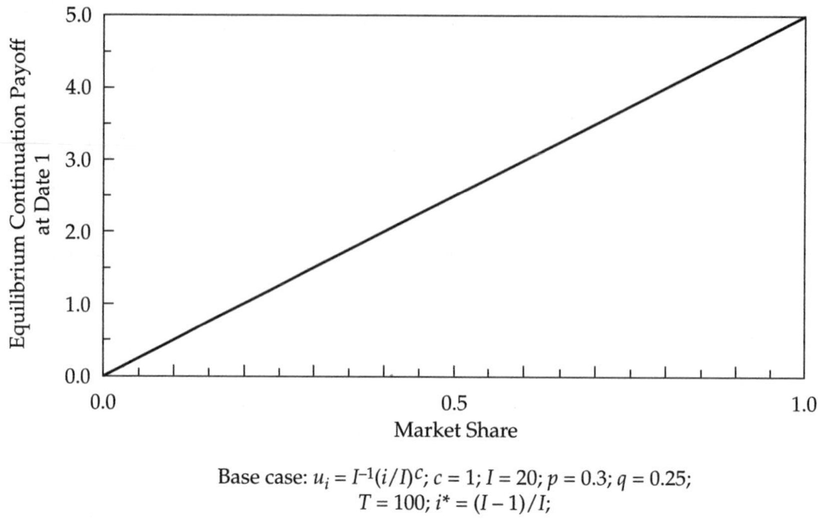

Figure 8.4
Absorbing barriers: equilibrium

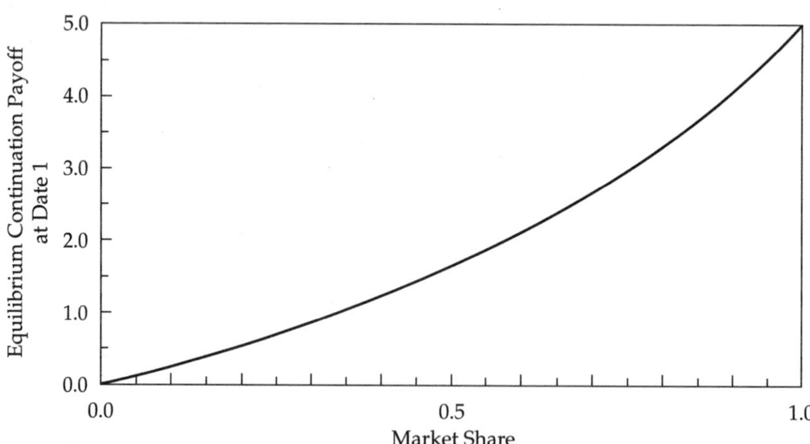

Figure 8.5
Absorbing barriers: equilibrium with $c = 2$

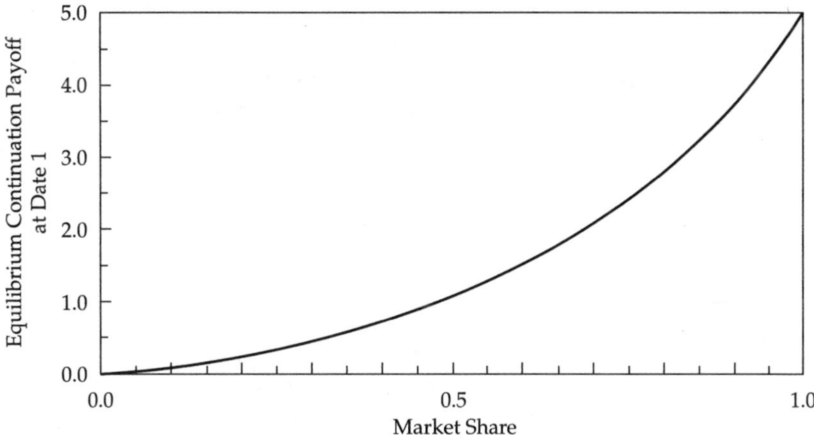

Figure 8.6
Absorbing barriers: equilibrium with $c = 4$

bankruptcy that limited the bank's downside risk and made the objective function convex. Here the counterpart to bankruptcy occurs in the model with an absorbing barrier, but this does not appear to increase the bank's incentive to take risk. The reason is that we have assumed that the bank's position can change only a little bit at a time. If we made the period length and the step size very small, the binomial process we are considering would approximate Brownian motion, which has continuous sample paths with probability one. It is the continuity of the movement of the bank's market share over time that eliminates the usual incentive for risk taking. The bank becomes "bankrupt" as soon as its market share hits zero. It cannot go below the line, and so it cannot shift risk to depositors or other creditors. The bank analyzed in the preceding section has the possibility of ending up with a significantly negative position because there are only two points at which the asset position is observed: before and after the return is realized. This can happen either because the bank is monitored at lengthy intervals or because it can make commitments to long-term investments that cannot be recalled once they are undertaken. If, on the other hand, the return were monitored continuously and the bank liquidates as soon as it became insolvent (had a liquidated net worth of zero), then that bank as well would lose the incentive to take risk in order to shift it to depositors. Although this point is analytically trivial, it has important implications for the regulation of banks.

Returning to the subject of absorbing barriers, we see that although their presence eliminates the positive incentive for risk taking that was found in the model with reflecting barriers, it also eliminates the incentive to avoid risk when market share is high that was found in the same model. Whether the incentive to take risk is greater or less is ambiguous.

Competition with Entry

With absorbing barriers, a bank that loses all of its market share effectively disappears from the market, leaving its rival in possession of the entire market for the remainder of the game. This prize that comes with the achievement of 100 percent market share may give banks an additional incentive to take risk when their market share is already large: if its market share goes down, it has lost only a small amount of income, but if it goes up, it secures the maximum income forever. To see whether this effect is an important incentive for risk taking, we change the model to ensure that a bank always has a rival. More precisely, we assume that when a bank exits the market, it is immediately replaced by an identical bank with the same market share. This model is halfway between the previous models with reflecting and absorbing barriers: to the successful bank it looks like the model with reflecting barriers, but to the failed bank it looks like a model with absorbing barriers. There is still a risk of bankruptcy if a bank is unsuccessful in competing with its rival, but a successful bank cannot hope to capture the market by eliminating the competition: as soon as one small bank is eliminated, another one springs up.

The results obtained in this case suggest that it is very similar to the model with absorbing barriers. In other words, it is the reflecting barriers that are important for generating risk-taking behavior. This is somewhat surprising because our entry assumption implies that there is in fact a reflecting barrier at the upper boundary $i = I$, so one might have thought this would encourage risk avoidance, as in the model with two reflecting barriers.

Asymmetric Equilibria

So far we have focused on symmetric equilibria, in which both banks use the same cutoff point. There also exist asymmetric equilibria, in which one bank will use the risky strategy over a wider range of the market positions than the other. Figures 8.7 through 8.9 show the asymmetric equilibria corresponding to the parameter values $c = 1, 2, 4$ for the model with two reflecting barriers. When the instantaneous payoff function is linear, the continuation payoffs are (roughly) linear for one bank and logistic for the other. The cutoffs are 0.45 for the first (the same as in the symmetric case) and 0.50 for the second. When the instantaneous payoff function is slightly convex ($c = 2$), one bank has a strictly convex continuation payoff and always chooses the risky strategy; the other has the usual logistic shape and has a cutoff of 0.65. The most convex case ($c = 4$) is qualitatively similar: the only difference is that the cutoff for the second bank has increased from 0.65 to 0.7. As far as one can tell from looking at these diagrams, asymmetric equilibria appear to encourage more risk taking.

Invariant Distributions

So far we have focused on the continuation payoff U_{it} and the relationship between the state of the market and the banks' choices. To see what is going on in equilibrium, however, we also need to know the distribution of the random state. Without this information it is hard to draw any firm conclusions about the amount of risk taking in equilibrium, because we do not know which states and hence which actions are relevant. For example, in the equilibrium corresponding to figure 8.1, both firms will sooner or later find themselves in the central region where both choose S. At that point, the state of the market becomes constant, and the rest of the strategy is irrelevant. (This conclusion is not robust to allowing a small probability of change when both banks choose S. In that case, the support of the invariant distribution is the entire set $\{0, 1, \ldots, I\}$.)

In other cases the invariant distribution is not trivial, but it turns out to be easy to calculate for any given equilibrium. Let $\{\mu_i\}$ denote the invariant distribution of a symmetric equilibrium, that is, μ_i is the probability that state i is observed in a stochastic stationary state. Recall that the critical value i^* indicates that the bank with market share i chooses the risky strategy in states $i = 0, \ldots, i^*$ and the safe strategy in states $i = i^* + 1, \ldots, I$. We assume that $i^* > I/2$. This implies that for extreme values of i, one bank chooses the safe strategy and one chooses the risky strategy; for intermediate values, both choose the risky strategy.

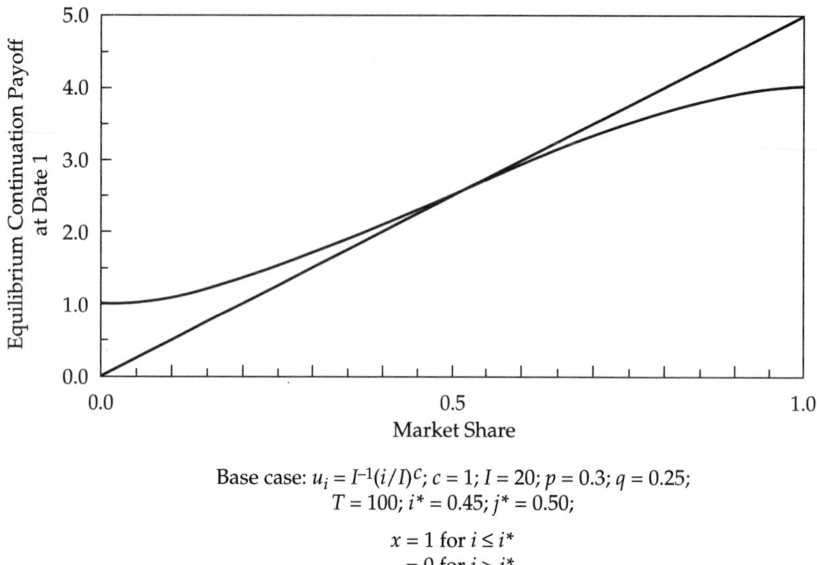

Figure 8.7
Reflecting barriers: asymmetric equilibrium

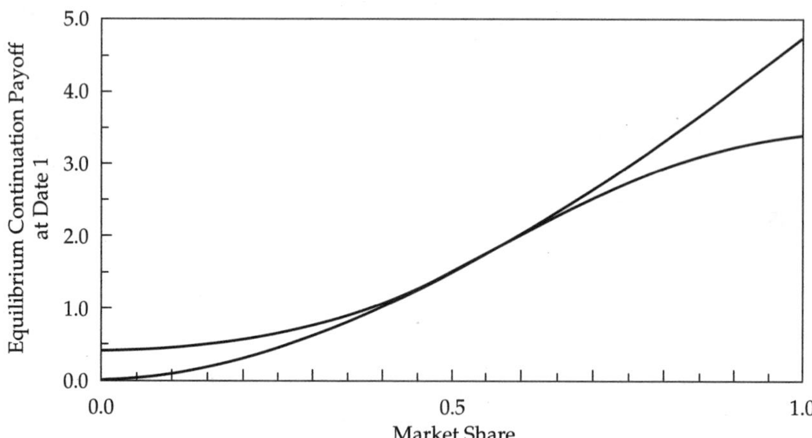

Figure 8.8
Reflecting barriers: asymmetric equilibrium with $c = 2$, $i^* = 0.65$, and $j^* = 1$

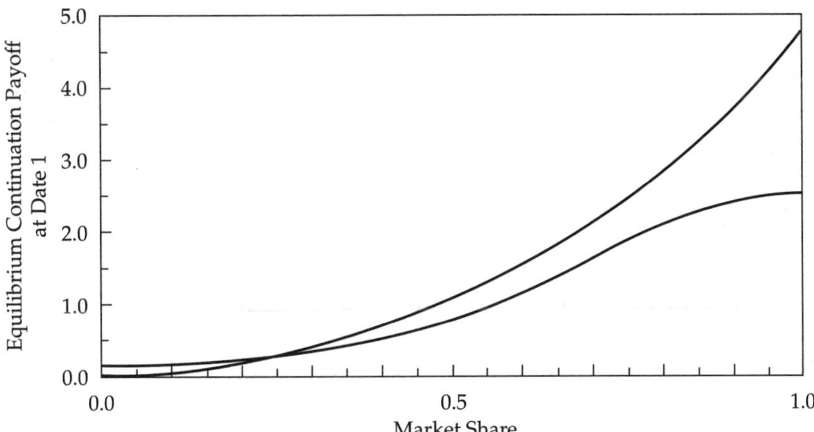

Figure 8.9
Reflecting barriers: asymmetric equilibrium with $c = 4$, $i^* = 0.7$, and $j^* = 1$

The probabilities that make up the invariant distribution satisfy a number of different conditions, depending on whether the associated state is on the boundary or in the interior of the state space and on the strategies chosen by the banks in that state and in neighboring states. First, consider the boundary states $i = 0$ and $i = I$. Here we have the conditions

$$\mu_0 = (1 - q)\mu_0 + q\mu_1$$

$$\mu_I = (1 - q)\mu_I + q\mu_{I-1},$$

since the probability of being in a boundary state is the invariant probability of being in that state last period and staying there plus the invariant probability of being in the neighboring state and moving to the boundary state. From these conditions it follows that

$$\mu_1 = \mu_0, \mu_{I-1} = \mu_I.$$

Next consider the states $0 < i \leq I - i^* - 1$ and $i^* + 1 \leq i < I$. We know that one bank is choosing the risky action and the other is choosing the safe action in any state i satisfying these conditions and also in the neighboring states $i - 1$ and $i + 1$. Then the invariant probabilities must satisfy

$$\mu_i = q\mu_{i-1} + (1 - 2q)\mu_i + q\mu_{i+1},$$

since the probability of entering i in the steady state is equal to the sum of the probabilities of being in $i-1$ and $i+1$, respectively, and making the transition to i plus the probability of being in i and staying there. From these conditions and the boundary conditions, it is easy to show that

$$\mu_i = \mu_0 \text{ for } i = 0 \ldots, I - i^* - 1$$

$$\mu_i = \mu_I \text{ for } i = i^* + 1 \ldots, I.$$

Similarly, for values of i in the intermediate range $I - i^* < i < i^*$, both banks are choosing the risky action in state i and in the neighboring states $i-1$ and $i+1$. Then the invariance condition is

$$\mu_i = p\mu_{i-1} + (1-2p)\mu_i + p\mu_{i+1},$$

which implies that

$$\mu_i = (\mu_{i-1} + \mu_{i+1})/2$$

for all i in this range. So the distribution is also linear in this range.

Now consider the state $i = I - i^* - 1$. In states i and $i-1$ the transition probability is q; in state $i+1$ it is p. The invariance condition is

$$\mu_i = q\mu_{i-1} + (1-2q)\mu_i + p\mu_{i+1},$$

and since $\mu_{i-1} = \mu_i$, we get

$$\mu_i = (q/p)\mu_0 \text{ for } i = I - i^*.$$

A similar argument for $i = i^* + 1$ yields

$$\mu_i = (q/p)\mu_I \text{ for } i = i^* + 1.$$

By symmetry and the uniqueness of the invariant distribution, we must have $\mu_0 = \mu_I$, which implies that $\mu_i = \mu_{i+1}$ for $i = I - i^* \ldots, i^*$. Putting all these results together,

$$\mu_i = \begin{cases} \mu_0 & \text{if } i \leq I - i^* - 1 \text{ or } i \geq i^* + 1 \\ (q/p)\mu_0 & \text{if } I - i^* \leq i \leq i^*. \end{cases}$$

Using the condition that the probabilities sum to one, we get the following expression for μ_0:

$$\mu_0 = \left(I + 1 - \frac{p-q}{p}(2i^* - I) \right)^{-1}.$$

The picture of the distribution that emerges is of two plateaux on either side of a valley in the middle. The middle section is lower because the higher transition probability $p > q$ implies that the system will pass through this part more rapidly and hence spend less time here on average. This means that although there is a region where both banks choose the risky action, the very fact that both are choosing the risky action will tend to reduce the likelihood of seeing this action. The mere size of the region in which the risky action is chosen by both does not tell the whole story.

For the asymmetric equilibrium, the story is similar, but the regions are asymmetric. Both banks choose the risky strategy if $i = 1 \ldots, i^*$; otherwise, one chooses the risky strategy and one the safe strategy. This means that the lower interval in which one bank chooses the safe strategy is restricted to the singleton $i = 0$. With this change, the calculation remains the same. This gives us the invariant distribution

$$\mu_i = \begin{cases} \mu_0 & \text{if } i = 0 \text{ or } i \geq i^* + 1 \\ (q/p)\mu_0 & \text{if } 1 \leq i \leq i^*. \end{cases}$$

Using the condition that the probabilities sum to one, we get the following expression for μ_0:

$$\mu_0 = \left(I + \frac{q}{p} - \frac{p-q}{p} i^* \right)^{-1}.$$

The invariant distribution gives us a theoretical characterization of the long-run behavior of the model, in the sense that the average frequency of any state i converges to the invariant probability of that state as the number of periods approaches infinity. But for any finite horizon, the initial conditions matter. As an illustration of how fast (or slowly) the average frequencies may converge, we have simulated the model over a number of horizons and calculated the average frequency of each state.

8.5 Competition and Financial Stability

Before leaving the analysis of competition, another aspect of competition policy must be mentioned. One of the central objectives of banking policy is the maintenance of financial stability. By comparison with other countries, where the banking sector is dominated by a few large banks, the United States, with its much more "competitive" banking sector, appears to have had a history of much greater financial instability. There are various reasons for this, including the late development of central banking in the United States, but it seems reasonable to suppose that the large number of small banks that characterized the U.S. banking system played a role. To the extent that there is a relationship between the size and number of banks and the stability of the financial system, there may be a conflict between competition policy and financial stability. The efficiency gains achieved by restricting the size of banks may be small compared to the costs incurred as a result of banks' failing. We have already seen that small banks may have greater incentives to take risky behavior. Problems of coordination and monitoring will also be greater in a system with a large number of small banks. Finally, it can be argued that larger banks are inherently more stable because of their greater ability to spread risks and because they are less subject to contagion when the banking sector is subjected to some external shock. One of the problems of any bank is that its assets may be illiquid because of asymmetric information about the value of the assets. To an outsider, it is not clear whether a bank is selling assets because they are "bad" assets that have low value or because of a need for liquidity that is unrelated to the value of the assets. Because of this lemons problem, a liquidity shock may cause an otherwise healthy bank to fail. For the same reason, the failure of one troubled bank can spread by contagion to other banks, which were previously sound. One of the benefits of merging banks is that the asymmetry of information is internalized, with the result that liquidity can be provided more efficiently.

Casual empiricism supports the notion that a more "competitive" banking sector, with large numbers of relatively small banks, may be more prone to financial instability than a concentrated banking sector with a few large banks. Surprisingly, the relationship between stability and competition has not been studied as extensively as one might expect. On the one hand, there are many models of competition in the literature, including models of bank regulation in a competitive environment (see Freixias and Rochet 1997, chap. 3, for a survey). On the other hand, there is a well-developed literature on bank crises, stemming from the seminal work of Diamond and Dybvig (1983), which typically assumes a competitive environment. But there is little on the impact of competition on stability. Two exceptions are the work of Matutes and Vives (1996), which assumes that greater size is associated with lower risk and studies the optimal policy in this context; and the work of Rochet and Tirole (1996), who develop a model of mutual bank monitoring in order to study the doctrine of "too big to fail." We have explored the relationship between competitive pressures and the incentives for risk taking, but only scraped the surface of a large and complex subject. Clearly much remains to be done.

8.6 Conclusions

This chapter has considered various aspects of competition in banking. The first result was to show that the focus in the United States of ensuring competition by having a large number of banks can in fact have the reverse effect. Having a small number of banks with large networks can lead to more competition in the provision of services than would occur with a large number of spatially isolated banks. This suggests that the traditional U.S. policy of having a large number of banks may have been misplaced, and the current consolidation of the banking industry is desirable. Current policies in the EU to extend the size of the market and have banks with larger networks may also lead to an improvement.

One possible effect of an increase in competition in the banking sector and an associated reduction in profits is to increase the incentive for banks to take risks in their investments. The reason is that banks' incentives are distorted by their use of debt contracts with depositors. This distortion is reduced the greater the degree of concentration and the higher is the level of profits. As a result, a concentrated banking system can be more efficient than a competitive one. These results were proved in a static context initially, but it was also shown that they hold in a dynamic context. The incentives to take risks can be involved in this case, however.

Finally, there is likely to be a relationship between competition and financial instability. A lower degree of competition can lead to higher profits, and hence a larger "buffer" should the financial system be hit by a shock. The subject of financial instability will be discussed in some detail in the next chapter.

References

Alhadeff, D. (1954). *Monopoly and Competition in Banking*. Berkeley: University of California.

Barth, J., D. Nolle, and T. Rice. (1997). "Commercial Banking Structure, Regulation and Performance: An International Comparison." Economics working paper 97-6, Office of the Comptroller of the Currency, Washington, D.C.

Berger, A., J. Leusner, and J. Mingo. (1997). "The Efficiency of Bank Branches." *Journal of Monetary Economics* **40,** 141–162.

Berger, A., and L. Mester. (1997). "Inside the Black Box: What Explains Differences in the Efficiencies of Financial Institutions?" *Journal of Banking and Finance* **21,** 895–947.

Cerasi, V., B. Chizzolini, and M. Ivaldi. (1997). "Sunk Costs and Competitiveness of European Banks after Deregulation." Working paper 16, Série Banque, Assurance, Finance, Institut d'Economie Industrielle, Toulouse.

Diamond, D., and P. Dybvig. (1983). "Bank Runs, Deposit Insurance, and Liquidity." *Journal of Political Economy* 91, 401–419.

Diamond, P. (1971). "A Model of Price Adjustment." *Journal of Economic Theory* **3,** 156–168.

Fischer, G. (1968). *American Banking Structure.* New York: Columbia University Press.

Freixas, X., and J. Rochet. (1997). *Microeconomics of Banking*. Cambridge: MIT Press.

Fudenberg, D., and J. Tirole. (1991). *Game Theory.* Cambridge: MIT Press.

Gilbert, R. (1984). "Bank Market Structure and Competition: A Survey." *Journal of Money, Credit and Banking* **16,** 617–644.

Keeley, M. (1990). "Deposit Insurance, Risk and Market Power in Banking." *American Economic Review* **80,** 1183–1200.

Matutes C., and X. Vives. (1996). "Competition for Deposits, Fragility and Insurance." *Journal of Financial Intermediation* **5,** 184–216.

Rhoades, S. (1982). "Welfare Loss, Redistribution Effects and Restriction of Output Due to Monopoly in Banking." *Journal of Monetary Economics* **9,** 375–387.

Rochet, J., and J. Tirole. (1996). "Interbank Lending and Systemic Risk." *Journal of Money, Credit and Banking* **28,** 733–762.

9 Financial Crises

In chapter 6 we studied one of the possible advantages of a financial system that relies heavily on banks and other institutions rather than markets. We argued that financial markets are excessively volatile and expose investors to market risk, especially when investors are subject to liquidity shocks. Banks and other financial intermediaries may be able to smooth returns over time in two ways. First, because their assets are not marked-to-market, they can eliminate market risk. Second, they may engage in intertemporal smoothing by accumulating reserves.

In chapter 8 we pointed out some ways in which banks and other financial institutions may increase risk in the financial system. In particular, like any investor with debt liabilities, banks have an incentive to engage in risk-shifting behavior when they are close to the waterline. There are other ways in which an intermediary-based financial system is prone to risk, however. Because banks have a mismatch between the maturities of liquid liabilities on the one hand and illiquid assets on the other, they are vulnerable to liquidity shocks. In particular, they are prone to bank runs, in which the bank's depositors attempt to withdraw their funds simultaneously. When this happens to several banks simultaneously, there is a banking panic or crisis. Banks may be seen as the victims of banking panics, but in other cases the banking system may actually be accused of creating the conditions that make a crisis inevitable. For example, when the banking system creates credit, this can lead to excessive borrowing that leads to a bubble in asset prices. The collapse of the bubble can then lead to defaults, which exacerbate the fall in prices and cause serious dislocation in the economy. Finally, it is often argued that the banking system is financially fragile, in the sense that a small shock in one part of the system can spread like a contagion to other parts of the system, leading to a cumulative effect that is many times larger than the size of initial shock.

In this chapter we focus on the origins and optimal management of financial crises. The first two sections describe a model of banking panics and use it to analyze optimal monetary policy. We argue that optimal policy should attempt to eliminate the allocative distortions caused by the crisis, particularly costly asset liquidations, rather than attempting to eliminating crises per se. The third section discusses how credit expansion and bank-financed investment can lead to bubbles that increase the extent and likelihood of a crisis. There is much more to be said about this topic than can be put into a single chapter, and, in particular, we do not consider the issue of financial contagion (see Allen and Gale 1998c for an analysis). However, we hope that readers are alerted to the interest and complexity of the subject.

9.1 Banking Panics

From the earliest times, banks have been plagued by bank runs, in which the bank's depositors attempt to withdraw their funds simultaneously. A financial crisis or panic occurs when depositors at many or all of the banks in a region or a country attempt to withdraw their funds simultaneously. One of the great achievements in the history of banking was the development of central banking techniques to eliminate crises. These were discovered in Europe in the nineteenth century, but effective central banking was not established in the United States until after the crisis of 1933.

Although banking panics appear to be a thing of the past in Europe and the United States, many emerging countries have had severe banking problems in recent years. Lindgren, Garcia, and Saal (1996) find that about three-quarters of the member countries of the International Monetary Fund (IMF) suffered some form of banking crisis between 1980 and 1996. In many of these crises, panics in the traditional sense were avoided by either central bank intervention or explicit or implicit government guarantees. This raises the issue of whether such intervention is desirable.

Given the historical importance of panics and their current relevance in emerging countries, it is important to understand why they occur and the policies that central banks should implement to deal with them. Although there is a large literature on bank runs, there is relatively little on the optimal policy that should be followed to manage runs. (But see Bhattacharya and Gale 1987, Rochet and Tirole 1996, and Bensaid, Pages, and Rochet 1996.) The history of regulation of the United States and other countries' financial systems seems to be based on the premise that banking crises are bad and should be eliminated. We argue below that optimal policy must weigh the costs and benefits of bank runs. Eliminating runs completely is unlikely to be optimal. An optimal response by the central bank must prevent the deadweight costs of asset liquidation while accommodating the contingent consumption allocation required by optimal risk sharing.

There are two traditional views of banking panics: the *sunspot view* and the *real business cycle view.* The classical form of the sunspot view suggests that panics are the result of mob psychology or mass hysteria (see, e.g., Kindleberger 1978). The modern version, developed by Diamond and Dybvig (1983) and Bryant (1980), is that bank runs are self-fulfilling prophecies. Given the sequential service constraint and costly liquidation of some assets, there are two equilibria. If depositors believe that a bank run is about to occur, it is optimal for each individual to try to withdraw his funds. If depositors believe that a run will not occur, then it is optimal for each to leave his funds in the bank. Which of these two equilibria occurs depends on extraneous variables, or "sunspots." (Postlewaite and Vives 1987 have shown how runs can be generated in a model with a unique equilibrium.)

An alternative to the sunspot view is that banking panics are a natural outgrowth of the business cycle. An economic downturn will reduce the value of bank assets, raising the possibility that banks are unable to meet their commitments. If depositors receive information about an impending downturn in the cycle, they will anticipate financial difficulties in the banking sector and try to withdraw their funds. This attempt will precipitate the crisis. According to this interpretation, panics are not random events but a response to unfolding economic circumstances (see, for example, Mitchell 1941).

A number of authors have developed models of banking panics caused by aggregate risk. Wallace (1988, 1990), Chari (1989) and Champ, Smith, and Williamson (1996) extend Diamond and Dybvig (1983) by assuming the fraction of the population requiring liquidity is random. Chari and Jagannathan (1988), Jacklin and Bhattacharya (1988), Hellwig (1994), and Alonso (1996) introduce aggregate uncertainty, which can be interpreted as business cycle risk. Chari and Jagannathan (1988) focus on a signal extraction problem where part of the population observes a signal about future returns. Others must then try to deduce from observed withdrawals whether an unfavorable signal was received by this group or whether liquidity needs happen to be high. Chari and Jagannathan are able to show that panics occur not only when the outlook is poor but also when liquidity needs turn out to be high. Jacklin and Bhattacharya (1988) also consider a model where some depositors receive an interim signal about risk. They show that the optimality of bank deposits compared to equities depends on the characteristics of the risky investment. Hellwig (1994) considers a model where the reinvestment rate is random and shows that the risk should be borne by both early and late withdrawers (see also von Thadden 1997, 1998). Alonso (1996) demonstrates using numerical examples that contracts where runs occur may be better than contracts that ensure runs do not occur because they improve risk sharing.

Gorton (1988) conducts an empirical study to differentiate between the sunspot view and the business cycle view of banking panics. He finds evidence consistent with the view that banking panics are related to the business cycle and difficult to reconcile with the notion of panics as random events. Table 9.1 shows the recessions and panics that occurred in the United States during the national banking era (1863–1914). It also shows the corresponding percentage changes in the currency/deposit ratio, which indicate the severity of the panics, and the change in aggregate consumption, as proxied by the change in pig iron production during these periods. The five worst recessions, as measured by the change in pig iron production, were accompanied by panics. In all, panics occurred in seven of the eleven cycles. Using the liabilities of failed businesses as a leading economic indicator, Gorton finds that panics were systematic events: whenever this leading economic indicator reached a certain threshold, a panic ensued. The stylized facts Gorton uncovered thus suggest that banking panics are intimately related to the state of the business cycle rather than some extraneous random variable. Calomiris and Gorton (1991) consider a broad range of evidence and conclude that the data do not support the sunspot view that banking panics are random events.

Allen and Gale (1998a) have described a model in which panics are caused by business cycle fundamentals rather than sunspots and used this model to analyze optimal monetary policy. We follow this paper closely in the next two sections.

A Fundamental Model of Bank Panics

As a benchmark, we first consider a model in which bank runs cause no misallocation of assets. Under the maintained assumptions, it can be shown that bank runs are optimal in the sense that the unique equi-

Table 9.1
National banking era panics

NBER cycle peak–trough	Panic date	%Δ (currency deposit)[a]	%Δ pig iron[b]
October 1873–March 1879	September 1873	14.53	−51.0
March 1882–May 1885	June 1884	8.80	−14.0
March 1887–April 1888	No panic	3.00	−9.0
July 1890–May 1891	November 1890	9.00	−34.0
January 1893–June 1894	May 1893	16.00	−29.0
December 1895–June 1897	October 1896	14.30	−4.0
June 1899–December 1900	No panic	2.78	−6.7
September 1902–August 1904	No panic	−4.13	−8.7
May 1907–June 1908	October 1907	11.45	−46.5
January 1910–January 1912	No panic	−2.64	−21.7
January 1913–December 1914	August 1914	10.39	−47.1

a. Percentage change of ratio at panic date to previous year's average.
b. Measured from peak to trough.
Source: Adapted from Gorton (1988, p. 233).

librium with bank runs supports a first-best allocation of risk and investment. There is no rationale for intervention by the central bank to prevent runs or change the allocation of resources. This model is quite special, as we shall see, but it makes the point that bank runs per se are not necessarily a bad thing. In order to provide a rationale for central bank intervention, we have to consider why bank crises entail deadweight costs. We pursue this point later, when we introduce assumptions under which bank runs are inefficient and analyze the optimal monetary policy for that case.

Time is divided into three periods, $t = 0, 1, 2$. There are two types of assets—a safe asset and a risky asset—and a consumption good. The safe asset can be thought of as a storage technology, which transforms one unit of the consumption good at date t into one unit of the consumption good at date $t + 1$. The risky asset is represented by a stochastic production technology that transforms one unit of the consumption good at date 0 into R units of the consumption good at date 2, where R is a nonnegative random variable with a density function $f(R)$. At date 1 depositors observe a signal, which can be thought of as a leading economic indicator. This signal predicts with perfect accuracy the value of R that will be realized at date 2.

There is a continuum of ex ante identical depositors (consumers) who have an endowment of the consumption good at the first date and none at the second and third dates. Consumers are uncertain about their time preferences. Some will be early consumers, who want to consume only at date 1, and some will be late consumers, who want to consume only at date 2. At date 0 consumers know the probability of being an early or late consumer, but they do not know which group they belong to. All uncertainty is resolved at date 1, when each consumer learns whether he is an early or late consumer and what the return on the risky asset is going to be. For simplicity, we assume that there are equal numbers of early and late consumers and that each consumer has an equal chance of belonging to each group. Then a typical consumer's utility function can be written as

$$U(c_1, c_2) = \begin{cases} u(c_1) & \text{with probability } 1/2 \\ u(c_2) & \text{with probability } 1/2, \end{cases}$$

where c_t denotes consumption at date $t = 1, 2$. The period utility functions $u(\cdot)$ are assumed to be twice continuously differentiable, increasing, and strictly concave. A consumer's type is not observable, so late consumers can always imitate early consumers. Therefore, contracts explicitly contingent on this characteristic are not feasible.

The role of banks is to make investments on behalf of consumers. Only banks have the expertise to invest in the risky asset, whereas anyone can hold the safe asset. By pooling the assets of a large number of consumers, the bank can offer insurance to consumers against their uncertain liquidity demands, giving the early consumers some of the benefits of the high-yielding risky asset without subjecting them to the volatility of the asset market.

Free entry into the banking industry forces banks to compete by offering deposit contracts that maximize the expected utility of the consumers. Thus, the behavior of the banking industry can be represented by an optimal risk-sharing problem. In the next two subsections we analyze the risk-sharing problems corresponding to different assumptions about the informational and regulatory environment.

There are two main differences between the model we have described and the original Diamond-Dybvig model. The first is the assumption that the illiquid, long-term assets that banks hold are risky and perfectly correlated across banks. Uncertainty about asset returns is intended to capture the impact of the business cycle on the value of bank assets. Information about returns becomes available before the returns are realized, and when the information is bad, it has the power to precipitate a crisis. The second is that we do not make the first-come, first-served assumption. This assumption has been the subject of some debate in the literature as it is not an optimal arrangement in the basic Diamond-Dybvig model (see Wallace 1988 and Calomiris and Kahn 1991). In a number of countries and historical time periods, banks have had the right to delay payment for some time period on certain types of account. This is rather different from the first-come, first-served assumption. Kroszner (1997) recounts how in the free banking era in Scotland in the eighteenth and nineteenth centuries, banks adopted an option clause, which allowed them to postpone convertibility. Sprague (1910) recounts how in the United States in the late nineteenth century, people could obtain liquidity once a panic had started by using certified checks, which traded at a discount. We model this type of situation by assuming the available liquidity is split on an equal basis among those withdrawing early. In the current context, this arrangement is optimal. We also assume that those who do not withdraw early have to wait before they can obtain their funds, and again what is available is split between them on an equal basis.

The Optimal, Incentive-Compatible, Risk-Sharing Problem

Consider the case where banks can write contracts in which the amount that can be withdrawn at each date is contingent on R. This provides a benchmark for optimal risk sharing. Since the proportions of early and late consumers are always equal, the only aggregate uncertainty comes from the return to the risky asset R. Since the risky asset return is not known until the second date, the portfolio choice is independent of R, but the payments to early and late consumers, which occur after R is revealed, will depend on it. Let E denote the consumers' total endowment of the consumption good at date 0, and let X and L denote the representative bank's holding of the risky and safe assets, respectively. The deposit contract can be represented by a pair of functions, $c_1(R)$ and $c_2(R)$, which give the consumption of early and late consumers conditional on the return to the risky asset.

The optimal risk-sharing problem can be written as follows:

$$(P1) \left\{ \begin{array}{lll} \max & & \mathrm{E}[u(c_1(R)) + u(c_2(R))] \\ \text{s.t.} & (1) & L + X \leq E; \\ & (2) & c_1(R) \leq L; \\ & (3) & c_2(R) \leq (L - c_1(R)) + RX; \\ & (4) & c_1(R) \leq c_2(R). \end{array} \right.$$

The first constraint says that the total amount invested must be less than or equal to the amount deposited. There is no loss of generality in assuming that consumers deposit their entire wealth with the bank, since anything they can do, the bank can do for them. The second constraint says that the holding of the safe asset must be sufficient to provide for the consumption of the early consumers. The bank may want to hold strictly more than this amount and roll it over to the final period, in order to reduce the consumption variability of the late consumers. The next constraint, together with the preceding one, says that the consumption of the late consumers cannot exceed the total value of the risky asset plus the amount of the safe asset left over after the early consumers are paid off. The final constraint is the incentive compatibility constraint. It says that for every value of R, the late consumers must be at least as well off as the early consumers. Since late consumers are paid off at date 2, an early consumer cannot imitate a late consumer. However, a late consumer can imitate an early consumer, obtain $c_1(R)$ at date 1, and use the storage technology to provide himself with $c_1(R)$ units of consumption at date 2. It will be optimal to do this unless $c_1(R) \leq c_2(R)$ for every value of R.

The following assumptions are maintained throughout this section and the next to ensure interior optima. The preferences and technology are assumed to satisfy the inequalities

$$\mathrm{E}[R] > 1$$

and

$$u'(0) > \mathrm{E}[u'(RE)R].$$

The first inequality ensures that investors will always hold a positive amount of the risky asset and the second that they will always hold a positive amount of the safe asset.

An examination of the optimal risk-sharing problem shows us that the incentive constraint (4) can be dispensed with. To see this, suppose that we solve the problem subject to the first three constraints only. A necessary condition for an optimum is that the consumption of the two types be equal, unless the feasibility constraint $c_1(R) \leq L$ is binding, in which case it follows from the first order-conditions that $c_1(R) = L \leq c_2(R)$. Thus, the incentive constraint will always be satisfied if we optimize subject to the first three constraints only and the solution to (*P1*) is the first-best allocation.

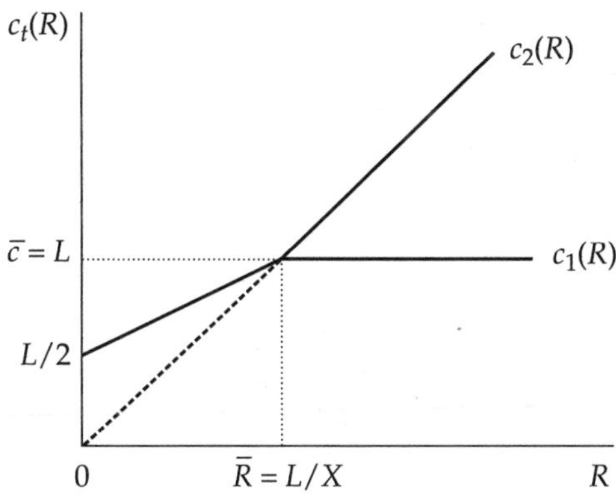

Figure 9.1
Optimal risk-sharing allocation and the optimal deposit contract with runs

The optimal contract is illustrated in figure 9.1. When the signal at date 1 indicates that $R = 0$ at date 2, both the early and late consumers receive $L/2$ since L is all that is available and it is efficient to equate consumption given the form of the objective function. The early consumers consume their share at date 1 with the remaining $L/2$ carried over until date 2 for the late consumers. As R increases, both groups can consume more. Provided $R \leq L/X \equiv \overline{R}$, the optimal allocation involves carrying over some of the liquid asset to date 2 to supplement the low returns on the risky asset for late consumers. When the signal indicates that R will be high at date 2 (i.e., $R > L/X \equiv \overline{R}$), then early consumers should consume as much as possible at date 1, which is L since consumption at date 2 will be high in any case. Ideally, the high date 2 output would be shared with the early consumers at date 1, but this is not technologically feasible. It is only possible to carry forward consumption, not bring it back from the future.

Optimal Risk Sharing Through Deposit Contracts with Bank Runs

The optimal risk-sharing problem (*P1*) discussed in the preceding subsection serves as a benchmark for the risk sharing that can be achieved through the kinds of deposit contracts observed in practice. The typical deposit contract is "noncontingent," where the quotation marks are necessitated by the fact that the feasibility constraint may introduce some contingency where none is intended in the original contract. We take a standard deposit contract to be one that promises a fixed amount at each date and pays out all available liquid assets, divided equally among those withdrawing, in the event that the bank does not have enough liquid assets to make the promised payment. Let $\bar{c}$ denote the fixed payment promised to the early consumers. We can ignore the amount promised to the late consumers since they are always paid whatever is available at the last date. Then the standard deposit contract promises the early consumers either $\bar{c}$ or, if that is infeasible, an equal share of the liquid assets L, where it has to be borne in mind that some of the late consumers may want to withdraw early as well. In that case, in equilibrium the early and late consumers will have the same consumption.

With these assumptions, the constrained optimal risk-sharing problem can be written as:

$$(P2)\left\{\begin{array}{lll} \max & & \mathrm{E}[u(c_1(R)) + u(c_2(R))] \\ \text{s.t.} & (1) & L + X \leq E; \\ & (2) & c_1(R) \leq L; \\ & (3) & c_2(R) \leq (L - c_1(R)) + RX; \\ & (4) & c_1(R) \leq c_2(R); \\ & (5) & c_1(R) \leq \bar{c} \text{ and } c_1(R) = c_2(R) \text{ if } c_1(R) < \bar{c}. \end{array}\right.$$

All we have done here is to add to the unconstrained optimal risk-sharing problem (*P1*) the additional constraint that either the early consumers are paid the promised amount $\bar{c}$ or else the early and late consumers must get the same payment (consumption).

Behind this formulation of the problem is an equivalent formulation that makes explicit the equilibrium conditions of the model and the possibility of runs. Constraint (5) in (*P2*) is a reduced form of these equilibrium conditions. Without loss of generality $\bar{c} \leq L$, so the bank will always be able to pay the early withdrawers the promised amount unless there is a run. In the event that there is a run, the early and late consumers must get the same consumption because the fraction of late consumers who join the run, denoted $\alpha(R)$, will be less than one except when $R = 0$, in which case the fraction is equal to one. To see this, note that if the late-withdrawing late consumers get to share $RX > 0$, their per capita consumption will be unbounded unless a nonnegligible fraction choose to withdraw late. So when there is a run, the equilibrium conditions require that late consumers be indifferent between joining the run and waiting, that is,

$$c_1(R) = \frac{L}{1 + \alpha(R)} = \frac{RX}{1 - \alpha(R)} = c_2(R).$$

The early consumers who are of measure 1 and the $\alpha(R)$ early-withdrawing late consumers receive a total of L at date 1, which is divided equally among them. The early-withdrawing late consumers carry their share over to date 2 using the safe asset. The $1-\alpha(R)$ late-withdrawing late consumers receive the total payoff from the risky asset RX at date 2, and this is divided equally between them. (See Allen and Gale 1998a for a fuller discussion of the equilibrating role of partial bank runs in this model.)

When we look carefully at the constrained risk-sharing problem (*P2*), we notice that it looks very similar to the unconstrained risk-sharing problem (*P1*) in the preceding section. In fact, the two are equivalent.

THEOREM 9.1 Suppose that $\{L, X, c_1(\cdot), c_2(\cdot)\}$ solves the unconstrained optimal risk-sharing problem (*P1*). Then $\{L, X, c_1(\cdot), c_2(\cdot)\}$ is feasible for the constrained optimal risk-sharing problem (*P2*). Hence, the expected utility of the solution to (*P2*) is the same as the expected utility of the solution to (*P1*), and a banking system subject to runs can achieve first-best efficiency using the standard deposit contract.

The easiest way to see this is to compare the form of the optimal consumption functions from the two problems. From (*P1*) we get

$$c_1(R) = \min\{\frac{1}{2}(L+RX), L\}$$

$$c_2(R) = \max\{\frac{1}{2}(L+RX), RX\},$$

and from (*P2*) we get

$$c_1(R) = \min\{\frac{1}{2}(L+RX), \bar{c}\}$$

$$c_2(R) = \max\{\frac{1}{2}(L+RX), L+RX-\bar{c}\}.$$

The two are identical if we put $\bar{c} = L$. In other words, to achieve the optimum, we minimize the amount of the liquid asset, holding only what is necessary to meet the promised payment for the early consumers, and allow bank runs to achieve the optimal sharing of risk between the early and late consumers. The risk sharing occurs because the lower the value of R, the greater is the proportion of late consumers $\alpha(R)$ who withdraw early and hence the less is the amount consumed by both early and late consumers.

The optimal deposit contract is illustrated by figure 9.1 with $\bar{c} = L$.

We have seen that the first-best outcome can be achieved by means of a "noncontingent" deposit contract together with bank runs that introduce the optimal degree of contingency. Thus, there is no justification for central bank intervention to eliminate runs. In fact, if runs occur in equilibrium, a policy that eliminates runs by forcing the banks to hold a safer portfolio must be strictly worse. It is possible, of course, to conceive of an equilibrium in which banks voluntarily choose to hold such a large amount of the safe asset that runs never occur. However, it can be shown that it is optimal for banks to choose contracts and portfolios such that runs will occur with positive probability if the support of R contains zero (see Allen and Gale 1998a). If the central bank nonetheless prevents runs by passing regulations that restrict the deposit contracts and portfolios that banks can choose, then depositors will be strictly worse off ex ante under these regulations.

9.2 Optimal Monetary Policy

The benchmark case in the preceding section shows that under certain conditions, laissez faire is optimal, and there is no rationale for intervention by the central bank to affect the incidence or severity of banking crises. This result is a useful antidote to simple-minded thinking about the costs of banking crises, but it is a very special case that depends on the following features of the model:

- There is no cost to liquidating the safe asset at date 1 and allowing the late consumers to hold it outside the banking system until date 2.
- The risky asset is completely illiquid. There is no possibility of liquidating it at date 1 even if a run occurs.

Relaxing either of these assumptions gives rise to a distortion in the allocation of assets whenever a bank run occurs with positive probability. This distortion provides a role for central bank policy. In this section, we consider the optimal policy when each of these distortions is relaxed.

Optimal Risk Sharing with Costly Liquidation

The simplest way to introduce a cost of withdrawing the safe asset prematurely is to assume that the return on the safe asset is higher within the banking sector than it is outside. Let $r > 1$ denote the return on the safe asset held by banks between dates 1 and 2. As before, one unit of consumption stored by individuals at date 1 produces one unit of consumption at date 2. Thus, premature withdrawal of one unit of the safe asset incurs a liquidation cost of $r-1>0$. To ensure that equilibria remain interior, it is assumed that the risky asset is more productive on average than the safe asset, that is,

$$\mathrm{E}[R]>r.$$

The characterization of the incentive-efficient deposit contract follows the same lines as before. The bank chooses a portfolio of investments (L, X) and offers the early (late) consumers a consumption level $(c_1(R))$ $(c_2(R))$, conditional on the return on the risky asset. The contract is chosen to maximize the ex ante expected utility of the typical consumer. Formally, the optimal risk-sharing problem can be written as:

$$(P3)\left\{\begin{array}{lll}\max & & \mathrm{E}[u(c_1(R))+u(c_2(R))] \\ \text{s.t.} & (1) & L+X\leq E; \\ & (2) & c_1(R)\leq L; \\ & (3) & c_2(R)\leq r(L-c_1(R))+RX; \\ & (4) & c_1(R)\leq c_2(R).\end{array}\right.$$

The only difference between this optimization problem and the original problem *(P1)* occurs in constraint (3), which reduces to the earlier formulation if we put $r=1$.

To solve problem *P3*, we adopt the same device as before: remove the incentive-compatibility constraint (4) and solve the relaxed problem. The consumption allocation is uniquely determined, given the portfolio (L, X), by the relations

$$u'(c_1(R))=ru'(c_2(R)) \text{ if } R<\bar{R},$$

$$c_1(R)=L,\ c_2(R)=RX \text{ if } R\geq\bar{R},$$

where $\bar{R}$ can be chosen to satisfy $u'(L)=ru'(RX)$. Figure 9.2 illustrates the form of the optimal contract. In figure 9.1 the two groups' consumption is equated whenever there is a run $(R<\bar{R})$. This is no longer the case because the first-order condition $u'(c_1(R))=ru'(c_2(R))$ implies that early consumers get strictly less than late consumers when $r>1$.

Standard Deposit Contracts with Costly Liquidation

The next step is to characterize an equilibrium in which the bank is restricted to use a standard deposit contract and, as a result, bank runs

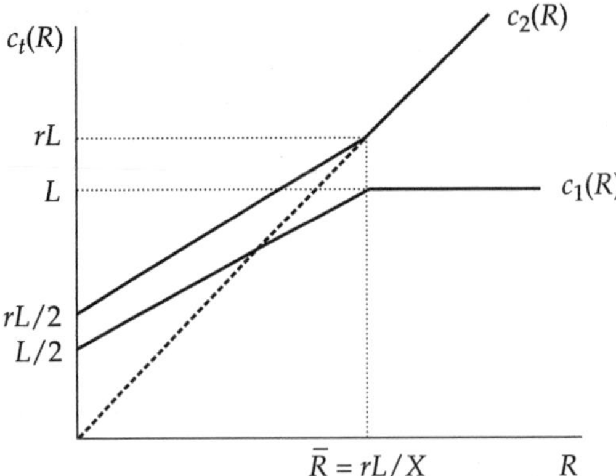

Figure 9.2
Optimal risk-sharing allocation with costly liquidation

become a possibility. With costly liquidation, we have to take explicit account of the fraction of late consumers' joining the run. This is because a unit of consumption withdrawn at date 1 reduces consumption at date 2 by $r - 1$. So here the size of the run affects the total amount of consumption available.

Let $\bar{c}$ denote the payment promised by the bank to anyone withdrawing at date 1, and let $c_1(R)$ and $c_2(R)$ denote the equilibrium consumption levels of early and late consumers, respectively, conditional on the return to the risky asset. Finally, let $0 \leq \alpha(R) \leq 1$ denote the fraction of late consumers who choose to "run," that is, withdraw from the bank at date 1.

The bank chooses a portfolio (L, X), the pair of consumption functions $c_1(R)$ and $c_2(R)$, the deposit parameter $\bar{c}$, and the withdrawal function $\alpha(R)$ to maximize the expected utility of the typical depositor, subject to the following equilibrium conditions. First, the bank's choices must be feasible, and this means that

$$L + X \leq E,$$

$$c_1(R) + \alpha(R)c_2(R) \leq L,$$

$$(1 - \alpha)c_2(R) \leq r(L - c_1(R) - \alpha(R)c_2(R)) + RX.$$

The first two constraints are familiar. The final constraint says that withdrawals in the last period, which equal the consumption of the late-withdrawing fraction of the late consumers, cannot exceed the sum of the returns on the risky asset and the returns on the part of the safe asset that is carried over to the last period.

The standard deposit contract requires the bank to pay the depositors who withdraw in the middle period either a fixed amount $\bar{c}$ or as much as it can from liquid assets. Formally, this amounts to saying that

$$c_1(R) \leq \bar{c},$$

$$c_1(R) + \alpha(R)c_2(R) = L \text{ if } c_1(R) < \bar{c}.$$

Finally, we have the incentive-compatibility condition:

$$c_1(R) \leq c_2(R),$$

and the equal-treatment condition:

$$c_1(R) = c_2(R) \text{ if } \alpha(R) > 0.$$

In other words, if some late consumers withdraw in the middle period, their consumption must be the same as the early consumers since they get the same payment from the bank and store it until the last period. In writing down these conditions, we have implicitly assumed that late consumers get the same consumption whether they withdraw early or late. This will be true in equilibrium, of course.

Having specified the constraints, the bank's problem is formally

$$(P4)\left\{\begin{array}{lll} \max & & \mathrm{E}[u(c_1(R)) + u(c_2(R))] \\ \text{s.t.} & (1) & L + X \leq E \\ & (2) & c_1(R) + \alpha(R)c_2(R) \leq L \\ & (3) & (1-\alpha)c_2(R) \leq r(L - c_1(R) - \alpha(R)c_2(R)) + RX \\ & (4) & c_1(R) \leq \bar{c} \\ & (5) & c_1(R) + \alpha(R)c_2(R) = L \text{ if } c_1(R) < \bar{c} \\ & (6) & c_1(R) \leq c_2(R) \\ & (7) & c_1(R) = c_2(R) \text{ if } \alpha(R) > 0. \end{array}\right.$$

The bank's decision problem can be simplified by noting that early and late consumers share the assets when there is a run ($R < R^*$) and the early consumers get $\bar{c}$ and the late consumers get whatever is left over otherwise ($R > R^*$). Then the decision problem can be reduced to the following:

$$\begin{array}{lll} \max & & \int_0^{R^*} 2u(\frac{L+RX}{2})f(R)dR + \int_{R^*}^{\infty}\{u(\bar{c}) + u(r(L-\bar{c}) + RX)\}f(R)dR \\ \text{s.t.} & (1) & L + X \leq E; \\ & (2) & R^* = \frac{(1+r)\bar{c} - rL}{X}, \end{array}$$

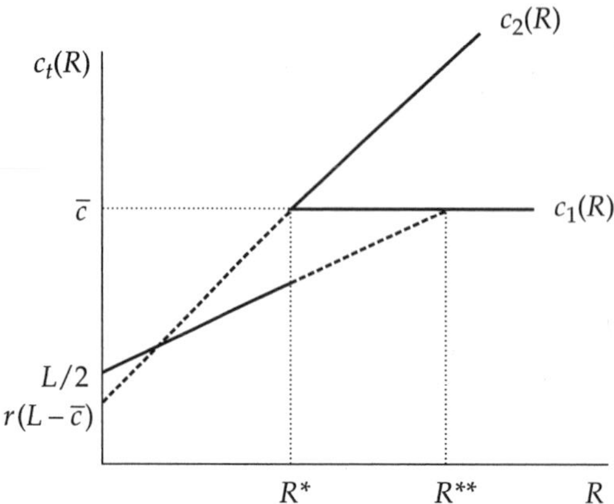

Figure 9.3
Optimal deposit contract with costly liquidation when $\bar{c} < L$

where constraint (1) is the familiar budget constraint and constraint (2) defines the critical return R^* at which runs occur.

There are two types of solution for this problem. The first possibility is $\bar{c} = L$. In this case, none of the safe asset is held over until the last period, and so there is no possibility of inefficient liquidation when a run occurs. The optimal deposit contract is the same as the solution to ($P2$), illustrated in figure 9.1. The second possibility is $\bar{c} < L$. In this case, an amount $L - \bar{c}$ of the safe asset is held over until the final period if a run does not occur and there is a loss of $(r-1)(L-\bar{c})$ from premature liquidation when a run does occur. This case is illustrated in figure 9.3. In both cases the solution is clearly different from and inferior to the optimal allocation shown in figure 9.2.

Monetary Policy with Costly Liquidation

The inefficiency of equilibrium with bank runs arises from the fact that liquidating the safe asset at date 1 and storing the proceeds until date 2 is less productive than reinvesting them in safe assets held by the bank. A simple monetary intervention by the central bank can remedy this inefficiency. Essentially it consists of giving the depositors money that is provided by the central bank instead of goods. In the event of a run at date 1, the central bank gives the representative bank a loan of M units of money. The bank gives depositors a combination of money and consumption whose value equals the fixed amount promised in the deposit contract. Since early consumers want to consume their entire wealth at date 1, they give the money to the early-withdrawing late consumers in exchange for consumption. The price level adjusts so that the early consumers end up with the first-best consumption level, and the early-withdrawing late consumers end up holding all the money. At date 2, the representative bank has to repay its loan to the central bank. For simplicity we assume that the loan bears zero interest. The money now held by late consumers is just enough to allow the bank to repay its loan, and the bank has just enough consumption from its remaining investment in the safe asset to give the early-withdrawing late consumers the first-best consumption level. The price level at date 2 adjusts so that the bank and the early withdrawers can exchange money for consumption in the correct ratio and the bank ends up with the amount of money it needs to repay the loan and the consumers end up with the first-best consumption level.

In order for this intervention to have the required effect on the choice of portfolio and the allocation of consumption, the deposit contract has to be specified in nominal terms. This means that a depositor is promised the equivalent of a fixed amount of money D if he withdraws in the middle period and whatever the representative bank can afford to pay in the final period. This intervention does not require the central bank to condition its policy on the return to the risky asset R. It is sufficient for the central bank to give the representative bank an interest-free line of credit that the representative bank can choose to draw on. Whatever part of the line of credit is used must be repaid in the last period. Without loss of generality, we can fix the size of the line of credit from the central bank and assume that the representative bank uses either none or all of it at date 1.

Suppose that $c_1(R)$ and $c_2(R)$ are the consumption functions derived from the optimal risk-sharing problem so that $c_1(R) < c_2(R)$. In states where $c_1(R) < L$, the price level adjusts so that

$$p_1(R)c_1(R) = D. \tag{9.1}$$

We do not want premature liquidation of the safe asset at date 1, so the late consumers must hold money only between dates 1 and 2. Since the nominal value of a withdrawal at date 1 is D, this implies that

$$\alpha(R)D = M. \tag{9.2}$$

Similarly, we want the early-withdrawing late consumers to be able to afford just $c_2(R)$ at date 2. To ensure this, we must have

$$\alpha(R)p_2(R)c_2(R) = M. \tag{9.3}$$

Clearly, there are many values of $\alpha(R)$, $p_1(R)$, and $p_2(R)$ that will satisfy these conditions. Furthermore, these conditions are sufficient for an equilibrium. At date 1, the bank hands out a mixture of goods and money to withdrawers. The early consumers do not want any money, so they exchange theirs with the late consumers. The late consumers do not want to hold any goods, since the return on money is greater than the return on goods:

$$\frac{p_1(R)}{p_2(R)} = \frac{c_2(R)}{c_1(R)} > 1,$$

where the equality follows from equations 9.1 through 9.3 and the inequality from the fact that in the solution to the optimal risk-sharing problem $c_2(R) > c_1(R)$. Consequently, the late consumers end up holding only money between dates 1 and 2. At date 2, the early-withdrawing late consumers supply all their money inelastically to the representative bank in exchange for goods. The representative bank gets back just enough money to repay its loan from the central bank, and has enough goods left over to give each late-withdrawing late consumer $c_2(R)$.

THEOREM 9.2 Suppose that the central bank makes available to the representative bank an interest-free line of credit of M units of money at date 1 that must be repaid at date 2. Then there exist equilibrium price levels $p_1(R)$ and $p_2(R)$ and an equilibrium fraction of early withdrawers $\alpha(R)$ for every value of R, which will implement the incentive-efficient allocation $\{(L, X), c_1(\cdot), c_2(\cdot)\}$.

Proof See Allen and Gale (1998a).

Although the central bank policy described in theorem 9.2 removes the deadweight costs of bank runs, it does not prevent the runs themselves. Injecting money into the banking system dilutes the claims of the early consumers so that they bear a share of the low returns to the risky asset. Without bank runs, first-best risk sharing would not be achieved.

Asset Trading and the Efficiency of Runs

In this section, we relax a second restrictive assumption of the benchmark model by introducing an asset market on which the risky asset can be sold at date 1. To simplify the analysis and distinguish the impact

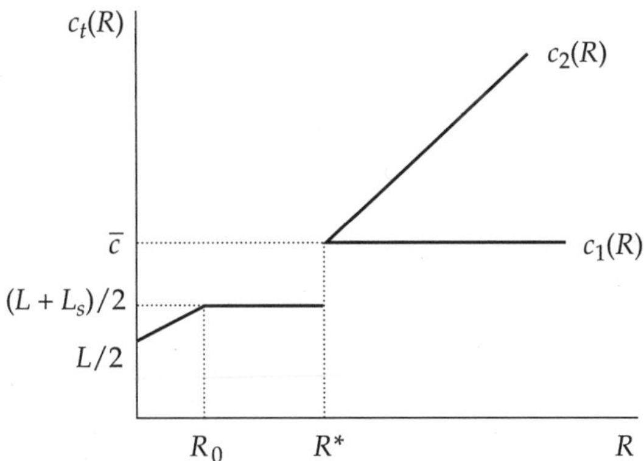

Figure 9.4
Optimal deposit contract when there is a market for the risky asset

of the asset market from the liquidation costs studied in the preceding subsections, we assume that $r = 1$ in what follows.

The impact of introducing the asset market can be illustrated using the consumption profiles in figure 9.4. The graphs in this figure represent the consumption levels of early and late consumers, respectively, as a function of the risky asset return R in the equilibrium with deposit contracts. For high values of R ($R \geq R^*$), there is no possibility of a bank run. The consumption of early consumers is fixed by the standard deposit contract at $c_1(R) = \bar{c}$, and the consumption of late consumers is given by the budget constraint $c_2(R) = r(L - \bar{c}) + RX$.

For lower values of R ($R < R^*$), it is impossible to pay the early consumers the fixed amount $\bar{c}$ promised by the standard deposit contract without violating the late consumers' incentive constraint, and a bank run inevitably ensues. However, there cannot be a partial run. The terms of the standard deposit contract require the bank to liquidate all of its assets at date 1 if it cannot pay $\bar{c}$ to every depositor who demands it. Since late withdrawers always receive as much as the early consumers by incentive compatibility, the bank has to liquidate all of its assets unless it can give at least $\bar{c}$ to all consumers. The value of R^* is determined by the condition that the bank can just afford to give everyone $\bar{c}$. Below R^* it is impossible for the bank to pay all the depositors $\bar{c}$, and the only alternative is to liquidate all its assets at the first date and pay all consumers less than $\bar{c}$. Since a late withdrawer will receive nothing, all consumers will choose to withdraw their deposits at the second date.

There is a discontinuity in the consumption profiles at the critical value of R^* that marks the upper bound of the interval in which runs occur. The reason is the effect of asset sales on the price of the risky asset. By selling the asset, the bank drives down the price, thus handing a windfall profit to the speculators and a windfall loss to the depositors. This windfall loss is experienced as a discontinuous drop in consumption.

To understand the pricing of the risky asset when there is a bank run, we have to distinguish two different regimes. For intermediate values of R ($R_0 < R < R^*$), the asset price is determined by the speculators' holdings of cash. Since one unit of the safe asset is worth r in the last period, the "fair" value of the bank's holding of the risky asset is RX/r. However, the amount of cash in the market is insufficient to pay the "fair" value of the risky asset, so the price is determined by the ratio of the speculators' cash to the bank's holding of the risky asset. This price is independent of R, which explains why consumption is independent of R in this interval. The consumption available at date 1 consists of the bank's holding of the safe asset, L, and the speculators' holding L_s. This is split among the early and late consumers, so each receives $(L + L_s)/2$.

For small values of R ($R < R_0$) the "fair" value of the risky asset is less than the amount of cash in the market, so the asset price is equal to the "fair" value.

To sum up, introducing a market for the risky asset has a number of important implications. It allows the bank to liquidate all its assets to meet the demands of the early withdrawers, but this has the effect of making the situation worse. First, because a bank run exhausts the bank's assets at date 1, a late consumer who waits until date 2 to withdraw will be left with nothing, so whenever there is a bank run, it will involve all the late consumers and not just some of them. Second, if the market for the risky asset is illiquid, the sale of the representative bank's holding of the risky asset will drive down the price, thus making it harder to meet the depositors' demands.

The all-or-nothing character of bank runs is familiar from the work of Diamond and Dybvig (1983). The difference is that in our model bank, runs are not sunspot phenomena: they occur only when there is no other equilibrium outcome possible. Furthermore, the deadweight cost of a bank run in this case is endogenous. When the representative bank is forced to liquidate the risky asset, it sells the asset at a low price. This is a transfer of value to the purchasers of the risky asset, not an economic cost. The deadweight loss arises because the transfer occurs in bad states when the consumers' consumption is already low. In other words, the market is providing negative insurance.

The Asset Market

The participants in the asset market are the banks, which use it to obtain liquidity, and a large number of wealthy, risk-neutral speculators, who hope to make a profit in case some bank has to sell off assets cheaply to get liquidity. Speculators consume only in the last period, and their objective is to maximize the expected value of their portfolio at date 2. The speculators are all identical, so they can be replaced by a representative individual who has an initial wealth W_s and chooses a portfolio consisting of L_s units of the safe asset and X_s units of the risky asset, subject to the budget constraint $L_s + X_s = W_s$.

Risk neutrality is often interpreted as meaning that an individual can have unboundedly negative consumption and hence supply unboundedly large amounts of the safe asset. Such an interpretation would make no sense here, because we want to emphasize the consequences of restricted liquidity in the market, so we impose the constraint $(L_s, X_s) \geq 0$. As a result, it will not be true that the price of the risky asset will be equal to its expected present value using the safe return $r = 1$ as the discount rate. Since the safe asset cannot be shorted, the speculators may not be able to buy as much of the risky asset as they would like. When this happens, the price of the asset is determined by the amount of cash the speculators supply in exchange for it. We call this "cash-in-the-market" pricing (Allen and Gale 1994).

Since the risky asset has a higher expected return than the safe asset, the safe asset will be held only if the speculators can make a profit by buying the risky asset at a low price at date 1. If bank runs occur with positive probability in equilibrium, speculators must hold a positive amount of the safe asset. If speculators do not have a positive holding of the safe asset at date 1, then when the banks try to sell the risky asset, the price will fall to zero in some states, which means that any speculator who had held the safe asset would make an infinite profit. (Note the importance for this argument of the assumption that speculators cannot short the safe asset.) Thus, $L_s > 0$ in an equilibrium where runs occur with positive probability.

The necessary and sufficient condition for holding both assets to be an optimum for the speculator is that

$$\mathrm{E}\left[\max\left\{1, \frac{R}{P(R)}\right\}\right] = \mathrm{E}[R],$$

where $P(R)$ is the price of the risky asset at date 1. In other words, the expected return from holding the safe asset and buying the risky asset at date 1 when the price of the risky asset falls below R is equal to the expected return from a buy-and-hold strategy, that is, buying the risky asset at date 0 and holding it until date 2. Note that $P(R) \leq R$ for all values of R, because $P(R) > R$ implies that no one is willing to hold the risky asset, and this cannot be an equilibrium. Therefore, we do not have to consider the possibility of switching from the risky to the safe asset at date 1, and the condition above reduces to

$$\mathrm{E}\left[\frac{1}{P(R)}\right] = \mathrm{E}[R]. \tag{9.4}$$

An equilibrium for the model with an asset market consists of a portfolio (L_S, X_S) for the representative speculator, a price function $P(R)$ that satisfies the no-arbitrage condition (equation 9.4), and a deposit contract $((L, X), \bar{c})$ that solves the bank's decision problem given the equilibrium pricing function $P(R)$.

Monetary Policy with Asset Trading

Once again, intervention by the central bank will be helpful, but the optimal policy will consist of eliminating the deadweight costs of runs that arise from premature liquidation rather than eliminating the runs themselves.

As a benchmark for judging the efficiency of the equilibrium with asset markets, we choose the allocation that solves (*P1*). This allocation can be implemented without relying on the asset market at all. It may not be the best the central bank can do, whatever one chooses to define as the "best," but it provides a lower bound for the second-best, and for some parameter values we can show that it is significantly better than the equilibrium allocation. The essential idea behind the policy that implements the solution to (*P1*) is similar to the monetary intervention described previously, but here the central bank is interpreted as supporting the risky asset's price rather than making an unsecured loan to the bank. Specifically, the central bank enters into a repurchase agreement (or a collateralized loan) with the representative bank, whereby the bank sells some of its assets to the central bank at date 1 in exchange for money and buys them back for the same price at date 2. By providing liquidity in this way, the central bank ensures that the representative bank does not suffer a loss by liquidating its holdings of the risky asset prematurely. Of course, an unsecured loan would also achieve the same end.

As before, we assume that the standard deposit contract promises depositors a fixed amount of money D in the middle period and pays out the remaining value of the assets in the last period. The price level at date t in state R is denoted by $p_t(R)$, and the nominal price of the risky asset at date 1 in state R is denoted by $P(R)$. We want the risky asset to sell for its "fair" value, so we assume that $P(R) = p_1(R)R$. At this price, the safe and risky assets are perfect substitutes. Let (X, L) be the portfolio corresponding to the solution of (*P1*), and let $(c_1(R), c_2(R))$ be the corresponding consumption allocations. For large values of R, we may have $c_1(R) = L < c_2(R) = RX$; for smaller values we may have $c_1(R) = c_2(R) = \frac{1}{2}(L + RX)$. Implementing this allocation requires introducing contingencies through price variation: $p_1(R)c_1(R) = D < p_2(R)c_2(R)$ for $R > \bar{R}$ and $p_1(R)c_1(R) = D = p_2(R)c_2(R)$ for $R < \bar{R}$. These equations determine the values of $p_1(R)$ and $p_2(R)$ uniquely. It remains only to determine the value of sales of assets and the size of the bank run.

In the event of a bank run, only the late consumers who withdraw early will end up holding cash, since the early consumers want to consume their entire liquidated wealth immediately. If $\alpha(R)$ is the fraction of late consumers who withdraw early, then the amount of cash injected into the system must be $\alpha(R)D$. For simplicity, we assume that the amount of cash injected is a constant M, and this determines the "size" of the run $\alpha(R)$. Since the safe asset and the risky asset are perfect substitutes at this point, it does not matter which assets the representative bank sells as long as the nominal value equals M. The representative bank enters into a repurchase agreement under which it sells assets at date 1 for an amount of cash equal to M and repurchases them at date 2 for the same cash value.

At the prescribed prices, speculators will not want to hold any of the safe assets, so $L_s = 0$ and $X_s = W_s$.

It is easy to check that all the equilibrium conditions are satisfied: depositors and speculators are behaving optimally at the given prices, and the feasibility conditions are satisfied.

THEOREM 9.3 The central bank can implement the solution to problem (*P1*) by entering into a repurchase agreement with the representative bank at date 1. Given the allocation $\{(L, X), c_1(R), c_2(R)\}$, corresponding to the solution of (*P1*), the equilibrium values of prices are given by the conditions $p_1(R)c_1(R) = D < p_2(R)c_2(R)$ for $R > \bar{R}$, and $p_1(R)c_1(R) = D = p_2(R)c_2(R)$ for $R < \bar{R}$. There is a fixed amount of money M injected into the economy in the event of a run, and the fraction of late withdrawers who "run" satisfies $\alpha(R)D = M$. The price of the risky asset at date 1 satisfies $p_1(R)R = P(R)$, and the optimal portfolio of the speculators is $(L_s, X_s) = (0, W_s)$.

While theorem 9.3 shows that the central bank intervention can achieve the planner's solution to (*P1*), it does not show that this is strictly better than the market equilibrium, since the market equilibrium allows for possibilities, such as liquidating the risky asset at date 1, that are not available in (*P1*). However, it is easy to show that the solution to (*P1*) is (strictly) Pareto preferred to the equilibrium of the model with asset markets.

COROLLARY 9.1 The solution to (*P1*), implemented by the policy described in theorem 9.3, is Pareto preferred to the laissez-faire equilibrium outcome of the model with asset markets.

9.3 Bubbles and Crises

The model of bank runs and crises already described represents a crisis as part of the real business cycle. Crises are endogenous to the extent that their incidence and size depend on equilibrium choices made by the banks. The cause of a crisis is a combination of negative information about bank assets and the noncontingent nature of deposit contracts. In this section we look at a different kind of model, in which bank lending can distort the asset values and increase the probability of a crisis.

History

Financial crises often follow what appear to be bubbles in asset prices. Historic examples of this type of crisis are the Dutch tulip mania, the South Sea Bubble in England, the Mississippi Bubble in France, and the Great Crash of 1929 in the United States. A more recent example is the dramatic rise in real estate and stock prices that occurred in Japan in the late 1980s and their subsequent collapse in 1990. Norway, Finland, and Sweden had similar experiences in the 1980s and early 1990s. In emerging economies, financial crises of this type have been particularly prevalent since 1980. Examples include Argentina, Chile, Indonesia, Mexico, and Thailand.

These bubbles in asset prices typically have three distinct phases. The first phase starts with financial liberalization or a conscious decision by the central bank to increase lending or some other similar event. The resulting expansion in credit is accompanied by an increase in the prices for assets such as real estate and stocks. This rise in prices continues for some time, possibly several years, as the bubble inflates. During the second phase, the bubble bursts and asset prices collapse, often in a short period of time (a few days or months), but sometimes over a longer period. The third phase is characterized by the default of many firms and other agents that have borrowed to buy assets at inflated prices. Banking and foreign exchange crises may follow this wave of defaults. The difficulties associated with the defaults and banking and foreign exchange crises often cause problems in the real sector of the economy that can last for a number of years.

The Japanese bubble in the real estate and stock markets that occurred in the 1980s and 1990s provides a good example. Financial liberalization throughout the 1980s and the desire to support the U.S. dollar in the latter part of the decade led to an expansion in credit. During most of the 1980s asset prices rose steadily, eventually reaching very high levels. For example, the Nikkei 225 index was around 10,000 in 1985; on December 19, 1989, it reached a peak of 38,916. A new governor of the Bank of Japan, less concerned with supporting the U.S. dollar and more concerned with fighting inflation, tightened monetary policy, and this led to a sharp increase in interest rates in early 1990 (Frankel 1993, Tschoegl 1993). The bubble burst. The Nikkei 225 fell sharply during the first part of the year and by October 1, 1990, it had sunk to 20,222. The next few years were marked by defaults and retrenchment in the financial system. The real economy was adversely affected by the aftermath of the bubble, and growth rates during the 1990s have been much lower than the average for the postwar period.

Many other similar sequences of events can be recounted. Norway, Finland, and Sweden also experienced this type of bubble. Heiskanen (1993) recounts that in Norway, lending increased by 40 percent in 1985 and 1986. Asset prices soared, and investment and consumption also increased significantly. The collapse in oil prices helped burst the bubble and caused the most severe banking crisis and recession since World War II. In Finland an expansionary budget in 1987 resulted in massive credit expansion. Housing prices rose 68 percent in 1987 and 1988. In 1989 the central bank increased interest rates and imposed reserve requirements to moderate credit expansion. In 1990 and 1991 the economic situation was exacerbated by a fall in trade with the Soviet Union. Asset prices collapsed, banks had to be supported by the government, and GDP shrank by 7 percent. In Sweden a steady credit expansion through the late 1980s led to a property boom. In the fall of 1990, credit was tightened and interest rates rose. In 1991 a number of banks had severe difficulties because of lending based on inflated asset values. The government had to intervene, and a severe recession followed.

Many other OECD countries experienced similar episodes, although they were not as extreme as in Japan and Scandinavia. Higgins and Osler (1997) consider eighteen OECD countries and document a significant rise in real estate and stock prices during the period 1984–1989. These prices subsequently fell during the period 1989–1993. Regression results indicate that a 10 percent increase in real residential real estate prices above the OECD average in 1984–1989 was associated with an 8 percent steeper fall than average in 1989–1993. Similarly, for equities, a 10 percent increase above the average in the earlier period is associated with a 5 percent steeper fall in the later period. Higgins and Osler interpret this as suggestive of the existence of bubbles. Investment and real activity were also sharply curtailed during the latter period.

Mexico provides a dramatic illustration of an emerging economy affected by this type of problem. In the early 1990s the banks were privatized, and financial liberalization occurred. Perhaps most significant, reserve requirements were eliminated. Mishkin (1997) documents how bank credit to private nonfinancial enterprises went from a level of around 10 percent of GDP in the late 1980s to 40 percent of GDP in 1994. The stock market rose significantly during the early 1990s. In 1994 the Colosio assassination and the uprising in Chiapas triggered the collapse of the bubble. The prices of stocks and other assets fell, and banking and foreign exchange crises occurred, followed by a severe recession.

Kaminsky and Reinhart (1996, 1999) study a wide range of crises in twenty countries—five industrial and fifteen emerging ones. A common precursor to most of the crises considered was financial liberalization and significant credit expansion, followed by an average rise in the price of stocks of about 40 percent per year above that occurring in normal times. The prices of real estate and other assets also increased significantly. At some point the bubble bursts, and the stock and real estate markets collapse. In many cases banks and other intermediaries were overexposed to the equity and real estate markets, and about a year later on average a banking crisis ensues. This is often accompanied by an exchange rate crisis as governments choose between lowering interest rates to ease the banking crisis or raising interest rates to defend the currency. Finally, a significant fall in output occurs. The recession lasts for an average of about a year and a half.

Although the episodes recounted share the same basic progression of the three phases outlined above, they also exhibit differences. One of the most important is the nature of the events associated with the bursting of the bubbles. In many cases, the trigger is a change in the real economic environment—for example, the collapse of oil prices in the case of Norway. In other cases the trigger is a result of the expectations about interest rates and the level of credit in the financial system not being fulfilled—for example, the collapse of the bubble in Japan in 1990.

There has been a considerable amount of work on bubbles (see Camerer 1989 for an excellent survey), but it can be argued that none convincingly captures the sequence of events outlined. Tirole (1982) argued that with finite horizons, bubbles in which asset prices deviate from fundamentals are not consistent with rational behavior. Tirole (1985) and many other authors showed that bubbles could exist in infinite horizon models in which all agents are rational. Weil (1987) has shown that bubbles can exist when there is a constant exogenous probability of the bubble's collapsing. In his model, bubbles crash in finite time with probability one. Santos and Woodford (1997) have argued that the conditions under which bubbles arise in standard general equilibrium frameworks are rather special. These types of models do not provide a good framework for analyzing events such as the Japanese, Scandinavian, and Mexican bubbles. In the special cases where bubbles occur, there is no explanation of what initiates and ends the bubble. Allen and Gorton (1993) constructed a model with continuous time but a finite horizon in which an agency problem between investors and portfolio managers could produce bubbles even though all participants were rational. Allen, Morris, and Postlewaite (1993) developed a discrete-time, finite-horizon model where the absence of common knowledge led to bubbles in asset prices. Although this work shows that bubbles can occur because of asymmetric information and agency problems, it fails to capture the typical development of bubbles recounted above. The role of the banking system and the relaxation and tightening of credit are not examined.

The model described in the rest of this section is based on Allen and Gale (1998b).

Asset Pricing with Real Shocks

To begin, we assume that the only source of uncertainty is the randomness of real asset returns. Later, the model is extended to allow us to study the dynamic effects of credit expansion.

- There are two dates, $t = 1, 2$, and a single consumption good at each date.
- There are two assets, a safe asset in variable supply and a risky asset in fixed supply. The safe asset pays a fixed return r to the investor: if x units of the consumption good are invested in the safe asset at date 1, the return is rx units of the consumption good at date 2. We can think of the risky asset as real estate or stocks. There is one unit of the risky asset at date 1. If an investor purchases $x \geq 0$ units of the risky asset at date 1, he obtains Rx units of the consumption good at date 2, where R is a random variable with a continuous positive density $h(R)$ on the support $[0, R_{MAX}]$ and mean $\bar{R}$.

The safe asset can be interpreted in a number of ways. One possibility is that it is debt issued by the corporate sector. Another is that it is capital goods leased to the corporate sector. The investors treat the rate of return as fixed because they are small relative to the size of the corporate sector. In equilibrium, competition will ensure that the rate of return on the bonds or the capital goods leased to the corporate sector is equal to the marginal product of capital. The return on the safe asset is determined by the marginal product of capital in the economy. The economy's productive technology is represented by an aggregate production function: $x \geq 0$ units of the consumption good at date 1 are transformed into $f(x)$ units of the consumption good at date 2. The production function $f(x)$ is assumed to satisfy the usual neoclassical assumptions, $f'(x) > 0$ and $f''(x) < 0$ for all x, $f'(0) = \infty$ and $f'(\infty) = 0$. There is a nonpecuniary cost of investing in the risky asset $c(x)$, which is incurred at the initial date 1. The cost function satisfies the usual neoclassical properties, $c(0) = c'(0) = 0$, $c'(x) > 0$ and $c''(x) > 0$ for all $x > 0$. The risky asset is initially owned by entrepreneurs who supply it inelastically in exchange for the consumption good at date 1.

The purpose of the investment cost $c(x)$ is to restrict the size of individual portfolios and to ensure that, in equilibrium, the borrowers make positive expected profits. There are alternative ways to do this, but this specification leads to a particularly simple analysis:

• There is a continuum of small, risk-neutral investors. Investors have no wealth of their own, but can borrow from banks to finance investments in the safe and risky assets.

• There is a continuum of small, risk-neutral banks. The representative bank has $B > 0$ units of the good to lend. Unlike investors, the banks do not know how to invest in the safe and risky assets, that is, they cannot distinguish between valuable and worthless assets. For this reason they have no choice but to lend to investors.

• The banks and the investors are restricted to using simple debt contracts. In particular, they cannot condition the terms of the loan on the size of the loan or on asset returns.

The assumptions under which it is optimal for banks to write simple debt contracts with investors are well known (see, e.g., Townsend 1979 or Gale and Hellwig 1985), and we do not discuss them here.

Since there is a continuum of investors and loans cannot be conditioned on their size, investors can borrow as much as they like at the going rate of interest. It follows that in equilibrium, the contracted rate of interest on bank loans must be equal to the return on the safe asset. If the rate of interest on bank loans were lower than the return on the safe asset, then the demand for loans by investors would be infinite. On the other hand, if the rate of interest on loans were higher, there would be no investment in the safe asset by investors, and so the return on the safe asset would be less than the marginal product of capital since $f'(0) = \infty$. This is inconsistent with our assumption of competition in the corporate sector. Thus, in equilibrium the rate of interest on loans must be equal to the return on the safe asset.

Although there is assumed to be a continuum of investors, we shall analyze the behavior of a representative investor in what follows. This is not just a matter of convenience. It implies that the equilibrium is symmetric and that all investors choose the same portfolio. The fact that all investors are identical ex post means that intermediaries cannot discriminate between borrowers by conditioning the terms of the loan on the amount borrowed or any other observable characteristic. X_S and X_R denote the representative investor's holdings of the safe and risky assets, respectively.

Since all investors are treated symmetrically, all will be charged the same rate of interest r. In principle, it might be possible to condition the interest rate on the amount borrowed, but we shall assume that the exclusive contracts this would require are not feasible. Hence there is linear pricing, that is, the same value of r applies to loans of all sizes. We assume that the banks supply the aggregate amount of loanable funds B inelastically and the rate of interest adjusts to clear the market, that is, to equate the total demand for loans to the amount of (real) credit available.

Because banks use debt contracts and cannot observe the investment decisions of the borrowers, there is a problem of risk shifting or asset substitution. An investor who has borrowed in order to invest in the risky asset does not bear the full cost of borrowing if the investment turns out badly. When the value of his portfolio is insufficient to repay the bank, he declares bankruptcy and avoids further loss. When the value of his portfolio is high, however, he keeps the remainder of the portfolio's value after repaying the bank. This nonconvexity generates a preference for risk.

The optimization problem that the representative investor faces is to choose the amount of borrowing and its allocation between the two assets to maximize expected profits at date 2. If the representative investor buys X_S units of the safe asset and X_R units of the risky asset, the total amount borrowed is $X_S + PX_R$, where P is the price of the risky asset. The repayment at date 2 will be $r(X_S + PX_R)$. The liquidation value of the portfolio is $rX_S + RX_R$ so the payoff to the investor at date 2 is

$$rX_S + RX_R - r(X_S + PX_R) = RX_R - rPX_R.$$

The optimal amount of the safe asset is indeterminate and drops out of the investor's decision problem, so we can write the investor's problem as follows:

$$\max_{X_R \geq 0} \int_{R^*}^{R_{MAX}} [RX_R - rPX_R]h(R)dR - c(X_R), \tag{9.5}$$

where $R^* = rP$ is the critical value of the return to the risky asset at which the investor defaults. Because the contracted borrowing rate is equal to the risk-free return, the investor earns no profit on his holding of the safe asset and the default return R^* is independent of the holding of the safe asset.

The market-clearing condition for the risky asset is

$$X_R = 1, \tag{9.6}$$

since there is precisely one unit of the risky asset. There is no corresponding condition for the safe asset, since the supply of the safe asset is endogenously determined by the investor's decision to invest in capital goods. The market-clearing condition in the loan market is

$$X_S + P = B, \tag{9.7}$$

since the total amount borrowed is equal to the amount invested in the safe asset X_S plus the market value of the risky asset P. Finally, we have the market-clearing equation for capital goods, which says that the return on the safe asset is the marginal product of capital,

$$r = f'(X_S). \tag{9.8}$$

An equilibrium for this model is described by the variables (r, P, X_S, X_R), where the portfolio (X_S, X_R) solves the decision problem (equation 9.5), given the parameters (r, P), and the market-clearing conditions (equations 9.6 through 9.8) are satisfied.

It is straightforward to show that there exists a unique equilibrium (r, P, X_S, X_R) if $\bar{R} > c'(1)$. In this equilibrium the banks supply a fixed amount of credit B inelastically. The contracted interest rate r adjusts to equate the quantity of funds demanded to the quantity supplied. Of course, the realized rate of return will be less than this amount. The typical borrower will default if $R < rP$, so the total return on a loan of one dollar is

$$r \Pr[R > rP] + \int_0^{rP} \frac{RX_R + rX_S}{B} h(R)dR < r.$$

The "loss" attributable to the difference between the contracted and the realized rates of return is borne by the banks (or their depositors). It can be thought of as an informational rent that accrues to the investors by virtue of their ability to hide their portfolio from the bank's scrutiny.

The investors' demand for credit is determined by the condition that they make zero profits on the last dollar borrowed. The first-order condition for the maximization problem (equation 9.5) equates the expected net return on a unit of the risky asset to the marginal cost of investment, thus ensuring that the zero-profit condition is satisfied for the risky asset. This condition uniquely determines the demand for the risky asset, given the contracted rate of interest r and the asset price P.

Since the rate of return on the safe asset is equal to the contracted rate, the investors make no profits on the safe asset and their demand for the safe asset is indeterminate. The equilibrium amount of the safe asset is determined by the condition that the return on the safe asset is equal to the marginal product of capital, which in turn is a function of the amount of the safe asset.

Substituting from the market-clearing condition $X_R = 1$, the decision problem (see equation 9.5) can be characterized by the first-order condition for the borrower's maximization problem,

$$\int_{R^*}^{R_{MAX}} [R - rP]h(R)dR = c'(1). \tag{9.9}$$

Substituting from the budget constraint $X_S = B - PX_R = B - P$, the market-clearing condition for the capital market (see equation 9.8) becomes

$$r = f'(B - P). \tag{9.10}$$

The two equations (9.9 and 9.10) in the two variables (r, P) determine the equilibrium.

The important components of the model, as far as asset pricing is concerned, are the risk-shifting problem and the fact that the risky asset is in fixed supply. Borrowers are attracted by the risky asset because they do not bear the loss if they receive a low return; the bank does. On the other hand, when the asset return is high, the borrowers receive the surplus, and the bank receives only its promised return. This means that the borrowers will bid up the price of the risky asset. As a result, the price of the risky asset is bid up above its "fundamental" value.

Establishing the fundamental value of the asset is typically a difficult task and depends on the particular circumstances, as Allen, Morris, and Postlewaite (1993) have argued. In the current context, where agents are risk neutral, it is natural to define the fundamental value as that which an individual would be willing to pay for one unit of the risky asset if there were no risk shifting, other things being equal. Suppose that a risk-neutral individual has wealth B to invest in the safe and risky asset. He would choose a portfolio (X_S, X_R) to solve the problem,

$$\max_{(X_S, X_R) \geq 0} \int_{0}^{R_{MAX}} [rX_S + RX_R]h(R)dR - c(X_R) \tag{9.11}$$

subject to $X_S + PX_R \leq B$.

Comparing the decision problem in equation 9.11 to the decision problem in equation 9.5, we see that the only differences are that there is no possibility of default in equation 9.11. The multiplier on the budget constraint takes the place of the interest rate r in equation 9.5. The first-order conditions for this convex problem are necessary and sufficient for a solution:

$$r = \lambda$$

and

$$\int_0^{R_{\text{MAX}}} Rh(R)dR - rP = c'(X_R). \tag{9.12}$$

Setting $X_R = 1$ in the first-order condition in equation 9.12, we can solve it for the fundamental price $\bar{P}$, that is, the price at which an agent who invests his own money would be willing to hold one unit of the risky asset:

$$\bar{P} = \frac{1}{r}(\bar{R} - c'(1)). \tag{9.13}$$

Equation 9.13 defines the fundamental value of the risky asset as the discounted value of net returns. We would like to show that the equilibrium price is greater than the fundamental, the classic definition of a bubble.

The equilibrium condition (see equation 9.9) can be rearranged to yield a similar expression:

$$P = \frac{1}{r}\left(\frac{\int_{R^*}^{R_{\text{MAX}}} Rh(R)dR - c'(1)}{\Pr[R \geq R^*]}\right). \tag{9.14}$$

Comparing the two pricing kernels (see equations 9.13 and 9.14), we see that both the numerator and the denominator of equation 9.14 are smaller than the corresponding elements of equation 9.13. However, the next proposition shows that the two prices can be ranked.

Proposition 9.1 There is a bubble in the intermediated equilibrium (r, P, X_S, X_R). More precisely, the equilibrium asset price P is at least as high as the fundamental price $\bar{P}$ and strictly higher as long as the probability of bankruptcy is positive, $\Pr[R < R^*] > 0$.

Proof See Allen and Gale (1998b).

Proposition 9.1 shows that the risk shifting that occurs because of the possibility of default leads to prices being higher than the fundamental, which is the discounted value of expected future payoffs.

Because investors are identical, everybody will default when $R < R^*$. This widespread default can be interpreted as a financial crisis. Of course, in more realistic models with heterogeneous agents, only a proportion will default, and the proportion defaulting will determine the extent of the crisis.

Proposition 9.1 illustrates the importance of shocks deriving from the real sector in generating financial crises. For example, Norway's financial problems following the oil price shock can be interpreted as a crisis precipitated by a low realization of R. What the proposition suggests is that the stage for these problems may have been set when risk shifting led to overinvestment in the risky asset, causing a bubble in asset prices and hence a greater probability of default. The widespread default following the collapse in asset prices caused banks to be insolvent, and it was this that led the government to intervene and bail out the banking system.

Because risk-shifting behavior is essential to the creation of a bubble in asset prices, it seems that an increase in the riskiness of the asset returns will increase the size of the bubble. There is a precise sense in which this is true: a mean-preserving spread in the returns to the risky asset increases both the size of the bubble and the probability of default (see Allen and Gale 1998b for a statement and proof of this result).

Asset Pricing with Financial Shocks

While in some cases it appears that a financial crisis was precipitated by a real shock, in other cases the crisis appears to have been triggered by an event in the financial sector. For example, in many cases, financial liberalization leads to an expansion of credit, which feeds a bubble in asset prices. These higher prices are supported by the anticipation of further increases in credit and asset prices. Any faltering of this cumulative process may lead to a crisis. Japan's tightening of credit in 1990, which precipitated the collapse in asset prices, provides an example.

Of course, if the collapse of asset prices were perfectly foreseen, the bubble would not have been possible in the first place. Backward induction would ensure that the market valuation of assets reflected the fundamental. However, the course of financial liberalization and credit expansion is never perfectly foreseen. The central bank has limited ability to control the amount of credit. In addition, there may be changes of policy preferences, changes of administration, and changes in the external environment, all of which may alter the extent and duration of the credit expansion that feeds the bubble. This uncertainty was particularly great in many emerging economies that underwent financial liberalization. A similar interpretation may be given to the credit expansions that occurred in developed countries like Japan and that subsequently were summarily cut off.

In the previous section we showed that there could be a bubble in the sense that the price of the risky asset was higher than its fundamental value. In this section we extend the horizon of the model and show how uncertainty about the extent of credit expansion can increase the magnitude of the bubble. There are now three dates, $t = 0, 1, 2$, and a single consumption good at each date. The final two dates 1 and 2 are essentially the same as in the previous model. The main addition is the prior date.

To allow for uncertainty about future credit expansion, we shall assume that B, the amount of credit available for lending to investors, is partially controlled by the central bank. The central bank sets reserve requirements and the quantity of assets available to be used as reserves. By altering one or other of these instruments, the central bank can influence the amount of credit available in the economy. This in turn affects the funds available for investors to purchase the two assets. Because of the uncertainty involved in this process—and this is crucial—investors rationally anticipate an expansion in B, but they are uncertain about its exact value. It is now the sequence of credit policies over time, that is, the levels of B_0 and B_1, and the amount of uncertainty associated with B_1, that matters. The following additional assumptions are required:

- At date 0, the level of B_1 is treated by agents as a random variable with a positive, continuous density $k(B)$ on the support $[0, B_{1MAX}]$. The price of the risky asset at date 1, $P_1(B_1)$, is therefore also a random variable.
- The safe asset pays $r_t x$ at date $t + 1$ if x is invested at date $t = 0, 1$. The owner of the risky asset receives a payoff of $\overline{R}x$ at date 2 if $x \geq 0$ is owned at that date.
- There is short-term borrowing at dates 0 and 1.
- Entrepreneurs initially own the asset in fixed supply. At date 0 they sell it to investors who hold the representative portfolio from date 0

to date 1. These new investors sell the risky asset at date 1 to the final group of investors, who own it until date 2. Investors in the risky asset incur the investment costs $c(x)$ at each date $t = 0, 1$.

As in the two-period model, we can show that the contracted borrowing rate must be equal to the return on the safe asset at each date $t = 0, 1$. Let r_t denote the return on the safe asset at date $t = 0, 1$.

To simplify the analysis and distinguish between the effects of real uncertainty about the asset returns and financial uncertainty about asset prices, we assume that the risky asset has a certain return $\bar{R}$. The risky asset remains risky only because it is a long-lived asset and hence is subject to fluctuations in its price at date 1. Since the safe asset is liquidated after one period, there is no uncertainty about its future value. From the analysis in the preceding section, we know that the equilibrium price of the risky asset at date 1 is given by the formula

$$P_1 = \frac{1}{r_1}(\bar{R} - c'(1)). \tag{9.15}$$

Since $r_1 = f'(B_1 - P_1)$ and $pf'(B_1 - p)$ is increasing in p, there is a unique value of P_1 satisfying this equation for each value of B_1. Let $P_1(B_1)$ denote the equilibrium value of the risky asset's price at date 1 when the level of available credit is B_1. Note that $P_1(B_1)$ is continuous and increases without bound if $f'(x) \to 0$ as $x \to \infty$.

Using this expression for the future asset price, we can define an equilibrium at date 0 in the same way we defined equilibrium in the two-period economy. Consider the representative investor's problem at date 0 (as before, the safe asset drops out of the investor's problem):

$$\max_{X_{0R} \geq 0} \int_{B_1^*}^{B_{1MAX}} [P_1(B_1)X_{0R} - r_0 P_0 X_{0R}] k(B_1) dB_1 - c(X_{0R}) \tag{9.16}$$

where P_0 is the price of the risky asset at date 0, (X_{0S}, X_{0R}) is the portfolio chosen at date 0, r_0 is the borrowing rate at date 0 and B_1^* denotes the value of B_1 at which the investor is on the verge of default at date 1:

$$P_1(B_1^*) = r_0 P_0. \tag{9.17}$$

The market-clearing conditions are

$$X_{0R} = 1, \tag{9.18}$$

$$X_{0S} + P_0 X_{0R} = B_0, \tag{9.19}$$

and

$$r_0 = f'(X_{0S}). \tag{9.20}$$

There is no market-clearing condition for the safe asset since its supply is endogenously determined by the investment X_{0S}.

An equilibrium is defined by the variables $(r_0, P_0, B_1^*, X_{0S}, X_{0R})$ satisfying equation 9.17, the market-clearing conditions (see equations 9.17–9.19), and such that (X_{0S}, X_{0R}) solves the decision problem (see equation 9.16) given the parameters (r_0, P_0, B_1^*).

Again, it is straightforward to show that there exists a unique equilibrium if $E[P_1(B_1)] > c'(1)$. Making the usual substitutions, we can reduce the set of equilibrium conditions to three:

$$\int_{B_1^*}^{B_{1MAX}} [P_1(B_1) - P_1(B_1^*) - c'(1)]k(B_1)dB_1 = 0 \tag{9.21}$$

$$r_0 = f'(B - P_0)$$

and

$$P_1(B_1^*) = r_0 P_0.$$

As a benchmark, we first consider an owner-investor with B units of wealth and ask at what price $\bar{P}_0$ such an agent would be willing to hold one unit of the risky asset. The decision problem faced by the owner-investor with wealth B_0 is to choose (X_{0S}, X_{0R}) to solve

$$\max_{(X_{0S}, X_{0R}) \geq 0} \int_0^{B_{1MAX}} [r_0 X_{0S} + P_1(B_1) X_{0R}]k(B_1)dR - c(X_{0R}) \tag{9.22}$$

subject to $X_{0S} + PX_{0R} \leq B$.

From the first-order conditions for this problem, we can find the fundamental value of the risky asset,

$$\bar{P}_0 = \frac{1}{r_0}\left(E[P_1(B_1)] - c'(1)\right). \tag{9.23}$$

Comparing equation 9.23 with the comparable expression for the equilibrium price,

$$P_0 = \frac{1}{r_0}\left(\frac{\int_{B_1^*}^{B_{1MAX}} P_1(B_1)k(B_1)dB_1 - c'(1)}{\Pr[B_1 \geq B_1^*]}\right), \tag{9.24}$$

we can prove the following result.

PROPOSITION 9.2 Let $(r_0, P_0, B_1^*, X_{0S}, X_{0R})$ denote equilibrium values for the intermediated economy, and let $\bar{P}_0$ be the fundamental price of the risky asset. Then $P_0 \geq \bar{P}_0$ and the inequality is strict if the probability of bankruptcy $\Pr[B_1 < B_1^*]$ is positive.

Proof See Allen and Gale (1998b).

The intuition behind proposition 9.2 is the same as for proposition 9.1, with uncertainty about B_1 taking the place of uncertainty about R. However, it can be argued that the scope for creating bubbles is much greater. The reason is that there is often a great deal of uncertainty about the course of credit expansion and hence how high the bubble may go and when it may collapse. This is particularly true when economies are undergoing financial liberalization. Thus, the variance of B_1 and $P_1(B_1)$, interpreted as the result of cumulative credit expansion over several years, may be very large. The uncertainty arising from government and central bank policies on credit expansion can dwarf the uncertainty associated with real payoffs on assets. It is the interaction between financial uncertainty and the agency problem in intermediation that leads to the possibility of large deviations of asset prices from fundamentals and subsequent severe financial crises.

9.4 Financial Fragility

Although proposition 9.2 shows how asset prices can become large relative to their fundamentals in intermediated financial systems, it has not yet been shown that credit policies can exacerbate a financial crisis (increase the probability of default). In addressing this issue, the important point is not the existence of the bubble at date 0 but rather the conditions that have to be satisfied at date 1 in order to avoid default by the investors. Even if credit expansion always occurs, that is, $B_1 > B_0$ with probability one, the variability of future credit availability may ensure that a financial crisis occurs. The point is that the expectation of credit expansion is already taken into account in the investors' decisions about how much to borrow and how much to pay for the risky asset. If credit expansion is less than expected, or perhaps simply falls short of the highest anticipated levels, the investors may not be able to repay their loans, and a crisis ensues.

To make this more concrete, consider the pricing equation (9.21) with the substitution of $P_1(B_1^*)$ for r_0P_0 and 1 for X_{0R}:

$$\int_{B_1^*}^{B_{1MAX}} (P_1(B_1) - P_1(B_1^*))k(B_1)dB_1 = c'(1).$$

As the transactions cost term $c'(1)$ becomes vanishingly small, the left-hand side must also vanish, which can occur only if $B_1^* \to B_{1MAX}$. Consequently, there will be a crash unless the expansion of credit is close to the upper bound. The intuitive explanation is that as transaction costs become less important, competition for the risky asset drives the price up, reducing profits and increasing the incentive for risk shifting.

Proposition 9.3 As $c'(1) \to 0$ the default level $B_1^* \to B_{1MAX}$. In other words, credit expansion must not merely be positive but must be close to the upper bound of the support of B_1 to ensure that a crisis is avoided.

Note that one does not have to go to this length to produce a high probability of crisis. If B_1 has a two-point support concentrated on $\{0, B_{1MAX}\}$ then the probability of a crisis will always be at least $\Pr[B_1 = 0]$, which we can choose as large as we like. The point we want to emphasize is that we can generate a high probability of crisis without resorting to a high probability of significant credit contraction. A crisis can occur even when credit is expanded.

To illustrate the operation of the model consider the following example:

B_1 is uniformly distributed on $[0, 2]$.

$B_0 = 1; \quad f(X_S) = 4X_S^{0.5}; \quad \bar{R} - c'(1) = 4.$

Restricting attention to positive prices, it can straightforwardly be shown that

$$P_1(B_1) = 2[(1 + B_1)^{0.5} - 1].$$

By varying the values of $c'(1)$ a number of cases of interest can be generated, as shown in table 9.2.

In each of the cases in table 9.2, the average level of credit expected by investors next period is the same as the level of credit currently. In the

Table 9.2
A numerical example

$c'(1)$	B_1^*	Probability of a crisis	Intermediated P_0	Fundamental $\bar{P}_0$	Bubble $P_0 - \bar{P}_0$
0.2	0.90	0.45	0.31	0.25	0.06
0.1	1.21	0.61	0.38	0.27	0.11
0.01	1.74	0.87	0.47	0.29	0.18

example with $c'(1) = 0.2$, the financial system is robust in the sense that if credit actually remains the same, so $B_0 = B_1 = 1 > B_1^* = 0.90$, there will be no default and a financial crisis will be avoided. In the second row, where $c'(1) = 0.1$, the financial system is fragile. The amount of credit must be expanded to $B_1 \geq B_1^* = 1.21$ if a financial crisis is to be avoided. It is not sufficient to hold it constant or increase it slightly. Finally, in the third case, where $c'(1) = 0.01$, the financial system is very fragile. Only a large increase in credit above $B_1^* = 1.74$ will prevent default. Here the probability of a crisis is very high. These examples illustrate that financial crises can occur in a wide variety of circumstances. It is not necessary for there to be a contraction in credit for a crisis to be triggered, or even that credit be at or above its expected level, an increase in credit that is simply too small may also result in a crisis.

9.5 Conclusion

Chapter 2 stressed the importance of financial crises in the historical development of financial systems. In the United Kingdom the South Sea Bubble in the eighteenth century led to regulation of the stock market, which was subsequently repealed, and banking crises in the eighteenth century led to the development of effective central bank policies. In the United States continual banking crises eventually led to a centralized Federal Reserve. The Great Depression led to the formation of the Securities and Exchange Commission and the development of a regulatory framework, much of it still in place. In Continental Europe the Mississippi Bubble, which occurred about the same time as the South Sea Bubble, created extreme skepticism about the role of markets. In the long run, financial systems were developed that relied primarily on banks rather than a combination of financial markets and banks as in the Anglo Saxon countries.

The formal analysis of financial crises is still at an early stage. A full understanding of how crises arise and their effects on real economic activity are of prime importance. We anticipate that this will be an active area of research in the future.

References

Allen, F., and D. Gale. (1994). "Liquidity Preference, Market Participation and Asset Price Volatility," *American Economic Review* **84,** 933–955.

———. (1998a). "Optimal Financial Crises." *Journal of Finance* **53,** 1245–1283.

———. (1998b). "Bubbles and Crises." *Economic Journal* (forthcoming).

———. (1998c). "Financial Contagion." *Journal of Political Economy* (forthcoming).

Allen, F., and G. Gorton. (1993). "Churning Bubbles." *Review of Economic Studies* **60,** 813–836.

Allen, F., S. Morris, and A. Postlewaite. (1993). "Finite Bubbles with Short Sale Constraints and Asymmetric Information." *Journal of Economic Theory* **61,** 206–229.

Alonso, I. (1996),"On Avoiding Bank Runs." *Journal of Monetary Economics* **37,** 73–87.

Bensaid, B., H. Pages, and J. Rochet. (1996). "Efficient Regulation of Bank's Solvency." Working paper, Institut d'Economie Industrielle, Toulouse.

Bhattacharya, S., and D. Gale. (1987). "Preference Shocks, Liquidity and Central Bank Policy." In W. Barnett and K. Singleton (eds.), *New Approaches to Monetary Economics.* New York: Cambridge University Press.

Bryant, J. (1980). "A Model of Reserves, Bank Runs, and Deposit Insurance." *Journal of Banking and Finance* **4,** 335–344.

Calomiris, C., and G. Gorton. (1991). "The Origins of Banking Panics, Models, Facts, and Bank Regulation." In R. G. Hubbard (ed.), *Financial Markets and Financial Crises.* Chicago: University of Chicago Press.

Calomiris, C., and C. Kahn. (1991). "The Role of Demandable Debt in Structuring Optimal Banking Arrangements." *American Economic Review* **81,** 497–513.

Camerer, C. (1989). "Bubbles and Fads in Asset Prices: A Review of Theory and Evidence." *Journal of Economic Surveys* **3,** 3–41.

Champ, B., B. Smith, and S. Williamson. (1996). "Currency Elasticity and Banking Panics: Theory and Evidence." *Canadian Journal of Economics* **29,** 828–864.

Chari, V. (1989) "Banking Without Deposit Insurance or Bank Panics: Lessons from a Model of the U.S. National Banking System." *Federal Reserve Bank of Minneapolis Quarterly Review* **13,** 3–19.

Chari, V., and R. Jagannathan. (1988). "Banking Panics, Information, and Rational Expectations Equilibrium." *Journal of Finance* **43,** 749–760.

Diamond, D., and P. Dybvig. (1983). "Bank Runs, Deposit Insurance, and Liquidity." *Journal of Political Economy* **91,** 401–419.

Frankel, J. (1993). "The Japanese financial system and the cost of capital," in S. Takagi, (ed.), *Japanese Capital Markets: New Developments in Regulations and Institutions.* Oxford: Blackwell, 21–77.

Gale, D., and M. Hellwig. (1985). "Incentive-Compatible Debt Contracts: The One-Period Problem." *Review of Economic Studies* **52,** 647–663.

Gorton, G. (1988). "Banking Panics and Business Cycles." *Oxford Economic Papers* **40,** 751–781.

Heiskanen, R. (1993). "The Banking Crisis in the Nordic Countries." *Kansallis Economic Review* **2,** 13–19.

Hellwig, M. (1994). "Liquidity Provision, Banking, and the Allocation of Interest Rate Risk." *European Economic Review* **38,** 1363–1389.

Higgins, M., and C. Osler. (1997). "Asset Market Hangovers and Economic Growth: The OECD During 1984–93." *Oxford Review of Economic Policy* **13,** 110–134.

Jacklin, C., and S. Bhattacharya. (1988). "Distinguishing Panics and Information-Based Bank Runs: Welfare and Policy Implications." *Journal of Political Economy* **96,** 568–592.

Kaminsky, G., and C. Reinhart. (1996). "Banking and Balance-of-Payments Crises: Models and Evidence." Working paper, Board of Governors of the Federal Reserve, Washington, D.C.

———. (1999). "The Twin Crises: The Causes of Banking and Balance-of-Payments Problems." *American Economic Review* **89,** 473–500.

Kindleberger, C. (1978). *Manias, Panics, and Crashes: A History of Financial Crises.* New York: Basic Books.

Kroszner, R. (1997). "Free Banking: The Scottish Experience as a Model for Emerging Economies." In G. Caprio, Jr., and D. Vittas, (eds.), *Reforming Financial Systems: Historical Implications for Policy.* New York: Cambridge University Press.

Lindgren, C., G. Garcia, and M. Saal. (1996). *Bank Soundness and Macroeconomic Policy.* Washington, D.C.: International Monetary Fund.

Mishkin, F. (1997). "Understanding Financial Crises: A Developing Country Perspective." In *Annual World Bank Conference on Development Economics 1996* (pp. 29-61). Washington, D.C.: International Bank for Reconstruction and Development.

Mitchell, W. (1941). *Business Cycles and Their Causes.* Berkeley: University of California Press.

Postlewaite, A., and X. Vives. (1987). "Bank Runs as an Equilibrium Phenomenon." *Journal of Political Economy* **95,** 485–491.

Rochet, J., and J. Tirole. (1996). "Interbank Lending and Systemic Risk." *Journal of Money, Credit, and Banking* **28,** 733–762.

Santos, M., and M. Woodford. (1997). "Rational Asset Pricing Bubbles." *Econometrica* **65,** 19–57.

Sprague, O. (1910). *A History of Crises Under the National Banking System.* Washington D.C.: U.S. Government Printing Office.

Tirole, J. (1982). "On the Possibility of Speculation Under Rational Expectations." *Econometrica* **50,** 1163–1181.

———. (1985). "Asset Bubbles and Overlapping Generations." *Econometrica* **53,** 1499–1528.

Townsend, R. (1979). "Optimal Contracts and Competitive Markets with Costly State Verification." *Journal of Economic Theory* **22,** 265–293.

von Thadden, E. (1997). "The Term Structure of Investment and the Banks' Insurance Function." *European Economic Review* **41,** 1355–1374.

———. (1998). "Intermediated versus Direct Investment: Optimal Liquidity Provision and Dynamic Incentive Compatibility." *Journal of Financial Intermediation* **7,** 177–197.

Tschoegl, A. (1993). "Modeling the behaviour of Japanese stock indices." In S. Takagi, (ed.), *Japanese Captial Markets: New Developments in Regulations and Institutions.* Oxford: Blackwell, 371–400.

Wallace, N. (1988). "Another Attempt to Explain an Illiquid Banking System: The Diamond and Dybvig Model with Sequential Service Taken Seriously." *Federal Reserve Bank of Minneapolis Quarterly Review* **12,** 3–16.

———. (1990). "A Banking Model in Which Partial Suspension Is Best." *Federal Reserve Bank of Minneapolis Quarterly Review* **14,** 11–23.

Weil, P. (1987). "Confidence and the Real Value of Money in an Overlapping Generations Economy." *Quarterly Journal of Economics,* **102,** 1–22.

10 Renegotiation and Relationships

10.1 Financial Systems and Relationships

One way of distinguishing financial markets and financial intermediaries is by the kind of relationship that is formed when two parties enter into a financial transaction. Any financial transaction involves time in an essential way, so any financial transaction establishes a relationship of some sort between the parties to the transaction. For example, if a firm sells bonds to investors, the investors become stakeholders in the company. But this is a rather loose kind of relationship. There may be a large number of investors, and they can sell their bonds at any time, so they have little incentive to monitor the firm and the firm has little incentive to find out about them. On the other hand, if the firm obtains a loan from a bank, a different sort of relationship may be established. In the first place, it is a one-to-one relationship, and it is more likely to be a long-term relationship. It may be a multifaceted relationship, as the bank may be providing many different services to the firm, and this gives the bank an opportunity to gather information about the firm. We should expect this kind of relationship to provide different information flows and different incentives to monitor, cooperate, and co-insure.

So we might conclude that one characteristic of financial systems that rely on banks and other intermediaries is the greater importance of long-term relationships compared to financial systems that rely on markets. As we saw in chapter 3, this turns out to be the case. The extensive use of the main bank system in Japan and the hausbank system in Germany means that long-lived relationships between large firms and banks are commonplace. At the other extreme, in the United States large firms have much more limited long-term relationships with banks. A growing literature on relationships in banking analyzes their advantages and disadvantages. (For theoretical analyses, see Diamond

1991; Boot, Greenbaum, and Thakor, 1993; Bhattacharya and Chiesa, 1995; von Thadden, 1995; Yosha, 1995; Boot and Thakor, 1996; Dinç, 1996; and Aoki and Dinç, 1997. For empirical analyses, see Berger and Udell, 1992; Petersen and Rajan, 1994, 1995; Berlin and Mester, 1997a, 1997b; and Elsas and Krahnen, 1997.)

Relationships are important not only in banking. They also play a role in many other parts of the financial system. Perhaps the most important of these is the private equity market. The United States has a much more sophisticated private equity market, including venture capital, than any other country. Lerner (1997) reports that in 1995, the ratio of the private equity pool to GDP was 8.7 times higher in the United States than in Asia and 8.0 times higher in the United States than in continental Europe. The literature on private equity and, in particular, venture capital has also been growing. (For theoretical analyses see Admati and Pfleiderer 1994; Berglof 1994; Bergemann and Hege 1997; Cornelli and Yosha 1997; Hellmann 1998; Black and Gilson, 1998; Repullo and Suarez 1998; and Trester 1998. For empirical analyses see Lerner, 1994a, 1994b, 1995; Gompers 1995, 1996; and Gompers and Lerner 1996, 1998.)

This chapter considers the role of renegotiation in financial relationships. Rather than focus on specific institutional details, we are interested in outlining the different aspects of renegotiation in general terms. We begin by reviewing some of the ideas presented by various authors concerning the costs and benefits of renegotiation in financial relationships. The theme of relationships is taken up again in chapter 15, where we focus on risk-sharing issues.

10.2 Renegotiation and Commitment

Credit markets are characterized by incomplete information, which gives rise to problems of adverse selection and moral hazard. Stiglitz and Weiss (1983) have argued that these problems are mitigated if lenders can threaten borrowers with punishment in the event of default or poor performance. For example, a firm that defaults on a bank loan may be refused credit in the future.

In analyzing the optimal use of threats, it is assumed that the lender can commit itself to a particular course of action in advance. From a purely economic perspective, the assumption of commitment is problematical. Although it is optimal to threaten to terminate the availability of credit in advance, once the borrower has defaulted, the first loan becomes a "sunk cost." As such, it should not affect future decisions. If the firm has another project that offers positive NPV, there exists an incentive-compatible contract that finances the project and makes both the borrower and the lender better off. In that case, it would be irrational not to take advantage of this opportunity. Thus, we should expect that the lender will continue to extend credit, even if the borrower defaults.

Renegotiation thus creates a time-consistency problem. The threat to terminate credit creates good incentives for the borrower to avoid the risk of default. Termination of credit is not Pareto efficient ex post, but the incentive effect makes both parties better off. However, if the borrower anticipates that the lender will not carry out the threat in practice, the incentive effect disappears. Although the lender's behavior is now ex post optimal, both parties may be worse off ex ante.

The time inconsistency of commitments that are optimal ex ante and suboptimal ex post is typical in contracting problems. The contract commits one to certain courses of action in order to influence the behavior of the other party. Once that party's behavior has been determined, the benefit of the commitment disappears, and there is now an incentive to depart from it. Whatever agreements have been entered into are subject to revision because both parties can typically be made better off by "renegotiating" the original agreement. The possibility of renegotiation puts additional restrictions on the kind of contract or agreement that is feasible (we are referring here to the contract or agreement as executed rather than the contract as originally written or conceived) and to that extent tends to reduce the welfare of both parties ex ante. Anything that gives the parties a greater power to commit themselves to the terms of the contract will, conversely, be welfare enhancing.

Dewatripont and Maskin (1995) have suggested that financial markets have an advantage over financial intermediaries in maintaining commitments to refuse further funding. If the firm obtains its funding from the bond market, then if it needs additional investment, it will have to go back to the bond market. Because the bonds are widely held, however, the firm will find it difficult to renegotiate with the bondholders. Apart from the transaction costs involved in negotiating with a large number of bondholders, there is a free-rider problem. Each bondholder would like to maintain his original claim over the returns to the project, while allowing the others to renegotiate their claims in order to finance the additional investment. The free-rider problem, which is often thought of as the curse of cooperative enterprises, turns out to be a virtue in disguise when it comes to maintaining commitments.

Although it is an interesting theoretical point, it is not clear how relevant Dewatripont and Maskin's argument is in practice. There does not appear to be convincing empirical evidence that intermediaries have a hard time making commitments to refuse further credit to borrowers who failed to repay in the past. (A possible exception is the case of sovereign debt, which lies outside the scope of this discussion.) There are a couple of theoretical reasons that this may be so. In the first place, the incentive effects of terminations depend critically on the assumption that the borrower is restricted to dealing with one lender. If it is possible to switch to other sources of funds, whether intermediaries or markets, it may be impossible to prevent the extension of credit in the future anyway. Of course, the initial lender still has a claim on the borrower, and this will lead to some sort of bargaining problem. However, this is no different from the renegotiation that would go on between a borrower and lender in any case. The point is that the lender cannot unilaterally prevent the financing of a positive NPV project if there is competition.

A second reason that intermediaries may not find it difficult to terminate a borrower with a bad history is asymmetric information. Renegotiation constrains the contracts only when there is complete information about the borrower's type. When the borrower's type is unknown and default is taken to be a bad signal, it may be possible to find beliefs that support the termination of credit as a perfect Bayesian equilibrium. For example, suppose that there are two types of borrowers, good and bad. A good borrower can choose either a safe project that produces a certain return R or a risky project that produces a return H with probability π and 0 with probability $1 - \pi$. A bad borrower can choose only worthless projects that produce 0 in every state. The lender cannot observe the outcome but can observe whether the loan is repaid. If good borrowers are expected to choose safe projects, then a good borrower who chooses the risky project runs the risk of being confused with the bad borrowers and being excluded from the credit market forever, whether he deals with an intermediary or a competitive financial market. This threat is credible and will discourage good borrowers from choosing risky projects. Note that the argument does not depend on the prior probability of the bad type. (For a formal model, see Diamond 1991, who analyzes reputation effects in credit markets.)

10.3 Renegotiation and Incomplete Contracts

Despite these theoretical caveats, it does seem plausible that renegotiation is more difficult in the case of a widely held security issue than in the case of a loan. More generally, renegotiation of a contract in the context of a long-term, multifaceted, one-to-one relationship would appear to be easier than in the context of a market relationship. To that extent, markets may have an advantage over intermediaries.

On the other hand, several authors (Huberman and Kahn, 1988, Hart and Moore, 1988) have argued that under certain circumstances, renegotiation is welfare improving. In that case, the Dewatripont-Maskin argument is turned on its head. Intermediaries that establish long-term relationships with clients may have an advantage over financial markets precisely because it is easier for them to renegotiate contracts.

The crucial assumption is that contracts are incomplete. Because of the high transaction costs of writing complete contracts, some potentially Pareto-improving contingencies are left out of contracts and securities. This incompleteness of contracts may make renegotiation desirable. The missing contingencies can be replaced by contract adjustments that are negotiated by the parties ex post, after they observe the realization of variables on which the contingencies would have been based. The incomplete contract determines the status quo for the ex post bargaining game (i.e., renegotiation) that determines the final outcome.

A good example of virtuous renegotiation is provided by the private equity market (professionally managed investments in unregistered securities of public and private companies). An important feature of the U.S. financial system is that the private equity market, which includes the venture capital sector, is much larger than in other countries. (The material in this section is drawn from Sahlman 1990 and Fenn, Liang and Prowse 1995.) The private equity market in the United States has grown very rapidly in the past fifteen years. In 1995 it was approximately one-sixth the size of the commercial paper and commercial bank loan markets. The organized private equity market consists largely of limited partnerships, which channel funds of wealthy individuals and institutional investors to companies that cannot raise funds in the debt market or in the public equity market: small start-up companies, midsized companies that have reached their borrowing limit in the debt market, and public companies going private through LBOs. The general partners in a limited partnership are professional investment managers whose job is to find opportunities for investment, structure the investments, and then take an active role in monitoring and advising the firms in which the partnership has invested.

Partnerships generally have a fixed life—typically ten years—with provision for one- or two-year extensions up to a maximum of four years. There is a period of three to five years when the partnership's capital is invested. After this initial period, the investments are managed and then gradually liquidated. The size of the partnerships varies, with LBO partnerships being the biggest. The portfolio of investments consists of ten to fifty companies, and there are typically six to twelve general partners (managers).

The need for managers arises from asymmetric information. Investing in new companies with little or no track record, often operating in an area of new technology, leads to serious adverse selection problems. Selecting the targets requires expert knowledge that may not be available to the investors; monitoring the firms also requires time and expertise. In effect, the limited partnership is an intermediary between the investors, the limited partners, and the investment targets, such as small start-up companies.

The private equity market exemplifies several of the features we have emphasized in discussing the role of intermediaries. One of the most important is the gathering and processing of information. Because of the lack of publicly available information and the asymmetry of information between insiders (the management of a small start-up, say) and outsiders, it is important to gather as much information as possible before investing. At the time that the limited partners buy a stake in the partnership, they do not know what investments the partnership will make. Their decision to invest has to be based on the history of the general partners. The general partners are required to exercise due diligence in selecting the firms in which to invest, which means that they screen large numbers of firms, selecting perhaps 1 percent of the initial proposals after extensive research on a short list of firms, including visits to the company, discussions with the management, suppliers, and creditors, and verification of accounting and other information submitted by the company. This process can take several weeks and obviously requires and produces a degree of expertise that would be impractical for all of the investors to possess or acquire.

A second important feature is the use of several different control mechanisms to overcome the moral hazard problems posed by the asymmetric information possessed by the management of the issuing firm. The management of a start-up company typically owns a large amount of stock, which may lead to risk-shifting behavior. To some extent this can be offset by altering the terms of the managers' employment contract. The use of convertible preferred stock provides incentives for the management, which typically holds common stock, to pursue the interests of the outside investors and also allows the partnership to share in the upside potential of the issuing firm. Holding positions on the board of the issuing firm and allocating voting rights to give the partnership more control may also be important control mechanisms.

The most interesting feature of the intermediary's role, from the point of view of this section, is the use of access of additional financing as a control mechanism:

> Venture capital is typically provided to portfolio companies in several rounds at fairly well defined development stages, generally with the amount provided just enough for the firm to advance to the next stage of development. Even if diversification provisions in the partnership agreement prevent the partnership itself from providing further financing, the general partners have the power, through their extensive contacts, to bring in other investors. Conversely, if the original partnership is unwilling to arrange for additional financing, it is unlikely that any other partnership will choose to do so; the reluctance of the original partnership is a strong signal that the company is a poor investment. (Fenn, Liang, and Prowse, 1995, p. 33)

This control of the access to additional finance is not restricted to the termination or extension of credit conditional on the partnership's assessment of the issuing company's prospects. The general partners monitor the issuing company and furnish managerial assistance in order to add value to their investment. Their influence is amplified by their control of access to additional funding.

Their general control of access to additional capital allows them to be much more flexible in aiding or restricting the flow of capital, something that would be difficult with an explicit contract. If more capital is needed to take advantage of unforeseen opportunities or to meet higher-than-anticipated expenses, the partnership can provide it or facilitate its provision by a third party. Similarly, if less is needed, they can scale back their planned investments. The information they get by actively participating in the management of the investment and the flexibility that comes from negotiating the amount of financing as they go along, together allow for a degree of "completeness" in providing contingent finance that would be very difficult to achieve in an explicit contract and certainly would be difficult to arrange if the issuing company had to deal with a large number of less-well-informed direct investors. Here the advantages of a long-term relationship with an intermediary seem clear.

At the same time, this part of the financial sector shares some of the characteristics of a market, principally the fact that there are large numbers of relatively small partnerships in operation and that potential investors can choose to spread their investments among different partnerships, just as they choose among different stocks in the organized exchanges.

10.4 Renegotiation in a Risk-Sharing Problem

A simple example based on Gale (1991) will illustrate the theoretical advantages of renegotiation referred to in the preceding section. Imagine the risk-sharing problem faced by a firm and an intermediary. We refer to the intermediary as a venture capitalist. The firm has borrowed money from the venture capitalist to invest in a risky project that yields a random payoff w sometime in the future. The venture capitalist and the firm write a complete contract to share the returns to the risky project. The risk preferences of the firm (resp. venture capitalist) are described by a von Neumann-Morgenstern utility function $u(x)$ (resp. $v(y)$) with the usual properties: both are C^2, increasing, and strictly concave. An optimal contract divides w between the venture capitalist and the firm to maximize a weighted sum of expected utilities:

$$\begin{array}{ll} \max & E[u(x) + \lambda v(y)] \\ \text{s.t.} & x + y \leq w \text{ a.s.} \end{array}$$

Since the utility functions are unique only up to an affine transformation, we can assume that $\lambda = 1$ without loss of generality. Then the necessary and sufficient condition for efficient risk sharing is that

$$u'(x) = v'(y)$$

for almost all values of x and y. This equation can be solved uniquely to give differentiable solutions $x(w)$ and $y(w)$ that solve the first-order condition $u'(x(w)) \equiv v'(y(w))$ and satisfy the feasibility condition $x(w) + y(w) \equiv w$ for all values of w. A simple calculation shows that $0 < x'(w) < 1$ and $0 < y'(w) < 1$ for all values of w. In other words, there is co-insurance.

We can think of the functions $x(w)$ and $y(w)$ as representing a complete contract between the firm and the venture capitalist. The contract contains every possible contingency in the sense that it specifies different levels of consumption—$x(w)$ for the firm and $y(w)$ for the venture capitalist—for each possible outcome w of the risky project. Conceptually this is not a very complex contract, but it might be very difficult to write down in words if the outcomes were not real numbers, but involved more or less complicated, qualitative descriptions. In any case, we can use this example to illustrate how a simpler contract, together with renegotiation, can replicate the more complicated complete contract.

The alternative to writing the complete contingent contract is for the venture capitalist and the firm to write a much simpler contract, say, a debt contract, and renegotiate the terms of the contract as more information becomes available. This requires a special information structure: information must become available gradually, in a sense to be made precise below. The debt contract chosen at the initial date sets the status quo for subsequent bargaining over the terms of the renegotiated contract. At each subsequent date, the contract is renegotiated: the firm proposes a new level of debt and a side payment, and the venture capitalist accepts or rejects the proposed renegotiation. As a result, the level of debt and the cumulative transfer evolve over time, gradually incorporating more and more information until, at the last date, the true value of w is known and the optimal division of the surplus is achieved.

Formally, we can show that in a subgame perfect equilibrium of a bargaining game, the renegotiation of a simple debt contract implements the optimal complete contract $\{x(w), y(w)\}$. This demonstrates that it is not necessary to write a complete contract in order to achieve the same effect in terms of risk sharing. However, it is important to remember that the equilibrium renegotiation strategies that implement the same allocation as the complete contract are just as complex as the complete contract itself. The unanswered question is whether the assumptions of an equilibrium theory of renegotiation are less demanding than the assumption of a complete contract.

Information Structure

Suppose that time is divided into T periods, $t = 1, \ldots, T$. The initial loan and investment are made before date 1, and the final outcome of the project is observed at date T. At each intervening date, some information about the eventual payoff arrives. Formally, we assume there is a sequence of random variables $\{w_t\}$ such that w_1 is a constant, $w_T = w$ is the outcome of the project, and the history $h_t = (w_1, \ldots, w_t)$ is common knowledge at each date t. In what follows we assume a binary information structure. Precisely, we assume the random variables $\{w_t\}$ satisfy

$$w_{t+1} = \begin{cases} w_t + a(h_t) & \text{with probability } p(h_t) \\ w_t + b(h_t) & \text{with probability } 1 - p(h_t), \end{cases}$$

for each $t = 1, \ldots, T-1$, where $a(h_t) > b(h_t)$ and $0 < p(h_t) < 1$ and the initial state $h_1 = w_1$ is a constant. At each date, there are only two possible outcomes of the information process. What this assumption captures is the notion that information arrives slowly, relative to the renegotiation process. For example, when there are many time periods and the steps $a(h_t)$ and $b(h_t)$ are very small, we can think of the binary process as an approximation to a diffusion process. As long as the length of the time periods is short, so that renegotiation proceeds quite quickly, this assumption is not too restrictive.

Contracts

In the model of renegotiation with incomplete contracts, we assume that the venture capitalist and the firm initially enter into a standard debt contract. The firm promises to pay the venture capitalist an amount of money d at date T if this is less than the outcome w and to pay the venture capitalist w otherwise. In addition, they can make side payments or lump-sum transfers. At each date $t = 1, \ldots, T$, the firm and the venture capitalist can agree to renegotiate the debt contract and make another side payment. Let d_t denote the face value of the debt chosen at date t and let m_t denote the cumulative transfers made to the firm up to and including date t.

The firm's liability is assumed to be limited to the revenue from the project. In other words, in the event of default, the venture capitalist can seize w, but it cannot seize the transfers that it has made to the firm. Presumably the defaulting managers have already used the side payments for their own consumption. If (d, m) is the prevailing contract at the last date, the venture capitalist receives the minimum of w and d. Since the venture capitalist has already paid m to the firm, its terminal income is $\min\{w, d\} - m$. Hence, the expected utility from the contract (d, m), evaluated at some date t with the history h_t, will be

$$E[u(\min\{w, d\} - m)|h_t],$$

assuming that it is not renegotiated before the last period. Call this value $V^*(d, m, h_t)$.

The contract (d, m) will give the firm a terminal income of $\max\{0, w - d\} + m$, and its expected utility evaluated at date t with history h_t will be

$$E[v(\max\{0, w - d\} + m)|h_t],$$

assuming the contract is not renegotiated before the final period.

The Bargaining Game

There are many ways in which renegotiations could be modeled. For the purposes of illustration, we take a simple bargaining game in which all offers are made by the firm. The crucial properties of the game studied here are that agreement is reached immediately and the outcome is efficient. Any game with these properties would lead to the same conclusions. For example, the analysis would be similar if the venture capitalist made all the offers or if the firm and the venture capitalist alternated in making offers. A different game would require a different initial contract and equilibrium path, but the terminal allocation of consumption would be the same as in the present case.

The rules of the game are as follows:

- The firm and the venture capitalist are assumed to have chosen an initial contract (d_0, m_0) before the first date.
- At each date t, there is a preexisting contract (d_{t-1}, m_{t-1}). The firm proposes a new contract (d_t, m_t).
- The venture capitalist accepts or reject the proposal.
- If the proposal is accepted, the venture capitalist makes a net transfer $m_t - m_{t-1}$ to the firm, and the firm's debt is changed to d_t. If the proposal is rejected, nothing happens and the preexisting contract at the next date will be $(d_t, m_t) = (d_{t-1}, m_{t-1})$.
- At the final date $t = T$, there is no scope for renegotiation. The firm receives the payoff $\max\{w_T - d_{T-1}, 0\} + m_{T-1}$, and the venture capitalist receives the payoff $\min\{d_{T-1}, w_T\} - m_{T-1}$.

Note that new information is arriving at each date, and the proposals that the firm makes will reflect this information. The firm's proposal at date t is a function of the history $h_t = (w_1, \ldots, w_t)$, and the venture capitalist's response is a function of the history h_t and the proposal (d_t, m_t). Thus, the sequence of contracts $\{(d_t, m_t)\}$ is a stochastic process adapted to $\{w_t\}$ and incorporates all the relevant information available to the two parties.

Spanning Conditions

Because the firm makes all the offers, it has all the bargaining power once the initial contract has been signed. Intuitively, we should not expect the venture capitalist to get any increase in expected utility as a result of the bargaining. This means that the venture capitalist cannot do better than to hang on to the existing contract. If he does that, the venture capitalist can guarantee that he will get at least $V^*(d_{t-1}, m_{t-1}|h_t)$ at date t, assuming that (d_{t-1}, m_{t-1}) is the preexisting contract and the information set is h_t. In other words, $V^*(d_{t-1}, m_{t-1}|h_t)$ is his security level at the information set h_t. If the first best is implemented by the equilibrium of the bargaining game, it must be the case that

$$V^*(d_{t-1}, m_{t-1}|h_t) = E[v(y(w_T)|h_t] \qquad (10.1)$$

for each date t and history h_t. If we can choose a contract (d_{t-1}, m_{t-1}) to satisfy equation 10.1 for each date and history, then we say that the spanning condition for implementation of the first-best risk-sharing allocation is satisfied.

It turns out that this condition is sufficient as well as necessary. If the spanning condition is satisfied, then the bargaining game has a subgame perfect equilibrium that implements the first best. Therefore, before investigating the equilibrium of the bargaining game, we have to see whether the spanning conditions can be satisfied.

We can use the spanning condition to define a sequence of contracts as follows. At the initial date, we have a preexisting contract (d_0, m_0) that is chosen to satisfy

$$V^*(d_0, m_0, h_1) = E[v(y(w))].$$

Given any history h_t, we know that next period the history will be either $(h_t, w_t + a(h_t))$ or $(h_t, w_t + b(h_t))$. The first-best expected utility of the venture capitalist will be

$$V^a(h_t) = E[v(y(w))|h_t, w_t + a(h_t)]$$

with probability $p(h_t)$ and

$$V^b(h_t) = E[v(y(w))|h_t, w_t + b(h_t)]$$

with probability $1 - p(h_t)$. If the preexisting contract (d_{t-1}, m_{t-1}) has the property that

$$V^*(d_{t-1}, m_{t-1}, h_t) = p(h_t)V^a(h_t) + (1 - p(h_t)V^b(h_t), \tag{10.2}$$

then we need to choose the next contract (d_t, m_t) to satisfy the following conditions:

$$V^*(d_t, m_t, (h_t, w_t + a(h_t))) = V^a(h_t) \tag{10.3}$$

and

$$V^*(d_t, m_t, (h_t, w_t + b(h_t))) = V^b(h_t). \tag{10.4}$$

If we can show that whenever the initial spanning condition (10.2) is satisfied, the analogous conditions for the following period (10.3 and 10.4) are satisfied, then we can recursively define the stochastic process of contracts $\{(d_t, m_t)\}$ to satisfy the general spanning condition, 10.1.

It remains to show that we can indeed choose (d_t, m_t) to satisfy the spanning conditions 10.3 and 10.4 at every date. Fix some date t and history h_t, and for $i = a, b$ let $F^i(w|h_t)$ denote the distribution of the random variable w conditional on the information set $(h_t, w_t + i(h_t))$. We have already assumed that $a(h_t) > b(h_t)$, and it seems natural to associate higher values of w_{t+1} with higher future values of w. Precisely, we assume that F^a dominates F^b in the sense of first-order stochastic dominance, that is, $F^a(w|h_t) \leq F^b(w|h_t)$ for all values of w and the inequality is strict for some values of w. This implies, among other things, that $V^a(h_t) > V^b(h_t)$.

We begin by noting that for every level of debt d, there exists a unique transfer $m(d)$ such that

$$V^*(d, m(d), h_t) = p(h_t)V^a(h_t) + (1 - p(h_t))V^b(h_t).$$

This follows from the continuity of v and the fact that the random variable w is bounded. Furthermore, it is easy to see that the function $m(d)$ is continuous, again because v and $\min\{d, w\}$ are continuous. If we choose $d = 0$, then $V^*(d, m(d), h_t) = v(-m(0))$, and we must have

$$V^b(h_t) < V^*(d, m(d), h_t + a(h_t)) = V^*(d, m(d), h_t + b(h_t)) < V^a(h_t).$$

Since the support of w is bounded, we can find an interval $[w_0, w_1]$ that contains the support in its interior. Now consider $d = w_1$. Then the venture capitalist's income under this contract will be $\min\{w_1, w\} - m(w_1) = w - m(\infty)$ for almost all values of w. Since the venture capitalist's income changes dollar for dollar with w, it is more sensitive under the contract $(w_1, m(w_1))$ than under the complete contract x. For this reason, it is reasonable to assume that

$$V^*(w_1, m(w_1), h_t + b(h_t)) < V^b(h_t) < V^a(h_t) < V^*(w_1, m(w_1), h_t + a(h_t)). \tag{10.5}$$

Since V^* is continuous in d, under this assumption, there must exist an intermediate value of d satisfying the desired spanning condition $V^*(d, m(d), h_t + i(h_t)) = V^i(h_t)$, for $i = a, b$. From now on, we assume that condition 10.4 is satisfied.

Subgame Perfect Equilibrium

Now we can define the subgame perfect equilibrium that implements the efficient risk-sharing contract $\{x(w), y(w)\}$. Prior to date 1, the venture capitalist and the firm have already chosen a contract (d_0, m_0) that gives the venture capitalist its first-best expected utility: $V^*(d_0, m_0, h_1) = E[v(x(w))|h_1]$. At date 1, the firm proposes a new contract (m_1, d_1) to the venture capitalist, which satisfies the spanning condition

$$V^*(d, m(d), h_1 + i(h_1)) = V^i(h_1), \quad \text{for } i = a, b,$$

and the venture capitalist accepts it. If the firm offers a contract that would give the venture capitalist a higher expected utility if held until date T, the venture capitalist will accept it. If the firm offers any other contract, the venture capitalist will reject it. Now suppose that we have defined the strategies for every history up to date $t-1$. At date t the prevailing contract will be (d_{t-1}, m_{t-1}). This may not be the equilibrium contract, in which case we have to solve the optimal risk-sharing problem over again, that is, we interpret (x, y) as the complete contract that maximizes the firm's expected utility, subject to the constraint that $E[v(x(w))|h_t] \geq V^*(d_{t-1}, m_{t-1}, h_t)$. With this convention we can proceed as before. The firm proposes a contract (d_t, m_t) that satisfies the spanning condition

$$V^*(d, m(d), h_t + i(h_t)) = V^i(h_t), \quad \text{for } i = a, b.$$

The venture capitalist accepts any contract (d, m) satisfying $V^*(d, m, h_t) \geq V^*(d_{t-1}, m_{t-1}, h_t)$ and rejects any other contract. Proceeding in this way, we can define strategies for every date and history. It is clear that these strategies implement the same allocation as the original complete contract (x, y).

To see that this is a subgame perfect equilibrium, we need to consider the strategies of the venture capitalist and the firm separately. The venture capitalist accepts any contract that gives it the same expected utility as the existing contract if each is held to date T and rejects any other contract. The venture capitalist's equilibrium payoff must be at least as great as the expected utility of this contract because it can always refuse to renegotiate. Since the firm holds the venture capitalist to its reservation expected utility, the equilibrium payoff will be exactly the expected utility of the preexisting contract held until date T. Thus, it is optimal for the venture capitalist to accept a proposal if and only if it guarantees an expected utility as great as the preexisting contract. It is clear that the specified strategy achieves the first-best allocation for the firm. Given that the venture capitalist starts out at the first-best utility and cannot be forced below this level, there is no way that the firm can do better than to achieve the first-best payoff. Thus, there does not exist a better strategy, so the specified strategy is optimal for the firm at every information set. This completes the proof that the specified strategies do constitute a subgame perfect equilibrium.

An Example

A parametric example illustrates the requirements of the theory and also allows us to see whether the spanning condition will be satisfied in a reasonable case. Suppose that both the firm and the venture capitalist have constant absolute risk aversion,

$$u(x) = -e^{-Ax}$$

$$v(y) = -e^{-By},$$

and suppose that $\{w_t\}$ follows a random walk:

$$w_{t+1} = \begin{cases} w_t + a & \text{w. pr. } \pi \\ w_t + b & \text{w. pr. } 1 - \pi, \end{cases}$$

for $t = 1, \ldots, T-1$, where w_1 is a known constant. The first-order condition for efficient risk sharing takes the form

$$Ae^{-Ax(w)} = Be^{-By(w)},$$

which implies that $x(w)$ is an affine function of $y(w)$. Then the fact that $x(w) + y(w) \equiv w$ implies that both $x(w)$ and $y(w)$ are affine functions of w.

Suppose that $y(w) = \lambda w + \mu$, where $0 < \lambda < 1$. Then in order to implement the first-best, risk-sharing scheme, the debt contract adopted at date $T - 1$ when w_{T-1} is observed must satisfy

$$\min\{w_{T-1} + a, d_{T-1}\} + m_{T-1} = \lambda(w_{T-1} + a) + \mu$$

$$\min\{w_{T-1} + b, d_{T-1}\} + m_{T-1} = \lambda(w_{T-1} + b) + \mu,$$

and since $0 < \lambda < 1$ this requires

$$d_{T-1} + m_{T-1} = \lambda(w_{T-1} + a) + \mu$$

$$w_{T-1} + b + m_{T-1} = \lambda(w_{T-1} + b) + \mu$$

or

$$d_{T-1} = w_{T-1} + \lambda a + (1 - \lambda)b$$

$$m_{T-1} = -(1 - \lambda)(w_{T-1} + b) + \mu.$$

So there are unique values of debt and transfers at date $T - 1$ that implement the first best. Obviously, the adding-up condition implies that the same values of d_{T-1} and m_{T-1} will give the firm $x(w)$.

At dates $t < T - 1$, the problem is more complicated, because we have to choose d_t and m_t to give the venture capitalist the equilibrium status quo utility level rather than to give it a particular income level. As a result, the calculations are more complicated. However, the critical problem, as we have seen, is to ensure that the spanning conditions are satisfied. Recall that (d_t, m_t) can be chosen so that

$$E[-\exp\{-B(\min\{w_T, d_t\} + m_t)\}|w_t] = E[-\exp\{-B(\lambda w_T + \mu)\}|w_t],$$

which is equivalent to

$$E[-\exp\{-B\min\{w_T, d_t\}\}|w_t] = e^{-B(\mu - m_t)}E[-\exp\{-B(\lambda w_T)\}|w_t].$$

We want to ensure that the analogous conditions hold at date $t + 1$, that is,

$$E[-\exp\{-B(\min\{w_T, d_t\} + m_t)\}|w_t + a] = E[-\exp\{-B(\lambda w_T + \mu)\}|w_t + a]$$

$$E[-\exp\{-B(\min\{w_T, d_t\} + m_t)\}|w_t + b] = E[-\exp\{-B(\lambda w_T + \mu)\}|w_t + b].$$

If we choose $d = \infty$, then $\min\{w_T, d_t\} = w_T$, and if we choose m_t so that the ex ante expected utility of (d_t, m_t) is equal to the ex ante first-best expected utility, then $m_t < \mu$ and $e^{-B(\mu - m_t)} < 1$. Clearly,

$$E[-e^{-Bw_T}|w_t + a] - E[-e^{-Bw_T}|w_t + b] > E[-e^{-B\lambda w_T}|w_t + a]$$

$$- E[-e^{-B\lambda w_T}|w_t + b] > e^{-B(\mu - m_t)}\Big(E[-e^{-B\lambda w_T}|w_t + a]$$

$$-E[-e^{-B\lambda w_T}|w_t + b]\Big),$$

so the ex ante condition implies that

$$E[-e^{-Bw_T}|w_t + a] > e^{-B(\mu - m_t)}E[-e^{-B\lambda w_T}|w_t + a]$$

$$E[-e^{-Bw_T}|w_t + b] < e^{-B(\mu - m_t)}E[-e^{-B\lambda w_T}|w_t + b]$$

as required. That is, the spanning condition is satisfied, so there exists a level of debt $0 < d_t < \infty$ that equates the expected utility of the debt contract with the first-best expected utility in each of the information sets at date $t + 1$.

10.5 Nonverifiability and Renegotiation

Another example of the usefulness of renegotiation is provided by the Aghion, Dewatripont, and Rey (1994) (ADR) framework, which makes use of a more sophisticated renegotiation mechanism to make the outcome completely contingent. ADR address the problem of optimal risk sharing in a context where states of nature are not verifiable. To use the previous example involving the venture capitalist and the firm, suppose that the two parties can write a complete contingent contract $\{x(w), y(w)\}$ but that the value of the random variable w is not verifiable by third parties. This means that the contract cannot be enforced by a court because the court cannot determine the true value of w. Although w is observed by the firm and the venture capitalist, the fact that $0 < x'(w) < 1$ means that each of them will have an incentive to lie. The firm will want to pretend w is lower than it is, and the venture capitalist will want to pretend that it is higher than it is.

This problem can be obviated by adopting a slightly more complicated contract, which is still rather simple. After w is observed by the two parties, each is required to announce to the court the value of w. If they agree, there is no difficulty: the contract is carried out as originally intended, that is, the firm pays $y(w)$ to the venture capitalist. If they disagree, the party that announces the higher value gets to take over the firm and must give the other party the first-best allocation. For example, if the venture capitalist announces $\hat{w}'$, which is greater than the firm's announcement $\hat{w}$, then the venture capitalist must give the firm $x(\hat{w}')$ in exchange for the output of the project. The payoffs are summarized as follows:

Announcements	Firm's payoff	Venture capitalist's payoff
$\hat{w} = \hat{w}'$	$w - y(\hat{w})$	$y(\hat{w})$
$\hat{w} > \hat{w}'$	$w - y(\hat{w})$	$y(\hat{w})$
$\hat{w} < \hat{w}'$	$x(\hat{w}')$	$w - x(\hat{w}')$

It is clear from inspection that truth telling is the unique Nash equilibrium.

In this account, the announcements being made by the parties to the contract do not actually change the terms of the contract, and in that sense they are different from the renegotiation discussed earlier. However, we can tell a different story. Suppose that w, which cannot be observed directly, is a function of some state of nature that can be observed by everyone and is very hard to describe. The reason the court cannot verify the value of w is that there is no description of the state in the contract. However, as long as the contract specifies the pairs (x, y) that are allowed in the contract, the same mechanism will work. The firm and the venture capitalist, by announcing the appropriate pair, are in effect making the contract contingent. Without their announcements, the contract does not specify a relationship between the outcomes and the states on which they are contingent and the court would have to choose a noncontingent default. In this sense, we can say that the firm and the venture capitalist are renegotiating the contract to make it more contingent, and the contract is much simpler than a contract that had to specify the relationship between the payments received by the parties and the states of nature.

10.6 Competition and Holdup Problems

One of the disadvantages of long-run relationships that has been emphasized in the literature (cf. Hart 1995) is the so-called holdup problem. In order to achieve all the potential gains from a long-term relationship, it may be necessary for one of the parties to make relationship-specific investments. Suppose two firms enter into a long-term agreement whereby the upstream firm, firm A, supplies a component that is used as an input by the downstream firm, firm B. Entering into this kind of relationship may be in the interests of both parties for a number of reasons. There may be increasing returns to scale or learning by doing, either of which implies gains from specialization and continuing production over a long period of time. If it is difficult to judge the quality of the component, it may be optimal to have a long-term relationship because it reduces the costs of monitoring. The disadvantage of this kind of relationship comes from the specific investments that are required in order to supply the component and the moral hazard problems to which this gives rise. If firm A has to make a large investment in machinery in order to supply the component cheaply, and this machinery has no alternative uses, then firm A runs the risk of substantial losses if firm B decides to cancel its order or switch to another supplier. Conversely, if firm A is the only supplier in the short run or has achieved a significant cost advantage, it can use its bargaining power to extract rents from firm B. Because of these moral hazard or holdup problems, firms may be unwilling to enter into a long-term relationship with another firm despite the technical advantages. For example, firms may insist on using multiple suppliers (multisourcing) to avoid being exploited by a single supplier.

A similar kind of problem arises in financial relationships. The cause of the problem is the information that is obtained by the parties in the relationship. Over time a bank may acquire a large amount of information about a firm to which it supplies funds, both because it has investigated the firm before it lent the money and because it obtains information while providing finance. This information will not be available to other intermediaries, except at a cost. This information asymmetry may give the lending bank bargaining power over the borrowing firm, allowing it to extract rents out of the firm. Although the firm has the option of going to other lenders, there may be a stigma attached since other intermediaries may assume that the previous relationship was terminated for cause—for example, because the firm had become a high risk. In that case, other intermediaries may not be willing to deal with the firm or may want to do so only after they have assured themselves at considerable cost that the firm has not become a bad risk. These barriers to finding competitive lenders can be exploited by the bank to charge higher-than-normal returns on funds provided or in some other way exploit the borrower. It has been suggested that this may be one reason that firms prefer to obtain funds from the corporate bond market as soon as they are able, rather than relying on bank finance (Hellwig 1991). It appears that dependence on bank finance is closely related to size. In the United States it is small and medium-sized companies, for which the fixed costs of going to the market are prohibitive, that are most dependent on bank loans for external finance. The extraction of informational rents could be one explanation why large companies in the United States do not rely on banks for external finance.

Although a number of authors have investigated this kind of theoretical argument, there does not appear to be much empirical evidence to support the claim. Some empirical evidence (Petersen and Rajan 1994) suggests the opposite: that firms with a long-term relationship with banks obtain more favorable treatment. The exact reason for this phenomenon is not known. It could be because the banks know them better.

One reason that the holdup problem may not be as severe as theoretical models suggest is that banks may have an incentive to build up a reputation. Banks deal with many clients and provide similar services to many of them. A bank that is known to exploit its information advantages is unlikely to attract potential borrowers if there are alternative sources of finance. It seems unlikely that a bank could keep such activities quiet—disgruntled firms can communicate their experiences with a bank to other firms—in which case the bank may have more to lose from exploiting long-term relationships than it gains. On the contrary, it may want to treat its current clients well precisely to encourage more firms to enter into long-term relationships.

10.7 Empirical Importance of Relationships

Turning aside from these interesting theoretical issues, we have to ask the question, How important are these relationships empirically? Here there does not seem to be a lot of evidence. As far as the importance of renegotiation in the sense of Dewatripont and Maskin (1995), the work of Asquith, Gertner, and Scharfstein (1994) suggests that little renegotiation occurs in the case of financially distressed firms. Conventional wisdom holds that banks are so well secured that they can and do pull the plug as soon as a borrower becomes distressed, leaving the unsecured creditors and other claimants holding the bag.

Petersen and Rajan (1994) suggest that firms that have a longer relationship with a bank do have greater access to credit, controlling for a number of features of the borrowers' history. It is not clear from their work exactly what lies behind the value of the relationship. For example, the increased access to credit could be an incentive device, or it could be the result of greater information or the relationship itself could make the borrower more credit worthy. Berger and Udell (1992) find that banks smooth loan rates in response to interest rate shocks. Petersen and Rajan (1995) and Berlin and Mester (1997a) find that smoothing occurs as a firm's credit risk changes. Berlin and Mester (1997b) find that loan rate smoothing is associated with lower bank profits and argue that this suggests the smoothing does not arise as part of an optimal relationship.

In conclusion, these surprising results underline that the issue of how important renegotiation and relationships are empirically, and the extent to which renegotiation is virtuous or vicious is an important area for future research.

References

Admati, A., and P. Pfleiderer. (1994). "Robust Financial Contracting and the Role of Venture Capitalists." *Journal of Finance* **49,** 371–402.

Aghion, P., M. Dewatripont, and P. Rey. (1994). "Renegotiation Design with Unverifiable Information." *Econometrica* **62,** 257–282.

Aoki, M., and S. Dinç. (1997). *Relational Financing as an Institution and Its Viability under Competition.* CEPR Publication No. 488. Stanford, CA: Stanford University.

Asquith, P., R. Gertner, and D. Scharfstein. (1994). "Anatomy of Financial Distress: An Examination of Junk-Bond Issuers." *Quarterly Journal of Economics* **109,** 625–658.

Bergemann, D., and U. Hege. (1997). "Venture Capital Financing, Moral Hazard and Learning." Discussion paper 1738, Center for Economic Policy Research (CEPR).

Berger, A., and G. Udell. (1992). "Some Evidence on the Empirical Significance of Credit Rationing." *Journal of Political Economy* **100,** 1047–1077.

Berglof, E. (1994). "A Control Theory of Venture Capital Finance." *Journal of Law, Economics, and Organization* **10,** 247–267.

Berlin, M., and L. Mester. (1997a). "Why Is the Banking Sector Shrinking? Core Deposits and Relationship Lending." Working paper 96-18/R, Federal Reserve Bank of Philadelphia.

———. (1997b). "On the Profitability and Cost of Relationship Lending." Working paper, Federal Reserve Bank of Philadelphia.

Bhattacharya, S., and G. Chiesa. (1995). "Proprietary Information, Financial Intermediation, and Research Incentives." *Journal of Financial Intermediation* **4,** 328–357.

Black, B., and R. Gilson. (1998). "Venture Capital and the Structure of Capital Markets: Banks Versus Stock Markets." *Journal of Financial Economics* **47,** 243–277.

Boot, A., S. Greenbaum, and A. Thakor. (1993). "Reputation and Discretion in Financial Contracting." *American Economic Review* **83,** 1165–1183.

Boot, A., and A. Thakor. (1996). "Can Relationship Banking Survive Competition?" Working Paper 96-6, School of Business Administration, University of Michigan.

Cornelli, F., and O. Yosha. (1997). "Stage Financing and the Role of Convertible Debt." Discussion paper 1735, Center for Economic Policy Research (CEPR).

Dewatripont, M., and E. Maskin. (1995). "Credit and Efficiency in Centralized and Decentralized Economies." *Review of Economic Studies* **62,** 541–555.

Diamond, D. (1991). "Monitoring and Reputation: The Choice Between Bank Loans and Directly Placed Debt." *Journal of Political Economy* **99,** 689–721.

Dinç, S. (1996). "Bank Competition, Relationship Banking and Path Dependence." Ph.D. dissertation, Stanford University.

Elsas, R., and J. Krahnen. (1997). "Is Relationship Lending Special? Evidence from Credit-File Data in Germany." Working paper, Institut für Kapitalmarktforschung/Center for Financial Studies, Johann Wolfgang Goethe-Universität Frankfurt am Main.

Fenn, G., N. Liang, and S. Prowse. (1995). "The Economics of the Private Equity Market." FRB1/2700/1095. Washington, D.C.: Board of Governors of the Federal Reserve System.

Gale, D. (1991). "Optimal Risk Sharing Through Renegotiation of Simple Contracts." *Journal of Financial Intermediation* **1,** 283–306.

Gompers, P. (1995). "Optimal Investment, Monitoring and the Staging of Venture Capital." *Journal of Finance* **50,** 1461–1489.

———. (1996). "Grandstanding in the Venture Capital Industry." *Journal of Financial Econmomics* **42,** 133–156.

Gompers, P., and J. Lerner. (1996). "The Use of Covenants: An Empirical Analysis of Venture Partnership Agreements." *Journal of Law and Economics* **39,** 463–498.

———. (1998). "Money Chasing Deals? The Impact of Fund Inflows on Private Equity Valuations." Working paper, Harvard Business School.

Hart, O. (1995). *Firms, Contracts, and Financial Structure.* New York: Oxford University Press.

Hart, O., and J. Moore. (1988). "Incomplete Contracts and Renegotiation." *Econometrica* **56,** 755–785.

Hellmann, T. (1998). "The Allocation of Control Rights in Venture Capital Contracts." *Rand Journal of Economics* **29,** 57–76.

Hellwig, M. (1991). "Banking, Financial Intermediation and Corporate Finance." In A. Giovannini and C. Mayer (eds.), *European Financial Integration* (pp. 35–63). New York: Cambridge University Press.

Huberman, G., and C. Kahn. (1988). "Limited Contract Enforcement and Strategic Renegotiation." *American Economic Review* **78,** 471–484.

Lerner, J. (1994a). "The Syndication of Venture Capital Investments." *Financial Management* **23,** 16–27.

———. (1994b). "Venture Capitalists and the Decision to Go Public." *Journal of Financial Economics* **35,** 293–316.

———. (1995). "Venture Capitalists and the Oversight of Private Firms." *Journal of Finance* **50,** 301–318.

———. (1997). "Venture Capital and Private Equity: A Course Overview." Mimeo. Harvard Business School.

Petersen, M., and R. Rajan. (1994). "The Benefits of Lending Relationships: Evidence from Small Business Data." *Journal of Finance* **49,** 3–37.

———. (1995)."The Effect of Credit Market Competition on Lending Relationships." *Quarterly Journal of Economics* **110,** 407–443.

Repullo, R., and J. Suarez. (1998). "Venture Capital Finance: A Security Design Approach." Working paper, Centro de Estudios Monetarios y Financieros (CEMFI), Madrid.

Sahlman, W. (1990). "The Structure and Governance of Venture-Capital Organizations." *Journal of Financial Economics* **27,** 473–521.

Stiglitz, J., and A. Weiss. (1983). "Incentive Effects of Terminations: Applications to the Credit and Labor Markets." *American Economic Review* **73,** 912–927.

Trester, J. (1998). "Venture Capital Contracting Under Asymmetric Information." *Journal of Banking and Finance* **22,** 675–699.

von Thadden, E. (1995). "Long-Term Contracts, Short-Term Investment and Monitoring." *Review of Economic Studies* **62,** 557–575.

Yosha, O. (1995). "Information Disclosure Costs and the Choice of Financing Source." *Journal of Financial Intermediation* **4,** 3–20.

III The Role of the Firm

11 Autonomous, Self-Financing Firms

Central to the literature on corporate governance is Berle and Means's (1932) observation that in practice there is a separation of ownership and control in large, widely held corporations. Shareholders have little voice in how the affairs of such firms are conducted because the managers make the important decisions. Inevitably they pursue their own interests, to some extent to the detriment of shareholders. Jensen and Meckling (1976) have stressed the agency relationship between shareholders and managers and suggest that the essential problem facing shareholders is to make managers act in the shareholders' interest.

Recent work in corporate finance has explored different aspects of the agency problem and shown how the structure of the firm has been shaped by the need to provide proper incentives for managers to act in shareholders' interest. The main internal control mechanism is the board of directors. It appears to be equally ineffective in all the countries considered, despite significant differences in the detailed operation (for example, the two-tiered structure of boards in Germany). It has been widely argued that the main external mechanism for corporate governance in the United States and United Kingdom is the market for corporate control, in particular, hostile takeovers. In the other countries considered in this book, hostile takeovers are rare or nonexistent. It is often suggested that monitoring by banks and other financial institutions performs the same role in these countries. In Japan, the main bank system involves long-term, close relationships between firms and banks. The same is true in Germany with the hausbank system. In addition, banks in Germany have the potential to exercise considerable control through their ability to vote their own shares and the proxies of their customers' shares. As we discussed in chapter 4, the evidence on the effectiveness of hostile takeovers and monitoring by financial institutions is mixed. We believe that they are effective in extreme circumstances, such as financial distress; however, provided a firm is solvent and there are no clear problems, the evidence suggests that managers have a great deal of autonomy in all five countries.

Another method of controlling managers' behavior that has received considerable attention in the recent literature is the use of debt. This creates an incentive for managers to work hard in order to avoid the risk of bankruptcy and the subsequent loss of their jobs and perquisites (Grossman and Hart 1982). Debt also prevents managers from squandering free cash flow by forcing them to pay out the firm's earnings to bondholders, who can then decide where to reinvest them (Jensen 1986). The threat of liquidation held by bondholders allows them to renegotiate with the manager over the optimal division of earnings between repayment of debt and reinvestment in the firm (Hart and Moore 1994). The structure of the debt can be designed to constrain management (Hart and Moore 1995). Finally, debt can serve as a mechanism for transferring control over the firm to bondholders in states of nature where the manager would overinvest, while leaving the manager free to determine investment in states where his interests are aligned with the shareholders (Aghion and Bolton 1992).

Although these theories have many appealing features, they are also problematic in a number of ways. First, they are not consistent with the basic stylized facts outlined in chapter 3 concerning how large corporations in modern developed countries actually obtain funds. As Mayer (1988, 1990) and others have stressed, large corporations in these countries typically obtain funds internally from retained earnings rather than externally from bond or equity issues or from banks. Second, the use of debt by large U.S. corporations has been relatively limited. Taggart (1985) has found that during the postwar period, long-term debt constituted about 35 percent of the market value of large U.S. corporations, with most of the remainder being equity. Although such firms have issued relatively little new equity, the significant level of internal finance through retained earnings has ensured that outside equity is the most important financing instrument. Third, the total return to equities in the United States and other countries has been high. According to Ibbotson Associates (1998) the (arithmetic) mean return on large company stocks in the United States for the period 1926–1997 was 13.0 percent. Of this, the average annual dividend yield during the period was 4.5 percent, with the remaining part of the return being capital gains. In comparison, corporate bonds yielded 5.7 percent during the same period. The total return on equity was thus much higher than on bonds. Even the dividend yield is not very far below the return on bonds. At least part of the difference between the return on equity and debt is due to a difference in risk between the instruments. However, the debate on the equity premium puzzle indicates that it is difficult to attribute all the difference in returns to differences in risk. In any case, these figures suggest that equity holders have not been prevented from obtaining good returns by lack of control.

Taken together with the evidence cited in chapter 4, these observations suggest that current theories of the firm do not provide a good explanation of the separation of ownership and control that Berle and Means emphasized. The importance of internal finance and the associated significance of outside equity suggest that managers are given a great deal of autonomy. Debt has not been used to control their behavior. Moreover, equity holders have fared well from the autonomy granted to managers. They have received a high dividend yield and high total returns.

By focusing on issues of manager-shareholder conflict, the corporate finance literature has made important advances in the theory of the firm, opening up the black box of the firm and revealing the numerous ways in which the organization and the financial structure of the firm affect performance. This fundamental contribution to economic theory has also left open a number of interesting possibilities that have not yet been as fully explored. Is it possible that firms perform well even without external controls? Are there good reasons that shareholders do not interfere in the running of the firm? If so, what is the role of financial structure? What role does growth through retained earnings have to play in providing incentives? Why is it that firms rely so heavily on internal finance? Can the relative autonomy provided by internal finance be consistent with good performance as evidenced by stock returns? What is the role of mergers and acquisitions? These are the issues considered here.

Our main theme in this chapter is that it can be optimal for shareholders to allow managers a significant degree of autonomy. In other words, separation of ownership and control can be optimal for shareholders. Although the interests of shareholders and managers are not the same, both do well if the firm does well. When there is asymmetric information and contracting opportunities are incomplete, trying to control managers' decisions may lead to lower returns for shareholders than giving them a large amount of discretion. We argue that the predominance of internal finance can be viewed as a way of ensuring that managers have an effective incentive system and is ultimately in the interests of shareholders. While recognizing the pervasive and fundamental importance of agency problems, we would argue that firms have the incentive and the ability to organize themselves in ways that promote growth, expansion of market share, and innovation. Although there is no reason to think that the interests of shareholders and other stakeholders are perfectly aligned, the way in which a semiautonomous firm operates may to some extent be in the interest of the shareholders.

11.1 The Theory of the Firm

The contemporary theory of corporate finance treats the manager as a self-interested agent who is constrained only by threats from external stakeholders. It is as if the managers themselves have become the owners and the original investors have become very junior claimants who may or may not get a share when all is said and done. The 1980s experience of highly leveraged management buyouts reinforces this idea that it is the managers who are in charge. After all, if owners cannot control the firm, it would seem that they might as well sell it to managers for whatever they can get. With managers as the official owners, at least one increases efficiency by eliminating the agency problem.

Hart's (1995) theory of the firm is based on the notion that a firm is defined by the control of assets. Ownership of an asset confers the residual right to make decisions—that is, any decision-making power that has not explicitly been signed away devolves to the owner. In a world of incomplete contracts, some patterns of ownership are more efficient than others, because ex post some individuals will have an incentive to make efficient decisions and others will not. Even if renegotiation is possible, so that ex post an efficient decision is always made, ex ante the anticipation of transfers necessitated by renegotiation will distort decisions, making some patterns of ownership inefficient ex ante. This is related to the well-known holdup problem, where sharing the gains from specific investments will lead to underinvestment. The existence of firms is explained by the fact that in the absence of complete contracts, it is efficient to invest the residual rights of control in certain managers.

One also must provide for the transfer of ownership when circumstances change, and this has led to a theory of debt as a means of making ownership and control state contingent (Aghion and Bolton 1992). Briefly, it may be efficient for the manager to exercise control when the firm is solvent and for bondholders to exercise control in adverse circumstances when the firm is insolvent. This provides us with a rationale for the transfer of ownership that occurs in bankruptcy.

This view of the firm has some sharp implications for the financing of investment. In the Hart-Moore (1994) theory of the debt, the only option open to the bondholders is to wrest control of the asset from the manager. They use this power to negotiate investment and dividend decisions ex post. This is best illustrated by example. Suppose there are three dates, $t = 1, 2, 3$, and at the initial date, the investors purchase an asset (a machine) that they put in the control of a manager. The machine produces a random return y_t at dates $t = 2, 3$ and can be liquidated for a fixed amount L in period $t = 2$ (it has no scrap value at the last date). All uncertainty is resolved at date $t = 2$ in the sense that (y_2, y_3) become known for sure. At the first date, the investors and the manager write a contract that specifies, among other things, the payments to be made by the manager in each period. The contract cannot be made conditional on the earnings of the firm because these are unverifiable; in fact, the only thing that can be verified is whether the manager has made a specified payment. If he has not, then the investors have the right to seize the asset and prevent the manager from using it.

Let D be the minimum payment required at the second date. If the manager makes a payment of at least D at $t = 2$, there is nothing the investors can do to stop him from using the rest of the firm's income for his own purposes after this. At the last date, the manager will simply consume y_3. There is nothing the investors can do to stop him. At the second-to-last date, the manager may lose control of the firm if he does not pay D to the investors, but he may get away with less. Clearly he will never pay them more than D. If he pays them only L, it will not be worthwhile seizing the asset. The exact division of the surplus is determined by a bargaining problem, but assuming the manager gets to make a take-it-or-leave-it offer, he will clearly pay the minimum of D and L if he can. If $y_2 < \min\{D, L\}$ then the investors will seize the asset, even though this is inefficient if

$$L < y_2 + y_3.$$

If $y_2 \geq \min\{D, L\}$ the manager will retain control, and his rents equal

$$y_2 + y_3 - \min\{D, L\}.$$

This story offers several lessons. First, the investors' power is restricted to the threat of taking away control of the asset. Second, this threat is credible only if the manager cannot pay the investors as much as they would get by taking away his control of the asset. (Different bargaining stories would lead to somewhat different conclusions here.) Third, because the manager cannot commit to pay the investors in the future, the transfer of control may be inefficient.

More important than the particular lessons we have been discussing is the general perspective on the theory of the firm that Hart and his coauthors have put forward. In their view, the owner-manager is in the driver's seat, and the outside claimants are forced to bargain for a share of the surplus. This is a useful complement to the traditional idea that managers maximize shareholders' preferences. It also throws into sharp relief the predicament of the shareholder in a modern corporation: If you do not like what the management is doing, what can you do about it? Even if it were possible to change the management (never an easy undertaking), is there any reason to think that the next management would behave any differently? If not, the threat to replace the management may not be credible, even if it is feasible. Similarly, one does not need to be persuaded by the idea that the manager can consume the firm's income. This is just a metaphor for the control of free cash flow, which generates private benefits for the manager.

On the other hand, this rather stylized view is in some respects unrealistic or inadequate as an account of the modern corporation. It is better suited as an account of an entrepreneurial firm in which the owner-manager's share is the only form of equity. The lack of any role for outside equity financing is a distinct limitation in a world where most large firms have a dispersed ownership. Moreover, the focus on the struggle between management and shareholders over the amount of the firm's earnings seems odd in a world in which the returns to equity (dividends plus capital gains) have historically been much higher than the returns to bonds. Even the dividend payments have been roughly two-thirds of the returns to bonds, but in the absence of any dividend payments, the capital gains would have offered an adequate return.

The specific issues raised by debt and renegotiation do not concern us here. We are more interested in the view of the manager as an independent operator and the implications this has for the financing of the modern corporation. The rest of this chapter has a more traditional focus on the division of ownership and control. We begin with the stylized facts that most large corporations rely on retained earnings to provide finance for investment and growth and that managers have a degree of independence from the shareholders who nominally control the firm. Given that there is not a perfect alignment of the interests of managers and shareholders, what rationale is there for a form of corporate control in which managers are independent agents running the firm? On the one hand, if the manager controls the internally generated funds, it seems natural that he would use them to expand his own firm or take over other firms, even if the shareholders could earn higher returns outside the firm. On the other hand, financial markets and intermediaries will be less likely to provide equity finance given their lack of control of the returns to their investment. Our answer is that given the imperfections of capital markets, there may be some justification for the tendency of the large, modern corporation to rely on self-financing and to allow the measure of independence for managers that this entails.

In the remainder of the chapter we pursue this theme in a number of settings. We analyze the costs and benefits of managerial discretion over internally generated funds when there is asymmetric information, discuss managerial discretion over internally generated funds and the provision of managerial incentives, and develop a framework for thinking about the allocation of internally generated funds, which is then used to discuss mergers and acquisitions.

11.2 Asymmetric Information and Managerial Discretion

Other things being equal, well-managed firms might be expected to generate larger amounts of cash than poorly managed firms. If well-managed firms also had better growth prospects, then one might think that investing retained earnings in the firms that generated them would be an efficient allocation of resources. Unfortunately, there does not seem to be any compelling reason to think that internally generated funds will perfectly match the efficient allocation of investment. On the contrary, it seems likely that start-up companies will have good growth prospects but negative cash flow and that mature companies may have a large cash flow but limited prospects for growth. The possibility of this kind of mismatch of funds has led some authors, such as Jensen (1986), to argue that firms should, as a matter of course, hand their earnings back to shareholders, who can then allocate them efficiently through the market rather than reinvest them in their own operations.

The apparent inefficiency of internal finance raises a number of questions. Foremost among them is the question of why financial markets are not used to reallocate the internally generated funds instead of leaving them in the hands of the manager. One possible explanation has to do with the costs of acquiring information. The fixed costs of acquiring information make it impractical for agents who have small investments in a firm to become fully informed. In principle shareholders could share the costs of becoming informed, but since this information is like a public good, the free-rider problem discourages the acquisition of costly information when agents can take advantage of the information acquired by other agents.

Suppose that there is a fixed cost of becoming informed and that a group of shareholders have to decide whether to obtain information. If they decide to become informed, they also have to decide how to share the cost. The shareholders have private information about their preferences (the value of information). For simplicity, suppose that there are only two possible values of information, high or low, and that the shareholders' types (value of information) are independently and identically distributed. Contributions to the cost of information are voluntary, so any institutional arrangements for sharing the cost of becoming informed must satisfy an individual rationality constraint. Formally, we can think of any institutional arrangement for sharing the cost of information as a mechanism for the provision of a public good (information). Since agents will have private information about their preferences, the mechanism must satisfy incentive compatibility constraints that ensure truthful reporting of preferences. Since agents are uncertain about their preferences ex ante, the ex ante optimal mechanism will include insurance. However, contributions are made after the agents know their types, so there must be an interim individual rationality constraint. Rob (1989), Mailath and Postlewaite (1990), and Neeman (1994) have studied this problem and show that when the number of agents becomes large, the costs of truthful revelation may be so large that it is impossible to acquire information. More precisely, if the low value of information is sufficiently low, the amount of the public good provided by any incentive-compatible and interim individually rational mechanism will converge to 0 in probability in the limit as the number of players becomes unboundedly large. This result captures the impossibility of cooperation among shareholders in the presence of private information when participation is voluntary: there simply do not exist institutions that will overcome the free-rider problem when the number of shareholders is large.

It makes sense to delegate the information-acquisition and investment process. A natural way to do this would be to use the services of a brokerage house or investment bank. Unfortunately, there are a number of obstacles that prevent financial institutions from fulfilling this function. The liquidity demanded of financial intermediaries forces these institutions to focus on short-term returns and diversification rather than the sort of long-term commitment that is required for carrying out mergers and acquisitions or restructuring a corporation. For this reason, decisions about takeovers, mergers and acquisitions, and large scale investment programs are delegated to the managers of firms. Second, intermediaries may not have the specialized information that is necessary to second-guess managers because of the large number of companies in which they have an interest. For example, it is sometimes argued that even in Germany, where banks have large stakes in major corporations and have positions on supervisory boards, they are not in a position to monitor the operations of these corporations effectively. For example, if Deutsche Bank, which has a major stake in Daimler-Benz, has thirty-five employees who monitor the performance of Daimler-Benz, it is very well informed relative to most investors, but even this does not put Deutsche Bank on the same footing as the Daimler-Benz management when it comes to the evaluation of detailed decisions. In principle, it might be possible for Deutsche Bank to replicate the information available to Daimler-Benz, but this would be too costly to be practical. In other cases, where the shareholding is even smaller, the cost of duplicating the managerial role would be even more impractical. The bottom line is that the shareholders delegate their portfolio decisions to the manager in order to overcome the problem posed by the size of the fixed costs of acquiring information.

The decision to delegate control of investment to the manager involves a trade-off between the costs and the benefits. From the shareholders' point of view, the benefits consist of the manager's ability to acquire information on their behalf. The costs consist of the distortions in the use of this information that result from the manager's preference for excessive investment. A simple example will help to clarify the trade-offs. The value of the firm is assumed to be a function $v(x, \theta)$ of the amount invested $x \geq 0$ and a random variable $\theta \geq 0$, which can be interpreted as the profitability of investment. We assume that v is quadratic in x

$$v(x, \theta) = (\theta - x/2)x$$

and that θ is uniformly distributed on an interval $[0, M]$. The manager's preferences are represented by a utility function,

$$u(x, \theta) \equiv v(x, \theta + a) = (\theta + a - x/2)x, \text{ where } a > 0.$$

In other words, the manager acts as if the state of nature were better than it is by a constant amount. Because of some private benefits he receives from investment, he acts as if he were overly optimistic and wants to invest more than is optimal for the investors for any state θ. If the shareholders could impose a Pigovian tax $t(x) = -ax$ on the manager, conditional on his investment, they could easily align his preferences with theirs and trivially solve the delegation problem. We do not observe such incentive schemes in practice, presumably because of the usual asymmetric-information and enforcement problems of implementing optimal incentives, so we shall assume that no such schemes are available.

In the absence of transfers conditional on the manager's actions, the problem for the shareholders is how to give the manager an incentive to reveal the information about profitability truthfully. Without loss of generality, we can treat the interaction between manager and shareholder as a problem of mechanism design. The manager observes the firm's type (the value of θ) and sends a message to the shareholders based on this signal. The shareholders then choose the level of investment as a function of the manager's message. We do not need to take this protocol literally. For example, it may be that the shareholders have instructed the manager how much investment to make in each state of nature. In any case, there is a strategic problem since the manager will not have an incentive to reveal his information truthfully. Truthful revelation will lead the shareholders to choose an investment level that is different from the manager's optimum and, anticipating this, the manager will have an incentive to misrepresent the firm's type.

We consider two versions of the delegation problem. In the first, we assume that the shareholders cannot commit themselves in advance to an optimal investment policy. Instead, they decide on the level of investment after the manager has become informed. In the second, corresponding to the classical mechanism design framework, they commit themselves ex ante to an optimal mechanism. We find that if the value of information is sufficiently high, the desirability of controlling the manager is limited. In the first case, the manager's decision is controlled to some degree. In the second case, it is optimal to allow the manager to choose the level of investment to maximize his own preferences within very broad limits.

We interpret the decision about how much the firm should invest as a metaphor for decision making within the firm. The lessons of these two exercises can then be applied to the firm's financial policy in general. Whether the decision being made relates to dividend policy, the growth of the firm, or mergers and acquisitions, the manager's information gives him an advantage in making the decision. Differences in objectives between the shareholders and the manager notwithstanding, the shareholders may be better off allowing the manager to make a relatively independent decision in order to take advantage of his superior information, rather than trying to micromanage the firm. The results shed some light on why managers are given such a great degree of autonomy in each of the countries considered in this book.

Delegation Without Commitment

Formally, the problem of delegation without commitment is a special case of the "cheap talk" game introduced by Crawford and Sobel (1982). Suppose that the shareholders cannot commit to a mechanism before the manager has observed the value of θ. Then the choice of x must be optimal for the shareholders, conditional on their beliefs about θ. By the revelation principle, we can assume that the manager makes an announcement about θ and that the shareholders then choose x to maximize their expected payoff. A strategy for the manager is a function $f : [0, M] \to [0, M]$, and the shareholders' strategy is a function $g : [0, M] \to \mathbf{R}_{+}$, with the obvious interpretations. The shareholders' beliefs are represented by a function $\mu : [0, M] \to \Delta[0, M]$, where $\Delta[0, M]$ denotes the set of probability distributions on $[0, M]$. Then $\mu(m)$ is the shareholders' probability distribution over possible values of θ when the manager announces m. The equilibrium conditions require that each player chooses a best response and that beliefs are consistent with Bayes' rule wherever possible:

1. $g(m) \in \arg\max \int_0^M (\theta - x/2)x d\mu(m)$;
2. $f(\theta) \in \arg\max(\theta + a - g(m)/2)g(m)$;
3. $\mu(m) = \text{unif} f^{-1}(m)$, for almost all m.

The first condition requires that the shareholders choose the level of investment given their beliefs about the firm's type based on the manager's announcement. The second condition requires that the manager chooses his announcement to maximize his expected utility given he knows how the shareholders react. The third condition requires that the shareholders' beliefs about firm type are consistent with the optimal announcement strategy of the manager.

If G is the range of the function g, then the manager is effectively choosing the level of investment from the set G and the second condition merely requires the manager to choose optimally from G for each value of θ. The concavity of the manager's objective function implies that the set $f^{-1}(x)$ is convex for every $x \in G$. Furthermore, the number of these sets must be finite, as the next lemma shows.

LEMMA 11.1 Suppose that x and x' belong to G and are chosen in equilibrium and $x < x'$. Then $x + a < x'$.

Proof The proof is by contradiction. Suppose that $x + a \geq x$. From the second and third conditions, it must be optimal for some type $\theta = x$ to choose a signal that causes the shareholders to choose x. But type θ's most preferred point is $x + a \geq x'$, so in view of the concavity of the objective function, this type would be strictly better off choosing a signal that caused the shareholders to choose x'. This contradicts the equilibrium condition (2) and establishes the desired result.

Without loss of generality, we can identify the manager's strategy with a finite list of intervals $\{(\theta_k, \theta_{k+1})\}_{k=1}^{K}$, where $\theta_1 = 0$ and $\theta_{K+1} = M$, such that all manager types $\theta \in (\theta_k, \theta_{k+1})$ send the same signal, which causes shareholders to choose an investment level x_k. From conditions 2 and 3, the kth investment level must satisfy

$$x_k = (\theta_k + \theta_{k+1})/2.$$

On the other hand, for any $1 \leq k < K - 1$, the marginal type θ_{k+1} must be indifferent between x_k and x_{k+1}:

$$(\theta_{k+1} + a - x_k/2)x_k = (\theta_{k+1} + a - x_{k+1}/2)x_{k+1}$$

$$(\theta_{k+1} + a)(x_k - x_{k+1}) = (x_k^2 - x_{k+1}^2)/2$$

$$(\theta_{k+1} + a) = (x_k + x_{k+1})/2.$$

Substituting the equilibrium values of x_k and x_{k+1}, we see that for each type $1 \leq k < K - 1$,

$$(\theta_{k+1} + a) = (\theta_k + \theta_{k+1} + \theta_{k+1} + \theta_{k+2})/4$$

or

$$\theta_{k+1} = (\theta_k + \theta_{k+2})/2 - 2a.$$

Using the two boundary conditions, $\theta_1 = 0$ and $\theta_{K+1} = M$, we can determine the intervals uniquely once we have decided how many of them there are.

THEOREM 11.1 Let $\{(\theta_k, x_k)\}_{k=1}^K$ be a sequence satisfying $\theta_1 = 0$ and $\theta_k < \theta_{k+1}$ and the following conditions:

(1) $x_k = (\theta_k + \theta_{k+1})/2,$ for $k = 1, \ldots, K,$ where $\theta_{K+1} = M;$

(2) $(\theta_{k+1} + a) = (x_k + x_{k+1})/2,$ for $k = 1, \ldots, K - 1.$

Then there exists a perfect Bayesian equilibrium (f, g, μ) such that $(\theta_k, \theta_{k+1}) \subset f^{-1}(m_k)$ and $g(m_k) = x_k$, for $k = 1, \ldots, K$. Conversely, for any perfect Bayesian equilibrium (f, g, μ), there exists a sequence $\{(\theta_k, x_k)\}_{k=1}^K$ satisfying conditions 1 and 2 and such that $(\theta_k, \theta_{k+1}) \subset f^{-1}(m_k)$ and $g(m_k) = x_k$, for $k = 1, \ldots, K$

Proof The first part of the theorem follows easily once we note that the equilibrium conditions are satisfied along the equilibrium path defined by $\{(\theta_k, x_k)\}_{k=1}^K$ and that off the equilibrium path we can easily define beliefs and optimal responses for the shareholders so that the manager does not have any incentive to deviate. The second part has already been established.

The theorem gives a fairly complete characterization of the set of possible equilibria. The equilibria vary a lot in terms of the amount of information that is revealed to the shareholders. At one extreme is the equilibrium with the trivial partition $\{(0, M)\}$; at the other extreme are equilibria in which the number of intervals K is quite large. What is not yet clear is how they compare in terms of the shareholders' payoffs. Is the information revealed by the manager in equilibrium valuable to the shareholders, or is the equilibrium with the trivial partition the best that can be achieved? For some parameter values, at least, the information revealed does have positive value for the shareholders, as the following example shows.

Assume that $M = 1$ and $a = 1/16$. Consider first the equilibrium with the trivial partition $\{(0, M)\}$. Since the shareholders have no information, they will choose $x = E[\theta] = 1/2$ and the payoff will be

$$E[(\theta - x/2)x] = (1/2 - 1/4)(1/2) = 1/8 = 0.125.$$

Now consider the case where $K = 2$. From the equilibrium conditions we know that $x_k = E[\theta|\theta_k < \theta < \theta_{k+1}]$, or that $x_1 = \theta_2/2$ and $x_2 = (\theta_2 + 1)/2$. Since type θ_2 is indifferent between x_1 and x_2, we have from $u(x_1, \theta_2) = u(x_2, \theta_2)$ that

$$\begin{aligned}\theta_2 &= (x_1 + x_2)/2 - a \\ &= (\theta_2/2 + (\theta_2 + 1)/2)/2 - 1/16 \\ &= 3/8.\end{aligned}$$

Then $x_1 = 3/16$ and $x_2 = 11/16$. The shareholders' expected utility will be

$$E[(\theta - x_1/2)x_1|\theta < 3/8] = (3/16 - 3/32)(3/16) = 0.0176$$

if $\theta < 3/8$ and

$$E[(\theta - x_2/2)x_2|\theta > 3/8] = (11/16 - 11/32)(11/16) = 0.2363$$

if $\theta > 3/8$, so the shareholders' expected utility is

$$E[u(x, \theta)] = (3/8)(0.0176) + (5/8)(0.2363) = 0.154.$$

Since 0.1543 is greater than 0.125, the shareholders are clearly better off in the equilibrium with more information.

It can similarly be shown that when $K = 3$,

$$\theta_1 = 0; \theta_2 = 1/12; \theta_3 = 5/12; \theta_4 = 1;$$

$$x_1 = 1/24; x_2 = 1/4; x_3 = 17/24;$$

$$E[u(x, \theta)] = 0.157.$$

The case with $K = 3$ is in fact the optimal solution. The expected utility of shareholders is lower with any number of intervals $K > 3$. Without commitment, shareholders have some degree of control. It is interesting to note that when profitability θ is low, shareholders get better information, in the sense of narrower intervals, than when it is high.

Delegation with Commitment

If the shareholders can benefit from the information revealed by the manager when there is no commitment, they can do even better when they are able to commit themselves to an optimal mechanism, since one possible mechanism is the investment function in the "cheap talk" equilibrium. In this case it turns out that the optimal mechanism restricts the manager's discretion even less than the optimal "cheap talk" mechanism.

By the revelation principle, we can restrict attention to direct revelation mechanisms. A direct revelation mechanism is a function $g: [0, M] \to \mathbf{R}_+$, where $g(\theta)$ is the investment specified by the shareholders when the manager reports his type to be θ. The manager will report his type truthfully if the mechanism is incentive compatible and the optimal (incentive-compatible) mechanism maximizes the shareholders' payoff, $E[(\theta - g(\theta)/2)g(\theta)]$, subject to the incentive-compatibility constraint. As in the case without commitment, the manager is effectively choosing an element from the range of g, $G = g([0, M])$. It will be convenient to use this representation of the mechanism in our analysis. To avoid pathological cases, we assume that G is a closed set.

LEMMA 11.2 If g is an optimal, incentive-compatible mechanism, the graph G is an interval.

Proof The proof is by contradiction. Suppose that G is not an interval. Since G is closed, there must exist a point $x \notin G$ such that $x' < x < x''$ for some $x', x'' \in G$. Since G is closed, we can choose a pair of points $x_0, x_1 \in G$ such that the interval $I = (x_0, x_1)$ does not intersect G. We shall argue that the incentive-compatible mechanism corresponding to $G \cup I$ dominates the original mechanism, and this will complete the proof.

If the manager is allowed to make an unconstrained choice, he will choose $x = \theta + a$ when his type is θ. The shareholders' payoff, conditional on the manager's type θ, is

$$\begin{aligned}\pi^*(\theta) &= (\theta - (\theta + a)/2)(\theta + a)\\ &= (\theta - a)(\theta + a)/2\\ &= (\theta^2 - a^2)/2.\end{aligned}$$

For any type of manager $\theta \in (\theta_0, \theta_1) \equiv (x_0 - a, x_1 - a)$, the manager's most preferred point will lie strictly between x_0 and x_1. Since his objective function is concave, this means that his most preferred point in G will be one of the two nearest points, x_0 and x_1. In fact, he will choose x_0 when $\theta \in (\theta_0, \bar{\theta})$ and x_1 when $\theta \in (\bar{\theta}, \theta_1)$, where $\bar{\theta} \equiv (\theta_0 + \theta_1)/2$. Conditional on $\theta \in (\theta_0, \bar{\theta})$, the shareholders' payoff is

$$\begin{aligned}\pi(\theta) &= (\theta - x_0/2)x_0\\ &= (\theta - (\theta_0 + a)/2)(\theta_0 + a)\\ &= (\theta - a + \theta - \theta_0)(\theta_0 - \theta + \theta + a)/2\\ &= (\theta^2 - a^2)/2 - (\theta - \theta_0)^2/2 + a(\theta - \theta_0)\\ &= \pi^*(\theta) - (\theta - \theta_0)^2/2 + a(\theta - \theta_0).\end{aligned}$$

A similar calculation shows that conditional on $\theta \in (\bar{\theta}, \theta_1)$, the shareholders' payoff is

$$\begin{aligned}\pi(\theta) &= (\theta - x_1/2)x_1\\ &= (\theta^2 - a^2)/2 - (\theta - \theta_1)^2/2 + a(\theta - \theta_1)\\ &= \pi^*(\theta) - (\theta - \theta_1)^2/2 + a(\theta - \theta_1).\end{aligned}$$

Let the difference be denoted by $\Delta(\theta) \equiv \pi^*(\theta) - \pi(\theta)$. Then conditional on the true type being in (θ_0, θ_1), the difference in the shareholders' payoff under the two mechanisms is

$$\begin{aligned}\int_{\theta_0}^{\theta_1} \Delta(\theta)d\theta &= \int_{\theta_0}^{\theta_1} (\pi^*(\theta) - \pi(\theta))d\theta\\ &= \int_{\theta_0}^{\bar{\theta}} \{(\theta - \theta_0)^2/2 - a(\theta - \theta_0)\}d\theta + \int_{\bar{\theta}}^{\theta_1} \{(\theta - \theta_1)^2/2 - a(\theta - \theta_1)\}d\theta\\ &= \int_{\theta_0}^{\bar{\theta}} \{(\theta - \theta_0)^2/2\}d\theta + \int_{\bar{\theta}}^{\theta_1} \{(\theta - \theta_1)^2/2\}d\theta > 0\end{aligned}$$

since

$$\int_{\theta_0}^{\bar{\theta}} \{a(\theta - \theta_0)\}d\theta = -\int_{\bar{\theta}}^{\theta_1} \{a(\theta - \theta_1)\}d\theta = \frac{1}{2}\left(\frac{\theta_1 - \theta_0}{2}\right)^2.$$

The concavity of the manager's objective function implies that for any type $\theta \notin (\theta_0, \theta_1)$, the end points x_0 and x_1 will always be strictly preferred to any point in the interval (x_0, x_1), so only the types $\theta \in (\theta_0, \theta_1)$ will be affected by the expansion of the set G to $G \cup (x_0, x_1)$. Thus, the change in the shareholders' payoff will be proportional to $\int_{\theta_0}^{\theta_1} \Delta(\theta)d\theta > 0$. This shows that the shareholders are strictly better off under the mechanism $G \cup (x_0, x_1)$, contradicting the optimality of G.

From now on we can assume the manager chooses his most preferred point from the interval $G = [x_0, x_1]$. As before, the manager will choose the investment $x = \theta + a$ if this belongs to G, and will choose the end point nearest to $\theta + a$ otherwise. So the manager will choose x_0 if and only if his type θ belongs to the interval $[0, x_0 - a]$, in which case the shareholders would prefer a smaller investment level. This implies it is optimal for them to put $x_0 = 0$. This leaves us with the constraint $x \leq x_1$ on the manager's choice. This constraint will be binding in the optimum mechanism, because the assumption of a compact support for θ implies that shareholders cannot benefit from managerial discretion for sufficiently high values of θ. Clearly it is optimal to choose $x_1 \leq M$, and this constraint will bind for all $\theta \geq M - a$. Our analysis of the optimal mechanism is summarized in the following result:

THEOREM 11.2 If $g^* : [0, M] \to \mathbf{R}_+$ is an optimal incentive-compatible mechanism for the shareholders, then for some value of $x_1 \leq M$, the mechanism has the form

$$g^*(\theta) = \min\{\theta + a, x_1\}, \forall \theta \in [0, M].$$

The optimal mechanism involves putting an upper bound x_1 on the amount of investment, but apart from that the manager can choose the level of investment that he wants. Although there is some constraint on managerial discretion, it will be very small when M is large or a is small. In other words, when uncertainty is large or the divergence between the interests of the manager and shareholders not too great, or both, the manager will be given almost complete discretion. We are led to speculate that if the support of θ were unbounded, the optimal mechanism could give managers complete discretion. In any case, this exercise indicates that there may be circumstances in which shareholders are best served by the separation of ownership and control, in spite of the existence of private benefits that distort the manager's decision.

It is important to distinguish the roles of the intervals in two theorems. The interval $[0, x_1]$ in the statement of theorem 11.2 is a range in which the manager can use his discretion; it does not correspond to the intervals $[\theta_k, \theta_{k+1}]$ in the statement of theorem 11.1, which are ranges of θ in which the shareholders choose the same value of x.

To illustrate the implications of the theorem, consider the same parameter values as in the previous example: $a = 1/16$ and $M = 1$. From the characterization in the theorem, we know the objective function is

$$E[u(x,\theta)] = \int_0^{x_1-a} [\theta(\theta+a) - \frac{1}{2}(\theta+a)^2]d\theta + \int_{x_1-a}^{1} [(\theta - x_1/2)x_1]d\theta. \quad (11.1)$$

Differentiating this expression with respect to x_1 and setting the result equal to zero gives us a first-order condition that can be solved for the optimal value of x_1:

$$\int_{x_1-a}^{1} [\theta - x_1(1 - x_1 + a)]d\theta = 0,$$

which implies that

$$x_1 = E[\theta|\theta > x_1 - a]$$
$$= \frac{1 + x_1 - a}{2}.$$

This equation is easily solved to give

$$x_1 = 1 - a = 15/16,$$

and, substituting back in equation 11.1,

$$E[u(x,\theta)] = 0.191.$$

Once x_1 is determined, the entire optimal policy is determined. In words, it tells us that the manager can choose any level of investment and any corresponding level of retained earnings and dividends, as long as the investment does not exceed $x_1 = 1 - a$. Since the maximum investment that the shareholders would ever want under complete information is $x = 1$ and the minimum is $x = 0$, it is obvious that they are committing themselves to give the manager a great deal of discretion. This is optimal because they gain from allowing the manager to make full use of his information (knowledge of θ), which he would not be willing to do, to the same extent, if they put more constraints on his actions.

The case with commitment provides an interesting contrast to the case without commitment. In the latter the manager could only choose among three levels of investment, $x_1 = 1/24$, $x_2 = 1/4$, or $x_3 = 17/24$. With commitment, the manager can choose a continuum of levels between 0 and 15/16. This flexibility allows an increase in expected utility from 0.157 to 0.191. Hence the precommitment of shareholders not to interfere with managers' investment decisions can be quite valuable, at least in the context of our quadratic example.

Another Argument for Managerial Discretion

In an important paper, Burkart, Gromb, and Panunzi (1997) give a similar kind of argument for the separation of ownership and control based on the provision of additional incentives for the manager to make an effort on behalf of the firm. This is a variant of solving the agency problem by "selling the firm to the agent." If the conflict of interest between shareholders and managers leads to inefficiency, reducing the claim of the shareholders may lead to greater efficiency. Too much control by shareholders is not a good thing. The manager must have some discretion to pursue his own interests and reap private benefits; otherwise he will not have an incentive to make an effort on behalf of the firm. The problem is that shareholders, once they start to micromanage, cannot commit themselves to reward the manager in a way that is consistent with optimal incentives, so the firm has to be constituted in a way that restricts shareholder power—in other words, commits them to leave some rents for the manager. Burkart, Gromb, and Panunzi argue that ownership structure can act as such a commitment device. By having dispersed ownership of outside equity, shareholders are effectively precommitting not to interfere with the managers. Each shareholder's ownership will be sufficiently small that there will be little incentive to monitor.

We have seen that precommitment not to micromanage is also an important issue in our framework. The lack of effectiveness of standard corporate governance mechanisms, documented at length in chapter 4 for all the countries considered can be viewed as a form of precommitment not to interfere. The standard view that the weakness of such mechanisms is undesirable is here turned on its head: it is a positive benefit that shareholders do not have much influence over the firm. The most effective governance mechanisms are the ones where the shareholders have the least direct influence! The separation of ownership and control that Berle and Means (1932) pointed out can in fact be optimal in a second-best sense.

11.3 Incentives, Growth, and Retained Earnings

Another possible way of precommitting to give the manager autonomy is by giving the manager discretion over dividend policy, that is, over how the firm's internally generated funds should be divided between dividends and retained earnings. There are reasons for thinking that the second best will require managers to retain a large fraction of the internally generated funds, which is what the manager is likely to do, left to his own devices. A version of the Laffer curve argument applies here. Dividends are like a tax on free cash flow from the manager's perspective. Raising the tax rate too high may actually reduce the revenue (dividends) because of the effect on incentives.

This is true even in a static context, but in a dynamic context, where capital gains may be the major source of the return to holding shares, the conflict between managers' interests and the shareholders' interests may be even less. As long as retained earnings are reflected in the value of the firm's equity (because, for example, of the possibility of liquidation), it is not necessary for any of the firm's earnings to be paid out as dividends in order for the shareholders to benefit. The conflict between the managers' desire to control free cash flow and the shareholders' desire for dividends disappears. The only remaining source of inefficiency is the difference between the internal and the external rates of return. If the incentive effect outweighs the difference in these rates of return, it may be optimal for both shareholders and managers to have the maximum level of retained earnings.

This perspective raises another question: the relationship between the market value of the firm and its fundamental value. Obviously we are not thinking of the share price as being equal to the present expected value of a stream of dividends, but there may still be a relationship between fundamentals and share price. On the other hand, the fact that share price cannot be described by the usual dividend discounting formula does suggest that a bubble may be more likely, and then the question of whether and how a particular dividend policy promotes the shareholders' interest becomes more difficult to answer. This is an important topic for future research.

The importance of managerial control over free cash flow depends on the absence of alternative incentive schemes. It has sometimes been argued that shareholders can always design an incentive scheme, using bonuses, stock options, and so forth to achieve the incentive-efficient operation of the firm. In that case, allowing managers to retain control of free cash flow may not be necessary. However, this assumes that the firm is transparent and that shareholders know how to motivate managers. The firm is a complex organization with many members. Shareholders may not know who is the most productive member of the team and who needs to be rewarded. The CEO may not have this information either; it is dispersed throughout the organization. Exactly how incentives are provided may be something of a mystery, but on the principle that a rising tide lifts all boats, it may be felt that growth and expansion are good for incentives, since they provide opportunities for rewarding those managers and workers who have been productive at all levels. This may be one of the strongest arguments for allowing the firm to retain earnings: the greatest incentive for entrepreneurship at all levels is the prospect of advancement, and this is possible only in a firm that is growing rapidly.

Commitment may be another reason that growth is necessary to provide incentives. Shareholders may not be able to commit to reward managers through pecuniary payments, even if they can observe a manager's effort and ability. Yet they can commit to promotion if it is necessary to have more top-level managers in order to operate the expanded firm. A high level of retained earnings is part of the arrangement between shareholders and managers, which allows shareholders to commit to providing opportunities for promotion, which in turn reward effort and create the sources of growth.

The idea that the growth from retained earnings provides incentives suggests that we view the firm as a tournament (Nalebuff and Stiglitz 1983) in which the prize is the control of free cash flow. Lower-level managers compete with each other by putting in effort in order to win promotion. The probability of a manager's being promoted to the top level of the organization depends on both his ability and the amount of effort he puts in. The tournament has two functions: it provides an incentive for junior managers to make more effort at their current tasks, and it screens managers according to ability. Both are necessary to increase the value of the firm. Greater effort by lower-level managers leads to greater efficiency; higher ability among top-level managers leads to better strategic planning. Furthermore, there may be a useful complementarity between these two functions of the tournament. Suppose that the performance measure used to promote managers becomes more informative of ability the higher the level of effort. Then making managers compete by putting in more effort will actually produce a more accurate screening mechanism, even though effort is a substitute for ability from the point of view of an individual manager.

Apart from the informational reasons, the fact that managers compete against each other in a tournament makes it a more effective incentive mechanism from the shareholders' point of view. Compare it to a profit-sharing scheme, for example. This has no screening function and will not produce the same incentive for effort. In a profit-sharing scheme, the manager's reward depends on a measure of group performance: profit. In the tournament, his reward depends not just on a message of group performance, but also on his own performance relative to his peers, as observed by other managers. In other words, he is rewarded if his effort or ability is high relative to other managers. Every manager has an incentive to increase group performance, as he would in a profit-sharing scheme; in addition he has an incentive to do well relative to his peers. This may lead to higher effort than in the case of a profit-sharing scheme. So the promotion tournament has advantages even if there is no constraint on the shareholders' ability to substitute pecuniary payments for promotion and even if growth is not necessary to create opportunities to reward managers.

The rewards of ability and effort may consist of the high salaries, bonuses, and similar rewards received by top management, but they may also consist of the intangible satisfaction of control and visible success. Growth of the firm increases these rewards. As lower-level managers compete more vigorously for promotion, they are simultaneously increasing the potential prize and thus increasing the incentives for making effort. The fact that the size of the prize depends positively on the effort of all the managers, which in turns depends positively on the size of the prize, suggests the possibility of multiple equilibria. If everyone chooses a high level of effort, the prize will be large, and it will be optimal to make a big effort. On the other hand, low effort produces a small prize, which generates a low level of effort.

Allen (1993) has applied these ideas in a macroeconomic context, arguing that high rates of economic growth create incentive opportunities, so that fast-growing economies such as Germany during the 1950s and 1960s and Japan during the 1960s through to the 1980s may have better incentives, which in turn feed back into higher growth rates. In a growing economy, failing to give people raises in line with the average per capita growth rate will have a large effect on their welfare. This threat provides good incentives to managers at all levels of the organization to work hard. For example, managerial salaries that grew at Japan's average per capita growth rate during the 1960s would have increased by 140 percent. By contrast, managerial salaries in the United States, which grew at the average during the same period, would have increased only by 28 percent. This difference means that Japanese managers who failed to receive the average wage because of a lack of effort would pay a much larger penalty than U.S. managers who adopted this course of action. Higher growth will therefore mean better incentives and better performance. High growth will be self-reinforcing since it will allow good incentives, which will help spur further growth.

11.4 The Market for Internal Funds

The observation by Mayer (1988, 1990) and others that retained earnings is the primary method of finance in all the countries considered in this book underlines the importance of internal capital markets. There is a large literature on the operation and rationale for such markets. Internal capital markets differ from external capital markets because of asymmetric information, investment incentives, asset specificity, control rights, or transaction costs (see, for example, Williamson 1975; Grossman and Hart 1986; Gertner, Scharfstein, and Stein 1994; and Stein 1997). There has also been considerable debate on the relationship between liquidity and investment (see, for example, Fazzari, Hubbard and Petersen 1988; Hoshi, Kashyap, and Scharfstein 1991; Whited 1992; Kaplan and Zingales 1997; Lamont 1997; and Shin and Stulz 1998). In this section we are interested in the situation where there are external financing constraints and resources are allocated through internal capital markets rather than external ones. We then use this model as a backdrop to interpreting the role of mergers and acquisitions in ensuring efficient investment.

In an Arrow-Debreu-Mackenzie world, it would not matter whether firms paid out all their earnings to shareholders. Funds would find their way to their most efficient uses, whether it was the managers or the shareholders who made the decision. In either case, value would be maximized, and value maximization is the necessary and sufficient condition for efficiency in a competitive world with complete markets. However, in a world of incomplete markets where external finance is limited, the resulting allocation of resources may be inefficient even if we assume that managers are value maximizers. We start by considering whether this is the case.

The External Finance Constraint

Consider an economy in which there is a finite number of firms, each controlled by a value-maximizing manager. To make the point as simply as possible, we assume that there is no external finance. This means that managers have to pay for all inputs up front, before production has taken place. One explanation for the absence of external finance might be that outsiders cannot obtain any credible information about the firm.

Formally, there is a finite number of physical assets $h = 1, \ldots, H$, a single liquid asset (money), and a finite number of managers $j = 1, \ldots, J$. Each manager j has an initial vector of physical assets $\omega_j \in \mathbf{R}^H_+$ and a cash position $\mu_j \geq 0$ representing the firm's internally generated funds.

Since money does not enter into the production process, the maximum value of the firm can be written as the sum of a term that depends on the assets of the firm $v_j(k_j)$ and the firm's cash position m_j. Thus, the manager's objective function is $v_j(k_j) + m_j$. Managers can exchange assets with other managers in order to maximize the value of their firm subject to their budget constraints; from this point of view, the model looks like a pure exchange economy with J agents and $H + 1$ commodities.

An asset allocation is now an ordered pair (k, m) where $k = (k_1, \ldots, k_J)$ and $m = (m_1, \ldots, m_J)$, and the allocation is attainable if $\sum_j k_j = \sum_j \omega_j = \omega$ and $\sum_j m_j = \sum_j \mu_j$. An attainable allocation is Pareto efficient if there does not exist another attainable allocation (k', m') such that $v_j(k'_j) + m'_j \geq v_j(k_j) + m_j$ for all j, with strict inequality for some j. An equilibrium for this model is an attainable allocation (k^*, m^*) and a price vector for the physical assets p^* such that, for every manager j, (k^*_j, m^*_j) maximizes $v_j(k_j) + m_j$ subject to the finance constraint $p^* \cdot k_j + m_j \leq p^* \cdot \omega_j + \mu_j$.

In spite of the external finance constraint, the equilibrium is Pareto efficient in the sense defined above. Since the objective function is strictly increasing in m_j, the finance constraint always holds exactly: $p^* \cdot k^*_j + m^*_j = p^* \cdot \omega_j + \mu_j$. Hence $v(k_j) + m_j \geq v_j(k^*_j) + m^*_j$ implies that $p^* \cdot k_j + m_j \geq p^* \cdot \omega_j + \mu_j$ and $v(k_j) + m_j > v_j(k^*_j) + m^*_j$ implies that $p^* \cdot k_j + m_j > p^* \cdot \omega_j + \mu_j$. Thus, if (k^*, m^*) is Pareto dominated by an attainable allocation (k, m), $\sum_j (p^* \cdot k_j + m_j) > \sum_j (p^* \cdot \omega_j + \mu_j)$, contradicting the attainability condition $\sum_j (k_j, m_j) = \sum_j (\omega_j, \mu_j)$.

The efficiency of equilibrium results from the fact that attainable allocations have been defined to take into account the incompleteness of markets. More precisely, we have implicitly assumed that the only commodities that can be exchanged (reallocated by the planner) are physical assets and money. We do not allow for the possibility that managers exchange future goods, such as the output of their production. Efficiency is being defined relative to an incomplete set of markets, so it does not bear the interpretation normally given to it: that a planner could not do better than the market.

If markets were complete, future output could be used to pay for resources given up in the present. In effect, this is how finance is provided in an Arrow-Debreu-Mackenzie model: managers sell the outputs from production to pay for the inputs, regardless of the date, and the difference in value is distributed as profit to the owners of the firm. If markets were complete in the present model, the value of the firm would be fungible and could be redistributed. In that case, a Pareto-efficient allocation would have to maximize the sum of the values of the firms.

An attainable allocation is Pareto efficient in the complete markets sense if and only if each manager maximizes $v_j(k_j) - p^* \cdot k_j$. To see this, note that for any other attainable allocation k, the maximum condition implies that

$$v_j(k_j^*) - p^* \cdot k_j^* \geq v_j(k_j) - p^* \cdot k_j.$$

Summing over j yields

$$\sum_{j=1}^{J} (v_j(k_j^*) - p^* \cdot k_j^*) \geq \sum_{j=1}^{J} (v_j(k_j) - p^* \cdot k_j).$$

But since both the allocations are attainable,

$$\sum_{j=1}^{J} k_j^* = \sum_{j=1}^{J} k_j = \omega,$$

so

$$\sum_{j=1}^{J} v_j(k_j^*) \geq \sum_{j=1}^{J} v_j(k_j).$$

Conversely, if k^* maximizes $\sum_{j=1}^{J} v_j(k_j)$ subject to the constraint $\sum_{j=1}^{J} k_j = \omega$, then under the usual convexity assumptions, there exists a vector of Lagrange multipliers p^* such that k^* maximizes $\sum_{j=1}^{J} (v_j(k_j) - p^* \cdot k_j)$. Then the classical decentralization theorem for production sets in the absence of externalities:

$$\sup \left\{ \sum_j p \cdot Y_j \right\} = \sum_j \sup\{p \cdot Y_j\}$$

implies that k_j^* maximizes $v_j(k_j) - p^* \cdot k_j$. This makes clear the sense in which the external finance constraint may constrain the efficiency of the equilibrium allocation. To maximize the sum of the firms' values, managers have to be able to choose the asset bundle that achieves an unconstrained maximum of the value of the firm net of the cost of acquiring assets. The budget constraint, in the form of the external finance constraint, may reduce the sum of the firm's values. A natural measure of the impact of the external finance constraint is the difference in the sum of values,

$$\sup_k \left\{ \sum_{j=1}^{J} (v_j(k_j) - p^* \cdot k_j) \right\} - \sum_{j=1}^{J} (v_j(k_j^*) - p^* \cdot k_j^*),$$

where k^* is the equilibrium allocation of assets. Note that the allocation of money does not enter into this calculation, since it affects only the sum of values through its effect on the allocation of physical assets k^*.

Another difference between the finance-constrained model and the complete markets model is that the initial pattern of liquid assets may affect the allocation of assets in the former but not in the latter. Lamont (1997) has used this fact to test for the existence of external finance constraints.

An Example

To make the comparison more concrete, suppose there is a single physical asset ("capital"), $v_j'(k_j) > 0$ and $v_j''(k_j) < 0$ and no liquid assets. Then the complete-markets efficient allocation k^{**} is determined by the first-order condition $v_j'(k_j^{**}) = v_i'(k_i^{**})$, for all i, j, and the attainability condition $\sum_j k_j^{**} = \sum \omega_j$, whereas the equilibrium allocation, subject to the external finance constraint, is $k^* = \omega$. Then the difference in the sum of values is $\sum_j (v(k_j^{**}) - v(\omega_j))$. From the gradient inequality, an upper bound for this expression is $\sum_j v_j'(\omega_j)(k_j^{**} - \omega_j)$.

Suppose, for example, that there are three firms $i = A, B, C$, satisfying the following conditions:

$$\mu_A > 0, \mu_B = \mu_C = 0,$$

$$v_A(k) = \frac{1}{2} v_B(k) > k, \forall k > 0; v_C(k) \equiv 0, \forall k,$$

$$\omega_A = \omega_B = \omega_C > 0.$$

In other words, only firm A has internally generated funds, but firm B is twice as productive as firm A and firm C is really a dummy that serves to supply capital to the other firms. In equilibrium, the price of capital is given by the equation

$$p^* = \min\{\max\{1, \mu_A/\omega_C\}, v_A'(2\omega_A)\}.$$

For very small values of μ_A, $p^* = 1$, firm A buys as much capital as it can, and the rest is held by firm C, which is indifferent between holding capital and money as a store of value at this price. For intermediate values of μ_A, $p^* = \mu_A/\omega_C > 1$, firm A supplies its money inelastically in exchange for capital and firm C supplies its capital inelastically in exchange for money. The price is determined by the amount of "cash in the market". For high values of μ_A, the price $p^* = v_A'(2\omega_A)$ is determined by marginal productivity. Firm C continues to supply capital inelastically, but at this price, firm A is indifferent at the margin between capital and money.

When $p^* = 1$, firm A ends up with a capital stock $k_A = \omega_A + \mu_A$. When $p^* > 1$, the entire initial capital held by firm C is transferred to A, so $k_A = \omega_A + \omega_C = 2\omega_A$. Thus, $k_A = \omega_A + \min\{\omega_A, \mu_A\}$. There are two sources of inefficiency. First, if firm A has insufficient internally generated funds, firm C ends up holding some of the capital, which it cannot put to productive use. Second, however much capital firm A acquires, the final allocation is inefficient because firm B, the more productive of the firms, has a smaller capital stock so $v_B'(\omega_B) > v_A'(k_A) = v_A'(\omega_A + \min\{\omega_A, \mu_A\})$.

While the first of these problems occurs whenever there are insufficient internally generated funds in the economy, the latter can occur even when the amount of internally generated funds is large, as long as it is not distributed correctly. An efficient allocation requires $v_A'(k_A) = v_B'(k_B)$. If $p^* < v_A'(k_A) = v_B'(k_B)$, both firms will supply money inelastically, and the efficient allocation can be achieved only if their money holdings are proportional to purchases:

$$\mu_i = p^*(k_i - \omega_i), \forall i = A, B,$$

an unlikely coincidence. If there is a lot of money in the economy, we may have $p^* = v_A'(k_A) = v_B'(k_B)$, which is consistent with the firms' retaining some of their initial money holdings in equilibrium. In that case, there may be many initial distributions consistent with the efficient allocation. However, the inequalities

$$\mu_i \geq p^*(k_i - \omega_i) = v_i'(k_i)(k_i - \omega_i), \forall i = A, B,$$

must still be satisfied and this restricts somewhat the possibility of achieving efficiency.

Liquidity Effects

The preceding treatment of the external finance constraint assumes that the value of the firm depends only on the physical assets associated with it. More precisely, one dollar of retained earnings held in the form of liquid assets adds exactly one dollar to the net value of the firm. But in the presence of an external finance constraint, we should expect that, at least some of the time, adding a dollar to liquid assets will add more than one dollar to the firm's future value. Let $v_j(k_j, m_j)$ denote the future value of the jth firm when it has a set of assets k_j and liquid assets equal to m_j. Then the manager's decision problem is to choose a set of assets k_j and a level of liquid assets m_j to maximize the net value of the firm $v_j(k_j, m_j)$ subject to the external finance constraint, $p \cdot k_j + m_j \leq p \cdot \omega_j + \mu_j$. This problem reduces to the previous one if we assume that $v_j(k_j, m_j) \equiv \tilde{v}_j(k_j) + m_j$. Typically we should assume that the marginal value of an extra dollar to the firm is greater than one, $\partial v_j(k_j, m_j)/\partial m_j > 1$, in which case the effect of the external finance constraint on efficiency is aggravated.

Private Benefits

Even if the interests of the manager and the shareholders (or the social planner) are perfectly aligned, the external finance constraint can lead to inefficiency. If there is some divergence between the interests of the manager and the interests of the shareholders, it is still less likely that Pareto efficiency will be achieved. There are many ways in which managers' interests can diverge from those of shareholders (and that constitutes a study in its own right). Because we want to focus on the macroeconomic implications of the external finance constraint, we make use of a shortcut that has been popularized in the corporate control literature and assume that managers receive "private benefits" from the activity of the firm they control. These private benefits of control are endogenous, but are treated as exogenous to simplify the analysis. To keep the story as simple as possible, we focus on one specification of private benefits: we assume that the private benefits are proportional to the value of the firm. This has two advantages. First, it minimizes the divergence between the interests of the manager and the shareholder to what is absolutely necessary to get a nontrivial tension between the two. With this specification, the manager still has an incentive to run the firm efficiently, that is, to maximize value. Second, because he ignores the opportunity cost of funds—that they could be given to shareholders instead—the manager tends to hold onto as much of the internally generated funds as possible. This is in accord with the free-cash-flow hypothesis of Jensen and others, which states that managers tend to overinvest because they do not consider the opportunity cost of funds.

In equilibrium, the manager chooses a set of assets and liquid assets to maximize his private benefits subject to the external finance constraint. Thus, an equilibrium consists of a feasible allocation $\{k_j^*\}$ and a price vector p^* such that for every j, (k_j^*, m_j^*) maximizes $v_j(k_j, m_j)$ subject to the finance constraint $p^* \cdot k_j + m_j \leq p^* \cdot \omega_j + \mu_j$. In any situation in which it is optimal for the manager to reinvest all of the internally generated funds in the firm, this specification of private benefits will lead to efficient choices subject to the external finance constraint; on the other hand, when it is optimal for the manager to pay some or all of the internally generated funds to the shareholders as dividends, he will overinvest in the firm and these actions will be inefficient subject to the external finance constraint.

11.5 Mergers and Acquisitions

In the 1960s and 1970s, a wave of corporate mergers and acquisitions swept the United States, creating a breed of corporate conglomerates whose value in terms of productivity was not always clear. In the 1980s, the process of conglomeration was in many cases reversed, as corporations were downsized, divisions were spun off, and companies focused on their core business. Bhagat, Shleifer, and Vishny (1990) have argued that this reversal provides evidence against the efficiency of conglomeration, in the sense that if there were genuine synergies behind the conglomerate mergers in the 1960s, the businesses would not have been broken up in the 1980s. However, the ideas developed in this chapter provide an alternative rationalization for the life cycle of these firms.

When markets do not provide capital for businesses, there is no guarantee that the distribution of internally generated funds will match the distribution of investment opportunities. In other words, there is no reason that firms should produce exactly the amount of funds that an efficient allocation of investment would require. Some reshuffling of the funds available for investment is required, but how is this to be achieved if the markets do not play a role?

Mergers and acquisitions may be an alternative channel for internally generated funds, in effect augmenting the capital market to allow firms that are cash rich but poor in investment opportunities to exploit the greater investment opportunities of firms that are cash poor.

There is a trade-off, however. This is not an arm's-length investment of the kind provided by the market. A takeover implies a change of management: the raider, which has been successful in the past, at least to the extent of producing a pile of cash, has poor prospects, yet it will take over the running of a possibly unrelated business. The target has good prospects, if only it can raise the cash, yet in this case the price of doing so is to accept management by a firm that may not be well suited to exploiting those prospects optimally. There is a balance of costs and benefits, which determines that the takeover will succeed if and only if the target is sufficiently strapped for cash or the incoming management is not too bad in the circumstances.

To make this more concrete, suppose that there are two firms, *A* and *B*. The management of each firm exerts effort in order to create value in its respective firm, which in this case we assume takes the form exclusively of a cash surplus at the end of the current period. At the end of the period, a free cash flow is realized (it depends on random factors as well as the effort and ability of the management). Then the two managements learn their new investment opportunities. If there is a good match between free cash and investment opportunities, each management will fund its own investment needs. However, if there is a bad match, there are gains from trade. The firm with too much cash, *A* say, will want to invest in the firm with too little, *B*, which we assume it can do only by taking over the finance-constrained firm. Firm *A* will reward its own lower-level managers by promoting the best of them to run firm *B*, even though these may not be the best suited, because of their background, to running firm *B*. Whether it is desirable for firm *A* to take over firm *B* depends on how valuable the new investment opportunities are relative to the cost of installing an inexperienced management. We are speaking now of private rather than social values. These values in turn feed back into the incentives for making efforts at the earlier stage. The reward to effort consists of two parts: the prospect of being promoted to take over another firm and the prospect of avoiding being taken over and losing one's job. In effect, the promotion tournament has been expanded to include the managers at both firms rather than just the one.

The rate of growth that can be achieved by conglomeration is naturally much higher than can be achieved through expansion of an existing company. To the extent that this provides incentives for managers to work hard, it may be a much more important mechanism than promotion through the ranks of a slowly growing firm. It is also a risky business, because it requires a firm either to produce large amounts of cash or to borrow, unless it can persuade the owners of the target firm to accept shares. Because of the lumpiness of the acquisition, there will be an incentive for risk-taking behavior, since the gains go to the firm that produces a lot more free cash flow than its target. The production of free cash flow may also be self-defeating, in the sense that it becomes a tournament in which the winner is the one that can produce the largest global investment, regardless of the rate of return.

Whether this incentive mechanism is socially optimal or close to it requires a detailed analysis of a model with specific parametric assumptions. There is no general presumption that it will do so, but it may do better than some alternatives. There may also be "bad" incentives in some cases—that is, private benefits from takeovers that lead to worse (Pareto inferior?) social outcomes. In some cases, there may be gains from preventing takeovers.

In any case, the benefits from merger and acquisition activity may be expected to be of finite duration. Once the investment has been made, there may be no further rationale for the two firms to be merged into one entity. Not only may the management be suboptimal, but the expanded scope of the combined firm may be inefficient, leading to loss of control, higher costs of information, coordination problems, and so forth. What we should expect over time is that the misallocation of investment funds, which provided the benefits for the original takeover, will disappear, leaving behind a firm that is greater than the optimal size. Then another takeover (change of management) is desirable, this one aimed at breaking up the firm and capturing the gains that result from downsizing and decentralization. So we can see the growth and dismemberment of firms as part of the natural life cycle in an economy with external finance constraints. Both may be optimal at different points in time. The fact that a firm is broken up at a later date does not necessarily mean that the earlier merger was a mistake, only that the gains from combining the two budget constraints could not have been realized without first gaining control.

References

Aghion, P., and P. Bolton. (1992). "An Incomplete Contracts Approach to Financial Contracting." *Review of Economic Studies* **59,** 473–494.

Allen, F. (1993). "Stock Markets and Resource Allocation." In C. Mayer and X. Vives (eds.), *Capital Markets and Financial Intermediation.* Cambridge: Cambridge University Press, 81–108.

Berle, A., and G. Means. (1932). *The Modern Corporation and Private Property.* Chicago: Commerce Clearing House.

Bhagat S., A. Shleifer, and R. Vishny. (1990). "Hostile Takeovers in the 1980s: The Return to Corporate Specialization." *Brookings Papers on Economic Activity: Microeconomics,* **Special Issue,** 1–72.

Burkart, M. , D. Gromb, and F. Panunzi. (1997). "Large Shareholders, Monitoring, and the Value of the Firm." *Quarterly Journal of Economics* **112,** 693–728.

Crawford, V., and J. Sobel. (1982). "Strategic Information Transmission." *Econometrica* **50,** 1431–1451.

Fazzari, S., R. G. Hubbard, and B. Petersen. (1988). "Financing Constraints and Corporate Investment." *Brookings Papers on Economic Activity,* 141–195.

Gertner, R., D. Scharfstein, and J. Stein. (1994). "Internal Versus External Capital Markets." *Quarterly Journal of Economics* **109,** 1211–1230.

Grossman, S., and O. Hart. (1982). "Corporate Financial Structure and Managerial Incentives." In J. McCall (ed.), *The Economics of Information and Uncertainty.* Chicago: University of Chicago Press.

———. (1986). "The Costs and Benefits of Ownership." *Journal of Political Economy* **94,** 691–719.

Hart, O. (1995). *Firms, Contracts and Financial Structure.* Oxford: Clarendon Press.

Hart, O., and J. Moore. (1994). "A Theory of Debt Based on the Inalienability of Human Capital." *Quarterly Journal of Economics* **109,** 841–879.

———. (1995). "Debt and Seniority: An Analysis of the Role of Hard Claims in Constraining Management." *American Economic Review* **85,** 567–585.

Hoshi, T., A. Kashyap, and D. Scharfstein. (1991). "Corporate Structure, Liquidity and Investment: Evidence from Japanese Industrial Groups." *Quarterly Journal of Economics* **106,** 33–60.

Ibbotson Associates. (1998). *Stocks, Bonds, Bills and Inflation 1998 Yearbook.* Chicago: Ibbotson Associates.

Jensen, M. (1986). "Agency Costs of Free Cash Flow, Corporate Finance, and Takeovers." *American Economic Review* **76,** 323–329.

Jensen, M., and W. Meckling. (1976). "Theory of the Firm: Managerial Behavior, Agency Costs and Ownership Structure." *Journal of Financial Economics* **3,** 305-360.

Kaplan, S., and L. Zingales. (1997). "Do Investment-Cash Flow Sensitivities Provide Useful Measures of Financing Constraints?" *Quarterly Journal of Economics* **112,** 169–215.

Lamont, O. (1997). "Cash Flow and Investment: Evidence from Internal Capital Markets." *Journal of Finance* **52,** 83–109.

Mailath, G., and A. Postlewaite. (1990). "Asymmetric Information Bargaining Problems with Many Agents." *Review of Economic Studies* **57,** 351–367.

Mayer, C. (1988). "New Issues in Corporate Finance." *European Economic Review* **32,** 1167–1188.

———. (1990). "Financial Systems, Corporate Finance, and Economic Development." In R. G. Hubbard (ed.), *Asymmetric Information, Corporate Finance and Investment.* Chicago: University of Chicago Press.

Nalebuff, B., and J. Stiglitz. (1983). "Prizes and Incentives: Towards a General Theory of Compensation and Competition." *Bell Journal of Economics* **14,** 21–43.

Neeman, Z. (1994). "Property Rights and Efficiency of Public-Good Mechanisms Under Asymmetric Information." *Discussion Paper 1092,* Northwestern University Center for Mathematical Studies in Economics and Management Science.

Rob, R. (1989). "Pollution Claim Settlements Under Private Information." *Journal of Economic Theory* **47,** 307–333.

Shin, H., and R. M. Stulz. (1998). "Are Internal Capital Markets Efficient?" *Quarterly Journal of Economics* **113,** 531–552.

Stein, J. (1997). "Internal Capital Markets and the Competition for Corporate Resources." *Journal of Finance* **52,** 111–133.

Taggart, R. (1985). "Secular Patterns in the Financing of U.S. Corporations." In Benjamin Friedman (ed.), *Corporate Capital Structure in the United States.* Chicago: University of Chicago Press.

Whited, T. (1992). "Debt, Liquidity Constraints, and Corporate Investment: Evidence from Panel Data." *Journal of Finance* **47,** 1425–1470.

Williamson, O. (1975). *Markets and Hierarchies: Analysis and Antitrust Implications.* New York: Collier Macmillan.

12 Objectives of Firms

12.1 Culture and the Organization of the Firm

In the previous chapter, we suggested that the firm's reliance on internal finance might be regarded as a solution to some of the imperfections of the financial system. In other words, the organization of the firm develops in a certain way because it is necessary to provide finance for investment and growth, and the result, although not as efficient as the complete markets paradigm would suggest, is not as bad as some critics may have argued. In this chapter, we look at some other deviations from the neoclassical theory of the firm that suggest solutions to some problems that have been identified in different countries' systems of corporate control. Of course, these alternative models have idiosyncratic disadvantages as well. We then apply these ideas to financial institutions and consider the implications for their special role as monitors of firms.

Neoclassical economics recognizes two sorts of institutions: the profit-maximizing firm and the government as omniscient central planner. But there is a third kind of organization, which is neither an altruistic central planner nor a profit-maximizing firm. Some of these organizations are explicitly not-for-profit and do not have well-defined objective functions—for example, universities, hospitals, and charities. We could also include in this group mutual insurance companies and savings and loan associations, which lack shareholders and cannot reduce the interests of the members to a single number. Even in the case of joint stock companies, which might be expected to operate in the interest of shareholders by maximizing profits or market value, it can be argued that their objectives are in fact more complex. Concern for their workers, the environment, and the communities in which they operate are often urged as appropriate goals for a modern corporation.

In some countries, the characterization of the firm as an institution exclusively concerned with maximizing some scalar measure of shareholder welfare would seem very strange. In Japan, for example, there is a very different tradition, in which the firm is expected to act in the public interest rather than in the interest of shareholders. The Japanese conception of the objectives of the firm has been shaped by Japan's postwar experience. In the aftermath of the war, with the Japanese economy in ruins and the repatriation of many people from countries formerly under Japanese control, creating employment was one of the highest goals of national policy and one that appears to have been embraced by Japanese corporations. The desire to create employment, which was a national imperative at one time, appears to have become internalized in the behavior of the firms over the succeeding decades. It is probably weaker now than it was then, but several aspects of the behavior of Japanese corporations suggest that it has not been supplanted by pure profit or value maximization. One example is the low rate of return on investment and the long repayment periods accepted by Japanese managers. Although this could be explained by long-term value maximization, it is also consistent with objectives other than value maximization. Similarly, their willingness to sacrifice short-term returns for market share is consistent with other objectives.

The decision-making structure of the Japanese firm is also different from that of the Anglo-Saxon corporation. In the United States and the United Kingdom, managers are given a large amount of freedom and then monitored and disciplined by the market or the corporate hierarchy if their performance is poor. Decision making in Japan relies much more on consensus and the use of committees than on the entrepreneurial model favored by the Anglo-Saxon corporation. The Japanese also make use of the seniority system: all managers have to pass through the ranks before they can achieve the top positions in the firm, and CEOs spend relatively little time at the top compared to their British and American counterparts. There is also a much lower degree of inequality in compensation in the Japanese corporation. This is indicative of the importance of teamwork and the use of group performance to determine rewards in the Japanese firm.

A considerable amount of research has been done to try to understand the operation of Japanese firms in the postwar period. Particularly important from the perspective taken in this book is the seminal work of Masahiko Aoki. In a sequence of contributions (Aoki 1984a, 1984b, 1988, 1992) and edited volumes (Aoki 1984c; Aoki, Gustaffson, and Williamson 1990; Aoki and Dore 1994; Aoki and Patrick 1994) great progress has been made in understanding the differences between Japanese and U.S. firms. Aoki (1990) contains an excellent survey of this literature and exposition of some of the main ideas it contains. He contrasts the traditional U.S. hierarchical firm, the "H-mode," with the Japanese firm structure, the "J-mode." The H-mode is characterized by hierarchical separation between planning and implemental operation and an emphasis on economies of specialization. The J-mode stresses horizontal coordination among operating units based on the sharing of ex post on-site information. Aoki also develops the relationship in Japan between internal organization aspects of the firm and bank-oriented financial control—the main bank system. When a firm is in financial distress, its main bank plays an important role in rescue operations. However, when a firm is financially sound, its main bank does not become involved. In addition, the existence of cross-holdings of shares among Japanese companies means there is no threat of hostile takeover. In the absence of outside control mechanisms, internal incentives are crucial. It is suggested that among other things lifetime employment, seniority advancement, and management discipline through competition over ranking by corporate profits are important. Also the fact that management decisions of Japanese corporations are subject to the influence of employees as well as owners is stressed.

When we look at German firms we see a similar departure from the pure value-maximizing model. The state has mandated the involvement of workers' representatives on supervisory boards, and this is indicative of the social objectives that have been imposed on German firms. Shareholders are only one group among several groups of stakeholders to whom the management of a German firm is responsible. The fact that many German firms are not publicly traded means that maximization of market value is not available as a guide to corporate decision making.

Some evidence of these cross-country differences in the organization and behavior of firms is provided by survey data on the attitudes of managements in different countries from the Institute of Fiscal and Monetary Policy (1996). Respondents were asked to choose between the following two alternative objectives:

a. *The only real goal of a company is making a profit.*

b. *A company, besides making a profit, has the goal of attaining the well-being of various stakeholders.*

Here are the percentages that selected choice a: Japan, 8 percent; United States, 40 percent; United Kingdom, 33 percent; Germany, 24 percent; and France, 16 percent.

Then they were asked to choose between the following alternative definitions of a company:

a. *A company is a system designed to perform functions and tasks in an efficient way. People are hired to fulfill these functions with the help of machines and other equipment. They are paid for the tasks they perform.*

b. *A company is a group of people working together. The people have social relations with other people and the organization. The functioning of the company is dependent on these relations.*

Here are the percentages that selected choice a: Japan, 29 percent; United States, 74 percent; United Kingdom, 55 percent; Germany, 41 percent; and France, 35 percent (Hampden-Turner and Trompenaars, 1993).

It is striking that profit maximization was not chosen as the only objective by a majority of respondents in any country. There is difficulty in interpreting this response because of the extreme narrowness of profit as an objective. Even neoclassical theory recognizes that NPV, or some similar concept, is the correct objective, not profit. It may be that a respondent, in rejecting profit as the only goal of the firm, is merely giving weight to growth, market share, or other aspects of the firm that affect future profitability and hence can be taken as proxies for the broader notion of NPV. If this is correct, then the low percentage of respondents choosing profit as the only goal does not necessarily indicate that the respondents rejected value maximization or shareholder interests, broadly defined, as the only proper objective of the firm.

Nonetheless, a significant difference appears among the respondents in different countries. To the extent that profit maximization can be identified with the neoclassical model of the firm, there appears to be much stronger support for this model in the United States and, to a lesser extent, in the United Kingdom than in the other countries. The weaker support for profit maximization in Germany, France, and especially Japan suggests that managers in those countries have a very different conception of the firm's objective function.

When we come to the more complex question of what a firm is, the differences are again striking. Although the two alternatives offered to the respondents are rather fuzzy, alternative a is clearly narrower and less cooperative than alternative b. The United States and the United Kingdom again support the narrower, more neoclassical conception of the firm, while Japan has the largest percentage supporting a more cooperative conception of the firm. These answers reflect not only differences in perceptions but also in the organization of the firm. Decisions made in a Japanese firm are more likely to be made by groups who have to pay attention to the rights and claims of a variety of different constituencies within the firm. In an American firm, decisions are likely to be made on a more entrepreneurial model by individuals who have the right to allocate workers to tasks with fewer constraints or to dispose of their services altogether and do so in the interest of an abstract notion of "the shareholders."

When we come to the question of who "owns" the company, the differences are even more marked. Companies were asked to choose between the following statements:

a. *Shareholder interest should be given the first priority.*

b. *A company exists for the interest of all stakeholders.*

The percentages choosing statement a were as follows: Japan, 2.9 percent; United States, 75.6 percent; United Kingdom, 55.0 percent; Germany, 17.3 percent; and France, 22.0 percent.

The responses to questions about job security and dividends were similar. Respondents were asked which was the more important:

a. *Dividends are more important.*

b. *Job security is more important.*

The percentages choosing statement a were as follows: Japan, 2.9 percent; United States, 89.2 percent; United Kingdom, 89.3 percent; Germany, 59.1 percent; and France, 60.4 percent (Yoshimori 1995).

In both cases, Japan is an outlier at one end, while the United States is an outlier at the other. The United Kingdom, France, and Germany are closer to the U.S. response on dividends but closer to Japan on ownership. In both cases the United Kingdom is closer to the American response.

The answers to all of these questions suggest a difference between the United States and the United Kingdom, on the one hand, and Japan, Germany, and France, on the other. Data of this sort are subject to many qualifications, relating to sample selection, the framing of the questions, and so forth. Furthermore, it is not clear what the responses mean in the sense that we cannot identify a formal model corresponding to the perceptions held by respondents in different countries. Nonetheless, it would be wrong to dismiss such data as meaningless.

Our tentative conclusion is that from the point of view of cultures as different as those of Japan, France, and Germany, the Anglo-Saxon emphasis on the rights of the shareholder and the fiduciary duties of the management (to the shareholder) appears to be only one way of organizing a firm, and perhaps a rather special one at that. In practice, we feel that even in the United States, the objectives of firms are much less clear-cut than the theory of the firm sometimes suggests. The firm is an ecosystem in which different species live and flourish. Trade unions, management, shareholders, suppliers, and customers all struggle to maximize their individual interests, which in some cases means the interests of their members, but they also have a common interest in the survival and prosperity of the firm, because they cannot pursue their individual objectives unless the firm survives and prospers. This community of interests may explain why the firm appears to have a coherent set of objectives. But each of these groups may have its own objective function, and the behavior of the firm, being the product of the interaction of many groups and individuals, cannot be reduced to the maximization of a single, simple objective.

Of course, it is often productive to simplify matters and pretend the firm has a single objective; but when we make this simplifying assumption, it is important to be aware of the ways in which actual institutions can differ from the neoclassical ideal. The neoclassical theory of the firm is useful and will remain the core concept for the foreseeable future, but this should not prevent other approaches from being considered.

Over the years many alternatives to the standard neoclassical paradigm have been suggested, including managerial theories of the firm (Baumol 1959, Marris 1964, Williamson 1964, and Alchian 1965), behavioral theories (Cyert and March 1963), transaction cost approaches (Williamson 1975, 1985, Klein, Crawford, and Alchian 1978), team organization views (Marschak and Radner 1972, Alchian and Demsetz 1972, Holmstrom 1982), a nexus of contracts approach (Jensen and Meckling 1976, Fama 1980), and survival (Winter 1982, Dutta and Sundaram 1992, Majumdar and Radner 1991, 1992, Radner 1995).

Recently theorists have begun opening the neoclassical "black box" and exploring a host of incentive problems in the theory of the firm. Pioneering work here was done by Oliver Hart and his coauthors Sanford Grossman and John Moore (Grossman and Hart 1986, Hart and Moore

1990, Hart 1995). Subsequent contributions have been made: MacLeod and Malcolmson (1993), Stole and Zwiebel (1996a, 1996b), Aghion and Tirole (1997), Hart, Shleifer, and Vishny (1997), DeMeza and Lockwood (1998) Rajan and Zingales (1998) and Rajan, Servaes, and Zingales (1998). Theorists, using a variety of models from principal agent theory, mechanism design, and contract theory, have begun to model the firm as a multiagent institution. The basic flavor of the profit-maximizing paradigm remains, however. In these models, there is usually some residual claimant, say an entrepreneur or a group of shareholders, who chooses the incentive scheme, mechanism, or contract in order to maximize a well-specified objective function. Compared to the neoclassical paradigm, in which an objective function is maximized subject to technological constraints, the new incentive-based theories are essentially adding incentive constraints to the usual technological constraints in the specification of the firm's maximization problem.

Despite the progress that has been made, by Aoki and others, it is not yet clear exactly what tools will be required to describe firms in countries such as France, Germany, and Japan. Certainly it is beyond the scope of this book to develop a complete theory of the role of national, corporate cultures in the organization and behavior of the firm. What we can do instead is explore one or two issues to indicate the way in which different types of organization may lead to different behavior, emphasizing in particular the role of consensus, teams, and hierarchy as they appear in the Japanese firm, among others. We begin by considering the time preferences that characterize different kinds of firms. As the debate on "short-termism" in the United States has suggested, this may be a major and important difference between U.S. and Japanese firms and one that may be traced to differences in organizational structure and culture. In the next two sections, we present a simple model of the firm's time preference and then apply these ideas to other aspects of the firm's behavior.

12.2 The Firm's Time Horizon

To see the kind of issues that are involved, we focus on one particular aspect of this problem: the discount factor implicit in the firm's decisions. The idea that a manager is a rent seeker, who dilutes the shareholders' property rights, is not necessarily antagonistic to the view that the firm is operated in the long-run interests of the shareholders. For example, the manager's rents may happen to give him an income stream similar to that of a shareholder, in which case his incentive is to maximize the value of the firm (present value of net earnings). The incentives might be even better if he owned all of the shares, but having a part share may be much better than the Grossman-Hart-Moore model, for example, suggests.

There is, however, a problem with this view of the firm. The manager has only a temporary interest in the firm. More precisely, his interest in the firm is limited to his tenure in the job. Once he ceases to run the firm, the rents will flow to his successor. Even if he owns part of the firm, he can liquidate this holding on the day he leaves. As a result, a manager-operated firm may have a horizon that is no longer than the tenure of the manager (assuming he does not have dynastic aspirations). If the manager has other interests he would rather pursue, the time horizon may be even shorter.

A large corporation, on the other hand, is run by a group of managers who, like the firm, may perpetuate itself more or less indefinitely. The interests of this group of managers, which is constantly renewing itself, will be quite different from those of any individual manager. The behavior of an individual manager, depending as it does on expectations about how other members of the group will behave, will be quite different from the behavior of an entrepreneur who controls all aspects of the firm's activities.

The difference between these two points of view, one of which identifies the behavior of the firm with the decisions of a single manager and the other of which regards the firm as being controlled by a sequence of overlapping generations of managers, can be illustrated by a simple example. Suppose that at any time two managers, one young and one old, are needed to run the firm. Each manager works for two periods, and each period a new (young) manager is hired. The managers have two options: they can put effort into running the firm on behalf of the shareholders, or they can engage in rent-seeking activities. Whatever they choose to do requires coordination. Unless they both cooperate in running the firm on behalf of the shareholders or, alternatively, both engage in rent seeking, the result will be worse for them than either of the alternatives just mentioned. The managers' rents depend on their allocation of effort to the shareholders' interests or to rent seeking. Let r be the aggregate flow of rents when the managers are making an effort on behalf of shareholders and R the rents when they are engaged in rent seeking. Naturally we assume that $R > r > 0$, where 0 is the managers' outside option. Suppose for simplicity that the rents are divided evenly between the two managers, and that managers are risk neutral and do not discount the future. Then they will seek to maximize the sum of lifetime rents.

We assume that the only action the shareholders can take is to replace the managers if they observe rent-seeking behavior. In practice it will be difficult to replace managers, and this will be done only with some delay, if at all. However, to make the point more strongly, let us assume that the shareholders are unusually powerful and can replace managers immediately if they observe rent seeking. This means that the managers can achieve at most one period of high rents before they will be replaced. The question then is, under what conditions the managers will choose to engage in rent-seeking behavior.

Recall that coordination between the managers is required if they are to achieve any rents at all. One interpretation of this requirement is that if anyone deviates from an agreed plan, the result is so disastrous that they all are worse off. Another interpretation is that the structure of decision making in the firm requires consensus. Another interpretation is that managers are able to monitor each other and enforce an agreed-on course of action. Whatever the interpretation, we will impose the requirement that the managers' actions will be changed only if everyone is willing to change. Thus, a given action is an equilibrium unless everyone can be made better off by a deviation.

Suppose that the managers are pursuing the shareholders' interests. The payoff to the young manager is $r/2 + r/2 = r$; the payoff to the old manager is $r/2$. If they were to switch to rent seeking, the payoff to the young manager would be $R/2 + 0 = R/2$, since he would be replaced next period. The payoff to the old manager would be $R/2$. Clearly the old manager is better off, since $R > r$, but the young manager would be no better off if

$$R/2 \leq r,$$

which becomes the condition for viability of the policy of pursuing the shareholders' interests.

As a benchmark, suppose that instead of imposing this overlapping generations (OLG) structure on the management, we had assumed that there existed a single, representative manager. To maintain comparability across the two models, we should assume that the choices available to the representative manager are the same and the aggregate rents are the same. This means that the manager can either exert effort on behalf of the shareholders or engage in rent seeking, that his per period rents in either case are r and R, respectively, and that he is replaced after two periods on average. Suppose that he exerts effort on behalf of shareholders. When he is young, his payoff from the given policy is $r + r = 2r$, and his payoff from rent seeking is $R + 0 = R$, so the condition for him to continue pursuing the shareholders' interests is

$$R \leq 2r,$$

which is equivalent to the viability condition given above. In the second period, however, his payoff from pursuing the shareholders' interests is only r, whereas the payoff from rent seeking is R. Since $R > r$, the policy is no longer viable.

The same argument extends immediately to a management structure involving N managers, each of whom lives for N periods. The lifetime rents to a manager who pursues the interests of shareholders is r, whereas the rents from deviating will only be R/N. The condition for viability becomes

$$R/N \leq r,$$

which becomes easier to satisfy as N becomes large. With a representative manager who runs the firm for N periods, the payoff in the last period from rent seeking is R, and the payoff from pursuing the shareholders' interests is r, so rent seeking will occur if $R > r$.

Similarly, distinguishing the rents of managers of different ages makes no real difference to the argument. Suppose that under rent seeking, a manager of age n receives R_n, and under a policy of pursuing the shareholders' interests he receives r_n, where $\sum r_n = r$ and $\sum R_n = R$. Then the viability condition for the policy of pursuing the shareholders' interests becomes

$$R_k \leq \sum_{n=k}^{N} r_n$$

for at least one manager $k = 1, \ldots, N$. If this condition is violated for all $k = 1, \ldots, N$, then summing the inequality over k implies $R > \sum r_n n$, so a sufficient condition for viability is

$$R \leq \sum r_n n.$$

This condition reduces to the one obtained earlier if we assume that $r_n = r/N$ for each n. As before, the representative manager will want to engage in rent seeking in the last period of his tenure.

12.3 The Management Game

It may be argued that this result depends crucially on the shareholders' being able to get rid of a lazy or self-serving management immediately and that in reality managements are rather hard to replace. But a variant of the preceding story works even if it is impossible to replace the management. We simply have to argue that rent seeking by management will ultimately have bad effects on the firm and that if the management structure is sufficiently farsighted, the managers themselves will choose not to go down this road. The reason is that ultimately it will become impossible to motivate enough effort to keep the firm going, even in rent-seeking mode, and the anticipation of this event will cause the management coalition to unravel. An interesting interpretation of this model is the Japanese corporation. Managers pursue the longevity of the firm. As a by-product shareholders do all right.

To make these ideas clear, we need a more formal model. The firm is assumed to have a finite number of states, indexed by $s = 0, 1, \ldots, S$. These states could represent market share or capital stock or successfully completed R&D or any other measure of the firm's well-being. The firm's management has a finite number of strategies available, which we assume they choose jointly. Again, this behavior could be represented as an equilibrium of a coordination game. The strategies or actions are indexed by $a = 0, 1, \ldots, A$. For simplicity, but also because it captures something important about the internal structure of the firm, we assume that all the managers are in effect playing the same strategy. This is partly because there is a complementarity, which requires every manager to be doing the right thing in order for the firm to succeed, and partly because managers can monitor one another and enforce performance of the required actions.

The self-perpetuating management is represented by the usual OLG structure. Each manager works for N periods, and the firm requires exactly N managers, whose ages are $1, \ldots, N$ as before. Each period, one of the managers retires and is replaced by a new manager. All the other managers shift up one place, like the guests at the Mad Hatter's tea party. Each period, a manager of age n receives a rent $r_n(a, s)$, if the action a is chosen and the state of the firm is s. A special case of this structure would be the one in which each manager receives the same rent, regardless of his rank in the firm.

The evolution of the state of the firm depends on the actions chosen by the managers and is described by the transition function $f(a, s)$. That is, $f(a, s)$ is the state of the firm next period if s is the state this period and a is the joint action chosen by the management this period. We do not allow for random transitions, though the model could clearly be extended to allow for this.

A policy function α associates an action $\alpha(s, t)$ with each possible state of the firm s and each date t. Let $V_{nt}(\alpha, s)$ be the equilibrium payoff in the continuation game of a manager of age n at date t if the firm's state is s and the policy is α. Since managers can always exercise an outside option, which we normalize to 0, a policy α is individually rational if and only if

$$V_{nt}(\alpha, s) \geq 0$$

for all n, t, and s. In addition, the managers are collectively rational and will not choose a dominated policy. A policy α is viable if it is individually rational and there does not exist another individually rational policy α' such that, for some date t and state s,

$$V_{nt}(\alpha, s) \geq V_{nt}(\alpha', s),$$

for all n, with strict inequality for some n. Thus, any manager has a veto on a change in policy.

Motivating Effort in the Long Run

Now let us see how rent-seeking behavior may be restricted by the OLG structure. Suppose that managers have three options: they can take effort on behalf of the firm (i.e., on behalf of the shareholders), take effort on their own behalf (i.e., rent seeking), or do nothing (i.e., shirking). Denote these strategies by a_E, a_R, and 0, respectively.

The transition function is defined by

$$f(a, s) = \begin{cases} s & \text{if } a = a_E \\ \max\{s - 1, 0\} & \text{otherwise.} \end{cases}$$

In other words, the state of the firm remains constant if and only if the managers all make effort on behalf of the shareholders. Otherwise the state of the firm deteriorates. Of course, we should realistically allow for strategies that could improve the state of the firm, but for the purposes of illustrating the mechanics of the model, this cruder version will suffice.

Now we need to make some assumptions about the payoffs to managers from following different policies. First, we set the payoff from shirking to 0, which is also the managers' outside option:

(A.1) $r(0, s) = 0$ for all n and s.

This assumption ensures that it is always possible to meet the individual rationality constraint. Alternatively, we could simply assume that the firm ceases to exist at some point, when it can no longer attract new managers.

Next recall that $r(a, s)$ measures the net rents received by a manager of age n when the action is a and the firm's state is s. This number may well be negative if the cost of acquiring firm-specific human capital and making effort is not fully compensated by the rents received in that state (compared to the outside option). Suppose that the state of the firm is constant over time and that a manager makes an effort on behalf of the firm for the whole of his life. We assume that the lifetime net rents are greater than the outside option if and only if the state of the firm is sufficiently high. More precisely, there exists a state $0 < k < S$ such that

(A.2a) $\sum_n r_n(a_E, s) < 0$ for $s = 0, \ldots, k-1$

and

(A.2b) $\sum_n r_n(a_E, s) > 0$ for $s = k, \ldots, S$.

We want to assume that even under rent-seeking behavior, new managers have to incur some setup costs. This may be necessary for incentive purposes, or it may be the result of some limitation on the managers' ability to redistribute rents. Formally, we assume that

(A.3) $r_1(a, s) < 0$ for $s = 0, \ldots, k-1$.

Finally, we assume that in the worst state, even rent-seeking behavior is not as good as the outside option:

(A.4) $\sum_n r_n(a, 0) < 0$.

Clearly any state $0 < s < k$ is not sustainable. In order to attract young managers, the firm has to offer them nonnegative lifetime net rents. But this means that they cannot choose $a = a_E$ all of the time, so the state of the firm is bound to deteriorate. The question then is what states are sustainable.

To answer this question we begin by showing that once the state of the firm drops below the critical level $s = k$, it is impossible to motivate any effort, even for rent seeking.

LEMMA 12.1 For any viable policy α, $V_{1t}(\alpha, s) = 0$ and $\alpha(s, t) = 0$, for any date t and for states $s = 1, \ldots, k-1$.

Starting at any date t and any given state $s = 1, \ldots, k-1$, let a^τ be the action chosen at date τ and s^τ the state at date τ, for any $\tau \geq t$. The sequence is defined recursively by putting

$$(a^t, s^t) = (\alpha(s,t), s)$$

$$s^\tau = f(a^{\tau-1}, s^{\tau-1}) \text{ for } \tau > t$$

and

$$a^\tau = \alpha(s^\tau, \tau) \text{ for } \tau > t.$$

In this notation, for any date $T > t$,

$$\sum_{\tau=t}^{T} V_{1\tau}(\alpha, s^\tau) = \sum_{\tau=t}^{T} \sum_{n=1}^{N} r_n(a^{\tau+n-1}, s^{\tau+n-1})$$

$$= \sum_{\tau=t+N-1}^{T-N+1} \sum_{n=1}^{N} r_n(a^\tau, s^\tau) + \sum_{\tau=t}^{t+N-2} \sum_{n=1}^{\tau-t+1} r_n(a^\tau, s^\tau) + \sum_{\tau=t-N+\tau}^{T} \sum_{n=N-T+\tau}^{N} r_n(a^\tau, s^\tau).$$

Since there is a finite number of actions, some pattern of N actions, $\{a^i\}_{i=1}^N$, must repeat itself infinitely often. Suppose that this pattern is observed between dates t and $t+N-1$. Then for some $T > t$, the same pattern must be observed between $T-N+1$ and T. That is, $a^{t+N-1} = a^{T-N+n}$ for $n = 1, \ldots, N$. In this case, the expression above reduces to

$$\sum_{\tau=t}^{T} V_{1\tau}(\alpha, s^\tau) = \sum_{\tau=t}^{T-N} \sum_{n=1}^{N} r_n(a^{\tau+n-1}, s^{\tau+n-1}).$$

Suppose that $s^t = 0$. Then $s^\tau = 0$ for all $\tau \geq t$, and by assumption

$$\sum_{n=1}^{N} r_n(a^{\tau+n-1}, s^{\tau+n-1}) \leq 0, \text{ for all } t.$$

Since $V_{1\tau}(\alpha, 0) \geq 0$ for all τ, we must have $V_{1\tau}(\alpha, 0) = 0$ for $\tau = t, \ldots, T$. Now suppose that at some date, the state of the firm becomes $s = 0$. Then we know that there is a later date at which $V_{1t} = 0$ and $a = 0$ at all subsequent dates. Suppose that $a^\tau \neq 0$ at some date preceding t, say, date $t - 1$. Then $V_{1,t-1}(0) = r_1(a^{t-1}, 0) < 0$, a contradiction. So $a^{t-1} = 0$ and by induction we can show that $a^\tau = 0$ whenever $s = 0$. In other words, $V_{1t}(0) = 0$ for all t.

Now suppose that this is true for states $s = 0, \ldots, h$, and suppose that the state of the firm is $s = h + 1$ at some date. We know that $a = a_E$ is not sustainable, so there must be some later date t, say, at which $a^t \neq a_E$. Consider the first such date t. Then we know that $a^t \neq a_E$, $s^t = h + 1$, and $s^{t+1} = h$. Then

$$V_{1t}(\alpha, h + 1) = r_1(a^t, h + 1) < 0,$$

a contradiction, since $a^\tau = 0$ for all $\tau > t$. Thus, we must have $a = 0$ whenever $s = h + 1$. By induction, this shows that $V_{1t}(\alpha, s) = 0$ and $\alpha(s, t) = 0$ for any t and any $s = 0, \ldots, k - 1$.

It now follows easily that $a = a_E$ is viable if the state is $s = k$. The reason is that this policy produces positive lifetime rents and that any deviation, even for one period, pushes the firm into the state $k - 1$, after which rents are 0. The first period in which this happens, the newest manager $n = 1$ will receive a negative rent, which makes him unwilling to join the firm.

Theorem 12.1 There exists a viable policy α such that $\alpha(s, t) = a_E$ for all t if $s = k$.

Whether higher states are sustainable depends on the exact comparison of rents under a_E and a_R.

Compare this result with what we should expect from the representative manager model. Let $r(a, s) \equiv \sum_n r_n(a, s)$ denote the total rents when the action is a and the state is s. A representative manager who retires at date T will look at the rents from engaging in rent-seeking behavior and compare

$$\sum_{\tau=t}^{T} r(a_R, k - \tau + t)$$

with the payoff from exerting effort on behalf of shareholders,

$$\sum_{\tau=t}^{T} r(a_E, k).$$

The gains from rent-seeking behavior will typically be much larger in this case, and so there is no reason to think that a state like $s = k$ is sustainable.

Extensions

In the preceding section we argued that the OLG structure greatly increased the incentives for management to take effort on behalf of shareholders, when compared with the incentives of a representative manager with a fixed horizon. However, the assumptions of the model were quite restrictive, even within the context of the management game.

One extension that is clearly needed is to expand the action set to allow for the possibility of increasing as well as decreasing the state of the firm. It may be possible to obtain the same result by showing that within the set $s = 0, \ldots, k-1$, managers will never have an incentive to use these actions. The argument will be made more complicated because the prospect of a higher future state may compensate young managers for the negative current rents, so the older managers will have to block these deviations.

An essential element of the argument is the existence of an absorbing state. There must exist some state or set of states that, once entered, will never be left because the incentives for effort are too low. The possibility of entering these states is then bootstrapped to undermine the incentive for effort in a larger set of states, which also makes it unattractive to enter the larger set of states. By making a large set of states out of bounds, we restrict the scope for rent-seeking activities.

There must also be some limitation on the distribution of rents. If older managers are free to bribe younger managers to join the firm in bad states, it may be possible to carry on rent-seeking activities without undermining incentives. In that case, the existence of an absorbing state may not lead to bootstrapping.

The assumption of a linear ordering of states and actions is quite special. It might be interesting to see if more general characterizations were obtainable. More general results might even be more intuitive, since they would appeal only to the structure provided by the basic ideas.

12.4 Value Maximization, Growth, and Risk Taking

The general ideas developed in the preceding section have broader application. Once we accept that the management of a firm is not a monolith but has the nature of an evolving coalition, engaged in a problem of social choice, it is clear that many of the simple intuitions about the behavior of the neoclassical firm may be revised. Of course, many modeling decisions remain to be made and a lot of analysis is required to work out the precise implications of this change of perspective in particular settings. A simple example suffices to illustrate some of the complexities that can arise, while demonstrating the fruitfulness of this way of looking at institutions.

Consider a firm or institution that is weighing a choice between two policies, A and B. Policy A generates profits Π_A for T periods and no profits thereafter. Policy B generates profits $0 < \Pi_B < \Pi_A$ in perpetuity. For concreteness, we assume that the present value of the profits from policy A, PV_A, is greater than the present value of the profits from policy B, PV_B, but this is not essential for much of what follows.

Value maximization requires the firm to choose policy A, and this may be what a representative manager will do if he does not have to worry about the sort of incentive or time-consistency problems discussed in the preceding section. However, such problems seem likely in this situation. Suppose that the rents available to managers are proportional to profits. Then policy A generates a stream of rents equal to R_A in the interval $[0, T]$ and 0 thereafter. Policy B generates a stream of rents equal to $0 < R_B < R_A$ in perpetuity. Although at the initial date, policy A may appear more attractive to managers, as time passes and the horizon T comes closer, the relative attractiveness of policy A diminishes and that of policy B increases. After T, policy B is clearly more attractive. Suppose that we thought of managers of different generations as making a decision in some initial position. Obviously they would have different preferences, depending on the time period in which they are going to be running the firm. The early managers would prefer A, and the later managers would prefer B. Side payments might lead to unanimity. For example, if the present value of rents available under A is greater than under B, then the late managers could be compensated for the choice of A. However, this may not be time consistent, in which case those managers would vote for B.

In practice, choices are made by current management, and this raises issues of time consistency. If the choice between the two policies, made at time 0, is irreversible, we do not need to consider the time consistency of the decision. The management in charge at time 0, having a shorter time horizon, is likely to choose policy A, and that is the end of the matter. If the present value of A is greater than the present value of B, then this choice is consistent with value maximization; if not, not.

Few decisions are completely irreversible, however, and if there is some possibility of reversing the initial decision and opting for B at a later date, the preferences of later managers become relevant. To analyze the dynamic choice of policies requires a more complete specification of the model; in particular, we need to specify what happens to the rents when there is a switch in policies.

Suppose that policy B can be adopted at any time, but policy A can be adopted only at time 0 and once abandoned cannot be restarted. There is a different manager at each point in time. In order to make the adoption of A time inconsistent, it is enough to assume that the rents from policy A are received with a lag, and only if A is maintained during the interval before the rents appear. That is, rents accruing at time t are received if and only if the policy is maintained throughout the interval $[t, t+\varepsilon]$, where $\varepsilon > 0$ is a fixed number. Once time T arrives and there are no further rents from A, the current manager will want to switch to B, in order to start receiving the rents from B as soon as possible. But this means that managers in the interval $[T-\varepsilon, T]$ do not receive any rents from A, so they also have an incentive to switch to B; in fact, it is a conditionally dominated strategy. Continuing to eliminate conditionally dominated strategies in this way, we find that the current manager optimizes by switching to B as soon as possible at every time $t > 0$, so A cannot be chosen in a subgame perfect equilibrium.

This example is very special, but similar kinds of unraveling will occur if there is an overlapping management structure, which progressively introduces younger managers as time passes, as long as there is some unrecoverable cost in the form of firm-specific investment in human capital. Suppose, for example, that managers work for $\tau > 0$ periods and that they must invest I_A in human capital under policy A and $0 < I_B < I_A$ under policy B. We can now assume that a switch from A to B can occur at any time and rents accruing under any policy are received up until the moment when the switch occurs.

In order to recover their investments, managers must receive rents from the corresponding policy for τ_i periods, where

$$\int_0^{\tau_i} e^{-\rho t} R_i = I_i, \text{ for } i = A, B.$$

A manager who starts work in the interval $(T - \tau_A, T]$ will evidently not recover his investment, and so they will not be prepared to undertake the required investment in human capital. In that case, we assume that the anticipated rents R_A are not produced. But this means that the managers who begin to work in the period $(T - 2\tau_A, T - \tau_A]$ will not be able to recover their investments either, so they will not invest in human capital, and the firm will not produce the anticipated rents. Continuing in this way, one sees that policy B conditionally dominates A at any time $t > 0$ and, without explicitly describing a game to choose the policy, we can conclude that the only subgame perfect equilibrium is to switch to B as soon as possible, that is, to choose B instead of A to begin with.

Leaving aside the technical details of these examples, the general lesson is that managers will naturally want to see the firm's activity continue after the date T at which the firm appears to shut down under policy A. The choice of A over B, which appears clear from the vantage point of date 0, therefore becomes progressively problematical as T approaches. Some form of commitment is required to keep the management on track and time consistent. Without commitment, a switch at a later date may be anticipated and this may lead to some kind of unraveling. For example, if higher effort is required under A than under B, then an anticipated switch to B at date $T' < T$ may cause managers to prefer to switch to B at $T'' < T'$, and so on.

Similar arguments apply even if we assume that the initial management can commit to this policy. That is, even if the initial management can commit the firm to policy A, so that there is no possibility of switching to policy B, the need to recover firm-specific investments may render the policy infeasible, so that the rents produced in equilibrium fall short of what is needed to make A preferable to B in the first place. As we saw above, in a firm where it is necessary to recruit successive generations of managers, the returns to working for the firm have to be big enough to reward the managers for acquiring firm-specific skills that are necessary to make them productive in the firm. If side payments are feasible and credible, this should not pose a problem. However, this again requires some kind of commitment, because once the manager's skills are acquired, the firm may have an incentive to "hold up" the manager by underpaying him. There may be other reasons that the firm is unable to make credible side payments as required. If the firm is constrained in the kind of payments it can credibly offer, then policy A may not be feasible. The argument is identical to the one given above. In the interval $(T - \tau_A, T]$ managers are not willing to undertake investment in necessary human capital, and we assume that no rents are produced. Then no one will undertake the investment in the interval $(T - 2\tau_A, T - \tau_A]$ and so on. The equilibrium rents from A are 0, even if there is no possibility of switching, so B will be chosen from the beginning.

None of these arguments depends on the present value of profits or managerial rents, so it is obvious that we cannot make any claim for value maximization based on these examples. On the contrary, there is little reason to think that value maximization will occur, except by accident, even if managerial interests happen to be aligned with shareholder interests. On the other hand, these examples do suggest that managements with this overlapping structure may tend to choose policies that appear to put weight on long-term rather than short-term returns. Japanese firms and financial institutions that appear to prefer low rates of return that offer prospects of large market share in the future and German banks that hold large hidden reserves in order to ensure the stability and future of the bank are behaving quite consistently with the examples outlined here. In fact, from the point of view of these examples, and it must be stressed that they are only examples, the puzzle is why American firms are so aggressive in pursuing short-term returns under the same circumstances.

The same kinds of arguments could be reworked in a setting where the management had to choose not between two policies that had different implications for the value of the firm but between two policies that had different implications for risk. A safe policy would be one that offered a steady stream of profits and rents with high probability; a risky policy would offer a high level of profits and rents for awhile, with the probability of bankruptcy at some finite date. This is just a stochastic version of the choice between A and B, where the date T has become a random variable. Assuming that there is some advance notice of bankruptcy before date T, the same arguments will be adduced to show that management will prefer to switch to B if this is feasible, or that a firm starting out under policy A will rapidly become unprofitable if a switch to B is not possible. Since the analysis is so similar, there is no need to pursue it here.

Finally, we turn to the question of growth. As we pointed out in the discussion of internal finance in chapter 10, growth provides opportunities for managers to advance, and this may be important to provide incentives for managerial effort. Regardless of the rationale in terms of the performance of the firm or financial institution, management may be expected to have a preference for growth that reveals itself in non-value-maximizing policies pursued by management. Consider, for example, an overlapping management structure in which time is discrete $t = 1, 2, \ldots$ and each manager works for two periods. In the first period, the manager acquires human capital while working in the bottom level of management; in the second period, he has a certain probability of promotion to the top level, where he will receive higher rents than in the lower level. We assume that managers who are not promoted remain in the bottom level. The probability of promotion equals the fraction of managers promoted. Suppose that the sizes of the two levels remain in fixed proportions. Then the probability of promotion will depend on the growth rate according to the arithmetical relationship

$$\begin{aligned}\lambda_t &= \frac{U_t}{L_{t-1}} \\ &= \frac{U_t}{L_t}\frac{L_t}{L_{t-1}} \\ &= k(1+g_t),\end{aligned}$$

where U_t and L_t are the size of the upper and lower levels of management at date t, respectively, k is the ratio of upper- to lower-level managers, and g_t is the proportional rate of growth at date t. So higher rates of growth lead to greater prospects of advancement. There may be a feedback loop from these greater incentives to the rate of growth, but that does not concern us here. Even without a positive relationship between growth, incentives, and effort, we can see that there may be a managerial preference for higher rates of growth than is consistent with value maximization. Furthermore, the overlapping, teamlike structure of management may increase this preference, since each generation of managers comes in with the expectation of growth and advancement, and if it were ever to stop, it might be difficult to retain or motivate the best managers. In a static environment, it may be possible to structure incentives so that managers will act in the best interest of shareholders, even if this means paying out all of the firm's earnings as dividends. In a more realistic environment, where we recognize that managements consist of large numbers of managers, that decision making is distributed among the different levels and individuals, and that this structure is to a large extent opaque to shareholders, the design of incentives to align the interests of management and shareholders is problematical. Promotion from one level to another and the linkage of rewards to particular positions in the firm are features of most corporate organizations. Whatever the rationale for this form of organization, it is something that may have to be taken as given by shareholders. In that case, the managerial preference for growth and the opportunities it brings may also present itself as an ineradicable feature of large firms and financial institutions.

12.5 Financial Institutions

The ideas that we have developed in this chapter have particular application to banks and other financial institutions. In addition to the issue of how efficiently they are run themselves, it is often suggested that they have an important role in monitoring other firms so how they are governed is particularly important for the operation of the financial system. There is a wide range of different corporate structures for financial institutions in different countries; they are sometimes partnerships, cooperatives, or mutual companies. Apart from the peculiar corporate structure of financial institutions, it also appears that they are, despite occasional catastrophes, long-lived and durable institutions.

Some well-known differences between financial institutions and firms are listed below.

Moral hazard. Because of the nature of the assets that financial institutions hold, moral hazard may always be a more serious problem than in industrial companies. Financial assets can be disposed of quickly without shareholders' being able to observe them. This means that shareholders are always at greater risk of losing their investment than if it were held in the form of assets like factories and stores. In the same way, bad judgment can lead to large losses very quickly, as we have recently seen in a number of celebrated cases, such as Barings Bank (Nicholas Leeson), Kidder Peabody (Joseph Jett), and Daiwa Bank (Toshihide Iguchi). For this reason, financial institutions that have lasted a long time may have an insurmountable reputational advantage, and the value of this advantage (in terms of the rents it generates) may provide a great incentive to play safe or take the long-run view. This is in addition to the safety effect of sheer size.

Liquidity and financial fragility. The value of financial assets depends on the liquidity of the markets that they can be sold on, and their value can change very rapidly if there is some shock to the system. The importance of exogenous, systemic shocks and the vulnerability of financial institutions may require a different form of organization than industrial companies.

Flexibility of financial institutions. Because of the nature of the services provided by financial institutions, we should expect them to be long-lived. Unlike producers of physical goods, which may disappear or be transformed rapidly because of technological progress or changing tastes, financial functions are fundamental to a capitalist system, and the financial institutions that provide these functions are capable of adjusting to provide analogous or comparable services and functions in widely changing circumstances. This does not mean that financial institutions do not disappear and cannot be taken over or merge with other firms. The recent history of financial innovation has led to a great deal of reorganization. However, because of the importance of reputation and access to capital, it seems more likely that existing financial institutions will adjust to changed circumstances rather than being replaced by start-up institutions.

There may be reasons of safety for organizing financial institutions in the Japanese manner rather than the entrepreneurial manner. A bureaucratic institution, with its complex system of checks and balances, may be more resistant to the kinds of moral hazard problems than an entrepreneurial company. Isolated rogue traders can be controlled more carefully when decisions are subject to extensive, hierarchical review. Misjudgments may be rarer when decisions are made collectively and require the agreement of large numbers of individuals. At the same time, the tendency toward a corporate mentality and group thinking may wipe out the independence that is essential if collective decision making is to avoid catastrophic losses. Finally, the natural bureaucratic tendency toward conservative strategies may be a source of safety in a world in which the lure of enormous profits biases decisions of agents with limited liability toward excessive risk taking. At the same time, in a rapidly changing environment such as we have seen in the financial world in the last twenty years, conservative strategies may themselves be extremely risky for an institution that hopes to survive.

The fact that financial institutions, as opposed to markets, are more important in France, Germany, and Japan than in the United States and United Kingdom is itself suggestive in this context. Perhaps it is because of the economic culture of these countries that financial institutions such as banks have played a larger role in providing financial functions than they have in the Anglo-American world.

12.6 Conclusion

The theme that runs through this chapter is that firms should be thought of as teams with many members whose identities change over time. As such, they acquire characteristics that may not be attributable to the preferences of the individual team members. One such characteristic is the priority of the survival of the firm, which may not serve the interests of a given individual at all times but in some sense serves the interests of the team as a whole. This point of view is also relevant to understanding how financial institutions work, since they are prime candidates to be understood as durable institutions with long horizons and also to understanding the role of financial institutions and financial markets in monitoring, financing, and advising firms, which may themselves be durable institutions.

We think these ideas have a natural application to corporations and nonprofits and can give insights into some of the cross-country differences in behavior that we observe. As we pointed out at the beginning of this chapter, there are significant differences between the attitudes to corporate governance in the United States, United Kingdom, France, Germany, and Japan. These differences may arise from cultural differences that are orthogonal to the models presented in this chapter, but they are compatible with our approach. The long horizons of Japanese and German firms, the tolerance of large, collusive arrangements, whether in the form of German cartels or Japanese, multi-industry conglomerates, the emphasis on market share and growth rather than profits—all of these can be seen as necessary conditions for the viability of the bureaucratic, employee-oriented capitalism found in France, Germany, and Japan, as opposed to the more entrepreneurial, shareholder-oriented variety found in the United States and United Kingdom. This conclusion has to be tempered by the realization that the economies of France, Germany, and Japan are steadily being invaded by more American financial practices (as the recent crisis in Japanese banking reminds us).

References

Alchian, A. (1965). "The Basis of Some Recent Advances in the Theory of Management of the Firm." *Journal of Industrial Economics* **14,** 30–41.

Alchian, A. and H. Demsetz. (1972). "Production, Information Costs, and Economic Organization." *American Economic Review* **62,** 777–795.

Aoki, M. (1984a). *The Co-operative Game Theory of the Firm.* Oxford: Clarendon Press.

———. (1984b). "Shareholders' Non-Unanimity on Investment Financing: Banks vs. Individual Investors." In M. Aoki (ed.), *The Economic Analysis of the Japanese Firm.* Amsterdam, North-Holland.

———. (ed.). (1984c). *The Economic Analysis of the Japanese Firm.* Amsterdam: North-Holland.

———. (1988). *Information, Incentives, and Bargaining in the Japanese Economy.* New York: Cambridge University Press.

———. (1990). "Toward an Economic Model of the Japanese Firm." *Journal of Economic Literature* **28,** 1–27.

———. (1992). "Decentralization-Centralization in Japanese Organization: A Duality Principle." In Shumpei Kumon and Henry Rosovsky (eds.), *The Political Economy of Japan,* Vol. 3: *Cultural and Social Dynamics* (pp. 142–169). Stanford: Stanford University Press.

Aoki, M., and R. Dore. (eds.). (1994). *The Japanese Firm: The Sources of Competitive Strength.* New York: Oxford University Press.

Aoki, M., B. Gustafsson, and O. Williamson (eds.). (1990). *The Firm as a Nexus of Treaties.* Newbury Park, CA: Sage Publications.

Aoki, M., and H. Patrick. (eds.). (1994). *The Japanese Main Bank System: Its Relevancy for Developing and Transforming Economies.* New York: Oxford University Press, 592–633.

Baumol, W. (1959). *Business Behavior, Value and Growth.* New York: Macmillan.

Cyert, R., and J. March. (1963). *A Behavioral Theory of the Firm.* Englewood Cliffs, NJ: Prentice Hall.

DeMeza, D., and B. Lockwood. (1998). "Does Asset Ownership Always Motivate Managers? Outside Options and the Property Rights Theory of the Firm." *Quarterly Journal of Economics* **113,** 361–386.

Dutta, P., and R. Sundaram. (1992). "Survival and the Art of Profit Maximization," Department of Economics, University of Rochester, unpublished.

Fama, E. (1980). "Agency Problems and the Theory of the Firm." *Journal of Political Economy* **88,** 288–307.

Institute of Fiscal and Monetary Policy. (1996). *Socio-Economic Systems of Japan, the United States, the United Kingdom, Germany and France.* Tokyo: Ministry of Finance, Japan.

Grossman, S., and O. Hart. (1986). "The Costs and Benefits of Ownership." *Journal of Political Economy* **94,** 691–719.

Hampden-Turner, C., and A. Trompenaars. (1993). *The Seven Cultures of Capitalism: Value Systems for Creating Wealth in the United States, Japan, Germany, France, Britain, Sweden, and the Netherlands.* New York: Currency Doubleday.

Hart, O. (1995). *Firms, Contracts and Financial Structure.* Oxford: Clarendon Press.

Hart, O., and J. Moore. (1990). "Property Rights and the Nature of the Firm." *Journal of Political Economy* **118,** 1119–1158.

Hart, O., A. Shleifer, and R. Vishny. (1997). "The Proper Role for Government: Theory and an Application to Prisons." *Quarterly Journal of Economics* **112,** 1127–1162.

Holmstrom, B. (1982). "Moral Hazard in Teams." *Bell Journal of Economics* **13,** 324–340.

Jensen, M., and W. Meckling. (1976). "Theory of the Firm: Managerial Behavior, Agency Costs and Ownership Structure." *Journal of Financial Economics* **3,** 305–360.

Klein, B., R. Crawford, and A. Alchian. (1978). "Vertical Integration, Appropriable Rents, and the Competitive Contracting Process." *Journal of Law and Economics* **21,** 297–326.

Macleod, B., and J. Malcolmson. (1993). "Investment, Hold-up and the Form of Market Contracts." *American Economic Review* **83,** 811–837.

Majumdar, M., and R. Radner. (1991). "Linear Models of Economic Survival Under Production Uncertainty." *Economic Theory* **1,** 13–30.

Majumdar, M., and R. Radner. (1992). "Survival Under Production Uncertainty." In M. Majumdar, (ed.). *Equilibrium and Dynamics: Essays in Honour of David Gale.* New York: St. Martin's Press, 179–200.

Marschak, J., and R. Radner. (1972). *The Theory of Teams.* New Haven, CT: Yale University Press.

Radner, Roy. *Economic Survival.* (Nancy L. Schwartz Memorial Lecture, 1955), Evanston, IL: Kellogg School of Management, Northwestern University.

Rajan, R., and L. Zingales. (1998). "Power in a Theory of the Firm." *Quarterly Journal of Economics* **113,** 387–432.

Rajan, R., H. Servaes, and L. Zingales. (1998). "The Cost of Diversity: The Diversification Discount and Inefficient Investment." Working paper, University of Chicago.

Stole, L., and J. Zwiebel. (1996a). "Organizational Design and Technology Choice Under Intra-Firm Bargaining." *American Economic Review* **86,** 195–222.

———. (1996b). "Intra-Firm Bargaining Under Nonbinding Contracts." *Review of Economic Studies* **63,** 375–410.

Williamson, O. (1975). *Markets and Hierarchies: Analysis and Antitrust Implications.* New York: Free Press.

———. (1985). *The Economic Institutions of Capitalism.* New York: Free Press.

Winter, S. (1982). "Competition and Selection." In J. Eatwell, J. Milgate, and P. Newman (eds.). *The New Palgrave.* Vol. 1. New York: Stockton Press, 545–548.

Yoshimori, M. (1995). "Whose Company Is It? The Concept of the Corporation in Japan and the West." *Long Range Planning* **28,** 33–44.

IV Markets and Intermediaries

13 Diversity of Opinion and Resource Allocation

Economic progress depends on the rate of technological change, the introduction of new products and processes that allow us to achieve a higher level of satisfaction with the same resources. Technological change can take place through the development of a new industry or the development of new technologies in existing industries. In either case, the financing of technological change is an important issue. New technologies are hard to evaluate, either because little information is available about their likely profitability or because the information itself is hard to evaluate without extensive expertise. Yet without such an evaluation, it may be difficult for the innovator, who has the knowledge about the new technology, to persuade the investor, who has the resources needed to implement the innovation, to make the necessary investment. In this chapter we are interested in comparing the performance of markets and intermediaries at financing new technologies. Not surprisingly, the comparison turns on their effectiveness at reducing the costs of acquiring and processing information, and it turns out that both markets and intermediaries have a comparative advantage at dealing with different kinds of information.

13.1 Common Priors and Common Knowledge

In chapter 7, we considered the role of information in resource allocation. The standard assumption underlying asset pricing models such as the CAPM is that agents share the same prior probability beliefs. When asymmetric information was introduced, we continued to assume that everyone had the same prior. Posterior probability beliefs differed because agents have different information sets. If everybody shared their information, their beliefs would be the same.

In an important paper, Aumann (1976) showed that if two people assign the same prior probabilities to a given event and their posterior probabilities (conditional on private information) are common knowledge, then the posterior probabilities must be identical. In other words, under the common prior assumption, they cannot agree to disagree. Geanakoplos and Polemarchakis (1982) demonstrated that if two agents receive different information, then, by communicating their posteriors back and forth, they will converge to a common posterior. McKelvey and Page (1986) extended these results to n individuals and showed that public announcement of posteriors was not necessary for convergence; the public announcement of aggregate statistics can have the same effect. However, if the information each person observes is sufficiently complex, the number of iterations required to obtain convergence can be large and the amount of information conveyed on each iteration may be small.

As Morris (1995) persuasively argues, there is nothing in Bayesian decision theory or standard theories of rationality that requires agents to have the same priors. There is a long tradition in economics of allowing for differences in prior beliefs. For example, the ADM model and the fundamental theorems of welfare economics allow for different priors. The model of Diamond (1967), discussed at length in chapter 7, has this feature. A number of important finance papers, such as Lintner (1965) and Ross (1976), have also allowed for differences in prior beliefs. A more recent example is Harris and Raviv (1993). Kandel and Pearson (1995) provide empirical evidence that trading around earnings announcements is due to differences in priors.

In this chapter, we consider contexts in which the common prior assumption is not appropriate. It can be argued that the common prior assumption is not appropriate when considering new industries and new technologies. Casual empiricism suggests that there is a wide variation in views on the effectiveness and value of innovations. Since the amount of data available based on actual experience with new products or technologies is nonexistent or small, such differences in views would appear to be due to differences in priors. There is diversity of opinion, and people agree to disagree. This is what distinguishes the approach taken in this chapter from the analysis in chapter 7.

Even if agents begin with different prior probability beliefs, their beliefs may eventually agree. The crucial requirement is that the prior probability beliefs have a common support. As more and more information becomes public, agents update their beliefs, and eventually they will converge to a common belief. Two situations of interest are thus that (1) relevant information is sparse and there is diversity of opinion, and (2) relevant information is plentiful and posterior beliefs have converged.

The first type of situation obtains when innovation has just occurred. The second obtains when a large amount of experience has been gained and things are no longer changing. It provides a justification for the standard finance approach since the common beliefs assumption is valid in this second type of situation. Diversity of opinion is appropriate in the first. The formal model developed below allows a continuous range of diversity of opinion. Nevertheless, it is helpful to start by initially discussing these two extremes.

When a new industry starts up, there are a number of different types of risk. In addition to the risk associated with the technology, there is very little knowledge that is relevant when it comes to deciding on the best management strategies to follow and the nature of the risks these entail. A wide variety of possibilities usually exist, and the merits and disadvantages of these alternatives are not clear. The wide range of possibilities and the lack of hard data mean that there is often considerable diversity of opinion. Potential providers of finance have different priors on the outcomes and agree to disagree. We argue here that markets have considerable advantages in such situations. They involve many people participating directly in the decision. This is costly because they have to acquire information to make the decision, but it has the great advantage that everybody can contribute or withhold their money according to their own views. This flexibility means that at least some innovative projects are likely to be financed.

The nature of intermediated finance is that the decision on whether to invest in a project is delegated to the manager of the intermediary. In this case funds can be allocated to a project even if the investors providing the funds have beliefs that it is a bad one; the decision to invest in a project is made by the manager, not the investors. The main advantage of an intermediary is the economizing on information acquisition. Only the manager needs to become informed. When there is wide agreement, this kind of delegation works well and can result in considerable savings (cf. Diamond 1984). The problem comes when there is diversity of opinion. Even if the manager does his best to choose projects he honestly believes are profitable (i.e., abstracting from the principal-agent problem), diversity of opinion implies that some of the providers of finance would disagree with those decisions if they had the same information as the manager. If the possibility of disagreement is sufficiently high, the investors may be unwilling to provide funds. Thus, intermediated finance may result in underfunding of innovative projects.

Our analysis suggests that diversity of opinion and the degree of risk are crucial in determining the relative performance of markets and intermediaries. Markets will be especially effective at financing industries that are new or where relatively little relevant data are generated, that is, industries in which information is sparse and diversity of opinion persists.

During the nineteenth and twentieth centuries, many new industries were introduced. In the nineteenth century, the most important perhaps was the railway industry. In the twentieth century, the automobile, consumer durables, aircraft, computer, and biotechnology industries are all examples of completely new industries.

A good example of a new industry where very little information was available initially is biotechnology. The lack of information was not only technological. Given the lack of similar existing industries, the business strategies to be pursued were also very unclear. All this led to great diversity of opinion. Nevertheless, this industry has been successfully funded through the stock market.

It is not just in entirely new industries that there can be diversity of opinion. In other situations in established industries, where there is only limited relevant experience, there is usually a wide range of views on the best way to proceed and on valuations. A good example is provided by the computer industry. IBM was clearly dominant during the 1950s, 1960s, and 1970s when mainframe machines were the primary technology. In the 1980s the development of the personal computer dramatically changed the industry. Initially, without the benefit of hindsight it was not at all clear how this change would affect the industry and what strategies companies should adopt. Indeed IBM lost its almost unchallenged dominance of the industry because it did not initially realize that personal computers represented a long-term competitive threat to mainframes. Even after IBM got into the personal computer market, it underestimated the value of the operating system and chip technology. Others in the industry, such as Intel and Microsoft, took a rather different view.

In general, the following are examples of factors that are likely to lead to a lack of relevant information and hence diversity of opinion:

1. Increasing returns to scale result in there being only a few firms in an industry.

2. There is often a long lag between the adoption of policies and the time that their success or failure is realized.
3. Technological change is important and rapid.

At the opposite extreme are industries where there is very little diversity of opinion because the amount of relevant information that is available is plentiful, and these data overwhelm differences in priors. Such circumstances are likely to occur when the following factors are present:

1′. The industry is competitive with many producers.
2′. Production cycles are relatively short.
3′. Technology is constant.

There are many industries with these kinds of features. One particularly good example is agriculture. Here a vast amount of information is available. There are many farmers. Production occurs in a matter of months and is repeated at least once a year. Technology changes slowly, and so information is relevant for many years. Many of the industries that start out characterized by factors 1–3 mature into industries better characterized by factors 1′–3′. For example, the automobile industry has developed into a competitive global industry. Producing new models is now a fairly short process. The technology does change, but this is fairly slow and involves gradual improvements in performance and reliability rather than substantial changes in the nature of the product.

The actual development of new industries and new technologies is an extremely complex process. The provision of finance is only one part of it. Establishing the historical importance of market-based versus bank-based finance empirically would be a lengthy and difficult exercise. However, as Allen (1993) notes, it is of some interest that many of the new industries we have mentioned were developed in the United Kingdom or United States. For example, railways were first developed in the United Kingdom, and to a large extent both the United Kingdom's and other countries' railways were financed through the London Stock Exchange in the nineteenth century. Even though the automobile was invented in Germany, it was in the United States that automobiles were first produced on a large scale. The aircraft, consumer durable, computer, and biotechnology industries were initially developed in the United States. It is not uniformly the case that all new industries were developed in the United Kingdom or United States. For example, some industries, such as the chemical industry, were initially developed on a large scale in Germany. Nevertheless, casual empiricism suggests that a surprising proportion of new industries have been developed in the United Kingdom and United States.

Although the other countries that we consider in this book—France, Germany, and Japan—are wealthy by any standards, their main strength has been in industries pioneered in other countries. They have traditionally been weak in terms of developing new industries. For example in the postwar years, France has done well in industries such as automobiles and other manufactured goods. Germany's automobile and machine tool industries have excelled. In Japan, automobiles and electronic goods have been very successful.

There has been an extensive literature over the years investigating the relationship between financial development and growth. An excellent survey is provided by Levine (1997). Numerous authors, including Bagehot (1873), Hicks (1969), McKinnon (1973), and Greenwood and Jovanovic (1990), have argued that financial development is an important factor in determining growth. On the other hand, many others, such as Robinson (1952) and Lucas (1988), argue that financial factors are not important in determining growth and that the causation can run the other way. Large financial sectors are the result of economic growth. In a survey of development economics, Stern (1989) does not mention the role of finance, even in the section on omitted topics. Levine's broad conclusion based on his review of the literature is that there are some linkages between financial development and growth and that a more developed financial system promotes a higher rate of growth.

Most of the literature on financial development and growth does not distinguish between intermediary-based and market-based systems. An exception is Gerschenkron (1968), who argues that the bank-based finance of Germany in the latter part of the nineteenth century allowed a faster rate of growth than the market-based United Kingdom system because of the closer ties banks can have with firms. We are also interested in the relationship between the type of finance, intermediary based versus market based, and the amount of innovation. In particular, we are interested in the question of whether intermediaries or markets are better for funding new activities when there is diversity of opinion.

A growing literature analyzes the ways in which different countries' financial systems operate and on the design of financial systems (see Boot and Thakor 1997a, 1997b, and for a survey Thakor 1996). In contrast, our focus is on financing new technologies rather than existing ones. Bhattacharya and Chiesa (1995) and Yosha (1995) consider the advantages of financing R&D using bilateral financing (one lender) compared to multilateral financing (many lenders). They do not consider the role of diversity of opinion. Berk, Green, and Naik (1997) analyze how R&D projects should be valued but are concerned with the extent to which risk is systematic rather than differences in views.

In the rest of the chapter, which is based on Allen and Gale (1999), we address the following questions:

- How can diversity of opinion be modeled consistently with a rational, Bayesian approach?
- What is the optimal institution for providing finance, markets or intermediaries, and what factors determine the optimal choice?
- What is the optimal architecture for a financial system?
- Will efficient financial institutions result from the uncoordinated behavior of rational maximizing agents?

13.2 A Model of Diversity

In this section, we describe a formal model of information acquisition in the presence of diversity of opinion. A new industry is being established in which there are large numbers of investment opportunities. Because investors have different prior beliefs, they will interpret information differently. Some investors will become pessimistic and refuse to invest even when presented with detailed information about a project. Others will interpret the same information as grounds for optimism. Before investors have seen the information, they do not know how they will react, and we can simplify the analysis by assuming that investors are ex ante identical, that is, they have the same probability of becoming optimists or pessimists. The importance of assuming heterogeneous priors is not that they imply different beliefs about the profitability of the project ex ante but rather that it allows investors, after being presented with evidence, to agree to disagree.

We start with the simplest case where there is just a single project, which is small relative to the amount of funds available:

- There is a continuum of risk-neutral investors with number (measure) MI, each with a single unit of capital to invest.
- There is a single project requiring an input of I units of capital. The project is initially owned by an entrepreneur who has no capital and seeks financing from investors.

• It is assumed that $MI > I$ so that the entrepreneur obtains all the surplus from the project, and investors obtain their opportunity cost. For simplicity, the investors' best alternative is assumed to be a safe asset with a zero rate of return, so for every unit invested at the beginning, one unit is obtained at the end.

• The investors initially have symmetric beliefs about the profitability of the project. They can obtain more information about the profitability of the project by paying a cost $c > 0$. After paying the cost, the investor is either in a state of optimism about the project, because he expects the return per unit of investment to be $H > 0$; or he is in a state of pessimism, because it has an expected return $L < 0$ per unit of investment. These returns are net of the original investment. The probability that an informed investor becomes an optimist is denoted by α. If no cost is paid, type is not discovered until after the investment decision.

Figure 13.1 shows the sequence of events. At the initial date, $t = 0$, all investors lack information about the detailed characteristics of the new project. At date $t = 1$ some details of the new project appear. An investor then has two possible courses of action. The first is to remain uninformed about the project. This option is represented by the left-hand branch in figure 13.1. The second is to pay a cost c to become informed about the details of the project. This option is represented by the right-hand branch. Paying the cost c allows investors to discover whether they are optimists or pessimists before the investment decision. Although the investors receive the same information, they interpret it differently. As a result, they have different beliefs and agree to disagree. The important point is that until they pay the cost c and acquire some information, they do not know whether they will react optimistically or pessimistically to the information available. All they can do is to assign probabilities to the expected payoffs H and L. Initially (at date 0), every investor assigns the same probability to becoming an optimist or pessimist because they do not yet know their true type.

The event "becoming an optimist" is not independent across investors. For example, suppose there are two equally likely states of the market, skepticism and euphoria. In a state of skepticism, four out of ten investors are optimistic. In a state of euphoria, eight out of ten investors are optimistic. Every investor has the same probability of being an optimist, but the total number of optimists is fixed: if there are ten investors, then exactly four or eight will be optimists.

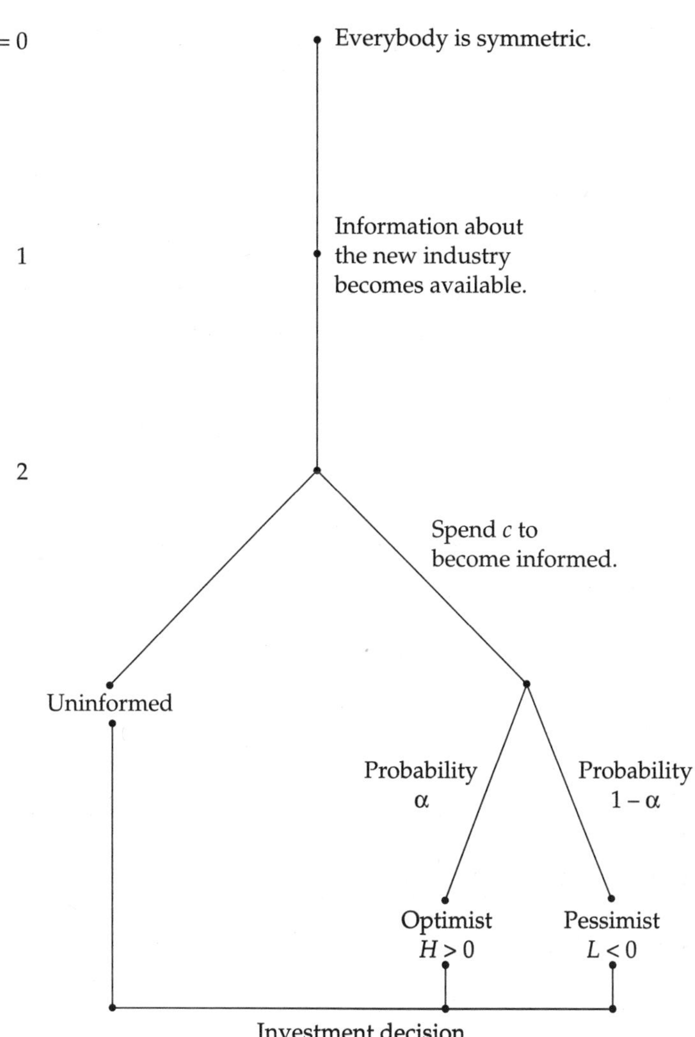

Figure 13.1
Time structure of beliefs

Diversity of information implies that informed investors do not necessarily agree. We can measure the amount of diversity by the probability that two investors will agree. In the example given, the ex ante probability of being an optimist is

$$0.5 \times 0.4 + 0.5 \times 0.8 = 0.6.$$

However, ex post, the probability that an informed investor is an optimist is either 0.4 or 0.8, depending on which state has occurred. We may not know which state has occurred, but if we know that a randomly selected, informed investor is an optimist, this makes the state of euphoria more likely and changes the probability that another, randomly selected, informed investor will also turn out to be an optimist. In fact, the posterior probability of a state of euphoria, given that a randomly selected, informed investor is optimistic, is given by Bayes' rule:

$$\frac{0.5 \times 0.8}{0.5 \times 0.4 + 0.5 \times 0.8} = \frac{0.4}{0.6} = \frac{2}{3}.$$

Using this posterior probability, the probability that a second, randomly selected, informed investor is optimistic is

$$\frac{1}{3} \times 0.4 + \frac{2}{3} \times 0.8 = \frac{2}{3}.$$

So the probability that two investors agree, given that the first is an optimist, will be 2/3.

The probability of agreement with a given investor depends on whether the investor is an optimist or a pessimist. If the investor is a pessimist, then the posterior probability of being in a state of euphoria is given by Bayes' rule,

$$\frac{0.5 \times 0.2}{0.5 \times 0.6 + 0.5 \times 0.2} = \frac{0.1}{0.4} = \frac{1}{4},$$

and the probability that a randomly selected, informed investor will also be a pessimist is

$$0.25 \times 0.2 + 0.75 \times 0.6 = \frac{1}{2}.$$

So the probability of agreeing with a pessimist is 1/2 and the probability of agreeing with an optimist is 2/3.

Diversity of opinion implies that informed investors do not necessarily agree. We measure the degree of diversity using the probability that a randomly selected informed investor will disagree with an optimist. If a randomly selected, informed investor is an optimist, the probability that another randomly selected, informed investor agrees with him is denoted by β. In other words, β is the probability that both investors are optimists, given that the first one is.

The profitability of delegating the investment decision to a manager of an intermediary depends on whether the beliefs of informed investors are correlated ex post. We can think of β as a measure of correlation among the investors' beliefs; alternatively, we can think of $1-\beta$ as a measure of diversity of opinion. To see this, suppose that we select two investors at random from the entire population. Their belief types (optimist or pessimist) can be represented by random variables X and Y that take the value 1 if the corresponding agent is an optimist and 0 if he is a pessimist. Then it is easy to show that

$$\begin{aligned} cov[X,Y] &= E[XY]-E[X]E[Y] \\ &= \alpha(\beta-\alpha), \end{aligned}$$

where $\alpha \leq \beta \leq 1$; the covariance is zero if and only if $\beta = \alpha$.

The parameter β is important because delegation is profitable if and only if the event "becoming an optimist" is correlated across investors. If these events are independent ($\alpha = \beta$) the manager's opinion is uncorrelated with the opinion of the investors in the intermediary. In that case, intermediated finance with delegated decision making is no better than uninformed finance. Conversely, a positive correlation between the manager's opinion and the opinion of the other investors ($\beta > \alpha$) allows for profitable delegation, because the informed manager can make a decision that is more representative of the agents' ex post beliefs than the (uninformed) agents can.

To see the exact relationship between α and β, it is helpful to develop a concrete stochastic structure with the required properties (this is a generalization of the numerical example given earlier). For a given project, suppose that the investors are randomly divided into two groups, one containing a fraction $1/2 \leq \gamma \leq 1$ of the population and the other containing $1-\gamma$. For example, we could imagine the population being distributed uniformly on a circle of radius $r = MI/2\pi$ as shown in figure 13.2, where MI is the measure of investors in the economy and the circumference of the circle. A point x is chosen randomly on the circle (x is uniformly distributed on the circle), and then γMI investors are counted off in a counter-clockwise direction and put into the majority group. The rest are put into the minority group. By symmetry, every investor has the same probability γ of being in the majority.

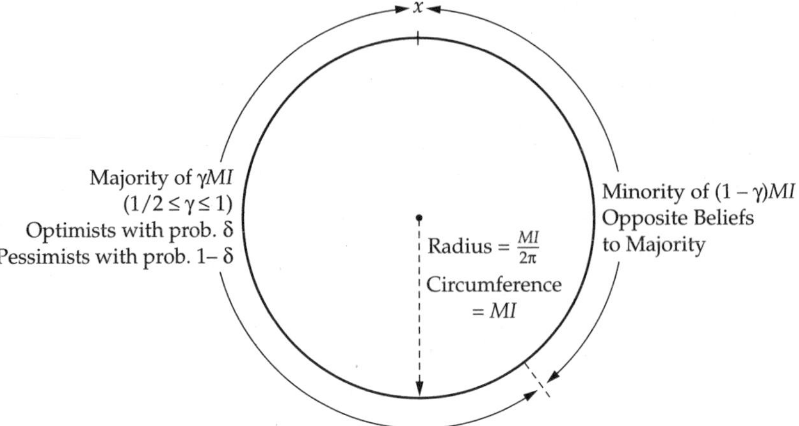

Figure 13.2
Stochastic structure of optimism and pessimism

The beliefs of the majority are the opposite of the minority's. If the majority are optimists, the minority are pessimists, and vice versa. Suppose that the majority is optimistic about the project with probability $0 < \delta < 1$. Then the unconditional probability of any investor's being optimistic is

$$\alpha = \gamma\delta + (1-\gamma)(1-\delta).$$

The first term is the probability of being in the majority and the majority being optimistic. The second term is the probability of being in the minority and the minority's being optimistic.

For a fixed value of γ, the probability α of being an optimist increases with δ and lies between $(1-\gamma)$ and γ. Intuitively, a lot of diversity (γ close to 1/2 so that the majority and minority are roughly equal) restricts the value of α to lie close to 1/2.

Now suppose that an informed investor is optimistic. What is the probability that he is in the majority? By Bayes' rule, it is equal to the probability that he is optimistic and in the majority, $\gamma\delta$, divided by the probability that he is optimistic, α. Then the probability that a randomly selected investor agrees with an optimist is

$$\beta = \frac{\gamma\delta}{\alpha}\gamma + \left(1 - \frac{\gamma\delta}{\alpha}\right)(1-\gamma),$$

since they agree if they are both in the majority or both in the minority, and the probability of the optimist's being in the majority is $\gamma\delta/\alpha$ and

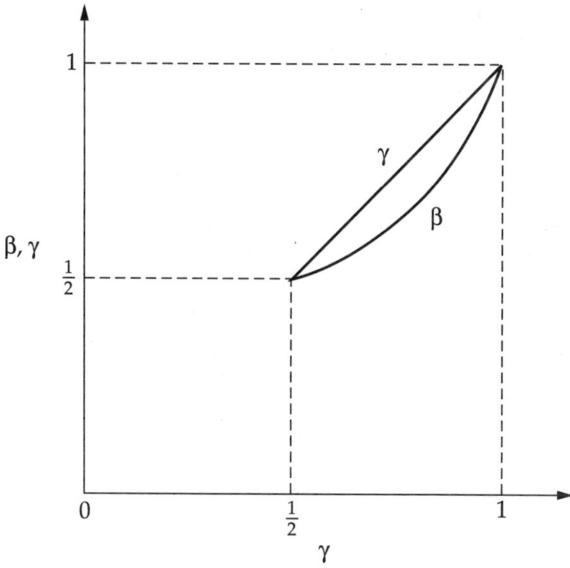

Figure 13.3
Relationship between β and γ

the probability of a randomly selected investor's being in the majority is γ. Substituting the expression for α we obtain

$$\beta = \frac{\gamma\delta}{\alpha}\gamma + \left(\frac{(1-\gamma)(1-\delta)}{\alpha}\right)(1-\gamma)$$

$$= \frac{\gamma^2\delta + (1-\gamma)^2(1-\delta)}{\gamma\delta + (1-\gamma)(1-\delta)}.$$

For a fixed value of δ, β is a convex function of γ. If γ is equal to 1/2 (resp., 1) then it is easy to see that β is equal to 1/2 (resp., 1). For any value of γ strictly between 1/2 and 1, the numerator is less than $\gamma(\gamma\delta + (1-\gamma)(1-\delta)) = \gamma\alpha$, since $\gamma > (1-\gamma)$, so $\beta < \gamma$. The relationship between β and γ is shown in figure 13.3.

13.3 Market versus Intermediated Finance

Direct or market finance is identified with a situation in which investors become informed and then decide individually whether to contribute to the funding of the project. Intermediated finance is identified with a situation in which I investors form a consortium. One of their number is designated as the manager. He becomes informed and, on the basis of that information, decides whether to invest in the project, while the rest of the group remains uninformed. The fact that there is a positive correlation between the manager's type and the types of the other members of the consortium means that, on average, he makes a representative decision for the group. If he finds out he is an optimist, it is likely that a majority of the rest of the consortium are optimists, so each uninformed person's expected utility as well as that of the manager is maximized by investing. On the other hand, if the manager finds out he is a pessimist, the expected utility of each member of the group is maximized by not investing. The assumption that only one member of the consortium becomes informed is clearly special. There might exist situations in which it would be optimal for any finite number between 1 and I to become informed. Here we simplify the problem by assuming that only one member becomes informed. One possible justification for this assumption is the existence of monitoring costs. The larger the number of managers (informed members of the consortium), the smaller the influence of any one manager's information and the greater the incentive to free-ride by not acquiring information at all. If managers have to be monitored in order to make sure that they actually become informed and if the marginal costs of monitoring additional managers are increasing, it may be optimal to have a small number of managers. A consortium with a single manager is a limiting case when monitoring costs are high.

Market finance can be thought of as raising money in public stock markets or in private markets. Intermediated finance can be thought of as bank finance. Since the bank provides all the finance and the entrepreneur has no collateral, there is no difference between risky debt and equity in the model.

Since there is only one project and a large number of potential investors, competition among investors ensures that all of the surplus will go to the entrepreneur. However, since we are interested only in determining the efficient form of finance, there is no loss of generality in assuming that the surplus goes to the investors.

An investor who does not finance the project receives a net return of 0. An uninformed investor expects the project to earn a net return of

$$V_U \equiv \alpha H + (1 - \alpha)L.$$

Even if this return is positive, the investor may be able to do even better by becoming informed.

Under market finance, each individual who wishes to become informed must pay the cost c. After becoming informed, an investor will invest in the project if and only if he is optimistic. Thus, the payoff to becoming informed is

$$V_M \equiv \alpha H + (1-\alpha)0 - c = \alpha H - c \tag{13.1}$$

since with probability α he becomes an optimist, expects a return $H > 0$, and invests in the project, with probability $(1-\alpha)$ he becomes a pessimist, expects a return $L < 0$, and does not invest, and in either case he pays the cost c.

Suppose next that a financial intermediary is formed. In order to be able to fund the project, the consortium must contain I members. The formation of an intermediary makes no difference if the intermediary does not become informed, so we always assume without loss of generality that the manager becomes informed.

The typical investor's views on the payoff to the intermediary are determined by considering his own possible beliefs if he were to become informed and weighting each possibility by the appropriate probability. In particular, the typical investor does not know whether he would agree with the manager if he (the investor) were to become informed, and this must be taken into account in evaluating the payoff to joining the consortium. If the manager is optimistic, then the expected return to investment for an uninformed investor is $\beta H + (1-\beta)L$ since the probability that the investor will agree (will be an optimist) is β. On the other hand, if the manager is a pessimist, the expected return to investment for an uninformed investor is $\beta' H + (1-\beta')L$, where β' is the probability of disagreement when the manager is a pessimist. We can calculate the value of β' to be

$$\beta' = \frac{\gamma(1-\delta)}{1-\alpha}(1-\gamma) + \left(1 - \frac{\gamma(1-\delta)}{1-\alpha}\right)\gamma$$

and show that

$$\beta' H + (1-\beta')L < \beta H + (1-\beta)L$$

because $\beta' < \beta$.

Information is valuable to the intermediary only if the investment decision depends on the outcome of obtaining information. We therefore focus on the case where

$$\beta' H + (1-\beta')L < 0 < \beta H + (1-\beta)L. \tag{13.2}$$

Thus, if it is worthwhile forming an intermediary at all, the return conditional on the manager's being optimistic (resp., pessimistic) is positive (resp., negative), and everyone agrees to invest in the project if and only if the manager is optimistic. Under this decision rule, the payoff is

$$V_I \equiv \alpha(\beta H + (1-\beta)L) + (1-\alpha)0 - \frac{c}{I} \tag{13.3}$$

$$= \alpha(\beta H + (1-\beta)L) - \frac{c}{I}, \tag{13.4}$$

since the manager is optimistic and decides to invest with probability α and, given that the manager is optimistic, the expected return to a randomly selected investor is $\beta H + (1-\beta)L$. With probability $1-\alpha$ the manager is pessimistic and does not invest. In every case the investor has to pay his share c/I of the information costs.

The payoffs from different forms of financing are summarized as follows:

1. No investment	0
2. Uninformed investment	$V_U = \alpha H + (1-\alpha)L$
3. Market investment	$V_M = \alpha H - c$
4. Intermediated investment	$V_I = \alpha(\beta H + (1-\beta)L) - c/I$

Comparing equations 13.1 and 13.4, market finance is preferred to intermediated finance if and only if the following inequality is satisfied:

$$\alpha H - c > \alpha(\beta H + (1-\beta)L) - \frac{c}{I}. \tag{13.5}$$

Then we have the following result.

PROPOSITION 13.1 Let $V^* = \max\{0, V_U, V_M, V_I\}$. Then no investment is optimal if $V^* = 0$; uninformed investment is optimal if $V^* = V_U$; market finance is optimal if $V^* = V_M$; and intermediated finance is optimal if $V^* = V_I$. Market finance is strictly preferred to intermediated finance if and only if

$$\alpha(1-\beta)(H-L) > c - \frac{c}{I},$$

and intermediated finance is strictly preferred to market finance if and only if the reverse inequality is satisfied.

The term $\alpha(1-\beta)(H-L)$ on the left-hand side of the inequality in the proposition can be interpreted as the difference in the expected returns under direct and intermediated finance, arising because of misalignment of the investor's preferences under intermediated finance. The term $\alpha(1-\beta)$ is the probability of investment in a project about which the investor is pessimistic. The term $H-L$ is the loss that results from investing in a project the investor is pessimistic about rather than one he is optimistic about.

The term $c - c/I$ on the right-hand side is the difference in the information costs of direct and intermediated finance. The inequality makes clear the trade-off involved in the two types of finance. It indicates that the factors that determine the form of finance that is preferred are as follows:

1. The ex ante degree of optimism, α.
2. The diversity of opinion, $1-\beta$.
3. The riskiness of the project, $H-L$.
4. The cost of information c and the number of people I.

An increase in the degree of ex ante optimism α, ceteris paribus, makes it more likely that market finance will dominate intermediated finance. An increase in α increases the left-hand side term of equation 13.5, $\alpha H - c$, by H, but it raises the right-hand side by only $\beta H + (1-\beta)L < H$. The higher the degree of ex ante optimism, the greater the expected payoff is when an investment is market financed, because everybody who is an investor is optimistic. On the other hand, with intermediated finance only a portion of investors agree with the managers' decision, and so the increase in the expected payoff to the investors is less.

The higher the degree of diversity of opinion $1-\beta$, ceteris paribus, the more likely it is that market finance is preferred. The payoff from direct or market finance (the left-hand side of equation 13.5) is independent of β, and the payoff from intermediated finance (the right-hand side of equation 13.5) is increasing in β, so there will be some critical value β^*, depending on the other parameters, such that market finance is preferred if $\beta < \beta^*$ and intermediated finance is preferred if $\beta > \beta^*$. When people disagree, markets work well because only those people who are optimistic end up investing, so the expected payoff of investors is high. In intermediated finance, investors rationally anticipate that there is a significant chance they would disagree with the manager who actually makes the decision. Of course, they do not actually acquire the information before the investment decision because it would be costly, so a disagreement does not occur at that time.

An increase in risk as measured by $H - L$, ceteris paribus, increases the left-hand side term $\alpha(1-\beta)(H-L)$ in the condition in proposition 13.1 but leaves the right-hand side term $c - c/I$ unaffected, so it makes market finance more likely to be preferred. With market finance, only upside risk H matters because only optimists invest. However, with intermediated finance, both upside and downside risk matter because the manager may invest even when an investor disagrees with his view. As a result, an increase in $H - L$ makes intermediated finance relatively less attractive.

The greater the cost of acquiring information c, and the larger the number of people required to provide finance I, ceteris paribus, the more likely it is that intermediated finance will be preferred. The whole advantage of intermediated finance is that it allows information costs to be shared by delegating the decision to the manager, while market finance requires everybody to become informed. The larger c and I are the greater the benefit from sharing the cost. An increase in c increases the right-hand side of the condition in proposition 13.1 but leaves the left-hand side unaffected, so there is a critical value c^* such that market finance is preferred if $c < c^*$ and intermediated finance is preferred if $c > c^*$. Of course, if the cost of information is high enough, it may be optimal to invest without information or it may be optimal not to invest at all.

In order to see the operation of the model consider example 1: $H = 10$; $L = -10$; $\delta = 0.5$; $\alpha = 0.5$; $I = 3$. The trade-off between diversity of opinion, β, and the cost of information, c, in the context of this example is illustrated in figure 13.4. Given $\delta = 0.5$, α is independent of γ and remains fixed at 0.5. As γ varies between 0.5 and 1, β also varies between 0.5 and 1. The first thing to note is that

$$V_U = 0.5 \times 10 + 0.5 \times (-10) = 0.$$

Hence there is no uninformed finance in this case. When there is significant diversity of opinion (i.e., β close to 0.5) and the cost of information is high, there will be no finance for the project rather than uninformed finance. This outcome occurs in the bottom right-hand region. Market finance occurs in the bottom left-hand region when diversity of opinion is high and the cost of information is low. Now

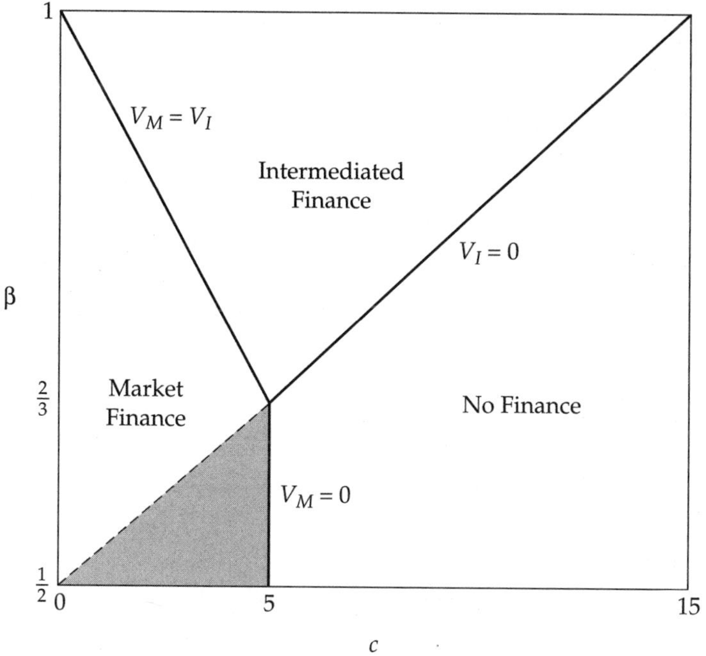

Figure 13.4
Optimal financing methods (example 1)

$$V_M = 0.5 \times 10 - c = 5 - c,$$

so the boundary between the market and no finance regions $V_M = 0$ is

$$c = 5.$$

Also,

$$V_I = 0.5[\beta 10 + (1 - \beta)(-10)] - \frac{c}{3} = 10\beta - 5 - \frac{c}{3},$$

so the boundary between the intermediated finance and no finance regions $V_I = 0$ is

$$\beta = \frac{1}{2} + \frac{c}{30}.$$

Finally, the boundary between intermediated and market finance $V_I = V_M$ is

$$\beta = 1 - \frac{c}{15}.$$

Thus intermediated finance is optimal in the top region where there is wide agreement and costs are high.

Figure 13.4 provides a graphic summary of the circumstances in which each type of financing is optimal. Market finance is superior when there is diversity of opinion and costs of information are low. Intermediated finance is best when costs of information are high and there is not much diversity of opinion. The project is not financed if there is diversity of opinion and costs of information are high.

The effect of increasing the ex ante degree of optimism α on figure 13.4 can easily be seen. When α is included explicitly, the three boundaries—$V_M = 0$, $V_I = 0$, $V_I = V_M$—become, respectively,

$$c = 10\alpha, \; \beta = \frac{1}{2} + \frac{c}{60\alpha}, \; \beta = 1 - \frac{c}{30\alpha}.$$

It follows that as α increases, the $V_M = 0$ boundary shifts to the right, the $V_I = 0$ boundary rotates downward, and the $V_I = V_M$ boundary rotates upward. The intersection of the three boundaries always occurs at $\beta = 2/3$. Hence the area where market finance is used increases, as does the area where intermediated finance is used. The area where no finance is made available shrinks. This change is illustrated in figure 13.5 with the higher value of α being represented by the dotted lines.

Next consider what happens if the degree of risk $H - L$ is increased. The simplest way to do this is to set $L = -H$ and increase H. Returning to the original values of the other parameters, the three boundaries $V_M = 0$, $V_I = 0$, and $V_I = V_M$ now become, respectively,

$$c = 0.5H, \; \beta = \frac{1}{2} + \frac{c}{3H}, \; \beta = 1 - \frac{2c}{3H}.$$

It can be seen that the effect of increasing risk is similar to the effect of increasing α. The changes can again be illustrated by the dotted lines in figure 13.5. The use of markets and intermediated finance is increased, while the circumstances where the project is not financed are reduced.

The remaining parameter is the number of people in the consortium, I. Obviously the $V_M = 0$ boundary is unchanged. The boundaries for $V_I = 0$ and $V_I = V_M$ now become, respectively,

$$\beta = \frac{1}{2} + \frac{c}{10I}, \; \beta = 1 - (1 - \frac{1}{I})\frac{c}{10}.$$

Both boundaries rotate downward as the number of people in the consortium is increased. As might be expected, the use of intermediated

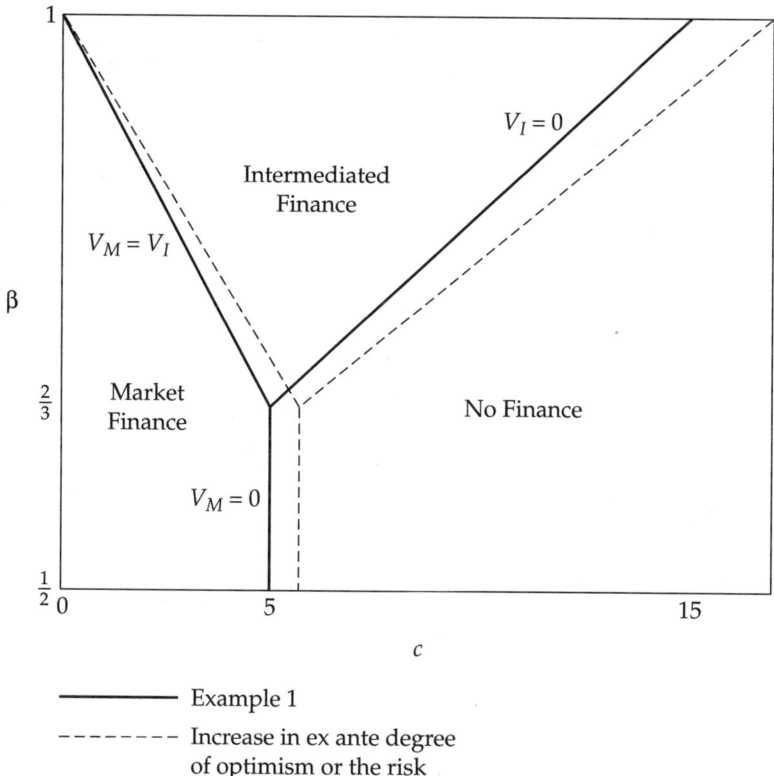

Figure 13.5
Effect of increasing the ex ante degree of optimism and the risk in example 1

finance increases, while market finance is used less. The no finance area is also smaller. The new boundaries are illustrated by the dotted lines in figure 13.6. As one might expect, increasing the size of the consortium increases the effectiveness of intermediaries.

It has so far been assumed that the optimal type of finance is used—market finance if that is superior and intermediated finance if that is superior. As indicated in chapter 3, the institutional settings in many countries are such that both systems do not exist side by side. For example, in Germany the possibilities for most companies to access capital markets are nonexistent or very limited. There are a number of possible explanations for the absence of markets, including government regulation or fixed costs that prevent markets from developing. One important implication of the analysis underlying proposition 13.1 is that if

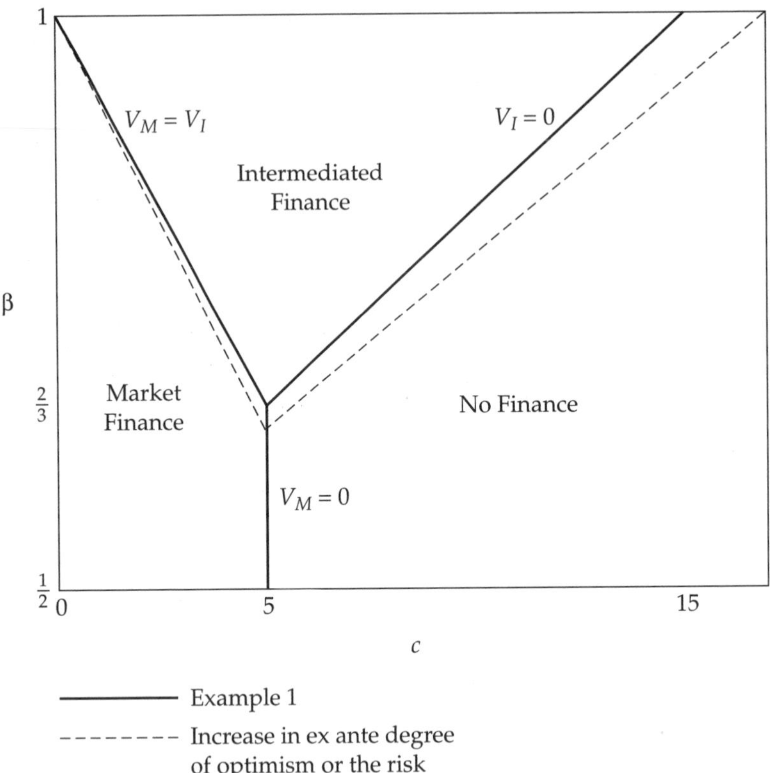

Figure 13.6
Effect of increasing the number of people in the intermediary in example 1

intermediated finance is used not because it is superior but because market finance has been artificially discouraged, innovative technologies where there is diversity of opinion and a high degree of risk is involved may be underfunded. In the context of example 1, an intermediary-based financial system would not fund projects in the shaded area in figure 13.4. In contrast, a market-based financial system would provide finance for these projects. This suggests that ensuring market finance is available can be important for establishing new high-technology industries where there is significant diversity of opinion and costs of becoming informed. The welfare properties of the model are discussed further in the context of a more fully developed model below. However, this observation is of interest from a positive perspec-

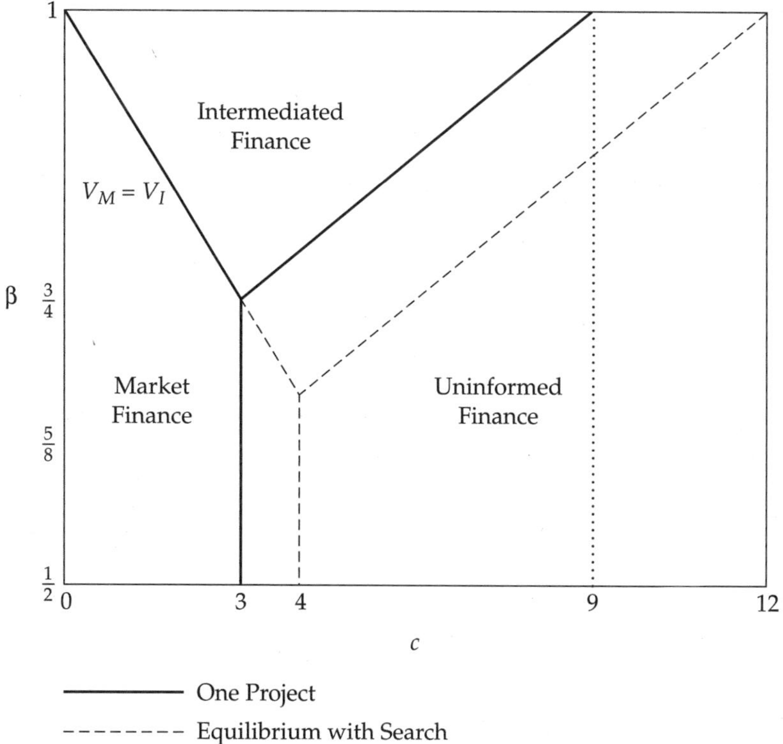

Figure 13.7
Optimal financing methods (example 2)

tive. Casual empiricism suggests that market-based financial systems do seem to be fairly effective at funding innovation.

Example 1 had the special feature that uninformed finance was not worthwhile. Now consider example 2, which is exactly like example 1 except $L = -6$. In this case

$$V_U = 0.5 \times 10 + 0.5 \times (-6) = 2.$$

The analysis is the same as before except now the best alternative is uninformed finance rather than no finance. The optimality of market and intermediated finance compared to uninformed finance is shown in figure 13.7. The effects of changing the other parameters are similar to those for example 1. Figure 13.7 illustrates that the difference between uninformed finance and no finance is not material in this context. It will be seen below that this is not the case when search is introduced.

13.4 Equilibrium

In the previous section, we analyzed the problem of choosing between direct finance and intermediated finance when there was a single project to be funded. Now we extend the analysis to a market in which there are many projects to be funded. This raises new questions and requires us to develop an account of search equilibrium where investors and projects are matched. We make the following assumptions to do this:

- There is a continuum of ex ante identical projects with the parameters (α, β).
- The number (measure) of consumers is MI, so that the total number of projects that can be funded is M, and the number (measure) of projects is $N > M$.

Since the number of projects is larger than the number that can possibly be financed, the investors will receive all the surplus and the entrepreneurs will receive their opportunity cost of zero for their projects. The investors' payoffs will be maximized in competitive equilibrium, subject to the entrepreneurs' participation constraint.

Because there is an excess supply of projects and the investors who have acquired information have heterogeneous beliefs about their profitability, investors must search in equilibrium to find the project they would like to invest in. To simplify the analysis, we impose assumptions that guarantee that the environment remains stationary over time:

- There is a sequence of dates $t = 1, 2, \ldots$ and at each date there is a continuum of N projects characterized by the parameters (α, β, c) and a continuum of MI identical investors. To keep the population of projects constant, we assume that as soon as a project is funded, it is replaced by an identical project. Similarly, to keep the population of investors constant, we assume that as soon as an investor funds a project, he is replaced by an identical investor.
- Entrepreneurs are passive. They simply allow investors to investigate the project and fund it when enough willing subscribers have been found.
- An investor can investigate one project per period and continues to search until he finds a project that he wants to finance. There is no

discounting, so investors are indifferent about how long it takes to find a project, but we assume that they do not delay unnecessarily.

- Investors, individually or in consortiums, are randomly matched with projects. Since there are more projects than can be financed with the available capital, every investor who wants to invest can find some project to invest in.

Generically there will be one optimal method of finance in equilibrium, so we only need to consider two types of equilibria: one with market finance and one with intermediated finance.

Equilibrium with a Single Project Type

Since there are many projects and any informed investor is optimistic about a given project with probability α, every investor will be optimistic about a fraction α of the projects, though he does not know ex ante which projects those are. This means that if an investor is pessimistic about one project after becoming informed, he can search for another, and the decision whether to become informed and whether to use market or intermediated finance will depend on the value of search. Let V^* denote the value of continuing to search in equilibrium, and suppose that an investor chooses market finance. Each time an investor evaluates a new project, a cost of c must be paid. Then his payoff will be

$$V_M = \alpha H + (1 - \alpha)V^* - c, \tag{13.6}$$

since with probability α he becomes optimistic and invests in the current project, with probability $1 - \alpha$ he becomes pessimistic and continues to search, and in either case he pays the cost c.

On the other hand, the payoff to intermediated finance is

$$V_I = \alpha(\beta H + (1 - \beta)L) + (1 - \alpha)V^* - \frac{c}{I}, \tag{13.7}$$

since with probability α the manager is optimistic and finances the project, given he finances the project the typical investor's expected return is $\beta H + (1 - \beta)L$, and with probability $(1 - \alpha)$ the manager is pessimistic and continues searching, and in any case the investor has to pay a share c/I of the cost of information.

As usual, an investor who does not finance a project gets 0, and the value assigned by an uninformed investor is

$$V_U = \alpha H + (1 - \alpha)L.$$

In an equilibrium with market finance, every investor becomes informed about a project; invests if he is optimistic and continues to search if he is pessimistic. Eventually every investor finds a project about which he is optimistic to invest in.

In order to describe the equilibrium in detail, we need to identify the decision that allows investors to achieve the equilibrium payoff $V^* = \max\{0, V_U, V_M, V_I\}$. From equation 13.6, it is clear that $V^* = V_M$ if and only if

$$V_M = H - \frac{c}{\alpha}.$$

Comparing this with the value of the project with market finance in the previous section in equation 13.1, it can be seen that the value is higher (provided it is positive). The reason is that every investor undertaking search will inevitably find a project that he is optimistic about. The expected payoff therefore rises from αH to H. In addition, costs are higher because on average, information will have to be acquired $1/\alpha$ times, but this effect is less than the increase in expected revenue provided the project has positive value.

Similarly, from equation 13.7, it is clear that $V^* = V_I$ if and only if

$$V_I = \beta H + (1 - \beta)L - \frac{c}{\alpha I}.$$

Again this is higher than the value in equation 13.3 because the investor knows the intermediary will fund a project for sure and will incur total expected costs of c/α so his share is $c/\alpha I$. Since the payoffs to no investment and uninformed financing are independent of V^*, we can generically characterize the equilibrium in the following proposition:

Proposition 13.2 Let V^* denote the equilibrium payoff and let

$$\hat{V}_M \equiv H - \frac{c}{\alpha}$$

$$\hat{V}_I \equiv \beta H + (1 - \beta)L - \frac{c}{\alpha I}.$$

Then, in any equilibrium, we have

$$V^* = \max\{0, V_U, \hat{V}_M, \hat{V}_I\},$$

and the optimal decision is no financing if $V^* = 0$, uninformed financing if $V^* = V_U$, market financing if $V^* = \hat{V}_M$, and intermediated financing if $V^* = \hat{V}_I$.

The proposition can be illustrated in terms of example 1 from the previous section. The expressions for the values of the projects with the different types of finance are the same as before except they are divided through by α. The boundaries are identical to those in figure 13.4. To see this, note that for the boundary between market finance and intermediated finance, both sides are divided by α, so it cancels. With the boundaries between market and no finance and between intermediated and no finance, the comparisons are with 0, so the α again drops out. The comparative statics of changing the other parameters are also similar to the previous section. When the best alternative is uninformed finance, as in example 2, there is a difference. Here the comparison of market and intermediated finance is with uninformed finance, which has a payoff of $V_U = 2$. Now the fact that the expressions are divided by α is significant and the boundaries are marked by the dotted lines rather than the solid lines shown in figure 13.7.

For simplicity, it was assumed that each time a new project was investigated, the investor or intermediary had to pay a cost c. This is the simplest case. Another possibility is to assume that acquiring information about the industry costs c_0, while investigating each project costs an additional amount c_1. Incorporating this change or some other cost structure for acquiring information will not alter the results significantly.

An important assumption was the stationarity of the search environment. This allowed particularly simple expressions for the value of search to be derived. The model could be enriched by allowing for a number of other approaches. One possibility would be to start with a fixed number of projects and investors and to suppose that these investors cannot observe each others' actions or beliefs. Initially an investor would be unaware of whether he was in the majority or minority. He could assign probabilistic beliefs to these possibilities, but he would not know for certain. In contrast to before, there would be no replacement of projects or investors. In this case, the dynamics of the system would be much richer than before. In particular, at each stage, investors would update their probabilities that they are in the majority or minority based on their experience in finding projects. Their estimates of the quality of projects that were available after each round would also change correspondingly. In this case, even though people agree to disagree, there would nevertheless be Bayesian updating because of these changes in beliefs.

Equilibrium with Multiple Project Types

When there are many types of projects characterized by the parameters (α, β, c), a number of new issues are introduced. Some projects will be more profitable than others, but since the number of these projects is limited, the entrepreneurs who own the projects are able to collect some rents. The shadow price of each project and the equilibrium payoff to the investors are jointly determined in equilibrium by the marginal type of project that is just worth financing.

The way that the investment process works here is that investors acquire information, and if they become optimistic and wish to invest, they have to provide p_k to the owner of a project of type k as well as the capital needed for the investment. The net price p_k is expressed in per capita terms, so the total revenue to an entrepreneur from I investors is $p_k I$.

Suppose that there are K different types of projects, $k = 1, \ldots, K$, defined by the parameters (α_k, β_k, c_k) for each k. There are N_k projects of type k and $N = \sum N_k > M$. Since projects and investors are automatically replaced as projects are financed, the total demand for finance in any period remains constant at NI and the supply remains constant at MI.

Investors, individually or in consortiums, are randomly matched with projects. The market clearing condition is that the demand for finance from entrepreneurs is equal to the supply of finance from investors. Entrepreneurs of type k will be indifferent about financing their projects if $p_k = 0$. Likewise, investors will be indifferent about supplying finance if the expected net return from the optimal form of finance is zero.

As before, the payoff to no investment is zero, and the payoff to uninformed investment in a type k project is

$$V_k^U = \alpha_k H + (1 - \alpha_k)L - p_k.$$

Let V^* denote the equilibrium payoff for the typical investor. Market financing of type k projects yields

$$V_k^M = \alpha_k(H - p_k) + (1 - \alpha_k)V^* - c_k,$$

and market finance is optimal if and only if $V^* = V_k^M$, that is,

$$V_k^M = H - p_k - \frac{c_k}{\alpha_k}.$$

Similarly, intermediated financing of a type k project yields

$$V_k^I = \alpha_k(\beta_k H + (1-\beta_k)L - p_k) + (1-\alpha_k)V^* - \frac{c_k}{I},$$

and intermediated financing is optimal if and only if $V^* = V_k^I$, that is,

$$V_k^I = \beta_k H + (1-\beta_k)L - p_k - \frac{c_k}{\alpha_k I}.$$

For any project type that does receive funding, we must have $p_k \geq 0$ and $V^* = \max\{V_k^U, V_k^M, V_k^I\}$. Let $\hat{V}_k^U = V_k^U + p_k$, $\hat{V}_k^M = V_k^M + p_k$ and $\hat{V}_k^I = V_k^I + p_k$. Then from the expressions above, it is clear that

$$p_k = \max\{\hat{V}_k^U, \hat{V}_k^M, \hat{V}_k^I\} - V^*.$$

To determine the equilibrium prices and the allocation of investments, we need only determine the equilibrium payoff for the investors V^*, since this immediately determines p_k, and that in turn tells us which projects are financed and the form of financing adopted in equilibrium.

For any value of V^*, there is a set of projects K^+ that are strictly profitable ($p_k > 0$) and a set of projects K^0 that are weakly profitable ($p_k = 0$). In order to have equilibrium in the market for firms, the number of investors searching must equal the number of profitable financing slots. This will be true if

$$\sum_{k \in K^+} N_k \leq M \leq \sum_{k \in K^+} N_k + \sum_{k \in K^0} N_k,$$

since the projects of type $k \in K^+$ must be financed and the projects of type $k \in K^0$ may or may not be financed in equilibrium. Since the price p_k is continuous and decreasing in V^*, we can find a unique value V^* such that the market-clearing inequality is satisfied if a weak profitability condition is satisfied, for example,

$$0 < \max\{V_k^U, \alpha_k \hat{V}_k^M, \alpha_k \hat{V}_k^I\},$$

for each k, or at least for enough types to provide more than M strictly profitable projects. Technically, one needs $\sum_{k \in K^+} N_k > M$ for $V^* = 0$, since individual rationality requires $V^* \geq 0$ in any equilibrium.

We can extend example 1 to illustrate how this kind of equilibrium works. In example 3, suppose that projects are identical except they possibly have different values of β_k and c_k. This means that the optimal type of finance is shown in figure 13.4. Consider first a situation with two types of project that are both optimally financed by markets and differ with regard to the degree of diversity of opinion. Example 3 is identical to example 1 except:

Project 1: $\beta_1 = 0.5$; $c_1 = 4$.

Project 2: $\beta_2 = 0.5$; $c_2 = 3$.

It can be seen from figure 13.4 that both projects will use market finance. Moreover $\hat{V}_1^M = 10 - 4/0.5 = 2$ and $\hat{V}_2^M = 10 - 3/0.5 = 4$. Here the initial owners of project 2 will earn a rent. The payments received by owners of project 1 are $p_1 = 0$ since they are the marginal project. The owners of project 2 are able to charge $p_2 = \hat{V}_2^M - \hat{V}_1^M = 4 - 2 = 2$. The investors receive a net return of $V^* = \hat{V}_1^M = 2$ from both projects.

There are, of course, many other possibilities even with only two groups. In addition to having both groups use the same method of finance it would be possible to have one using intermediated finance and the other market finance with the rents earned by entrepreneurs depending on which is the marginal project. An illustration is given in example 4 which is different from example 1 as follows:

Project 3: $\beta_3 = 2/3$; $c_3 = 4$.

Project 4: $\beta_4 = 3/4$; $c_4 = 3$.

For project 3, $\hat{V}_3^M = 10 - 4/0.5 = 2$ and $\hat{V}_3^I = (2/3)10 + (1/3)(-10) - 4/(0.5 \times 3) = 2/3$, so market finance will be used. For project 4, $\hat{V}_4^M = 10 - 5/0.5 = 0$ and $\hat{V}_4^I = (3/4)10 + (1/4)(-10) - 5/(0.5 \times 3) = 5/3$, so intermediated finance will be used. It can be seen that project 4 is the marginal project, so $p_4 = 0$. The owners of project 3 are able to charge $p_3 = 2 - 5/3 = 1/3$, and the investors receive $V^* = 5/3$.

Examples 3 and 4 illustrate two possible equilibria when there are many types of project. There are, of course, many other possible examples that could be developed. However, these two examples illustrate the main features of this type of equilibrium: the determination of the rents p_k received by the owners of the different types of project and the return received by investors V^*.

Efficiency of Equilibrium

At the initial date, all investors hold the same beliefs concerning their type. After the new industry technology has been discovered and after the investors have expended a cost to acquire information, they discover whether they are optimistic or pessimistic. This structure simplifies the welfare analysis of the model since ex ante everybody has the same expected utility. It is sufficient therefore to focus on the representative investor at the initial date.

Since all investors are risk neutral, an equilibrium is efficient if the method of financing each type of project in equilibrium maximizes the surplus. The surplus is the sum of the price paid to the entrepreneur p_k and the payoff to the typical investor. Since

$$V^* = \max\{\hat{V}_k^U, \hat{V}_k^M, \hat{V}_k^I\} - p_k,$$

the surplus from financing the project is

$$V^* + p_k = \max\{\hat{V}_k^U, \hat{V}_k^M, \hat{V}_k^I\},$$

so the method of financing is clearly chosen efficiently in equilibrium.

There is no reason to think that one method of financing will be optimal for all projects. On the contrary, different parameters (α_k, β_k, c_k) will make different types of finance optimal, as example 4 in the previous section illustrated. So a predominance of one type of financing, market or intermediated, throughout the economy is unlikely to be efficient, at least in the context of the current model. In some countries, such as Germany, there appears to be a predominance of intermediated finance. In other countries, such as the United States, markets play a more prominent role. In order to explain this phenomenon using our model, we would have to assume that the set of projects available in Germany was different from the set of projects available in the United States. This does not seem to be a very plausible explanation. At least, we have no reason to think that diversity of opinion is higher in the United States than in Germany.

There are other possible explanations, however. One is that restrictive regulations may have prevented the development of markets in Germany. Another is that fixed costs of setting up markets may result in multiple equilibria—one in which market finance predominates and another in which intermediated finance predominates (see Pagano 1993 and Subrahmanyam and Titman 1999). Once one institutional form has been established, perhaps as a result of historical accident, increasing returns to scale give it an advantage that may prevent the establishment of a competing form. In this kind of situation, there is no reason to think that the observed predominance of one form of finance is optimal. If the German financial system developed in this way, the absence of markets may represent a significant loss of welfare.

An illustration of the possible welfare loss is provided by a comparison of two economies, economy *A* and economy *B*, which are identical except for the form of financing allowed. In economy *A* only intermediated finance is allowed by regulators, whereas in economy *B* markets and intermediaries coexist. In the context of example 1 it was pointed out that under certain conditions, innovative new projects will not be financed by intermediaries but will be financed by markets. Although there is disagreement about the projects financed, the expected returns from investment will be higher in economy *B* than in economy *A*. If there is any rationality in these beliefs, it must be expected in the long run that development and technology will advance in economy *B* more than in economy *A*. Ex post utility will be improved through time. If each generation is weighted equally, then in the long run the system with markets will predominate because of technological progress. Economy *B*, which allows only intermediated finance, will stagnate at a low level of utility.

13.5 Conclusion

Allen (1993) has suggested that stock market–based economies, such as the United Kingdom in the nineteenth century and the United States in the twentieth century, have been more successful in developing new industries than intermediary-based economies such as Germany and Japan. For example, railways were first developed in the United Kingdom in the nineteenth century and were financed largely through the London Stock Exchange. In the twentieth century, the United States has been the most successful country at developing new industries. At the turn of the century, the United States successfully developed the automotive industry even though the automobile was invented in Germany. After World War I, the commercial aircraft industry was mainly developed in the United States. The United States had a similar success with the computer industry after World War II and more recently with the biotechnology industry. There are counterexamples, such as the development of the chemical industry on a large scale in nineteenth-century

Germany, but it is interesting to note that the chemical industry had existed on a small scale before, so the degree of diversity of opinion might be expected to be less than for entirely new industries.

The model developed above is consistent with these observations. Markets work well, in the sense that providers of finance anticipate high expected profits, in the development of new industries and new technologies. In such circumstances, evidence based on experience is sparse, and there is wide diversity of opinion. The riskiness of the payoffs is also high. Some new firms have very high payoffs, but most do not succeed. Finally, stock market–based economies such as the United States and United Kingdom also tend to have well-developed systems for the acquisition and distribution of information, so the cost of information is low. In contrast, the delegation employed by intermediaries does not work well when there is diversity of opinion and high risk. Investors rationally anticipate that they may well disagree with the manager and are less willing to provide funds as a result.

In addition to providing insights into the relationship between financial markets and the development of new industries and technologies, the model is consistent with the observation that intermediary-based economies such as Germany and Japan are very good at traditional industries. Recent examples in this context would be automobiles in both countries and electronics in Japan. It is precisely in these types of situation that intermediaries excel because of the economies of scale in information acquisition achieved through delegation.

It is often argued that one of the reasons the United States has been so successful in recent years in developing new industries is the existence of a strong venture capital sector. For example, Kortum and Lerner (1997) have documented a strong relationship in the United States between the extent to which venture capital is used in an industry and the rate of patenting. Venture capital should be thought of as being market finance rather than intermediated finance. It is because venture capitalists can easily cash out by selling firms in IPOs in the market that makes them willing to provide seed capital initially. The high price that can be obtained in the market is consistent with the theory in this chapter that it is only people with favorable beliefs that are providing the funding.

The difference in assumptions between the previous literature and our work is that we are not assuming common priors. In our model there is no updating when other people's beliefs are revealed because people agree to disagree. If there are common priors and the information that people have is sufficiently complex, the amount of updating may be close to zero. Another way of interpreting our model is that it is an approximation to the case of common priors but very complex information where there is almost no updating.

The delegation model of intermediation developed in this chapter is essentially a form of principal-agent model. This observation suggests that the techniques used in this chapter may be applicable in a wide range of principal-agent relationships. The basic assumption of the standard approach is that priors are common. However, in many of the standard applications, it is not at all clear that this is valid. For example, in many of the classic principal-agent relationships, such as those between doctors and patients, lawyers and clients, and managers and shareholders, there may well be diversity of opinion between different parties because of a lack of actual data. We believe that incorporating the possibility for differences in beliefs into the standard principal-agent model and its many applications is an important area for future research.

References

Allen, F. (1993). "Stock Markets and Resource Allocation." In C. Mayer and X. Vives (eds.). *Capital Markets and Financial Intermediation.* Cambridge: Cambridge University Press.

Allen, F. and D. Gale. (1999). "Diversity of Opinion and the Financing of New Technologies." *Journal of Financial Intermediation* **8,** 68–89.

Aumann, R. (1976). "Agreeing to Disagree." *Annals of Statistics* **4,** 1236–1239.

Bagehot, W. (1873). *Lombard Street.* Homewood, IL: Irwin, (1962 ed.).

Berk, J., R. Green, and V. Naik. (1997). "Valuation and Return Dynamics of R&D Ventures." Working paper, (GSIA), Carnegie Mellon University.

Bhattacharya, S., and G. Chiesa. (1995). "Financial Intermediation with Proprietary Information." *Journal of Financial Intermediation* **4,** 328–357.

Boot, A., and A. Thakor. (1997a). "Financial System Architecture." *Review of Financial Studies* **10,** 693–733.

———. (1997b). "Banking Scope and Financial Innovation." *Review of Financial Studies* **10,** 1099–1131.

Diamond, P. (1967). "The Role of a Stock Market in a General Equilibrium Model with Technological Uncertainty." *American Economic Review* **57,** 759–776.

Geanakoplos, J., and H. Polemarchakis. (1982). "We Can't Disagree Forever." *Journal of Economic Theory* **28,** 192–200.

Gerschenkron, A. (1968). *Continuity in History and Other Essays.* Cambridge, MA: Harvard University Press.

Greenwood, J., and B. Jovanovic. (1990). "Financial Development, Growth, and the Distribution of Income." *Journal of Political Economy* **98,** 1076–1107.

Harris, M., and A. Raviv. (1993). "Differences of Opinion Make a Horse Race." *Review of Financial Studies* **6,** 473–506.

Hicks, J. (1969). *A Theory of Economic History.* Oxford: Clarendon Press.

Kandel, E., and N. Pearson. (1995). "Differential Interpretation of Public Signals and Trade in Speculative Markets." *Journal of Political Economy* **103,** 831–872.

Kortum, S., and J. Lerner. (1997). "Does Venture Capital Spur Innovation?" Working paper, Harvard University.

Levine, R. (1997). "Financial Development and Economic Growth: Views and Agenda." *Journal of Economic Literature* **35,** 688–726.

Lintner, J. (1965). "Security Prices, Risk, and Maximal Gains from Diversification." *Journal of Finance* **20,** 587–615.

Lucas, R., Jr. (1988). "On the Mechanics of Economic Development." *Journal of Monetary Economics* **22,** 3–42.

McKelvey, R., and T. Page. (1986). "Common Knowledge, Consensus, and Aggregate Information." *Econometrica* **54,** 109–128.

McKinnon, R. (1973). *Money and Capital in Economic Development.* Washington, D.C.: Brookings Institution.

Morris, S. (1995). "The Common Prior Assumption in Economic Theory." *Economics and Philosophy* **11,** 227–253.

Pagano, M. (1993). "The Flotation of Companies on the Stock Market: A Coordination Failure Model." *European Economic Review* **37,** 1101–1125.

Robinson, J. (1952). "The Generalization of the General Theory." In *The Rate of Interest, and Other Essays* (pp. 67–142). London: Macmillan.

Ross, S. (1976). "The Arbitrage Theory of Capital Asset Pricing." *Journal of Economic Theory* **13,** 341–360.

Stern, N. (1989). "The Economics of Development: A Survey." *Economic Journal* **99,** 597–685.

Subrahmanyam, A., and S. Titman. (1999). "The Going Public Decision and the Development of Financial Markets." *Journal of Finance* **54,** 1045–1082.

Thakor, A. (1996), "The Design of Financial Systems: An Overview." *Journal of Banking and Finance* **20,** 917–948.

Yosha, O. (1995). "Information Disclosure Costs and the Choice of Financing Source." *Journal of Financial Intermediation* **4,** 3–20.

14 Costly Markets

In an earlier book, *Financial Innovation and Risk Sharing*, we pointed out that despite the enormous pace of financial innovation in the 1980s, the opportunities for hedging many of the risks that affect individuals most directly have been largely unaffected. The risk of unemployment, of drastic changes in the value of one's home, of inflation, and of changes in the value of one's human capital cannot be hedged on any of the markets introduced in the last fifteen years. There are good reasons that such markets do not exist—reasons having to do with moral hazard, adverse selection, and transaction costs—but the fact remains that in terms of financial innovation, we have a long way to go before we achieve the complete set of markets envisioned in the ADM model.

In his recent book, *Macro Markets: Creating Institutions for Managing Society's Largest Economic Risks*, Robert J. Shiller makes a similar point: "The major economic risks that our society faces are dealt with individually: each person bears his or her own misfortunes. Society does share some risks, such as risks of natural disaster, medical emergencies, or temporary unemployment; society takes care of many sudden or extreme misfortunes. Still, most of the risk that individuals face about their lifetime well-being is not shared. We allow our standards of living to be determined substantially by a game of chance." He goes on to argue that creating markets for securities to hedge risks such as changes in the value of real estate, or changes in the level of national, regional, or occupational incomes, is in fact a practical undertaking, which would lead to a significant improvement in the welfare of individuals by allowing them to hedge the major risks that affect their lives.

Much of Shiller's book is concerned with technical issues, such as the definition of indexes on which the futures, options, swaps, and other forward contracts would be based. Some more fundamental issues, such as the economic obstacles to the existence or efficient operation of these markets, are given less attention. We focus here on what is perhaps one of the most important barriers: the knowledge required to use these markets effectively. One of the biggest obstacles to the effective hedging of risk is the difficulty of making effective decisions. Taking into account the cost of gathering and processing information and the sophistication required to make optimal hedging decisions, it is not clear that individuals will be able to use macro and other markets effectively to hedge their individual risks.

In this chapter and in chapter 15, we make an important distinction between a system in which individuals participate directly in markets and one in which intermediaries provide insurance contracts to individuals and use markets to reinsure the risks they have incurred. Obviously direct participation requires a certain sophistication on the part of individuals, and it may be beyond the capacity of the average person to develop an adequate hedging strategy. In that case, intermediation by financial institutions may be an essential ingredient to ensure that firms and individuals can benefit from markets. The markets for options, futures, indexes, and swaps that grew so enormously in the 1980s are used by financial professionals to hedge risks that arise naturally in their business of managing portfolios of stocks, bonds and securitized loans, mortgages, and receivables. If macro markets are used exclusively by professionals, for the purpose of laying off the risks incurred in providing insurance to ordinary individuals, then Shiller's scheme would seem to be much more practical: with sophisticated professionals forecasting and analyzing the macro risks involved and packaging insurance in the form of simple contracts that ordinary individuals can understand, it seems that macro markets might make a significant contribution to risk sharing.

However, even with the help of intermediaries, there is a difficulty in providing insurance against the risk of changes in national or industrial income or changes in house prices. This kind of insurance requires a different kind of economic calculation from the life or casualty insurance with which most of us have some experience. When an individual purchases insurance against the possibility of her house burning down, she is insuring against an unlikely event with fairly precisely specified parameters. The purpose of the policy is to offset or make whole the damage that she will suffer in this singular event. Once she has the insurance, she does not have to worry about the risk of fire or consequent fluctuations in her standard of living. Deciding whether and how much insurance she wants is a nontrivial, but feasible, task for the average householder.

Now consider the use of insurance against fluctuations in the value of housing. Housing is a very lumpy asset, and because of the moral hazard problem (an owner-occupier will maintain and care for his house better than someone who does not have a substantial equity stake), most house owners are underdiversified with respect to their equity position in real estate. There are several reasons why someone might want insurance against fluctuations in property values. A person who has not yet bought a house may want to insure against increases in the price of real estate. A person who has just purchased a house may want to insure against fluctuations in the value of his equity, or he may want to insure against the possibility of having to move to another area after there has been an adverse change in the relative costs of housing in the two areas. Unfortunately, the contracts traded in macro markets will not ensure the value of the owner's house or a particular house that he would like to buy. On the contrary, the macro market will insure only against fluctuations in aggregate indexes. There are two reasons that this must be so. First, only a market based on some broad index will have the depth needed to guarantee liquidity. Second, moral hazard and adverse selection will make it impossible to offer insurance on individual assets, whose value depends critically on the actions taken by the owner and on information available only to the owner. Because a macro market is based on a macro index—say, the value of the average house sold in the northeastern United States—the relationship between the value of the index and the risks to be hedged by the individual are complex and changeable. Unlike the case of fire insurance, the consequences of insuring against fluctuations in the value of property are not very clear. However simple the contract offered by the intermediary, the individual is effectively buying a derivative of a macro index and bears the responsibility of deciding what position or portfolio of positions to take in these securities in order to hedge his risks optimally. What is the statistical relationship between the index and the derivative? What is the statistical relationship between the derivative and the risks that the individual wants to hedge? How do these relationships change over time? How often does the individual need to alter his position, and how does he predict the movements of the index and other relevant variables? These questions make the use of macro markets, even with the help of an intermediary, sound more like trading in sophisticated financial markets than buying property and casualty insurance.

Furthermore, this is not a decision that can easily be delegated, for a number of reasons: the principal-agent relationship between the individual and her financial adviser, the private information the individual has, which may be hard to communicate to the intermediary, and the expense of hiring an adviser.

Similar comments apply to the difficulty of using macro markets based on indexes of national income or industry sales to hedge individual risks. However these indexes are packaged, there remains a highly nontrivial, dynamic, portfolio choice problem for the individual to solve. In principle, the individual can solve this problem, just as he does in the ADM model with complete markets. In practice, the costs of using markets, which are essentially costs of acquiring and processing information, may make these markets impractical.

These comments concerning the viability of macro markets for hedging individual risk also have significant relevance for financial markets that do exist. Often a great deal of sophistication is required to transact in them. One of the most important differences between market-based and intermediary-based financial systems is the difference in the costs of using the financial instruments they offer. At one extreme, bank accounts are particularly simple to use. Bonds, particularly those issued by governments, are easier to understand than equities. At the other extreme, derivatives markets are quite difficult to use. In chapter 3 we noted that in Japan, a high proportion of assets are held in the form of bank accounts, which have low information costs. In the United States, a large amount of equity is held directly by individuals, and the information costs of equity are high. Unfortunately, there is no well-developed theory of costly markets, but it is clearly an important issue to consider when comparing financial systems.

In this chapter we make some initial attempts to model the costs of using markets. We make the classical assumption that individuals invest directly in markets, without the help of intermediaries. In chapter 15 we consider the difficulties of using intermediation to overcome some of the informational problems of operating successfully in complex markets.

14.1 Viability of Markets

One of the first issues that must be faced when the costs of markets are introduced is the fact that however the markets are designed, their operating characteristics are to a greater or lesser extent endogenous.

There may be good equilibria and bad equilibria. Since some of the costs of establishing a market are in the nature of fixed costs, it requires a certain minimum size to make the market successful. If the contract traded is not properly designed, the market will not attract enough volume to cover its fixed costs, and it will not survive long. However, even if the contract is well designed, there may be equilibria in which the market does not provide an effective hedge.

One aspect of this problem, first analyzed by Pagano (1989), concerns liquidity. Liquidity in Pagano's theory is equivalent to market depth. Suppose that every trader's demand for the asset is subject to some idiosyncratic liquidity shock. These shocks will be incorporated in the equilibrium asset price, which will tend to be more volatile than information about asset returns would predict. However, if the liquidity shocks are independent across agents and the number of agents is large, the law of large numbers ensures that the aggregate effect of these liquidity shocks will be small relative to the aggregate demand for the asset. As a result, when there is a large number of traders active in the market, the asset-price volatility attributable to liquidity shocks will be small and the market will be relatively liquid. Thus, depth produces liquidity.

The causality runs both ways, however. The willingness of traders to enter the market depends on the liquidity of the market. If the market is illiquid, that is, if the volatility of the asset price is very high, some investors will not want to hold the asset. This raises the possibility of multiple equilibria. If the market is expected to be illiquid, few traders will participate, and because the market lacks depth, the asset price will be sensitive to liquidity shocks. In this way, the expectation of low liquidity can become a self-fulfilling prophecy. By the same token, if liquidity is expected to be high, a large number of traders will participate, the market will have greater depth, and the liquidity shocks will tend to cancel out, justifying the expectation of high liquidity.

Thus, even if there exists an equilibrium in which an asset market attracts large numbers of traders and achieves a high degree of liquidity, there may be other equilibria in which the market fails to be used by most potential traders. In extreme cases, the lack of sufficient liquidity may cause the market to close.

Allen and Gale (1994) have investigated a related phenomenon, which depends not on the number of traders but rather on the types of traders who choose to participate. Because most important markets involve large numbers of traders, it seems unlikely at first glance that liquidity shocks are a crucial determinant of asset price volatility. However, different traders will hold different portfolios and, in particular, will want portfolios with different degrees of liquidity, where liquidity is identified with the proportion of liquid assets, such as cash, held in those portfolios, rather than the number of traders in the market. The crucial assumption in the Allen and Gale theory is that participating in markets is costly and that traders cannot change their participation quickly in response to information about prices. In the short run, which is relevant for price fluctuations, only the traders who are already participating in markets are able to react quickly to stabilize prices. Further, the ability of these agents to stabilize prices depends on their own liquidity. If they hold large cash positions, they will be able to offset sudden waves of selling by buying an undervalued asset. If they are illiquid, they will be able to do nothing. How much of the liquid asset these traders have in their portfolios depends on their liquidity preference, that is, the likelihood that they will need liquidity for their own purposes. Different types of traders have different degrees of liquidity preference, and the composition of the market will therefore affect the liquidity of the market as a whole.

Again, there is a possibility of sustaining multiple equilibria because of the self-fulfilling expectation of different degrees of liquidity. If the market is expected to be illiquid, in the sense of having high asset-price volatility, only traders with a low liquidity preference will enter. Since these agents have low liquidity preference, they hold a small fraction of their wealth in the form of liquid assets, and so they are not able to smooth the fluctuations in asset prices caused by liquidity shocks when they arise. Conversely, if the market is expected to be liquid, other types of traders, who have high liquidity preference, will participate in the market. Because these traders have a higher liquidity preference, they hold a larger fraction of their wealth in the form of liquid assets, so the market becomes more liquid and the volatility of asset prices is correspondingly smaller.

Another possible source of market failure is explored by Gale (1992), this time related to the informational costs of participating in markets. If potential investors have to pay a fixed cost to acquire information about a new security, they may decide to trade a security without becoming informed. In that case, they bear greater risk, and the price they are willing to pay will be lower than it would be in the presence of better information. Now suppose that there is a fixed cost of issuing a security or opening a market. Then if the price of the security is low, because investors have not become informed, the issuer may decide not to issue the security or the market organizer may decide not to open the market.

Gale (1992) relates this phenomenon to a coordination failure in the design of new securities. In order to generate this failure, information must be of a particular kind. First, the information required is idiosyncratic to individuals. Second, the information they require is generic, in the sense that it relates not to a single security but rather to whole classes of securities. For example, individuals may have different risks to hedge. In that case, in order to evaluate the security they will need to know the correlation between the returns of the security they are thinking of purchasing and their own individual risk. This information is clearly idiosyncratic, since each individual's risks are different, and it is generic to different securities, to the extent that once one has identified one's personal risk factors, one is able to use that information to evaluate a range of securities. Similarly, consider the problem of acquiring information about accounting practices or company law or general investment principles. This information is, almost by definition, generic, and it is idiosyncratic in the sense that each individual has to acquire the information at some personal cost. No one can give me this information for free.

The characteristic of idiosyncraticity guarantees that investors cannot economize by sharing the costs of acquiring information, and, in particular, they cannot acquire this information by observing prices. The characteristic of genericity ensures that the incentive to become informed depends on the availability of a whole class of securities, not just one. Because of risk aversion, investors will want to diversify. If few securities of a particular type are available, they may not be able to diversify. They may still hold a small quantity of the securities that are issued, and so avoid exposing themselves to a significant risk, but in that case the amount of the security they hold will not justify the investment in generic information needed to evaluate the security.

The factors discussed can be used to demonstrate the existence of multiple equilibria sustained by self-fulfilling beliefs when markets are costly. If many securities of a given class are simultaneously issued, or if many markets of a given type are simultaneously opened, the potential investors will find it worthwhile to invest in generic information, they will be able to evaluate securities appropriately, and the prices of securities will be high enough to justify the initial issues or market openings. On the other hand, if the securities are not issued or the markets are not opened, potential investors will not become informed, the anticipated prices of securities will remain too low to justify the initial issues or market openings, and their initial pessimism becomes self-justifying.

14.2 Information and the Uncertainty Premium

Shiller (1993) considers whether individuals would be willing to use the macro markets he proposes in order to hedge their risks. The evidence is mixed: some kinds are readily purchased by most individuals (life insurance, casualty insurance), but other kinds of insurance are ignored (e.g., disability insurance), and undiversified risks are the rule in real estate. Of course, there are many reasons that individuals may choose some types of insurance and not others; cost and availability may be a factor in some cases. The lumpiness of housing makes it difficult for individuals to diversify their home equity positions, and the moral hazard problem and favorable tax treatment make it advantageous to be an owner in spite of the risk. Nonetheless, it seems intuitively plausible that even if more hedging opportunities were available, there would still be some reluctance on the part of individuals to diversify or hedge because of a lack of information about portfolio choice techniques and the benefits of diversification and hedging. Many individuals may purchase insurance with limited knowledge of the nature of the transaction. In more complex decisions, where some sophisticated knowledge is required, it may be impossible for them to make the necessary decisions. For example, it is easy to reach the conclusion that one needs life insurance because everyone else has it. Likewise, one can adopt some rule of thumb offered by a neighbor or an insurance agent about the relationship between one's income and the optimal amount of life insurance. Relating the balance of income and growth funds in one's personal portfolio to one's planning horizon is more difficult, but still the individual may be able to rely on rules of thumb that cover a broad class of individual circumstances. But hedging against fluctuations in housing prices or interest rate changes is much more complex, and it is not clear that individuals will be able to take an active role in hedging these risks. This leaves us with the question of what an individual is to do and how a decision is to be arrived at.

The classical theory of rational expectations equilibrium (REE) (Lucas 1972, Radner 1979) makes very different assumptions about individuals' abilities to process information. In the theory of REE, agents are assumed to be able to infer information about asset returns from asset prices. In fact, under certain circumstances, all the relevant information can be inferred from prices. This is a very strong result, and, not surprisingly, some strong assumptions are needed to obtain it. Two particular assumptions are of interest here. First, it is assumed that agents have a large amount of general information to start with. Each agent receives a private signal, but in order to make use of this signal, he also needs to know the joint distribution of the signal and the asset returns. Similarly, in order to infer information about asset returns from the equilibrium asset prices, an agent needs to know the mapping from agents' signals to prices. This relationship depends on preferences, endowments, and information structures. Finally, in case there exist multiple REEs, the agent needs to know which equilibrium he is in. While an agent in a rational expectations equilibrium may not require strictly all of this information, it is hard to think of a smaller information set that would suffice in all circumstances. If this prior information is not available to agents or is not common knowledge, it is not clear that the fully revealing REE is an appropriate model.

A second important assumption is that all the agents are interested in the same information. This may seem innocuous—after all, who wouldn't be interested in knowing the returns of the assets being traded—but it is easy to imagine situations in which different agents are interested in quite different kinds of information. Suppose that agents want to hedge some idiosyncratic risks, for example, their future incomes from employment. Then each agent will want to know the correlation between the return to a particular asset and his own labor income. Or it may be that different agents have different theories about how the world works, different world views, in which case they may process information differently and draw different conclusions from the same data. Under these conditions, not all the relevant information may be revealed by prices.

How should markets be modeled when investors do not have the initial information assumed by the REE theory? One possibility is that there is an uncertainty premium that discourages investors from participating in markets with which they are unfamiliar. This is not a concept that makes sense in the usual REE framework. An agent who has a well-defined prior probability distribution over the returns to some asset should always be willing to take a nonzero position (long or short) regardless of the risk or his degree of risk aversion. If there are fixed transaction costs or short sales are not allowed, then sufficiently high variance of asset returns may discourage an investor from taking a nonzero position in the asset. Similar reticence can be explained by appealing to theories of nonexpected utility maximization (Dow and Werlang 1992, Mukerji and Tallon 1998). Even so, if we believe that agents have well-defined (and sensible) priors and can infer information easily from prices and other signals, it may be hard to convince ourselves that the empirical magnitudes are consistent with the existence of a significant uncertainty premium. On the other hand, if we believe that agents are genuinely uncertain—they do not know enough to engage in Bayesian inference, and are therefore unable to infer information from publicly available signals—the idea of an uncertainty premium becomes more plausible. This uncertainty premium may be an important obstacle to participation in markets.

In the remainder of this chapter, we offer some suggestions for describing and analyzing the costs of making difficult decisions in markets. We do not have a complete theory to offer; in fact, we offer only some simple examples. But we think they shed some light on the issues of interest. The conclusion to which we tentatively come is that there may be substantial barriers to the effective use of markets and that other kinds of institutions may have a role to play.

14.3 Random Search

It is a truism that markets provide information, but it is less often remarked that in order to make use of the information provided by markets, economic agents need to have a great deal of information to start with. The classical model of REE is not an isolated case. Models of incomplete information typically assume that agents know a great deal about the structure of the economy and the equilibrium strategies in order to infer a relatively small amount of information from prices or other endogenous variables. This is true of models of principal-agent relationships, adverse selection, markets for experience goods, and many other examples.

In practice, agents often have much less information than this. Think of a naive investor who is confronted for the first time with the bewildering variety of securities traded in financial markets. Even a sophisticated investor is uncertain about the value of these securities, because she cannot perfectly predict the returns of the underlying assets. The naive investor faces an additional source of uncertainty because he is unfamiliar with the securities, the markets, the behavior of the traders, and the underlying assets. Prices will not tell this investor the difference between an interest rate future and a convertible bond. This is information that he must acquire before he trades, perhaps at considerable cost. Moreover, much of this information takes the form of education or general knowledge. For example, it is easy for a sophisticated investor to assimilate the information in a stock's beta. An unsophisticated investor, with no knowledge of statistics or the CAPM, may not be able to make any use of this information. Another problem for the naive investor is that until he has some general knowledge and training, he does not really know what information he needs. A framework for organizing information about the securities available is extremely valuable, perhaps essential, even if it takes the form of charting or some other investment philosophy.

Our basic point is that the assumption implicit in most models of equilibrium with incomplete information—that agents know the structure of the model and can observe all but a small set of exogenous variables—is inappropriate in some important situations. We need to recognize that there are situations in which agents have very limited information to start with, and this affects how they go about acquiring the information they need in order to make a rational decision. Consider the naive investor who is faced with a large number of mutual funds to choose from and scant information on which to base his choice. He may know little more than the names of the funds and a few adjectives that the marketing department has chosen to attract his attention. He really has no idea where to begin his search or what he is likely to find. Furthermore, even after he has begun to learn about some of the funds available, he may have only fragmentary knowledge about some of the other funds available, in which case his continuing search may not be very systematic.

All of this argues for a model of information acquisition that departs from the Bayesian ideal of a maximizing agent with a well-defined prior over every relevant variable. On the other hand, without adopting a Bayesian approach, it is very hard to model the investor's decision in a precise way. The compromise adopted in this chapter is to accept Bayesian decision making, but to make the process of information acquisition more costly. In particular, we want to get away from the assumption that the investor's prior gives him a lot of free information about the securities that he trades. Formally, this is achieved by assuming that an investor searches randomly for information about the set of securities available in the market. Each time he samples a security, he learns the expected utility that he will get from that security, but the randomness of his search scrambles his prior information in a way that makes it unusable for guiding his future search. This means that the investor cannot easily exploit the information encoded in his prior distribution over the characteristics of different securities. He may know that there are good securities but does not know where to find them. If the market situation in which investors find themselves is too complex, and too many choices are available, the costs of coping with incomplete information may be very high and the outcome highly inefficient.

In this section, we introduce a simple model, based on Gale (1997), in which agents search randomly for information. The agents in this model are all Bayesian maximizers. In particular we assume that they have correct priors over the unknown parameters in the model. In this sense we are assuming substantive rationality. However, we prevent them from using this information as effectively as they might by assuming that there is a lot of randomness in the process by which they acquire information. This randomness is a substitute for the uncertainty about the structure of their world, which is what we would really like to model. Although this is the only nonstandard assumption, it takes us quite a long way in the direction of a more realistic theory. For example, we can show in what sense investors may prefer to have fewer choices, because it simplifies their informational problem.

Consider an economy in which there is a continuum of securities, denoted by $X=[0,1]$. There is a continuum of agents, and it is assumed that each investor wants to purchase at most one unit of at most one security. This is a crude assumption, but one that has proved fruitful in studying the microstructure of markets (cf. Glosten and Milgrom 1985).

The supply of securities is assumed to be perfectly elastic—for example, a small mutual fund can expand without changing the prices of its component securities—so the equilibrium price of every security is uniquely determined by its marginal cost. To simplify notation, the marginal cost of each security is normalized to zero and references to prices are suppressed in what follows. This rules out learning from prices, of course.

For most purposes, it is sufficient to work with a finite number of types of securities, $n=1,\ldots,N$. Let E_n denote the set of securities of type n. The security space X is partitioned by the intervals $\{E_n\}$, where E_n is the set of type n securities. Letting λ denote Lebesgue measure on $[0,1]$, we denote the measure of type n securities by $\lambda_n=\lambda(E_n)$.

There is a finite number of types of investors, indexed $i=1,\ldots,I$, and a unit measure of each type, so we can identify the investors of type i with the interval $(i-1, i]$. Let u_{in} denote the expected utility that an investor of type i derives from one unit of a security of type n. Since the true value of the security may not be realized until many years later, the expected utility of the security u_{in} may incorporate a great deal of uncertainty. An investor's type can be identified with the utility vector $u_i = (u_{i1}, \ldots, u_{iN})$. When an investor acquires information about securities, he is really learning about his type, that is, his true preferences over the set of securities.

If an investor knows which securities are which, his choice problem is trivial. He simply chooses a security of the type that maximizes u_{in}. This is an example of the way in which the prior information assumed by the Bayesian framework goes too far in its assumption of how much investors know about the world around them. To make the behavior of the model more realistic, we assume that although investors know the expected payoffs, they cannot identify the types of individual securities. In order to find out which securities yield which expected returns, they must acquire costly information.

The costly acquisition of information is modeled as a search process. Each time the agent searches, he samples the set of securities and discovers the expected utility he can derive from one of the securities. Let $\gamma_i > 0$ be the cost of a single search for an agent of type i, measured in terms of utils.

The Optimal Search Problem

Suppose that an investor has already sampled a finite number of securities. He has perfect recall, so he will never sample these securities again, but since the set of sampled securities has measure zero, the distribution of unsampled securities remains the same: it is like sampling with replacement. Since the cost of search is constant, the expected utility of search is independent of the number of searches made so far. Let v_i^* denote the maximum expected utility in equilibrium for an investor of type i, assuming that he has not yet found a satisfactory security, and let v_i denote the maximum expected utility of search. The expected utility of search satisfies the usual functional equation:

$$v_i = \sum_{n=1}^{N} \lambda_n \max\{u_{in}, v_i\} - \gamma_i.$$

If he decides to search one more time, he will encounter a security of type n with probability λ_n. If this security offers a higher expected utility than continued search, he will stop searching and accept the payoff u_{in}; otherwise he continues searching.

We distinguish v_i^* from v_i because there are alternatives to searching. One alternative is to choose a security without first becoming informed. In that case, all the investor knows is that the chosen security belongs to type n with probability λ_n. The expected utility from a randomly chosen security is therefore $v_i^0 \equiv \sum_{n=1}^{N} \lambda_n u_{in}$. Note the distinction between random search, which is the process of becoming informed about the payoffs from individual securities, and random choice of a security, which means choosing a security without first becoming informed about it. A second alternative is not to buy a security at all. In that case the expected utility is 0. Clearly, $v_i^* = \max\{v_i, v_i^0, 0\}$.

The most interesting case is where $v_i^* = v_i$, and for most purposes this is the case under consideration.

The Efficiency of Search

Agents do not interact in any way in this model. Each agent solves his own decision problem, and that is all there is to equilibrium. Taking the set of securities and the search technology as given, the agents' decisions must be efficient (they are maximizing expected utility), and so the equilibrium is efficient. The only way we can improve the effectiveness of the agents' decisions is by changing the set of securities or reducing the cost of search. An example will make this clear.

There are two types of investors $i = 1, 2$ and three types of securities $n = 1, 2, 3$. The expected utility of the first security $u_{i1} = \bar{u}$ is the same for each type of investor i, whereas the expected utilities of the second and third securities differ:

$$u_{in} = \begin{cases} u_H & \text{if } (i, n) = (1, 2), (2, 3) \\ u_L & \text{if } (i, n) = (1, 3), (2, 2), \end{cases}$$

where $0 < \bar{u} < u_H$ and $\bar{u} + u_L + u_H < 0$. All investors have the same cost of search, $\gamma_i = \gamma > 0$ and $\lambda_n = 1/3$ for $n = 1, 2, 3$.

Because the example is symmetric, we look at everything from the point of view of investors of type 1. Note that the assumptions imply that $\sum \lambda_n u_{in} = v_i^0 < 0$, so investors will never make an uninformed choice, and that $u_L < 0$, so investors will never choose the less preferred of the second and third securities. There are three cases that need to be distinguished.

In case A, $(u_H - \bar{u})/3 > \gamma$. Even if the investor has found a security that yields $\bar{u}$, the expected gain from searching again in the hopes of finding a security that yields u_H is $(u_H - \bar{u})/3$, which by assumption is greater than the cost of search. The investor will continue searching until he eventually finds a security that yields u_H. Hence,

$$\begin{aligned} v^* &= \frac{1}{3}u_H + \frac{2}{3}v^* - \gamma \\ &= u_H - 3\gamma. \end{aligned}$$

Now suppose that search were restricted to the set $S = E_2 \cup E_3$. Again, the investor will continue until he finds a security that yields u_H, so

$$\begin{aligned} v^* &= \frac{1}{2}u_H + \frac{1}{2}v^* - \gamma \\ &= u_H - 2\gamma, \end{aligned}$$

which is obviously better.

In case B, $(u_H - \bar{u})/3 < \gamma < (u_H + \bar{u})/3$. An investor will stop if he finds a security that yields u_H, but if he finds one that yields only $\bar{u}$, he will also stop, since the option value of continuing, $(u_H - \bar{u})/3$, does not compensate for the cost of search γ. In this case,

$$\begin{aligned} v^* &= \frac{1}{3}u_H + \frac{1}{3}\bar{u} + \frac{1}{3}v^* - \gamma \\ &= \frac{1}{2}u_H + \frac{1}{2}\bar{u} - \frac{3}{2}\gamma. \end{aligned}$$

Now suppose that his search were restricted to the set $S = E_1$. In that case, $v^* = \bar{u}$, since no search is necessary, and that implies that the equilibrium payoff is higher with the smaller set of securities:

$$\begin{aligned} \bar{u} - (\frac{1}{2}u_H + \frac{1}{2}\bar{u} - \frac{3}{2}\gamma) &= \frac{1}{2}(\bar{u} - u_H) + \frac{3}{2}\gamma \\ &> \frac{1}{2}(-3\gamma) + \frac{3}{2}\gamma = 0. \end{aligned}$$

So again, restricting choice improves the welfare of both types of investors.

In case C, $\gamma > (u_H + \bar{u})/3$, it is not optimal to search. Since we have assumed that the expected utility of random choice is negative, the investors will choose not to trade. Even in this case, we could do better by choosing $S = E_1$, which yields an expected utility of $\bar{u} > 0$. If the expected utility of random choice were positive, investors would still opt for a random choice whenever γ is sufficiently high, but this would still be inefficient since, as long as $\bar{u} > (\bar{u} + u_H + u_L)/3$, we could do better by putting $S = E_1$.

One aspect of this example may strike the reader as odd. In case B all securities are purchased by some investors, but in case A, the securities of type 1 are never chosen by any investors. If no one ever buys these securities, why do they exist? There are two ways of answering this question. One is to introduce a third type of investor, who is indifferent among all types of securities. These investors choose securities at random and, in equilibrium, provide some demand for each security. Since they are indifferent among all securities, their utilities will not be affected by any restrictions on the set of available securities, so the same welfare conclusions will continue to hold.

Another way of providing positive demand for all securities is to allow the costs of search to increase with the number of searches. Then, even in case A, some unlucky investors will not find a security yielding u_H until the costs of search have become so high that they give up and accept $\bar{u}$. Assuming that the costs do not rise until k is very large, the equilibrium expected utilities of the investors will not be affected very much by this change in the model, and the same welfare conclusions will continue to hold.

What this example suggests is that the inability of the investors to identify the nature of securities in advance, without resorting to costly search, makes it most likely that they will waste resources on search or, alternatively, make an uninformed and hence suboptimal choice. They would be better off if a regulator or planner were to restrict their choice set. Of course, this is true only when the regulator or planner has superior information. In fact, it can be shown that superior information is necessary in the precise sense that random restrictions of the choice set cannot improve the efficiency of search (see Gale 1997).

If a regulator needs superior information in order to be able to improve on the market allocation, why does he not simply make the information available to investors and allow them to make whatever choices they like? In some cases, restricting choices is equivalent to providing information. If communication is costless, the regulator might just as well announce the set S and leave the investors to make their own choices. On the other hand, it may be difficult or costly to transmit this information. For example, if investors have difficulty identifying which securities belong to the approved set, it may be easier to restrict the set of securities than by giving general instructions to investors.

It could also be argued that the market will provide the necessary information. In that case, we need to ask what incentives financial institutions have to share information when communication is costly. Is it incentive compatible for them to tell the truth? If information is generic, in the sense that it helps investors to evaluate more than one security, there will be a free-rider problem: each institution may underprovide information in the hope that other institutions will provide it instead. In extreme cases, we may not be able to rely on institutions to provide this information at all. There may also be an incentive for institutions to dissemble and pretend that their securities are all things to all people. These issues go beyond the scope of this chapter, but prima facie it is not obvious that the market will provide the information that investors need.

14.4 Redundant Securities

Example 1 shows that with some additional information, a regulator can improve the welfare of all the investors. How general is this result, and what is the best that can be achieved? With a single type of investor the answer is trivial: simply choose $S = E_x$, where x is the best type of security for this type of investor. When there are many investor types, the problem becomes complicated. Different investor types want different securities, so there is a trade-off between maximizing surplus, which requires variety, and reducing search costs, which requires uniformity.

This section provides a characterization of an efficient set of securities. When there are many types of investors and securities, the restrictions are somewhat hard to interpret, although the mathematical characterization is simple and elegant. However, in particular cases, the characterization has a natural interpretation: it requires the number of types of securities to be matched to the number of types of investors (there is at most one security for each type of investor). In this sense, there is a case for requiring uniformity within broad classes of securities.

For the purposes of this analysis, the preferences of type i investors are represented by an arbitrary, Lebesgue-integrable function u_i: $[0, 1] \to \mathbf{R}$, where $X = [0, 1]$ is the set of securities and $u_i(x)$ is the expected utility of security x.

Necessary Conditions

We assume that every type of investor finds it optimal to search in equilibrium, so $v_i = v_i^*$. Then the value of search is characterized by the equation

$$v_i^* = \int_0^1 \max\{u_i(x), v_i^*\}dx - \gamma_i,$$

which can be written equivalently as

$$\int_0^1 [\max\{u_i(x) - v_i^*, 0\} - \gamma_i]dx = 0.$$

Let $\phi_i(x) \equiv \max\{u_i(x) - v_i^*, 0\} - \gamma_i$, for every i and x. An equilibrium is defined by an I-tuple of values (v_i^*), which determine the optimal search rules for each type of investor. In the obvious way, we can define an equilibrium relative to any set of securities $E \subset X$. For each security set E there is a unique equilibrium payoff $v_i^*(E)$ for investor type i. An equilibrium (relative to X) is Pareto efficient if it is impossible to find a measurable set $E \subset X$ such that every type of investor has a higher equilibrium payoff when the securities are restricted to the set E, that is, $v_i^*(E) > v_i^*(X)$ for $i = i, \ldots, I$.

THEOREM 14.1 Suppose that an equilibrium (v_i^*) is Pareto efficient. Then there exists a vector $a = (a_1, \ldots, a_I) > 0$ such that

$$\sum_{i=1}^{I} a_i \phi_i(x) = 0$$

for each i and almost every x.

Proof For each i and n, define $\zeta_i(x)$ by putting $\zeta_i(x) = \{z_i : z_i \leq \phi_i(x)\}$ for every i and then put $\zeta(x) = \zeta_1(x) \times \ldots \times \zeta_I(x)$ and $\hat{\zeta}(x) = \zeta(x) \cup \{0\}$, for every x. We claim that

$$0 \notin \text{int}\{\int \hat{\zeta}(x)dx\}.$$

If not, there exists a measurable selection $z(x) \in \hat{\zeta}(x)$ such that $0 = \int z(x)dx$. Let E be the support of $z(\cdot)$, so that $z(x) \in \zeta(x)$ for every $x \in E$. Then, by construction,

$$\int_E \phi_i(x)dx > 0 \text{ for } i = 1, \ldots, I,$$

which, incidentally, proves that E has positive measure. Now this inequality can be rearranged to give

$$v_i^* < \lambda(E_i)^{-1} \int_{E_i} u_i(x)dx - \gamma_i \lambda(E)/\lambda(E_i), \quad \text{for } i = 1, \ldots, I,$$

where $E_i = \{x \in E | u_i(x) \geq v_i^*\}$. The expression on the right-hand side can be interpreted as the expected utility of the following decision rule: search randomly in the set E and accept the first security $x \in E_i$. What the inequality shows is that this rule gives a higher expected utility than v_i^* for every i, contradicting the assumed Pareto efficiency of the equilibrium. This contradiction shows that $0 \notin \text{int}\{\int \hat{\zeta}(x)dx\}$ as claimed.

By Lyapunov's theorem, we know that the set $\int \hat{\zeta}(x)dx$ is convex, and by construction it contains $-\mathbf{R}^I$. Also, $0 \in \int \hat{\zeta}(x)dx$, so Minkowski's lemma implies that there exists a vector $a = (a_1, \ldots, a_I) > 0$ such that

$$0 = \sup\{a \cdot \int \hat{\zeta}(x)dx\}.$$

Since $0 \in \hat{\zeta}(x)$ for every $x \in [0, 1]$, this in turn implies that

$$0 = \sup\{a \cdot \hat{\zeta}(x)\} \text{ a.e.} \Rightarrow$$

$$0 \geq \sup\{a \cdot \zeta(x)\} \text{ a.e.} \Rightarrow$$

$$0 = \sup\{a \cdot \zeta(x)\} \text{ a.e.}$$

since $\int \phi_i(x)dx = 0$ for every i. Thus,

$$\sum_{i=1}^{I} a_i \phi_i(x) = 0 \text{ a.e.}$$

The theorem extends immediately to the case where some agents do not trade. Simply put $\phi_i(x) = 0$ for this type of investor. If some type i chooses a security randomly, without searching first, the theorem can be extended by putting $\phi_i(x) = u_i(x) - v_i^*$, for each x, and using the same argument as before.

This theorem provides quite a strong necessary condition for efficiency, one that is unlikely to be satisfied in practice for an arbitrarily specified set of utility functions $\{u_i(\cdot)\}$. Whenever this condition is not satisfied, we can find some nonnegligible set $E \subset [0, 1]$ such that allowing investors to search in the restricted set E will make each of them better off. Further, when we have found an efficient set of securities E, that is, a set with the property that no other set will make everyone better off, then in particular it will be true that no further restriction will make everyone better off and, consequently, the characterization will apply to the set E as well.

Of course, there will be many efficient sets, and some of them may not be very attractive from a distributional point of view. For example, let E consist of the security that is most preferred by type i. This set maximizes the expected utility of type i but may not be very good from the point of view of other investor types. Nonetheless, it will be Pareto efficient, because any other set will either not give type i their most preferred choice or else will involve costly search.

To understand better the implications of theorem 14.1, consider the case where there are only two types of investors, $i = 1, 2$. Then the characterization obtained in the theorem implies that, for $i \neq j$,

$$a_i(\max\{u_i(x) - v_i^*, 0\} - \gamma_i) = -a_j(\max\{u_j(x) - v_j^*, 0\} - \gamma_j), \forall x \in E_i.$$

Let $E_i = \{x | u_i(x) \geq v_i^*\}$ denote the set of securities that are optimal for type i investors to buy. Then

$$u_i(x) - v_i^* - \gamma_i = \begin{cases} a_j\gamma_j/a_i & \text{if } x \in E_i \backslash E_j \\ -a_j(u_j(x) - v_j^* - \gamma_j)/a_i & \text{if } x \in E_i \cap E_j. \end{cases}$$

This yields the following restrictions on the expected utilities of the securities in E_i:

$$u_i(x) = \begin{cases} \text{constant} & \text{if } x \in E_i \backslash E_j \\ \alpha + \beta u_j(x) & \text{if } x \in E_i \cap E_j. \end{cases}$$

Suppose that we rule out the affine relationship between u_i and u_j by assumption, that is, assume that there does not exist a non-null set E and constants α and $\beta \neq 0$ such that

$$u_i(x) = \alpha + \beta u_j(x), \forall x \in E.$$

Then $E_i \cap E_j = \phi$, and we are left with a simple picture of the investors' preferences. The set of securities X is partitioned (modulo a set of measure zero) by E_i and E_j, and u_i (resp. u_j) is constant on E_i (resp. u_j). There is no restriction of u_i on E_j, but since $u_i \leq v_i^*$ on E_j, these preferences are not relevant in equilibrium. In effect, there are only two types of securities, one for each type of investor.

Clearly this is a rather restrictive condition, suggesting that, in general, equilibrium is unlikely to be efficient unless the set of securities is restricted. Moreover, the fact that efficiency requires essentially one type of security per investor provides a rationale for uniform regulations on the securities that can be offered.

On the other hand, for general preferences $\{u_i\}$ the business of identifying an efficient set of securities will be far from trivial, and one may doubt whether a regulator has the necessary information to select a Pareto-improving set E.

Sufficient Conditions

Theorem 14.1 provides a necessary condition for efficiency. As a partial converse, suppose that there is a set, E and an equilibrium $\{v_i^*\}$ relative to this set, and define the functions ϕ_i in the preceding way and let $\phi \equiv (\phi_1, \ldots, \phi_I)$. Suppose that a vector $a = (a_1, \ldots, a_I) > 0$ satisfies $a \cdot \phi \leq 0$ for a.e. x and $E = \{x | a \cdot \phi(x) = 0\}$. Then we claim that E is an efficient set of securities, in the sense that there exists no other set E' such that every type of investor is better off in an equilibrium in which search is restricted to E'.

To see this, suppose, contrary to what we want to prove, that there is such a set E'. Let $\{v_i^{**}\}$ be the equilibrium values corresponding to the set E'. Then, assuming that every agent finds it optimal to search (the other cases can be dealt with by an obvious extension),

$$v_i^{**} = \lambda(E')^{-1} \int_{E'} \max\{u_i(x), v_i^{**}\} dx - \gamma_i$$

or

$$0 = \int_{E'} [\max\{u_i(x) - v_i^{**}, 0\} - \gamma_i] dx.$$

Since by assumption $v_i^{**} > v_i^*$, we have

$$0 < \int_{E'} [\max\{u_i(x) - v_i^*, 0\} - \gamma_i] dx$$

$$= \int_{E'} \phi_i(x) dx.$$

Multiplying by a_i and summing over i we get

$$0 < \sum_{i=1}^{I} \int_{E'} a_i \phi_i(x) dx$$

$$= \int_{E \cap E'} a \cdot \phi(x) dx + \int_{E' \setminus E} a \cdot \phi(x) dx$$

$$= 0 + \int_{E' \setminus E} a \cdot \phi(x) dx < 0,$$

since by assumption $a \cdot \phi(x) < 0$ for almost every $x \in E' \setminus E$ and $a \cdot \phi(x) = 0$ for almost every $x \in E \cap E'$. This contradiction proves the desired result.

THEOREM 14.2 Suppose that $\{v_i^*\}$ defines an equilibrium relative to a set of securities E and define the functions ϕ_i in the usual way. Suppose that there is a vector $a = (a_1, \ldots, a_I) > 0$ such that $a \cdot \phi_i \leq 0$ for a.e. x and $E = \{x | a \cdot \phi_i(x) = 0\}$. Then E is a Pareto-efficient set of securities, that is, there exists no other set E' such that every type of investor is better off in an equilibrium in which search is restricted to E'.

In the discussion so far, it has been implicitly assumed that any restrictions of trading must apply uniformly across all types of investors. In other words, the regulator cannot restrict investors of type i to a set S_i and investors of type j to a set S_j, where $S_i \neq S_j$ if $i \neq j$. We have in mind a situation in which investors' types are private information. If some of the investors' characteristics could be publicly observed and some were private, the regulator could condition his restrictions on the public characteristics. Then the analysis presented here would apply to subgroups of investors with identical public characteristics but different private characteristics. The investor types in the present model correspond to these private characteristics.

If investors knew their types, the regulator might be able to design a mechanism to extract this information from the investors. However, aside from the cost of such an undertaking, there is another obstacle insofar as investors are unlikely to know their own types. An investor's type is simply a way of denoting his true preferences over securities. As long as he is uncertain about the nature of the securities available in the market, he will be uncertain about his type. To say that investors appear ex ante identical is just another way of saying that they are all equally uncertain about the available securities and does not imply that a lack of heterogeneity in (true) preferences over securities. Investors' types will be revealed, perhaps slowly, as they observe the payoffs from different types of securities. The only way for the investors' to obtain information about their types is through search, so the regulator cannot restrict their trading conditional on their types. In fact, any restrictions the regulator imposes may prevent the accumulation of information.

14.5 Search and Social Learning

In the model of random search, there is no interaction among different agents. Equilibrium is just a collection of single-agent decision problems. In a complex environment, there is an obvious incentive to learn from others. However, individuals' ability to take advantage of others' information is limited, by contrast with the model of REE, and in equilibrium the attempt to exploit the information of others can lead to inefficiency. These ideas are illustrated in the recent literature on social learning (Banerjee 1992; Bikhchandani, Hirshleifer, and Welch 1992; Smith and Sorensen 1996). The model of random search can also be extended to allow for learning from others (see Gale 1997 for details).

Unlike the REE theory, which assumes that the agents solve the model to infer information from prices, the theory of social learning assumes that agents observe the actions of other agents directly and use that information to guide their own decisions. Like the REE theory, agents are assumed to be perfect Bayesians and to that extent they are substantively rational, but the flavor of these models is different, insofar as it focuses on simpler models and on examples of informational failure. This is an attempt to capture the flavor of bounded rationality using the tools of substantive rationality. (There are also examples of successful social learning, but that is less relevant to our concerns.)

One of the early lessons of this literature is the possibility that rational agents will ignore their own information and rely exclusively on the information provided by others. This is an example of an informational cascade, which is a special form of herd behavior. (More precisely, consider a sequence of agents who make decisions one after the other and can condition their decisions on both private information and the decisions of previous movers. Herd behavior arises when all the agents make the same choice from some point onward; an informational cascade arises if all agents make a choice that is independent of their private information from some point onward. Smith and Sorensen 1996 have shown that informational cascades are harder to support than herd behavior.) The problem with herd behavior and informational cascades is that although each agent is behaving rationally, the outcome may not be optimal with respect to the sum of the agents' information. By failing to share their information optimally, the agents' condemn themselves to a suboptimal allocation. When agents must acquire information at some cost, the problem of herd behavior is exacerbated by the free-rider problem, and there is little hope that informational efficiency will result (see Gale 1996 for an elementary survey).

Suppose that a large number of economic agents have to make some financial decision—perhaps the choice of which mutual fund or stock to invest in or which insurance policy to buy. For simplicity, we are going to assume that agents make their decisions sequentially and that each agent can observe the decisions of all the agents who have chosen previously. We also assume that each agent chooses one element from a finite set; prices and quantities do not enter explicitly into the story. As a model of a financial market, this is pretty crude, but the point of the exercise is to capture something of what happens when agents have limited ability to process the information provided by price signals and one way to do that in a Bayesian framework is to limit the choices and the information available to them.

As above, we consider a finite set of choices (securities, funds, etc), $n = 1, \ldots, N$. Agents' preferences are represented by a random utility model. The utility of security n is a random variable $\tilde{u}_n$, and the vector of utilities is $\tilde{u} = (\tilde{u}_1, \ldots, \tilde{u}_N)$. The sample space is denoted by $U = \mathbf{R}^N$, the set of possible utility vectors, and the joint cumulative distribution function is denoted by F, with marginal distribution functions F_n.

There are I agents, indexed by $i = 1, \ldots, I$. Agents make their decisions sequentially and in the natural order—first agent 1, then agent 2, and so on. Each agent can observe the choices of all the previous agents when he makes his choice, but this is all that he observes. He does not observe the search procedures adopted by previous agents, nor does he observe the information collected during their search.

Before choosing a security, the agent has the opportunity to gather costly information about the securities. Specifically, he can discover the true expected utility of security n by paying a fixed cost $\gamma > 0$. This leads to a standard sequential sampling problem that can be solved by dynamic programing.

Common Values

We begin by considering the case where all agents have the same preferences, that is, they have the same prior distribution $F_n = \tilde{F}$ over expected utility vectors, and the expected utility of any security is in fact the same for any two agents. Agent 1 does not observe anyone else's choice, so he faces a standard search problem: he collects information about some subset of N and chooses the security that offers the highest expected utility. Denote his choice by x_1. When agent 2 comes to make his choice, he observes that agent 1 has chosen x_1. Since agent 1 has chosen optimally and all agents have the same preferences and search costs, it is clearly optimal for agent 2 to make the same choice, without incurring the cost of gathering any information for himself. By the same reasoning, every subsequent agent does the same. This outcome is not necessarily optimal. If it were possible to make transfers among agents, the cost of search could be spread among a large number of agents, making the effective cost negligible. So the Pareto optimum, if the number of agents is sufficiently large, is to obtain complete information, and this will not necessarily be the case in the equilibrium outcome, since agents ignore the value of their information to other agents.

Of course, in a common values environment, it would be a trivial matter to design a policy to achieve the Pareto optimum, but in practice agents are heterogeneous, and this makes the problem more difficult.

Measurement Error

Now suppose that agents cannot observe the true expected utility from any particular choice, but instead learn the expected utility with error. For example, they might observe $\tilde{u}_n + \epsilon_{in}$, where ϵ_{in} is the random error made by agent i when observing the return to security n. These observation errors are assumed to be independent across individuals, but are fixed for each individual: this is like some kind of bias in the judgment of the individual and will affect each observation in exactly the same way. Otherwise there would be nothing to stop the individual agent from eliminating this noise by making multiple observations.

With this alteration in the model, there is an incentive for agents $2, 3, \ldots$ to continue searching. Since previous agents might have made mistakes, later agents have an incentive to replicate their efforts. Eventually, however, the cumulative effect of the earlier agents' choices will render further search suboptimal. If k agents have made the same choice, then an agent knows that even if he obtains a noisy signal, it will not be sufficiently reliable to offset the effect of seeing k other agents selecting the same security, so he will not bother to become informed. This is the by-now-familiar informational cascade or herd behavior popularized by Banerjee (1992) and Bikchandhani, Hirshleifer, and Welch (1993), but with the added cost of acquiring information to discourage later agents from becoming informed.

Private Values

When agents have idiosyncratic preferences, for example, because they have different horizons, different private risks to hedge, or different wealths, there is an incentive to continue searching even after a large number of agents have made choices. In the case of measurement error, the incentive to gather information must eventually disappear because the law of large numbers implies that the measurement errors have a zero mean in a large sample. Although the choices made by previous agents limit the set of choices from which an agent may sample, with idiosyncratic preferences, each agent must find the best choice for himself from among the set of choices observed in equilibrium. However, although the agents go on searching, there will still be inefficiency because of the presence of externalities. In the limit, after many choices have been observed, each agent will limit his search to a (possibly small) set of choices repeatedly made by previous agents. The selected set will not be the optimal one in general. For the same reason that herd behavior occurs with common values, there will be herd behavior with respect to the set of choices when there are private values. There may be too few elements in the asymptotic set, or the wrong elements, or both.

Private Values with Measurement Error

If we add measurement error to idiosyncratic preferences, efficiency requires repeated sampling. Individuals have an incentive to sample repeatedly for two reasons now: the noisy signals of their predecessors and the heterogeneity of their preferences. However, herd behavior may limit the amount of search to be less than the optimal amount, and even if there is a diffuse support, agents may mistake measurement error for idiosyncratic preference shocks and vice versa.

14.6 Conclusion

In this chapter, we have followed the traditional approach to modeling asset markets by assuming that the market consists of a large number of individual investors, who manage portfolios on their own account. Where we have extended the model is in introducing information costs to show how markets may fail to be efficient when information is hard to acquire and, in particular, where investors do not initially have a large amount of information about how the market works. The main result was to show that having a restricted set of investments in which to invest may be better than allowing unlimited numbers of investments. This has important implictions for comparing financial systems. It suggests that the vast array of possibilities available to investors in the United States and United Kingdom may not be an unmixed blessing when compared to the quite limited choice sets of investors in Japan, Germany, and France. In recent years, total participation in equity markets, including both direct and indirect holdings, has increased enormously in the United States and, to a lesser extent, in the United Kingdom. It remains to be seen whether this increase in participation is accompanied by an increase in welfare in the long run.

The view that asset markets are primarily for individual investors is, of course, dated. Today's markets are dominated by institutions such as mutual funds, pension funds, brokerage houses, and the like, which are run by professional managers controlling large amounts of money on behalf of shareholders and clients. And it could be argued that the role of professional managers overcomes the informational problems that face ordinary investors. This optimistic view overlooks two points. The first is the agency problem that always exists when portfolio management is delegated (Bhattacharya and Pfleiderer 1985, Heinkel and Stoughton 1994, Admati and Pfleiderer 1997). The second is that even if their funds are managed by professionals, individuals bear the ultimate risk, and this means that the manager cannot optimize for them unless they have somehow conveyed their preferences to the manager. How this can be done is not at all clear, especially if the investor does not know enough about the market to tell the manager precisely what he would like done. Another way of looking at this problem is to take the policies of the managers as given and ask how the investor finds the "right" fund for her (the investor's) preferences. Since there are currently more mutual funds than stocks traded on the NYSE, the informational problems of the investor searching for a mutual fund are not necessarily smaller than those of an investor searching for a stock or a small portfolio of stocks.

The analysis of models of individual investor decisions therefore remains relevant for two reasons. First, some decisions are still made by the individual investor, and, second, the need for the investor to be informed (in order to instruct the manager to whom he delegates decisions) cannot be avoided simply by having a well-informed manager.

Nonetheless, there is a need to extend these models to explore the role of delegation and intermediation in markets. The informational costs of operating in markets make it unlikely that most individuals can operate directly in markets without considerable assistance. So, as we have suggested throughout this book, in order to make use of markets, we need to have intermediaries. But we pointed out that exactly how intermediaries can solve some of the informational problems is not clear. These issues will be explored in chapter 15.

References

Admati, A., and P. Pfleiderer. (1997). "Does It All Add Up? Benchmarks and the Compensation of Active Portfolio Managers." *Journal of Business* **70,** 323–350.

Allen, F., and D. Gale. (1994). *Financial Innovation and Risk Sharing*. Cambridge, MA: MIT Press.

———. (1994). "Limited Market Participation and Volatility of Asset Prices." *American Economic Review* **84,** 933–955.

Banerjee, A. (1992). "A Simple Model of Herd Behavior." *Quarterly Journal of Economics* **107,** 797–817.

Bikhchandani, S., D. Hirshleifer, and I. Welch. (1992). "A Theory of Fads, Fashion, Custom, and Cultural Change in Informational Cascades." *Journal of Political Economy* **100,** 992–1026.

Bhattacharya, S., and P. Pfleiderer. (1985). "Delegated Portfolio Management." *Journal of Economic Theory* **36,** 1–25.

Dow, J., and S. Ribeiro da Costa Werlang. (1992). "Uncertainty Aversion, Risk Aversion, and the Optimal Choice of Portfolio." *Econometrica* **60,** 197–204.

Gale, D. (1992). "Standard Securities." *Review of Economic Studies* **59,** 731–755.

———. (1996). "What Have We Learned from Social Learning?" *European Economic Review* **40,** 617–628.

———. (1997). "Spoiled for Choice: Variety and Efficiency in Markets with Incomplete Information." *Ricerche Economiche* **51,** 41–67.

Glosten, L., and P. Milgrom. (1985). "Bid, Ask, and Transaction Prices in a Specialist Market with Heterogeneously Informed Traders." *Journal of Financial Economics* **14,** 71–100.

Heinkel, R., and N. Stoughton. (1994). "The Dynamics of Portfolio Management Contracts." *Review of Financial Studies* **7,** 351–387.

Lucas, R., Jr. (1972). "Expectations and the Neutrality of Money." *Journal of Economic Theory* **4,** 103–124.

Mukerji, S., and J. Tallon. (1998). "Ambiguity Aversion and Incompleteness of Financial Markets." Working paper, CNRS-EUREQUA Université Paris I.

Pagano, M. (1989). "Trading Volume and Asset Liquidity." *Quarterly Journal of Economics* **104,** 255–274.

Radner, R. (1979). "Rational Expectations Equilibrium: Generic Existence and the Information Revealed by Prices." *Econometrica* **47,** 655–678.

Shiller, R. (1993). *Macro Markets: Creating Institutions for Managing Society's Largest Economic Risks.* Oxford: Clarendon Press.

Smith, L., and P. Sorensen. (1996). "Pathological Outcomes of Observational Learning." Working paper, MIT.

15 Relationships and Risk Sharing

In parts of this book, we have contrasted the characteristics of financial markets and financial intermediaries, showing that each has advantages and disadvantages in performing similar tasks. This focus suggests that policymakers face a choice between markets and intermediaries as alternative components from which to build a financial system. The contrast between market-oriented systems, such as the United States and United Kingdom, and intermediary-oriented systems, such as Germany and Japan, emphasizes this contrast by suggesting that two alternative paths were historically followed by the different economies. However, as Hellwig (1998) has recently emphasized, intermediaries are often necessary for the existence and efficient functioning of markets. Similarly, it is obvious that intermediaries benefit from the existence of markets, in which to hedge risks, for example. So there is also an argument for a symbiotic relationship between markets and intermediaries, which is supported by the analysis of the immediately preceding chapters where we emphasized the importance of informational barriers to participation in markets. Intermediaries are needed to overcome these barriers.

In chapter 13 we discussed the relative merits of markets and financial institutions as mechanisms for allocating resources for investment when there is diversity of opinion. In chapter 14 we presented several models to argue that using markets is costly—so costly that occasionally it is infeasible for economic agents to make use of markets for risk sharing. In this chaper, we continue the discussion of the problems presented by uncertainty and asymmetric information for the efficient allocation of risk sharing. As we have already pointed out, it takes expert knowledge to make effective use of sophisticated risk management techniques. An individual who lacks this knowledge can go to an expert for advice, but this creates a new problem: How does the individual know that he is getting good advice? There is a moral hazard problem inherent in this unequal relationship, because the expert may not make sufficient effort on behalf of his uninformed client. Furthermore, even if we ignore the moral hazard problem, it is not clear that the individual will get appropriate advice unless he is able to communicate effectively his preferences and beliefs to the expert. We explore the possibilities for using long-term relationships to overcome some of these informational barriers to using sophisticated risk management techniques. In the context of a long-term relationship, an intermediary can overcome the asymmetry of information that exists with a less expert investor and use its expertise to guide the investor toward a more effective risk management strategy. The chapter is based on Allen and Gale (1999).

15.1 Changing Paradigms

The financial services industry has undergone a dramatic transformation recently. What might be termed the traditional paradigm for intermediation is illustrated in figure 15.1. Banks and insurance companies convey funds from low-wealth households to firms. High-wealth households and large companies (with the help of investment banks) mostly use financial markets directly. The primary role of intermediaries is perceived to be reducing transaction costs and providing information. Markets and intermediaries are alternative ways of channeling funds.

One aspect of the transformation has been the increase in importance of traditional financial markets in the United States, such as those for equity and debt. For example, the market capitalization of corporate equity in the United States has risen steadily as a percentage of GDP, from around 50 percent in 1975 to nearly 75 percent in 1994 (OECD, 1995). Another aspect is that the range of markets available has widened with the development of liquid options, financial futures, and other derivative markets.

Despite a significant fall in the direct costs of trading after the deregulation of stock commissions in 1975, the increased availability of information about corporations and access to price data and standard valuation models through services such as Bloomberg, this expansion in the importance of financial markets is not because of higher participation by individuals or firms. In fact, the share of individual ownership of corporate equity in the United States fell between 1967 and 1995. There was a particularly sharp change in the early 1980s, when individual

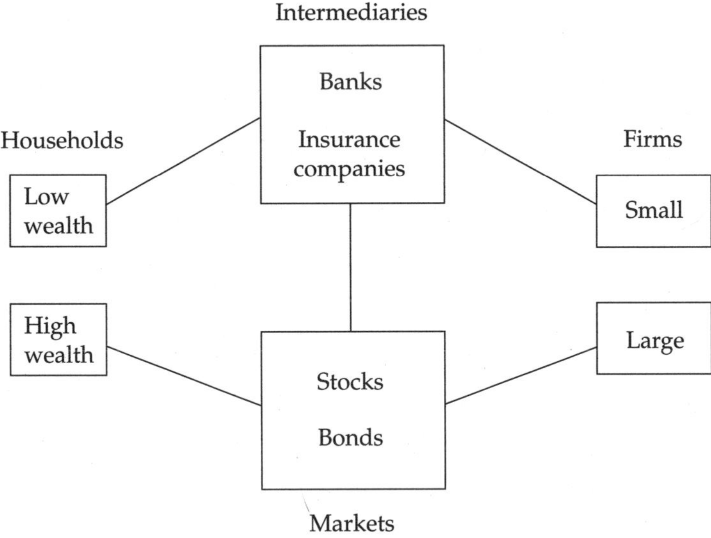

Figure 15.1
Traditional paradigm

ownership fell from over 75 percent to around 50 percent in only a few years (Board of Governors of the Federal Reserve System, 1996).

The change occurred because intermediaries are using markets more extensively than before. Between 1967 and 1995, the share of pension funds' ownership of equity in the United States rose from less than 10 percent to over 20 percent. In the same period, the share of mutual funds' ownership of equity in the United States grew from around 5 percent to nearly 25 percent (Board of Governors of the Federal Reserve System, 1996). In derivatives markets, intermediaries play an even more significant role. As of 1995, financial institutions accounted for 82 percent of the notional amounts of OTC derivatives outstanding, while nonfinancial institutions accounted for the remaining 18 percent (Bank for International Settlements–Central Bank Survey of Derivatives Market Activity 1995).

Figure 15.2 illustrates what might be termed the emerging paradigm for intermediation that these changes are leading to. Most households increasingly deal with intermediaries, such as pension and mutual funds that invest on their behalf in markets. Even among the very wealthy, the use of private banking services and hedge funds, where advisers make investment decisions on behalf of their clients, has become increasingly common. Small firms deal with banks and other

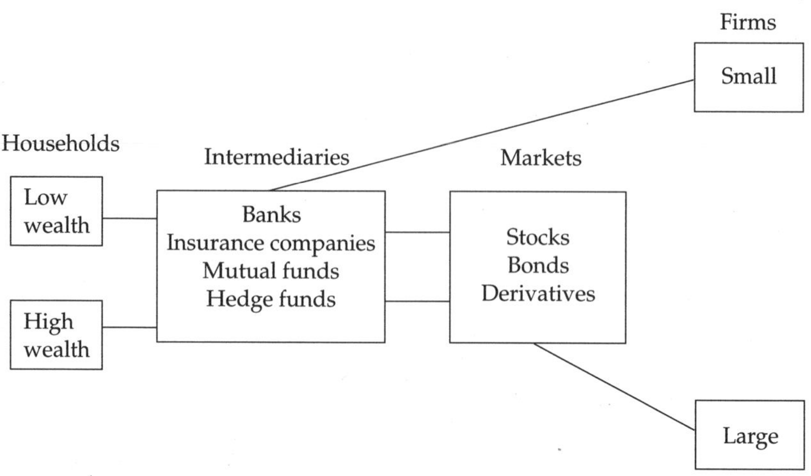

Figure 15.2
Emerging paradigm

entities, such as limited partnerships providing venture capital and other forms of private equity. Only the very largest firms (with the help of investment banks) deal directly in financial markets.

Allen and Santomero (1997) have suggested that the focus of intermediaries' activities has shifted away from reducing transaction costs and providing information. Instead, risk management has become an increasingly important activity. Intermediaries are using the wide range of markets available to them to transfer, transform, and redistribute risk. Understanding the practice and role of risk management has become the center of a growing literature (see Allen and Santomero 1997). Figure 15.2 illustrates that in the emerging paradigm of intermediation, the increased importance of risk management is only one part of the change in the financial services industry that has occurred. Another part is the increase in the interaction of intermediaries with households and firms.

To understand these changes in the financial services industry, we have to revise the traditional view of the comparative advantages of financial markets and financial intermediaries. The traditional paradigm stresses three differences between financial markets and financial intermediaries. First, markets offer the opportunity to trade standard securities, whereas intermediaries can tailor securities to the needs of the individual investor or firm. A market needs a certain amount of depth (liquidity) to attract traders. As a result, there exist viable markets for a relatively small fraction of the set of all conceivable securities.[1] On the other hand, intermediaries can design securities for specific customers and specific needs. Investment banks such as Goldman Sachs provide a wide range of securities for a price.[2] In short, there is an inherent trade-off between liquidity and customization.[3]

Second, markets are more competitive and offer services at lower cost. This may result from greater concentration in the intermediary sector or from the existence of holdup problems and lock-in effects. The intermediary may have information about the customer or about the financial product that allows it to extract surplus. Switching costs and lemons problems may lead to lock-in effects, which the intermediary can use to extract rents (Sharpe 1990, Rajan 1992). In addition, markets may actually be cheaper because they can tap a larger pool of resources and so reduce the cost of raising funds. The junk bond market was successful initially because it allowed a significant reduction in the cost of funds compared to bank finance.[4]

Third, the traditional role of intermediaries is explained in terms of the existence of increasing returns to scale in executing transactions, monitoring investments, and acquiring information. Because fixed costs are involved in each of these activities, a specialist institution can reduce the per unit expense for investors. Intermediaries may also be able to lower the costs of its customers by providing information. Here the advantage comes from increasing returns to scale. Once the intermediary has paid the fixed cost of acquiring information, it can provide it to all its customers at nearly zero marginal cost (Diamond 1984).[5] An alternative is to package risk in such a way that it is easier to evaluate than the securities provided by the market. Markets can also do this to some extent (cf. Boot and Thakor 1993, Duffie and DeMarzo 1995), but since different individuals have different information available, it may be impossible for markets to duplicate this function in the form of standard securities.

The development of more sophisticated markets has provided a new and somewhat different role for intermediaries. As new markets have opened up and made new hedging opportunities available, they have increased the expertise necessary to devise strategies and make effective use of these opportunities. So while tangible transaction costs such as fees and the cost of observing prices may have fallen, some types of information costs have increased. To evaluate a complex security, a complex portfolio, or a complex strategy requires more than just knowing the facts about a firm's balance sheet. It requires financial expertise that an ordinary investor usually does not possess. Even large firms may lack this expertise. So intermediaries assume the role of advisers, bridging the gap between the investors' lack of knowledge and the expertise required to get the most out of sophisticated markets.

Thus, intermediaries play a crucial role in allowing firms and investors to participate in financial markets and, at the same time, ensure that financial markets have enough depth to survive. In this sense, financial markets and financial intermediaries have a symbiotic relationship, each necessary to the other. Without intermediaries, the informational barriers to participation would prevent investors from reaping the benefits of the new markets, and the markets themselves might not survive. At the same time, financial markets reduce costs for the intermediaries and their customers and allow them to hedge risks more effectively than they previously could.

In this chapter, we focus on one aspect of the emerging paradigm and consider the role of intermediaries in reducing the risk to investors and firms of operating in the new and highly sophisticated markets. In an Arrow-Debreu world with complete markets and complete information, there would be no role for intermediaries, but in the world we live in there are numerous reasons why the risk-sharing opportunities offered by markets are incomplete:

- *Complexity*. It may be very expensive to write complex contracts, so the market provides only simple contracts, which is what most investors want.

- *Liquidity*. In order to maintain a viable market, the volume of trade must be large enough to allow the market makers to cover their fixed costs and ensure sufficient market depth to avoid excessive price volatility. This may not possible for very exotic securities, with the result that we tend to observe a limited set of securities (Pagano 1989, Allen and Gale 1994).

- *Legal uncertainty*. One of the barriers to the introduction of new securities is the uncertainty about how the legal system will treat them. As a result, there is a preference for securities on which there is a settled body of case law. This necessarily limits the selection of contracts on offer.

• *Gains from standardization*. Trading securities requires general knowledge about classes of securities, stocks, bonds, options, futures, and other instruments, as well as specific knowledge about individual securities, mean return, variance, beta, and so forth. As a result, information costs are reduced by dealing in standard securities, and this may also discourage the introduction of new securities (Gale 1992).

We begin our analysis of risk sharing in costly markets by looking at a standard risk-sharing problem when an intermediary can provide risk-sharing opportunities that are missing from the market. This provides a role for the intermediary, but it does not explain why the intermediary has an advantage over the market. Why can the intermediary provide a risk-sharing contract at lower cost than the market? The subsequent sections attempt to provide an explanation.

15.2 Explicit Risk-Sharing Contracts

As a benchmark, we study a simple example with incomplete markets. A customer can hedge an idiosyncratic risk in the market, but the risk-sharing opportunity is incomplete. This means that there is the potential for an intermediary to increase the customer's welfare by offering a supplementary risk-sharing contract. It is assumed that the intermediary can write an explicit contract, that is, a written contract that can be enforced by third parties such as the courts. It is also assumed that the contract is complete, that is, it is the optimal contract under the assumption that there is complete information and no transaction costs. In this case, the intermediary is able to increase welfare because we assume that it can do something that the market cannot do: provide an explicit, complete risk-sharing contract.

Suppose that the customer, which could be a firm or an investor, wants to hedge the risk of a random income. Risk preferences are represented by von Neumann-Morgenstern utility functions $u(x)$ for the customer and $v(y)$ for the intermediary. The customer receives income $w(s)$ in state s. There is a market in which a security f is traded. This security pays a net return $f(s)$ in state s, where the net return includes the price of the security as well as any commissions and fees. Without loss of generality, we can scale the security's payoffs so that the customer wants to trade exactly one unit in equilibrium. Then, if it trades the security f on the market, its net income will be $f(s) + w(s)$ in state s and its expected utility will be

$$E[u(f+w)] = \sum_s p(s)u(f(s)+w(s)),$$

where $p(s)$ is the probability of state s.

Now suppose the customer went instead to the intermediary and wanted to hedge the risk w. We ignore other income for the intermediary, so if the intermediary wants to sell a security g to the customer, its income is simply $-g(s)$ in state s. Without further information, the expected utilities of the customer and intermediary, conditional on trading the security g, will be $E[u(g(s)+w(s))]$ and $E[v(-g(s))]$, respectively. The particular security chosen by the intermediary has two functions: to share risks efficiently and to provide the maximum payoff to the intermediary. If the intermediary has all the bargaining power, it maximizes its own payoff subject to the constraint that the customer can always go to the market:

$$\max_g \quad E[v(-g(s))]$$

$$\text{s.t.} \quad E[u(g(s)+w(s))] \geq E[u(f(s)+w(s))].$$

In other contexts, the customer may have some bargaining power. For example, the customer may be able to extract informational rents if the intermediary does not know its reservation utility. In that case, the surplus will be shared in a less extreme way. In any case, the contract chosen will be efficient. The bottom line is that the intermediary can improve risk sharing by tailoring the security to the customer's needs, but may or may not share the gains with the customer.

This may not be the whole story, however. The intermediary may have higher costs than the market. For example, if there is a fixed cost $c > 0$ of writing a tailor-made security (i.e., a complete contract), then the intermediary's payoff is $E[v(-g(s)-c)]$, and if the intermediary's reservation utility is $v(0)$, then even if the customer has all of the bargaining power, the most that it can obtain is

$$\max \quad E[u(g(s)+w(s))]$$

$$\text{s.t.} \quad E[v(-g(s)-c)] \geq v(0),$$

which may be less than $E[u(f(s)+w(s))]$. Even if there is positive surplus, the intermediary needs something less than full bargaining power to make the firm no better off than it would be dealing in the market. A similar issue arises if the intermediary's cost of funds is greater than the market's. That will also appear as a cost that must be subtracted from g in order to define the intermediary's payoff.

The essential issue in this situation is the trade-off between the costs and benefits of markets and intermediaries. For some investors and firms, intermediaries may be superior, while for others markets are superior. The existence of both intermediaries and markets allows all agents to choose the least-cost method of lending or borrowing funds.

15.3 Self-Enforcing Implicit Contracts

In this section, we take the argument a step further by assuming that writing explicit contracts is costly. The market provides a limited set of securities (and hence a limited set of hedging opportunities) because it is too costly to provide a broader set of securities. However, intermediaries have an advantage over the market because they can offer risk sharing through implicit contracts, that is, contracts that are unwritten and hence unenforceable by the courts. The problem with implicit contracts, of course, is that they must be self-enforcing. The intermediary must have an incentive to carry out the terms of the implicit contract. In the static model studied in the last section, the intermediary would have no incentive to keep the terms of an implicit contract. If the investor suffers a loss in some state of nature, it would not be rational for the intermediary to make good the loss. However, the intermediary may have an incentive to abide by the terms of the implicit contract in the context of a long-term relationship rather than renege and put an end to the relationship. In this section, we show how an implicit contract can be made self-enforcing in a long-term relationship. The degree of risk sharing that can be sustained by an implicit contract will be limited by the value of the ongoing relationship. If the amount of money transferred between the parties ex post is greater than the value of the relationship, the party that is required to pay will dissolve the relationship rather than abide by the contract, so the need for the implicit contract to be self-enforcing implies that the contract will be incomplete. This has the further implication that an increase in competition, which reduces ex post payoffs to the intermediary, will reduce the completeness of the implicit contract. In analyzing the risk-sharing problem, we have assumed that the customer and the intermediary write an explicit and enforceable contract. However, the costs that make complete markets an implausible assumption may also make complete explicit contracts unrealistically expensive too. One way of getting around this problem is to assume that the intermediary and the customer do not have an explicit (written) contract, but rather have an implicit (unwritten) understanding about what might happen if a bad outcome occurs.

This solution raises another problem, however. If the implicit contract between the intermediary and customer is unwritten and hence unenforceable by a third party, why should either the customer or the intermediary believe the other will keep the terms of the implicit contract? In a one-shot contracting problem, unenforceability may prevent any insurance from being offered by the intermediary. In the context of a long-term relationship, however, it may be possible to sustain risk sharing through a self-enforcing implicit contract, in which the value of the ongoing relationship to both parties provides incentives to abide by the terms of the agreement rather than renege and end the relationship. However, the amount of insurance that can be offered in a self-enforcing way will be limited by the value of the ongoing relationship. We study this next.

Sustainable Relationships

The model in the previous section is extended to allow for the possibility of long-term relationships and implicit contracts. As before, there are two parties to a risk-sharing contract: a customer and an intermediary. There is a sequence of dates $t = 1, 2, \ldots$ and a new risk-sharing opportunity at each date. The states $\{s_t\}_{t=1}^{\infty}$ are assumed to be independently and identically distributed random variables with probability density $p(s_t)$. The customer's random income is $w(s_t)$ if the state s_t is observed at date t. The written contract is a function $f(s_t)$, where $f(s_t)$ is the amount of money paid by the intermediary to the customer in state s_t. In the absence of any other transfers, the expected utility of the customer at date t is $E[u(w(s_t) + f(s_t))]$, and the expected utility of the intermediary, ignoring other risks, is $E[v(-f(s_t))]$. The contract f is taken as given, that is, it has been designed by the intermediary and represents the best hedge that the intermediary could write for the customer. The question now is how much better can the intermediary and the customer do by entering into an implicit risk-sharing arrangement.

Let $h(s_t)$ be the transfer that is paid by the intermediary to the customer in state s_t as a result of this implicit agreement. In order to make the implicit contract self-enforcing, there must be some threat of punishment for either party if it reneges on the agreement. Sometimes concern for reputation is sufficient to sustain the relationship. If the intermediary reneges on its part of the bargain, it will lose its reputation and the possibility of future business. In the same way, a customer that reneges on its part of the bargain will find it difficult to get an intermediary to offer implicit insurance in the future. Without modeling this part of the story formally, we assume that if either party reneges on its part of the implicit contract, it will be impossible to find another partner. On the other hand, we assume that the customer can always resort to the formal contract as a security level. For this reason, even if the customer is restricted to dealing with its current intermediary, the customer has a level of expected utility below which the implicit contract cannot push it in any state of nature.

The participation constraints that both the customer and intermediary face are similar. For ease of exposition, we will illustrate the operation of these constraints by focusing on those faced by the customer and assume in what follows that the intermediary can commit itself to the implicit agreement. Let

$$u^* = E[u(w(s_t) + f(s_t) + h(s_t))]$$

be the ex ante expected utility of the customer in each period when there is an implicit risk-sharing agreement, and let

$$u^{**} = E[u(w(s_t) + f(s_t))]$$

be the corresponding value without the implicit agreement. Then the participation constraint for the customer is

$$u(w(s_t) + f(s_t) + h(s_t)) + \frac{u^*}{r} \geq u(w(s_t) + f(s_t)) + \frac{u^{**}}{r}$$

where r is the customer's discount rate. The left-hand side of the inequality is the expected utility of continuing the implicit agreement, while the right-hand side is the expected utility of deviating this period and ending it. This inequality puts a lower bound on the value of $h(s_t)$ that is a function of s_t and u^*, call it $H(s_t, u^*, u^{**})$. Assuming that competition among intermediaries leads them to maximize the expected utility of the customer subject to some period opportunity cost v^{**} (we assume for simplicity that each intermediary can deal with at most one customer), the equilibrium implicit contract has to solve the following problem:

$$\max \quad u^* = E[u(w(s_t) + f(s_t) + h(s_t))]$$
$$\text{s.t.} \quad h(s_t) \geq H(s_t, u^*, u^{**}), \forall s_t$$
$$E[v(-f(s_t) - h(s_t))] \geq v^{**}.$$

This is an equilibrium problem, since the participation constraint $h(s_t) \geq H(s_t, u^*, u^{**})$ depends on the expected utility that is available from continuing the relationship, which in turn is the value of the maximization problem.

The first-order conditions that must be satisfied by the solution to this problem are

$$u'(s_t + f(s_t) + h(s_t)) = \lambda v'(-f(s_t) - h(s_t)) \text{ if } h(s_t) > H(s_t, u^*, u^{**})$$
$$u'(s_t + f(s_t) + h(s_t)) \geq \lambda v'(-f(s_t) - h(s_t)) \text{ if } h(s_t) = H(s_t, u^*, u^{**}),$$

where λ is the Lagrange multiplier on the intermediary's participation constraint. The first condition applies in states where the optimal insurance payment is consistent with the customer's participation constraint. The second condition applies if the risk-sharing transfer is constrained by the future surplus obtained from the relationship.

Effect of Competition on Relationships

The value of the implicit insurance contract is revealed by the fact that $u^* > u^{**}$ whenever $f(s_t)$ is not itself an optimal contract. However, there may be other constraints on the contract. The more opportunities either party has to renege, the tighter the ex post participation constraint will be and the lower the value of u^* relative to u^{**}. Possibilities for reneging reduce the future surplus and hence the level of transfer that the implicit agreement can involve.

In the preceding section, we assumed that the only alternative to complying with the terms of an implicit contract was for the customer to renege and accept the loss of implicit insurance. Neither the customer nor the intermediary was allowed to abandon the relationship and take up with another party. This could be equilibrium behavior if every other customer and intermediary were willing to punish a customer or intermediary who reneged on such an agreement, but it is not entirely clear (because we have not explicitly modeled it) that this would be supported by an equilibrium. In any case, it seems likely that in most explicit formulations, the more competitors there are on each side of the market and the more anonymous the market becomes, the less likely it is that any customer or intermediary will be punished for reneging on an implicit agreement. The more outside options each party has available, the tighter the (ex post) participation constraints become and the lower the (ex ante) expected utility from the implicit contract.

Suppose, to take an extreme case, that customers can switch intermediaries whenever it suits them. This requires in particular that the written contract f does not include any penalties for terminating the relationship or any bonding devices such as payment of fees and commissions to the intermediary in advance. Then the ex post participation constraint takes the form

$$u(w(s_t) + f(s_t) + h(s_t)) + \frac{u^*}{r} \geq u(w(s_t) + f(s_t)) + \frac{u^*}{r},$$

or $h(s_t) \geq 0$. In other words, the implicit agreement can never require the customer to make a transfer to the intermediary. This is a tighter constraint, as long as $u^* > u^{**}$, and so it reduces the expected utility that can be achieved for the customer. Increased competition, in the form of easier switching between intermediaries, makes it harder to enforce agreements and causes a real efficiency cost in terms of reduced risk sharing. Another way of saying the same thing is that the set of self-enforcing contracts is smaller and excludes the contracts that offer better risk sharing.

We can take this argument one step further and consider the effect of competition from financial markets. Since intermediaries can duplicate anything markets can offer, the introduction of a market does not introduce any new opportunities for risk sharing. Furthermore, since intermediaries can provide products at least as good as those provided in financial markets, there is no tightening of the ex post participation constraint. What markets may do is to change the distribution of surplus between the customer and the intermediary. To make this very clear, consider the case where there is initially either a monopolistic intermediary or a collusive cartel of intermediaries that can extract all the surplus from the customer. In that case, the implicit contract solves the problem:

$$\begin{aligned} \max \quad & v^* = E[v(-f(s_t) - h(s_t))] \\ \text{s.t.} \quad & h(s_t) \geq H(s_t, u^*, u^{**}), \forall s_t \\ & u^* = E[u(w(s_t) + f(s_t) + h(s_t))] \geq u^{**} = E[u(w(s_t))]. \end{aligned}$$

Now suppose that a financial market opens up, in which the security k is traded competitively. This security may be identical to f except for the fees and commissions that are incorporated in the definition of the security and are assumed to be lower than those charged by the intermediary. Then the customer's reservation utility changes from $u^{**} = E[u(w(s_t))]$ to $u^{***} = E[u(w(s_t) + k(s_t))]$. This change has two effects. First, it makes the customer better off. Second, it changes the ex post participation constraint. The first is a distributional change and comes at the expense of the monopolistic intermediaries. The second has efficiency repercussions, because it restricts the risk-sharing properties of the implicit contract being offered by the intermediaries. So there is a trade-off between efficiency and distribution. A reduction in monopoly rents may lead to a reduction in risk sharing.

15.4 Reducing the Costs of Market Participation

We now turn to the central question of the chapter, which is how an intermediary can reduce investors' participation costs, particularly their cost of acquiring information. The problem the investor in the market faces is not so much one of risk as one of uncertainty. The investor simply does not know what he is getting into. He lacks the expertise needed to evaluate the security, derivative, or risk-sharing contract that the intermediary wants him to trade. The intermediary can reduce the uncertainty that the investor faces by offering implicit insurance against unforeseen contingencies or misunderstandings.

We model uncertainty by assuming that the outcome of a security depends on two different types of states of nature. We distinguish between salient states, which correspond to the kinds of risk that everyone, including investors and firms, can understand, and obscure states, which correspond to uncertainty about the nature of the security that can be eliminated only by acquiring costly expertise. Writing a complete contingent contract does not solve this problem, because including more contingencies simply increases the number of obscure states and makes it harder for the customer to evaluate the contract.

We model the cost of becoming informed by a fixed cost of evaluating the security in each state. Investors take an attitude of extreme risk aversion toward obscure states and hence toward any security or contract that contains contingencies based on obscure states. The intermediary can reduce participation costs by providing an implicit agreement to insure the customer. If things turn out badly, there is the possibility of compensation. In effect, the intermediary, by providing insurance against unforeseen contingencies (obscure states), reduces the security's contingency on obscure states and hence reduces the need for the investor to have information in the first place.

Insurance Against Unforeseen Contingencies

One of the things that discourages small investors and firms from making use of financial markets is the information needed to operate successfully in volatile and sophisticated markets. Quite apart from the risk attached to the underlying variables that are being hedged, there is uncertainty about the exact nature of the securities being traded, the behavior of the markets, the dealing process, and so forth. Unsophisticated investors and firms do not know what they are getting into.

Intuitively, dealing with a trusted adviser or intermediary seems to avoid some of this risk because the intermediary can give advice on the choice of securities. Beyond this it can offer some assurance that there will be no unpleasant surprises. If something unexpected does occur, the intermediary may be willing to bear the cost or, at least, share the cost with the customer. In short, dealing with an intermediary provides insurance against nonspecific risks. Were an agent to operate directly in a financial market, however, there would be no such insurance. The agent gets what the security specifies, no more and no less. For this reason, investors and firms may feel much more comfortable dealing with an intermediary. This is not an appeal to irrationality. The fact that one has a relationship with the intermediary provides insurance.

It is not easy to model the kind of uncertainty that the customer faces in trying to make decisions in an unfamiliar environment. Here we try to develop a model that distinguishes this uncertainty from ordinary risk associated with asset returns. One of the costs of going to the market is the cost of becoming informed about the securities traded and about the market mechanism itself. Suppose that the customer does not know what the security f is, that is, he is uncertain not just about the state of nature s that will eventually be revealed, but also about the value of the security in state s. In this case, the intermediary may be able to offer the customer insurance about the nature of the security by promising to compensate the customer for any unpleasant surprises.

This has the additional advantage that the intermediary is taking advantage of the market's lower costs by piggybacking on the standard security f, so the customer is trading f indirectly through the intermediary and getting an additional security $h = g - f$ that has two functions: to customize the standard security f to the customer's individual needs and to relieve the customer of the need to obtain extra information about the nature of the security f.

How are we to interpret the transfers $h = g - f$? They could take the form of cash payments but need not. They could take the form of some readjustment of the terms of the contract f. Or, if the customer and the intermediary do business repeatedly, h may take the form of an adjustment in the terms of a subsequent transaction. If the customer gets burned on one deal, it may receive favorable terms on the next deal as compensation. Or the intermediary may provide services in lieu of direct compensation, for example, by arranging a loan if the customer is facing liquidity problems because the last deal turned out badly. Or the intermediary may pay for the cost of some action to make the customer whole after suffering some damage because of an unanticipated outcome from a previous transaction. On occasion the customer may require compensation in cash. In some cases this may involve legal action, but this does not have to be the norm.

Risk, Uncertainty, and Implicit Insurance

To clarify some of the ideas introduced above, it will be necessary to have a slightly richer model. Suppose that f is the security traded in the market and that the outcome of f depends on two types of contingencies or states. The first type of state we call *salient* and the second we call *obscure*. The salient states consist of contingencies the individual investor or firm is likely to think of and understand when evaluating a security; the obscure states consist of those that are not consciously brought to mind at the time a decision is made. Ex post, both kinds of states are observable. In fact, we may consider both to be salient ex post because it will be clear that they have affected the outcome in a particular way. Let S denote the finite set of salient states. For each state $s \in S$ the finite set of obscure states is $T(s)$. The probability of a salient state s is $p(s)$, and the conditional probability of an obscure state t given s is $\pi(t|s)$. It is important to note that the division of contingencies into salient and obscure states is subjective, that is, it depends on the firm or individual in question and may vary from one to another.

For simplicity, we assume that the customer's income risk depends on only the salient states and that the customer has well-defined probabilities attached to these states. The customer behaves like a von Neumann-Morgenstern expected utility maximizer with respect to states $s \in S$ where $T(s)$ contains one element, so there is no obscurity. On the other hand, when $T(s)$ contains more than one element, the obscure states represent a source of uncertainty in the Keynesian sense, precisely because they are not being consciously scrutinized. It is less clear how the customer should respond to this uncertainty. We assume that for obscure states, the customer attaches a very low utility denoted $\underline{u}$. There are a number of formal ways this can be justified. For simplicity and the sake of illustrating the general idea, suppose that the customer acts like an infinitely risk-averse individual when confronted with this kind of uncertainty, that is, if $f(s,t)$ is the payoff to the security in the combined state (s,t), then the customer acts as if the outcome were $f_0(s) \equiv \inf_{t \in T(s)}\{f(s,t)\}$ in state s and proceeds to calculate the expected utility of the security f_0 in the usual way. The utility of f_0 in state s is $\underline{u}(s)$. This rather pessimistic way of evaluating the security is not likely to make the customer very keen to trade the security. In many cases, the optimum response may be to choose the quantity $\theta = 0$. Note that infinite risk aversion does not lead the customer to sell the security short: when $\theta < 0$, the customer's pessimism will take the form of replacing $f(s)$ with $f_0(s) \equiv \sup_{t \in T}\{f(s,t)\}$. Hence, unlike standard expected utility theory, the model is consistent with the fact that a large proportion of potential investors do not participate in standard financial markets at all (cf. Dow and Werlang 1992). For example, Mankiw and Zeldes (1991) find that only a small proportion of investors participate in the stock market; in their sample of those with liquid assets in excess of \$100,000, only 47.7 percent held stocks.

The existence of obscure states and the uncertainty to which they give rise is a barrier to the participation of unsophisticated individuals in financial markets. But why should securities depend on obscure states in the first place? There are at least two reasons. First, it may not be possible to provide securities that avoid obscure states altogether. Salience and obscurity are subjective: what is salient to one individual may not be salient to another because of a difference in background or expertise. Second, the incompleteness of the set of securities exacerbates the problem by reducing the set of securities from which the individual has to choose. The formulas that can be written down in a legally enforceable contract may inevitably involve contingencies that are obscure to some individuals; the case law that is likely to determine how contracts are enforced in practice may be obscure to all but a few lawyers specializing in an area; and so on.

This is where the intermediary can provide a valuable service. It can insure the individual or firm against obscure contingencies, thus reducing or eliminating the uncertainty that lowers the value of the security. Note that this does not require the intermediary to write a contract that is in some sense more detailed or complete than the security offered in the market. The insurance can be implicit in the relationship between the intermediary and the customer. What the intermediary is offering the customer is a substitute contract that pays the customer the certain amount $f_1(s)$ in state s rather than the uncertain amount $f(s, t)$. For example, $f_1(s)$ may be the mean of $f(s, t)$ according to the intermediary's beliefs about the distribution of t. This security f_1 can do a perfectly adequate job of hedging against the risk in $y(s)$, which depends on only the salient state s. Of course, the legally binding contract is f; the difference between f and f_1 is something that the customer cannot quite understand, but that does not matter since only f_1 needs to be taken into account in the outcome. The important point is that the implicit contract is based on states that the customer and the intermediary can both fully distinguish. The extent to which customers can rely on the implicit contract will depend on the profitability of the ongoing relationship versus the benefit of reneging, as before. The difference now is that customers are unaware of the benefit of reneging. In making their decision, customers must rely on the information available to them, such as previous experience on reneging with contracts of this type.

In the next subsection, we extend this simple view of implicit insurance to allow for information acquisition.

Operation of Markets with Ex Ante Information

Consider an (implicit) contracting problem between an intermediary and a customer. As before, suppose that the intermediary is designing a risk-sharing arrangement with the customer. The intermediary has the expertise to identify both salient and obscure states; the customer can identify only salient states. This has the important implication that explicit contracts cannot be used to provide insurance to the unsophisticated against obscure states. The customer has no idea how to interpret such contracts and will simply assign a low utility to them. Implicit contracts must therefore be used to insure against outcomes in obscure states.

Consider the use of securities traded in the market first. As usual, the unsophisticated customer faces a random income $w(s)$ in state s so if it trades the security f, its net income will be $f(s, t) + w(s)$ in state (s, t). We ignore other income for the intermediary in the usual way, so its income is simply $-f(s, t)$ in state (s, t). With no further information, the expected utilities of the customer and intermediary, conditional on trading the randomly chosen security f, will be

$$E[u(f(s,t)+w(s))]$$

and

$$E[v(-f(s,t))],$$

respectively. There are two sources of uncertainty here—one arising from the uncertainty about the salient state and the other arising from uncertainty about the obscure state t. The uncertainty about the salient state of nature will be resolved at some time in the future, and we shall have no more to say about it here. On the other hand, we assume that for some cost, information is available to customers about the obscure states t for each salient state s. One way of capturing the possibility of reducing uncertainty about the nature of $f(s,t)$ is to assume that for some fixed cost $c>0$ and for some state s, the customer can observe the true value of $f(s,t)$ for all states t. If the number of salient states is large, it will never be optimal to pay this cost and learn the entire security $f(s,t)$; but depending on the circumstances, it may pay to learn in some states. For each state s where information is acquired, it is possible to calculate expected utility in the standard way. For other states where the cost c is not incurred, the utility assigned is $\underline{u}(s)$.

The problem of evaluating f can be regarded as a search problem. If the security is evaluated in a subset of states $\Phi \subset S$, then the expected utility of the contract to the customer is

$$U(f\,|\,\Phi)=\sum_{s\in\Phi}\sum_{t\in T(s)} p(s)\pi(t|s)u(w(s)+f(s,t)-\#\Phi c)+\sum_{s\in S\backslash\Phi} p(s)\underline{u}(s),$$

where $\#\Phi$ denotes the number of elements of Φ. The value of information comes from the possibility of making the trade conditional on the information, in which case the customer gets the maximum of $U(f\,|\,\Phi)$ and $E[u(w(s)-\#\Phi c)]$. The optimal choice of Φ maximizes

$$E[\max\{U(f\,|\,\Phi), E[u(w(s)-\#\Phi c)]\}].$$

Investing in information makes sense only if it sometimes changes the decision to buy the security. If it does not, there is no gain, and the customer would be better off not paying the cost of evaluating the contract. For this reason, there is the usual well-known nonconvexity in the objective function. If there is a large number of individually insignificant states of nature, information about any one state is unlikely to make a difference to the decision whether to accept the contract. Therefore, a small amount of information—for example, about the contract's payoff in a single state—may have no value. Clearly an intermediate amount of information may affect the decision and therefore has a positive value, so there must be increasing returns to information over some range. On the other hand, when a large amount of information has been collected, getting information about an additional state is unlikely to have much effect on the decision, so the marginal value of information is decreasing beyond some point.

For $c = 0$ complete contingent contracts will be optimal. Both sides will understand exactly how the contract will work in each state, and all possibilities for risk sharing will be exploited by the contract. In that case relationships will have no role to play.

For moderate c, the security will be evaluated at states that are likely to occur but not at other states. Ex post there will be surprises in the sense that for those states at which the security was not evaluated, the utility obtained will be different from that expected. The optimal expenditure on evaluating how the contract will work involves trading off the transaction costs against the risk of surprises.

For sufficiently high c, the security will never be evaluated. In this case the basic underlying risk (salient states) will be compounded by the uncertainty about how the contract will work (obscure states). Surprises will occur frequently.

Depending on the level of c and the cost of surprises in terms of the risk, there may be no trade at all if

$$E_{\pi}[u(f(s) + w(s))] + E_{\pi}[v(-f(s))] < E[u(w(s)] + v(0).$$

This might be true in spite of the fact that the security does have some genuine risk-sharing benefits, simply because of the customers' uncertainty about the actual outcome in some states and the costs of eliminating this uncertainty.

Intermediaries and Ex Ante versus Ex Post Security Evaluation

The essential problem with using contracts in the framework developed is that the costs of evaluation are borne ex ante. This means that the security is evaluated in many states even though ex post only one will occur. This raises the obvious possibility of improving the allocation of resources by dispensing with ex ante evaluation and having some type of insurance should a surprise occur. The difficulty is how this type of insurance can be provided. Explicit contracts based on obscure information cannot be evaluated by unsophisticated investors. When confronted with contracts that attempt to condition on obscure states, they will simply assign $\underline{u}$ unless they incur the costs of evaluation. This is where the implicit insurance allowed by relationships is important. Customers may be willing to forgo ex ante evaluation because they understand that if there is a problem, the intermediary will eliminate or share the risk of any surprises. As a result they may be willing to trade even though explicit contracts alone would not provide any surplus. The implicit ex post insurance allowed by relationships means that the ex ante costs of complex explicit contracts can be avoided.

To illustrate this in terms of the model developed, suppose the explicit written contract provides a payoff $f(s,t)$. The implicit contract is such that the net payment to the customer is

$$f_1(s) = f(s,t) - h(s,t).$$

In other words, the customer is provided with a payoff that can be understood ex ante. There is no need to undertake complex evaluation ex ante. The implicit insurance provided by the intermediary means customers do not have to incur the costs of investigating obscure possibilities. By insuring against these possibilities, the intermediary can potentially provide a huge saving in costs or increase the funds people are willing to invest in markets, or both.

There are various ways in which implicit insurance contracts can be executed. After an unexpected outcome, the aggrieved party may engage in bargaining with the counterparty, threatening to take his business elsewhere or create unfavorable publicity until the intermediary makes amends. In some cases, a legal action may be brought against the intermediary. Whatever form the renegotiation takes, it is part of the implicit contract that is played out over time. We can imagine that all of this is anticipated by the parties when they write the explicit contract. The real contract is the anticipated mapping from states of nature to payoffs, not the written contract, and it is the real contract that has to be evaluated and enforced. Formally, this is equivalent to an explicit contract with the same contingent payoffs, but the crucial difference is the cost of writing and enforcing the contract. The long-term relationship with its implicit insurance is just a cheaper way of achieving a particular pattern of state-contingent payoffs.

15.5 Strategies for Implementing Relationships

The ex ante costs of explicit contracts can sometimes be avoided by the development of long-lasting relationships and implicit insurance between intermediaries and firms or consumers. A question of some interest to providers of financial services is how relationships can best be structured to maximize these benefits from implicit insurance.

In the United States in recent years, a number of intermediaries have tried to construct financial supermarkets where consumers can obtain a whole range of financial services from the same providers. For example, in the 1980s Sears bought Dean Witter and a number of other specialist financial service firms. At one point it was offering a full range of services, including FDIC-insured deposits, consumer loans, credit cards, mortgage banking, commercial lending, mutual funds, brokerage services for securities, and insurance. American Express combined with Shearson and Lehman and a number of other firms and offered a similar range of financial services. Ultimately these strategies were unsuccessful in the sense that the groups were broken up and returned to competing separately. Prudential thought that insurance agents and stockbrokers could sell each other's products and merged with Bache. However, they do not appear to have been particularly successful at implementing this idea. A recent and extreme example of the trend to provide consumers with a full range of financial products from one firm is the combination of Citibank and the Travelers Group to form Citigroup. In addition to attempts to extend relationships between intermediaries and consumers, there have also been attempts to extend relationships between intermediaries and firms. One example is the recent creation of Section 20 subsidiaries to perform investment banking services by many large commercial banks. The merger between Banker's Trust and Alex Brown in 1997 is another. Citigroup may benefit from the combination of investment banking and commercial banking allowed by links between Salomon Smith Barney within Travelers and Citibank.

In many European countries such as Germany, it has long been the case that universal banks have provided a whole array of services to consumers and firms. On the consumer side, in addition to standard banking accounts and loans, insurance and other types of financial service are offered. On the firm side, loans and underwriting services are often provided. Relationships are wider in scope and much more important than in the United States.

The model of relationships developed above can be used to shed some light on when strategies of extending the scope of relationships are likely to be successful. That increased competition reduces the amount of implicit insurance that is possible with relationships indicates that it is essentially the available future surplus that is important. The more future surplus at stake, the higher the transfers that are incentive compatible, and hence the more implicit insurance there can be. By extending the scope of relationships and putting a greater amount of future surplus at stake, the more valuable the relationships can be made. For example, suppose a bank is providing loans to consumers, and a mutual fund is providing investment products. Both have long-term relationships with their customers. The extent of risk sharing through implicit contracts that can be achieved by both firms is limited by the future stream of profits each will separately expect to earn in the future. To the extent the current outcomes in each, and hence the need for transfers under the implicit insurance arrangement, are independent, there will be a gain to combining the two and forming a more extensive relationship with customers. Now the transfer to provide the implicit insurance that can take place in each division will depend on the future profits in the combined entity. In states where both divisions need transfers simultaneously, it cannot be worse to have the two combined, and in states where only one division requires a transfer, a strict improvement in the implicit insurance can be obtained.

This argument is consistent with the observation that extensive relationships involved in universal banking have been successful in Europe while financial supermarkets have been unsuccessful in the United States. In Europe there is not much competition in financial services, while in the United States there typically is. Combining relationships will be successful only to the extent that large future streams of profits are put at risk, which happens in Europe but not in the United States.

In order for intermediaries in the United States to be successful when creating broader relationships, the objective should be to put together profitable services and not just give consumers a wide range of products. The financial supermarkets that have been constructed have really just given consumers convenience through one-stop shopping; they have not provided more implicit insurance because each individual line is fairly competitive. For consumers one-stop shopping for financial services does not appear to be very valuable, and thus the mergers have been unsuccessful. The results above suggest that combining commercial banking and investment banking in the United States may be more successful. The reason is that there are areas of both that are highly profitable, and hence extended implicit insurance should be possible.

15.6 Conclusion

Financial markets have become increasingly important, although they have mostly become markets for intermediaries rather than markets for individuals and firms. We have argued that one of the main reasons for this change is that increased participation costs in markets have meant that individuals and firms have withdrawn from markets and rely increasingly on intermediaries. If complex complete contracts were used between intermediaries and their customers, there would be no gain because of the extensive ex ante costs of evaluating how the contracts will operate. Instead, customers can rely on the implicit insurance made possible by long-term relationships. Households and firms know that if there is a surprise, the intermediary will share the risk. Such risk sharing is possible only if both parties will benefit from the relationship in the future. This means that competition by intermediaries may be undesirable if it reduces future profits and, hence, the amount of risk sharing that can occur. It also suggests that when choosing strategies to maximize the benefits of relationships, firms should be concerned with offering a range of profitable services rather than simply expanding the number of services available.

Throughout the discussion of explicit and implicit contracts, we took the explicit written contracts as exogenously given. This is obviously a gross oversimplification. There are complex issues to be discussed about how these contracts are written and how they interact with the implicit contract. Only one issue will be mentioned here, but it illustrates a wider class of issues. There are gains to locking in the customer in order to provide better insurance to both the customer and the intermediary. One way of doing this is by getting the customer to post a bond by paying fees and commissions up front. These can be thought of as an "insurance premium" that the customer will forfeit if it switches to another intermediary or reneges on the implicit contract and reverts to the written contract. However, the customer may have difficulty paying this premium up front because it lacks liquidity. In that case, the written contract can easily be amended to provide a stream of payments to the intermediary. Since this stream of payments is noncontingent, there is no problem writing it into the contract, and since the written contract is enforceable it serves as a bonding device. Further, since the payments are spread over time, it solves the firm's liquidity problem. However, this change in the contract makes the ex ante value of the written contract lower and so reduces the value of the relationship and may adversely affect the ex post participation constraint. So the problem of contract and security design cannot be separated from the problem of providing optimal implicit insurance. We do not pursue this issue here since it raises the question of how to write down the problem in a satisfactory way—for example, to specify the constraints on what contracts can be written and what contracts cannot. This is an important problem for future research.

Many of the arguments developed in this chapter may have applications to a wider range of economic phenomena. In many principal-agent relationships the principal employs an agent precisely because the principal lacks relevant knowledge and expertise. For example, informational problems that are similar to those of an investor trading a complex security may arise in the relationship between a doctor and patient, a lawyer and client, a computer manufacturer and computer user. However, we believe that the informational problems arising from financial transactions are serious, so it is important to consider this issue in a financial setting. Financial transactions are often concerned with risk sharing and the outcomes are typically unpredictable. A firm or investor buying a complex security faces a wide range of possible outcomes, and the intermediary cannot insure against all of them. For example, if a change in interest rates may affect most of the derivatives sold by the firm. Indeed, it is rarely optimal for one party to bear all of the risk. Because each party has a lot of private information—for example, information about their idiosyncratic risks—it is hard to be clear about what they expect as a result of a complex financial transaction. Financial arrangements seem to be more opaque and to offer more scope for problems than other kinds of transactions.

The topic we discuss in this chapter is related to a number of strands of the literature. Merton (1989) justified the use of continuous time techniques, which assume no frictions, by distinguishing between intermediaries and individual investors and firms. He suggested that intermediaries could trade at almost zero marginal costs in markets. These intermediaries could rebundle payoff streams for individual investors, who would pay a price for this service. He focused on intermediaries' activities in markets, whereas we focus on their interaction with unsophisticated investors. The existing literature on the importance of relationships and implicit contracts for intermediaries has a rather different focus from ours. Sharpe (1990) and Rajan (1992) consider the generation of information during relationships between banks and borrowers and the possibility for ex post exploitation of the monopoly rents these contracts lead to. They show how ex ante competition limits the potential amount that can be extracted and the effect this has on loan rates and choices of financing. In contrast, in our model there is not a problem with opportunistic behavior. Instead, relationships are beneficial because they can provide implicit insurance. Boot and Thakor (1996) consider the effect of competition on the composition of bank lending between transaction loans, which are like capital market funding, and relationship loans, which are like traditional lending. They are able to show the surprising result that relationship lending increases with competition. Their focus is thus on the composition of banks' activities, whereas ours is on the interaction between explicit and implicit contracts.

Notes

1. Even though markets provide a limited number of securities, it may be argued that it is possible to synthesize a large number of different securities by adopting dynamic trading strategies involving a small number of actively traded securities; but this requires a lot of expertise, which a small investor or firm may not have. An intermediary can provide the security directly, saving the investor or firm the trouble of figuring out the trading strategy (Merton 1989).

2. Even when the product being offered by the intermediary is "vanilla-flavored," the intermediary may still be able to offer services tailored to the needs of the customer that a market cannot. For example, in the United Kingdom and other European countries, the relationship with the bank manager is important, because even small depositors and borrowers expect the privileges of relationship banking, although the products being offered are not very sophisticated.

3. A good illustration is provided by a comparison of futures, which offer the liquidity that is possible in an exchange market, and forwards, which offer greater opportunities for customization. The exchanges have recognized the value of customization by offering a broader menu of instruments such as LEAP and FLEX options on the CBOE, which attempt to afford greater customization and liquidity.

4. A related issue is that the investor or firm may be the victim of moral hazard because it lacks information about what the intermediary is doing. In that case, too, intermediaries may turn out to be costly.

5. An example is provided by information intermediaries such as Reuters, Bloomberg, or the internet, which can provide a platform that enables information vendors to reap the advantages of economies of scale in information distribution. As a result of these economies, "standard" financial information, such as stock and bond prices, can be distributed more cheaply to market participants.

References

Allen, F., and D. Gale. (1994). "Limited Market Participation and Volatility of Asset Prices." *American Economic Review* **84,** 933–955.

———. (1999). "Innovations in Financial Services, Relationships and Risk Sharing." *Management Science* (forthcoming).

Allen, F., and A. Santomero. (1997). "The Theory of Financial Intermediation." *Journal of Banking and Finance* **21,** 1461–1486.

Boot, A., and A. Thakor. (1993). "Security Design." *Journal of Finance* **48,** 1349–1378.

———. (1996). "Can Relationship Banking Survive Competition?" Mitsui Life Financial Research Center working paper 96-6, University of Michigan.

Diamond, D. (1984). "Financial Intermediation and Delegated Monitoring." *Review of Economic Studies* **51,** 393–414.

Dow, J., and S. Ribeiro da Costa Werlang. (1992). "Uncertainty Aversion, Risk Aversion, and the Optimal Choice of Portfolio." *Econometrica* **60,** 197–204.

Duffie, D., and P. DeMarzo. (1995). "A Liquidity-Based Model of Market Design." Working paper, Stanford University.

Gale, D. (1992). "Standard Securities." *Review of Economic Studies* **59,** 731–755.

Hellwig, M. (1998). "Banks, Markets, and the Allocation of Risks in an Economy." *Journal of Institutional and Theoretical Economics* **54,** 328–345.

Mankiw, N., and S. Zeldes. (1991). "The Consumption of Stockholders and Nonstockholders." *Journal of Financial Economics* **29,** 97–112.

Merton, R. (1989). "On the Application of the Continuous-Time Theory of Finance to Financial Intermediation and Insurance." *Geneva Papers on Risk and Insurance Theory* **14,** 225–261.

OECD (1995). *Financial market trends #62.* Paris: Organisation for Economic Cooperation and Development.

Pagano, M. (1989). "Endogenous Market Thinness and Stock Price Volatility." *Review of Economic Studies* **56,** 269–288.

Rajan, R. (1992). "Insiders and Outsiders: The Choice Between Informed and Arm's Length Debt." *Journal of Finance* **47,** 1367–1400.

Sharpe, S. (1990). "Asymmetric Information, Bank Lending and Implicit Contracts: A Stylized Model of Customer Relationships." *Journal of Finance* **55,** 1069–1087.

16 Afterword

The instability of financial markets at the beginning of the eighteenth century, in particular the South Sea and Mississippi bubbles, led to the introduction of onerous regulations in the United Kingdom and France. In the United Kingdom these restrictions were removed just over a century later, and London became the center of a market-oriented financial system. The United States also developed a market-oriented financial system, both because of its close ties to the United Kingdom and because of its aversion to powerful financial institutions. In France, financial markets remained heavily regulated, and a liquid market for the stocks of firms did not develop until the 1980s. Instead, France developed a bank-based financial system, which was subsequently adopted by Germany and other European countries as well as Japan.

In recent years there has been a widespread move in both Europe and Japan to supplement bank-based systems with financial markets. Is this a good idea? Conventional neoclassical theory does not provide a good framework for answering this question. We have tried to develop alternative models that might provide insight into the operation of the two types of financial system. There are no simple conclusions. We have derived a number of results that go against what many might regard as the conventional wisdom. The most important of these are the following:

- Financial markets may be bad for risk sharing.
- Competition in banking can be undesirable.
- Financial crises can be good as well as bad.
- Separation of ownership and control can be desirable.
- Financial markets work well and traditional intermediaries work poorly when there is diversity of opinion in the financing of new technologies.

• Participation costs are high in financial markets, and intermediaries are necessary complements rather than substitutes for financial markets.

The standard justification for financial markets has traditionally been that they provide liquidity and allow investors to share risk. However, in bank-oriented economies such as Japan, Germany, and France, households hold predominantly safe assets and very little equity. As a result, they are exposed to relatively little risk. In the market-oriented economies of the United States and United Kingdom, households hold around half of their assets in equities and bear substantial amounts of market risk, that is, risk associated with changes in the market value of assets. How can this paradox be understood? The answer is that (incomplete) markets do not do a very good job of dealing with nondiversifiable risk. An intermediated financial system, where reserves are acquired to provide intertemporal smoothing, can be superior under certain circumstances.

The United States has long encouraged competition in banking. Other countries have had much more concentrated banking sectors. Recently, both the European Union and Japan have adopted policies to increase competition. We have argued that the traditional U.S. policy of encouraging a large number of banks by imposing geographical restrictions may reduce rather than increase competition in the provision of services. Perhaps more important, an increase in competition and a consequent reduction in banking profits can lead to risk-taking behavior. As a result, a concentrated banking system can (under certain circumstances and in certain respects) be more efficient than a competitive one.

Financial crises were endemic in Europe until the middle of the nineteenth century and in the United States until well into the twentieth century. In recent years, financial crises have reemerged as an important problem, particularly in emerging economies. It is often argued that banking crises are undesirable and should be eliminated by central banks. However, an inflexible avoidance of financial crises can be harmful. Optimal risk sharing requires that low returns be spread over as large a group as possible. By making returns to bank deposits contingent, a bank crisis can be beneficial and improve risk sharing. This is not to say that banking crises do not involve deadweight costs. Careful intervention by the central bank can reduce these costs while at the same time allowing optimal risk sharing. In addition to banking crises, there are also crises associated with financial markets. When central banks allow credit to expand too rapidly, either because of financial liberalization or for some other reason, there may be a bubble in asset prices. When there is a real shock to the economy or credit is tightened, the bubble can burst and impose severe costs on the economy. The actions of the central bank are crucial in both causing and correcting the effects of these bubbles.

It has long been suggested that when a corporation's equity is widely held, there is an (undesirable) separation of ownership and control. In the United States and United Kingdom, it is usually argued that the market for corporate control and, in particular, hostile takeovers limit the inefficiencies associated with this separation. In Japan and Germany, the main bank and hausbank systems are supposed to achieve the same result through monitoring of firms. The empirical evidence for the effectiveness of these mechanisms is far from compelling, however. We argue that, in fact, separation of ownership and control can be optimal in a second-best world. Managers have access to much better information than shareholders, and as long as the two groups' interests are somewhat aligned, it may be best to give managers considerable discretion. Managers are naturally concerned with the survival of the firm, and this can create a convergence of interests between them and shareholders.

One of the main determinants of the success of an economy is the way in which new technologies are financed. Innovations are often characterized by diversity of opinion, since there is very little previous information available on which to base judgments. In such circumstances, the hierarchical form of intermediaries does not work well: intermediaries can economize on the gathering of information through delegation, but they cannot cope with fundamental differences of opinion. Markets allow individual investors who are enthusiastic about a discovery to come together to finance it. As a result, markets can be much more effective in funding new technologies.

In many markets for products and services, the costs of market participation are low, and it is safe to ignore them to a first approximation. In financial markets this is not the case. Participation costs are of first-order importance because of the complexity of financial decisions. Allowing for this fact significantly changes the standard analysis. When individuals make decisions, a reduction in the choices available to them can be an improvement. Perhaps more important, though, is the result that intermediaries may be able to reduce participation costs significantly. In modern financial systems, financial markets and intermediaries are not substitutes but complements.

How, then, should financial systems be designed? It is unfortunate that the advocates of different systems exaggerate the benefits of markets and intermediaries. With the end of the cold war, Eastern Europe was to be transformed by the introduction of financial markets. Never mind that these countries had no system of company law and no accounting standards, that there was no tradition of trading in financial markets or of the regulation that is required to ensure fairness and equity. Never mind that there was no system of corporate control and no way of safeguarding shareholders' property rights. Never mind that privatization was often undertaken with no concern for obtaining value for the state or ensuring competent management. It is not surprising that the results have been less than miraculous. What is amazing is that virtual miracles should have been expected by writers who pretended to be hard-headed realists. Markets presume well-defined (and protected) property rights, and, as we have constantly emphasized, they require a lot of information on the part of the participants to be effective. Furthermore, markets do not by themselves create efficient, well-run companies, producing the goods that society demands. There is no substitute for competent managers and skillful workers.

In the 1980s, many prominent academics proclaimed the superiority of financial intermediaries, typified by the universal banks of Germany and Japan. These farsighted institutions were the antithesis of the short-sighted American money managers, who focused exclusively on quarterly returns. With long time horizons and low rate-of-return targets, these financial institutions encouraged managers to invest in new technology and better products, with the expectation that greater market share and long-term growth would be their own reward, unlike the accountants in charge of U.S. companies, who ran them according to financial criteria, ignoring R&D and investment in favor of short-term gains from cutting unprofitable activities. Now the same Japanese financial institutions are out of favor, having amassed billions of dollars of nonperforming loans and shown themselves incapable of cleaning house. The German banks are solvent, but as the disastrous attempt to turn Daimler-Benz into a diversified conglomerate showed, they have not proved themselves adept at monitoring firms or exercising corporate control. Obviously, banks are no better than their management, which, given the wrong incentives, can make the same mistakes as other managers.

The truth about financial systems is complicated. Neither markets nor intermediaries provide a silver bullet that can protect us against stupidity or corruption. Prudent regulation, transparent accounting, a reliable legal system, and a predominance of well-trained professionals are the least that is required to make any financial system work.

Markets and intermediaries have both advantages and disadvantages, and the choice of whether to favor one or the other is bound to depend on the specific parameters of each economy. Ultimately the choice of structure also depends on what is desired. If a reduction of nondiversifiable risk through intertemporal smoothing is given a high priority, then a bank-based system will be best. On the other hand, if the funding of new industries is regarded as more important, then a market-based system will be preferable.

In any case, in advanced economies, markets and intermediaries have a symbiotic relationship. Where a large investment in human capital is required to operate in a market, intermediaries can help to achieve wider participation and allow firms and individuals to enjoy the benefits of the market. This is only one example of the way in which intermediaries make markets possible. Conversely, markets are valuable to financial institutions because they allow for the hedging of risks that these institutions incur in the course of providing services to the public. So markets make life easier for intermediaries.

Finally, since neither markets nor intermediaries seem to work in exactly the way theory suggests, we would do well to exercise some humility in making recommendations about policies to reform our financial systems.

Index